The Law Commission
Consultation Paper No 153

The Scottish Law Commission
Discussion Paper No 105

COMPANY DIRECTORS: REGULATING CONFLICTS OF INTERESTS AND FORMULATING A STATEMENT OF DUTIES

A Joint Consultation Paper

London: The Stationery Office

ISBN 0 11 730237 8 4

Printed in the United Kingdom for The Stationery Office
J58462 9/98 C12 10170

EXECUTIVE SUMMARY

1.   This project falls into two parts. The first part is a *review of Part X of the Companies Act 1985*. This regulates self-dealing by directors and contains provisions as to what information concerning transactions in which directors are interested should be disclosed, and to whom, what the role of shareholders should be, and when such transactions are prohibited.

2.   There are many transactions entered by a company in which directors (or persons connected with them) have an interest. The provisions in Part X are diverse and complex, and they lack overall coherence and consistency. Moreover, since they were enacted, there have been important developments in corporate governance. What this consultation paper aims to do is to obtain a wide range of views on the ways in which these complex and important statutory rules can be modernised and rationalised.

3.   The second half of the project considers the case for having *a statutory statement of the duties of directors to their company*. This would include fiduciary duties and the duty of care. This issue has been considered before but it is time to look at it at again. There have been many calls to make the law in this area more accessible and transparent. This consultation paper puts forward a range of possibilities for making directors' duties under the general law more widely understood.

4.   Appendix A contains a draft statement of the duties of directors under the general law. It also contains a draft clause setting out a possible new statutory duty of care in line with recent developments in the general law.

5.   This project aims to contribute to the DTI's recently announced review of company law.

6.   This project contains an economic analysis of the law and proposes empirical research in the consultation period.

7.   A summary of questions for consultees is set out in Part 18. The consultation period will end on 24 November 1998.

ACKNOWLEDGEMENTS

J E Parkinson, *Corporate Power and Responsibility* (1993) by permission of Oxford University Press.

The King Report on Corporate Governance (29 November 1994) reproduced with permission of the Institute of Directors in South Africa.

Principles of Corporate Governance ©1994 by The American Law Institute. Reprinted with permission. All rights reserved.

Edward S Herman, *Corporate Control, Corporate Power* (1981) by permission of Cambridge University Press.

The Companies Act 1993, New Zealand ©The Crown. Reproduced with permission of the Crown.

Review of the Hong Kong Companies Ordinance - Consultancy Report (March 1997) reproduced with permission of The Government of the Hong Kong Special Administrative Region.

The Listing Rules, ©London Stock Exchange Limited 1998. Reproduced with permission.

The Combined Code (1998). Reproduced with permission of the Publishers of the Combined Code, Gee Publishing Ltd, 100 Avenue Road, Swiss Cottage, London NW3 3PG.

The Report of the Committee on the Financial Aspects of Corporate Governance ("the Cadbury Report") (24 May 1995). Reproduced with permission of the Publishers of the Cadbury Report, Gee Publishing Ltd, 100 Avenue Road, Swiss Cottage, London NW3 3PG.

Directors' Remuneration, Report of a Study Group chaired by Sir Richard Greenbury ("the Greenbury Report") (17 July 1995). Reproduced with permission of the Publishers of the Greenbury Report, Gee Publishing Ltd, 100 Avenue Road, Swiss Cottage, London NW3 3PG.

The Committee on Corporate Governance ("the Hampel Committee"), Final Report (January 1998). Reproduced with permission of the Publishers of the Final Report of the Hampel Committee, Gee Publishing Ltd, 100 Avenue Road, Swiss Cottage, London NW3 3PG

Financial Reporting Standard 8 and *Financial Reporting Standards for Smaller Entities* reproduced with permission of the Accounting Standards Board.

True and Fair Joint Opinions reproduced with permission of Mrs Justice Arden and the CCAB.

The Australian Corporations Law and the *Corporate Law Economic Reform Bill 1998* (and Explanatory Memorandum) ©Commonwealth of Australia. Reproduced with permission.

The Canada Business Corporations Act 1974-75-76, reproduced with permission of the Canadian Government.

THE LAW COMMISSION

THE SCOTTISH LAW COMMISSION

COMPANY DIRECTORS: REGULATING CONFLICTS OF INTERESTS AND FORMULATING A STATEMENT OF DUTIES

CONTENTS

SECTION A: PART X OF THE COMPANIES ACT 1985

PART 4: SUBSTANTIVE IMPROVEMENTS 1: SECTIONS 312-323 OF THE COMPANIES ACT 1985

PART 5: SUBSTANTIVE IMPROVEMENTS 2: DISCLOSURE OF DIRECTORS' SHARE DEALINGS (SECTIONS 324-326, 328-329 AND SCHEDULE 13)

PART 6: SUBSTANTIVE IMPROVEMENTS 3: LOANS AND SIMILAR TRANSACTIONS (SECTIONS 330-342)

PART 7: SUBSTANTIVE IMPROVEMENTS 4: DISCLOSURE OF TRANSACTIONS IN WHICH DIRECTORS AND THEIR CONNECTED PERSONS ARE INTERESTED IN THE ANNUAL ACCOUNTS (SCHEDULE 6, PART II) AND THE SPECIAL PROVISIONS FOR BANKS (SECTIONS 343 AND 344)

PART 8: SUBSTANTIVE IMPROVEMENTS 5: CONNECTED PERSONS (SECTION 346) AND REMAINING SECTIONS OF PART X OF THE COMPANIES ACT 1985

PART 9: FURTHER OPTIONS: (1) CAN SECTIONS IN PART X BE REPEALED? (2) WOULD PART X BE IMPROVED IF IT WAS REWRITTEN?

PART 10: SHOULD PART X OF THE COMPANIES ACT 1985 BE DECRIMINALISED

SECTION B: THE CASE FOR A STATUTORY STATEMENT OF DIRECTORS' DUTIES UNDER THE GENERAL LAW

PART 11: FIDUCIARY DUTIES: THE CURRENT LAW

PART 12: DUTY OF CARE: THE CURRENT LAW

PART 13: PREVIOUS PROPOSALS FOR A STATUTORY STATEMENT OF DIRECTORS DUTIES

PART 14: A STATEMENT OF DIRECTORS' DUTIES: OPTIONS FOR REFORM

PART 15: DUTY OF CARE: OPTIONS FOR REFORM

SECTION C: MISCELLANEOUS MATTERS

PART 16: EMPIRICAL SURVEY OF DIRECTORS

PART 17: HOW SHOULD THE LAW APPLY TO DIFFERENT CATEGORIES OF DIRECTOR?

GLOSSARY OF ABBREVIATIONS

AGM - Annual general meeting

AIM - Alternative Investment Market

AktG - the German Stock Corporation Act

CBCA - Canada Business Corporations Act 1974-75-56

the Cadbury Committee - the Committee on the Financial Aspects of Corporate Governance, chaired by Sir Adrian Cadbury

the Cadbury Report - Report of the Committee on the Financial Aspects of Corporate Governance (December 1992)

the Cadbury Code of Best Practice - incorporated in the Report of the Committee on the Financial Aspects of Corporate Governance (December 1992)

CBI - Confederation of British Industry

CISCO - the City Group for Smaller Companies

the City Code - The City Code on Takeovers and Mergers

CJA - Criminal Justice Act 1993

CLERP - the Australian Corporations Law and Economic Reform Programme

the Combined Code - the London Stock Exchange's Principles of Good Governance and Code of Best Practice

CSLRC - Companies and Securities Law Committee (Australia)

the Cohen Committee - the Committee on Company Law Amendment, chaired by Mr Justice Cohen

the Cohen Report - the Report of the Committee on Company Law Amendment, chaired by Mr Justice Cohen (1945) Cmd 6659

the Davey Committee - Report of the Departmental Committee to enquire what amendments are necessary in the acts relating to joint stock companies incorporated with limited liability under the Companies Acts, 1862-1890, chaired of Lord Davey (1895)

the Dickerson Report - Proposals for a New Business Corporations Law for Canada (1971)

D&O insurance - Directors and officers liability insurance

Draft Civil Proceedings Rules - Access to Justice, Draft Civil Proceedings Rules (July 1996)

DTI - the Department of Trade and Industry

the DTI's Consultative Paper - Modern Company Law for a Competitive Economy (March 1998)

the DTI's company law review - the DTI's review of company law launched in March 1998

EGM - extraordinary general meeting

ESRC Centre for Business Research - Economic and Social Research Council, Centre for Business Research at the University of Cambridge

FRS - Financial Reporting Standard

FTSE 100 & 350 - the FTSE International compiled indices of, respectively, the top 100 and 350 companies, by market capitalisation, quoted on the London Stock Exchange. FTSE International is jointly owned by the Financial Times and the Stock Exchange

Greene Committee - the Company Law Amendment Committee 1925/26, chaired by Sir Wilfred Greene

the Greenbury Committee - the study Group on Directors' Remuneration, chaired by Sir Richard Greenbury

the Greenbury Report - Directors' Remuneration: the Report of a study Group, chaired by Sir Richard Greenbury (July 1995)

the Hampel Committee - the Second Committee on the Financial Aspects of Corporate Governance, chaired by Sir Ronald Hampel

the Hampel Report - Final Report of the Committee on Corporate Governance, chaired by Sir Ronald Hampel (January 1998)

the Hong Kong Consultancy Report - The Review of the Hong Kong Companies Ordinance - Consultancy Report (March 1997)

the Jenkins Committee - the Company Law Committee, chaired by Lord Jenkins

the Jenkins Report - the Report of the Company Law Committee, chaired by Lord Jenkins (1962) Cmnd 1749

the King Committee - Committee set up by the Institute of Directors in Southern Africa under the chairmanship of Mervyn E King SC to consider various areas of corporate governance

the King Report - the King Report on Corporate Governance (29 November 1994)

the Listing Rules - the Listing Rules for the official list of the London Stock Exchange

the Model Code - a code of dealing for transactions in securities by directors, certain employees and connected persons, which appears in an appendix to chapter 16 of the Listing Rules

OECD - the Organisation of Economic Co-operation and Development

PIRC - Pensions and Investment Research Consultants Ltd

plc - public limited company

the Registrar - the registrar performing the duty of registering companies under the Companies Act 1985 in England and Wales or Scotland

SAS - Statement of Accounting Standards

Table A - Companies Act 1985, Table A (SI 1985/805, Schedule)

Woolf Interim Report - *Access to Justice, Interim Report to the Lord Chancellor on the Civil Justice System in England and Wales* (June 1995)

Woolf Report - *Access to Justice, The Final Report to the Lord Chancellor on the Civil Justice System in England and Wales* (July 1996)

PART 1
INTRODUCTION

THE DTI'S REVIEW OF COMPANY LAW

1.1 In March 1998 the Department of Trade and Industry ("DTI") launched a wide-ranging review of company law ("the DTI's company law review") and issued a consultation document entitled *Modern Company Law for a Competitive Economy* ("the DTI's Consultative Paper"). This states that the DTI's objectives in undertaking this review include the promotion of "a framework for the formation and constitution of British businesses which, through an effective combination of the law and non-statutory regulation: ... provides straightforward, cost-effective and fair regulation which balances the interests of businesses with those of shareholders, creditors and others ... [and] promotes consistency, predictability and transparency and underpins high standards of company behaviour and corporate governance".[1] The consultation document refers to the fact that the Law Commissions were currently examining whether the duties of directors should be put into the Companies Acts so that they should be more widely known and understood. That examination forms part of the current project and is one of the issues with which this consultation paper deals.

TERMS OF REFERENCE

1.2 The role of the Law Commissions, which are independent statutory bodies established by the Law Commissions Act 1965, is to keep under review the law with which they are respectively concerned with a view to its systematic development and reform.[2] This includes the simplification and modernisation of the law. This project constitutes the Law Commission's second full law reform project in core company law. This project is the Scottish Law Commission's first in core company law although it was consulted on and contributed to the Law Commission's first project in this field.[3]

1.3 The terms of reference for this project are as follows:

- to review Part X of the Companies Act 1985 with a view to considering how the provisions can be simplified and modernised

- to consider the case for a statutory statement of the duties owed by directors to their company under the general law, including their fiduciary duties and their duty of care

- to review additional provisions of the Companies Acts which the Commissions consider should be reviewed at the same time as part of the above work

---

[1] Paragraph 5.1.

[2] Law Commissions Act 1965, s 3(1). The Law Commission is concerned with the law of England and Wales and the Scottish Law Commission is concerned with the law of Scotland.

[3] The first was Shareholder Remedies (1997) Law Com No 246.

and to make recommendations.

1.4 We deal with the two main parts of this project, namely the review of Part X and the consideration of the case for a statutory statement of directors' duties, in sections A and B respectively.[4] In section C we deal with a number of miscellaneous matters.

CONTENTS OF THIS PART

1.5 In this part we deal with a number of preliminary matters relating to the project. Together with Part 2 (Guiding principles for reform) and Part 3 (Economic considerations) it sets out the background to the project and the underlying issues and principles which have guided our approach to it.

1.6 We begin by explaining the reasons for the project, and the legislative history of Part X. Next we set out the methodology we have adopted in reviewing Part X. We then set out what we regard as the central general questions to which we are seeking answers in this consultation paper, and explain the approach to company law reform which we have adopted. This is followed by an outline of the DTI's own work in the field of company law reform in recent years. Next we examine the role of self-regulation in modern company law, give a brief overview of the various sources of rules in this context, and give an explanation of the legal consequences of a breach of these rules. Linked to this is the question of accounting standards which we also consider briefly. We then give a brief overview of the typology of companies incorporated in the United Kingdom, and the framework of regulation of directors. Finally, we mention a number of other matters (territorial scope of the project, the influence of European Community law, and the areas which we regard as outside the project) before setting out in more detail the structure of the consultation paper.

REASONS FOR THIS PROJECT

1.7 In broad outline Part X of the Companies Act 1985 contains a variety of provisions[5] designed to deal with situations in which a director has a conflict of

---

[4] We have also included in Section A consideration of Sched 6, Pt II and Sched 13 to the Companies Act 1985. Note that, unless stated otherwise, section references throughout this paper are to the Companies Act 1985.

[5] The provisions in Part X include a prohibition on paying remuneration to directors tax-free (s 311); various prohibitions on making undisclosed side-payments to directors when they leave office (ss 312-316); a provision which makes it obligatory for directors to disclose certain interests to their board (s 317); provisions for making directors' service contracts open for inspection by members (s 318); restrictions on transactions which a company can enter into with a director or a person connected to him (ss 320-322); a provision imposing liability on directors who cause their company to breach the terms of its constitution by entering into a transaction with him or a person connected with him (s 322A); an obligation on sole member companies to record contracts with the member when he was also a director (s 322B) a prohibition on directors dealing in options in the company's shares (s 323); an obligation on the director to keep the company informed of interests in shares and on the company to keep a register of those interests and if the company is listed to notify them to the Stock Exchange (ss 324-329); extensive restrictions on the loans and other financial transactions that a company can enter which benefit a director or in some cases a person who is connected with him (ss 330-342).

interest. It covers an important and sensitive area namely the statutory rules which regulate dealings by directors which affect their company. It is widely perceived as being extremely detailed, fragmented, excessive, and in some respects defective, regulation of directors, and many criticisms have been made of its provisions to the DTI by directors and other users of company law. In those circumstances the DTI requested the Law Commissions to examine the area in detail to see if the provisions could be reformed, made more simple or dispensed with altogether. As respects the second half of the project, consideration of the case for a statutory statement of the duties of directors, this has been attempted on several previous occasions and it seemed that the matter ought to be canvassed fully and publicly. The two main parts of the project are linked since increased awareness, and accessibility of directors' duties under the general law, may enable Parliament to dispense with some of the detailed provisions of Part X.

1.8   Part X raises, within a short compass, many of the issues affecting the reform of core company law as a whole. In particular it raises the issue of *efficiency*, that is the extent to which the current rules are the most effective way of regulating the key relationship in a company between the directors and their shareholders; the issue of potential *over-regulation*, that is whether legislation of this complexity is the only option; or whether there should be *self-regulation* in certain areas; the issue of *legislative drafting*, that is whether statutory material can usefully be rewritten in a more understandable way; the issue of *codification*, viz whether important areas of general law should be codified; the issue of non-statutory guidance, viz whether users of companies should be given *authoritative*[6] *non-statutory guidance* as to the law; the issue of *decriminalisation*, that is whether the criminal sanctions in Part X should be removed; the *future handling* issue, that is how policy on company law reform should be arrived at in future;[7] the effect of *EC harmonisation* on the Companies Acts and so on.

LEGISLATIVE HISTORY OF PART X

1.9   Part X is relatively recent in origin. Much of the Companies Act 1985 is derived from provisions first enacted in 1900 or earlier. Part X of the Companies Act 1985 is an exception. As can be seen from the Table of Derivations in Appendix C these provisions only go back to the Companies Act 1928, and many of them come from the Companies Act 1980. The provisions then enacted for the first time and now forming part of Part X are sections 319-322 and 329-347, other than section 330(1) which is derived from section 190 of the Companies Act 1947. The reason for many of the legislative changes in 1980 was the large number of financial scandals that had then recently occurred which led to inspections by inspectors appointed under the Companies Act by the DTI. In many cases the reports were published and so these events were made public. Many of the provisions of Part X represented a hasty legislative response to these

---

[6]   This consultation paper refers to the draft statement of duties suggested below (see paras 14.32-14.40) as "authoritative" because it would be propounded by the DTI, and not by a private body. The statement would not, however, have legal force.

[7]   Discussion of this issue is, however, beyond the scope of this project.

events. One example of the findings of inspectors' reports is given in the next paragraph.

1.10   The inquiry into the affairs of Peachey Property Corporation Limited was triggered as a result of concern about certain financial irregularities in relation to the company by the late Sir Eric Miller, Chairman and Managing Director. Examples of transactions that were considered by the inspectors[8] included the purchase of an emerald and diamond necklace for £42,000 at the company's expense. Sir Eric described this as an investment. It was subsequently sold and the proceeds used to reduce Sir Eric's personal overdraft. He told a series of lies and sent a misleading letter to conceal this. There are many other examples of what the report terms "very grave acts of wrongdoing."[9] The term "professional fees" was used to conceal a loan to pay another person's income tax bill. A number of other large scale transactions were entered into which were clearly not to the company's benefit. A yacht was hired to entertain business friends and undertake family holidays. Furthermore a company helicopter was used for private use. The Company had an account with a London hotel, the purpose of which seemed to be to extract money for the chairman's own use. Purely personal items such as entertaining and domestic bills were paid for by the company.[10] He entertained lavishly and gave gifts at company expense.

METHODOLOGY ADOPTED IN REVIEWING PART X

1.11   Having regard to the piecemeal way in which Part X has been enacted, we consider that the primary objects of this review must be:

- to examine all the provisions in detail;

- to investigate whether there were any deficiencies in the detailed wording of the provisions;

- to consider whether there is any duplication of regulation;

- to consider ways in which the substance of the provisions can be simplified;

- to consider whether the language can be made clearer and simpler;

- to consider the provisions of Part X in conjunction with the Stock Exchange Listing Rules, accounting standards and voluntary codes; and

- generally to consider whether the restrictions imposed by Part X fairly balance the interests of directors on the one hand and those of shareholders on the other.

---

[8]   Raymond Kidwell QC and Stanley Samwell FCA. See *Peachey Property Corporation Limited, investigation under s 165(6) of the Companies Act 1948*, HMSO, 11 December 1978.

[9]   Paragraph 167.

[10]   Indeed section 13 in the report is headed "His Private Bank".

1.12 To achieve these objects, we have in Parts 4-8 proceeded by first setting out the relevant section (or group of sections) and then reviewing it.[11] This enables the reader to review the precise text at the same time. The rules in Part X vary in their gravity. In some cases a criminal sanction is imposed.[12] In other cases there is a potential consequence of voidability if a statutory rule which requires disclosure/approval of a transaction is infringed. Different regulatory mechanisms have been used.[13] In no case is there a need on the face of Part X to justify the wisdom of the transaction. Likewise the wisdom of the transaction is not made a defence. That question is left to the normal processes within the company. Part X is concerned with what is done and the way in which it is done rather than with the merit of what is proposed.

CENTRAL GENERAL QUESTIONS

1.13 In this paper, we shall be asking consultees many detailed questions. But in reading the paper and in considering those questions, it is important that consultees have in mind, and do not lose sight of, the central *general* questions that underpin this work. The seven general questions are:

(1) **Should detailed substantive amendments be made to Part X?**

(2) **Should large parts of Part X be repealed (for example, because they duplicate areas covered by the general law)?**

(3) **Should Part X be disapplied where appropriate self-regulatory rules exist?**

(4) **Should Part X be rewritten in simple language?**

(5) **Should Part X be decriminalised?**

(6) **Should directors' duties under the general law be codified? (This involves deciding on the standard of the duty of care).**

(7) **Should there be a non-binding but authoritative statement of directors' duties under the general law?**

APPROACH TO COMPANY LAW REFORM

1.14 In view of the DTI's wider review of company law, it is right that we articulate for consultees' consideration and views the approach to company law reform on which this consultation paper proceeds. We do this in detail in Part 2 (Guiding Principles for Reform). At this point we would emphasise two points. First, we

---

[11] The statutory material is included in the form now in force. Brackets are used to indicate repeals or amendments made since the Companies Act 1985. References to the amending or repealing provision are not included but can be found in *Butterworths Company Law Handbook*, (11th ed, 1997).

[12] Sections 314(3), 317(7), 318(8), 322B(4), 323(2), 324(7), 326(2)(3)(4) and (5), 328(6), 329(3), 342(1), 342(2), 342(3) and 343(8).

[13] See para 3.32 below.

recognise that directors bear heavy responsibilities to investors, employees, customers and the community. They have many considerations in mind in making their decisions: for instance, they must assess the benefits to the company, form a view as to the changing market and competitive environment, deploy the company's resources to best advantage, make cost savings, watch for business opportunities, see that creditors are paid, supervise organisational change, institute research, maintain good relations with employees, suppliers, lenders, shareholders, governments, regulators and the community and ensure proper financial controls. Directors must also often make up their minds quickly. With all these demands on them, the law regulating their relationship to the company must, as well as being principled and appropriate,[14] be as accessible and as clear as possible and in general the minimum necessary to safeguard stakeholders' legitimate interests. Unclear law creates unnecessary costs and inhibits decision-making and thus competitiveness. Unnecessary litigation over points of company law is not now, and should not be permitted to become, part of the commercial process in the United Kingdom.[15]

1.15 Second, we recognise that company law is not simply the preserve of legal practitioners and academics. It is a functional area of law: it must facilitate commercial activity and enable, or at least not prevent, the delivery of benefits to all the company's stakeholders.[16] Effective company law reform must have that vision. With this in mind, we hope very much that the response to this consultation paper will come not simply from the legal community but also from others. We therefore particularly need assistance from directors and stakeholders. We would encourage them to tell us where they disagree with what this document says. We propose that, unless consultees inform us to the contrary, their responses should be available to the DTI so that they can be taken into account in the course of the DTI's wider review. Consultees' responses to this paper will in that way also contribute to the wider review. Moreover, to enable us to see how the area of company law with which this project is concerned impacts on directors

[14] Appropriate law in this context must draw a balance. It must reflect the responsibilities which directors are expected to discharge to the company and other constituencies, but not prevent them from managing the company's business so that it performs well, taking account of the demands placed on directors by commercial life.

[15] There are a number of reasons why this is so, including the general absence in fact of contingency fees, the costs shifting rules, the sheer expense of litigation and the lack of juries in civil trials. Moreover the courts in general seek to stop tactical litigation: see for example *R v Takeover Panel, ex p Datafin Plc* [1987] 1 QB 815 (CA) and also the restrictions placed by the courts on the remedies of unfair prejudice and derivative actions described in Shareholder Remedies (1997) Law Com No 246, paras 3.5-3.7 and 6.1-6.4, and Appendix D, and our recommendations in that report would retain that approach. We are not saying that tactical litigation does not occur but rather that it is not as prevalent a feature of commercial life in this country as it is in some other jurisdictions and should not be permitted to become more prevalent. We do not wish to suggest that a party should be criticised for enforcing a right that he has for commercial advantage, or that judicial scrutiny does not serve a valuable process; our comments are directed to what is in reality speculative litigation designed to bring a negotiating advantage.

[16] We use the term stakeholder to describe all those with whom a company has some form of relationship. The term includes shareholders, employees, customers, suppliers, lenders, creditors and the community.

and companies in practice, we have commissioned the economic research which is set out in Part 3, and supported the empirical survey described in Part 16 below.

DEPARTMENTAL REVIEW OF COMPANY LAW 1991-98

1.16 Some work has already been done on the area covered by this project. In recent years the DTI has reviewed selected areas of company law. Relevant projects have been as follows.

(a) DTI's consultative document on the Companies Act 1985, Schedule 6 (October 1991)

1.17 In October 1991 the DTI published a consultative document *Amendments to Schedule 6 to the Companies Act 1985: Disclosure by Companies of Dealings in Favour of Directors*. The document contained proposals to simplify the rules in Schedule 6, Parts II and III, regarding the information which must be disclosed in company accounts about loans to directors and connected persons and other arrangements in which directors have an interest.[17] Draft regulations amending the Schedule were annexed to the proposals. Action was not however taken to implement the proposals in advance of a wider review of Part X of the Companies Act 1985.

(b) DTI Working Party 1993-95 on directors' duties

1.18 In 1993 a working party was set up by the DTI to examine how best to clarify the duties of company directors and to simplify the provisions of Part X of the Companies Act 1985. The members of the working party included business representatives, academics and legal and accounting practitioners. The working party had several meetings but in the event no proposals were published.

(c) The Law Commission's feasibility study on private companies (November 1994)

1.19 The DTI invited the Law Commission, in consultation with the Scottish Law Commission, to carry out a three month feasibility study into the reform of the law applicable to private companies in the context of the needs of small business. This was published by the DTI in 1994.[18] Although this was not primarily concerned with directors' responsibilities, it was noted that the majority of respondents to one study had supported a proposal to clarify directors' responsibilities.[19]

(d) DTI's consultative document on disclosure of directors' shareholdings (August 1996)

1.20 In August 1996 the DTI published a consultative document *Disclosure of Directors Shareholdings*, which contained detailed proposals for an Order under the Deregulation and Contracting Out Act 1994. The aim of the proposals was to

---

[17] The provisions regulating the matters form part of Part X.

[18] Company Law Review: The Law Applicable to Private Companies. A consultative document (November 1994). URN 94/529.

[19] *Ibid*, para 5.42.

7

reduce the burden imposed by current disclosure requirements relating to directors' interests in their company's shares and debentures, but without introducing scope for abuse.

ROLE OF SELF-REGULATION IN MODERN COMPANY LAW

1.21   We referred in paragraph 1.8 above to the role of self-regulation. Company law is not simply the provisions of the Companies Act, nor even the provisions of the Companies Act as supplemented by the large volume of delegated legislation that supplements it. It also consists of various rules, codes and statements of principle which are binding either because they are generally accepted in that part of the business community to which they apply or because they have some authoritative source other than Parliament.[20] This project demonstrates that a significant interdependency now exists between voluntary codes and formal law but this in turn raises questions as to the way in which they should work together.

1.22   So far as relevant these rules include:

- the listing rules of the Stock Exchange

- the rules of the Alternative Investment Market.

The Alternative Investment Market ("AIM") was established by the Stock Exchange in 1995 and it provides a market place for dealings in the securities of smaller companies than are listed on the Stock Exchange and with lower costs and requirements.

1.23   The relevant codes are the Cadbury, Greenbury and Hampel codes, now replaced by the Stock Exchange's Combined Code and the City Code on Takeovers and Mergers. We describe the status of these Codes below. There is a high level of compliance with the City Code, and according to the Hampel report,[21] for the most part larger listed companies have implemented the codes on corporate governance fully.[22]

The Stock Exchange's Listing Rules

1.24   The Stock Exchange has responsibility for admitting to listing securities that are covered by Part IV of the Financial Services Act. It also admits to listing, on a non-statutory basis, securities to which Part IV does not apply, principally gilt-edged securities. To that end it makes rules governing admission to listing ("the Listing Rules"),[23] the continuing obligations of issuers, the enforcement of those obligations[24] and suspension and cancellation of listing. They reflect requirements

---

[20]   See Arden, "The Changing Face of Company Law" (1995) 10 BJIB & FL 210.

[21]   Final Report of the Committee on Corporate Governance, chaired by Sir Ronald Hampel (28 January 1998); see paras 1.32-1.33 below.

[22]   Hampel Report, para 1.10.

[23]   For example the Listing Rules lay down, *inter alia*, requirements relating to incorporation, accounts, nature and duration of business activities, directors, and working capital.

[24]   See para 1.25 below.

that are mandatory under European Community Directives,[25] additional requirements of the Exchange under its powers as competent authority in relation to securities covered by Part IV of the Financial Services Act and corresponding requirements in relation to other securities admitted to listing.

1.25 The Stock Exchange may refuse an application for listing. Where an issuer contravenes the Listing Rules, the Stock Exchange[26] may censure it or suspend or cancel the listing, in whole or part, of the issuer's securities. Moreover where any contravention of the Listing Rules is due to a failure of all or any of the issuer's directors to discharge their responsibilities it may censure the relevant director. In the case of wilful or persistent failure of a director following censure, the rules provide that it may be stated publicly that in its opinion the director's continued retention of office is prejudicial to investors.[27] Where the director remains in office following such a statement it may suspend or cancel the listing of the issuer's securities.[28]

The Stock Exchange's Model Code for transactions in securities by directors, certain employees and connected persons

1.26 The Model Code, which appears in an appendix to Chapter 16 of the Listing Rules ("the Model Code"), sets out a code of dealing that restricts the freedom of directors and certain employees of issuers from dealing in their company's securities. Under Rule 16.18 of the Listing Rules a company is required to ensure that its directors and relevant employees comply with a code of dealing no less exacting than the Model Code, taking all proper and reasonable steps to secure compliance.

1.27 If a company fails to secure the compliance of its directors and employees with a dealing code no less exacting than the Model Code, it will be subject to sanctions for breach of Rule 16.18 of the Listing Rules. If contravention of the Rule is due to the failure of directors to "discharge their responsibilities under the Listing Rules", they too will be subject to penalties. The sanctions for the breach of Rule 16.18 are the same as those for all other Listing Rules breaches.[29]

---

[25] Such as the Admissions Directive (Council Directive 79/279/EEC co-ordinating the conditions for the admission of securities to official stock exchange listing).

[26] Rule 1.10. Technically the Quotations Committee is the principal actor save where the issuer or director concerned agrees to a private censure by the Stock Exchange and the Stock Exchange considers that to be the appropriate sanction.

[27] Rule 1.10.

[28] In addition to the sanctions described in this paragraph, the Government has stated that legislation is being prepared which will give the Stock Exchange the power to fine issuers and directors for breach of the Listing Rules; see Written Answer *Hansard* (HC), 6 May 1998, vol 311, cols 383-384; and Financial Services and Markets Bill: A Consultation Document (July 1998), para 13.4. See also paras 5.32 n 39 and 10.34 nn 65 and 67 below.

[29] See para 1.25 above.

The Rules of the Alternative Investment Market (AIM)

1.28   Issuers on AIM and their directors[30] are required to comply with the AIM rules. Issuers are also required to take steps to ensure that their directors' comply with a code of dealing no less exacting than its Model Code.[31] Both the rules and AIM's Code regulate transactions involving directors. The provisions are similar to or the same as those of the Listing Rules.[32] However the AIM rules are less demanding than those of the Official List.[33]

1.29   As part of its regulatory function in relation to AIM, the Stock Exchange deals with breaches of the AIM rules.[34] If the Stock Exchange decides that dealings in securities are affecting the integrity or reputation of the market, are being conducted in a "disorderly manner" or threaten investors, it may suspend or discontinue the admission of those securities to trading.[35] It also has the authority to levy fines against issuers in certain circumstances.[36] If the Stock Exchange considers that a breach of the AIM Rules is the fault of a director, it may exercise the same sanctions as those available under the Listing Rules.[37]

Cadbury Report

1.30   The Committee on the Financial Aspects of Corporate Governance (known after its chairman, Sir Adrian Cadbury, as "the Cadbury Committee") was formed in May 1991 by the Financial Reporting Council, the Stock Exchange and the accountancy profession.[38] Its final report ("the Cadbury Report"), incorporating a Code of Best Practice for all listed companies ("the Cadbury Code of Best Practice"), was published on 1 December 1992. Recommendations of the Cadbury Committee were underpinned by a disclosure requirement to the Listing Rules.

---

[30]   Who can be personally censured for breach of AIM rules. See Rule 16.36(a).

[31]   See Rule 16.9(b). The Model Code for AIM Companies is set out in Appendix 12 of the AIM Rules.

[32]   Compare, for example, paragraphs 2 to 21 of the Model Code in the Stock Exchange's Listing Rules with paragraphs A 12.2 to A12.20 of the Model Code for AIM Companies.

[33]   See Rule 16.11(c).

[34]   Decisions of the exchange can be appealed to the AIM Appeals Committee.

[35]   See r 16.35.

[36]   For breaches of r 16.32 (see r 16.36).

[37]   See r 16.37 of the AIM Rules and r 1.10 of the Stock Exchange Listing Rules.

[38]   Considerable interest in corporate governance has since developed in many parts of the world. For example, in November 1994, South Africa's King Committee published a report and recommendations on the financial aspects of corporate governance. The report contained a Code of Corporate Practices & Conduct intended to apply to all companies listed on the Johannesburg Stock Exchange's main board as well as large public entities, banks, financial and insurance bodies and large unlisted public companies (The King Report on Corporate Governance, November 1994). More recently an advisory group established by the Organisation of Economic Co-operation and Development (OECD) has recommended that the OECD should draw up a code of corporate governance: see Public Law for Companies (1998) vol IX , May 1998, pp 10-11.

Greenbury Report

1.31　The Study Group on Directors' Remuneration, chaired by Sir Richard Greenbury ("the Greenbury Committee"), was formed on the initiative of the Confederation of British Industry ("CBI") in January 1995 in response to widespread concern about the level of directors' remuneration, in particular following the privatisation of a series of public utility companies.[39] Its terms of reference were to identify good practice in determining directors' remuneration and prepare a code of such practice for use by UK plc's. Its report ("the Greenbury Report") was published on 17 July 1995.

Hampel Report

1.32　The Committee on Corporate Governance, known as "the Hampel Committee" after its chairman, Sir Ronald Hampel, was established in November 1995 on the initiative of the Chairman of the Financial Reporting Council. It produced a preliminary report in August 1997 and a final report ("the Hampel Report") in January 1998. Its sponsors were the Stock Exchange, the CBI, the Institute of Directors, the Consultative Committee of Accountancy Bodies, the National Association of Pension Funds and the Association of British Insurers. Its remit extended only to listed companies. The Committee was inter alia to keep under review the role of directors, executive and non-executive, recognising the need for board cohesion and the common legal responsibilities of all directors and to address as necessary the role of shareholders in corporate governance issues.

1.33　The Committee's final report stated that the Committee intended to produce a set of principles and code embracing its work and that of the Cadbury and Greenbury Committees and that compliance with this code would be underpinned by the Listing Rules. The objective of the new principles and code would be to secure sufficient disclosure so that investors and others could assess companies' performance and governance practice and respond in an informed way.[40] In January 1998, the Hampel Committee delivered its code to the Stock Exchange.

The Stock Exchange's Combined Code of Corporate Governance

1.34　Following publication of the Hampel Report, a consolidated Code for corporate governance, combining the Cadbury and Greenbury Codes with the recommendations of the Hampel Committee, was adopted by the Stock Exchange (the "Combined Code"). The Combined Code is appended to but does not form part of the Listing Rules. The Code is also published by the Exchange as a free standing document.

1.35　Paragraphs (a) and (b) of Rule 12.43A of the Listing Rules require companies to make a statement in their annual report and accounts in relation to their compliance with the Combined Code. The Listing Rules also require some

---

[39]　As noted in the comment at para 1.7 of the Hampel Report.

[40]　Hampel Report, para 1.25.

aspects of this compliance statement to be reviewed by the auditors.[41] This statement must explain how the company has applied the principles in the Code,[42] and give an explanation of why it has failed to comply with any of its provisions during any part of the relevant accounting period.[43]

The City Code on Takeovers and Mergers

1.36   The City Code on Takeovers and Mergers ("the City Code") is issued by the Panel on Takeovers and Mergers. The Panel is an unincorporated association without legal personality. In a case which establishes that the circumstances in which decisions of the Panel may be reviewed by the Court are restricted, Sir John Donaldson MR described the panel as a "truly remarkable body - both literally and metaphorically it oversees and regulates a very important part of the United Kingdom financial market."[44] The Code[45] and the panel operate principally to ensure fair and equal treatment of all shareholders in relation to takeovers. The Code also provides an orderly framework within which takeovers are conducted.[46]

1.37   The City Code is based upon a number of general principles[47] and also contains a number of more detailed rules. The Code has not, and does not seek to have, the force of law. However, as was noted by the Court of Appeal in *R v Takeover Panel, Ex p Datafin Plc*,[48] although lacking any authority de jure it exercises immense power de facto by way of sanction, principally through the withholding of the facilities of the markets. If a person, authorised by the Financial Services Authority, certain relevant self-regulating associations and certain professional bodies recognised under the Financial Services Act 1986, fails to comply with the Code or a ruling of the Panel, its regulator may in certain circumstances, take disciplinary or other action against it, including withdrawal of its authorisation.[49]

---

[41]   Rule 12.43A, final paragraph; but see now *Auditors' Responsibility Statements* and *Auditors' Reports on Corporate Governance* issued by the Auditing Practices Board (June 1998) which proposes a comprehensive auditors' responsibility statement to be included in annual accounts, and removal from the Listing Rules of the requirement for auditors to review compliance with certain aspects of the Combined Code.

[42]   Rule 12.43A(a). The Principles are contained in Part 1 of the Combined Code.

[43]   Rule 12.43A(b). The Provisions are set out in Part 2 of the Combined Code. Although the Combined Code and new r 12.43A were published on 25 June 1998, the compliance disclosure requirements in 12.43A(a) and (b) will first come into effect in relation to annual reports and accounts published in respect of accounting periods ending on or after 31 December 1998.

[44]   *R v Takeover Panel, Ex p Datafin Plc* [1987] QB 815, 824. In general the court will only intervene in decisions of the Panel by making declaratory orders in retrospect, thereby allowing contemporary decisions to stand.

[45]   The current edition of the City Code was updated on 23 July 1998.

[46]   The Introduction to the City Code provides fuller details on its nature, membership, procedure and enforcement.

[47]   Such as the principle that all shareholders of the same class must be treated equally (General Principle 1) and the principle that shareholders must be given sufficient information and advice to enable them to reach a properly informed decision (General Principle 4).

[48]   [1987] QB 815.

[49]   See para 1(c) of the Introduction to the City Code, Appendix M below.

Legal consequences of a breach of the self-regulatory rules

1.38 Non-compliance by a company or one of its directors with a self-regulatory rule cannot of itself result in the commission of a criminal offence or give rise to an action for damages or other relief under the general law. The question arises whether there are any situations arising in company law in which the court will grant relief on the basis that the matter of which complaint is made is a breach by a director of a self-regulatory rule, or alternatively whether there are circumstances in which the court will attach weight to that factor.[50]

1.39 Non-compliance with a voluntary code or self-regulatory rule may, in future, be a matter to which the court has regard when deciding whether a director is unfit to be a director or ought to be disqualified under the provisions of the Company Directors (Disqualification) Act 1986 but, so far as we are aware, there is no decided case in which this question has arisen thus far.

1.40 There appears to be a conflict of authorities on the question whether non-compliance with a self-regulatory rule can be unfair prejudice for the purposes of section 459 of the Companies Act 1985. Under that section a shareholder can apply to the court for relief (of any kind) where the company acts in a manner which is unfairly prejudicial. The courts have given guidance on what constitutes unfairly prejudicial conduct for this purpose. Thus in *Re Saul D Harrison plc*[51] the Court of Appeal held that in general a legal wrong, for example a breach of duty by a director, must be shown, though there is a category of cases where it is sufficient for the applicant to show that he has a legitimate expectation that the affairs of the company will be conducted in a particular way. The question is whether this guidance excludes the possibility of unfair prejudice where a company breaches a voluntary code. In *Re Astec(BSR) plc*,[52] where it was held that in a public company no question of legitimate expectations could arise and moreover that the exercise by a majority shareholder of its legal rights contrary to the Cadbury Code of Best Practice was not capable of giving rise to a claim for unfair prejudice, even though investors expect companies to comply with voluntary codes on corporate governance, Jonathan Parker J said:

> So far as corporate governance is concerned, members of the public buying shares in a listed company may well expect that all relevant rules and codes of best practice will be complied with in relation to the company. But that expectation cannot, in my judgment, give rise to an equitable constraint on the exercise of legal rights conferred by the Company's constitution (of which the Listing Rules, the City Code and the Cadbury Code form no part) so as to found a petition under s 459. It is in essence little more than an expectation that the company's affairs will not be conducted in a manner which is unfairly prejudicial to the interests of the members generally, or some part of

---

[50] It is outside the scope of this project to consider whether there ought to be some statutory underpinning for voluntary codes of conduct but this may be a matter which is considered in the course of the DTI's wider review of company law.

[51] [1995] 1 BCLC 14.

[52] (Unreported) 7 May 1998, Jonathan Parker J.

its members, an expectation which one would expect to be present in virtually every case.

1.41 These views may be contrasted with what was said in *Re BSB Holdings Ltd (No 2) Ltd*[53] in which the court said:

> ... in my judgment, it is not the effect of *Re Saul D Harrison & Sons plc* that a remedy under s 459 can be given only if the directors have acted in breach of duty or if the company has breached the terms of its articles or some other relevant agreement. These matters constitute in most cases the basis for deciding what conduct is unfair. But the words of the section are wide and general and, save where the circumstances are governed by the judgments in *Re Saul D Harrison & Sons plc*, the categories of unfair prejudice are not closed. The standards of corporate behaviour recognised through s 459 may in an appropriate case thus not be limited to those imposed by enactment or existing case law.

1.42 On this basis it would follow that in certain circumstances a breach of a voluntary code is capable of constituting by itself conduct which was unfairly prejudicial to the interests of a complaining shareholder, even in a public company. On that basis the courts could give some legal underpinning to the voluntary codes.

1.43 It is however clear that the codes can at the very least constitute benchmarks by which the courts can determine whether conduct is unfairly prejudicial. Thus in *Re Macro (Ipswich) Ltd*[54] the question was whether a majority shareholder in a private company and director could properly appoint an employee as his sole co-director. The court held:

> Given the presence of minority interests, the absence of an independent director would in my judgment be prejudicial to the position of the plaintiffs as shareholders in the companies. If support were needed for such proposition, it can be found in the recent report of the Committee on the Financial Aspects of Corporate Governance (the Cadbury Committee) published in December 1992. This report, which has been accepted by, inter alia, the Stock Exchange, emphasises that no one individual within a company should have unfettered powers of decision and that, where the chairman is also chief executive, there should be a strong and independent element on the board. While that report is directed to listed companies, the desirability of having a truly independent board is applicable to all cases where there are minority shareholders.[55]

---

[53] [1996] 1 BCLC 155, per Arden J.

[54] [1994] 2 BCLC 354. On appeal, appeal dismissed 22 May 1996 (unreported). This ground was not considered. See also *Re a Company* [1986] BCLC 376, 389 *per* Hoffmann J.

[55] See also *Re Chez Nico (Restaurants) Ltd* [1992] BCLC 192, 209, where Sir Nicolas Browne-Wilkinson VC said:

> The [City] Code does not have the force of law. But in considering for the purposes of s 430C whether the court should exercise its discretion, in my judgment the code is a factor of great importance. One of the purposes of the code is to provide protection to the shareholders whose shares are the subject of a bid.

1.44   In conclusion, while self-regulation has many advantages in that it offers flexibility and the ability to act more speedily than where legislation is required, when it comes to seeking remedies for breaches of self-regulatory rules in a court of law, the civil and criminal remedies available are far less than those available for a breach of a rule of the general law or of some legislative provision.

ACCOUNTING STANDARDS

1.45   The Companies Act 1985 provides for "accounting standards", that is statements of standard accounting practice, to be issued by bodies prescribed by regulations.[56] The Accounting Standards Board has been prescribed for this purpose.[57] Accounting standards do not have the force of law. However, the annual accounts of a company (other than a small or medium-sized company)[58] must state whether the accounts have been prepared in accordance with applicable accounting standards[59] and give particulars of any material departure from those standards and the reasons for the departure.[60] The balance sheet included in the annual accounts must show a true and fair view of the state of affairs of the company as at the end of the financial year and the profit and loss account must show a true and fair view of the profit or loss of the company as at the end of that year.[61] Whether a true and fair view is given is a question of law but the court will take account of the views of the practices and the views of accountants. The fact that a standard has been issued increases the likelihood of the court saying that compliance with the standard is necessary for the purpose of showing a true and fair view. The issue of standards has in itself created an expectation on the part of users that accounts will comply with accounting standards except where there is good reason why they should not do so.[62] In the field of accounting standards there is therefore a measure of underpinning in the Companies Act.

> Where, under the code, the bidder is himself under a duty to provide such information, substantial infringements of the provisions of the code as to disclosure in my judgment provides strong evidence that the offer is not fairly made: it certainly negatives any presumption that the offer is fair because 90% of the shareholders have accepted it: see *Re Lifecare International plc* [1990] BCLC 222. I am not suggesting that any infringement of the code (however small) will necessarily lead the court to exercise its discretion in favour of the non-assenting shareholder. But substantial failure by the bidder to comply with the code's provisions as to disclosure should, in my view, be a very major factor operating against the compulsory acquisition of the non-assenting shareholders' shares.

[56]   Section 256.

[57]   Accounting Standards (Prescribed Body) Regulations 1990, SI 1990 No 1667.

[58]   See para 6.14 below.

[59]   Applicable accounting standards are defined in s 256(2) as standards relevant to the company's circumstances and to the accounts.

[60]   Sched 4, para 36A.

[61]   Section 226(2). This requirement overrides the other requirements of the Act and supplementary information may have to be given or the accounts may have to depart from the relevant provisions of the Act; see ss 226(4) and (5).

[62]   See generally on the true and fair view the joint opinions (1983 and 1984) for the Accounting Standards Committee by Leonard Hoffmann QC (now the Rt Hon Lord Hoffmann) and Mary Arden (now The Hon Mrs Justice Arden DBE) published in

TYPOLOGY OF COMPANIES

1.46 In considering the issues raised by this consultation paper, consultees should bear in mind that there are several different types of company.[63] The vast majority of companies incorporated in Great Britain and Northern Ireland are private companies. As at May 1998 there were 1,201,089 companies on the active register for Great Britain.[64] This includes 66,098 active companies registered in Scotland. There are 11,700 public companies on the register for Great Britain of which 507 are registered in Scotland. As at the same date there were 15,529 companies registered in Northern Ireland of which 51 were public companies. There are 2,136 listed companies on the UK market at the Stock Exchange and 521 on the International market.[65] There are 310 companies in AIM.[66]

1.47 Very many private companies are owner-managed, that is to say they have a small number of shareholders many of whom also participate in the management of the company. In these companies, there are fewer outside factors to impact on the conduct of directors. For instance, the Listing Rules and voluntary codes do not apply. Thus, despite their participation in the business, the shareholders continue to need legal safeguards and effective remedies.[67] But there is a higher level of involvement and informality in owner-managed companies and this has to be taken into account. High standards of corporate behaviour need to be promoted in companies of all types.

1.48 There are no statistics for the number of subsidiary companies.[68] However, it is common knowledge that many companies are members of groups of companies. The law has to take account of this. It means, for instances, that disclosure to shareholders is often unnecessary, and shareholder approval a formality,[69] where one company is a wholly-owned subsidiary of another body corporate, wherever incorporated, and is fully solvent.

Accounting Standards 1984/5 at p 178 by the Institute of Chartered Accountants in England and Wales; the opinion (1983) for the Institute of Chartered Accountants in Scotland by J A D Hope QC (now the Rt Hon Lord Hope), and the opinion (1993) for the Accounting Standards Board by Mary Arden QC published as an appendix to the Foreword to Accounting Standards produced by the Accounting Standards Board (June 1993).

[63] This paper does not deal with a type of company not mentioned in the text, namely the charitable company.

[64] The figures as to numbers of registered companies in Great Britain and Northern Ireland were supplied by Companies House and the DTI.

[65] All Stock Exchange figures are for 30 April 1998.

[66] The total market capitalisation for AIM companies is £6.5bn (as at 30 April 1998).

[67] See, for instance, Shareholder Remedies (1997) Law Com No 246.

[68] However, in R I Tricker, *Corporate Governance* (1984) p 55, it was estimated that the top 50 UK companies had over 10,000 subsidiaries, and other companies in the top 500 UK companies had on average 25 subsidiaries each (excluding dormant companies). This was based on 1981/82 data. (At the end of 1982, there were 807,817 registered companies).

[69] This is recognised already in, eg, Companies Act 1985, s 321(1).

REGULATION OF DIRECTORS

Duties of directors

1.49   Numerous duties are imposed on directors by statute and by the general law. There are no formal qualifications for company directors, though a number of organisations and some employers provide training courses. Reference is made below[70] to the statutory liability for wrongful trading to which directors have been subject since 1985[71] to contribute to the assets of their company in the event of its liquidation if the company continued to trade after they knew or ought to have known that there was no reasonable prospect of its paying its liabilities to creditors. This liability can be imposed on directors by the court on the application of the liquidator unless they took every step which they ought to have taken to minimise the loss to creditors.[72]

Enforcement of directors' duties

1.50   In October 1997 the Law Commission, in consultation with the Scottish Law Commission, published its final report on Shareholder Remedies.[73] It recommended *inter alia* that there should be for England and Wales a new rule of court and for Scotland a new statutory provision which sets out in modern and accessible form the circumstances in which the courts will permit a derivative, or in Scotland a shareholder's, action[74] to be brought. This would facilitate such an action where the cause of action arises out of a breach, or threatened breach, of duty by a director to his company, including negligence. It also recommended that there should be a statutory presumption in unfair prejudice proceedings[75] for smaller companies so as to make the outcome of litigation more certain and help encourage parties to settle claims at an early stage.[76] In the consultation paper the Commission set out six guiding principles[77] which we set out below[78] and which were used in framing the recommendations in the final report.

---

[70]   Eg para 12.9.

[71]   Now the Insolvency Act 1986, s 214.

[72]   Liability is imposed on the basis that the director should take such actions as would be taken by a reasonably diligent person having both the knowledge skill and experience reasonably to be expected of a person in the same position, *and* the director's own general knowledge skill and experience. This prevents a director from relying on his own ignorance, and also means that he will be judged by any special qualifications that he had.

[73]   Shareholder Remedies (1997) Law Com No 246. The DTI's Consultative Paper states: "So far as civil sanctions are concerned the Law Commissions have made a valuable contribution in their recent report on shareholder remedies" (para 6.3).

[74]   That is, by one or more shareholders on behalf of the company. The Lord Chancellor's Department has since issued "Access to Justice - Specialist Jurisdictions: Proposed New Procedures - A Consultation Paper" (December 1997), in which it sought views on the Commission's recommendation for the derivative action and certain other recommendations which can be implemented in conjunction with the new Civil Procedure Rules. These are being introduced as part of the current civil justice reforms.

[75]   Under Companies Act 1985, s 459.

[76]   *Ibid*, at paras 3.26-3.64.

[77]   *Ibid*, at paras 1.9-1.12; see also Shareholder Remedies, Consultation Paper No 142, paras 14.11-14.13.

Disqualification of company directors for unfitness

1.51 Disqualification[79] was first introduced by the Companies Act 1929. After various legislative changes a specific piece of legislation, what is now the Company Directors Disqualification Act 1986, was enacted. The Act requires the court to disqualify a director for a minimum two year period if it makes a finding of "unfitness."[80] It is a question of fact whether a director is unfit, though past decisions of the court may be helpful in identifying particular circumstances in which a director would clearly be unfit.[81] A second important area is that a disqualification order[82] may be made[83] in respect of a person convicted of an offence in connection with the formation, promotion, management or liquidation of a company or with the receivership of the company's property. In the year ended 31 March 1997, 1219 disqualification orders were notified to the Secretary of State.[84]

PART X AND THE LAW RELATING TO DIRECTORS' DUTIES AND ITS APPLICATION TO ENGLAND, WALES AND SCOTLAND

1.52 This project is concerned with Part X of the Companies Act 1985 and with the case for a statutory statement of directors' duties. The Companies Act 1985 applies to England, Wales and Scotland and the questions which we have been asked to consider are not areas in which material differences currently exist between the law of England and Wales and that of Scotland.

NORTHERN IRELAND

1.53 This project is not strictly concerned with the review and reform of Northern Ireland law. However the law of Northern Ireland in this context is for all practical purposes the same as that applying in England, Wales and Scotland. The equivalent of Part X of the Companies Act 1985 is to be found in Part XI of the Companies (Northern Ireland) Order 1986. The Law Reform Advisory Committee for Northern Ireland, which in the field of civil law carries out functions similar to the Law Commissions in England and Wales and Scotland, is taking a close interest in this project and any reform of English law is likely to lead

---

[78] Paragraphs 2.14-2.15.

[79] This subject is considered at length in Mithani & Wheeler, *The Disqualification of Company Directors* (1996).

[80] Section 6; *Re Grayan Building Services Ltd* [1995] Ch 241. The maximum period of disqualification is 15 years.

[81] *Re Sevenoaks Stationers (Retail) Ltd* [1991] Ch 164 at p176. As regards the period of disqualification the Court of Appeal provided guidance and introduced a concept of "banding" depending on the seriousness of the complaint. *Ibid* at 174. There are disqualification periods of over 10 years for the most serious cases, 6 to 10 years for less serious cases, and 2 to 5 years where the case is not very serious.

[82] For a period not exceeding 15 years.

[83] Under s 2(1).

[84] See *Companies in 1996-97*, Department of Trade and Industry, The Stationery Office (October 1997), Table D1. Figures for the year to 31 March 1998 will be published in October of this year.

to equivalent changes in Northern Ireland law which normally closely follows developments in English company law.

EUROPEAN COMMUNITY LAW

1.54 Since 1972 a driving force in amendments in the Companies Acts has been the need to implement directives of the European Community.[85] There are examples of this in sections 322A and 322B in Part X. We have considered whether there is any pending harmonisation measure in the field of company law which might affect the area covered by this project, but we are not aware of any at this stage. The draft fifth directive[86] on company law contains provisions on the structure and liability of the board of directors but this proposal is effectively dormant and there is as we understand it no early prospect of its being moved forward. The Court of the European Communities has recently confirmed that the first EC directive on company law,[87] which restricts the circumstances in which a company can rely on the lack of authority of one of its organs, does not affect national rules as to the effect of transactions authorised by directors having a conflict of interest.[88]

MATTERS OUTSIDE THIS PROJECT

1.55 Certain matters affecting the duties of directors are outside the project though they may be dealt with in the course of the DTI's wider review of company law. They include the question whether directors should owe duties to persons other than the company such as employees and the community,[89] and the question whether the duties should be for other reasons altered. Likewise this project is not concerned with any duties of good citizenship the company may owe to the

---

[85] Company law is one of the few areas of private law to be directly referred to in the Treaty of Rome 1957. The main provisions on company law are to be found in the chapter on freedom of establishment, namely Articles 52, 54 and 58. The principal reference is in Article 54, which empowers Community institutions to harmonise national company laws by means of directives. There are also references to company law in articles 220, 235 and 100a. Some 9 directives have now been adopted. However as European economic integration as progressed, reliance has also been placed on articles 235 and 100a in order to create uniform instruments in the interests of a single (European) single market. Where the purpose of an enactment is to make UK law conform to the requirements of a directive, the provisions of the enactment will be construed, if they can reasonably be construed so to do, in a manner which accords with the directive in question even if that involves a departure from the strict interpretation of the provisions (see *Pickstone v Freemans plc* [1989] AC 66; *Litster v Forth Dry Dock & Engineering Co Ltd* [1990] 1 AC 546).

[86] See OJ C240/2 9 September 1998, as published in *Harmonisation of Company Law in the European Community - Measures Adopted and Proposed - Situation as at 1 March 1992*, Office of the Official Publications of the European Community, ISDN 92-286-4314-X.

[87] 68/151.

[88] *Cooperative Rabobank "Vecht en Plassengebied" B A v Minderhoud* (Case C-104/96) [1998] 1 WLR 1025.

[89] The DTI's Consultative Paper states that this is an issue for the wider review (Consultative Paper, p 10, para 3.7). Readers should be aware that this debate exists. The Law Commissions' view is that the value and significance of this project is not undermined by that debate (important though it is) since it is still important to analyse and clarify the duties owed to the company under the current general law and to consider the means by which that law may be made more accessible. However it means that the precise form of any statement of duties may change.

community[90] or with the question whether companies should support philanthropic or charitable causes. This project assumes that the board is structured on the present UK model and therefore contains no discussion of two-tier boards such as are found in Germany and does not examine the issues of who should be directors. The project does not discuss insider dealing, or review the general law on remedies for breach of duty or examine the amount of directors' remuneration[91] or the law relating to the disqualification of directors or with any special rule applying to charitable companies.

STRUCTURE OF THIS CONSULTATION PAPER

1.56 This consultation document deals with the subject matter of the project in the following manner:

- we start by identifying principles for the reform of the relevant law (Part 2);

- we then include discussion of the economic considerations underlying the relevant law and its reform (Part 3);

- the rest of the paper falls into three parts:

  Section A deals with Part X of the Companies Act 1985-

  Substantive Improvements 1: sections 312-323 (Part 4);

  Substantive Improvements 2: sections 324-329 (Part 5);

  Substantive Improvements 3: sections 330-342 (Part 6);

  Substantive Improvements 4: disclosure requirements (Part 7);

  Substantive Improvements 5: "connected persons" etc (Part 8);

  Further options: repeal and rewriting (Part 9);

  Decriminalising Part X of the Act (Part 10);

  Section B deals with the case for a statutory statement of directors' duties-

  fiduciary duties: the current law (Part 11);

  duty of care: the current law (Part 12);

  previous proposals for a statutory statement of duties (Part 13);

  statement of directors' fiduciary duties: options for reform (Part 14);

---

[90] See eg, Handy, *The Hungry Spirit* (1997) p 179.

[91] The DTI's Consultative Paper states that the wider review will provide an opportunity to examine the responsibilities of shareholders in relation to directors' pay (p 10, para 3.7).

duty of care: options for reform (Part 15);

Section C deals with miscellaneous issues, namely-

the proposed empirical survey (Part 16); and

the different categories of director (Part 17).

1.57   A list of the questions for consultees appears in Part 18.

ACKNOWLEDGEMENTS

1.58   We gratefully acknowledge the assistance we have received from the persons and bodies listed in Appendix O. We would like to express our particular thanks to Professor D D Prentice of the University of Oxford, Richard Nolan of St John's College, Cambridge and Robert Bertram, visiting Professor at Edinburgh and Heriot-Watt Universities, who have acted as our consultants on the project. We should also like to thank Dr Deakin of ESRC Centre for Business Research at the University of Cambridge who carried out the study of the economic considerations applicable to this project which is set out in Part 3 and who is assisting us with the empirical research described in Part 16. We are also grateful to Professor Wooldridge of Notre Dame University in London for permitting us to use the summary of German law which appears in Part 12.

21

PART 2
GUIDING PRINCIPLES FOR REFORM

INTRODUCTION

2.1 In this part we aim to deduce the general principles which should guide the reform of the law in this area and to obtain consultees' views on them. Formulation of these principles involves standing back from the detail and complexity of the provisions of Part X, and the problems which they seek to address, and asking in somewhat abstract terms what policy approach the law should seek to adopt. This in turn requires an understanding of the role of the legal system in regulating directors, and of the contribution which the different organs within the company can make to the successful management of the company's business, and how this is best achieved. We seek consultees' views as to whether we have identified what they see as the right objectives to guide reform in this area.

2.2 This is not an academic exercise. The announcement of the DTI's Company Law Review means that there is both an opportunity to consider the contribution which each part of the Companies Acts makes to the whole and in addition a need to ensure that the policy basis for reform in any given area is properly understood. The reform suggested for any particular area of company law must blend in with the reforms being suggested for company law as a whole. The Law Commissions are placed in the difficult and challenging position of issuing the first consultation paper during the currency of this review. We hope that the exposition of the issues in this paper will assist in stimulating an open debate on the optimal shape of our company law for the foreseeable future.

AIMS OF COMPANY LAW REFORM

DTI's Company Law Review

2.3 We have already referred to this Review in Part 1. The DTI's Consultative Paper describes the Department's objectives in undertaking the review. They are:[1]

> to promote a framework for the formation and constitution of British businesses which through an effective combination of law and non-statutory regulation:

> - supports the creation, growth and competitiveness of British companies and partnerships;

> - promotes an internationally competitive framework for business, so that the UK continues to be an attractive place to do business;

---

[1] DTI's Consultative Paper, para 5.1.

- provides straightforward, cost-effective and fair regulation which balances the interests of business with those of shareholders, creditors and others; and

- promotes consistency, predictability and transparency and underpins high standards of company behaviour and corporate governance.

2.4 The DTI proposes that the terms of reference for the review should include the following:

(1) To consider how far core company law can be modernised in order to provide a simple, efficient and cost-effective framework for carrying out business activity which:

(a) permits the maximum amount of freedom and flexibility to those organising and directing the enterprise;

(b) at the same time protects, through regulation where necessary, the interests of those involved with the enterprise, including shareholders, creditors and employees; and

(c) is drafted in clear, concise and unambiguous language which can be readily understood by those involved in business enterprise.[2]

2.5 The review is to be conducted with openness and independence and on the basis of wide consultation.[3] The final report is to be published in the year 2000.[4] The consultative paper states that the Government also intends to publish a white paper in the year 2000 outlining the Government's proposals for legislation in the light of the outcome of the review.[5]

The Australian Corporations Law and Economic Reform Programme (CLERP)

2.6 In March 1997 the Australian Government announced a sweeping program of company law reform called the Corporations Law and Economic Reform Programme (CLERP) as part of the Government's drive to promote business and economic development. The intention is to provide a much stronger economic focus. The current law is deemed too prescriptive, legalistic and in many respects out of touch with modern commercial practice.[6] There was previously a plan to re-write the Corporations Law in more understandable English. It has been decided that this alone is inadequate to address underlying problems, though a second Corporate Law Simplification Bill will nonetheless be introduced into the Australian Parliament. The Australian Treasury is committed to providing

---

[2] *Ibid*, at para 5.2.

[3] *Ibid*, at para 7.2.

[4] *Ibid*, at para 8.2.

[5] *Ibid*, at para 8.2-8.3.

[6] *Corporate Law Economic Reform Program, A strategy document*, Australian Treasury, March 1997.

substantial resources to statutory agencies to enforce corporate law. As part of CLERP, draft bills were published on 8 April 1998 dealing with capital raising, takeovers, futures and securities, directors' duties, electronic commerce and accounting standards.

Recent Company Law Reform initiatives in Canada, New Zealand and Hong Kong

2.7 There have been a number of company law reform initiatives in the Commonwealth in the past twenty years. Prior to then most company law in the Commonwealth was based on the UK Companies Acts. We mention three of these initiatives.

Canada

2.8 In 1971 the Dickerson Committee published its report, "Proposals for a New Business Corporations Law for Canada" ("the Dickerson Report"). The report contained the draft for a new federal corporations Act that drew on both American and Commonwealth precedent. Following its publication, in 1975 a new federal corporate law statute was implemented that adopted the Dickerson Committee's draft virtually unchanged. Harmonising legislation was subsequently introduced in the majority of Canada's provinces.[7] Extracts from the federal Canadian Business Corporations Act ("CBCA") appear in Appendix J to this paper.

New Zealand

2.9 In 1989, the New Zealand Law Commission published its 9th Report,[8] "Company Law - Reform and Restatement".[9] The report proposed a basic law to govern the creation, operation and termination of all companies and contained a recommended draft Companies Act. The Commission produced a supplementary report in 1990, "Company Law Reform: Transition and Revision",[10] which contained recommendations for a variety of improvements to its 1989 draft Companies Act. The report also contained recommendations for and drafts of transitional and consequential legislation so that comprehensive company law reform could be implemented.[11] Although its revised draft was not based on any

---

[7] The detailed provisions of the different statutes vary, but overall the provincial Acts are drafted in similar terms to the CBCA.

[8] The Commission was established by the Law Commission Act 1985 to promote the systematic review, reform and development of the law of New Zealand. Its remit is also to advise on ways in which the law can be made as understandable and accessible as practicable.

[9] NZLC R9 (June 1989).

[10] NZLC R16 (September 1990).

[11] Recommendations for draft legislation to replace the Companies Act 1955 (the Act having been based on the UK Companies Act 1948) had also appeared in the Commission's 8th Report, "A Personal Property Securities Act for New Zealand" (NZLC R8, April 1989).

24

one overseas model, the Commission acknowledged the assistance it had derived from the (US) Model Business Corporations Act and the Dickerson Report.[12]

2.10   Following the Commission's reports, New Zealand enacted the Companies Act 1993.[13] The Law Commission's draft was used as a basis for the new Act, although significant changes were introduced. Extracts from the Companies Act 1993 appear in Appendix I to this paper.

Hong Kong

2.11   When Hong Kong was a British colony the Companies Ordinance was adopted and it was based upon UK companies legislation. The ordinance continues to apply, but in 1994 the Hong Kong Government initiated a review of the ordinance. In the course of the review a consultancy report was prepared and published recommending widescale changes ("the Hong Kong Consultancy Report"). The Government of Hong Kong has yet to respond to this report. A combination of factors prompted a review of the ordinance. The last review of the Companies Ordinance had been commenced 25 years ago. Concerns were expressed about the redomiciling/overseas domicile phenomenon of listed companies and the Companies Registry had raised a number of practical problems with regard to the enforcement of the ordinance. Also changes to the UK legislation resulting from harmonisation with European Union Company Law Directives raised the issue of the continued suitability of the United Kingdom as a model for Hong Kong Companies law. The recommendations in the report are based on modern companies legislation in the United States, Canada and New Zealand. Extracts from the Hong Kong Consultancy Report appear in Appendix L to this paper.

ROLE OF SHAREHOLDERS AND DIRECTORS IN COMPANIES

2.12   Shareholders are owners of the enterprise: the directors manage it and control day-to-day decision-making.[14] Directors have to have regard to shareholders' interests and to a certain extent[15] to those of third parties. However, directors and shareholders are mutually interdependent. Directors rely on shareholders to maintain their investment in the company and exercise their powers in respect of decision-making reserved to them in a favourable manner. Shareholders rely on directors to manage the enterprise competently, without taking personal benefits, loyally and on the basis that so far as practicable shareholders are kept in the picture about any matter which is relevant to them.

---

[12]   See NZLC R16, p xvii.

[13]   It came into effect on 1 July 1994, although parts of the old legislation remained in force until 1 July 1997.

[14]   This is the starting point. As stated in paras 1.47 and 2.17, in some cases the directors are also owners of the enterprise and the roles of directors and shareholders are then often treated as merged.

[15]   See para 11.28 below.

FUNCTION OF PART X AND DIRECTORS' DUTIES

2.13   The provisions of Part X and (in some respects) the rules relating to directors'
        basic duties under the general law are designed to ensure that directors do not act
        in a way which confers an unacceptable benefit on them or persons who are close
        to them. The provisions of Part X are essentially a series of prescriptive rules: it
        epitomises the movement in UK company law since 1862 from what was
        originally conceived of as an enabling statute to a regulatory one with the
        tendencies of what is sometimes called "Christmas tree legislation".[16] To achieve
        its purpose, Part X employs a number of techniques including absolute
        prohibition,[17] a requirement for disclosure of interests to the board,[18] a
        requirement for prior disclosure to all members whether they have voting rights or
        not,[19] a requirement for prior disclosure to and approval by the company in
        general meeting, a requirement for disclosure to the Stock Exchange,[20] disclosure
        by maintenance of a register which is open to inspection and disclosure in the
        annual accounts. A relevant question is always going to be whether the right
        technique has in fact been employed, and indeed whether there are other
        appropriate techniques not yet used in Part X.

WHAT ARE THE GENERAL PRINCIPLES THAT SHOULD GUIDE REFORM OF THE LAW IN THE AREA OF PART X AND DIRECTORS' DUTIES?

Law Commission Report on Shareholder Remedies

2.14   As already explained, the Law Commission produced a report on this topic, in
        consultation with the Scottish Law Commission, in October 1997. The approach
        which we adopt in this part builds on the approach that the Commissions adopted
        in that report. In it the Commissions identified a number of guiding principles for
        the purposes of that reform exercise. We thus start by considering whether any of
        those principles is also relevant here: there is a very clear relationship between
        shareholder remedies, which are the means by which the aid of the court is
        invoked, and the present field of law which regulates the duties which directors
        owe to their companies and the terms on which they will be allowed to enter
        transactions which affect the company or its shareholders. So far as possible the
        principles underlying reform in both areas should be homogenous and
        harmonious. Indeed, as we have indicated above,[21] there should in general be
        consistency between different areas of core company law.

2.15   The principles which were identified in the context of shareholder remedies were:

---

[16]   Ie once it became the policy to include in the Act some very specific prohibitions, it became
        difficult to resist the argument that it should not contain a number of further prohibitions in
        the same style.

[17]   See eg ss 330-343.

[18]   See eg s 317.

[19]   See eg ss 312, 323.

[20]   See eg s 324-9.

[21]   Para 2.2 above.

(i)   **The proper plaintiff principle:** that is, that normally it is only the company which should be able to bring proceedings to enforce a cause of action to which it is entitled.[22] This principle as such is specific to shareholder remedies and has no application here. However it is indicative of the relationship between those who control a company and individual shareholders. The latter have invested in the company and have sunk their monies into a common pool which it is likely that others will control. The duties which directors owe are owed to the company and not to individual shareholders.

(ii)   **The internal management principle:** that is, that the court should not be involved in the resolution of disputes that under the company's constitution are determined by the vote of the majority. This principle is concerned with the relationship between an individual shareholder and the general body of shareholders and therefore as such it has no application to the field with which this project is concerned. However it again indicates the fundamental premise on which company law is based, namely that individual shareholders having taken shares in a company have contributed to a common pool which they are unlikely to control.

(iii)   **The commercial judgment principle:** that is, that the courts should not substitute their judgment for that of the directors on commercial matters provided that the directors' decision is itself arrived at by a satisfactory process. The threshold requirements which were identified for such a judgment were that the directors should have acted in good faith, on proper information and in the light of the relevant considerations and that it appears to be a reasonable decision for the directors to have taken. This principle is one which affects the field of action delegated to directors and in our view this policy issue here is an issue also in the field of Part X and directors' duties.

(iv)   **The principle of sanctity of contract:** this is well known to lawyers and means the principle whereby a person is bound by the terms of the agreement that he made and the court is not given power to relieve him from that contract. In commercial life there is a high premium on certainty and this principle is conducive to certainty. This principle is not specific to shareholder remedies and thus an issue arises as to whether it is correct for directors' duties and dealings as well. It does not mean that the principle may never be modified. There are situations in which it is fair to give the court some discretion to relieve a party to a contract from the consequences of their action but those situations will be limited and form the exceptions rather than the rule.

(v)   **The principle of freedom from unnecessary shareholder interference:** we explained that shareholders should not be able to involve the company in litigation without good cause or where they intend to cause the company or other shareholders embarrassment or harm rather than genuinely pursue the relief claimed. Otherwise the company may be "killed by kindness",[23]

---

[22] In Scots law the rules on title to sue achieve a similar result. See, Shareholder Remedies (1997) Law Com No 246, Appendix D.

[23] *Prudential Assurance Ltd v Newman Industries Ltd (No2)* [1982] Ch 204, 221.

or waste money or management time on dealing with unwarranted proceedings. We took the view that the way ahead was not that there should be a bar on shareholders bringing derivative proceedings save in very exceptional circumstances, but rather that the requisite control should be exercised by the courts. In that way the delicate balance of power between shareholders and their companies could be maintained.

(vi)   The principle of efficiency and cost-effectiveness: We took the view that all shareholder remedies should be made as efficient and cost-effective as can be achieved in the circumstances. This principle is obviously a general principle and it clearly ties in with the emphasis on competitiveness in the DTI's Company Law Review. We see it as a principle of general application, and certainly as one that is capable of being applied to directors' duties and dealings.

2.16   The guiding principles summarised above were set out in the consultation paper on Shareholder Remedies, issued in October 1996. Consultees views were sought on them and they were well supported on consultation. The principles were criticised in legal journals[24] as not articulating the fundamental values which company law ought to achieve and in this respect being insufficiently penetrating and analytical. We understand and respect those criticisms but consider that the task of this project is to formulate recommendations with respect to a limited part of company law which will form a contribution to the DTI's wider review of company law. Thus we have to work on the basis (so far as this project is concerned) that companies will continue to perform the same economic and societal role that is currently permitted by law. The debate as to any wider or new role is one which is of value but does not fall within the confines of this project.

Guiding principles for directors' dealings and duties?

2.17   We suggest for consideration by consultees that the following are the key principles that should apply in the area of core company law covered by this project:

(1)   **A principle of separate but interdependent roles for shareholders and directors:** We provisionally consider that any reform of the law in this area should recognise that the roles of shareholders and directors are separate but interdependent. Of course, the precise roles may be varied by the articles in some companies such as joint venture companies, or in practice where the shareholders are all directors and the distinction between their two roles is blurred. But the law should start from the recognition that usually directors and shareholders have quite separate roles in the company.[25] Directors manage the business while shareholders

---

[24]   D Sugarman, "Shareholder Remedies and the Law Commission's consultation paper" (1997) PIC 3 and "Reconceptualising company law: reflections on the Law Commission's consultation paper on shareholder remedies: Part 2" (1997) Co Law 274; Report from the CCLP, IALS by Dr Leslie Moran, "Shareholder Remedies Workshop" (1997) Co Law 93; Professor William Rees, "Shareholder Remedies" [1997] 5 ICCLR 155; CA Riley, "The values behind the Law Commission's consultation paper" (1997) Co Law 260.

[25]   See para 2.12 above.

monitor their stewardship. However the roles of shareholders and directors are *mutually interdependent* and the law should strike an appropriate *balance* between their respective interests. Shareholders are not in a position to control the activities of directors on a day to day basis, and this means that the law has to impose some restrictions on the activities of directors. On the other hand management must also have freedom from unnecessary shareholder interference. This freedom is one of the principles identified in the Law Commissions' Shareholder Remedies project.[26] In the context of shareholder remedies, this principle was left to be mediated through the courts. That is less likely to be the route available in this context and therefore care has to be taken to see that where it is absent there are other mechanisms to subject directors to appropriate scrutiny and sanctions.

(2) **Law as facilitator principle:** Law in this area should facilitate and not impede the conduct of proper business transactions. We have already referred to this in paragraph 1.14 above.

(3) **Appropriate sanctions principle:** There must be a flexible range of sanctions and consideration should be given to whether the existing sanctions for any particular breach are effective and realistic. This raises the sub-issue of decriminalisation of Part X, which we discuss in Part 10 below.

(4) **A company-specific principle:** The rules which emanate from this project must be tested against the different sorts of companies to which they apply and where appropriate different rules should be devised for different types of company. This raises the question of how companies are appropriately classified in this area.

(5) **An inclusive principle:** In Part X generally and in the formulation of directors' duties under the general law, due regard must be paid, to the extent to which the law from time to time allows this,[27] to the obligation of directors to consider other constituency interests apart from those of shareholders. In this respect, the law must have an inbuilt elasticity to permit organic growth and development.

(6) **A usability principle:** The law in this area must be accessible, comprehensible, clear and consistent with common sense. It must also meet business needs and be built on a proper understanding of how business works.

(7) **A certainty principle:** The prescriptive rules of Part X must be clear and certain so that directors can be advised or decide for themselves without difficulty whether a particular transaction falls within their ambit or not. There is rather a special need for certainty in this area because generally there is no time to go to court to determine the question of law: the

---

[26] See para 2.15(v) above.

[27] But no further, because the stakeholder issue is outside this project: see para 1.55 above.

opportunity which it was desired to pursue will no longer be capable of being pursued if the parties have to wait for a court decision. But the principle of certainty as we see it has to be applied with caution. First, the existence of prescriptive rules can sometimes be self-defeating: because they are construed very literally, it is often possible, with a little ingenuity, to "drive a coach and horses" through them.[28] In circumstances such as these the courts have sometimes, but not often, been prepared to recharacterise the transaction[29] and in tax law the courts have gone further and devised rules to disregard artificial transactions.[30] Second, it is also the case that even in the Companies Acts Parliament has had to include provisions which are very general and imprecise, such as "shadow director",[31] "subsidiary undertaking",[32] "financial assistance",[33] directors' "interests" in transactions.[34] While therefore we see that in general the rules of Part X should be abundantly clear in their scope, we consider that users of company law must recognise that there are going to be situations where, from the nature of the subject matter, this is not achievable.

(8)   **An "enough but not excessive" principle:** Part X must strike the right balance between necessary regulation and freedom for directors to make business decisions. It should not be criticised simply for failing to deal with every possible permutation of facts or eventuality. Part X should ideally seek to regulate in those areas and in those ways in which legal regulation can be effective. If consultees agree with this statement in principle, we invite them to give us their views as to how effective regulation might be achieved. It may be difficult to apply the ideal without research which may not be currently available. This ideal also leads to the question of what legal doctrines should be developed and/or legislated for to achieve the most effective regulatory result.

(9)   **A principle of ample but efficient disclosure:** Disclosure, like sunlight in Justice Brandeis' famous phrase,[35] is the best disinfectant. It is one of the best ways of achieving high standards, since, although directors are not prohibited from doing that which they have to disclose, they will not in general be willing to see disclosed that which, though not illegal, may subject them to criticism. On the other hand disclosure carries its own cost, both direct and indirect, and the consequences of information being

---

[28]   See for example the practice of "rolling contracts" referred to under s 319 at para 4.169 below.

[29]   See for example the doctrine of sham in relation to mortgages (applied in eg *Welsh Development Corporation v Export Finance Co* [1992] BCLC 148.

[30]   See eg *Ramsay(WT) Ltd v IRC* [1982] AC 300.

[31]   Section 741(2).

[32]   Section 258.

[33]   Sections 151-158.

[34]   Section 317.

[35]   Louis D Brandeis, *Other People's Money* (1914) p 92. Justice Brandeis was a Justice of the Supreme Court of the United States of America from 1916 to 1939.

available in the public domain. Care must be taken to ensure that the costs of disclosure do not outweigh its utility.

(10) **The principle of efficiency and cost effectiveness:** As with the law relating to shareholders' remedies, the law in the field covered by this project too must be made as efficient and cost-effective as can be achieved in the circumstances. Thus in the context of disclosure it is important to bear in mind not merely the need to avoid the risk of information overload, but also the waste of costs and management resources which may result from an obligation to disclose information to shareholders which shareholders do not need to perform their function. Such waste tends to diminish a company's ability to perform well and to be competitive.

(11) **The commercial judgment principle:** There are areas of company law in which the courts pass judgment on what are essentially commercial matters, such as whether putting a company into administration is likely to lead to its survival as a going concern.[36] But the general principle, in a review of an act said to have constituted a breach of duty, should be that the courts do not substitute their judgment for that of the directors made in good faith. In the context of this project the rationale for such a principle may be more a need to provide the right incentives to directors to take proper commercial risks, than because the courts would not be able to review the commercial wisdom of the decision. On the other hand there will be circumstances where despite this general approach the court has to reject the view of the directors, for instance because they acted for an irrelevant purpose.[37]

(12) **The principle of sanctity of contract:** This principle, and its importance as a commercial matter, are explained above.[38] There are, however, examples within the scope of this project where the company is relieved of a contract because some mandatory rule in Part X or the general law is not complied with. In addition, the court has power under section 727 of the Companies Act 1985[39] in limited circumstances, to relieve a director from the consequences of breach of duty. The matter can be approached on the basis that these points only illustrate the principle. The starting point is that the law will generally uphold contractual relationships .

Consultees are asked whether, in their view, the appropriate principles to guide reform in this area are those set out at paragraph 2.17 above; and/or

---

[36]   See Insolvency Act 1986, s 8.

[37]   Similarly, the court would probably not be bound by the directors' view on a commercial matter if it was manifestly unreasonable or was made on the basis of inadequate information: cf *Charterbridge Corporation Ltd v Lloyds Bank Ltd* [1970] Ch 62: see para 11.29 below.

[38]   See para 2.15(iv) above.

[39]   See paras 11. 41-11.45 below.

whether some other, and if so what, principles should apply for that purpose.

2.18   It can be seen that law reform in this field has in many respects to be tested against the efficiency of the relevant legal rules in achieving the desired measure of control. Because of that, we consider that the questions to which this project gives rise are not purely legal ones: in many respects they are also economic ones. We are not alone in seeing a role for economics in company law. Much important work in company law using economic analysis has already been done in this country.[40] We turn next in the next Part to a study of the economic considerations applicable to this project, which we believe give an added dimension to this law reform exercise. The study has been carried out for the Law Commissions by the ESRC Centre for Business Research at the University of Cambridge.[41]

---

[40]   See for example Prentice, "The Theory of the firm: minority shareholder oppression: sections 459-461 of the Companies Act 1985" (1988) OJLS 55; Ogus, "Economics and Law Reform: Thirty years of Law Commission endeavour" (1995) LQR 407; B R Cheffins *Company Law: Theory, Structure and Operation* (1997); Parkinson, *Corporate Power and Responsibility* (1993); and Ogus, *Regulation: Legal Form and Economic Theory* (1994).

[41]   The Report was prepared by Simon Deakin and Alan Hughes, respectively Assistant Director and Director of the ESRC Centre for Business Research.

PART 3
ECONOMIC CONSIDERATIONS

INTRODUCTION

3.1 The purpose of this part is to undertake an economic analysis of the present law contained in Part X of the Companies Act 1985, and to consider economic implications of possible changes to the law resulting from the review of Part X and from the introduction of a statutory statement of directors' duties.

3.2 The discussion is arranged as follows. We firstly consider the contribution which an economic analysis can make to the understanding of legal rules and of their reform (paragraphs 3.3-3.9). This is followed by a very brief overview of the economic approach to company law (paragraphs 3.10-3.18) and by a more extensive economic analysis of the fiduciary principle as it applies to company directors (paragraphs 3.19-3.50). We then look at a number of specific areas of law from an economic viewpoint, namely the detailed requirements of Part X of the Companies Act 1985 (paragraphs 3.51-3.72); the civil sanctions (paragraphs 3.73-3.78) and criminal sanctions (paragraphs 3.79-3.84) which are attached to Part X and to related aspects of directors' liability; and directors' duties of skill and care (paragraphs 3.85-3.91).The main conclusions are summarised at the end of this part (paragraph 3.92).

THE CONTRIBUTION OF ECONOMIC ANALYSIS

3.3 The economic analysis of law can fulfil two purposes. Firstly, it can be used to *evaluate* particular legal provisions in terms of how far they enhance efficiency, or, in other words, how far they contribute to the wealth or well being of society as a whole. Secondly, it can be employed to *predict* the effects of changes in the law.[1]

3.4 The first type of analysis generally assesses legal rules according to how far they promote *allocative efficiency*, or the allocation of scarce resources in a way which maximises their value to society. It is also concerned with *technical efficiency*, or the minimisation of costs which are involved in the use of resources.

3.5 Also relevant here is the concept of *dynamic efficiency*, which is widely used in the economic analysis of industrial organisation. This idea refers to the capacity of a given system or organisation to innovate and survive in a changing and uncertain environment. The emphasis here is on how far legal rules, and other mechanisms, can contribute to the efficient production of information and the management of risk and uncertainty.

3.6 The second type of economic analysis is concerned with predicting the impact of legal rules on commercial or social practices. The effects of a given legal provision

---

[1] These types of economic analysis are termed 'normative' and 'positive' analysis, respectively. See A I Ogus, "Economics and Law Reform: Thirty Years of Law Commission Endeavour" (1995) 111 LQR 407.

may well be marginal when set against wider economic forces.[2] However, changes in legal rules can alter incentives and so can change the ways in which markets operate. It will often be important to assess how legal rules may work in conjunction with incentives which operate through the market or, where relevant, through self-regulation.

3.7 Equally, economic analysis may help to predict when wider social and economic forces may render a rule ineffective. For example, the intended aim of a rule may be offset by 'second-order effects' as the parties adapt to a new legal environment.[3]

3.8 The type of analysis used in this part is important, then, for achieving a better understanding of the consequences of legal rules. It is not being suggested that economic analysis is always capable of making clear-cut predictions of the economic and social effects of legal change. While it may not provide a conclusive answer in most cases, it can, nevertheless, inform policy makers of some of the possibly unintended consequences of changes to the law.

3.9 It is also important to be aware of the limitations of a purely conceptual analysis. In the present context of the discussion of reforms to Part X of the Companies Act 1985 and the effects of introducing a statement of directors' duties, the range of factors affecting corporate decision-making is sufficiently wide that a change in the framework of legal rules could, in principle, have one of many different possible effects, the likelihood of which can only be more clearly established through empirical research. As a result, **the contribution of economic analysis in this part is three-fold: to identify economic rationales for the existing body of law; to identify possible outcomes of legal reform; and to indicate the main areas in which further, empirical research would be desirable.**[4]

COMPANY LAW AND ECONOMIC EFFICIENCY

Company law and agency costs

3.10 One of the functions which economic analysis attributes to company law is the reduction of agency costs. Agency costs have been described as 'the costs

---

[2] The Rt Hon Lord Hoffmann, "The Fourth Annual Leonard Sainer Lecture" (1998) Co Law 194.

[3] '[I]n designing solutions to legal problems, law reformers should not overlook behavioural responses which may vitally affect the efficacy of those solutions and which economics, in particular, can be used to predict': Ogus, op cit, at p 417. For example, second-order effects may frustrate the redistributive intention of a rule: landlords may respond to rigid rent controls by withdrawing their properties from the market, leaving tenants, as a group, worse off (Ogus, *ibid*, at p 418). A more positive implication of this type of analysis is that a rule may be designed with the aim of *inducing* certain desired second-order effects. For example, in the context of commercial relationships, legal rules may have the effect of enhancing the flow of economically valuable information as a preliminary step to further bargaining between the parties. This is a point directly relevant to the law governing directors' duties, to which we will return below.

[4] We identify in this part certain issues on which empirical research would be useful; see also Part 16, below.

associated with having your property managed by someone else'.[5] They are the inevitable consequence of the 'separation of ownership and control',[6] or the separation of the company's shareholders from the management of its business, which to some degree characterises all companies above a certain size.

3.11 The economic benefits of specialisation make it desirable for the responsibility for management to be vested in the board of directors, which in turn delegates to the senior officers and employees of the company. In economic terms, the problem with such *agency relationships* is that the 'principal' cannot costlessly observe or monitor the performance of the 'agent'.[7] Delegation gives rise to costs of monitoring and to costs which are incurred in bargaining over the terms upon which responsibilities are divided up and tasks carried out. In principle, the law can assist in the reduction of the agency costs and in making bargaining more effective, thereby contributing to both technical and allocative efficiency in the senses defined in paragraph 3.4 above.

3.12 In particular, efficiency will be increased if an incentive structure can be put in place which will align the interests of the parties as far as possible. This set of incentives may be thought of, in a loose sense, as a contract or governance structure which is the result, in part, of bargaining between the parties, even though not all aspects of the arrangement would be regarded as contractual in the juridical sense of constituting a legally binding agreement.

3.13 Some aspects of the relationship between shareholders and senior managers, for example, may be expressly spelled out. The shareholders can seek to minimise the risks to them of managerial self-dealing and under-performance through the inclusion of express terms in directors' service contracts, ranging from the linking of executive remuneration to performance indicators, to provisions explicitly governing conflicts of interest. Certain provisions of the articles of association, which may deal with the powers and remuneration of directors, can similarly be understood as forming part of the loose or extended incentive 'contract' between shareholders and managers. Shareholders' agreements and resolutions of the company in general meeting may also perform a contractual effect in the loose sense of a consensual arrangement.

3.14 In economic theory, a perfectly efficient or optimal incentive contract is one which would completely specify the mutual rights and obligations of the parties in the event of all relevant contingencies. In long-term relationships based on complex,

---

[5] Rt Hon Lord Hoffmann, op cit. For a valuable review of theories of the firm in economics and their relevance to corporate law (mainly in the US context) see W Bratton Jr, "The New Economic Theory of the Firm: Critical Perspectives from History", in S Wheeler (ed) *A Reader on the Law of the Business Enterprise* (1994).

[6] See generally A Berle and G Means, *The Modern Corporation and Private Property* (1932) (perhaps the prime example of interdisciplinary collaboration between a lawyer and economist in the field of company law).

[7] The economic terms 'principal' and 'agent' do not bear the same meaning as their juridical counterparts: in English law, directors are agents of the company and not of the shareholders, nor are the officers and employees the agents of the board. The economic concept of 'agency' is concerned with the costs which arise from delegation, rather than with the precise nature of the juridical relationship to which delegation gives rise.

repeated exchange, such as the shareholder-manager relationship, there will come a point when the costs of anticipating and dealing with future contingencies outweigh the benefits of explicit contracting. Hence, any express agreement is bound to be incomplete to some degree, and to that extent less than 'perfectly' efficient. Here, company law performs an important role in supplying a set of background rules which fulfil a number of functions, including filling in the gaps in express contractual arrangements and facilitating bargaining between the parties.[8]

A typology of rules within company law

3.15 *Default rules* may be defined as optional terms and conditions which apply in the absence of specific agreement on a certain point. They specify the parties' rights and obligations in situations which are not covered by an express agreement. At the same time, they can be customised or modified by the parties if they see it as in their interest do so. Such rules therefore allow for flexibility in adapting to particular circumstances.

3.16 *Mandatory rules* which limit or restrict the scope for bargaining may, for that reason alone, have adverse economic effects; they may lock the parties into an inefficient allocation of resources, or unnecessarily raise the costs of avoiding the rule by requiring the parties to go to certain lengths to contract around it. Alternatively, where bargaining is likely to be extremely costly or where there is an imbalance of power or information between the parties, a mandatory rule may be justified. Thus shareholders are protected, in some instances, by mandatory rules.[9] Moreover, where bargaining produces *externalities*, that is to say, *unbargained-for effects upon third parties*, a restriction of contractual autonomy may be appropriate in order to prevent an overall welfare loss to society. An example of an externality is the potential loss caused to creditors of the company by transactions which corporate insiders (managers and shareholders) may, under certain circumstances, see as being in their interests, such as loans to directors or other transactions which have the effect of depleting corporate assets. This may help to explain why, for example, certain loans to directors are prohibited under sections 330-342 of the Companies Act 1985.[10]

3.17 In practice, the distinction between default rules and mandatory rules may not be clear cut. Certain rules of company law can be avoided but only at a cost in terms of time and resources. The circumstances under which a rule or liability may be avoided are complex; they may include requirements of prior or subsequent disclosure of information, prior permission, ratification after the event, and/or release from liability. Rules of this kind are referred in the economic literature as *penalty default rules*. Their economic importance lies in their use to provide

---

[8] There is an extensive literature on the role of the law in supporting contractual cooperation. For recent contributions, see D Campbell and P Vincent Jones, *Contract and Economic Organisations: Socio-Legal Initiatives* (1996); S Deakin and J Michie, *Contracts, Cooperation and Competition* (1997).

[9] See our discussion of Part X Companies Act 1985, para 3.51 *et seq* below.

[10] See below, paras 3.54-3.56. Another example is the rule that dividends must be paid out of realised profits (Companies Act 1985, s 263).

36

incentives for the sharing of information (see below). Their economic purpose is related to the need to overcome obstacles to cooperation, and hence to the promotion of dynamic efficiency as defined in paragraph 3.5 above.

3.18 To sum up our discussion so far, **company law can be seen as having a number of economic purposes, in particular: (1) promoting efficient bargaining between corporate actors; (2) protecting the interests of third parties such as creditors; and (3) providing incentives for cooperation, thereby promoting competitiveness.**

THE FIDUCIARY RELATIONSHIP

3.19 Before we examine the statutory rules relating to self-dealing and other conflicts of duty and interest in Part X of the Companies Act 1985, we must first consider the economic aspects of the general law relating to the fiduciary obligations of company directors. The central question to be addressed is whether an economic rationale can be found for the application to directors of the fiduciary principle. The fiduciary principle does not, at first sight, conform to the type of efficient default rules which economic theory would predict for this situation. This is because fiduciary duties of loyalty are imposed upon directors by law and cannot easily be excluded by agreement.[11] Moreover, the common law provides for 'supracompensatory' remedies for breach of fiduciary duty, that is, remedies which do more than simply compensate the beneficiary for losses flowing from the breach of duty. In particular the fiduciary's liability to account for profits - the so-called 'disgorgement' or restitution measure of damages - departs from the rule in contract law, to the effect that restitutionary damages are not normally available for a breach of contract. If, as economic theory suggests, the underlying nature of the relationship between directors and the company (and, at one remove, the shareholders) is essentially contractual, then is such a rule efficient?

3.20 Notwithstanding the points made in the preceding paragraph, it has been argued by some law and economics scholars that the fiduciary principle is efficient, since 'the duty of loyalty must be understood as the law's attempt to create an incentive structure in which the fiduciary's self-interest directs her to act in the best interest of the beneficiary'.[12] The application of a duty of loyalty which consists of a vague, open-ended standard is said to be justified by the high costs of express contracting over the terms of the fiduciary's performance. These costs arise from the wide variety of circumstances under which the fiduciary may be presented with the opportunity for self-dealing or other conflicts of duty and interest.

3.21 A second factor is the high cost of monitoring the fiduciary's performance; this is said to justify certain deterrent or 'prophylactic' features of the law relating to the duty of loyalty. The rule that a fiduciary must not place him or herself in a

---

[11] As we shall see below, fiduciary duties can, in practice, be modified or excluded by various means, but even then it is arguable that certain residual elements of the director's duty to act bona fide in the interests of the company cannot be excluded. See para 3.29 below.

[12] R Cooter and B Freedman, "The Fiduciary Relationship: Its Economic Character and Legal Consequences" (1991) 66 NYU Law Review 1045, 1074. See also R Campbell Jr, "A Positive Analysis of the Common Law of Corporate Fiduciary Duties" (1995-96) 84 Kentucky L J 455.

position where their duty to the company conflicts with their own interests, or with their duty to another, is one of these. Some commentators see this rule as, in effect, inferring a breach of the duty of loyalty from the *appearance* of disloyalty or wrong-doing.[13] The civil sanctions associated with fiduciary law, in particular the liability to account for profits, are also relevant here, since they can be seen as having a deterrent effect.[14]

3.22 Shareholders are, arguably, particularly vulnerable to the risks of disloyalty by the fiduciaries upon whom they depend.[15] The following factors have been identified in the theoretical literature. *Firstly*, even where shareholders are 'repeat players' such as institutional investors, they will almost certainly be less well informed about the nature of the company's business than the managers who are employed to run it. Day to day control of management is, by definition, not feasible. This factor adds to the inherent costs of monitoring managerial performance.

3.23 *Secondly*, concerted shareholder pressure on management will be costly to achieve because of 'free rider' effects, in companies where shareholdings are widely dispersed. In companies with concentrated shareholdings (such as small family businesses and also companies which have undergone a management buy-out), problems of monitoring may be reduced, but not entirely eliminated. However, there is some evidence to suggest that shareholder activism has increased in both Britain and the United States since the early 1990s.[16] This is an issue requiring further empirical research.

3.24 Against these considerations, the application to directors of the fiduciary duty of loyalty also entails potential costs for shareholders and potential efficiency losses. *Firstly*, there are, without doubt, *some* instances in which the open-ended fiduciary principle, if unqualified in any way, would deter the exploitation of corporate opportunities by directors and senior managers in such a way as to harm shareholder wealth.

3.25 For example, a manager who was presented with the possibility of exploiting a business opportunity might choose to forego the chance to do so, rather than seek to negotiate an arrangement with the company which would be mutually

[13] Cooter and Freedman, op cit 1054-55.

[14] See paras 3.73-3.78 below for further discussion of civil remedies for breach of directors' duties.

[15] See V Brudney, "Corporate Governance, Agency Costs, and the Rhetoric of Contract' (1985) 85 Col LR 1403; V Brudney, "Contract and Fiduciary Duty in Corporate Law" (1997) 38 Boston College LR 595; M Whincop, "An Economic Analysis of the Criminalisation and content of Directors' Duties" (1996) 24 Australian Business Law Review 273. The question of whether corporate constituencies other than shareholders can be regarded as the ultimate beneficiaries of directors' fiduciary duties is outside the scope of our present discussion; however, it should be noted that there are economic arguments for acknowledging the existence of duties to take into account the interests of creditors, employees and others under certain circumstances, as, indeed, is currently the case in UK company law. See S Deakin and G Slinger, "Hostile Takeovers, Corporate Law, and the Theory of the Firm" (1997) 24 J Law & Soc 124.

[16] See T Ghilarducci, J Hawley and A Williams, "Labour's Paradoxical Interests and the Evolution of Corporate Governance" (1997) 24 J Law & Soc 26.

advantageous, if he or she could not be confident of that arrangement being respected by the courts. Similarly, companies may avoid transactions which would otherwise be beneficial to them, because of the risk of placing a director in a situation of self-dealing, or of a conflict of duty and interest. At the very least, then, clear rules allowing for an exemption from liability in the case of disclosure of information and approval and ratification of directors' conduct are needed by way of qualification to the basic principle.[17]

3.26 *Secondly*, the imposition of a too-strict duty of loyalty may give rise to undesirable 'second-order effects'. In the context of directors' duties, these might include premature resignations from office by directors, or a reluctance of potential directors to serve.[18] It is also conceivable that directors may demand side-payments or additional compensation as protection against the risk of incurring certain fiduciary liabilities, thereby increasing bargaining costs.

3.27 *Thirdly*, it is argued that shareholders are already adequately protected against the risk of disloyalty (as certain other de facto beneficiaries of the performance of fiduciary duties are not) by market forces: 'the high powered incentives provided by markets protect [shareholders], making the use of a governance structure - the open-ended fiduciary duty adjudicated by a court - unnecessary'.[19] For example, the existence of an active labour market for senior managers may provide incentives for managers to maintain high levels of probity and performance. The threat of hostile takeover, or the 'market for corporate control', may have a similar effect, since the possibility of takeover may act as a means of raising the performance of managerial teams. In so far as these effects operate in practice, the imposition of strict legal standards in addition to market forces would, it is suggested, give rise to unnecessary duplication.[20]

3.28 A more fully-informed picture of the potential costs and benefits of the fiduciary principle is only obtainable through empirical research. Nevertheless, it can be seen from the short review undertaken here that economic arguments for imposing the fiduciary principle upon directors are not all one way. It is likely, then, that in some situations, the parties to corporate transactions will seek to adapt or contract around the basic rule. Alternatively, where it cannot be avoided, we would expect to find compensating 'side payments' to managers, the costs of

[17] In practice, the application of these rules is not always very clear: see Shareholder Remedies, Consultation Paper No 142, at paras 5.16-5.17, and (1997) Law Com No 246, at paras. 6.80-6.85.

[18] See R Daniels, "Must Boards Go Overboard? An Economic Analysis of the Effects of Burgeoning Statutory Liability on the Role of Directors in Corporate Governance" (1994-95) 24 Canadian Business LJ 229; B Chapman, "Corporate Stakeholders, Choice Procedures and Committees" (1995-96) 26 Canadian Business LJ 211.

[19] R Romano, "Comment on Easterbrook and Fischel, 'Contract and Fiduciary Duty'" (1993) 36 Journal of Law and Economics 446, 450.

[20] Romano, op cit. It should be noted that Romano's argument is only valid if the market forces to which she refers in fact have an appreciable effect of the kind suggested, which is a matter for empirical research. For recent reviews of the empirical evidence, see Romano, "A Guide to Takeovers: Theory, Evidence, and Regulation" (1992) 9 Yale Journal of Regulation 119; and Deakin and Slinger, op cit. For present purposes, it is sufficient to note the general argument which Romano makes.

which would have to be met, at least in part, by the shareholders. The expense of contracting around the rule would, in this situation, give rise to unnecessary or 'deadweight' bargaining costs.

3.29 There is a case in principle, then, for constituting the duty of loyalty as a *default rule* which applies only if it is not varied, modified or customised through a consensual arrangement of some kind. This analysis is compatible with the general thrust of UK company law relating to the fiduciary duties of company directors, although not necessarily with all of its detailed provisions. Although the fiduciary duty of loyalty does not originate in contract and there is a formal statutory bar on agreements which seek to derogate from it in advance,[21] it is normally possible to avoid liability for breach of fiduciary duty in respect of a particular transaction or set of transactions through the processes of disclosure, approval, release and ratification;[22] hence the duty is *not* unqualified. The substantial difficulties which, under the present state of UK company law,[23] face shareholders who wish to bring a derivative action in respect of a breach of directors' duties, give the fiduciary duty of loyalty even more of the quality of a default rule.

3.30 The analysis given above would be compatible with the view that **the underlying principle of legal regulation in this area should be the achievement of procedural fairness in the regulation of self-dealing and other conflicts of duty and interest. In other words, the law should be concerned to ensure that there are adequate procedures for dealing with self-dealing and conflicts of interest, for example through disclosure of information and ratification. This would be preferable to a complete prohibition** for the reasons just given.

3.31 It also follows that **any restatement of the fiduciary duties of directors should make some reference to the role of disclosure, approval, release and ratification in enabling liability for breach of fiduciary duty to be avoided in appropriate circumstances. The rules on disclosure and ratification also need to be clearly stated.** Otherwise, any such statement of duties could be perceived as placing excessive emphasis on the deterrent elements of fiduciary obligation, and an insufficient stress on the circumstances under which the obligation may be qualified in the interests of both the company (understood here as the general body of shareholders) and the director or manager concerned.

---

[21] Companies Act 1985, s 310; although, even here, there is scope for derogation as a consequence of the decision of Vinelott J in *Movitex Ltd v Bulfield* [1988] BCLC 104. On the conflict between s 310 and art 85 of Table A (1985), which, contrary to the Act, appears to envisage *ex ante* agreements to allow self-dealing by directors, see P Davies, *Gower's Principles of Modern Company Law* (6th ed, 1997) at pp 623-626.

[22] *Ibid*, at pp 620-621 and 645-648.

[23] See *ibid*, ch 23, and Shareholder Remedies (1997) Law Com No 246.

Efficient default rules: Some general considerations

3.32 A number of different types of default rules, with different effects in each case, may be identified.[24] Three of these are *straightforward default rules*, *penalty default rules* and *strong default rules*; their effects are described in the following paragraphs.

3.33 A *straightforward default rule* is akin to a standard form contract which applies in the absence of contrary agreement. Its purpose is two-fold: to save the parties the time and trouble of negotiating over all points of detail, and to allow them to customise or vary particular terms as they see fit. The model set of articles of association contained in Table A is the classic example, in this context, of a set of straightforward default rules.[25]

3.34 By contrast, a *penalty default rule* sets out to induce the parties to cooperate by sharing risk and information, by providing one or both of them with an incentive to alter or shift a rule which would otherwise impose an unwelcome liability. Hence, 'efficiency-minded lawmakers should sometimes choose penalty defaults that induce knowledgeable parties to reveal information by contracting around the default penalty'.[26] However, the costs of renegotiating, avoiding or otherwise modifying the rule must be comparatively low; otherwise the rule may have the effect of locking the parties into an inefficient allocation of rights and obligations.

3.35 Many of the rules under Part X can be characterised as penalty default rules in the sense just identified. For example, under section 317, a director may incur criminal liability if he or she has an interest in a contract entered into by the company, unless he or she makes disclosure of that interest to the board. The purpose of the 'penalty' here is not necessarily to bar self-dealing, but rather to encourage the disclosure of information by the more knowledgeable party. The rule therefore has an economically beneficial 'information-inducing' or 'cooperation inducing' effect.

3.36 In the case of a *strong default rule*, by contrast, the court or legislator sets a high procedural barrier to contracting out. Strong default rules are therefore close to being immutable or mandatory rules. They may be based on the assumption that certain transactions are potentially highly disadvantageous to one party, and should therefore require a high degree of formality to be surmounted in order to be legally effective. Another purpose of a strong default may be to avoid a negative externality, or unbargained for cost, arising from the contract. Strong default rules nevertheless allow for the possibility of contracting-out by parties who perceive the high costs of doing so to be outweighed by significant benefits to them. The form of the rule then allows their interests to override the negative effect which

---

[24] See I Ayres and R Gertner, "Filling Gaps in Incomplete Contracts: An Economic Theory of Default Rules" (1989) 99 Yale LJ 87. A further analysis of the different types of default rules within company law and their relationship to property rights lies outside the scope of this paper; for an analysis of these issues see M Whincop, "Painting the Corporate Cathedral: the Protection of Entitlements in Corporate Law" forthcoming, OJLS.

[25] Table A (1985) is the 'default' set of articles in the sense that it applies where a company fails to register separate articles of its own: Companies Act 1985, s 8(2).

[26] Ayres and Gertner, op cit, at p 94.

their contract or arrangement may impose on the third party, on the grounds that, in this case, the aggregate wealth or well being of society would be enhanced.[27]

3.37   Under Part X, sections 320-322, governing substantial property transactions between directors and their companies, are an example of a strong default rule. There is a risk of depletion of the company's assets which may detrimentally affect both shareholders and creditors. Such transactions are accordingly voidable at the instance of the company, unless one of a number of conditions apply, one of which is that the transaction was affirmed within a reasonable period of time by a general meeting of the shareholders (section 322(2)(c)). Requiring a vote in general meeting amounts to imposing a costly and inconvenient precondition of the validity of the transaction. Shareholders are thereby given a high degree of protection against this type of transaction. Creditors, on the other hand, may potentially be exposed to risk if shareholders vote to approve transactions of this kind, since they may lead to a depletion of corporate assets. In that regard, sections 320-322 may be contrasted with the absolute prohibition on a director receiving a loan from the company (section 330); this can be seen as a *mandatory rule* which operates principally for the protection of third parties, that is, creditors, although the rule can also be seen as protecting the interests of shareholders too (see below, Part 6).

3.38   Policy makers have a choice, then, in where to set the initial standard for a default rule and in how far to impose procedural costs or obstacles when enabling the parties to contract around the rule. This requires an assessment to be made of the costs and benefits for particular parties of contracting around, *and not contracting around,* particular default rules. Some parties will consider it worth their while to contract around, or to modify, a default rule. Where this occurs, a wide variation of practices will result. This resulting situation is known as a *separating equilibrium.* By contrast, in a *pooling equilibrium,* the costs of contracting out or around a rule are so considerable that they deter a large number of contracting parties from customising the default rule to their particular circumstances, when they might otherwise have done so.

3.39   The point can be illustrated by reference to the rules concerning the length of directors' service contracts in section 319 of the Act. A term which has the effect that a director must be employed by the company for a period of more than five years, where the contract cannot be terminated by notice or can be so terminated only in specified circumstances, is only valid if given the prior approval of the shareholders in general meeting. A leading authority on company law has suggested that prior to the recommendations of the Cadbury and Greenbury Reports which recommended a shorter period still for service contracts, this provision of the Act had 'largely eradicated long-term service agreements not determinable by the company until the directors reach retirement age', at least in the case of public companies. However, the Act did not outlaw the use of 'five year roller' contracts which can have the effect of guaranteeing that notice of at least five years is nearly always required if the company wishes to terminate the

---

[27]   In other words, here the gain to the contracting parties would outweigh the loss to the third party.

contract.[28] The effect of section 319, then, appears to have been to create a 'pooling equilibrium': for whatever reason, 'directors of public companies have a rooted antipathy to exposing their service agreement to debate and possible rejection by the general meeting of the members'; so the default rule became in effect a general standard. However, account must also be taken of the use of 'five year rollers'. Where companies considered it worth their while to adopt such devices, a degree of 'separation' or variation in practice between companies was introduced.

3.40   It can be seen from this analysis that the setting of a default rule has effects on both distribution and economic efficiency. Where there are high costs to recontracting or contracting around a rule, or where there are externalities, the allocation of liabilities under a default rule will tend to lock the parties in. Thus it will affect the private wealth of the parties concerned. The choice of rule will also have efficiency effects: these depend upon the incentives for information-sharing and for contractual cooperation which these rules create.

The fiduciary principle should in general operate as a *penalty default rule*

3.41   We may now place the analysis of default rules in the context of directors' fiduciary duties. As we saw, the arguments for applying the strict and open-ended duty of loyalty to senior managers are finely balanced. It is possible to show that shareholders, as a group, are in need of the deterrent protection which the open-ended rule provides, but that some flexibility in the application of the rule is also needed. The uneven or asymmetric division of information between investors and managers means **there is a case for constituting the fiduciary principle in the form of a *penalty default rule* which places the onus of avoiding liability on the fiduciary.**

3.42   This is broadly the effect of the current equitable rule, which enables a director or other senior manager to avoid an otherwise onerous liability through prior disclosure of their interest to the board or, in some circumstances, the shareholders, or through subsequent approval, release or ratification by the shareholders. These rules have an 'information-inducing' effect which, according to the arguments presented above, could be compatible with contractual efficiency under certain conditions.

3.43   However, the advantages of this information-inducing effect would be offset if the rule created a significant disincentive on fiduciaries to seek out the information which the rule required them to disclose in order to avoid liability. Shareholders and managers alike would be worse off if fiduciaries were deterred from investing time and effort in seeking out valuable business opportunities in the first place. This issue could be clarified by empirical research.

3.44   It is also possible that executive directors and other managers would receive implicit compensation in the terms of their service contracts for the limits imposed by the law on their right to exploit corporate opportunities for private

---

[28]   Davies, op cit, at p 361.

gain. The shareholders, in other words, would implicitly be paying more for the right to hold managers to account.[29]

3.45 However, even if this were so, the resulting combination of incentives arguably leaves shareholders better off than they would be with a rule which allowed managers full discretion to exploit opportunities as they saw fit and so obviated the need for a compensating side-payment in the service contract. This is because the combination of the fiduciary rule and the provisions of the service contract provide for a superior flow of information between the parties than the alternative. Again, this is a possible area for empirical research.

3.46 Non-executive directors, whose role is principally that of monitors rather than managers, are unlikely to come across valuable business information as a result of the investment of their own personal time and effort; a default rule penalising them for self-dealing would not, therefore, result in a diminution in the acquisition of valuable information.

How onerous should the disclosure and/or ratification requirements be?

3.47 If the aim of policy were to induce directors to release information to other corporate actors concerning their exploitation of business opportunities or the possibility of self-dealing, the threshold for disclosure should be set at a reasonably low level - in other words, it should be reasonably straightforward to comply with the disclosure requirements as it is, for example, in respect of the requirement to make disclosure to the board under section 317. Otherwise, both sides might find themselves locked into an inefficient allocation: directors would not disclose information where the private costs of doing so outweighed the gains to them. Shareholders would be less well informed, and the opportunity would be unexploited.

3.48 Consider the situation in which a manager approaches the board with a proposal to be allowed to set up a separate company to exploit an opportunity which he or she has developed.[30] Disclosure is induced by the threat that the manager will otherwise have to account for the profits which he or she subsequently makes from the deal. However, it is better for all parties, and for society, for the opportunity to be taken up either inside or outside the corporation, rather than to be left unexploited. If the manager sets up on his or her own, the company can set the price for letting them go. Alternatively, it may be possible for the manager to negotiate terms for the exploitation of the opportunity within the company. Whatever the outcome, in principle it is preferable for the parties to make their own contract, assuming bargaining costs are low, than for the court to set the price for them.

3.49 On the other hand, a *strong default rule* may be thought necessary to protect investors against unilateral behaviour by managers if the prospects of bargaining over corporate opportunities are, in practice, remote. In this context, it is often

---

[29] See F Easterbrook and D Fischel, "Contract and Fiduciary Duty" (1993) 36 Journal of Law and Economics 425, 428.

[30] This example is given by Easterbrook and Fischel, op cit, at pp 444-445.

suggested that the form of articles of association and the terms of directors' service contracts are frequently determined by board members themselves, with limited scope for direct negotiation with investors.[31] In large public companies, shareholders are in effect expected to rely on the non-executive directors to oversee the negotiation of service contracts. However, in such companies, the addition of a further layer of monitoring within the structure of the corporation itself creates further agency costs.

3.50　The question of whether to set high procedural requirements under Part X depends crucially, then, on the nature of bargaining or negotiation between the different corporate actors. In principle, different patterns of relationships could be found according to whether a company is a public company with a stock exchange listing, at one extreme, or a small private company or 'quasi partnership' at the other. The role of non-executives as monitors acting on the shareholders' behalf also needs to be taken into account. These aspects of the shareholder-director relationship are matters which could be clarified further by empirical research. **A central aim of empirical research should therefore be to clarify the precise nature of the relationship between shareholders, non-executive directors and senior management in companies of different types and sizes, and in particular to ascertain the extent to which bargaining over the exploitation of corporate opportunities is a realistic possibility.**

ANALYSIS OF THE DISCLOSURE AND RATIFICATION REQUIREMENTS UNDER PART X OF THE COMPANIES ACT

3.51　It follows from our earlier analysis that while it is important for the law to allow for the principle of disclosure and ratification in respect of the exploitation of corporate opportunities, the procedures for disclosure and ratification may justifiably differ according to the subject matter being considered. However, it is not clear whether the current rules in Part X reveal a coherent set of justifications. The following different requirements are currently imposed in respect of the provisions of Part X and other relevant legal provisions:

(1)　Absolute prohibitions (sections 323 and 330-342).

(2)　Prohibitions which may be avoided through disclosure (in some cases prior to, and in other cases within a period following, the transaction) to:

(a)　the board (sections 317 and 322B);

(b)　the shareholders in general meeting, or via the company accounts, or via a register (sections 314, 318, 324, 325 and 328);

(c)　the Stock Exchange (section 329; and certain derogations from corporate governance rules under the Combined Code).

---

[31]　See M Eisenberg, "The Structure of Corporate Law" (1989) 89 Col LR 1461, discussing US practice.

(3) Prohibitions which may be avoided by consent[32] (through either approval, in advance, or ratification or release, after the event) of:

    (a) the board;

    (b) the shareholders (sections 312-313, 315, 319, 320, 322, 322A and 337);

    (c) the Stock Exchange

3.52 These rules relating to disclosure and consent can be illustrated in tabular form, as follows:

---

[32] Consent may, for this purpose, be effective if there has not been adequate prior disclosure, so there may be a considerable overlap between categories (2) and (3).

TABLE

Rules governing disclosure and consent through approval, release and ratification under Part X of the Companies Act 1985

	Disclosure (General meeting*) (Notice to shareholders**) (Notification to company***) (Company accounts†) (Inspection††)		Consent	
	Before	**After**	**Before (Approval)**	**After (Release, Affirmation Ratification)**
Board	*s 317(1), (2)(a),(3), (4),(8)*	*s 317(2)(b)* *s 322B*		
Share-holders	*s 312** *s 313(1)** *s 314(2)*** *s 319(5) ††* *s 337(3)(a)**	*s 318††* *s 324 and Sched 13, Pt II**** *s 325 and Sched 13, Pt IV††* *s 328(3) **** *Sched 6, Pt II †* *ss 343-344††*	*s 312* *s 313(1)* *s 315(1)(b)* *s 319(3)-(4)* *s 320(1)* *s 337(3)*	*s 322(2)(c)* *s 322A(5)(d)*
Stock Exchange		*s 329*		

3.53   What criteria should guide policy makers in determining whether a particular matter should be prohibited outright, disclosed to the board alone, disclosed to shareholders, disclosed to the Stock Exchange, or approved or ratified by shareholders?

Absolute prohibitions: Sections 323 and 330

3.54   **With regard, firstly, to absolute prohibitions, we would suggest that these can be justified only where there is a significant risk that the transactions in question would give rise to a negative externality or third party effect (such as harm to the interests of creditors, sufficient to outweigh the gains to the internal corporate actors) or a significant public interest (such as the need to maintain market integrity).** (See paragraph 3.16 above)

3.55   The complete prohibition on certain loans to directors (sections 330-342) is a rare example, in this context, of a mandatory rule. While it is difficult to envisage circumstances where a loan from the company, as opposed to one from a third party, would be justified, the possibility that such circumstances might exist could be respected by allowing ratification under strict limits (such as the need for unanimity). However, if creditors' interests would be adversely affected by this, the presence of such an externality would justify the retention of the mandatory rule. It should also be noted that as the law currently stands, there is an exception for loans made to directors to meet expenditure incurred or to be incurred for the purposes of the company; these may lawfully be made as long as they are approved by the company in general meeting.[33] In addition, there are disclosure requirements in respect of certain loans and quasi-loans which are lawful under the exceptions to section 330.[34] These provisions allow for a degree of flexibility in the application of the principle that shareholders and creditors need to be protected against transactions which can lead to the depletion of the company's assets. Whether the law strikes the right balance between outright prohibitions, in some cases, and requirements for approval and/or disclosure in others, is not a question which can be answered without further research into the operation of these laws in practice.[35]

3.56   The prohibition on directors' options dealings (section 323) raises issues of market integrity in so far as it can be viewed as part of the law governing insider trading. With regard to its role in regulating the internal relationship of directors and shareholders, it is arguable that little purpose would be served by varying the current outright prohibition to allow ratification by the shareholders, given that this form of trading by directors is highly speculative and could be seen as in some circumstances trading against the company. There is also an argument to the effect that it is not beneficial to the company to allow directors to take up short-term trading positions in their companies' shares.

---

[33]   Companies Act 1985, s 337.

[34]   *Ibid*, Sched 6 and, in the case of banks, ss 343-344.

[35]   For a critical analysis of the argument that mandatory rules are needed to protect the interests of creditors, see B R Cheffins, *Company Law: Theory, Structure and Operation* (1997) p 245.

General principles governing disclosure

3.57 With regard to disclosure, the general guiding principle should be **that each organ of the company (board, shareholders) should be presumptively entitled to receive from management the information which it needs to have in order to be confident that it has carried out its particular monitoring function.**[36] For example, the shareholders must have sufficient information to enable them to decide whether the directors are acting in good faith in the best interests of the company. **Two further factors place a limit on efficient disclosure; firstly, the need for confidentiality, that is to say, the problem that excessive disclosure of information may destroy the value of that information; and, secondly, the costs incurred in the process of dissemination.**

Disclosure to the board: Sections 317 and 322B

3.58 In some cases, disclosure of information to the board only is required. Hence, disclosure to the board alone (in the form of a formal declaration) is needed in the case of a director who has an interest in a transaction or proposed transaction with the company (section 317). Under section 322B, in the case of a company with a sole member, contracts between the company and the member which are neither in writing nor set out in the form of a written memorandum must be recorded in the minutes of a board meeting.

3.59 The purpose of section 322B is to provide evidence of a contract which may be important in the context of a winding up or administration order. In the context of a sole member company, it is arguable that the section adequately meets this need.

3.60 The efficiency of requiring disclosure to the board alone under section 317 is unclear, however. Because of the information costs which attach to identifying a case of self-dealing, the shareholders may not even be in a position to know whether the board is acting in the company's interests if disclosure of a conflict of interest to them is not required. Nevertheless, this consideration must be balanced against the need to preserve confidentiality. Disclosure of certain contracts or transactions in which directors have an interest could destroy their value. For this reason, it might be felt to be unfeasible to replace the requirement of disclosure to the board with a rule requiring full disclosure to the shareholders. The degree of shareholder protection would depend, then, on the effectiveness of monitoring of directors by one another.

3.61 Alternatively, this problem could be overcome by the maintenance of a register of such transactions which shareholders could consult if they wished, as is already the case with directors' share dealings under section 324; or legislation could require shareholders to give periodic approval to conduct by directors which would fall under section 317.

---

[36] This is not to suggest that each organ of the company has the *same* monitoring function, either in law or in practice. In particular, a distinction may be drawn between directors, who are under a certain legal duty to monitor each other's activity, and shareholders, who monitor the directors out of self-interest rather than legal obligation.

3.62   Consideration could also be given to extending section 317 to cover not just cases in which a director or shadow director has an interest in a contract or proposed contract with the company (or its subsidiary), but to other transactions where there is a conflict of interest or which involve the use of a corporate opportunity.[37]

3.63   The approach to be taken is also affected by the question of how far non-executive directors can effectively perform a monitoring role on shareholders' behalf with regard to conflicts of interest and duty. It is also likely that in many companies, the question of such conflicts is approached through express terms, governing non-competition and the use of corporate opportunities, in directors' service contracts. These are therefore issues which need to be clarified by empirical research.

Disclosure to shareholders: Sections 314, 318, 324, 325 and 328

3.64   A number of provisions in Part X are concerned with the disclosure to shareholders of information concerning the contracts of employment of directors (section 318) [38] and certain payments to directors (section 314). In the case of publicly listed companies, these requirements operate in conjunction with the provisions of the Stock Exchange Listing Rules. It follows from the economic nature of the 'agency relationship' between shareholders and senior managers that the former have an interest in both the implicit and explicit incentives which operate on the behaviour of management. As a result, statutory requirements for disclosure of the contents of directors' service contracts and payments in respect of loss of office have a clear economic purpose in aiding monitoring, and hence in reducing agency costs. The extension of these disclosure rules to cover senior managers who are not directors would also fulfil this purpose,[39] although the advantages in terms of disclosure might be outweighed by the costs of delimiting the scope of those covered by such a rule. It could also be argued that the board is capable of dealing adequately with the case of managers and officers who are not directors, although the possibility of too close an identification of interests between board members and senior employees should also be borne in mind.

3.65   Monitoring costs are also reduced by the requirement for the compulsory disclosure of directors' share dealings (sections 324-328). Again, as a matter of general principle, this type of provision can be seen as assisting the monitoring of directors by shareholders, in particular from the viewpoint of how far directors are observing the duty to act in good faith in the company's interests.

---

[37]   Disclosure to the board may suffice to avoid liability under the general principles of fiduciary law (*Queensland Mines Pty Ltd v Hudson* (1978) 18 ALR 1), so giving rise to a general incentive to disclose information concerning corporate opportunities. However, the scope of the judge-made rule is unclear; clarification by statute could be considered to be beneficial.

[38]   Section 318 requires disclosure of the terms of directors' service contracts.

[39]   Officers and senior managers of the company are caught, in principle, by general fiduciary duties, but only directors (and sometimes shadow directors) are affected by Part X.

Approval and ratification by shareholders: Sections 312, 315, 316, 319, 320, 322, 322A and 337

3.66   The approval and ratification provisions of Part X fall into a number of categories. In some cases, prior approval is needed. This is so in relation to directors' service contracts for a term (without notice) of five years or more in length (section 319), although shareholder approval is not required for 'golden parachutes' in service contracts under the Privy Council's decision in *Taupo Totara Timber* v *Rowe*.[40] Prior approval is also required in the case of uncovenanted compensation payments to directors for loss of office (sections 312 and 316), certain substantial property transactions involving directors (section 320), and loans or quasi-loans to directors in relation to expenses incurred in relation to work for the company (section 337). Shareholder ratification, after the event, suffices to avoid liability in the case of certain transactions with the company in which a director has an interest and which are beyond the powers of the board (section 322A) and also certain types of substantial property transactions (section 322).

3.67   There are substantial costs to approval and ratification, in particular in the case of large listed companies. As a result, then, these rules operate as *strict default rules*; we would expect there to be only a limited degree of contracting around the rule. Such rules could be justified if there were a risk of particularly extensive damage to shareholders from conflicts of interest, or of unilateral action by the board which goes beyond the limits set by the constitution of the company and thereby exposes the shareholders to a particularly high risk of loss. Transactions involving substantial property interests come into the first category; unconvenanted service payments and transactions beyond the board's powers under the articles of association - and which therefore threaten to undermine the agreed division of powers between the board and the company in general meeting - come into the second.

3.68   The rules relating to long-term service contracts and golden parachutes have the effect, in each case, of protecting shareholders against the consequences of senior managers receiving excessively large pay-outs on the termination of their employment. It is not clear, given their similar purpose, why ratification is currently needed in the case of contracts beyond five years but not (under *Taupo*) for golden parachutes. In principle, the two sets of rules could be harmonised. Moreover, the question inevitably arises, in this context, of why these particular terms have been singled out for regulation, and not others. In practice, directors can be compensated for the loss of flexibility over these aspects of the contract by increased benefits of another kind.

3.69   Along with other aspects of the remuneration of senior managers, these questions are also dealt in greater detail with by the Listing Rules and by the Combined Code on Corporate Governance. In effect, these provisions impose a set of disclosure requirements for publicly quoted companies which have taken the question of remuneration outside the immediate control of the company in general meeting, and placed the responsibility for monitoring more clearly on the non-executive directors. Although they involve much reduced compliance costs,

---

[40]   [1978] AC 537.

the standards set by the Combined Code are stricter than those set by Part X of the Act and cover a broader range of issues. Nevertheless, compliance with the Code is, in the end, voluntary, and further empirical research is needed before its effects can be fully assessed.

3.70   Under these circumstances, the question of what purpose is served by having separate statutory standards could usefully be addressed. A coherent scheme of statutory controls could serve as a 'backstop' to the provisions of the Code and the Listing Rules, and would be particularly important, in this respect, for non-listed companies. However, in the absence of clearly agreed criteria for placing any particular limit on senior managers' pay, a regime of disclosure, as opposed to one of ratification, may function adequately to protect shareholder interests.[41] However, without further research on the role of non-executive directors in overseeing service contracts, it is difficult to draw firmer conclusions on this question.

General conclusions on Part X

3.71   To conclude this part of the discussion, the provisions of Part X do not constitute a consistent approach to the imposition of disclosure and ratification requirements in cases of self-dealing, conflicts of interest and duty, and directors' service contracts. In particular, it is not clear why, in the context of section 317, disclosure of self-dealing is currently required only to the board, as opposed to being made available to the shareholders through a register or made subject to their periodic approval. Nor do the rules governing shareholders' approval for certain terms of service contracts reveal a coherent scheme, since the basis on which certain terms but not others are singled out for approval is not apparent. This means that the regulatory intent of the legislation can be avoided through contracting, which in itself may be costly and serve no purpose.

3.72   These considerations suggest that **there may be merit in moving towards a general principle of disclosure to the shareholders of information concerning self-dealing and directors' contracts. Only in relation to a smaller number of transactions would shareholder approval and/or ratification be required. This would be the case where there was a danger of depletion of corporate assets from particular types of transactions (as is currently the case in regard to sections 320-322) or where the agreed division of powers between the board and the shareholders was in danger of being undermined (as in the case, currently, of section 322A).**

CIVIL REMEDIES FOR BREACH OF FIDUCIARY DUTY

3.73   Law and economic scholars have questioned whether an economic justification can be found for the pattern of civil remedies for breach of fiduciary duty, and in particular for the restitutionary basis of the remedy of account of profits. A restitutionary award, it is argued, may under certain circumstances unduly

---

[41] We do not consider here the question of whether the maintenance of a certain relationship between senior managers' pay and the pay of other employees is conducive to more effective performance within the organisation, and hence in the shareholders' longer-run interests.

penalise a fiduciary who diverts a corporate opportunity; the result will be over-deterrence of fiduciaries in general. The correct measure of damages from an economic point of view, it is suggested, is that based on the principal's loss, as in the case of damages for breach of contract.[42]

3.74 Even if the correctness of the basic economic position with regard to the 'efficiency' of certain breaches of contract is accepted,[43] the remedy of account of profits in cases of breaches of fiduciary duty may nevertheless be justified on economic grounds. Because of difficulties of detecting disloyalty by fiduciaries (see our analysis above, in particular at paragraph 3.41), economic theory suggests that there is a low probability that breaches of fiduciary duty will be detected and sanctioned. Hence, fiduciaries would be under-deterred from disloyalty by a regular contract measure of damages which merely sought to compensate the beneficiary for losses flowing from breach.[44]

3.75 More precisely, damages for breach of fiduciary duty should ideally be set 'at the level required both to offset enforcement error and to achieve deterrence'.[45] Where enforcement error - the failure to detect and sanction breach - is thought to be extensive, a restitutionary element to damages may be justified. Requiring *full* restitution of profits may have a highly deterrent effect, since it might make the fiduciary *worse off* than he or she would have been had they not committed the breach. This is because the fiduciary will incur various costs in making the gain which may not be taken into account in his or her favour, and they will also most likely suffer additional losses (such as dismissal and harm to reputation) from a finding of breach of duty.

3.76 In practice, however, it is not clear how far the current state of the law in the UK conforms to this analysis, since it is possible that a court would grant the fiduciary an allowance for expenses incurred which would considerably reduce the extent of his or her liability; the manner in which the court calculates the net profits of the fiduciary may also go to reduce their liability and hence the deterrent effect of this type of civil remedy. It should also be borne in mind that for certain types of breach of fiduciary duty involving self-dealing, as opposed to the diversion of a corporate opportunity, a remedy requiring the fiduciary to account to the

---

[42] See F Easterbrook and D Fischel, op cit. Their argument would apply *a fortiori* to the use of proprietary remedies for breach of fiduciary duty, such as the remedial constructive trust, in the context of corporate opportunities. For reasons of space, a full economic analysis of the different remedies which may be available, and the implications of the conceptual distinction between property rights and liability rules in this context (which, it should be noted, does not correspond precisely to the distinction between personal and proprietary claims), cannot be undertaken here. See M Whincop, op cit (forthcoming) for an extended analysis of these issues.

[43] The economic theory of 'efficient breach' has, indeed, been the subject of substantial criticism, not least by restitution scholars: see GH Jones, "The Recovery of Benefits Gained from a Breach of Contract" (1983) LQR 443, cited with approval by the Court of Appeal in *A-G v Blake* [1998] 1 All ER 833.

[44] See Cooter and Freedman, op cit, for further elaboration of this argument.

[45] *Ibid*, p 1070.

principal for profits arising from the transaction may not be available.[46] These tendencies within the law support the view of some commentators to the effect that the economic case for restitutionary damages is uncertain; enforcement errors may instead be minimised and costs of detection overcome by the rule which infers disloyalty from its appearance (that is to say, from the conflict of interest and duty). Given the willingness of the law to allow a cause of action where disloyalty is inferred from its appearance, it might be more efficient to restrict damages to a purely compensatory amount, since this would increase the number of disloyal fiduciaries who would then be caught (and also reduce the costs of wrongly penalising honest fiduciaries).

3.77 **On balance, the presence of a restitutionary element in civil damages for breach of fiduciary duty by directors may be seen as efficient in the sense of helping to overcome difficulties in detecting breaches of duty by directors.**[47] This is particularly so given the costs which face shareholders considering bringing a civil claim, and hence by the low likelihood that such claims will be mounted. This argument would no longer be so persuasive if procedural barriers to the initiation of derivative suits (in Scotland shareholder actions) were reduced.

3.78 Notwithstanding the difficulties facing civil litigants, the present rule could give rise to the possibility of opportunistic litigation by undeserving plaintiffs, and hence of a waste of resources.[48] *Regal (Hastings) Ltd v Gulliver*[49] is, arguably, just such a case, since it produced a windfall for the new owners of the company.[50] In this context, the possibility, after the event, of the court granting a director absolution for breach of duty (Companies Act 1985, section 727), may reduce the likelihood of a speculative claim being brought against him or her. The decision in *Regal*, by providing the company with a cause of action in the event of the directors profiting from a conflict of duty and interest, may also offer an important source of protection for the company's creditors. Moreover, the court can, in an appropriate case, fashion relief so that an undeserving party does not gain a windfall.[51]

THE EFFICIENCY OF CRIMINAL SANCTIONS FOR BREACH OF FIDUCIARY DUTY

3.79 Similar considerations apply to the attachment of criminal sanctions to certain breaches of fiduciary duty which needs to be considered in the context of Part X

---

[46] *Re Cape Breton Co* (1885) 29 Ch D 795; see R C Nolan, "Conflicts of Interest, Unjust Enrichment and Wrongdoing", in W R Cornish, R C Nolan, J O'Sullivan and G Virgo (eds) *Restitution: Past, Present and Future: Essays in Honour of Gareth Jones* (1998).

[47] For arguments against full restitution in the context of directors' duties, and references to US jurisdictions in which the normal rule has been varied for corporate transactions, see Easterbrook and Fischel, op cit, at p 442.

[48] The costs which arise from opportunistic litigation are considered in the context of antitrust law by W Baumol and J Ordover, "Antitrust: Source of Static and Dynamic Inefficiencies?", in T Jorde and D Teece, *Antitrust, Innovation and Competitiveness* (1994).

[49] [1942] 1 All ER 378.

[50] Davies, op cit, at p 616.

[51] See *Selangor United Rubber Estates v Cradock (No 4)* [1969] 1 WLR 1773, 1776.

of the Companies Act 1985. The efficiency of criminal sanctions depends upon the balance between the harm caused to society by the activity in question and the likelihood of wrongdoers being caught.[52] In the context of conflicts of interest and duty on the part of directors, this perspective suggests that a criminal penalty may be justified by high detection costs and by the limited incentives of private parties to initiate litigation. However, to the extent that effective civil sanctions are available, in the form of the restitutionary remedy of account of profits (see above paragraphs 3.72-3.77), criminal sanctions may not be needed.

3.80   Economic theory also suggests that criminal sanctions should not be excessively severe where the aim is to overcome problems of detection. Severe sanctions may be levied less often by courts, so reducing the probability of the sanction being applied and, hence, of wrongdoers being deterred.[53]

3.81   Disproportionate remedies may give rise to perverse incentives on the part of wrongdoers, who may have no reason to pay regard to the threat of further criminal liability if a criminal sanction is attached to a trivial or technical breach of the law.[54] Conversely, a nominal fine, which in itself, imposes a minimal cost upon the individual concerned, may be appropriate, given that conviction entails wider costs to the reputation of the individual.[55]

3.82   The form of a rule is relevant to the application of criminal sanctions. There is a danger of over-deterrence, for example, if criminal sanctions are attached to open-ended standards, such as the general duty of loyalty, as opposed to clearly defined bright-line rules. This point argues against the criminalisation of the general duty of loyalty,[56] as opposed to particular instances of self-dealing such as those currently contained in Part X of the Companies Act 1985.

3.83   These considerations suggest that **a role for criminal sanctions in the enforcement of fiduciary duties may be defended on economic grounds. However, this point is subject to certain qualifications: first, the limits of criminal liability must be clearly set, and, secondly, low-level sanctions, such as fines, are probably appropriate.**

3.84   **Conversely, there would be a strong case for decriminalisation in respect of Part X of the Companies Act 1985 if more effective alternative means were to be found for monitoring and detecting illicit conduct of directors, such as lower-cost civil litigation by shareholders, or improved internal monitoring (for example, by non-executive directors).** This would be so, in particular, if it were the case that the criminal sanctions envisaged by Part X were

---

[52]   Daniels, op cit.

[53]   Cooter and Freedman, op cit at p 1071, applying the analysis of G Becker, "Crime and Punishment: An Economic Approach" (1968) 76 Journal of Political Economy 169.

[54]   Daniels, op cit, at p 235.

[55]   *Ibid*, at p 236; for empirical analysis, see J Karpoff and J Lott, "The Reputational Penalty Firms Bear from Committing Criminal Fraud" (1993) 36 Journal of Law and Economics 757.

[56]   See M Whincop, op cit, discussing s 232 of the Australian Corporations Law.

not used in practice, or were not seen as having a significant deterrent effect. These are matters requiring empirical investigation.

THE DUTY OF CARE

3.85 Different economic considerations may apply to the duty of care than those which apply in the case of the fiduciary duty of loyalty. Monitoring of managers' performance is subject, as before, to high information costs and to the costs of specifying a complete set of contractual obligations. However, because lack of care by managers is arguably easier to detect than disloyalty, and the potential gains from breach are less, there is less of a clear justification for a strong prophylactic element in the duty of care or in the sanctions for its breach.[57] Hence, a tort or delictual remedy, restoring the victim to the position which he or she occupied prior to the tort or delict being committed, is likely to be more efficient than a remedy based on restitutionary damages.[58]

3.86 It has been argued that a good initial case exists for aligning directors' general duties of care with the standard set by section 214 of the Insolvency Act 1986,[59] on the basis that the board is the organ which is best placed, within the structure of the corporation, to collate information and monitor the employees' performance. **However, if the standard of care is raised, possible problems are that directors may be deterred from taking normal business risks; in particular if there are limits to the availability of insurance; non-executive directors may be unable to overcome insider domination by executive directors and officers, so reducing the effectiveness of the board as the principal organ for monitoring the performance of employees; and internal systems of communication, through which the board ensures internal compliance with its general instructions, may break down, again preventing the board from being an effective monitor. We now consider these points in greater detail.**

3.87 There is empirical evidence from Canada that the introduction of personal liabilities for directors has led to directors' resignations,[60] and also that liability insurance has not consistently been available to cover the full extent of directorial liabilities.[61] In so far as the risks of liability cannot be shifted through insurance,

---

[57] See Cooter and Freedman, op cit. However, their argument about ease of detection would not apply to carelessness brought about through an omission to act.

[58] Cooter and Freedman, op cit at pp 1059-1061, consider that this measure of 'perfect compensation' contains an element of punishment since managers found personally liable for negligence will suffer additional reputational losses and, most likely, loss of employment; these punitive elements may be justified, they suggest, since in the case of negligence actions, there is no reversal of the burden of proof as there is, in effect, in cases of breach of fiduciary duty under US law.

[59] See *Re D'Jan of London* [1994] 1 BCLC 561; Rt Hon Lord Hoffmann, op cit. For a more sceptical view, see Cheffins, op cit pp 537-548.

[60] Precisely, this is said to have occurred in order to avoid possible personal liability for back wages owed to employees, in the event of the insolvency of the company: Daniels, op cit.

[61] R Daniels and S Hutton, "The Capricious Cushion: The Implications of the Directors and Officers' Insurance Liability Crisis on Canadian Corporate Governance" (1993) 22 Canadian Business LJ 182.

directors may be inhibited more generally from condoning commercially risky ventures. There is a danger here of dampening incentives for innovation, although the magnitude of this effect is difficult to specify with any precision.

3.88 Even if insurance is made available, claims against directors may, for that reason alone, increase.[62] Although the protection of insurance may ensure that directors do not have to face personal ruin, potential damage to the reputation of directors involved in litigation, as well as costs in terms of their time and effort, may deter capable directors from taking office. This consideration may apply particularly to non-executives, whose role is limited to monitoring and who necessarily have limited control over matters of internal organisation.

3.89 Some second-order effects stemming from a raising of the standard of care can be envisaged, not all of which are necessarily adverse. If directors are to be held liable for failing to adequately scrutinise the performance of employees, it is possible that they will respond by requiring tighter internal monitoring and reporting systems. In principle it is not clear whether this would lead to an improvement in internal reporting, which would assist compliance with external regulatory standards, or to unnecessary costs. Empirical research would be of assistance here.

3.90 In the present state of research in this area, it is not possible to predict with certainty the consequences of restating the duty of care in such a way as to raise the standard of care and skill expected of all directors. Even if insurance is made more generally available, an increase in litigation could have adverse consequences for the willingness of capable individuals to take office as directors. On the other hand, the raising of the legal standard of care could have beneficial effects in terms of improving internal communication and monitoring systems within organisations.

3.91 **To avoid possible adverse effects, consideration should be given to the adoption, within a restatement of the duty of care, of a general 'business judgement' defence, the effect of which would be to provide some protection with regard to decisions within the range of normal business risks, that is to say, decisions taken on the basis of a reasonable weighing of the risks involved. A role for more specific limits on directors' personal liability, in the form of checklists for compliance with due diligence, could also be considered here. The content of such 'safe havens' could be informed by auditing standards.**

CONCLUSIONS

3.92 The main conclusions of this part may be restated:

(1) The contribution of this economic analysis has been three-fold: to identify economic rationales for the existing body of law; to identify possible outcomes of legal reform; and to indicate the main areas in which further, empirical research would be desirable.

---

[62] Daniels, op cit.

(2) Company law can be seen as having a number of economic purposes, in particular: (1) promoting efficient bargaining between corporate actors; (2) protecting the interests of third parties (such as creditors) who may be affected by negative externalities, that is to say, unbargained for costs which are imposed upon them by transactions between others; and (3) providing incentives for cooperation, thereby promoting innovation and competitiveness.

(3) The underlying principle of legal regulation in this area should be the achievement of procedural fairness in the regulation of self-dealing and other conflicts of duty and interest, that is to say the specification of the conditions under which disclosure, approval, release and ratification are needed in order to avoid liability, rather than an outright prohibition on all conflicts of duty and interest.

(4) A restatement of the fiduciary duties of directors should make some reference to the possibility of the avoidance of liability through disclosure, approval, release and ratification.

(5) There is a case for constituting the fiduciary principle in the form of a *penalty default rule* which places the onus of avoiding liability through disclosure, ratification etc, on the fiduciary.

(6) Absolute prohibitions on certain types of transactions can be justified only where there is a significant risk that the transactions in question would give rise to a negative externality or unbargained for effect imposed upon a third party (such as harm to the interests of creditors, sufficient to outweigh the gains to the internal corporate actors) or where they would harm a significant public interest (such as the need to maintain market integrity).

(7) The guiding principle for disclosure should be to ensure that each organ of the company (board, shareholders) receives from management the information which it needs to have in order to be confident that it has carried out its monitoring function. Hence, the shareholders must have sufficient information to enable them to decide whether the directors are acting in good faith in the best interests of the company. Two further factors place a limit on efficient disclosure; firstly, the need for confidentiality, that is to say, the problem that excessive disclosure of information may destroy the value of that information; and, secondly, the costs incurred in the process of dissemination.

(8) On this basis, the provisions of Part X do not constitute a consistent approach to the imposition of disclosure and ratification requirements. In particular, the rules governing shareholders' approval for certain terms of service contracts do not reveal a coherent scheme, since the basis on which certain terms but not others are singled out for approval is not apparent. This means that the regulatory intent of the legislation can be avoided through contracting, which in itself may be costly.

(9) These considerations suggest that there may be merit in moving towards a general principle of disclosure to the shareholders of information concerning self-dealing and other conflicts of duty and interest and directors' contracts. Shareholder approval and/or ratification etc would be required only in a smaller number of cases, where there was a danger of the depletion of corporate assets from particular types of transactions or where the agreed division of powers between the board and the shareholders was in danger of being undermined.

(10) Under the present state of both English and Scots law, the existence of a restitutionary element in civil damages for breach of fiduciary duty by directors can be justified as providing an efficient incentive against disloyalty.

(11) A role for criminal sanctions in the enforcement of fiduciary duties may be defended on economic grounds. However, this point is subject to certain qualifications: first, the limits of criminal liability must be clearly set, and, secondly, low-level sanctions, such as fines, are probably appropriate.

(12) Conversely, there would be a strong case for decriminalisation in respect of Part X of the Companies Act 1985 if more effective alternative means were to be found for monitoring and detecting illicit self-dealing, such as lower-cost civil litigation by shareholders, or for improved internal monitoring (for example, by non-executive directors).

(13) If the standard of care for directors' duties of care and skill is raised, possible problems are that directors may be deterred from taking normal business risks, in particular if there are limits to the availability of insurance; non-executive directors may be unable to overcome insider domination by executive directors and officers; and internal systems of communication, through which the board ensures internal compliance with its general instructions, may break down, in each case preventing the board from acting as an effective monitor of employees' performance.

(14) To avoid possible adverse effects, consideration should be given to the adoption, within a restatement of the duty of care, of a general 'business judgement' defence, the effect of which would be to provide some protection with regard to decisions within the range of normal business risks. A role for more specific limits on directors' personal liability, in the form of checklists for compliance with due diligence, could also be considered.

SECTION A
PART X OF THE COMPANIES ACT 1985

PART 4
SUBSTANTIVE IMPROVEMENTS 1:
SECTIONS 312-323 OF THE COMPANIES
ACT 1985

INTRODUCTION

4.1 In this part, we review sections 312-323.[1] In the following three parts (Parts 5-7) we review the other main groups of sections: disclosure of directors' share dealings (sections 324-329[2] and Schedule 13); loans and similar transactions (sections 330-342); and disclosure in the annual accounts and elsewhere of loans etc in which directors are interested (sections 343-344 and Schedule 6). Part 8 contains a review of section 346 (which defines "connected persons" and like expressions) and the remaining sections of Part X. We put forward in these parts a number of suggestions for amending the relevant provisions. In Part 9 we consider two further approaches, namely the repeal or rewriting of some or all of these provisions. In Part 10 we consider the question of decriminalising the provisions.

4.2 The project involves a review of each of the sections of Part X and this means that we must critically examine almost every section in turn, both in terms of its substance and textually. This is not our normal approach, so we begin by outlining how this review proceeds. Of necessity, the complete exercise is a lengthy process.

4.3 We set out the wording of each of the sections (or groups of sections) in the text of the paper. This is followed by a commentary, and then by specific questions for consultees to consider on the relative section or group of sections. The examination of each section varies in length and complexity. In some cases, we simply ask whether consultees have experienced any difficulties with the relevant provisions;[3] in others, we set out a number of detailed suggestions for reform.

4.4 Turning to the provisions reviewed in this part, we have raised in respect of many of the sections a considerable number of different suggestions - which we call "*options*" - as to the way in which the sections might be dealt with or amended. In some cases these are fundamental changes, in others they are small changes

---

[1] We also deal with s 327 in this part which extends the application of s 323; see para 4.216 below. We deal with s 311, which we provisionally recommend should be repealed in Part 9 (see paras 9.30-9.32 below).

[2] With the exception of s 327 which is included in this part; see n 1 above.

[3] Eg ss 322A and 322B (paras 4.209 and 4.213), and ss 343-344 (para 7.17).

designed to deal with specific problems. *Thus it is possible in many cases to choose more than one option.*

4.5 In all cases where we have put forward suggestions for reform,[4] we have included as option 1 *"no change"*. This is to provide an opportunity for those respondents who reject any change, perhaps because they take the view that the section should have only its existing limited operation. If a respondent chooses option 1 he or she of necessity rejects all the ideas for change considered in the succeeding options on that section, but we do not duplicate those ideas or the arguments for and against them under the "no change" option.

4.6 In choosing options consultees are asked whether the relative section would actually be *improved* if the option were reflected in the section. In some cases, consultees may conclude that the legislation would be more flexible if the section covered a particular - though exceptional - situation and feel that the added complexity is inevitable and essential. In other cases, consultees may reject change not because the option is not technically sound, but on the grounds that the complexity which it would introduce would render the legislation yet more unwieldy. It should be borne in mind that it has traditionally been difficult to obtain amendments to the Companies Acts which were needed in practice. It is possible that the method of reforming company law will to some extent be improved in the future so that the law can be amended more much speedily, and with a much greater level of consultation with users of company law in particular than has been the case in the past. The issue of future handling of company law reform is outside the scope of this project, but may fall for consideration in the DTI's wider review of company law.[5]

4.7 As indicated above, the question of repealing individual sections or groups of sections is considered in Part 9 below. Obviously, if consultees take the view that any of the sections discussed there should be repealed, the question of substantive amendments does not arise. The sections discussed in this part in respect of which repeal is considered in Part 9 are sections 312-316,[6] section 319,[7] sections 320-322,[8] and section 323.[9] We would be grateful for consultees views on the options set out in this part even if consultees consider that the section should be repealed.

4.8 We consider the sections in turn under the following heads:

- Sections 312-316: Payments to directors for loss of office, etc

- Section 317: Disclosure by directors to their board

---

[4] In two cases we have not put forward options for reform, but simply asked consultees if they are aware of any deficiencies in respect of the sections. These are ss 322A and 322B; see paras 4.205-4.213 below.

[5] See para 1.1 above.

[6] See paras 9.3-9.28 below.

[7] *Ibid.*

[8] *Ibid.*

[9] See para 9.33 below, where we provisionally recommend that the section should be repealed.

- Section 318: Directors' service contracts (1)

- Section 319: Directors' service contracts (2)

- Sections 320-322: Substantial property transactions involving directors etc

- Section 322A: Transactions beyond the directors' powers

- Section 322B: Contracts with sole member directors

- Sections 323 and 327: Prohibition of option dealing by directors and their near families

Impact of the economic considerations discussed in Part 3

4.9   In Part 1, the view was expressed that Part X was concerned with what was done and the way in which it was done rather than the merit of what was proposed.[10] The economic analysis in Part 3 is consistent with this.[11] The economic analysis also shows that there are different ways in which Part X regulates self-dealing: most particularly, so far as this part is concerned by imposing an obligation to make disclosure to the shareholders or the board, an obligation to obtain approval of the shareholders as well or an absolute prohibition.[12] There are examples of all these methods in the sections considered in this part. The choice of method depends on the policy behind the rule. For example in sections 320-322, which we consider in this part,[13] the purpose of the rule would seem to be to protect shareholders from the risk of detrimental depletion of assets and accordingly these transactions when significant in general require the approval of shareholders. The general conclusion in Part 3 is that the general principle ought to be one of disclosure to the shareholders, with approval or ratification being required only in exceptional situations. Part 3 identified these situations as being where there is a risk of a depletion of corporate assets or where the agreed division of powers between the board and shareholders is in danger of being undermined.[14]

Impact of the general principles provisionally identified in Part 2

4.10   As already stated, Part X sets out the procedure for permitting self-dealing by directors in a number of specific cases. The basic approach of Part X thus illustrates the first general principle that we provisionally identified in Part 2 - the principles of separate but interdependent roles for directors and shareholders. The method of controlling self-dealing has to make best use of their respective roles. Deciding whether and if so how to regulate self-dealing also calls for the application of other of the principles that we have provisionally identified,

---

[10]   See para 1.12 above.

[11]   See para 3.30 above.

[12]   See the Table at para 3.52 above.

[13]   See para 4.172 *et seq* below.

[14]   See para 3.72 above.

including the law as facilitator principle,[15] the usability principle,[16] the certainty principle,[17] the "enough but not excessive" principle of regulation,[18] and the principle of ample but efficient disclosure.[19] We ask consultees, if they agree with the principles set out in Part 2, to have regard to those principles in addressing the options for reform presented in this part, and in particular to the multiples options in:

paragraphs 4.42-4.61 (sections 312-316);

paragraphs 4.94-4.118 (section 317);

paragraphs 4.131-4.152 (section 318);

paragraphs 4.163-4.171 (section 319); and

paragraphs 4.190-4.204 (sections 320-322).

SECTIONS 312-316: PAYMENT TO DIRECTOR FOR LOSS OF OFFICE, ETC

312.— It is not lawful for a company to make to a director of the company any payment by way of compensation for loss of office, or as consideration for or in connection with his retirement from office, without particulars of the proposed payment (including its amount) being disclosed to members of the company and the proposal being approved by the company.

313.— (1) It is not lawful, in connection with the transfer of the whole or any part of the undertaking or property of a company, for any payment to be made to a director of the company by way of compensation for loss of office, or as consideration for or in connection with his retirement from office, unless particulars of the proposed payment (including its amount) have been disclosed to members of the company and the proposal approved by the company.

(2) Where a payment unlawful under this section is made to a director, the amount received is deemed to be received by him in trust for the company.

314.—(1) This section applies where, in connection with the transfer to any persons of all or any of the shares in a company, being a transfer resulting from—

(a)   an offer made to the general body of shareholders; or

---

[15]   See for example the question whether s 312 should cover covenanted payments, para 4.14 *et seq* below; and the question whether s 317 should impose a duty to disclose non-material interests, para 4.97 below.

[16]   See for example the question whether s 317 should contain a code of civil remedies for breach of the duty imposed by the section: see 4.106 below; and the question whether s 320 should prohibit conditional agreements: see para 4.192 below.

[17]   See for example the question whether s 320 should apply to payments which are within s 312-6: see para 4.193 below.

[18]   See for example the question whether s 317 should apply to sole director companies: see para 4.100 below.

[19]   See for example the consideration of the possibilities of informing shareholders and allowing them to call for a meeeting in paras 4.54 and 4.200 below, and the possibility of approval by independent non-executive directors of substantial property transactions.

(b) an offer made by or on behalf of some other body corporate with a view to the company becoming its subsidiary or a subsidiary of its holding company; or

(c) an offer made by or on behalf of an individual with a view to his obtaining the right to exercise or control the exercise of not less than one-third of the voting power at any general meeting of the company; or

(d) any other offer which is conditional on acceptance to a given extent,

a payment is to be made to a director of the company by way of compensation for loss of office, or as consideration for or in connection with his retirement from office.

(2) It is in those circumstances the director's duty to take all reasonable steps to secure that particulars of the proposed payment (including its amount) are included in or sent with any notice of the offer made for their shares which is given to any shareholders.

(3) If—

(a) the director fails to take those steps, or
(b) any person who has been properly required by the director to include those particulars in or send them with the notice required by subsection (2) fails to do so,

he is liable to a fine.

315.—(1) If in the case of any such payment to a director as is mentioned in section 314 (1) —

(a) his duty under that section is not complied with, or
(b) the making of the proposed payment is not, before the transfer of any shares in pursuance of the offer, approved by a meeting (summoned for the purpose) of the holders of the shares to which the offer relates and of other holders of shares of the same class as any of those shares,

any sum received by the director on account of the payment is deemed to have been received by him in trust for persons who have sold their shares as a result of the offer made; and the expenses incurred by him in distributing that sum amongst those persons shall be borne by him and not retained out of that sum.

(2) Where—

(a) the shareholders referred to in subsection (1)(b) are not all the members of the company, and
(b) no provision is made by the articles for summoning or regulating the meeting referred to in that paragraph,

the provisions of this Act and of the company's articles relating to general meetings of the company apply (for that purpose) to the meeting either without modification or with such modifications as the Secretary of State on the application of any person concerned may direct for the purpose of adapting them to the circumstances of the meeting.

(3) **If at a meeting summoned for the purpose of approving any payment as required by subsection (1)(b) a quorum is not present and, after the meeting has been adjourned to a later date, a quorum is again not present, the payment is deemed for the purposes of that subsection to have been approved.**

316.—(1) **Where in proceedings for the recovery of any payment as having, by virtue of section 313 (2) or 315 (1) been received by any person in trust, it is shown that—**

    (a)   **the payment was made in pursuance of any arrangement entered into as part of the agreement for the transfer in question, or within one year before or two years after that agreement or the offer leading to it; and**

    (b)   **the company or any person to whom the transfer was made was privy to that arrangement,**

the payment is deemed, except in so far as the contrary is shown, to be one to which the provisions mentioned above in this subsection apply.

(2) **If in connection with any such transfer as is mentioned in any of sections 313 to 315—**

    (a)   **the price to be paid to a director of the company whose office is to be abolished or who is to retire from office for any shares in the company held by him is in excess of the price which could at the time have been obtained by other holders of the like shares; or**

    (b)   **any valuable consideration is given to any such director,**

the excess or the money value of the consideration (as the case may be) is deemed for the purposes of that section to have been a payment made to him by way of compensation for loss of office or as consideration for or in connection with his retirement from office.

(3) **References in sections 312 to 315 to payments made to a director by way of compensation for loss of office or as consideration for or in connection with his retirement from office, do not include any bona fide payment by way of damages for breach of contract or by way of pension in respect of past services.**

"Pension" here includes any superannuation allowance, superannuation gratuity or similar payment.

(4) **Nothing in sections 313 to 315 prejudices the operation of any rule of law requiring disclosure to be made with respect to such payments as are there mentioned, or with respect to any other like payments made or to be made to a company's directors.**

General

4.11   These sections are derived from sections 191-194 of the Companies Act 1948, which re-enact earlier provisions in the Companies Acts of 1947, 1929 and 1928.[20]

---

[20]   Elements of all the sections, apart from s 312 which was introduced in 1947 on the recommendation of the Committee on Company Law Amendment 1945 (the "Cohen

4.12   The object of sections 312-316 is to make payments to directors for loss of office or as consideration for or in connection with retirement from office unlawful unless there has been prior disclosure and approval. The sections do not apply to any other form of side payment to a director (eg. a bribe not connected with retirement from office), and they exclude the possibility of ratification after the payment has been made. The sections deal with three situations: (i) payment by the company on a director's[21] retirement, resignation or removal;[22] (ii) payment by the company or a third party in the event of a transfer of the whole or part of the company's undertaking or property;[23] and (iii) payment by any person in connection with the types of share offer specified in section 314, primarily general offers or offers for control.[24] In the case of (i) and (ii), the Act requires disclosure to all the members whether they hold voting shares or not[25] and approval by the company in general meeting. In the case of (iii), the Act requires the director to take all reasonable steps to secure disclosure of the payment in the offer document.[26] Section 316(3) excludes from all these sections "any bona fide payment by way of damages for breach of contract or by way of pension for past services".

The Jenkins Committee

4.13   In 1962 the Jenkins Committee considered the predecessor provisions of what are now sections 312 to 316. The Committee recommended that:[27]

(1)   sections 312-315 should be amended to cover payments to former directors;

(2)   sections 312-315 should be amended to cover payments for the loss, while a director of the company or on the occasion of or in connection with loss of office as a director of the company, of any other office in connection with the management of the company's affairs or of any office as director or otherwise in connection with the management of the affairs of a subsidiary;

(3)   sections 312 and 313 should require the approval of a special resolution and section 315(1)(b) should refer to an equivalent majority of the members concerned; and

---

Committee") (see Cmd 6659, Recommendation VI, p 52), were present in the Companies Act 1928.

[21]   For the meaning of director see paras 17.2-17.3 below, which discusses the question whether these sections should apply to shadow directors.

[22]   Section 312.

[23]   Section 313.

[24]   See s 314(1).

[25]   Section 312; see *Re Duomatic Ltd* [1969] 2 Ch 365.

[26]   Section 314(2).

[27]   See Report of the Company Law Committee ("the Jenkins Report") (1962) Cmnd 1749, paras 92, 93, 99(h)(i) and (j).

(4)   where disclosure was required it should include disclosure of any payments for which approval was not required.

Sections 312-316 have not been amended as recommended by the Jenkins Committee.

The distinction between covenanted and uncovenanted payments and the Privy Council's decision in *Taupo Totara Timber v Rowe*[28]

4.14   As already noted,[29] bona fide payments by way of damages for breach of contract are excluded from sections 312-316. The view of the Cohen Committee was that these sections should not extend to the giving up of executive offices for example as managing director:

> 92. ...(a)... Our attention has been drawn to cases where the powers of "settling" claims by a director who is also an executive and who is asked to give up his executive office, are exercised by a board in a manner open to invidious comment, eg where a contract is entered with a managing director with the very intention of terminating the contract and paying compensation in the form of capital not income. The practice is open to obvious objections, but numerous cases must occur where a board desire to dispense with the services of an executive director and where it is to the advantage of the company to negotiate a resignation, on the footing of paying compensation rather than to dismiss the executive director and face legal proceedings and in our view, it would not be right to interfere with the exercise by the board of such a power merely because a minority abuse it.[30]

The Cohen Committee envisaged that as now the compensation would be disclosable in the notes to the annual accounts. The Jenkins Committee also thought that payments to which directors were legally entitled should remain outside these sections and not require approval by the company or members concerned.[31] Clearly if a case such as the Cohen Committee envisaged occurred there would be likely to be a remedy open to the company against its directors for breach of duty.

4.15   The wording of section 316(3) is not however wide enough to exclude payments which a company is bound to pay to a director on his retirement or other loss of office because it has made some prior agreement to that effect or it otherwise has some legally binding obligation to do so.[32] The question whether sections 312-316 apply to such payments (which we will call covenanted payments) has arisen, however, in a decision of the Privy Council namely *Taupo Totara Timber v Rowe*,[33]

---

[28]   [1978] AC 537, PC.

[29]   See para 4.12 above.

[30]   Para 92(a).

[31]   See para 93.

[32]   For example, because he has a claim under a quantum meruit.

[33]   [1978] AC 537, PC.

and in a case before the Outer House of the Court of Session, *Lander v Premier Pict Petroleum Ltd*.[34]

4.16 *Taupo Totara Timber v Rowe* was an appeal from New Zealand's Court of Appeal to the Privy Council, concerned with whether a payment agreed to be made under the terms of a service contract to a managing director on loss of office was unlawful by virtue of section 191 of the New Zealand Companies Act 1955, as it had not been approved by the company in a general meeting. Section 191 is identical to section 312 of the Companies Act 1985.

4.17 Lord Wilberforce, giving the advice of the Privy Council, held that section 191 made payments illegal only where they were uncovenanted and made to directors in connection with their loss of office as director alone. He referred to the judgment of Hudson J in the Australian case of *Lincoln Mills (Aust) Ltd v Gough*.[35] In that case, the provision in question section 129 of the Companies Act 1961 (Victoria), which was the same as section 191 but added after the words "compensation for loss of office" the words "as director" and referred to "retirement from *such* office", but Lord Wilberforce considered the additional words of the Australian provision to be clarificatory rather than restrictive.

4.18 Lord Wilberforce continued:

> The respondent, as well as being a director, was an employee, and, as other employees with this company, had the benefit of a service agreement: he was described as 'employee' in it. In certain events, which might not happen, he could become contractually entitled to a sum of money, on resignation or dismissal, the amount of which was not fixed by the agreement and could only be ascertained if and when the event happened. The directors had full power under art 116 to appoint him as managing director on such terms as they thought fit. There was no obligation on them to seek approval of this agreement by the company in general meeting; to do so indeed would be both unusual and possibly undesirable. Then, if the agreement was, as (subject to any point as to vires, see below) it undoubtedly was, valid in itself, does s 191 require the directors to seek the approval of a general meeting for carrying it out? Presumably this approval would be sought at a time when the obligation to make the payment had arisen and when its amount was known, but meanwhile the position of the employee would be uncertain and difficult. In their Lordships' view the section imposes no such requirement. The section as a whole read with ss 192 and 193 which are in similar form and the words 'proposed payment' and 'proposal' point to a prohibition of uncovenanted payments as contrasted with payments which the company is legally obliged to make. Their Lordships note that this contrast is drawn by the authoritative report of the Jenkins Committee; there is also textbook support for it.[36]

---

[34] 1997 SLT 1361.

[35] [1964] VR 193; see Hudson J at p 199.

[36] [1978] AC 537, 546.

4.19 Although, as a decision of the Privy Council, the decision is persuasive rather than binding, it is commonly thought that section 312 would be held to have the same effect. On this basis sections 312-315 is of much reduced importance. As respects that part of the decision which excludes from the requirement for shareholder approval payments to a director for the loss of an executive position (under a service contract) rather than his office as director, Gower notes that the effect of the decision is to make section 312 inapplicable where it is most needed. He concludes that "the loopholes with which sections 312-316 are riddled enable their obvious purpose to be easily defeated and they are in urgent need of review."[37]

4.20 We provisionally consider, however, that, provided section 316(3) is properly applied in practice,[38] as a matter of policy the effect of the *Taupo* decision is right. The other terms of a service agreement generally[39] are not subject to shareholder approval, and in practice they cannot be. The shareholders have the power to remove the directors, and if the payments are not justified, the company[40] can sue the directors for breach of duty.

4.21 If it is considered that the position established by the *Taupo* decision ought to be or is the position under UK law, then arguably sections 312-314 should be amended to make it clear that they do not apply to covenanted payments.

4.22 In addition to pre-determined contractual payments, covenanted payments include:

- payments to directors who though executive have no service agreement

- payments to non-executive directors who are given a sum to compensate them for extra work done[41]

if, in each case, the company has a legally enforceable obligation to pay the sum in question, for example by way of quantum meruit.

Later authorities

4.23 The decision of the Privy Council was followed by Lord Osborne in *Lander v Premier Pict Petroleum Ltd.*[42] This case concerned a company director who was employed under a contract of service as a managing director. Under the terms of the contract, if the director gave notice to terminate his employment in the event of a change in the company's ownership, he became entitled to payment of a compensatory sum, sometimes referred to as a "golden parachute" payment. The

---

[37] *Gower's Principles of Modern Company Law* (6th ed, 1997) p 815.

[38] This is considered below; see paras 4.25-4.27.

[39] Cf section 319 post.

[40] And in certain circumstances individual shareholders: see generally Shareholders Remedies (1997) Law Com No 246.

[41] Eg on a takeover.

[42] 1997 SLT 1361; [1998] BCC 248.

company refused to pay the sum, arguing that the effect of section 312 of the Companies Act 1985 was to require such a payment to have been approved by its members.

4.24   Rejecting this argument, Lord Osborne said:

> It is to my mind quite clear that in this case the Privy Council decided that the section they were considering applied only to payments made in connection with the office of director ... Further, their Lordships considered that the language of the section and, in particular, the words "proposed payments" and "proposal" pointed to a prohibition of uncovenanted payments, as contrasted with payments which the company was legally obliged to make.[43]

Is section 316(3) properly applied?

4.25   In many cases approval for compensation for loss of office is not sought for compensation payments on the basis that they are bona fide payments by way of damages for breach of contract, and that accordingly section 316(3) applies. Because these payments often appear to be excessive, there is concern that section 316(3) may not be properly applied in practice.[44] It may be that to obtain a quiet and confidential settlement the company takes rather a generous view of what are the appropriate damages bearing in mind that this will involve some difficult estimates of what mitigation for further employment a director should be allowed.

4.26   The subsection clearly permits a payment made in good faith on the grounds that it represents damages for breach of contract, and to ensure that a payment meets this description, legal advice will often be sought. Directors will have the protection of the section if they seek proper advice. The exception does not cease to apply because the apparently proper advice in the event is wrong.

4.27   We invite consultees' views as to whether the provision is being properly applied and call for any evidence on this point. In the case of listed companies it may be that in future the remuneration committee will be required to express a view as to whether they consider that the payment was within the exception and give reasons in the case of payments which, for example, exceed one year's salary for the director involved. We invite consultees' views below on possible solutions for both listed and unlisted companies.[45]

Consultees are asked whether section 316(3) is being properly applied in practice and, if not, to produce, where possible, evidence to support their answer.

---

[43]   1997 SLT 1361, per Lord Osborne at p 1365G-I.

[44]   "...there are many instances where well-known individuals, whose experience and reputation have been quickly recruited by outsiders, have been able to continue being remunerated during what would otherwise have been the balance of their contract. Nevertheless, judging from published information, this factor is by no means always taken into account". Letter A J Mezzetti, *Times Business News*, 4 October 1994.

[45]   See paras 4.59 and 10.40 below.

Role of self-regulation

(i) Hampel Committee: Pre-determined compensation clauses encouraged

4.28   In its final report the Hampel Committee recommended that the sum to be paid to a director if he is removed from office before his contract expires (except for misconduct) should be agreed in advance as a term of his service contract.[46]

4.29   The Committee concluded that this solution would overcome the difficulties of negotiating compensation:

> Such provision would be effective whether or not the director found other employment. The arrangement would provide certainty for both sides, be operationally convenient for the employer, recognise the dislocation to the director inherent in summary dismissal, but avoid the problems of mitigation and inevitably subjective arguments about performance, conducted at the time of departure. Shareholders would of course see these provisions as they would be part of the director's service contract available for inspection.[47]

(ii) The Combined Code: Role of remuneration committees explained

4.30   Remuneration committees have a role both at the time a director's service contract is negotiated and when the question of making a payment of damages to an executive director for loss of office arises. Provisions B.1.9 and B.1.10 of the Combined Code state:

B.1.9:

> Remuneration committees should consider what compensation commitments (including pension contributions) their director's contracts of service, if any, would entail in the event of early termination. They should in particular consider the advantages of providing explicitly in the initial contract for such compensation commitments except in the case of removal for misconduct.

B.1.10:

> Where the initial contract does not explicitly provide for compensation commitments, remuneration committees should, within legal constraints, tailor their approach in individual early termination cases to the wide variety of circumstances. The broad aim should be to avoid rewarding poor performance while dealing fairly with cases where departure is not due to poor performance and to take a robust line on reducing compensation to reflect departing directors' obligations to mitigate loss.

---

[46]   See the Hampel Report, para 4.10.

[47]   Hampel Report, para 4.10, pp 35-36. See the Scottish Law Commission's discussion paper on Penalty Clauses (1997) Scot Law Com No 103.

4.31 The last sentence does not refer to the procedure for approving compensation payments, which is that shareholder approval must be sought if the damages are not payments in good faith by way of damages for breach of contract.[48]

4.32 The Combined Code states that the board should report to shareholders each year on remuneration. It leaves it to companies to decide whether the company in general meeting should be asked to approve the policy in the report.[49] Apart from that provision, the Combined Code does not envisage that shareholders shall have any voice on directors' compensation for loss of office in addition to that given by the Companies Act.

(iii) The City Code

4.33 The City Code requires disclosure and approval of any contracts made from the point at which an offeree board "has reason to believe that a bona fide offer might be imminent", if, for example, they involve the disposition of assets "of a material amount"[50] or entry into or amendment of any contract "otherwise than in the ordinary course of business".[51] This includes a service contract which provides for an abnormal increase in emoluments.

4.34 In addition, Rule 24.5 states:

> unless otherwise agreed with the Panel, the offer document must contain a statement as to whether or not any agreement, arrangement or understanding (including compensation arrangement) exists between the offeror or any person acting in concert with it and any of the directors, [or] recent directors ... of the offeree company having any connection with or dependence upon the offer, and the full particulars of any such agreement, arrangement or understanding.[52]

Overlap with section 320

4.35 The question has arisen whether payments which do not require approval under sections 312-314 because of the application of section 316(3) or because they constitute covenanted payments may still require approval under section 320. As a matter of policy section 320 should not apply to damages for breach of contract or to covenanted payments if they are outside sections 312-316, since those latter sections constitute the special statutory regime for approval of payments for loss of office. Lord Osborne in the *Lander* case[53] considered that section 320 did not apply to a golden parachute payment. There is a first instance decision in England to the same effect regarding damages for breach of contract.[54] However, in practice

---

[48] See section 316(3).

[49] See B.3.5 in Appendix D below.

[50] Rule 21, (d). "Material amount" is defined for this purpose in Note 2 to the Notes on Rule 21.

[51] Rule 21(e).

[52] See also Chapter 11 of the Listing Rules, referred to in para 4.182 below.

[53] See para 4.23 above.

[54] *Gooding v Cater* (unreported) 13th March 1989.

the position is still regarded as unclear. Accordingly, we consider below the question whether section 320 should be amended to make this clear.[55]

Takeover offers and sections 314-315

4.36 The world of takeover offers has moved on since sections 314-315 were first enacted. There are at least two types of takeover with which section 314 does not deal. It does not deal with those that are achieved by a scheme of arrangement involving a reduction of the capital paid up on the offeree's shares. This is a common method for an agreed takeover and has several advantages for the offeror, including the knowledge that when the scheme is sanctioned the shares in the offeree will all have been effectually acquired. Section 426 requires disclosure in the explanatory statement sent to shareholders in the offeree with the notice convening the meeting to consider the scheme of all "material interests of directors". The explanatory statement must also state the scheme's effect on directors' interests, in so far as that differs from the scheme's effect on the like interests of other persons.[56] However, there is no provision which makes a payment to a director in connection with loss of office unlawful if the scheme is a cancellation scheme, or imposes on him any trust of the benefit received for former shareholders.

4.37 Furthermore, section 314(1) appears to apply only to offers conditional on acceptance for example by 51 per cent of the shareholders.[57] In some cases, offers (for example offers to acquire outstanding minority shareholdings) are unconditional. It is therefore questionable whether section 314 should be restricted to conditional offers.

4.38 A further point that arises in connection with takeover offers is that the wording of section 315(1)(b) appears to permit the offeror and his associates[58] to vote at a meeting convened to consider a loss of office payment to which section 314 applies in respect of shares in the offeree shareholders which they already hold. Such shareholders should arguably be excluded from voting at a meeting of the offeree shareholders.

Conflicting claims

4.39 The question also arises whether a claim could arise under both sections 312 and 314 on the same facts, for example because a company offers a payment to a director for loss of office in connection with a takeover. If section 312 applies but not section 314, the refunded payment would benefit the company and not the offeree shareholders. In either case, the director should not keep the payment unless the requisite disclosure and approval has taken place. On the other hand, where it was paid by the offeror, it would be a windfall to him if the claim under

---

[55] See para 4.193 below.

[56] Section 426(2). Directors have a duty to supply the relevant information to the company, and in default are liable to a fine: s 426(7).

[57] See s 314(1)(d) which speaks of "any *other* offer which is conditional on acceptance to a given extent".

[58] See n 73 below.

section 312 superseded any claim under section 315 and the price paid by the offeror for the offeree's shares had taken account of the payment. In those circumstances, it would seem that the claim under section 315 should prevail.

Civil remedies

4.40 Section 315 sets out civil remedies for breach of section 314. However unlike sections 320-322, sections 312 and 313 do not set out the effect of a payment in breach of these sections. Under sections 312 and 313, the payment will be unlawful, and the consequences of this on the agreement for payment are explained in Part 10.[59] Under section 314, however, the payment is not unlawful, and accordingly a contract to make a loss of office payment in a takeover will be enforceable.

4.41 It is for consideration whether sections 312 and 313 should specifically provide that where a payment is made in breach of these sections, the director who receives it is liable to account to the company, and the directors who authorised it are liable to indemnify it against loss.

Options for reform and issues reviewed

4.42 We set out 12 options for reform in respect of sections 312-316, including option 1 which is to leave the sections unchanged. Options 2 and 3 concern the extent to which the provisions should apply to covenanted payments and are alternatives. Most of the other options suggest extensions to the scope of the provisions (options 4, 5, 7 ,9 and 12), clarification of the consequences of a breach of the provisions (options 10), or additional disclosure requirements (option 11), and consultees may choose more than one of these options. Options 6 and 8 concern the manner in which shareholders must give approval of relevant transactions and are mutually exclusive. Finally we ask consultees whether any further reform of sections 312-316 should be considered. The question whether these sections should be repealed in their entirety is considered in Part 9 below.[60] The question whether sections 312-316 should be criminalised is considered in Part 10 below.[61] In considering the options for reform, consultees are asked to have regard to the principles set out in Part 2 above.

Option 1: No Change

4.43 The sections arguably provide sufficient protection for companies and their members. It can additionally be said that a boards' freedom to determine departing directors' compensation with appropriate speed (that is not hindered by any additional requirement to seek shareholder approval) should not be further curtailed, but existing controls are necessary and familiar. This view assumes that there are no problems in those sections which require to be addressed.

---

[59] See para 10.25 below.

[60] See paras 9.22-9.28 below.

[61] See para 10.37 below.

Consultees are asked whether, if retained, sections 312-316 should be retained without amendment.

Option 2: Reverse the effect of the decision in Taupo Totara Timber v Rowe

4.44 The *Taupo* decision is only persuasive authority but, assuming that the same result applies in the UK, payments of damages for breach of a service contract and predetermined compensation clauses, such as golden parachute payments do not require either disclosure or approval. While this has reduced the apparent effectiveness of sections 312 to 316, the negotiation of service contracts may be regarded as a management matter in which shareholders should not be involved. This would be an application of the principle identified above that shareholders and directors should have separate but interdependent roles.[62] Moreover it would be consistent with the recommendation of the Hampel Report for a remuneration committee to consider these and other matters relating to the remuneration of directors.[63] Furthermore, it would be odd if approval was only required when a liability to make the payment had arisen. Shareholders are not required to approve the terms of an executive director's service contract before he commences, and even if *Taupo* does not apply in UK law there is no requirement for approval of such terms as the amount of the salary or any golden hello payment.[64] If approval is required, it may deter suitable candidates from becoming directors. Moreover, if the terms which the board negotiates are over-generous, the board may be in breach of duty and the shareholders will have remedies against them irrespective of the requirement for prior approval. In other words these matters are regulated to some extent by the general law.[65]

4.45 However, as against those points, it may be said that there is a potential inconsistency in Part X between, on the one hand, section 319, which regulates the period of service contracts[66] and gives shareholders a voice if they exceed a certain length, and sections 312 and 316, assuming that the result in *Taupo* applies and that those sections are not amended to give shareholders any voice when it comes to covenanted payments.[67] The solution to this problem might be to impose a limit on covenanted payments over a certain amount. This would then mirror the scheme in section 319. Such a limit might lead to directors' remuneration packages in effect being limited because companies would, as they are with service contracts, be unwilling to seek shareholder approval for a higher amount. A major difficulty would be in fixing that amount: if it was pegged to the director's legal entitlement to damages in the event of early termination, it would be difficult to know precisely when that limit had been reached[68] and that is not therefore a limit

---

[62] Para 2.17(1) above.

[63] See para 4.28 above.

[64] By "golden hello" payment we mean a lump sum payment made to a director to induce him to take up employment with the company.

[65] But see the more detailed discussion in Part 9 below.

[66] See section 319 and paras 4.153-4.171 below.

[67] See paras 3.67-3.69 above.

[68] This would be in conflict with our certainty principle in para 2.17(7) above.

which we have put forward. In view of the fact that the DTI's Consultative Paper states that directors' pay is a controversial issue and that the Government is watching developments closely, and further that the review will provide an opportunity to examine the responsibilities of shareholders in this area, the question of imposing a scheme on covenanted payments which involves shareholder approval in certain circumstances has not been pursued in this consultation paper.

4.46   As we indicated in paragraph 4.20 above, our provisional view is that provided section 316(3) is properly applied in practice, as a matter of policy the effect of the *Taupo* decision is right. Accordingly, we do not consider that sections 312-316 should apply to covenanted payments. This would also seem to be the likely starting point even if a change in the law to give shareholders increased responsibility in this sphere is recommended by the review, and it would represent a principled starting point for any future development of the law of that kind.

Consultees are asked whether they agree with our provisional view that sections 312-316 should not apply to covenanted payments.

Option 3: Amend sections 312-316 to make it clear that they do not apply to covenanted payments

4.47   If it is accepted that *Taupo* is right, sections 312-314 should be amended to make clear that they only apply to uncovenanted payments. Covenanted payments would include:

- payments to directors who though executive have no service agreement

- payments to non-executive directors who are given a sum for extra work that they do for the company

if in each case the company has a legally enforceable obligation to pay the sum in question. As indicated above, our provisional view is that the effect of the *Taupo* decision is correct, and we consider provisionally that sections 312-316 should be amended to make it clear that they do not apply to covenanted payments.

Consultees are asked whether they agree with our provisional view that sections 312-316 should be amended to make it clear that they do not apply to covenanted payments.

Option 4: Extend the provisions of sections 312-316 to former directors

4.48   This option seeks consultees' views on one of the recommendations of the Jenkins Committee.[69] So far as former directors are concerned, our provisional view is that if the sections were extended to former directors, they might unfairly catch proper transactions. For example, ex gratia payments made to directors who have had to retire because of illness, to relieve financial hardship. Moreover, there is no

---

[69]   See para 4.13 above.

evidence that directors are resigning before they make any arrangement to receive compensation and they are unlikely in fact to do so.

Consultees are asked whether they agree with our provisional view that sections 312-316 should not be amended so as to apply to payments to former directors.

Option 5: Extend the provisions of sections 312-316 to cover payments to connected persons

4.49 Sections 312-316 do not in terms apply to payments to connected persons occasioned by a director ceasing to hold office, although in other sections of Part X, transactions or arrangements involving connected persons are included.[70] The definition of "connected person" is in section 346, which we review below. Where the payment is made to the connected person as a nominee for the director, the courts are likely to hold that the sections apply anyway. If the payment is made to a connected person on some other basis, for example to the spouse of a retiring director who retires from some other position in the company at the same time as his or her spouse who is a director, the company is already protected by the fact that the director must act in good faith in the best interests of the company. We are not aware that such payments are made to connected persons. If sections 312-316 were extended to cover payments to a connected person of a director in connection with the connected person's loss of office, consideration would have to be given for a provision which exculpates either the payer or the recipient because they did not know the facts which made the person connected. In any event, the provisions applying to connected persons could be no wider than those applying to directors, and so (for example) section 316(3) would apply.

Consultees are asked whether sections 312-316 should cover payments made to connected persons, and, if so, in what circumstances.

Option 6: Require approvals by company in general meeting under sections 312 and 313 to be by special resolution and where disclosure under those sections or section 314 is required, stipulate that disclosure should cover payments made on the same occasion for which disclosure is not required by those sections

4.50 These were recommendations made by the Jenkins Committee which was concerned that a director might receive contractual damages (not disclosable) as well as an ex gratia payment.[71] Our provisional view is that a special resolution is inappropriate because the special resolution procedure is reserved for fundamental corporate changes, and that there is no need for any special statutory rules as to the circular for members.[72]

---

[70] See ss 317(6), 322A(1)(b) and 328(3)(b) for example.

[71] Jenkins Report para 93.

[72] Under the general law, the circular must give full and proper disclosure of the purpose of the meeting: *Kaye v Croydon Tramways* [1898] 1 Ch 358.

Consultees are asked whether they agree with our provisional views that:

(i) it should not be a requirement that the approval by the company in general meeting required by sections 312 and 313 should be by special resolution;

(ii) it should not be a requirement of approval under those sections or section 314 that there should be a stipulation that details of payments which do not require approval should be disclosed when approval of those which require disclosure is sought.

Option 7: Non-contractual payments received for loss of other offices

4.51 As stated in paragraph 4.13 above, the Jenkins Committee recommended that sections 312-315 should be amended to cover payments for the loss, while a director of the company or on the occasion of or in connection with loss of office as a director of the company, of any other office in connection with the management of the company's affairs or of any office as director or otherwise in connection with the management of the affairs of a subsidiary.

4.52 Where a director, in addition to being a director, holds some other position in a company or its group, it is possible for a company to circumvent the requirement for approval of uncovenanted payments by making such a payment to the director in connection with his loss of that position. Under paragraph 8 of Schedule 6 to the Companies Act 1985, such a payment would require to be aggregated in the figure for compensation to directors for loss of office to be shown in the notes to the annual accounts.

4.53 Payments for loss of other offices would appear to be caught by section 316(2)(b) for the purposes of sections 313 and 314, but not by section 312. That section therefore allows some scope for avoidance, and it may be anomalous that the Act considers the figure sufficiently important to be the subject of (aggregated) disclosure but does not require approval of it.

Consultees are asked:

(i) whether they consider that section 312 should require approval of uncovenanted payments made to a director in respect of the loss of some other position in the company, or its group, apart from that of director (a) if he loses that position at the same time as he loses his office as a director, or (b) whenever he receives such a payment;

(ii) whether they consider that sections 312-316 should apply to any such payments which are covenanted as well.

Option 8: Deem payments approved if notified and members raise no objection to the proposed payment within a stipulated period

4.54 The argument raised against shareholder approval is that it may be costly, cumbersome and create uncertainty. One answer to this objection (and indeed to the requirement for approval under, for example, section 319) would be to make the payment subject to "negative approval", ie to deem it approved if the company gave notice of the intention to make it to shareholders unless a specified proportion of members, say shareholders holding shares carrying the right to 5 per cent of the votes capable of being cast on the resolution, objected to it within, say, three weeks of the notice. If an objection was received, the company would have to call a meeting to approve the payment. This option could be in addition to, or in lieu of, the additional requirement for a meeting. We are provisionally of the view that this option should be rejected for the reasons given in 4.171 below.

Consultees are asked whether they agree with our provisional view that sections 312-314 should not be amended so as to permit a company to dispense with approval of the company in general meeting if notice is given to members and there is no objection from a specified proportion of members within a specified period.

Option 9: Amend sections 314 and 315 to cover acquisitions by way of a cancellation of shares under schemes of arrangement etc

4.55   We have noted above that there are deficiencies in sections 314 and 315: in particular that they do not apply to takeovers that proceed by way of a scheme of arrangement involving a cancellation of shares rather than an acquisition of shares, that the offer must be a conditional one and that the offeror and his associates[73] are permitted to vote at the meeting convened pursuant to section 315. It is also the case that there is no remedy at all under the section unless the offer becomes unconditional. If the obligation to make the payment is unconditional, section 315(1) will not apply unless the offer also becomes unconditional. Moreover, if the offer does become unconditional the selling shareholders get the whole of the benefit even if the offer was only a partial one.

Consultees are asked whether they consider that sections 314 and 315 should be amended:

(i) to cover acquisitions by way of a cancellation of shares under a scheme of arrangement;

(ii) to cover unconditional offers;

(iii) to prevent the offeror or his associates from voting at the meeting convened pursuant to section 315;

(iv) in any other way to remove deficiencies in their application to takeovers in accordance with modern practice.

---

[73]   There is no provision for excluding any holder of shares of the same class, as there would be if the court convened a meeting under section 425 of the Companies Act 1985: see *Re Hellenic & General Trust Ltd* [1976] 1 WLR 123. For definitions of "associate", see s 430E of the Companies Act 1985 and the definition of "associate" in the City Code.

Option 10: Amend sections 312-314 to provide civil remedies against the directors and section 315 so that a claim under this section has priority where the amount paid to the director was taken into account in determining the price to offeree shareholders

4.56   We have observed already that section 314 contains provision for recovery of the amount of the payment by former shareholders but that sections 312 and 313 make no such provision. In the case of these sections, the recovery should logically be by the company of which the director was a director since (a) in the case of section 312 it was the payer, and (b) in the case of section 313 it may have been the payer, but in any event the membership of the company is unaffected and if there was any loss it (or the totality of its members) would have been the loser. In the case of section 315, it is appropriate that the remedy should be in favour of the offeree shareholders since if the offer is successful they will no longer be able to claim through the company.

4.57   The provision that would seem appropriate if any provision is to be inserted into section 312 and 313 to deal with civil remedies, is a simple provision that the director is liable to account to the company for the benefit of the payment and the directors who authorised it are liable to indemnify the company against any loss. If the provisions are extended to cover payments to connected persons they should be liable in the same way as recipient directors.

4.58   The insertion of a civil remedy would assist users in understanding the effect of a breach. We are provisionally in favour of it.

4.59   So far as section 314 is concerned, it is possible that the payment may be made by the company rather than say, the offeror, and that accordingly a claim pursuant to section 312 (on the basis that the payment was a breach of duty by the directors involved) may lie as well as a claim under section 315. We suggest that it is clear that the director should not retain the payment if the appropriate disclosure and approval does not occur. In addition, if the company made the payment in circumstances where the shareholders parted with their shares to the offeror, on the face of it the benefit of the remedy should not reside with the company and through its new owner, the offeror, because the former shareholders would get nothing. On the other hand, it may be that they should not get anything if the price for their shares took into account that the company would be making payment rather than the offeror direct. In those circumstances the remedy should lie with the offeror.

Consultees are asked:

(i) whether they agree with our provisional view that sections 312 and 313 should be amended to provide for civil remedies on the lines suggested in paragraph 4.50;

(ii) whether section 315 should be amended so as to provide that, unless the court otherwise orders, the claim of former shareholders under section 315 should prevail over that of any of the company in section 312 in respect of the same payment.

***Option 11: Reinforce section 316(3) by requiring companies to disclose in
their annual accounts particulars of the calculation of compensation paid
to a director***

4.60   While no doubt any prudent board would wish to have the benefit of legal advice
when approving a severance payment to ensure that it was properly calculated,
there is a certain amount which turns on the precise facts when poor conduct or
misconduct is alleged or other factual questions arise as to the proper allowance to
be made for mitigation. In the last mentioned case, the directors can take the
obvious step in the case of damages for breach of contract of paying the director
his contractual entitlement and waiting to see when he gets a new post. But there
is some evidence[74] that directors need to be encouraged, as exhorted by the
Combined Code, to take a robust line and one way of achieving this would be
through a requirement for disclosure.[75] In larger companies directors' claims for
compensation following early termination of their contracts will be considered by
the remuneration committee. At the present time, the notes to the annual
accounts show the aggregate amount paid to all directors for loss of office in the
year in question.[76]

**Consultees are asked whether they consider that particulars of a
severance payment made to a director should be included in the annual
accounts and, if so, what in their view those particulars should cover and
when the disclosure requirement should arise.**

***Option 12: Extend section 312 to cover the situation where the payment is
made by a company to a director of its holding company in connection
with loss of office as such director***

4.61   Section 312 does not deal with the situation where a payment is made by say a
wholly-owned subsidiary to a director of its parent company. The director may
have been employed as a director of the holding company by the subsidiary,
especially if the subsidiary is the company which employs all employees in the
group. Section 320, by contrast, deals with the situation where a company enters
into a substantial property transaction with a director of a parent company. In that
situation the Act presently requires a resolution of both the subsidiary and the
parent company, unless the subsidiary is a wholly owned subsidiary. In that case
its shareholders do not need to be protected by a requirement for disclosure or the
passing of a resolution.

**Consultees are asked whether section 312 should apply to payments made
by a company to a director of a holding company in connection with his
loss of office as such director and, if so, whether the requirement for
disclosure and approval should be satisfied in both companies (other than
a wholly-owned subsidiary).**

---

[74]   See above paras 4.30 - 4.32.

[75]   In para 10.40 below, we consider whether the payment of funds in breach of ss 312-314
should be a criminal offence.

[76]   Companies Act 1985, Sched 6, para 8.

Generally

Finally, consultees are asked whether any further reform of sections 312-316 should be considered.

SECTION 317: DISCLOSURE BY DIRECTORS TO THEIR BOARD

317.—(1) It is the duty of a director of a company who is in any way, whether directly or indirectly, interested in a contract or proposed contract with the company to declare the nature of his interest at a meeting of the directors of the company.

(2) In the case of a proposed contract, the declaration shall be made—

(a)   at the meeting of the directors at which the question of entering into the contract is first taken into consideration; or

(b)   if the director was not at the date of that meeting interested in the proposed contract, at the next meeting of the directors held after he became so interested;

and, in a case where the director becomes interested in a contract after it is made, the declaration shall be made at the first meeting of the directors held after he becomes so interested.

(3) For purposes of this section, a general notice given to the directors of a company by a director to the effect that—

(a)   he is a member of a specified company or firm and is to be regarded as interested in any contract which may, after the date of the notice, be made with that company or firm; or

(b)   he is to be regarded as interested in any contract which may after the date of the notice be made with a specified person who is connected with him (within the meaning of section 346 below),

is deemed a sufficient declaration of interest in relation to any such contract.

(4) However, no such notice is of effect unless either it is given at a meeting of the directors or the director takes reasonable steps to secure that it is brought up and read at the next meeting of the directors after it is given.

(5) A reference in this section to a contract includes any transaction or arrangement (whether or not constituting a contract) made or entered into on or after 22nd December 1980.

(6) For purposes of this section, a transaction or arrangement of a kind described in section 330 (prohibition of loans, quasi-loans etc to directors) made by a company for a director of the company or a person connected with such a director is treated (if it would not otherwise be so treated, and whether or not it is prohibited by that section) as a transaction or arrangement in which that director is interested.

(7) A director who fails to comply with this section is liable to a fine.

(8) This section applies to a shadow director as it applies to a director, except that a shadow director shall declare his interest, not at a meeting of the directors, but by a notice in writing to the directors which is either—

    (a)   a specific notice given before the date of the meeting at which, if he had been a director, the declaration would be required by subsection (2) to be made; or

    (b)   a notice which under subsection (3) falls to be treated as a sufficient declaration of that interest (or would fall to be so treated apart from subsection (4)).

(9) Nothing in this section prejudices the operation of any rule of law restricting directors of a company from having an interest in contracts with the company.

General

4.62   In the words of Lord Templeman, "Section 317 shows the importance which the legislature attaches to the principle that a company should be protected against a director who has a conflict of interest and duty."[77] This section is derived from section 199 of the Companies Act 1948.[78] The duty on a director to disclose to the company, through its board, any interest in its contracts first appeared in section 81 of the Companies Act 1928,[79] later re-enacted as section 149 of the Companies Act 1929. This duty is in addition to the general law which makes voidable a contract between a company and a director where the latter has a conflict of interest for which he does not have the fully informed consent of the company in general meeting.[80] The statutory duty of disclosure to the board under section 317, and the duty under the general law to make full diclosure to the company in general meeting for its consent, are easily confused but must be kept separate.

4.63   The effect of section 149 was reviewed by the Cohen Committee. The focus of the Cohen Committee's concern was the question whether directors should be prohibited from voting at board meetings on contracts in which they had an interest, and additionally, if it was desirable to require disclosure to shareholders, through the director's report, of "exceptional contracts" in which they had some personal stake. Having concluded that neither of the foregoing should be dealt with by statute, the Committee limited its recommendations to "one relatively small matter". It recommended that where disclosure was to be made by a general

---

[77]   *Guinness plc v Saunders* [1990] 2 AC 663, at 694E-F.

[78]   As amended by sections 60, 63(3) and Sched 3, para 25 of the Companies Act 1980 and (s 80 and Sched 2 of the 1980 Act so far as they affected the fine imposed by s 199(4) of the 1948 Act).

[79]   Before 1928, statute law, although dealing with the issue of directors' interest in contracts with the company, had not sought to impose any duty of disclosure. See s 29 of the Joint Stock Companies Act 1844, which disqualified the director from acting or voting as a director in relation to any contract in which he was interested, and required shareholders' approval of the same, and s 85 of the Companies Clauses Consolidation Act 1845, which disqualified a director with a conflict of interest from voting or acting.

[80]   See para 4.69 below.

written notice of a director's membership of another company, so that he might be regarded as interested in any contract made with that company after the date of the notice:[81]

> it should be provided that the notice of disclosure should be deemed to be part of the proceedings of a meeting of directors so that the obligation to keep minutes of a meeting of directors laid down by section 120 shall apply.[82]

This recommendation was implemented by section 41(5) of the Companies Act 1947.[83] Section 149 of the Companies Act 1929, as amended by the Companies Act 1947, was re-enacted as section 199 of the Companies Act 1948.

4.64   In 1962, the Jenkins Committee recommended that section 199 be limited, so that, rather than require a director to disclose an interest, however small, only in contracts that came before the board, the requirement should fix on the disclosure of "material interests in contracts, whether or not any such contracts come before the board of directors."[84] However, it also recommended that there be a saving provision:

> for cases where a director can show that he had no knowledge of the contract and that it was unreasonable to expect him to have had such knowledge.[85]

4.65   In addition, it recommended that section 199(3)[86] should be extended in order that a director could give a general notice of a broader range of interests than simply those related to his membership of another firm, and to require the nature of the interest to be stated.[87] It rejected as not "desirable or practicable" the notion that a director's interests should be disclosed to the general body of shareholders. At most, in the particular circumstances of a director having a material interest in a managing agency approved to manage the whole or a substantial part of the company's business, the Committee saw merit in that interest being disclosed in the directors' report and the relevant contract being filed with the Registrar of Companies.[88] However, none of its principal recommendations were enacted.[89]

---

[81] Pursuant to provisions then found in s149(3) of the Companies Act 1929 and now in s 317(3), excluding the later added s317(3)(b), of the Companies Act 1985.

[82] The Cohen Report, para 95, p 50. See also Recommendation V, p 52. Section 120 of the 1929 Act is now in s 382 of the 1985 Act.

[83] Now s 317(4).

[84] The Jenkins Report, para 95, p 33 and Recommendation (l), para 99, p 36.

[85] The Jenkins Report; Recommendation (l), p 36.

[86] Now s 317(3).

[87] The Jenkins Report, para 95.

[88] In particular because the director would be drawing part of his remuneration for managing the company "indirectly through the agency". See the Jenkins Report, para 96, pp 33-34.

[89] Although by ss 15-24 of the Companies Act 1967, the contents of directors' reports were expanded to include declarations as to directors' interests in subsisting and pre-existing

4.66 The Companies Bill 1973 contained provisions which, although adopting the Jenkins Committee's suggestions in relation to contracts not coming before the board and the extension of section 199(3), did not incorporate its "materiality" threshold or the saving provision in relation to a director's "reasonable knowledge" of the existence of a contract.[90]

4.67 In addition, disclosure of the interests of members of a director's family in contracts or proposed contracts was also required.[91] The Bill was lost, however, as a consequence of the first 1974 general election.

4.68 In 1977[92] a White Paper, "the Conduct of Company Directors", again addressed disclosure of directors' interests in contracts with the company. It proposed inter alia fuller disclosure in the annual accounts of certain transactions involving possible conflicts of interests.[93] The following year, another White Paper, "Changes in Company Law",[94] set out clauses in a draft Bill that sought to give statutory effect to the recommendations in "The Conduct of Company Directors", focusing, in clause 52, on the increased disclosure of transactions involving directors in the company accounts.[95] However the 1978 Bill was lost as a consequence of the general election of 1979.

4.69 The Companies Act 1980[96] widened the scope of the duty of disclosure in section 199 so that it attached to shadow directors[97] and made the first express reference

---

contracts: see s16(1)(c) of the 1967 Act (repealed by the Companies Act 1980, its provisions becoming part of s 54 of the 1980 Act).

[90] Clause 47, subsections (1) and (2) of the Bill stated:

(1) Subject to the provisions of this section, it shall be the duty of a director of a company who is in any way, whether directly or indirectly, interested in a contract or proposed contract with the company (whether or not a contract coming before a meeting of the directors of the company) as soon as practicable to declare the nature of his interest to the other directors.

(2) Where a director gives to the directors of the company a general notice stating that, by reason of the facts specified in the notice, he is to be regarded as interested in contracts of any description which may subsequently be made to the company, that notice shall be deemed for the purposes of this section to be a sufficient declaration of his interest, so far as attributable to those facts, in relation to any contract of that description which may subsequently be made by the company: but no such general notice shall have effect in relation to any contract unless it is given before the date on which the question of entering into the contract is first taken into consideration on behalf of the company.

[91] See clause 47(4).

[92] The Report of the Committee of Enquiry on Industrial Democracy (the "Bullock Report"), of January 1977, touched on the question of a director's fiduciary duty to the company in the context of outside interests, but only in the specific context of employee representatives on boards.

[93] See The Conduct of Company Directors (1977) Cmnd 7037, paras 16-18, pp 4-5.

[94] Changes in Company Law (1978) Cmnd 7291.

[95] Interestingly, the Bill adopted the Jenkins Committee's "material interest" threshold; see clause 52(1)(a).

[96] See ss 60, 63(3) and para 25 of Sched 3.

to the possibility of directors being interested in contracts made between the company and persons "connected" with them.[98] It also extended reference to a "contract" to include any "transaction or arrangement" entered into after 22nd December 1980,[99] whether or not constituting a contract, thus increasing the disclosure that needed to be given.

4.70 Pursuant to the joint recommendations of the Law Commission and the Scottish Law Commission in relation to the consolidation of the Companies Acts,[100] section 63(3) of the 1980 Act was clarified to ensure that general declarations of interest by shadow directors were properly recorded in board minutes, and this clarification is reflected in the current section 382(2) of the Act.

Effect of section 317

4.71 Section 317 imposes a statutory duty on directors,[101] including shadow directors,[102] to disclose[103] to the board[104] any interest[105] they[106] may have in any proposed or subsisting contract or any proposed or subsisting transaction or arrangement with it[107] (in the case of a transaction or arrangement, provided that the latter was made or entered into on or after 22nd December 1980);[108] subject to the penalty of a fine[109] for any failure to comply with the statutory duty in the section.[110]

---

[97] See ss 317(8) and 741(2) of the Companies Act 1985 and s 63(3) of the Companies Act 1980.

[98] See ss 317(3)(b) and 346 of the Companies Act 1985 and para 25, Sched 3 of the Companies Act 1980, and para 4.115 below.

[99] See ss 317(5) and (6) of the Companies Act 1985 and s60 of the Companies Act 1980.

[100] See Law Com No 126 and Scot Law Com No 83 (1983) Cmnd 9114, Amendment No 50, pp 34-35.

[101] Section 317(1).

[102] Section 317(8).

[103] Although the duty is one of disclosure, it is satisfied only by "declaration", apart from the instances in which the use of a notice is permissible. The degree of detail required to satisfy the requirement for disclosure will depend on the circumstances of the case. See *Gary v New Augarita Porcupine Mines Ltd* [1952] 3 DLR 1 PC.

[104] Section 317(2) and (3). See also *Guinness plc v Saunders* [1988] 1 WLR 863.

[105] Even if the benefit is only nominal: see *Todd v Robinson* (1884) 14 QBD 739, CA.

[106] For the position in respect of interests of connected persons, see paras 4.110 and 4.115 below.

[107] Including their own contract of service and any variation in it (see *Runciman v Walter Runciman plc* [1992] BCLC 1084 and, further ss 317(1), (5), (6) and (9) and s 330 of the Companies Act 1985) and transactions and arrangements described in s 330 of the Act. There is authority to suggest that that the section is not restricted only to contracts that come before the board (see *Neptune v Fitzgerald* [1995] 1 BCLC 352).

[108] Section 317(5).

[109] See s 730 and Sched 24 of the 1985 Act. The fine is unlimited on conviction on indictment, but limited to the statutory maximum of £5000 on summary conviction. See further Part 10 below.

[110] Section 317(7).

4.72   In relation to proposed contracts, the duty of disclosure is discharged either by making a declaration or by giving a general notice. If it is discharged by making a declaration, this must be made at the board meeting on the occasion that entering the contract is first "taken into consideration".[111] If the director acquires his interest subsequently, the declaration must be made at the first board meeting after he became interested in the contract. However, a shadow director[112] may only declare his interest in a contract (either proposed or subsisting) by a notice in writing to the directors (having the same effect as a verbal declaration and being duly deemed to be and minuted as part of the proceedings),[113] which must be given to them prior to the date of the meeting at which an ordinary director would have needed to give notice under subsection (2).[114]

4.73   Disclosure may alternatively be made by a general notice given to all the directors that the director is a member of a specified company or firm,[115] and should be treated as interested in any contract made with it subsequent to the date of the notice, or that he should similarly be regarded as interested in any contract the company may make with a specified person with whom he is "connected" within the definitions set out in section 346 of the 1985 Act.[116] A shadow director may similarly give a general notice under section 317(8)(b), which must be in writing.[117] In the case of a director other than a shadow director, the notice is of no effect unless it is either given at a meeting of directors or the director takes reasonable steps to secure that it is brought in and read at the next board meeting after it is given.[118]

4.74   In relation to contracts that the company has already concluded, but in which a director acquires an interest, the director must declare his interest the first full board meeting following the date on which the director becomes so interested. A shadow director must declare that he has acquired an interest in a contract already concluded by written notice to the directors.

4.75   Section 317(9) states that the obligation to make disclosure to the board does not alter the general law. Under the general law a director cannot vote on any matter in which he is interested or receive any benefit without the informed consent of shareholders. This informed consent is frequently given in the articles of

---

[111]   Section 317(2)(a).

[112]   See definition in s 741(2) and para 17.11 below.

[113]   See ss 317(8) and 382(3).

[114]   A difficulty here is that a shadow director may not be aware of the point at which the board first considers entering the contract, particularly if that consideration is sufficiently informal not to be minuted.

[115]   Section 317(3)(a). Thus an interest in addition to membership of the other company (apart from a link with a connected person as envisaged in s317(3)(b)) will not be deemed sufficiently declared if made by general notice.

[116]   Section 317(3)(b). For the meaning of "connected persons", see para 4.110 below.

[117]   Section 317(8).

[118]   Section 317(4).

association, but contingent on disclosure which complies with section 317. Thus articles of association commonly provide:

> Subject to the provisions of section 199 of the Act a Director may contract with and participate in the profits of any contract or arrangement with the Company as if he were not a Director. A Director shall also be capable of voting in respect of any such contract or arrangement where he has previously disclosed his interest to the Company ... .[119]

4.76 The current version of Table A[120] also makes the permission given to directors to have an interest in contracts with the company subject to proper disclosure of such interests, but in this case the disclosure requirement is modified in accordance with the Jenkins Committee recommendations:

> 85. Subject to the provisions of the Act, and provided that he has disclosed to the directors the nature and extent of any material interest of his, a director notwithstanding his office—
>
> (a) may be a party to, or otherwise interested in, any transaction or arrangement with the company or in which the company is otherwise interested;
>
> (b) may be a director or other officer of, or employed by, or a party to any transaction or arrangement with, or otherwise interested in, any body corporate promoted by the company or in which the company is otherwise interested; and
>
> (c) shall not, by reason of his office, be accountable to the company for any benefit which he derives from any such office or employment or from any such transaction or arrangement or from any interest in any such body corporate and no such transaction or arrangement shall be liable to be avoided on the ground of any such interest or benefit.
>
> 86. For the purposes of regulation 85—
>
> (a) a general notice given to the directors that a director is to be regarded as having an interest of the nature and extent specified in the notice in any transaction or arrangement in which a specified person or class of persons is interested shall be deemed to be a disclosure that the director has an interest in any such transaction of the nature and extent so specified; and
>
> (b) an interest of which a director has no knowledge and of which it is unreasonable to expect him to have knowledge shall not be treated as an interest of his.

---

[119] Taken from *Palmer's Company Precedents* (17 ed, 1956) p 556. *Ireland Alloys Ltd v Dingwall & Others* (unreported) 9 December 1997; *Re BSB Holdings Limited* [1996] 1 BCLC 155, 249-50.

[120] SI 1985/805.

4.77 It has been held in Australia that the breach of section 317 does not of itself give rise to an action for damages for breach of statutory duty.[121] The point has not arisen in the United Kingdom but it is considered that the same would be held to be the position under UK law.

4.78 There is then the question of the effect of a breach of section 317 on the contract which the board subsequently approves. In *Hely-Hutchinson v Brayhead*[122] this point was not contested but it was considered by the Court of Appeal. Their conclusion was that breach of the section did not of itself render the contract unenforceable. Where the director ought under the general law to have disclosed his interest, the consequence was that the contract was voidable.[123] The contract would therefore be binding on the company unless it exercised its right under the general law to avoid it and that right had not been lost, for instance by affirmation or because the rights of a third party, who had no notice of the breach of section 317 and had acquired his rights for value, had intervened. Lord Pearson said:

> The section merely creates a statutory duty of disclosure and imposes a fine for non-compliance.[124]

4.79 In *Guinness Plc v Saunders*,[125] Lord Goff, obiter, approved Lord Pearson's approach in *Hely-Hutchinson* adding that:

> On this basis[126] I cannot see that a breach of section 317, which is not for present purposes significantly different from section 199 of the Act of 1948, had itself any effect upon the contract ... As a matter of general law, to the extent that there was failure by Mr Ward to comply with his duty of disclosure under the relevant article of Guinness ... the contract (if any) between him and Guinness was no doubt voidable under the ordinary principles of the general law to which Lord Pearson refers.[127]

4.80 In the same case, Lord Templeman in passing suggested that *Hely-Hutchinson* decided that section 317 rendered the contract voidable.[128] However, Harman J, reviewing these decisions in the later case of *Lee Panavision Ltd v Lee Lighting Ltd*,[129] concluded that Lord Templeman was incorrect in this and that "section 317 itself does not invalidate any contract"[130] and was not "the foundation for the

---

[121] *Castlereagh Motels v Davies-Roe* (1967) 67 SR (NSW) 279.

[122] [1968] 1 QB 549.

[123] [1968] 1 QB 549; *per* Lord Denning MR at p 585, on the basis that the situation was analogous to non-disclosure in a contract *uberrimae fidei*; *per* Lord Wilberforce at p 589-591 and *per* Lord Pearson at p 594.

[124] [1968] 1 QB 549 at p 594.

[125] [1990] 2 AC 633. See also [1988] 1 WLR 863, CA for the contrasting view of Fox LJ.

[126] Approving the text of Lord Pearson's speech at [1968] 1 QB 549, p 594D-G.

[127] [1990] 2 AC 633, *per* Lord Goff, 697F-H.

[128] At 694E.

[129] [1991] BCC 620.

[130] [1991] BCC 620, at p 627C.

rule of law that a director or other fiduciary may not be concerned in a contract in which he also has a duty or an interest."[131] That arose from the general law.

Stock Exchange requirements

4.81 The Stock Exchange Listing Rules require[132] that listed company articles of association must:

> prohibit a director from voting on any contract or arrangement or any other proposal in which he has an interest which (together with any interest of any person connected with him) is to his knowledge a material interest otherwise than by virtue of his interests in shares or debentures or other securities of, or otherwise in or through, the listed company.[133]

4.82 Exceptions to this prohibition are permitted in respect of resolutions relating to the giving of security, guarantees or indemnities in relation to debts or other corporate obligations incurred or assumed by the director, or another person at the company's request, on behalf of the company or its subsidiaries;[134] offers of securities in which a director may be entitled to participate;[135] contracts or arrangements with other companies in which the director or persons connected with him have, to their knowledge, a 1 per cent or less share of the equity or voting rights;[136] arrangements for the benefit of company or subsidiary company employees, where the directors entitlement is generally no more than that of other employees[137] and Directors & Officers ("D&O") insurance cover.[138]

Requirements of the Codes

(a) The corporate governance reports

4.83 The Cadbury Committee made no recommendations as to what a company's articles should contain, but stated that its Code of Best Practice was founded on the principles of "openness, integrity and accountability".[139] In the context of contracts in which directors had an interest, it confined its explicit recommendations to directors' service contracts, noting that "executive directors should play no part in decisions on their own remuneration".[140]

---

[131] [1991] BCC 620, at p 627D-E.

[132] Rule 13.8.

[133] Para 20, Appendix 1 to Chapter 13.

[134] Para 20(a)(i) and (ii).

[135] Para 20(b).

[136] Para 20(c).

[137] Para 20(d).

[138] Para 20(e).

[139] See the Cadbury Report paras 3.2-3.4, p 16.

[140] See para 4.42, p 31.

4.84   The Greenbury Committee, which focused exclusively on director's remuneration, echoed the Cadbury Committee's conclusion on this particular conflict of interest,[141] and the Hampel Report supported its approach, emphasising that directors "should not participate in the decisions on their own remuneration packages".[142]

(b) The Combined Code

4.85   Principle A.1.5 of the Combined Code simply states:

> All directors should bring an independent judgement to bear on issues of strategy, performance, resources (including key appointments) and standards of conduct.

4.86   In relation to non-executive directors only, the Combined Code further identifies their "independent judgement" as being impliedly undermined where they are not "independent of management" or might be "materially" influenced by a "business or other relationship".[143]

What must a director disclose?

4.87   Section 317(1) requires the director to disclose "the nature of his interest". It is not enough for him merely to state that he has an interest. He must also state what that interest comprises.[144] Dealing with the same phrase in section 94 of the Canadian Companies Act 1937, Lord Radcliffe, giving the advice of the Privy Council said:

> There is no precise formula that will determine the extent of detail that is called for when a director declares his interest or the nature of his interest. The amount of detail required must depend in each case upon the nature of the contract or arrangement proposed and the context in which it arises. His declaration must make his colleagues "fully informed of the real state of things" (see *Imperial Mercantile Credit Assn v Coleman* (1873) LR 6 (HL) 189 at p 201, per Lord Chelmsford). If it is material to their judgment that they should know not merely that he has an interest, but what it is and how far it goes, then he must see to it that they are informed (see Lord Cairns in the same case at p 205).[145]

---

[141]   See the Greenbury Report, para 1.12, Code of Practice Provision A.1 and Action Point 4.8.

[142]   See the Hampel Report, Principles II, 2.11, p 19, and IV, 4.11-13, p 36.

[143]   Materiality and independence from management are not further defined in Principle A.3.2, Part 2 or in provision B.2.2 in relation to non-executive directors, which echoes para 4.12 of the Cadbury Report. It should be noted that the Cadbury Report had recommended that whether a non-executive director had the necessary independence was a matter for the board (see para 4.12, p 22); but see also its comments on matters that impliedly undermine independence at para 4.13. See also, generally, Action Point 4.8 of the Greenbury Report.

[144]   *Imperial Mercantile Credit Association v Coleman* (1873) LR 6HL 189.

[145]   *Gray v New Augarita Porcupine Mines Ltd* [1952] 3 DLR 1.

Disclosure of interests already known to the board

4.88 In *Runciman v Walter Runciman plc*[146], a director's service contract had been extended by the board. The company's articles required that a director with an interest in a contract should disclose his interest at a directors' meeting in accordance with section 199 of the Companies Act 1948. No declaration in accordance with the terms of section 317 ever took place in relation to the director's interest in the extended term. Simon Brown J held that both a director's service contract and contractual variations of it would be caught by the provisions of the section.[147]

4.89 However, the court held that in relation to the particular circumstances of the case, there was no requirement for a declaration.[148] Simon Brown J held that:

> Whatever may be the suggested advantages of a strictly formal approach to the section, such as a record of the proceedings and a reduced risk of directors abusing their position, no such advantage would have accrued here. It is certainly not suggested in this case that the plaintiff or his fellow directors in any way abused their position.[149]

4.90 On this basis, and on the grounds that all affected parties were aware of the nature of the plaintiff's contract and his interest in its extension, his conclusion was that the "balance of justice" did not require that "a merely technical breach" of the statutory duty of disclosure should render the variation unenforceable.[150]

Disclosure by a sole director

4.91 In *Neptune (Vehicle Washing Equipment) Ltd v Fitzgerald*,[151] the director was the sole member of the board and the question arose as to whether a declaration was required under these circumstances.

4.92 Emphasising the importance of section 317, Lightman J held that the object of the section was to ensure that the issue of a director's interest in a contract became an "item of business at a meeting of the directors".[152] Thus, a sole director, holding a meeting at which only he was present:

> must still make a declaration to himself and have a statutory pause for thought, though it may be that the declaration does not have to be out

---

[146] [1992] BCLC 1085.

[147] [1992] BCLC 1085, *per* Simon Brown J at pp 1093g-i and 1094c-f.

[148] [1992] BCLC 1085, at p 1095h-i.

[149] [1992] BCLC 1085, at p 1096e. The contract may, however, be voidable under the general law: see paras 5.69-5.71 below.

[150] [1992] BCLC 1085, at p 1097b-d. This approach was taken by the Court of Appeal (obiter) in *Lee Panavision Ltd v Lee Lighting Ltd* [1992] BCLC 22, 33 c-d, and by Knox J in *Re Dominion International Group plc (No 2)* [1996] 1 BCLC 572, 600a.

[151] [1995] 1 BCLC 352.

[152] [1995] 1 BCLC 352, *per* Lightman J at p 359a.

loud, and he must record that he has made the declaration in the minutes.[153]

Voting by the interested director

4.93 In the United Kingdom the question whether a director can vote on a matter in which he is interested is usually dealt with in the articles. If the articles are silent, there is nothing in section 317 to prevent the director from voting.[154] The position is the same in New Zealand where the matter may be dealt with by the articles but if it is not so dealt with the director may vote.[155] In Australia however there is a provision, which applies only to public companies, which prevents a director of a public company from voting on any matter in which he has a material personal interest. What constitutes such an interest is not defined, but the prohibition on voting does not apply where the director's interest is held as a member of the company and in common with other members of the company, or where the transaction is a directors' insurance policy unless the company is the insurer. Moreover the prohibition does not apply if the board passes a resolution which specifies the director, the interest and the matter and states that the directors are satisfied that the interest of the director should not disqualify him from voting on the matter.[156] The effect of the recommendations in the Hong Kong Consultancy Report would be that no director could vote on a matter in which he was interested.[157]

Options for reform

4.94 We proceed generally on the basis that the Cohen Committee's views remain valid, that disclosure of contracts in which a director is interested should be mandatory, and if mandatory, as a practical matter, must be to the board so far as the statutory duty is concerned. This was the view of both the Cohen Committee and the Jenkins Committee. Below, we set out 13 options for reform (including, as option 1, no change to the current wording). Some of these suggest possible exemptions to the disclosure requirements (options 3, 4, 5, 6, 7, and 8) or other ways in which the requirements may be limited (option 2); others suggest ways in which the requirements could be tightened up (options 10, 11, 12 and 13). Option 9 concerns the consequences of breach of the provisions. With the exception of option 1 (no change) consultees may choose any number of these options. In considering the options for reform, consultees are asked to have regard to the principles set out in Part 2 above.

Option 1: No change

4.95 Consultees may take the view that the disclosure requirements contained in section 317 are operating satisfactorily in practice. The arguments in favour of

---

[153] [1995] 1 BCLC 352, *per* Lightman J at p 360c.

[154] But, if he votes, there may be consequences under the general law: s 317(7).

[155] Section 144 of the Companies Act 1993, which is set out in Appendix I below.

[156] See s 232A of the Australian Corporations Law.

[157] See para 6.20 of the Consultancy Report set out in Appendix L below.

creating exceptions to the requirements, or tightening up the provisions in certain respects, are discussed under the relevant options below.

Consultees are asked whether section 317 should be retained as it is.

Option 2: Limit the duty of disclosure to material interests only

4.96   On the face of it, it seems unnecessary that a director should have to disclose any interest however trivial. The alternative would be to confine the obligation to disclose to material interests.[158] If that were to be done, how should "material" be defined? It is difficult to see how it could be defined in terms of a monetary amount. The choice would appear to be whether it means:

- material in the sense that the board would normally consider a transaction of this type;

- material to the director; or

- material to the company.

4.97   Financial Reporting Standard 8 on Related Party Disclosures in the annual accounts states that:

> Transactions are material when their disclosure might reasonably be expected to influence decisions made by users of general purpose financial statements. The materiality of related party transactions is to be judged, not only in terms of their significance to the reporting entity, but also in relation to the other related party when that party is
>
> > (a) a director, key manager or other individual in a position to influence, or accountable for stewardship of, the reporting entity; or
> >
> > (b) a member of the close family of any individual mentioned in (a) above; or
> >
> > (c) an entity controlled by any individual mentioned in (a) or (b) above.

By analogy to the first sentence quoted above, section 317 could define "material interests" as those whose disclosure might reasonably be expected to affect the decisions of the board.[159] In the above passage materiality is to be judged both in

---

[158]   Regulation 85 of Table A (as now in force) permits a director to be interested in a contract provided he discloses any material interest in it. See para 4.74 above. Section 232A of the Australian Corporations Law (referred to in para 4.91 above) refers to "material personal interest" of a director, but does not define this term.

[159]   See generally the discussion of materiality in Part 7 below, and compare the meaning of "material" contract for the purpose of the disclosure of material contracts in a prospectus in accordance with para 14 of Sched 4 to the Companies Act 1948. This was interpreted as meaning any contract which, "whether deterrent or not, an intending investor ought to have the opportunity of considering": see *Buckley on the Companies Acts* (13 ed, 1957) p 96 and the authorities there cited.

terms of significance to the company and in terms of significance to the director concerned. By contrast, the recent Financial Reporting Standard for Smaller Entities does not require disclosure in the annual accounts of transactions which are not material to the company, thus making the financial amounts involved generally a critical factor. Section 139 of the Companies Act of New Zealand[160] sets out a non-exhaustive list of situations which will result in a director being interested in a transaction with the company for the purposes of their section 317, but this approach is also likely to result in situations arising in which a director should be taken to be interested but which fall outside the statutory list.

Consultees are accordingly asked whether they consider that section 317 should only apply to material interests in a contract; and if so (a) whether "material" should be defined by statute, and (b) if so, whether it should mean those interests whose disclosure might reasonably be expected to affect the decision of the board or some other meaning.

Option 3: Exempt from the obligation of disclosure transactions or arrangements which either do not come before the board or a committee of the board, or do not require approval by the board or a committee of the board

4.98   The director's duty to disclose an interest in a contract[161] in section 317 has been held to be a general obligation applying to all contracts and not only those that come before the company's board.[162] In many large companies only contracts of very high value or policy importance require board approval. Section 317 thus places a heavy disclosure burden on directors in large companies who may have no knowledge, through their office, of minor contracts in which a disclosable interest of theirs has arisen. The burden is all the heavier as section 317 contains no de minimis threshold. The duty on directors to disclose very minor interests imposes, in turn, administrative burdens on companies in relation to the recording of those interests. The effect of this option would be that there would be no statutory duty to disclose interests in contracts which do not qualify for consideration by the board.

4.99   On the other hand, this option may result in there being insufficient protection or information for creditors or members, or may open up areas for dispute and litigation. For this reason, our provisional view is that there should be no exemption along the lines suggested above.

Consultees are asked whether they agree with our provisional view that section 317 should not exempt directors from the need to disclose their interests in transactions or arrangements which either do not come

---

[160]   Set out in Appendix I below. The final category is other direct or indirect material interests (s 139(1)(e)).

[161]   "Contract" is defined as including all transactions and arrangements, whether or not constituting a contract. See s 317(5).

[162]   See *Neptune (Vehicle Washing Equipment) Ltd v Fitzgerald* [1995] 1 BCLC 352, *per* Lightman J at p 359f-h.

before the board, or a committee of the board, or do not require approval by the board, or a committee of the board.

Option 4: Exempt sole director companies

4.100   Both Cheffins and Gower criticise the *Neptune* case. Gower described it as "the apotheosis of meaningless disclosure".[163] Cheffins said "the judiciary again adopted a highly technical and arguably unnecessary strict interpretation of legislative measures".[164]

4.101   Does a disclosure of interest by a director to himself serve any useful purpose? It may have little effect on the director's decision.[165] However it may facilitate record keeping and thus the process of liquidation, should the company become insolvent.[166] The further question is whether, in this one case, disclosure should be to the shareholders.[167] Our provisional view is that in a single director company there should be no obligation on a director to make any disclosure to the board. On the other hand, we consider that it would be appropriate for this information to be made available to the shareholders of such a company. At paragraph 4.118 we consider whether there should be disclosure of directors' interests to shareholders (for all companies - not just single director companies) both by means of a register of directors' interests and a report to shareholders in the annual accounts. This would serve a similar purpose to a requirement that directors of single director companies should disclose interests to the company in general meeting, and would in our view render such an additional requirement for single director companies unnecessary. If, however, the suggestion put forward at paragraph 4.118 is not adopted, then we provisionally consider that there should be a requirement that a director of a single director company should disclose interests to the company in general meeting. However, we would allow shareholders to waive or vary this duty by resolution or in the articles.[168]

Consultees are accordingly asked whether they agree with our provisional views that:

(i) section 317 should not apply where there is only one director; and

(ii) if the suggestion put forward at paragraph 4.118 is not adopted, there should be a requirement that where there is only one director, the director should disclose interests to the company in general meeting,

---

[163]   *Gower*, p 629.

[164]   Brian R Cheffins, *Company Law, Theory, Structure and Operation* (1997) p 354.

[165]   The draft Bill to amend the Corporation Law published in Australia on 8 April 1998 disapplies the requirement for disclosure by directors of interests to single director companies: New Directors' Duties and Corporate Governance Provisions, s 13.

[166]   Compare section 322B: see paras 4.210-4.213 below.

[167]   Gower argues (p 629) that the plaintiff's argument in *Neptune,* that disclosure where there is a sole director should be to shareholders, "has a lot to commend it."

[168]   This should be expressly provided for in the statute because of s 310. See below paras 11.49-11.52.

unless this requirement is waived by shareholders or varied by resolution or in the articles.

Option 5: Exempt from the obligation of disclosure interests in director's own service agreement

4.102   This option would be consistent with developing case law.[169] In addition, there are already separate provisions for ensuring that shareholders can inspect directors' service contracts[170] and for regulating the length of directors' service contracts.[171] Our provisional view is therefore that there should be an exemption for a director's own service contract. The exemption would have to cover variations to service agreements, as well as the service agreement itself.

Consultees are accordingly asked whether they agree with our provisional view that section 317 should exempt directors from the need to make formal disclosure of their interest in their own service contracts.

Option 6: Exempt from the obligation of disclosure executive directors' interests in contracts or arrangements made for the benefit of all employees

4.103   The argument that a director should disclose his interest in a contract or arrangement diminishes if the interest which he has is as an employee and the benefit is one which is ordinarily made to the "company's" employees and on terms no less favourable.[172] It is suggested that it is likely to be obvious to fellow directors that executive directors have an interest. On the other hand that will be obvious to executive directors too so it is hardly burdensome, and probably prophylactic, for them to make disclosure of their interest.

Consultees are accordingly asked whether there should be an exemption from disclosure under section 317 for benefits which a director receives which are ordinarily made to employees on terms no less favourable.

Option 7: Exempt from the obligation of disclosure interests arising by reason only of a directorship of, or non-beneficial shareholding in, another group company

4.104   It has been suggested that this exemption would be useful particularly where cross-guarantees are being taken from several members of a group[173] in connection with banking facilities. However there is often a divergence between the interests of the different companies in this type of situation: they may for example be obtaining different benefits from the arrangements and be giving disproportionate

---

[169]   See *Runciman v Walter Runciman plc* [1992] BCLC 1084.

[170]   Section 318: see below paras 4.119-4.152.

[171]   Section 319: see below paras 4.153-4.171.

[172]   Compare s 388(6) and see *IRC v Educational Grants Association Ltd* [1967] Ch 993.

[173]   Viz a group of companies consisting of a holding company and one or more subsidiaries, as defined in s 736 of the Companies Act 1985, as amended.

amounts of security.[174] Accordingly there is the possibility that this exemption would operate to the detriment of creditors. For this reason, we are provisionally against such an exemption.

(i) Consultees are asked whether they agree with our provisional view that there should not be excepted from disclosure under section 317 interests which a director has by reason only that he is a director of another company in the same group or has a non-beneficial shareholding in it.

(ii) If consultees disagree, do they consider that this exception should only apply to directorships and shareholdings in (a) wholly-owned subsidiaries, or (b) all subsidiaries (whether or not wholly-owned)?[175]

Option 8: Exempt from disclosure an interest of which a director has no knowledge and of which it is unreasonable to expect him to have knowledge

4.105　　While it is reasonable to expect a director to make himself aware of interests of which he ought to inform the board where that is reasonably possible, there would seem to be no point in putting him under a duty to disclose that of which he could not reasonably be aware. Still less is there any basis for subjecting him to criminal liability in these circumstances. It is to be noted that article 86(b) in the current Table A quoted in paragraph 4.76 above excludes this kind of interest. Our provisional view is therefore that there should be an exemption from disclosure for an interest of which a director has no knowledge and of which it is unreasonable to expect him to have knowledge.

Consultees are asked whether they agree with our provisional view that section 317 should exempt from disclosure an interest of which a director has no knowledge and of which it is unreasonable to expect him to have knowledge.

Option 9: Make any contract voidable where the requisite disclosure has not been made and provide a civil remedy for compensation or disgorgement, or alternatively provide that the section does not affect any resulting contract

4.106　　At present, non-compliance with section 317 has no effect on the resulting contract. It is for consideration whether a failure by directors to disclose their interest in a contract with the company to the board in breach of section 317 should of itself render any such contract voidable at the instance of the company, subject to loss of the right of rescission under the general law. We discuss below the scheme which applies in relation to substantial property transactions under sections 320-322.[176] An arrangement in contravention of section 320 is voidable,

---

[174]　However the transaction may be caught by s 238 of the Insolvency Act 1986 (Transactions at an undervalue).

[175]　The terms "subsidiary" and "wholly-owned subsidiary" are defined in s 736(2) of the Companies Act 1985.

[176]　Set out above at paras 4.173-4.181. Cf ss 141-142 of the New Zealand Companies Act 1993, Appendix I.

but section 322(2) sets out circumstances in which the company's right to avoid the arrangement is lost. This is essentially where:

> (a) restitution is no longer possible or the company has been indemnified, or
>
> (b) rights acquired by a third party would be affected, or
>
> (c) the arrangement is affirmed by the company within a reasonable period.[177]

4.107 If section 317 were to be amended so that breach of the section would render the contract voidable, a provision could also be included that the contract would cease to be voidable in similar circumstances to those set out (in relation to substantial property transactions) in section 322(2). As regards third party rights ((b) above) under section 322(2) the party must not be a party to the arrangment which breaches the section. Arguably, however, under section 317 it should be sufficient if the third party acted in good faith, for value and without actual notice of the breach of section 317, because the director's interest is indirect and it may be difficult for the counterparty to know of it.

4.108 Likewise, following the pattern in section 322(3), it is for consideration whether section 317 should also provide that where a director does not make the disclosure required by section 317, he should be liable to account to the company for any gain he makes from the breach or to indemnify it against any loss from the breach.

4.109 There may be cases, however, where the need for disclosure in accordance with section 317 serves no useful purpose, for example because the board is fully aware of the interest in any event. One possibility for making section 317 operate in a way which draws a fairer balance between the interests of members and directors would be to give the courts a dispensing power in relation to the consequencese of a breach of the section where a director had (without any intention to deceive) failed to make disclosure where it would have served no useful purpose. So far as the liability of a director is concerned (if the proposal in paragraph 4.108 is adopted), there would be no need for a new dispensing power, since the director could apply for relief under section 727 of the Companies Act 1985.[178] However, it may be appropriate to give the court discretion to disapply any new provision rendering the contract automatically voidable (ie if the proposal in paragraphs 4.106-4.107 is adopted). This was in effect what happened in the *Runciman* case.[179] However, the disadvantage of this course is that it would be uncertain when the contract was made, whether the court would (later) grant relief under such a discretionary power.

---

[177] Under the Hong Kong Consultancy Report recommendations, a special resolution would be necessary; see Appendix L, para 6.21.

[178] See para 11.41 below.

[179] [1992] BCLC 1085. See para 4.88 above.

4.110 One final point to consider is the position of connected persons. We discuss below[180] the extent to which a director is obliged to disclose transactions in which a person connected with him is interested. We provisionally recommend that section 317 should be amended to provide that a director should disclose the interests of connected persons if he is aware of them and if they would have to be disclosed if they were interests of his. If that proposal is adopted, the liability discussed in paragraph 4.108 could be extended to connected persons if, in addition, the connected person cannot show that he did not know of the failure to discharge that obligation. The company in general meeting would have power to release a claim to enforce any such liability against a director (or a connected person) in the usual way.

4.111 The issues we have raised in paragraphs 4.106-4.109 would lead to a considerable increase in the length of section 317.

4.112 If consultees are of the view that a breach of section 317 should not have the consequences described in paragraphs 4.106-4.109 above, then the question arises whether section 317 should be amended so as to include expressly a statement that a breach of the section has no effect on the resulting contract. This is the effect of the current law but it might make section 317 clearer and easier to understand if that was stated.

4.113 Our provisional view is that a breach of section 317 should render the contract voidable unless (a) one or more of the conditions set out in section 322(2) (in relation to substantial property transactions) apply, or (b) the court otherwise directs. We are also of the provisional view that a breach of section 317 should result in the director being personally liable to account for any profit he makes, and to indemnify the company for any loss it incurs as a result of the breach. We have not formed a provisional view on the extension of this liabiltiy to connected persons as this depends on the view taken in relation to option 11 below.

Consultees are accordingly asked:

(i) whether they agree with our provisional views that:

> **(a) a breach of section 317 should automatically result in the contract or arrangement being voidable unless the court otherwise directs;**
>
> **(b) the contract or arrangement should cease to be voidable in the same circumstances as those set out in section 322(2);**
>
> **(c) a breach of section 317 should result in the director being personally liable (a) to account for any profit he makes, and (b) to indemnify the company for any loss it incurs as a result of the breach.**

---

[180] See para 4.115 below.

(ii) whether, if the answer to (i)(a) is no, section 317 should be amended to state that it has no effect on the contract or arrangement.

(iii) whether, if section 317 is amended so as to require the disclosure of the interests of connected persons, the liability referred to in paragraph (i)(c) above should extend to connected persons, and if so whether connected persons should have a defence if they can show that they did not know of the director's failure to comply with the section.

Option 10: Disqualify directors of public companies from voting on matters in which they have an interest or a material interest

4.114 As already noted,[181] in Australia there are provisions which prevent directors of public companies from voting on matters in which they are interested though this prohibition may be lifted by the board. In the United Kingdom, this matter is left to be dealt with by the articles. The Listing Rules require articles of listed companies to prohibit (subject to specified exceptions) an interested director from voting in respect of matters in which he has a material interest. We are not aware that the present situation is unsatisfactory. The City Group for Small Companies ("CISCO") has commented that smaller companies face particular difficulties in recruiting non-executive directors.[182] They may thus face greater problems when directors can only vote in relation to issues in which they are disinterested or where they might be regarded as "independent".

Consultees are asked whether they consider that the Companies Act should prohibit directors of public companies from voting on matters in which they have a material interest and, if so, whether there should be any exceptions to this general rule.

Option 11: Require directors to disclose material interests of their connected persons of which they are aware

4.115 Under section 317 the present position as regards the interests of connected persons is as follows: (1) in the case of a transaction to which section 330 applies, a director is deemed to be interested in it if a connected person of his is interested in it[183] and (2) in other cases he may be interested in a transaction because one of his connected persons is interested in it.[184] Thus section 317 recognises that a director's judgment may be affected by the interests of his connected persons. The difficulty about the present section is that where test (2) applies it is uncertain when a director would be taken to be interested in a transaction because one of his connected persons is interested in it; indeed the existence of the second test seems to us to be well hidden and that the drafting of the section could usefully be clarified in any event. To resolve the disadvantage of uncertainty we provisionally consider that it would be better to provide that a director should disclose the

---

[181] See para 4.93 above.

[182] See *The Financial Aspects of Corporate Governance; Guidance for Smaller Companies*, CISCO, 1993, para 8, p 7.

[183] Section 317(6))

[184] See section 317(3) (b).

interests of connected persons if he is aware of them and if they would have to be disclosed if they were interests of his.

Do consultees agree with our provisional view that section 317 should be amended to provide that a director should disclose the interests of connected persons if he is aware of them and if they would have to be disclosed if they were interests of his?

Option 12: Require that general notice under section 317(3) include details of the interest concerned

4.116   At present the subsection enables a director to give general notice of certain interests but does not require details of those interests to be given. It has been suggested that the formula in Table A (article 86(a)) could be followed, requiring disclosure of the "nature and extent" of any material interest. This would follow a recommendation made previously by the Jenkins Committee.[185] It would also mean that the board would have to be informed if there was a change in that interest. Our provisional view is that this would be desirable because the present requirment does not reasonably give sufficient information to enable the board to assess the weight to be given to the views of the director having the interest.

Consultees are accordingly asked whether they agree with our provisional view that a general notice under section 317(3) should be required to state the nature and extent of the interest, and that the director should give notice amending these particulars if they change.

Option 13: Require a register of directors interests to be kept which would be open to inspection by members or require a report to be made to shareholders in the annual accounts of the nature of interests which directors had disclosed

4.117   In Part 3, it is suggested for reasons there given[186] that there may be merit in moving towards a general principle of disclosure to shareholders of information concerning self-dealing and directors' contracts. This could be achieved by having a register of directors' interests along the lines of the register of directors' service contracts[187] and/or a report to shareholders on the lines of a remuneration committee report. The information given could be subject to audit.[188] There might have to be an exemption for information if the directors reasonably considered that disclosure of it would be harmful to the company.[189] This would reduce some of the value of disclosure. The idea of disclosure to shareholders still however has considerable merit. First, as already noted in Part 2, disclosure can often lead to reticence about entering into transactions in which directors are interested and where this is desirable this may have the effect of raising standards of corporate

[185]   See para 4.64 above.

[186]   See paras 3.72 and 3.91 above.

[187]   Sections 318 to 319 below.

[188]   Cf s 237(4) of the Companies Act 1985.

[189]   Cf s 150(2) of the Companies Act 1948.

behaviour. Second, it may often happen that all the board has an interest but yet is permitted to vote[190] and in those circumstances the disclosure mandated by section 317 to the board alone seems to have little point. Third, section 317 is rightly criticised as giving no protection where all the board is dishonest, but it is difficult to devise any solution to meet that particular situation.[191]

4.118   As against the view expressed in the preceding paragraph, paragraphs 15(c) and 16(c) of Schedule 6 to the Companies Act 1985, which we consider in Part 7 below,[192] require the disclosure in the notes to the annual accounts of specified particulars of transactions and arrangements in which a director had directly or indirectly a material interest. However as we shall see this disclosure requirement is subject to a number of broad exemptions. Moreover these requirements only apply if the transactions or arrangements are actually entered into. Apart from Schedule 6, there are also requirements in the Listing Rules concerning related party transactions,[193] and FRS 8 requires the disclosure in annual accounts of related party transactions: the exemptions provided by FRS 8 are not the same as those provided by Schedule 6.[194] It is for consideration whether an additional requirement for a register of directors interests, which sets out particulars of interests which the directors have declared[195] on a permanent and ongoing basis might not be a better way of monitoring compliance with section 317 and indeed compliance with Schedule 6, paragraph 15(c) and 16(c). The register would not necessarily cover the same ground as the Schedule 6/ FRS 8 disclosure, and it may be thought to convey more meaningful information than the details required to be disclosed under Schedule 6. The register would be open for inspection by members at the same times and in the same places as the section 318 register. The register would not wholly obviate the desirability of a report to shareholders as well since not every shareholder would wish or be able to exercise his right of inspection. As against these arguments, however, it would be inconsistent with the guiding principles which we have provisionally identified above[196] to require the disclosure of too much information or the disclosure of information which is not useful to shareholders in performing their monitoring function, and to impose unwarranted cost burdens on companies.

Consultees are asked:

---

[190]   Either because the transaction or arrangement falls within paragraphs (a) to (d) of art 94 of Table A or other provisions to like effect applicable to the company, or because, as is common in private companies, directors are permitted by the articles to vote on any matter even if they are interested in it.

[191]   J E Parkinson, *Corporate Power and Responsibility* (1993) p 22.

[192]   See para 7.6 *et seq.*

[193]   See paras 4.81-4.82 above.

[194]   See FRS 8, para 17.

[195]   Subject to any appropriate need for confidentiality of the board's proceedings.

[196]   Para 2.17 (9) and (10).

(i) whether a register of directors interests should be required to be kept which would be open to inspection by members;

(ii) whether a report should be required to be made to directors in the annual accounts of the nature of interests which directors had disclosed;

(iii) if the answer to (i) or (ii) is yes:

> (a) whether there should be an exemption from disclosure for information which the directors reasonably consider it would be harmful to the company to disclose; and

> (b) whether any information disclosed in the register or report should be audited.

SECTION 318: DIRECTORS' SERVICE CONTRACTS (1)

318. —(1) Subject to the following provisions, every company shall keep at an appropriate place—

(a) in the case of each director whose contract of service with the company is in writing, a copy of that contract;

(b) in the case of each director whose contract of service with the company is not in writing, a written memorandum setting out its terms; and

(c) in the case of each director who is employed under a contract of service with a subsidiary of the company, a copy of that contract or, if it is not in writing, a written memorandum setting out its terms.

(2) All copies and memoranda kept by a company in pursuance of subsection (1) shall be kept at the same place.

(3) The following are appropriate places for the purposes of subsection (1)—

(a) the company's registered office;

(b) the place where its register of members is kept (if other than its registered office);

(c) its principal place of business, provided that is situated in that part of Great Britain in which the company is registered.

(4) Every company shall send notice in the prescribed form to the registrar of companies of the place where copies and memoranda are kept in compliance with subsection (1), and of any change in that place, save in a case in which they have at all times been kept at the company's registered office.

(5) Subsection (1) does not apply to a director's contract of service with the company or with a subsidiary of it if that contract required him to work wholly or mainly outside the United Kingdom; but the company shall keep a memorandum—

(a) in the case of a contract of service with the company, giving the director's name and setting out the provisions of the contract relating to its duration;

(b)   in the case of a contract of service with a subsidiary, giving the director's name and the name and place of incorporation of the subsidiary, and setting out the provisions of the contract relating to its duration,

at the same place as copies and memoranda are kept by the company in pursuance of subsection (1).

(6) A shadow director is treated for purposes of this section as a director.

(7) Every copy and memorandum required by subsection (1) or (5) to be kept shall, ... , be open to inspection of any member of the company without charge.

(8) If—

(a)   default is made in complying with subsection (1) or (5), or
(b)   an inspection required under subsection (7) is refused, or
(c)   default is made for 14 days in complying with subsection (4),

the company and every officer of it who is in default is liable to a fine and, for continued contravention, to a daily default fine.

(9) In the case of a refusal of an inspection required under subsection (7) of a copy or memorandum, the court may by order compel an immediate inspection of it.

(10) Subsections (1) and (5) apply to a variation of a director's contract of service as they apply to the contract.

(11) This section does not require that there be kept a copy of, or memorandum setting out the terms of, a contract (or its variation) at a time when the unexpired portion of the term for which the contract is to be in force is less than 12 months, or at a time at which the contract can, within the next ensuing 12 months, be terminated by the company without payment of compensation.

General

4.119   Section 26 of the Companies Act 1967 introduced, for the first time, statutory provisions whereby the members of a company could inspect the service contracts of its directors. This was not in response to any Jenkins Committee recommendation. Section 26 of the 1967 Act was extended by the Companies Act 1980,[197] to require disclosure of contracts of service between directors of the company and its subsidiaries.

4.120   Section 318 requires a company to keep a copy of any service contract[198] between it (or a subsidiary of it) and any of its directors,[199] or a written memorandum of terms of any such contract if not itself in writing, or a variation of any such

---

[197] Section 61.

[198] The section only deals with contracts of service and not contracts for services: see para 4.137 below.

[199] Including shadow directors: see s 318(6).

contract,[200] at either its registered office or the place where its register of members is kept or its principal place of business,[201] provided the latter is "situated in that part of Great Britain[202] in which the company is registered"(section 318(2)(c)).[203]

4.121   All documents required to be kept under this section must be kept in the same place (sections 318(2) and 318(5)). This place must be notified[204] to the registrar of companies (section 318(4)), together with any change of location, if it is not the company's registered office. Further, all such documents must be open to inspection and copying by any member of the company without charge (section 318(7)).[205]

4.122   If an inspection is refused, the member can obtain a court order[206] compelling the company to allow it access,[207] and the company and every officer in default is liable to a fine and, for continued contravention, a daily default fine.[208] Likewise, default in complying with subsection (4),[209] or default in complying with subsections (1) and (5) may also result in the commission of an offence.[210]

4.123   Copies of contracts of service requiring directors to work "wholly or mainly" outside the UK need not be kept, but the company must keep a memorandum setting out minimum stipulated information. In the case of contracts of service with the company itself, the memorandum merely has to name the director and set out the provisions governing the duration of the contract,[211] with contracts with

---

[200]   See s 318(10).

[201]   This is a question of fact. See *De Beers Consolidated Mines Ltd v Howe* [1906] AC 445.

[202]   Great Britain is defined as England, Scotland and Wales; see the Union with Scotland Act 1706, preamble, art I, vol 10, title Constitutional Law (Pt 1), as read with the Interpretation Act 1978, s 22(1), Sched 2, para 5(a), vol 41, title Statutes. Therefore the effect of s 318(3)(c) is that a company can have the information available for inspection at its principal place of business if (a) it is registered in England and Wales, and its principal place of business is either in England or Wales, and (b) if it is registered in Scotland, and its principal place of business is in Scotland.

[203]   This may prove to be in a director's interest should he wish to prove his status as an employee of the company. See *Parsons v Albert J Parsons & Sons Ltd* [1979] ICR 271.

[204]   The prescribed form is form 318: Companies (Forms) (Amendment) Regulations 1995, SI 1995/736, reg 3, Sched 2.

[205]   Inspection must be possible for a minimum of two hours each working day (ie excluding weekends and bank holidays) between the hours of 9am and 5pm. The person inspecting may copy any information made available for inspection by taking notes or a transcription of the information. See Companies (Inspection and Copying of Registers, Indices and Documents) Regulations 1991 (SI 1991 No 1988).

[206]   See RSC Ord 102, r 2(1). In Scotland a court order can be obtained by petition under the Rules of the Court of Session, Rule 14.2.

[207]   See s 318(9)). The contempt not only attaches to the company but also any director of the company responsible for its failure to comply with the court's order; see *A-G for Tuvalu v Philatelic Distribution Corporation Ltd* [1990] 1 WLR 926.

[208]   See s 318(8)(b) and (c).

[209]   A delay of 14 days or more.

[210]   See s 318(8)(a) and (c).

[211]   See s 318(5)(a).

subsidiaries needing only to add the name and place of the subsidiary's incorporation.[212] Although "mainly" presumably bears its normal meaning of more than half,[213] it is not clear how the section applies to a director who works abroad during part of the contract and then wholly in the UK.

4.124 Further, contracts with less than 12 months to run and contracts that can be terminated with 12 months[214] notice without payment of compensation are exempted from the provisions of the section.[215]

The Stock Exchange Listing Rules

4.125 Rules 16.9 to 16.11 of the Listing Rules contain additional disclosure requirements:

> (i) Rule 16.9 requires that directors' service contracts[216] should be available[217] for inspection by any person, whereas section 318 disclosure is restricted to members of the company;[218]
>
> (ii) Rules 16.9 to 16.11 make no distinction between UK and foreign based directors, thus not adopting the exemption in section 318(5);
>
> (iii) Rules 16.9 to 16.11 do not exempt from disclosure contracts which require a director to work wholly or mainly outside the UK;[219]
>
> (iv) Rule 16.11, unlike s 318,[220] requires not only the director's service contract itself be available for inspection, but if that document does not contain:
>
>> (a) the name of the employing company;
>>
>> (b) the date of the contract, the unexpired term and details of any notice periods;
>>
>> (c) full particulars of the director's remuneration including salary and other benefits;

---

[212] See s 318(5)(b).

[213] See *Fawcett Properties v Buckingham County Council* [1961] AC 636 HL, *per* Lord Morton of Henryton at 667.

[214] Calendar months; see the Interpretation Act 1978, s 5, Sched 1, vol 14, title Statutes.

[215] See s 318(11). However, directors of a company listed on the London Stock Exchange will need to ensure its adherence to the more extensive disclosure requirements of paragraphs 16.9 to 16.11 of the Listing Rules (September 1997 edition).

[216] The Stock Exchange treats service contracts as including contracts for services.

[217] At the registered office during business hours and at the annual general meeting, including at least 15 minutes before the meeting starts.

[218] See s 318(7).

[219] Cf s 318(11).

[220] Although it should be noted that s 318(5), unlike s 318(1), requires that directors' names and the duration of their service contracts must be included in the memoranda held for inspection.

(d) any commission or profit sharing arrangements;

(e) any provision for compensation payable upon early termination of the contract; and

(f) details of any other arrangements which are necessary to enable investors to estimate the possible liability of the company upon early termination of the contract;"

then that information must be attached to the service contract and also made available for inspection. In contrast, s 318(1)[221] merely requires the service contract (if in writing) or a written memorandum of its terms be disclosed.

4.126   Rule 16.11(f)[222] is significant, and catches for example golden parachute clauses.[223]

The Combined Code

4.127   Listed companies are also required[224] to make a statement in their annual report and accounts in relation to their compliance with the Combined Code.

4.128   Schedule B to the Combined Code requires that the remuneration package of each director, identified by name, should be disclosed,[225] including pension entitlements earned during the year.[226]

The City Code

4.129   Rule 25.4 of the City Code requires that certain particulars of the current or proposed offeree board's service contracts[227] be included in its first major circular advising shareholders on an offer. The particulars required to be given are the directors' name, the contract's expiry date and the amounts of both fixed and variable remuneration. Service contracts are not required to be put on display. Particulars of contracts with less than 12 months to run need not be disclosed. If there are no service contracts with less than 12 months to run, this fact must be stated in the circular. There is no exemption equivalent to section 318(5).

4.130   If any service contracts of which particulars are required to be given have been entered into or amended within 6 months of the date of the document, particulars must also be given of the earlier arrangements. Again, if there were no earlier arrangements, this fact must be stated.

---

[221] Note above the comments in relation to s 318(5).

[222] See para 4.125(iv) above.

[223] See para 4.23 above.

[224] See paras (a) and (b) of r 12.43A of the Listing Rules, Appendix E below.

[225] See para 1.

[226] See para 4.

[227] Including service contracts with subsidiaries.

Options for reform

4.131 The possible deficiencies of section 318 seem to us to be:

(1) it is restricted to contracts of service;[228]

(2) it does not require disclosure of all documents or terms collateral to the service contract;

(3) it does not conform to the Listing Rules;

(4) the exemption contained in subsection (5);

(5) the exemption contained in subsection (11); and

(6) it is over-complex.

4.132 We set out below 7 options for reform which (with the exception of option 1 which proposes no change) suggest ways of dealing with these problems. In considering the options for reform, consultees are asked to have regard to the principles set out in Part 2 above.

Option 1: No change

4.133 It can be argued that the level of disclosure required by section 318 is sufficient. We deal with the reasons for each suggested extension of section 318 under the relevant options below.

4.134 It can also be argued that any reform requiring a greater degree of disclosure would serve to increase company costs.

Consultees are asked whether section 318 should be retained as it is.

Option 2: The Secretary of State should have power to disapply section 318 to the extent that, in the Secretary of State's opinion, a company is already bound by sufficient comparable disclosure obligations under the Listing Rules

4.135 This option offers a limited change to avoid listed companies being subject to both statutory and Stock Exchange control. The cost saving value of this measure is likely to be small. The sanctions for breach of the Listing Rules are discussed in Part 1. If this option were followed, the criminal sanctions in section 318 would not apply to listed companies.

4.136 This option would not act to increase the disclosure requirements for unlisted companies and should not therefore be seen as an alternative to options 3 to 7.

Consultees are asked whether the Secretary of State should be able to disapply section 318 to the extent that, in the Secretary of State's opinion,

---

[228] Compare s 318(1) with the width of s 319(1) which applies to "any term of an agreement".

a company is already bound by sufficient comparable disclosure obligations under the Listing Rules.

Option 3: Extend section 318 to contracts for services and non-executive directors' letters of appointment

4.137 The section currently requires that only contracts of service be disclosed, not contracts for services. Under section 319, "employment" includes employment under a contract for services.[229]

4.138 The question also arises whether the section applies where non-executive directors are appointed by means of letters of appointment. We do not consider that this is generally a service contract.[230]

4.139 It is arguably anomalous that contracts for services and non-executive directors' letters of appointment are not already within section 318. Any increase in costs is likely to be marginal. Our provisional view is that section 318 should be extended to contracts for services and letters of appointment of non-executive directors.

Consultees are asked whether they agree with our provisional views that:

(i) section 318 should require the disclosure of contracts for services and not just contracts of service; and that

(ii) section 318 should apply to letters of appointment for non-executive directors.

Option 4: Repeal of subsection (5) (Director to work abroad)

4.140 The subsection (5) exemption was introduced at a time when few company directors could take advantage of its provisions. It is unclear whether there was a particular reason for its introduction as opposed to a general concern to keep the section restricted. There may have been a concern that directors based in countries where they may have been at risk of kidnap or extortion might have derived some benefit from keeping the details of their remuneration secret. Nonetheless, it is difficult to conceive of a situation in which, in the absence of the exemption, kidnappers from (say) South America, for example, would have acquired shares in an English company[231] and then travelled to its registered office in (say) Bradford in order to inspect directors' service contracts and assess a director's ransom potential, before returning home to abduct their target.

---

[229] See s 319(7)(a).

[230] This is because a non-executive director has a relatively limited degree of involvement in the company and the company does not exercise control over him. However, the characterisation of a non-executive director's letter of appointment as a contract for services, and thus not one of employment, will depend on the circumstances in each case. See *O'Kelly and Others v Trusthouse Forte Plc* [1984] 1 QB 90.

[231] The statutory register only being accessible to members of a company under the provisions of s 318(7).

4.141   In any event, the exemption has been lost for directors of listed companies due to the disclosure requirements of the Listing Rules. These make no distinction between directors based in the UK or abroad (in fact, requiring that listed overseas companies disclose details of their directors' service contracts (see Rule 16.9(a)). Moreover, section 318(5) never provided any protection to any UK based director who was (for example) subject to a risk of kidnapping because of the ransom that could be extracted.

4.142   The benefit offered to directors of non-listed companies to avail themselves of the subsection (5) exemption is therefore the only issue to be considered in assessing the value of its retention. There seems no reason why directors of non-listed companies need protection if directors of listed companies do not require it.

4.143   Further, as business becomes increasingly global, the exemption may be applicable to a growing number of directors and may be used to avoid disclosure more frequently. If there is concern that certain information about directors working abroad should not be disclosed, the Seceretary of State could be given power to exempt prescribed information from disclosure. Our provisional view is therefore that the subsection (5) should be repealed.

4.144   If the section is not repealed, or if the Secretary of State is given the power suggested in the preceding parargraph, it should be made clear that the question whether a director works "mainly abroad" should be determined by assessing whether, at the material time, he is working mainly abroad. It should not be sufficient that in some periods he works mainly or exclusively abroad and in others in the UK.

Consultees are asked:

(i) whether they agree with our provisional view that section 318(5) should be repealed, and, if so, whether the Secretary of State should be given power to exempt prescribed information from disclosure in the case of directors working wholly or mainly abroad; and

(ii) whether, if there continues to be an exemption or a power to give exemption in respect of service contracts which require a director to work wholly or mainly abroad, it should be made clear that, in the case of a contract which requires a director to work abroad and in the UK for different periods of the contract, the exemption or power applies only in relation to the period for which he actually works mainly abroad.

Option 5: Repeal of subsection (11) (Contract with less than 12 months to run)

4.145   It has been said that, the equivalent exemption under the Stock Exchange's pre-1993 Listing Rules to section 318(5)[232] was used as a widespread means of

---

[232]   The equivalent exemption was in s 5, ch 2, para 42(a) of the Admission of Securities to Listing.

directors keeping their pay secret; thus it may be that, in relation to unlisted companies, the exemption in section 318(11) is being used in a similar way.[233]

4.146 Further, the exemption will become increasingly important given the pressure that now exists to reduce the length of fixed-term contracts to a duration of less than 12 months.[234]

4.147 As with subsection (5), the exemption will in practice only apply to directors in companies not subject to the Listing Rules.[235] Many directors in these companies have fixed-term contracts in excess of 12 months in any event. Our provisional view is that subsection (11) should be repealed.

Consultees are asked whether they agree with our provisional view that section 318(11) should be repealed.

Option 6: Amend section 318 to require disclosure of particulars of terms collateral to the service contract

4.148 The need only to disclose the contract or a memorandum of its terms, without making available for inspection collateral documents or terms referred to therein, may result in shareholders being unable to assess, by inspection under section 318, the full value of the directors' remuneration.

4.149 On the other hand, to require disclosure of all collateral documents may be unduly burdensome. In addition, there may be some information that ought, arguably, to remain outside the public domain. A particular concern might attach to the disclosure of D&O insurance or kidnap and ransom insurance. Disclosure of these kinds of insurance may encourage claims. D&O insurance is now increasingly common.[236] The answer here may be to give the Secretary of State power by order to grant exemptions from disclosure for prescribed information, for example, information which relates to insurance designed to ensure the personal safety of directors or their families.

4.150 This option would also increase the administrative costs on companies, and listed companies already undertake extensive disclosure.[237]

Consultees are asked whether section 318 should require disclosure of particulars of terms collateral to the service contract, and, if so, whether the Secretary of State should have power to exempt prescribed information from disclosure.

---

[233] See Brian R Cheffins, *Company Law, Theory, Structure and Operation* (1997) p 664, n 83.

[234] See Option 2, paras 4.165-4.168 below.

[235] Note comments in the Hampel Report at para 4.9, pp 34-5.

[236] See paras 11.53-11.57 below.

[237] See r 16.11 above, para 4.126. But r 16.11(f) is limited to information relevant to the company's potential liability if the director's service contract terminates early.

Option 7: Allow public inspection of directors' service contracts

4.151   Unlike the Listing Rules, section 318 only gives members a right of inspection. Arguably, there are today others, such as potential investors, creditors and employees who also have a legitimate interest in inspection. This option thus proposes for consideration public inspection of directors' service contracts.

4.152   This option would increase administrative costs for unlisted companies.

> **Consultees are asked whether the statutory register ought to be open to public inspection (a) in the case of all companies, or (b) in the case of companies listed on the Stock Exchange or AIM only.**

SECTION 319: DIRECTORS SERVICE CONTRACTS (2)

319. —(1) This section applies in respect of any term of an agreement whereby a director's employment with the company of which he is a director or, where he is the director of a holding company, his employment within the group is to continue, or may be continued, otherwise than at the instance of the company (whether under the original agreement or under a new agreement entered into in pursuance of it), for a period of more than 5 years during which the employment—

(a)   cannot be terminated by the company by notice; or

(b)   can be so terminated only in specified circumstances.

(2) In any case where—

(a)   a person is or is to be employed with a company under an agreement which cannot be terminated by the company by notice or can be so terminated only in specified circumstances; and

(b)   more than 6 months before the expiration of the period for which he is or is to be so employed, the company enters into a further agreement (otherwise than in pursuance of a right conferred by or under the original agreement on the other party to it) under which he is to be employed with the company or, where he is a director of a holding company, within the group,

this section applies as if to the period for which he is to be employed under that further agreement there were added a further period equal to the unexpired period of the original agreement.

(3) A company shall not incorporate in an agreement such a term as is mentioned in subsection (1), unless the term is first approved by a resolution of the company in general meeting and, in the case of a director of a holding company, by a resolution of that company in general meeting.

(4) No approval is required to be given under this section by any body corporate unless it is a company within the meaning of this Act, or is registered under section 680, or if it is a wholly-owned subsidiary of any body corporate, wherever incorporated.

(5) A resolution of a company approving such a term as is mentioned in subsection (1) shall not be passed at a general meeting of the company unless a

written memorandum setting out the proposed agreement incorporating the term is available for inspection by members of the company both—

(a) **at the company's registered office for not less than 15 days ending with the date of the meeting; and**

(b) **at the meeting itself.**

(6) A term incorporated in an agreement in contravention of this section is, to the extent that it contravenes the section, void; and that agreement and, in a case where subsection (2) applies, the original agreement are deemed to contain a term entitling the company to terminate it at any time by the giving of reasonable notice.

(7) In this section—

(a) **"employment" includes employment under a contract for services; and**

(b) **"group", in relation to a director of a holding company, means the group which consists of that company and its subsidiaries;**

and for purposes of this section a shadow director is treated as a director.

General

4.153 This section is derived from sections 47 and 63(1)[238] of the Companies Act 1980, and contains controls to prevent directors arranging for themselves long-term service contracts with their companies. A White Paper on "The Conduct of Company Directors" issued in 1977[239] recommended that directors' service contracts for longer than 5 years should be approved by the company in general meeting.[240] A clause to implement this recommendation was contained in the draft Companies Bill 1978[241], but the bill that was subsequently introduced was lost because of the 1979 General Election.

4.154 Section 319 requires shareholder approval to be obtained[242] for any proposed term in any agreement[243] whereby a director's employment[244] with the company, or, if he

---

[238] Section 63(1) provided that shadow directors would fall within the definition of a "director" for certain purposes, including s 47.

[239] (1977) Cmnd 7037.

[240] *Ibid*, para 14, p 5.

[241] See clause 47 of the 1978 Bill, as contained in Changes in Company Law (1978) Cmnd 7291, p 53-4.

[242] Section 319(3). The shareholders' approval required is that of the company in general meeting, or, where the director is the director of a holding company, by resolution of that company in general meeting.

[243] Not necessarily one to which the director is a party, thus ensuring that the section cannot be avoided by use of an agreement with a company controlled by the director.

[244] Under a contract of service or for services: s 319(7)(a).

114

is a director of a holding company, the group[245] is to continue or may be continued, otherwise than at that company's instance for a period in excess of 5 years (see sections 319(1) and (3)) during which the company cannot terminate his employment by notice or can only do so in certain circumstances. Section 319 provides for aggregation of periods of employment where a new contract is to be entered into more than six months before the expiration of a previous agreement.[246]

4.155   By section 319(6), failure to obtain the necessary shareholder approval renders the term in question void and the company can terminate the agreement (and, where section 319(2) applies, the previous agreement) by notice. Thus section 319(6) can apply to a previous agreement even if it would have fallen outside section 319 but for the company's entry into a new agreement.

4.156   If a company[247] wishes to enter any fresh agreement, containing a term to which section 319(1) applies, the necessary approvals process is set out in subsections (3) and (5). First, subsection (3) stipulates that the subsection (1) term must be approved by a resolution of the company,[248] or the holding company, in general meeting. Subsection (5) then provides that the resolution may not be passed unless a written memorandum which sets out the proposed agreement incorporating the term has been available for inspection by members of the company, not only at its registered office for a period of not less than 15 days[249] culminating with the date of the meeting, but also at the meeting itself. Alternatively, a private company[250] can use the written resolution procedure permitted by section 381A but in that case the document referred to in subsection (5) must be given to members of the company eligible to sign the resolution either at the time of signature or before.[251] Thus although all members of the company, irrespective of their voting rights, will have access to the text of the proposed

---

[245]   "Group" is defined in relation to the director of a holding company, as both that company and its subsidiaries; subsection (7)(b).

[246]   The subsection prevents a director who is coming to the end of a fixed-term 4 year contract (which the company cannot terminate by notice, or can only terminate by notice in specified circumstances), from for example, gaining another with the company on the same terms a year before the original contract's expiry date - effectively creating a 7 year period during which time the directors' employment cannot be terminated by the company by notice.

[247]   For the purposes of the section, approval is only required if the company is a company within the meaning of the Companies Act 1985, or a company registered under s 680 of the Act. Approval is not required if the company is a wholly-owned subsidiary of another body corporate.

[248]   Tolley's Company Law (p D50/10) suggests that the object of approval by members, to check the self interest of the board, might be defeated by a weighted voting rights article, such as that upheld by the House of Lords in Bushell v Faith [1970] AC 1099. However, weighted voting rights are not within the scope of this project.

[249]   The Companies (Inspection and Copying of Registers, Indices and Documents) Regulations 1991 (SI 1991/1998) does not apply to access to the documents held open for inspection by members under subsection (5)(a), see s 3(1) of the Regulations.

[250]   Any company which is not a public company, see s1(3) of the 1985 Act.

[251]   A company probably cannot approve the term by means of informal unanimous consent, even if members see a subsection (5) memorandum before giving consent. Cf Re RW Peak (Kings Lynn) Ltd [1998] 1 BCLC 193.

agreement if approval is to be obtained at a general meeting of the company,[252] only members entitled to attend and vote at the meeting if one had been held will have access to its text if the approval is to be by written resolution.

Listed companies and self-regulation

4.157   Since section 319 was first introduced, there have been a number of self-regulatory developments affecting the service contracts of directors of listed companies.

(a) Recommendations of the Cadbury, Greenbury and Hampel Committees

4.158   The Cadbury Committee recommended that directors' service contracts should not exceed three years without shareholder approval. The Greenbury Committee thought that there was a strong case for setting notice or contract periods at, or reducing them to, one year or less, and that provisions for predetermined compensation on termination which exceeded one year's salary and benefits should be disclosed and the reasons for the longer notice periods explained.[253]

The Hampel Committee recommended that:

> boards should set as their objective the reduction of directors' contract periods to one year or less, but the committee recognises that this could not be achieved immediately.[254]

(b) The Combined Code

4.159   Paragraphs B.1.7 and B.1.8 of the Combined Code state:

B.1.7

> There is a strong case for setting notice or contract periods at, or reducing them to, one year or less. Boards should set this as an objective; but they should recognise that it may not be possible to achieve it immediately.

B.1.8

> If it is necessary to offer longer notice or contract periods to new directors recruited from outside, such periods should reduce after the initial period.

4.160   Paragraph 7 of Schedule B in Part 2 of the Combined Code, which contains provisions on what should be included in the Remuneration Report, adds:

---

[252]   In harmony with the views of Buckley J in *Re Duomatic Ltd*, *ibid* at p 374F-G and the Court of Appeal in *Re George Newman & Co* [1895] 1 Ch 674, *per* Lindley LJ at p 686

[253]   The Cadbury Report, para 4.14, p 31.

[254]   The Hampel Report, summary point 24, p 60.

Any service contracts which provide for, or imply, notice periods in excess of one year (or any provisions for predetermined compensation on termination which exceed one year's salary and benefits) should be disclosed and the reasons for the longer notice periods explained.[255]

"Rolling" contracts, fixed-term contracts and long notice periods

4.161 The purpose of section 319 is to ensure that a company is not put under an obligation to employ a director for more than five years unless its members have approved the relevant term. Section 319 does not regulate the length of notice that the company can be required to give. However, the directors approving the contract may be in breach of duty under the general law if this is excessive.

4.162 Section 319 is not treated as prohibiting "rolling contracts". This is not a term of art. It appears to include contracts for periods of up to 5 years which might, for example, be replaced at the end of their first year with a new fixed term contract. The contract may be replaced either by agreement or automatically, subject to the company not giving notice that the replacement was not to take place. The view is taken that this practice is outside section 319 on the basis that as the old contract is brought to an end and is replaced by a new contract, there is no period of the old contract which is unexpired for the purposes of section 319(2). It also includes contracts for an indefinite duration terminable by the company on (say) two years notice. The agreement can be characterised as a contract for the notice period which rolls over daily. The contract may require the notice to be given on a particular day or in a particular period of the year.

Options for reform

4.163 We set out below 4 options for reform in respect of section 319 (including option 1 which is for no change to the wording). The question of repeal of section 319 is considered in Part 9.[256] If consultees reject option 1 (no change) and are against repeal, they may choose more than one of the remaining options. In considering the options for reform, consultees are asked to have regard to the principles set out in Part 2 above.

Option 1: No change

4.164 It is arguable that section 319 is now well understood and confers adequate protection to shareholders, and therefore should not be changed in any of the ways specified below or at all.

Consultees are asked whether section 319 should be retained in its current form.

---

[255] See also r 12.43A(c)(vi) of the Listing Rules in Appendix E below.
[256] See para 9.3-9.28 below.

Option 2: Reduce the statutory period in section 319(1) from 5 years to 1, 2 or 3 years

4.165 The importance of limiting the length of fixed term contracts has been recognised in the reports of the Cadbury, Greenbury and Hampel Committees, as well as by the Stock Exchange through its adoption of the Combined Code. The final report of the Hampel Committee concluded that most companies had reduced directors' contracts from 3 years to 2, without cost to the company and that a general reduction to one year could not be achieved immediately.[257] Research published in 1997 noted that 62 per cent of directors in 68 FTSE 100 companies had service contracts with notice periods of 2 years or more.[258] However, data supplied to the Hampel Committee (by the Association of British Insurers) on compliance with the Cadbury and Greenbury codes in the 1994/5 and 1995/6 company reporting seasons indicated a marked decrease in, but not elimination of, the number of directors with rolling contracts of more than 3 years between the two years. This reducing trend is corroborated by PIRC's research which states that less than 5 per cent of directors in the largest 296 companies had contracts for 3 years or longer by 1996.[259] Change is therefore occurring, and there is a question whether section 319 should be amended to force the pace of change or simply to reflect it.

4.166 Although the Combined Code now favours notice or contract periods being set at one year or less, its Provision B.1.8 notes that longer periods may be initially acceptable, in particular in the case of new directors recruited from outside the company. Shareholders could be asked to approve a longer period, though this may involve some cost and delay.

4.167 The position of smaller listed companies and unlisted companies must be considered.[260] CISCO was established in 1992 as an independent organisation[261] to voice the concerns of the smaller company sector of the London stock market.[262] It has produced responses[263] to the Cadbury and Greenbury Committee's reports and has most recently commented on the Stock Exchange's new Combined Code and related Listing Rules amendments. In its response to the Greenbury Report, CISCO supported a reduction in the length of service contracts to one year as a way of avoiding directors' being compensated for failure. However, its view was

---

[257] Hampel Report, para 4.9, p 35.

[258] See Jason Nissé, "Cadbury Notice Period Broken by 60% of Directors", *The Times*, 25 September 1997 (Business News, p 26).

[259] After Greenbury: Directors' Contracts and Compensation (1996) pp 16-17.

[260] It is worth noting that the Greenbury committee's recommendations were not simply intended to apply to listed companies, although this corporate form was its main focus (see para 1.18, p 12. Compliance for listed companies was to be "to the fullest extent practicable"; see the Code of Best Practice, para 2.3, p 13). Compliance with the Code of Best Practice was also recommended to "others ... as they see fit" (see para 1.18, p 12).

[261] Entirely funded by its membership of over 100 City firms.

[262] CISCO normally defines "smaller quoted companies" as those not included in the FTSE 350 indices.

[263] See "The Financial Aspects of Corporate Governance; Guidance for Smaller Companies", CISCO, 1993; and "Greenbury, The Smaller Company Perspective, Objectives for the next stage of corporate governance", CISCO, 1995.

that most service contracts in smaller companies would typically be for two years, particularly due to the "higher risk of employment in a smaller company."[264]

4.168   The protection offered by section 319 to unlisted companies may be as important as that offered to listed ones; on the other hand it may be in smaller companies that in order to attract directors it is necessary to give them longer contracts without shareholder approval. Apart from the potentially larger costs that may initially accrue to unlisted companies if the law is changed there is arguably no reason for listed and unlisted companies to be treated any differently under the section.

Consultees are asked:

(i) whether the statutory period in section 319(1) should be reduced to (a) one year, (b) two years, or (c) three years;

(ii) whether any reduction of the statutory period should apply either (a) to both listed and unlisted companies, or (b) only to listed companies.

Option 3: Amend section 319 to prohibit (without shareholder approval) the creation of "rolling contracts" having a notice or contract period in excess of the period permitted by section 319

4.169   As is described above, section 319 is treated as not prohibiting "rolling contracts".[265] Thus a director may in practice be able to maintain a security of tenure for, effectively, in excess of five years without the company needing to seek shareholder approval for this arrangement. Section 319 would need to be amended to prevent a company giving valid notice beyond a maximum length. Shareholders would be free to approve a longer period. In addition, section 319 would need to be amended so that the length of the term of the prior contract is aggregated with the new contract, in a similar way to that which already occurs for contracts with 6 months still to run under section 319(2)(b), and with the same consequences. However this may catch situations which ought not to require shareholder approval, for example where a director who has a 5 year service contract as an executive director is promoted to finance director and offered a new 5 year contract. Moreover, this may cause a rise in remuneration levels, if the practice of rolling contracts is widespread.

Consultees are asked whether section 319 should be amended to prevent "rolling contracts" for a period exceeding the maximum term permitted by section 319 unless they are first approved by ordinary resolution.

---

[264]   See "Greenbury, The Smaller Company Perspective, Objectives for the next stage of corporate governance", CISCO, 1995, p 6.

[265]   See paras 4.161-4.162 above.

Option 4 : Deem terms approved if notified and members raise no objection to the proposed term within a stipulated period

4.170 The argument raised against shareholder approval is that it may be costly, cumbersome and create uncertainty. One solution to terms requiring approval under section 319 is to make them subject to "negative approval". Thus the term could be made subject to an obligation on the part of the company to give notice to shareholders and to a notice by shareholders holding a specified percentage of shares carrying the right to vote to object with a set time limit. If no objection was raised, the term could then be deemed approved. If an objection was received, the term would require shareholder approval.[266] This option could be in addition to, or in lieu of, the existing requirements for shareholder approval.

4.171 This solution would not eliminate uncertainty. It might in some cases offer a cheaper and quicker method of obtaining approval. However, if a meeting was required there would be a longer interval of time before it was held. There is also the problem of shareholder apathy. Shareholders may very well fail to consider the proposals with the result that the time for requiring a meeting passes by. In these circumstances the requirement for a meeting would not be an effective scrutiny of the transaction. We are provisionally against a "negative approval" procedure along these lines.

Consultees are asked whether they agree with our provisional view that section 319 should not be amended so as to permit a company to dispense with approval of the company in general meeting[267] if a notice was given to members and there is no objection from a specified proportion of members within a specified period.

SECTIONS 320-322: SUBSTANTIAL PROPERTY TRANSACTIONS INVOLVING DIRECTORS ETC

320.—(1) With the exceptions provided by the section next following, a company shall not enter into an arrangement—

    (a)   whereby a director of a company or its holding company, or a person connected with such a director, acquires or is to acquire one or more non-cash assets of the requisite value from the company; or

    (b)   whereby the company acquires or is to acquire one or more non-cash assets of the requisite value from such a director or a person so connected,

unless the arrangement is first approved by a resolution of the company in general meeting and, if the director or connected person is a director of its holding company or a person connected with such a director, by a resolution in general meeting of the holding company.

---

[266] Cf para 4.54 above.

[267] A like option could be given with respect to approval of the holding company, when that is required.

(2) For this purpose a non-cash asset is of the requisite value if at the time the arrangement in question is entered into its value is not less than [£ 2,000] but (subject to that) exceeds [£100,000] or 10 per cent of the company's asset value, that is—

    (a)   except in a case falling within paragraph (b) below, the value of the company's net assets determined by reference to the accounts prepared and laid under Part VII in respect of the last preceding financial year in respect of which such accounts were so laid; and

    (b)   where no accounts have been so prepared and laid before that time, the amount of the company's called-up share capital.

(3) For purposes of this section and sections 321 and 322, a shadow director is treated as a director.

321.—(1) No approval is required to be given under section 320 by any body corporate unless it is a company within the meaning of this Act or registered under section 680 or, if it is a wholly-owned subsidiary of any body corporate, wherever incorporated.

(2) Section 320 (1) does not apply to an arrangement for the acquisition of a non-cash asset—

    (a)   if the asset is to be acquired by a holding company from any of its wholly-owned subsidiaries or from a holding company by any of its wholly-owned subsidiaries, or by one wholly-owned subsidiary of a holding company from another wholly-owned subsidiary of that same holding company, or

    (b)   if the arrangement is entered into by a company which is being wound up, unless the winding up is a members' voluntary winding up.

(3) Section 320(1)(a) does not apply to an arrangement whereby a person is to acquire an asset from a company of which he is a member, if the arrangement is made with that person in his character as a member.

[(4) Section 320(1) does not apply to a transaction on a recognised investment exchange which is effected by a director, or a person connected with him, through the agency of a person who in relation to the transaction acts as an independent broker.

For this purpose an "independent broker" means—

    (a)   in relation to a transaction on behalf of a director, a person who independently of the director selects the person with whom the transaction is to be effected, and

    (b)   in relation to a transaction on behalf of a person connected with a director, a person who independently of that person or the director selects the person with whom the transaction is to be effected;

and "recognised", in relation to an investment exchange, means recognised under the Financial Services Act 1986.]

322.—(1) An arrangement entered into by a company in contravention of section 320, and any transaction entered into in pursuance of the arrangement (whether by the company or any other person) is voidable at the instance of the company unless one or more of the conditions specified in the next subsection is satisfied.

(2) Those conditions are that—

(a) restitution of any money or other asset which is the subject-matter of the arrangement or transaction is no longer possible or the company has been indemnified in pursuance of this section by any other person for the loss or damage suffered by it; or

(b) any rights acquired bona fide for value and without actual notice of the contravention by any person who is not a party to the arrangement or transaction would be affected by its avoidance; or

(c) the arrangement is, within a reasonable period, affirmed by the company in general meeting and, if it is an arrangement for the transfer of an asset to or by a director of its holding company or a person who is connected with such a director, is so affirmed with the approval of the holding company given by a resolution in general meeting.

(3) If an arrangement is entered into with a company by a director of the company or its holding company or a person connected with him in contravention of section 320, that director and the person so connected, and any other director of the company who authorised the arrangement or any transaction entered into in pursuance of such an arrangement, is liable—

(a) to account to the company for any gain which he has made directly or indirectly by the arrangement or transaction, and

(b) (jointly and severally with any other person liable under this subsection) to indemnify the company for any loss or damage resulting from the arrangement or transaction.

(4) Subsection (3) is without prejudice to any liability imposed otherwise than by that subsection, and is subject to the following two subsections; and the liability under subsection (3) arises whether or not the arrangement or transaction entered into has been avoided in pursuance of subsection (1).

(5) If an arrangement is entered into by a company and a person connected with a director of the company or its holding company in contravention of section 320, that director is not liable under subsection (3) if he shows that he took all reasonable steps to secure the company's compliance with that section.

(6) In any case, a person so connected and any such other director as is mentioned in subsection (3) is not so liable if he shows that, at the time the arrangement was entered into, he did not know the relevant circumstances constituting the contravention.

122

4.172 As noted in paragraph 1.9 above, the main provisions of these sections were introduced by the Companies Act 1980[268] following a number of DTI inspectors' reports of the 1970s. The section overrides provisions which enable directors to acquire assets from their company or to transfer assets to them. We are not aware that the provisions now cause any great hardship or inconvenience

Section 320

4.173 Section 320 prohibits an arrangement for the transfer of a non-cash asset of the requisite value between companies and directors or directors of their holding companies (including shadow directors) or persons connected with them,[269] unless those arrangements have been first approved by a resolution of the company and (where the director is a director of its holding company) the holding company in general meeting. Assets are "of the requisite value" if at the time the arrangement is made, they are worth more than the lower of £100,000 or a 10% share of the relevant company's net asset value, subject to a minimum of £2,000.

4.174 The definition of "non-cash asset" is contained in section 739(1). It means any property other than cash (including foreign currency). Section 739(2) provides:

> A reference to the transfer or acquisition of a non-cash asset includes the creation or extinction of an estate or interest in, or a right over, any property and also the discharge of any person's liability, other than a liability for a liquidated sum.

This provision extends the meaning of transfer and acquisition of an asset so as to include the creation of interests over assets,[270] such as the grant of a lease over land. The final words cover the case where a payment is made to discharge a sum other than an unliquidated amount. This sum may be owed by any person, which would in the absence of contrary indication include the company itself. However it has been held that the discharge by the company of a liability for damages for breach of a service contract to a director does not require approval under this section.[271] It also appears that the section does not apply to covenanted payments under a director's service agreement, such as golden parachute payments.[272]

---

[268] See ss 48 and 63(1). The re-enacted sections have been subject to amendment by the Companies (Fair Dealing by Directors)(Increase in Financial Limits) Order 1990 (SI 1990/1393) (which increased the financial limits in s 320(2)) and the Companies Act 1989 (which inserted s 321(4)).

[269] In contrast with s 322A(7), where the arrangement is with a director or connected person jointly with another party outside the definitions in the section, s 320 would appear not to apply.

[270] The question whether this wording includes the novation of a contract to acquire an asset was left open by the Court of Appeal in *Re Duckwari plc (No 1)* [1997] 2 BCLC 713 at 722. In that case the company (D plc) acquired either the benefit of the contract or the purchaser's beneficial interest in the property. On either basis the asset acquired was a non-cash asset for the purposes of s 739(2), and it was of the requisite value because the amount of the deposit paid by the purchaser exceeded 10% of the assets of D plc.

[271] *Gooding v Cater* (unreported), 13 March 1989, Chancery Division.

[272] See *Lander v Premier Pict Petroleum Ltd* 1997 SLT 1361. On the question of the overlap between s 320 and ss 312-316, see para 4.35 above and para 4.189 below. We recommend

Section 321

4.175   Section 321 provides exceptions to the prohibition in section 320:

(1)   approval is required only if the company is a company within the meaning of the Companies Acts[273] and even then approval is not required if the company is a wholly-owned subsidiary of a body corporate wherever incorporated;

(2)   approval is not required if the transfer is between members of the same wholly-owned group;

(3)   approval is not required if the arrangement is entered into by a company which is in compulsory or voluntary winding up, unless it is a members' voluntary winding up;

(4)   approval is not required if the arrangement is one whereby a member acquires an asset from the company in his capacity as a member, such as where the company makes a bonus issue of shares to him;

(5)   approval is not required for a transaction effected by a director or a connected person on a recognised stock exchange through an independent broker as defined in section 321(4).

4.176   It has been said that the exception for intra group transactions does not adequately protect the assets of companies given that the same directors may be standing on both sides of the transaction.[274] We think that this criticism is misplaced. Section 320 at most requires a shareholder resolution and this is unnecessary in the case of a transaction between members of a wholly-owned group as the exception recognises. The fourth exception has also been criticised on the basis that it does not prevent share issues to directors.[275] Again we do not see this as a substantial criticism since that exception will only apply where the issue is to a director as shareholder, for example a bonus issue or a rights issue.

Section 322

4.177   Section 322 sets out the liabilities arising from contravention of section 320. First, arrangements in contravention of section 320, or linked transactions, are voidable

below that s 320 should be amended to make it clear that it does not apply to covenanted payments under service agreements with directors or to payments to which s 316(3) applies (ie bona fide payments by way of damages for breach of contract); see para 4.193.

[273]   Section 735(1), or if the company is a joint stock company which has been registered under s 680 of the Companies Act 1985.

[274]   See J H Farrar, N E Furey and B M Hanningan, *Farrar's Company Law* (3rd ed, 1991) p 418, n 17. The rationale behind the exception was the feeling that directors of a holding company would exert sufficient control over directors of its subsidiaries.

[275]   See *Farrar's Company Law* (3rd ed, 1991) p 417, n 4 (see also now 4th ed, 1998, p 411, n 19), referring to the criticism of the subsection by Leigh and Edey in *Companies Act 1981* (1981) at para 376.

at the instance of the company. However, the transaction is not void *ab initio*[276] or illegal by reason of section.[277] The right to recission is lost if one of the conditions in section 322(2) is satisfied. Thus for instance it is lost if the arrangement is affirmed by the company in general meeting within a reasonable period.

4.178 Directors and their connected persons who enter into the arrangement or a linked transaction, directors whose connected persons enter into such an arrangement or transaction and directors who authorise the arrangement or transaction are liable to account to the company for any direct or indirect gains made as a result,[278] or indemnify the company for any resulting loss or damage.[279] Under subsection (4), this liability arises irrespective of whether the relevant arrangement or transaction has been avoided and acts without prejudice to any other concurrent liabilities.[280]

4.179 A director who would otherwise be liable under subsection (3) because a connected person of his entered into a transaction or arrangement with the company has a defence if he can show that he took all reasonable steps to secure the company's compliance with section 320.[281] Both connected persons and merely authorising directors have a defence if they can show that at the time the relevant arrangement was entered into they did not know of the relevant circumstances constituting the contravention of section 320.[282]

4.180 The nature of the profit to be accounted for under section 322(3) depends on the circumstances.[283] However it is now clear that the liability to indemnify the company against loss extends to any subsequent decline in the market value of an asset after its acquisition.[284] This result is consistent with what the position would be under the general law if the director entered into a transaction in breach of duty.

4.181 The mischief to which sections 320-322 are directed is not simply to prevent acquisitions at an inflated value and disposals at an under value. As Carnwath J

---

[276] Thus assets received from the company will not be held by the recipient on trust (see *Guinness v Saunders* [1990] 2 AC 663, *per* Lord Goff at 698E). However, if the transaction is rescinded the company may retain equitable title sufficient to support a tracing claim (see *El Anjou v Dollar Land Holdings plc* [1993] 3 All E R 717 at p 743d-e). In Scotland a personal right of restitution of the property would be available based on unjustified enrichment. A tracing claim may be available at least against a director under the remedy of constructive trust (see *Sutman International Inc v Herbage* (unreported) 2 August 1991, Lord Cullen (1991 GWD 30-1772); *Huisman v Soepboer* 1994 SLT 684).

[277] See *Niltan Carson Ltd v Hawthorne* [1988] BCLC 298, 322.

[278] Section 322(3)(a).

[279] Section 322(3)(b).

[280] Section 322(4).

[281] Section 322(5).

[282] Section 322(6).

[283] See Aggravated, Exemplary and Restitutionary Damages (1997) Law Com No 247, paras 3.28-3.32 and 3.59-3.63.

[284] *Duckwari plc v Offerventure Ltd, The Times* 18 May 1998 (CA). The position is similar to the situation where a trustee makes an unauthorised investment.

said in *British Racing Drivers' Club v Hextall Erskine*[285] as to the purpose of the section:

> It is necessary to look at the purpose of s 320. The thinking behind that section is that if directors enter into a substantial commercial transaction with one of their number, there is a danger that their judgment may be distorted by conflicts of interest. The section is designed to protect a company against such distortions. It enables members to provide a check. Of course, this does not necessarily mean that the members will exercise a better commercial judgment; but it does make it likely that the matter will be more widely ventilated, and a more objective decision reached.

The Stock Exchange Listing Rules

4.182　Chapter 11 of the Stock Exchange's Listing Rules sets out requirements for all transactions between a listed company and any of its directors (and other related parties).[286]

4.183　When a transaction[287] between a listed company, or a subsidiary, and a relevant "related party"[288] is proposed,[289] the principal requirements of Chapter 11 are that, subject to the exceptions in paragraph 4.184 below, the company concerned must:

> (a) send a circular to its shareholders[290] containing specific information in addition to full particulars of the transaction.[291] The circular must also contain a statement by the directors (excluding any "related party" director) that:
>
> > ... the transaction is fair and reasonable so far as the shareholders of the company are concerned and that the directors have been so advised by an independent adviser acceptable to the Exchange.

---

[285] [1997] 1 BCLC 182, 198.

[286] Chapter 10 also contains provisions in respect of transactions concerning non-cash assets, particularly during takeovers or mergers, but unlike ss 320-322 and Chapter 11, is not specifically concerned with transactions involving directors or their connected persons.

[287] "Transactions with a related party" means a transaction between the company (or a subsidiary) and a related party, arrangements for investment by the company (or a subsidiary) and a related party in the same undertaking or asset, and arrangements with controlling shareholders.

[288] These include current and former directors and shadow directors and substantial shareholders. The full definition is set out in Appendix N below.

[289] The variation or novation of an existing agreement is also subject to the requirements of r 11.4, even if the related party was not so classifiable when the original agreement was made. See r 11.6.

[290] It may, in addition, also need to make a Chapter 10 announcement, if applicable; see r 11.14(a).

[291] Rules 11.4(b) and 11.10 generally, but in particular 11.10(c) regarding the full particulars requirement.

(b) obtain shareholder approval for the transaction either prior to it being entered into, or if that is conditional upon such approval, before its completion; and

(c) take all reasonable steps to ensure that the related party's associates abstain from voting on the relevant resolution, and ensure that the related party itself abstains.[292]

4.184 The following transactions are exempted from Chapter 11:

(1) transactions of a revenue nature in the ordinary course of business;[293]

(2) where the company does not have any listed equity securities;[294]

(3) where the company is an overseas company with a secondary listing on the Exchange;[295]

(4) transactions involving the issue of new securities either for cash, the offer being made on the same terms for all existing securities holders, or relates to the exercise of conversion or subscription rights in a listed class of securities or previously approved in general meeting;[296]

(5) transactions involving the receipt of cash by a director or the issue of options to him under an employees' share scheme or long-term incentive scheme;[297]

(6) transactions involving the grant of credit to or by a related party on normal commercial terms in the ordinary course of business or on no more favourable terms than those offered to employees;[298]

(7) the grant of indemnities to directors;[299]

(8) underwriting of a securities issue on normal commercial terms;[300]

(9) joint investment arrangements which in the opinion of an independent adviser are no less favourable to the company than the related party;[301] and

---

[292] Under the provisions of rr 11.4(d) and 11.5, the requirement to ensure that the related party abstains is absolute on the company, and is not conditioned by the taking of "all reasonable steps".

[293] Rule 11.1 (a)(ii).

[294] Rule 11.7(a).

[295] See r 11.7 (b).

[296] See r 11.7(c).

[297] See r 11.7(d).

[298] See r 11.7(e).

[299] See r 11.7(f).

[300] See r 11.7(g).

[301] Rule 11.7(h).

(10) small transactions, assessed according to a series of percentage ratio formulas.[302] There are stipulated calculations for 5 different ratios.[303] In relation to assets, for example, the percentage ratio is calculated by dividing the net assets that are the subject of the transaction by the net assets of the listed company.[304] A small transaction is one where each of the percentage ratios is less than or equal to 0.25%.[305]

4.185 There are key differences between the provisions in the Listing Rules and sections 320-322. These can be identified as follows:

(1) Rule 11.1(i) exempts all transactions "of a revenue nature"[306] made in the ordinary course of business from any need for shareholder approval.[307]

(2) The definition of "related party" differs from that of "connected person" in section 346.[308]

(3) Rule 11.4 requires that a related party that is also eligible to vote on a relevant transaction approval resolution should abstain from doing so. There is no such requirement in sections 320-321.

(4) Rule 11.4 (c) requires that shareholder approval must take place prior to the transaction being either entered into or completed. There is thus no provision equivalent to that of section 322(2)(c).

(5) Rule 11.7 (d) exempts transactions involving employee share schemes and directors' long term incentive schemes. These exemptions are not present in sections 320-322.

AIM Rules

4.186 The AIM rules do not require shareholder approval of related party transactions.

The City Code

4.187 The City Code contains further restrictions on transactions by offeree companies, or "those in which control (as defined) may change or be consolidated",[309] during

---

[302] See r 11.7(I), r 10.5 and r 11.8. The same percentage ratio calculations are used to determine transaction class (Class 3, 2, Super Class 1 etc) under Chapter 10.

[303] Assets, profits, consideration to assets, consideration to market capitalisation and gross capital. See r 10.5(a) to (e).

[304] See r 10.5(a).

[305] Where the 0.25% de minimus threshold is exceeded in relation to one or more of the percentage ratios, but all are calculated to be less than 5%, a modified disclosure and approval system operates under Chapter 11; see r 11.8.

[306] This phrase is not defined in the Listing Rules, but would appear to narrow the scope of the ordinary course of business transaction exemption only to those where a net gain will accrue to the company or its subsidiary.

[307] See also the similar exemptions in r 11.7(e), (g) and (h).

[308] See para 8.10 below.

the course of a takeover or merger offer. These apply whether or not the other party is related to the company.

4.188   Its Rule 21 sets out:

> During the course of an offer, or even before the date of the offer if the board of the offeree company has reason to believe that a bona fide offer might be imminent, the board must not, except in pursuance of a contract entered into earlier, without the approval of shareholders in a general meeting:–
>
> (a) issue any authorised but unissued shares;
>
> (b) issue or grant options in respect of any unissued shares;
>
> (c) create[310] or issue, or permit the creation or issue of, any securities carrying rights of conversion into or subscription for shares;
>
> (d) sell, dispose of or acquire, or agree to sell, dispose of or acquire, assets of a material amount;[311] or
>
> (e) enter into contracts otherwise than in the ordinary course of business.
>
> The notice convening such a meeting of shareholders must include information about the offer or anticipated offer.
>
> Where it is felt that an obligation or other special circumstance exists, although a formal contract has not been entered into, the Panel must be consulted and its consent to proceed without a shareholders' meeting obtained.

Overlap with section 316(3) and the effect of the definition of "non-cash asset" in section 739

4.189   As is noted at paragraph 4.35 above, there is some doubt whether a payment made in settlement of a claim for contractual damages, not requiring shareholder

---

[309]   Defined by r 4 as including all listed and unlisted public companies considered by the Panel on Takeovers and Mergers as resident in the UK, Channel Islands or Isle of Man, as well as certain categories of private companies.

[310]   It should be noted that the wording of s 739 of the Companies Act 1985, whilst dealing with the creation or extinction of rights or interests in property, does not deal with the creation of the property itself.

[311]   Guidance on the definition of "material amount" is contained in the Notes on r 21. Whilst the factors identified therein are not decisive, given that the Panel will only "in general, have regard" to them, it is notable that materiality is flexibly assessed according, for the most part, to a comparative test of the value of the asset transferred against the remaining assets of the offeree company.

approval under section 316(3), requires approval under section 320. We seek consultees' views on this at paragraph 4.193 below.[312]

Options for reform

4.190 We set out below 9 options for reform in respect of sections 320-322 (including option 1 which proposes no change). The question whether these sections should be repealed in their entirety is considered at Part 9 below.[313] Option 2 concerns conditional contracts and option 3 concerns the overlap with sections 312-316. Options 6, 7 and 8 suggest ways in which, effectively, shareholder approval under the section could be replaced and can be viewed as alternatives. Consultees may choose any number of the other options which concern administrative receivers and court appointed administrators (option 4), listed companies (option 5), and remedies (option 9). In considering the options for reform, consultees are asked to have regard to the principles set out in Part 2 above.

Option 1: No change

4.191 One option would be to leave sections 320-322 as they stand and without any amendment. We would be grateful if consultees would please tell us if there are any difficulties with these sections apart from those specifically mentioned below.

Consultees are asked:

(i) whether they are aware of any difficulties in the operation of these provisions which ought to be addressed; and

(ii) whether they would favour retaining sections 320-322 as they stand.

Option 2: Amend section 320 so that it does not prohibit a company from making a contract which is subject to a condition precedent that the company first obtains approval under section 320

4.192 A practical difficulty pointed out to us is that the section does not enable a company to make a provisional arrangement to buy or sell an asset if approval under section 320 is required. This puts the company at a commercial disadvantage as it may not be able to rely on the other party remaining willing to enter into the transaction in the period necessary to hold a shareholders' meeting. Our provisional view is that section 320 should be amended to make it clear that contracts are possible subject to a condition precedent, under which the company comes under no liability whatever unless shareholder approval is first obtained.

Consultees are asked whether they agree with our provisional view that section 320 should be amended so that a company is able to enter into a

---

[312] There is also a question whether s 320 applies to covenanted payments under service agreements with directors (see paras 4.35 and 4.174 above) on which we also seek consultees views.

[313] See paras 9.3-9.28 below.

contract which only takes effect if the requisite shareholder approval is obtained.

Option 3: Amend section 320 to make it clear that it does not apply to covenanted payments under service agreements with directors or to payments to which section 316(3) applies

4.193 We have indicated above,[314] that as a matter of policy we consider that section 320 should not apply to damages for breach of contract or to covenanted payments if they are outside sections 312-316. This is because those sections constitute the special statutory regime for approval of payments for loss of office. If it is considered that certain payments for loss of office need not be subject to approval by shareholders under those sections, then it would not seem appropriate for similar approval requirements to be imposed by the more general provision of section 320. It appears that this is the position under the law at present, but there remains some doubt.[315] We consider provisionally that section 320 should be amended to make the position clearer.

Consultees are asked whether they agree with our provisional view that section 320 should be amended to make it clear that it does not apply to covenanted payments under service agreements with directors or to payments to which section 316(3) applies.

Option 4: A safe harbour for transactions with administrative receivers and court-appointed administrators

4.194 At the present time transactions between a director and a liquidator are exempt except where the company is in members' voluntary winding up. It has been suggested to us that there should be a similar exemption for transactions with administrators and receivers.[316] We can see that in the case of administrative receivers it would have been an objection that it was possible that the receiver was appointed by the director or a connected person since that situation might facilitate the activities of "phoenix" companies, which become insolvent, and then transfer their assets to a new creature company of the directors so that they can carry on trading. However, since the Insolvency Act 1986 receivers have had to be insolvency practitioners. Accordingly this objection is less strong. The objection does not in any event hold good in the case of a court-appointed administrator. However, the position of administrative receivers and administrators is not entirely analagous to that of a liquidator since the appointment of a liquidator (except in a members' voluntary winding up) would involve insolvency, while the appointment of an administrative receiver or administrator may not do so and members may continue, therefore, to have an interest in giving approval.

---

[314] See para 4.35.

[315] See paras 4.35 and 4.189 above.

[316] See *Demite Ltd v Protec Health Ltd* [1998] BCC 638, where it was held that section 320 applied to a transaction with an administrative receiver.

Consultees are asked whether they consider that an exception should be permitted in section 321 for administrators or receivers.

Option 5: Give the Secretary of State power to exempt listed companies from section 320

4.195 The view can be taken that in the case of listed companies the Listing Rules adequately specify the sort of related party transaction for which shareholder approval is required. In these cases it can be argued that the protection provided by the Listing Rules or AIM rules for shareholders is more complete than that provided by sections 320-322 since it disenfranchises the director and his related parties from voting on the transaction in question if the matter has to be put to the shareholders in general meeting.

4.196 It would also mean that in those cases where the company did not obtain shareholder approval but ought to have done so, the remedies contained in section 322 would no longer be available. The sanctions for breaches of the Listing Rules have been explained at paragraph 1.25 above.

Consultees are accordingly asked whether the Secretary of State should have the power to exempt listed companies from sections 320-322.

Option 6: Dispense with the requirement for shareholder approval where the independent non-executive directors approve the transaction

4.197 We appreciate that cost and delay is involved in calling a meeting to obtain shareholder approval. Moreover the requirement for shareholder approval may prevent directors from entering transactions which would be in the company's interests.[317] These disadvantages could be eliminated if the company had an independent group of non-executive directors to whom the task of approving the transaction could be delegated.

4.198 While this alternative would no doubt be convenient and cost saving, there are several dangers in it. In particular, the transaction is not subject to beneficial disclosure to shareholders. It would be necessary to define independence. We suggest that in this context independence means two things. It means freedom from any business or other relationship which would materially interfere with their independent judgement.[318] It also involves the ability to bring an independent mind to bear on a problem.[319] It cannot of course in this field mean "unpaid". The greater difficulty would be in ensuring that the independent directors had in fact decided the matter in an independent way.[320] Moreover there may not be the same full disclosure as would be required in a circular to shareholders.

---

[317] See para 3.66 above.

[318] See the Cadbury report, para 4.12, p 22 with which the Hampel Report agreed: para 3.9, p 25.

[319] See *Potato Marketing Board v Merricks* [1958] 1QB 317,335 per Devlin J.

[320] Compare the approach in *Smith v Croft (No 3)* [1988] Ch 114.

4.199   In addition there are other practical difficulties with this suggestion. The statute would have to say what is to happen if not all the non-executive directors are available to approve the transaction or only a majority do so or some are not independent for the purposes of this transaction. Our provisional view is that the disadvantages outweigh the advantages of this proposal and that it should not be adopted.

Consultees are asked whether they agree with our provisional view that section 320 should not be amended so as to provide that alternative approval could be provided by a specified minimum number of non-executive directors of the company.

Option 7: Deem payments approved if notified and members raise no objection to the proposed payment within a stipulated period

4.200   The benefits of this change would be that it might save the costs of a meeting in some cases. On the other hand, as already stated,[321] if a meeting was required there would be a longer interval of time before it was held. There is also the problem of shareholder apathy. Shareholders may very well fail to consider the proposals with the result that the time for requiring a meeting passes by. In these circumstances the requirement for a meeting would not be an effective scrutiny of the transaction. We are provisionally against this proposal.

Consultees are asked whether they agree with our provisional view that section 320 should not be amended so as to permit a company to dispense with approval of the company in general meeting if notice is given to members and there is no objection from a specified proportion of members within a specified period.

Option 8: Provide that shareholder approval is not required if an expert reports that in his opinion the transaction is fair and reasonable

4.201   Again this option is intended to reduce the cost of convening and holding a meeting. But there are difficulties in it. In particular how could shareholders be satisfied that the expert had the appropriate expertise and was independent of the company? His report would have to be open to inspection by shareholders and the transaction and his advice would have to be reported in the next financial statements.

4.202   A more fundamental objection is we believe this; the object of the section is to enable shareholders to take the decision whether a transaction should go ahead if the director has a conflict of interest and the transaction meets other conditions. We do not see that the expert's report on the terms would really address the problem which is whether the company should go ahead with the transaction at all given the conflict of interest. The expert would have no expertise in this. For all these reasons, we provisionally reject this option.

---

[321] Paragraph 4.171, above. As in relation to the option considered there, so here if the option were supported on consultation, it could be extended to approval by the holding company where that was required.

Consultees are asked whether they agree with our provisional view that companies should not be able to obtain an independent expert's report as an alternative to having to obtain shareholder approval under section 320.

Option 9: Provide that the statutory consequences of breach apply only where the company suffers prejudice

4.203   This option would deal with the hardship that might occur if the transaction were not prejudicial to the company but the company nonetheless sought to enforce some of its remedies under section 322. For instance, it might choose to sue the director for an account of profits.

4.204   One of the difficulties of this option would be that it would make it necessary to show whether the transaction was beneficial. It would accordingly reduce the certainty of the legal position as a result of the transaction. In addition, as explained in paragraph 3.21 the liability of the director to account for profit is a powerful incentive to him to fulfil his duty. We are provisionally against this option.

Consultees are asked whether they agree with our provisional view that section 322 should not be amended to the effect that a company will have no remedy under the section where the defendant or defender shows that it was not prejudiced by the transaction.

SECTION 322A: TRANSACTIONS BEYOND THE DIRECTORS' POWERS

322A.—(1) This section applies where a company enters into a transaction to which the parties include—

    (a)   a director of the company or of its holding company, or
    (b)   a person connected with such a director or a company with whom such a director is associated,

and the board of directors, in connection with the transaction, exceed any limitation on their powers under the company's constitution.

(2) The transaction is voidable at the instance of the company.

(3) Whether or not it is avoided, any such party to the transaction as is mentioned in subsection (1)(a) or (b), and any director of the company who authorised the transaction, is liable—

    (a)   to account to the company for any gain which he has made directly or indirectly by the transaction, and
    (b)   to indemnify the company for any loss or damage resulting from the transaction.

(4) Nothing in the above provisions shall be construed as excluding the operation of any other enactment or rule of law by virtue of which the transaction may be called in question or any liability to the company may arise.

(5) The transaction ceases to be voidable if—

(a) restitution of any money or other asset which was the subject-matter of the transaction is no longer possible, or

(b) the company is indemnified for any loss or damage resulting from the transaction, or

(c) rights acquired bona fide for value and without actual notice of the directors' exceeding their powers by a person who is not party to the transaction would be affected by the avoidance, or

(d) the transaction is ratified by the company in general meeting, by ordinary or special resolution or otherwise as the case may require.

(6) A person other than a director of the company is not liable under subsection (3) if he shows that at the time the transaction was entered into he did not know that the directors were exceeding their powers.

(7) This section does not affect the operation of section 35A in relation to any party to the transaction not within subsection (1)(a) or (b).

But where a transaction is voidable by virtue of this section and valid by virtue of that section in favour of such a person, the court may, on the application of that person or of the company, make such order affirming, severing or setting aside the transaction, on such terms, as appear to the court to be just.

(8) In this section "transaction" includes any act; and the reference in subsection (1) to limitations under the company's constitution includes limitations deriving—

(a) from a resolution of the company in general meeting or a meeting of any class of shareholders, or

(b) from any agreement between the members of the company or of any class of shareholders.

4.205 Section 322A was inserted by the Companies Act 1989 to create liabilities in relation to transactions involving directors, which exceed the powers under the company's constitution. The ultra vires doctrine was abolished by sections 35 and 35A of the Companies Act 1985, as amended by the 1989 Act, both as regards the company or a person who deals with the company, with the result that both can acquire rights and obligations with respect to an act which is not authorised by the company's objects clause. The validity of an act cannot now be called into question on the grounds of a company's lack of capacity.[322] Section 35A creates a statutory presumption that the power of the board of directors to bind the company or to authorise others to do so is free of any limitation under the company's constitution unless the other party is shown not to have been acting in good faith.[323]

4.206 Section 322A(1) renders voidable at the instance of the company a transaction whose parties include a director of the company or its holding company, and

---

[322] Section 35.

[323] See s 35A(1), (2)(c).

which exceeds any limitation on the director's powers under the company's constitution.[324]

4.207 A transaction within the section ceases to be voidable if:

    (a) restitution is no longer possible;

    (b) the company has been indemnified;

    (c) rights acquired by a person not party to it who acts in good faith for value and without actual notice of the excess of powers would be affected by the avoidance; or

    (d) the transaction is ratified by the company in general meeting by ordinary or special resolution or otherwise as the case may require.

4.208 Under section 322A(3), the other party to the transaction (if a director of the company or its holding company or a connected person of, or company associated with, a director) and directors who authorised the transaction, are liable to account to the company for any profit and to indemnify it against any loss. This applies even if the transaction is not avoided.

4.209 We are not aware of any deficiency in section 322A.

Consulteees are asked whether they are aware of any deficiency in section 322A.

SECTION 322B: CONTRACTS WITH SOLE MEMBER DIRECTORS

322B.—(1) Subject to subsection (2), where a private company limited by shares or by guarantee having only one member enters into a contract with the sole member of the company and the sole member is also a director of the company, the company shall, unless the contract is in writing, ensure that the terms of the contract are either set out in a written memorandum or are recorded in the minutes of the first meeting of the directors of the company following the making of the contract.

(2) Subsection (1) shall not apply to contracts entered into in the ordinary course of the company's business.

(3) For the purposes of this section a sole member who is a shadow director is treated as a director.

(4) If a company fails to comply with subsection (1), the company and every officer of it who is in default is liable to a fine.

(5) Subject to subsection (6), nothing in this section shall be construed as excluding the operation of any other enactment or rule of law applying to contracts between a company and a director of that company.

---

[324] It also extends to transactions between the company and a person connected with a director or a company associated with him as defined in Part X of the Companies Act 1985.

(6) Failure to comply with subsection (1) with respect to a contract shall not affect the validity of that contract.

4.210 This section[325] relates to a company limited by shares and having only one member. Where an oral contact is entered into between the company and a sole member director[326] its terms must be either set out in a written memorandum or recorded in the minutes of the first directors meeting following the making of the contract.

4.211 The Twelfth Company Law Directive, which this section is designed to implement,[327] sought to harmonise divergences that had occurred between member states permitting single-member private limited liability companies. The aim of the directive was to encourage enterprise amongst small firms. The directive allowed member states to take action to lay down restrictions on the use of single-member companies. In fact the preamble to the directive specifically states that contracts between a sole member and his company as represented by him must be recorded in writing. From the United Kingdom point of view, this provision is likely to have most relevance in the context of winding up or administration. Those contracts entered into, not in the ordinary course of business, will be of particular interest to the liquidator, hence the need for them to be adequately evidenced. If there is a breach of the section, the company and every officer in default is liable to a fine.

4.212 There is a parallel section in Part XI of the Act, dealing with oral decisions by a single member which have the same effect as a resolutions of the company in general meeting.[328] These decisions must also be recorded. In default a criminal offence is again committed. Both sections provide that the transaction is not affected by a failure to comply with the section.

4.213 We are not aware of any deficiency in this section.

Consultees are asked whether they are aware of any deficiency in section 322B.

SECTIONS 323 AND 327: PROHIBITION ON OPTION DEALING BY DIRECTORS AND THEIR NEAR FAMILIES

323.—(1) It is an offence for a director of a company to buy—

(a) a right to call for delivery at a specified price and within a specified time of a specified number of relevant shares or a specified amount of relevant debentures; or

---

[325] Inserted by the Companies (Single Member Private Limited Companies) Regulations 1992, SI 1992/1699, reg 2, Sched, para 3 as from 15 July 1992, pursuant to art 5, Twelfth Company Law Directive [1989] OJ L395/40.

[326] The provision does not apply to contracts entered into in the ordinary course of the company's business.

[327] See generally the DTI's paper: Twelfth Company Law Directive, a consultative document, November 1991.

[328] See s 382 of the Companies Act 1985.

(b)   a right to make delivery at a specified price and within a specified time of a specified number of relevant shares or a specified amount of relevant debentures; or

(c)   a right (as he may elect) to call for delivery at a specified price and within a specified time or to make delivery at a specified price and within a specified time of a specified number of relevant shares or a specified amount of relevant debentures.

(2) A person guilty of an offence under subsection (1) is liable to imprisonment or a fine, or both.

(3) In subsection (1) —

(a)   "relevant shares", in relation to a director of a company, means shares in the company or in any other body corporate, being the company's subsidiary or holding company, or a subsidiary of the company's holding company, being shares as respects which there has been granted a listing on a stock exchange (whether in Great Britain or elsewhere);

(b)   "relevant debentures", in relation to a director of a company, means debentures of the company or of any other body corporate, being the company's subsidiary or holding company or a subsidiary of the company's holding company, being debentures as respects which there has been granted such a listing; and

(c)   "price" includes any consideration other than money.

(4) This section applies to a shadow director as to a director.

(5) This section is not to be taken as penalising a person who buys a right to subscribe for shares in, or debentures of, a body corporate or buys debentures of a body corporate that confer upon the holder of them a right to subscribe for, or to convert the debentures (in whole or in part) into, shares of that body.

327.—(1) Section 323 applies to—

(a)   the wife or husband of a director of a company (not being herself or himself a director of it), and

(b)   an infant son or infant daughter of a director (not being himself or herself a director of the company),

as it applies to the director; but it is a defence for a person charged by virtue of this section with an offence under section 323 to prove that he (she) had no reason to believe that his (her) spouse or, as the case may be, parent was a director of the company in question.

(2) For purposes of this section—

(a)   "son" includes step-son, and "daughter" includes step-daughter ("parent" being construed accordingly),

(b)   "infant" means, in relation to Scotland, [person under the age of 18 years], and

(c)   a shadow director of a company is deemed a director of it.

General

4.214 Section 323[329] makes it a criminal offence for directors (including shadow directors) of a company to buy "put" and "call" options in listed shares or debentures in that company or a company of the same group. The prohibition extends to the spouses and minor children of directors.[330]

4.215 In Part 9, we provisionally recommend the repeal of section 323. In this part we set out various substantive improvements which might be made if that provisional recommendation is not accepted.

4.216 Section 327 extends the prohibition in section 323 to spouses and minor children (not themselves being board members) or directors. In this section "director" includes a shadow director. However, it is a defence for a person charged under this section to show that he had no reason to believe his spouse or parent was a director of the company in question. This extension was first enacted in 1967. It does not derive from any recommendations of the Jenkins Committee but it can be inferred that the purpose was to prevent the mischief to which the prohibition was directed being circumvented by spouses and children dealing in options instead of the director. Section 327, like section 346, refers to spouses but not to persons with whom a director may be living as man and wife. We discuss under section 346 below in the context of connected persons whether the references to spouses and minor children should be extended to include cohabitants and natural children and other children of the cohabitant who is not a director.

Insider dealing

4.217 The Jenkins Committee considered that a victim of insider dealing by a director of a company "who, in any transaction relating to the securities of his company or of any other company in the same group, made improper use of a particular piece of confidential information which might be expected materially to affect the value of those securities" should have a civil remedy. However, this recommendation was not implemented. Indeed, until 1980,[331] there was no specific statutory regulation of insider dealing. However, the Jenkins Committee recommendation on dealings by directors in options to purchase securities of their own company was implemented by section 25 of the Companies Act 1967, from which section 323 is derived.[332]

4.218 The Jenkins Committee thought that directors' dealings in put and call options should generally be prohibited because:

---

[329] Which re-enacts s 25 of the Companies Act 1967, as amended by s 42(1) and Sched 2 of the Companies Act 1976 and s 80(1) and Sched 2 of the Companies Act 1980.

[330] See s 327, below.

[331] Part V of the Companies Act 1980 introduced provisions making insider trading a criminal offence. These were subjected to minor amendment and re-enacted in the Company Securities (Insider Dealing) Act 1985. This was, in turn, repealed and replaced by the provisions of the Criminal Justice Act 1993.

[332] Jenkins Report; Recommendation at para 99 (b), p 35.

[a] director who speculates in this way with special inside information is clearly acting improperly, and we do not believe that any reputable director would deal in such options in such circumstances.[333]

The Criminal Justice Act 1993

4.219   The Criminal Justice Act 1993 ("CJA"), Part V, implementing provisions of the European Council Directive Co-ordinating Regulations on Insider Dealing (89/592/EEC), now makes it an offence for an individual who has information as an insider,[334] to deal, on a regulated market or whilst acting as or through a professional intermediary,[335] in price-affected securities in relation to that information.[336] An individual is also guilty[337] of insider dealing if he encourages another to deal in the same circumstances or improperly discloses inside information to another.[338]

4.220   Under section 60(1), the Act defines a "regulated market" as:

> any market, however operated, which, by an order made by the Treasury, is identified (whether by name or by reference to criteria prescribed by the order) as a regulated market for the purposes of this part.

4.221   Currently, regulated stock exchanges in relation to the Act include major exchanges in EU states as well as NASDAQ in the USA, although the New York Stock Exchange is not included.[339]

4.222   Section 323 however applies to the purchase of options whether on or off market.

The Stock Exchange Model Code

4.223   The Model Code,[340] which is set out in Appendix E below restricts the freedom of directors in listed companies dealing in the securities of the companies concerned. The Model Code imposes "closed periods" within which directors cannot deal in the securities of their company, including options (although in some special

---

[333] Jenkins Report, para 90, p 31.

[334] Insider is defined in s 57, subsection (2) which states that a person will have knowledge as an insider, or from an inside source, if they have it through "being a director, employee or shareholder of an issuer of securities" (s 57(2)(a)(i)). In relation to the s 327 extension, note a person may have information as an insider if one of the aforementioned group was the source of the information (s 57(2)(b)).

[335] See s 52(3).

[336] See s 52, and Sched 2 of the Act for the width of the types of securities within the purview of the offence.

[337] Subject to the defences in s 53.

[338] See s 52(2).

[339] See Insider Dealing (Securities and Regulated Markets) Order 1994 (SI 1994/187) and the Insider Dealing (Securities and Regulated Markets (Amendment) Order 1996 (SI 1996/1561).

[340] Listing Rules, Ch 16, Appendix.

circumstances options dealing is permitted).[341] Rule 16.18[342] of the Listing Rules requires companies to ensure that their directors, and employees and directors in the same group likely to have unpublished price-sensitive information, comply with a code no less exacting than the Model Code.

4.224 In *Chase Manhattan Securities v Goodman*,[343] Knox J held that the obligation to operate internal dealing codes fell on companies and not on individual directors. Nevertheless, it was the view of Knox J that directors were under an obligation to the company to comply with the Model Code[344] if aware of its terms, even in the absence of their company adopting a code of its own.[345]

Options for reform

4.225 Our provisional recommendation is in fact that section 323 should be repealed, and this is discussed in Part 9 below.[346] However, we put forward below two suggestions for substantive improvements on the basis that that provisional recommendation is not in due course adopted (options 2 and 3). We also include an option of no change (option 1).

Option 1: No change

4.226 It could be argued that section 323 should be retained as it has a more restricted application than the CJA. Section 323 and the Listing Rules are only applicable to companies listed on the Stock Exchange. The purchase of put and call options trading is highly geared trading in the company's securities,[347] and is imprudent for directors.

Consultees are asked whether section 323 should be left unchanged.

Option 2: Make off-market dealings in options with inside information an offence

4.227 If the section is retained, another option would be to ensure that its provisions were reformed in order to be consistent with both the policy of the CJA and the Model Code requirements. Thus section 323 could be limited to making off-

---

[341] See paras 14 and 15 of the Model Code.

[342] See Appendix E below.

[343] [1991] BCLC 897.

[344] See Appendix E below.

[345] [1991] BCLC 897 *per* Knox J at p 924-9.

[346] See para 9.33 below.

[347] For a small investment, the purchaser can make a large profit or incur a large loss. The effect of the s 323 prohibition on contracts is not dealt with in the Companies Act 1985 and falls to be determined under the general law. See also s 63(2) of the CJA, where different considerations apply. The Law Commission is reviewing the effect of illegality on transactions. See the Law Commission's 6th Programme of Law Reform; Law Com No 234, Item 4, p 29. The Commission hopes to issue a consultation paper in the second half of this year.

market dealing in put and call options with inside information a criminal offence. The overlap between the CJA and section 323 could then be reduced.

4.228   A disadvantage in relation to this option would be that even though the legislation would be more consistent, section 323 would become a third source for prohibitions on insider dealing and it would be illogical to restrict it to directors and for it not, for example, to apply to employees with access to unpublished price-sensitive information. Now that insider dealing is an offence, it may not be justified to retain section 323 in this restricted form.

Consultees are asked whether, if section 323 is not repealed, it should be amended so that it applies only to off market dealings in options on the basis of inside information.

Option 3: No change, but exempt dealings in options under a scheme for the benefit of employees

4.229   It has been suggested that the purchase of options from the trustees of an employee share trust should be exempted from any retained prohibition.[348] Employee share trusts are common. The section does not apply to options to subscribe for shares[349] and incentive schemes involving the grant of options to subscribe are therefore not affected. Arguably there is no reason why schemes which provide for options to purchase shares should not also be excluded. Indeed, they may well be preferable, because they do not involve the dilution of existing shareholdings since no new shares are required to be issued to participants. The exclusion would be limited to the purchase of options under schemes offering comparable benefits to directors and employees in general.[350] Only an executive director could therefore benefit.

Consultees are asked whether, if section 323 is not repealed, it should be disapplied in relation to the purchase of options under a scheme for the benefit of employees.[351]

---

[348]   See the Model Code, para 14, which is set out in Appendix E.

[349]   See section 323(5).

[350]   Compare the definition of "employees' share scheme" in s 743, which provides:

   ... is a scheme for encouraging or facilitating the holding of shares or debentures in a company for the benefit of-

   (a) the bona fide employees or former employees of the company, the company's subsidiary or holding company or a subsidiary of the company's holding company, or

   (b) the wives, husbands, widows, widowers or children or step-children under the age of 18 of such employees or former employees.

[351]   Including former employees and near relatives as in s 743, see n 350 above.

PART 5
SUBSTANTIVE IMPROVEMENTS 2: DISCLOSURE OF DIRECTORS' SHARE DEALINGS (SECTIONS 324-326, 328-329 AND SCHEDULE 13)

INTRODUCTION

5.1 In Part 4 we saw that there are some prohibitions on share dealing by directors. The prohibitions include section 323 which prohibits dealings by directors in options to buy and sell their company's shares.[1] Dealings by directors in their company's shares on the basis of unpublished price-sensitive information are also prohibited by the Criminal Justice Act 1993.[2] There are self-regulatory rules which lead to restrictions on the times when a director may deal in company's shares, most notably in the Stock Exchange's Model Code.[3] But except where these restrictions apply, a director may properly acquire an interest in his company's shares. The law does not seek to prohibit him from doing so[4] but rather seeks to ensure *transparency*, more specifically to ensure that members of the company have the requisite information about these dealings and to ensure that where a company's shares are listed the information is made available promptly to the market.

5.2 This part is concerned with sections 324-326, 328-329 and Schedule 13. These provisions deal with the duty of a director to notify interests in shareholdings to his company and impose an obligation on the company to record interests in a register and to disclose them to the relevant exchanges. They can be seen as merely ministerial provisions but they are important because they are the means of achieving the transparency referred to in the preceding paragraph. To achieve their purpose, these provisions involve the successful application of several of the guiding principles which we have provisionally identified, particularly the principle that the law should seek to achieve ample but efficient disclosure (principle 9),[5] the principle of "enough but not excessive" regulation (principle 8)[6] and the principle of efficiency and cost-effectiveness (principle 10).[7] As we see it there are several reasons for the provisions with which this part deals. The interests which a director has in his company and his acquisitions and disposals of such interests

---

[1] See para 4.214 above.

[2] See para 4.219 above.

[3] See para 4.223. There is a similar Model Code for AIM listed companies: see Appendix 12 of the AIM rules.

[4] Indeed many would argue that benefits flow from directors owning shares in their own companies.

[5] See para 2.17(9) above.

[6] See para 2.17(8) above.

[7] See para 2.17(10) above.

convey information about the financial incentives that a director has to improve his company's performance and accordingly these provisions form part of the system put in place by the Companies Acts to enable shareholders to monitor the directors' stewardship of the company. In addition where the shareholdings are substantial the information also conveys important information about the ability of the directors to control the affairs of the company in general meeting. They also have a separate function of providing through disclosure an additional incentive to directors to comply with the prohibitions which the law imposes on directors' share dealings.[8] The economic importance of these provisions, as Part 3 explains, lies in providing efficient incentives for the sharing of information.[9] This reduces the costs that shareholders have to incur in monitoring the activities of directors and no doubt by like token in the public interest they make it more likely that the rules are complied with and that the criminal sanctions do not have to be enforced. We do not think that there is any reasonable ground for seeking to remove these provisions from the Companies Act.

5.3 We consider the provisions in turn under the following heads:

- The *obligation of disclosure* in sections 324 and 328[10] - these deal with the director's duty to disclose interests in shareholdings in his own company. Section 328 is dealt with alongside section 324 because it attributes to a director the interests of his spouse and infant children for the purposes of section 324.

- The *meaning of "interest"* and the *mechanics of disclosure* - Schedule 13, Parts I-III.[11] These supplement section 324 and for example amplify the meaning of interest and specify the period within which a director must notify an interest.

- The *company's register of directors' interests* - sections 325 and 326, and Schedule 13, Part IV[12] - these deal with the register which the company is bound to keep of the interests notified to it by directors.

- *Notification to the exchanges* - section 329[13] - this deals with the obligation of a listed company to notify interests notified to it by directors to the exchange on which its shares are listed.

5.4 Section 327 extends the prohibition on option dealing and so it is dealt with in Part 4 above.[14] The criminal sanctions created by section 324(7) and 326 are considered in Part 10 below.

---

[8] See para 5.1 above.

[9] See paras 3.34, 3.41-43 and 3.64 above.

[10] See paras 5.6-5.19 below.

[11] See paras 5.20-5.26 below.

[12] See paras 5.27-5.29 below.

[13] See paras 5.31-5.39 below.

[14] Para 4.216.

5.5 In August 1996, the DTI issued a consultative document[15] in which it made proposals for changes to sections 324 and 329, which would be made by secondary legislation using the powers under section 1 of the Deregulation and Contracting Out Act 1994. The proposals are outlined below with a summary of consultees' responses and the DTI's conclusions as communicated to us. As a result, few issues remain. Our review of the sections dealt with in this part has thus been a limited one.

THE OBLIGATION OF DISCLOSURE: SECTIONS 324 AND 328 – DUTY OF DIRECTOR TO NOTIFY OWN AND ATTRIBUTED SHAREHOLDINGS IN COMPANY

324.—(1) A person who becomes a director of a company and at the time when he does so is interested in shares in, or debentures of, the company or any other body corporate, being the company's subsidiary or holding company or a subsidiary of the company's holding company, is under obligation to notify the company in writing—

(a) of the subsistence of his interests at that time; and

(b) of the number of shares of each class in, and the amount of debentures of each class of, the company or other such body corporate in which each interest of his subsists at that time.

(2) A director of a company is under obligation to notify the company in writing of the occurrence, while he is a director, of any of the following events—

(a) any event in consequence of whose occurrence he becomes, or ceases to be, interested in shares in, or debentures of, the company or any other body corporate, being the company's subsidiary or holding company or a subsidiary of the company's holding company;

(b) the entering into by him of a contract to sell any such shares or debentures;

(c) the assignment by him of a right granted to him by the company to subscribe for shares in, or debentures of, the company; and

(d) the grant to him by another body corporate, being the company's subsidiary or holding company or a subsidiary of the company's holding company, of a right to subscribe for shares in, or debentures of, that other body corporate, the exercise of such a right granted to him and the assignment by him of such a right so granted;

and notification to the company must state the number or amount, and class, of shares or debentures involved.

(3) Schedule 13 has effect in connection with subsections (1) and (2) above; and of that Schedule—

(a) Part I contains rules for the interpretation of, and otherwise in relation to, those subsections and applies in determining, for

---

[15] Disclosure of Directors' Shareholdings - Proposal for an Order under the Deregulation and Contracting Out Act 1994.

145

145

purposes of those subsections, whether a person has an interest in shares or debentures;

    (b)   Part II applies with respect to the periods within which obligations imposed by the subsections must be fulfilled; and

    (c)   Part III specifies certain circumstances in which obligations arising from subsection (2) are to be treated as not discharged;

and subsections (1) and (2) are subject to any exceptions for which provision may be made by regulations made by the Secretary of State by statutory instrument.

(4) Subsection (2) does not require the notification by a person of the occurrence of an event whose occurrence comes to his knowledge after he has ceased to be a director.

(5) An obligation imposed by this section is treated as not discharged unless the notice by means of which it purports to be discharged is expressed to be given in fulfilment of that obligation.

(6) This section applies to shadow directors as to directors; but nothing in it operates so as to impose an obligation with respect to shares in a body corporate which is the wholly-owned subsidiary of another body corporate.

(7) A person who—

    (a)   fails to discharge, within the proper period, an obligation to which he is subject under subsection (1) or (2), or

    (b)   in purported discharge of an obligation to which he is so subject, makes to the company a statement which he knows to be false, or recklessly makes to it a statement which is false,

is guilty of an offence and liable to imprisonment or a fine, or both.

(8) Section 732 (restriction on prosecutions) applies to an offence under this section.

328.—(1) For the purposes of section 324—

    (a)   an interest of the wife or husband of a director of a company (not being herself or himself a director of it) in shares or debentures is to be treated as the director's interest; and

    (b)   the same applies to an interest of an infant son or infant daughter of a director of a company (not being himself or herself a director of it) in shares or debentures.

(2) For those purposes—

    (a)   a contract, assignment or right of subscription entered into, exercised or made by, or a grant made to, the wife or husband of a director of a company (not being herself or himself a director of it) is to be treated as having been entered into, exercised or made by, or (as the case may be) as having been made to, the director; and

    (b)   the same applies to a contract, assignment or right of subscription entered into, exercised or made by, or grant made to, an infant son or infant daughter of a director of a company (not being himself or herself a director of it).

(3) A director of a company is under obligation to notify the company in writing of the occurrence while he or she is a director, of either of the following events, namely—

    (a)   the grant by the company to his (her) spouse, or to his or her infant son or infant daughter, of a right to subscribe for shares in, or debentures of, the company; and

    (b)   the exercise by his (her) spouse or by his or her infant son or infant daughter of such a right granted by the company to the wife, husband, son or daughter.

(4) In a notice given to the company under subsection (3) there shall be stated—

    (a)   in the case of the grant of a right, the like information as is required by section 324 to be stated by the director on the grant to him by another body corporate of a right to subscribe for shares in, or debentures of, that other body corporate; and

    (b)   in the case of the exercise of a right, the like information as is required by that section to be stated by the director on the exercise of a right granted to him by another body corporate to subscribe for shares in, or debentures of, that other body corporate.

(5) An obligation imposed by subsection (3) on a director must be fulfilled by him before the end of 5 days beginning with the day following that on which the occurrence of the event giving rise to it comes to his knowledge; but in reckoning that period of days there is disregarded any Saturday or Sunday, and any day which is a bank holiday in any part of Great Britain.

(6) A person who—

    (a)   fails to fulfil, within the proper period, an obligation to which he is subject under subsection (3), or

    (b)   in purported fulfilment of such an obligation, makes to a company a statement which he knows to be false, or recklessly makes to a company a statement which is false,

is guilty of an offence and liable to imprisonment or a fine, or both.

(7) The rules set out in Part I of Schedule 13 have effect for the interpretation of, and otherwise in relation to, subsections (1) and (2); and subsections (5), (6) and (8) of section 324 apply with any requisite modification.

(8) In this section, "son" includes step-son, "daughter" includes step-daughter, and "infant" means, in relation to Scotland, [person under the age of 18 years].

(9) For purposes of section 325, an obligation imposed on a director by this section is to be treated as if imposed by section 324.

General

5.6   Section 324 requires that, on becoming a director (including a shadow director) of a company, a person must give a company written notice of any interest they have in its shares or debentures or any shares or debentures of any company in the same group or fellow subsidiary of the same holding company.[16] Under section 324(2), whilst he remains in office, a director is under a continuing obligation to notify the company of any alteration in his interests, together with the entry into any contract for sale or the assignment of a right to subscribe granted to him by the company[17] or the grant to him by another group company or a fellow subsidiary of a right to subscribe for its shares or debentures. The notification requirements are strict. Not only must the notice be in writing; it must also be expressed to be given in fulfilment of the director's obligation under the section. Failure to notify an interest, or the knowing or reckless making of a false statement in respect of either, is a criminal offence (see subsection (7)), although in England and Wales the prosecution cannot be brought without the consent of the Secretary of State or the DPP. Prosecutions in Scotland are in the hands of the Lord Advocate and of subordinate public prosecutors under his control.

5.7   Section 328 attributes to directors, for the purposes of the disclosure obligations imposed by section 324, the interests held by, and transactions undertaken by, their spouses and minor children who are not also directors of the company concerned. The attribution is limited to these interests and does not cover, for example the interests of cohabitants who are not spouses. We consider these questions under section 346 below, where the same issue arises.[18] No exception is made for the interests of separated spouses. However, the obligation to give notice does not arise until the director knows of the event which gives rise to the obligation to notify.[19]

The DTI's August 1996 proposals

5.8   The DTI proposed that section 324 should be made less onerous by allowing directors the option of giving aggregate disclosure of small transactions in shares or debentures of companies whose shares were publicly traded, allowing postponement of the aggregate disclosure whilst it remained below a set threshold or until the end of the financial year. Shares listed on a stock exchange in any member state of the European Union or admitted to trading on a market operated by a recognised investment exchange in the UK would be publicly traded for this purpose. The DTI proposed that, in order to qualify for the exemption from disclosure, the aggregated transactions would, if they involved shares, have to be

---

[16]   There is an exception for interests in the shares of wholly-owned subsidiaries: s 324(6). Such interests could only be interests held as nominee for some other group company.

[17]   A director need not notify the company of a right to subscribe which it grants to him, and the company automatically comes under an obligation to insert particulars of any such option in the register maintained under s 325. But a director must give notice of rights to subscribe granted to persons whose interests are attributable to him under s 328: see s 328(3)(a).

[18]   See Part 8 below.

[19]   Sched 13, para 14(2).

both below a monetary amount (£10,000 was suggested) and below a specified percentage (1% was suggested) of the company's total share capital, whereas if they involved debentures, it would be sufficient if they met a monetary limit of the same amount.

5.9 It was proposed that the aggregate disclosure thresholds should apply to directors' interests in each individual company within a group, provided that this option did not create too much opportunity for avoidance.

5.10 The DTI also proposed that directors should be permitted to "net off"[20] transactions over the course of a business day, this proposal having received support from consultees responding to its previous paper in relation to the disclosure requirements under Part VI of the Companies Act 1985.

5.11 In addition, it was proposed that directors' non-beneficial interests in company shares and debentures (eg as trustees for pension funds) should be entirely exempted from disclosure. The rationale for the proposal was that disclosure appeared "inappropriate as changes in such non-beneficial interests will not be significant in terms of the director's personal financial interests in the success of the company"[21] and might even prove misleading. It is important to note that the DTI's proposals were limited to non-beneficial interests strictly so-called, that is where the director did not stand to benefit directly or indirectly, for instance through a close family member, from the performance of the trust fund.

5.12 The DTI's proposals also covered scrip dividends. The DTI did not think that these transactions should be the subject of an outright exemption because this could lead to significant transactions being concealed and to the company's register being inaccurate. However the DTI thought that an intermediate approach would be appropriate. This would exempt transactions from anything other than obligatory year end disclosure. Discretionary PEPs[22] (where a director has no control over which securities are held) concerning publicly traded companies were also thought appropriate for this approach in order to help reduce disclosure burdens. However, self-selected and single company PEPs were in a different position because of the degree of control a director could exercise when making equities transactions in these cases.

Consultees' response and the DTI's conclusion

5.13 A majority of respondents to the consultation thought that the disclosure threshold, if introduced, should not apply to disclosure by the director to the company. Many respondents argued that aggregation would in practice impose an additional burden on the director, as it would be necessary to keep a running tally to know when the threshold had been reached. Several listed companies also argued that in practice it was essential for company secretaries to have accurate

---

[20] Ie where directors undertook buy and sell transactions on the same day, those transactions could be offset and disclosure only required in relation to the net purchase or sale.

[21] DTI consultative document, para 4.33, p 15.

[22] Ie Personal Equity Plans.

data on directors' interests, and expressed concern that the proposed amendment would make this more difficult.

5.14 In view of the lack of support for the proposal as a deregulatory measure, the DTI is no longer proposing to amend section 324. Taken in conjunction with the retention of the requirement under section 325,[23] this will also ensure that shareholders and creditors continue to have access to accurate information through the company's register of directors' interests.

5.15 Respondents were split as to whether "netting off" within a business day should be permitted. Many respondents argued that there could be a strong market interest in the different prices at which a director had dealt in the company's shares, and that the market would wish to be aware of occasions where the exercise of share options by a director had been followed by a sale of the company's shares on the same day. In light of these concerns, the DTI is not proposing to permit "netting off".

5.16 A majority of respondents supported the proposal that directors' non-beneficial interests in a company should be entirely exempted from disclosure. However, some respondents argued that there might be considerable market interest if, in cases where the directors are acting as trustees, the holding represented a significant degree of control in the company. The DTI has requested us to invite further views on this issue.

5.17 A majority of respondents supported the proposals that publicly traded companies should be permitted to disclose directors' scrip dividends and directors' interests held via discretionary PEPs only at the end of the financial year.

5.18 There was one aspect of the DTI's August 1996 proposals regarding section 324 which was supported by respondents,[24] but as we have indicated above the DTI have asked us to seek further views on this, which we do in the next paragraph. Apart from that matter, there are, as we see it, no further questions under this section at this stage,[25] though we invite consultees below[26] to inform us if they disagree.

Option for reform: Exempt from disclosure under section 324 directors' non-beneficial interests

5.19 A director may be a trustee of a trust which holds shares or debentures in a company of which he is a director. The effect of section 324 is that (unless he is a bare trustee) he must disclose his interest in those securities and any changes in the holding. There are arguments for saying that this information is not of value. If he has no beneficial interest in the holding whatever, then details of it will not

---

[23] See paras 5.27-5.29 below.

[24] See para 5.16 above.

[25] As indicated above, we deal with the question of the persons whose interests should be attributed under s 346 in Part 8 below and the question whether the section should be decriminalised in para 10.37 below.

[26] See the questions following para 5.19 below.

150

convey any meaningful information about the financial incentives which he has to cause the company's performance to improve. The position is unlikely to be any different if he has a beneficial interest in law (as many trustees do) simply because he is entitled to recover his expenses or remuneration or is entitled to an indemnity for liabilities properly incurred.[27] We provisionally consider that such limited beneficial interests should not prevent a holding being treated as non-beneficial. The director may indeed not have been involved in the transaction if the company is a listed or AIM company because the Model Code applies to dealings by a director as a trustee as they do where he is dealing on his own account, unless the decision to deal is taken by other trustees acting independently of the director.[28] However this may be, there will be cases where a director-trustee has an influence on a dealing by a trust and accordingly it would seem likely that the market will be interested in the information unless the transaction is small in value. If an exception is provided for small transactions, it is for consideration whether the aggregate limit proposed above[29] is appropriate.

Consultees are asked if non-beneficial holdings should be exempt from section 324 and if so:

(i) whether non-beneficial holdings should be defined as excluding any beneficial interests which the director may have by reason of any right to expenses, remuneration or indemnity;

(ii) whether the exemption should apply irrespective of the size of the transaction or only if the transaction (when aggregated with other transactions in non-beneficial holdings) does not exceed a certain size;

(iii) if they consider that the exemption should only apply if the transaction does not exceed a certain size, how should such size be ascertained.

Consultees are also asked if they consider that there are deficiencies in section 324 not considered above.

THE MEANING OF "INTEREST" AND THE MECHANICS OF DISCLOSURE:
SCHEDULE 13, PARTS I-III
PART 1: RULES FOR THE INTERPRETATION OF SECTIONS 324-326, 328 AND 346
1.—(1) A reference to an interest in shares or debentures is to be read as including any interest of any kind whatsoever in shares or debentures.

(2) Accordingly, there are to be disregarded any restraints or restrictions to which the exercise of any right attached to the interest is or may be subject.

---

[27] Compare Companies Act 1985, Sched 2, para 4(1).

[28] See the Model Code in Appendix E, para (10).

[29] See para 5.8 above.

2.— Where property is held on trust and any interest in shares or debentures is comprised in the property, any beneficiary of the trust who (apart from this paragraph) does not have an interest in the shares or debentures is to be taken as having such an interest; but this paragraph is without prejudice to the following provisions of this Part of this Schedule.

3.—(1) A person is taken to have an interest in shares or debentures if—

(a) he enters into a contract for their purchase by him (whether for cash or other consideration), or

(b) not being the registered holder, he is entitled to exercise any right conferred by the holding of the shares or debentures, or is entitled to control the exercise of any such right.

(2) For purposes of sub-paragraph (1)(b), a person is taken to be entitled to exercise or control the exercise of a right conferred by the holding of shares or debentures if he—

(a) has a right (whether subject to conditions or not) the exercise of which would make him so entitled, or

(b) is under an obligation (whether or not so subject) the fulfilment of which would make him so entitled.

(3) A person is not by virtue of sub-paragraph (1)(b) taken to be interested in shares or debentures by reason only that he—

(a) has been appointed a proxy to vote at a specified meeting of a company or of any class of its members and at any adjournment of that meeting, or

(b) has been appointed by a corporation to act as its representative at any meeting of a company or of any class of its members.

4.— A person is taken to be interested in shares or debentures if a body corporate is interested in them and—

(a) that body corporate or its directors are accustomed to act in accordance with his directions or instructions, or

(b) he is entitled to exercise or control the exercise of one-third or more of the voting power at general meetings of that body corporate.

As this paragraph applies for the purposes of section 346(4) and (5), "more than one-half" is substituted for "one-third or more".

5.— Where a person is entitled to exercise or control the exercise of one-third or more of the voting power at general meetings of a body corporate, and that body corporate is entitled to exercise or control the exercise of any of the voting power at general meetings of another body corporate ("the effective voting power"), then, for purposes of paragraph 4(b), the effective voting power is taken to be exercisable by that person.

As this paragraph applies for the purposes of section 346(4) and (5), "more than one-half" is substituted for "one-third or more".

6.—(1) A person is taken to have an interest in shares or debentures if, otherwise than by virtue of having an interest under a trust—

    (a)   he has a right to call for delivery of the shares or debentures to himself or to his order, or

    (b)   he has a right to acquire an interest in shares or debentures or is under an obligation to take an interest in shares or debentures;

whether in any case the right or obligation is conditional or absolute.

(2) Rights or obligations to subscribe for shares or debentures are not to be taken, for purposes of sub-paragraph (1), to be rights to acquire, or obligations to take, an interest in shares or debentures.

This is without prejudice to paragraph 1.

7.— Persons having a joint interest are deemed each of them to have that interest.

8.— It is immaterial that shares or debentures in which a person has an interest are unidentifiable.

9.— So long as a person is entitled to receive, during the lifetime of himself or another, income from trust property comprising shares or debentures, an interest in the shares or debentures in reversion or remainder or (as regards Scotland) in fee, are to be disregarded.

10. —A person is to be treated as uninterested in shares or debentures if, and so long as, he holds them under the law in force in England and Wales as a bare trustee or as a custodian trustee, or under the law in force in Scotland, as a simple trustee.

11.— There is to be disregarded an interest of a person subsisting by virtue of—

    [(a)   any unit trust scheme which is an authorised unit trust scheme within the meaning of the Financial Services Act 1986];

    (b)   a scheme made under section 22 [or 22A] of the Charities Act 1960 [or section 24 or 25 of the Charities Act 1993], section 11 of the Trustee Investments Act 1961 or section 1 of the Administration of Justice Act 1965; or

    (c)   the scheme set out in the Schedule to the Church Funds Investment Measure 1958.

12. — There is to be disregarded any interest—

    (a)   of the Church of Scotland General Trustees or of the Church of Scotland Trust in shares or debentures held by them;

    (b)   of any other person in shares or debentures held by those Trustees or that Trust otherwise than as simple trustees.

"The Church of Scotland General Trustees" are the body incorporated by the order confirmed by the Church of Scotland (General Trustees) Order Confirmation Act 1921; and "the Church of Scotland Trust" is the body incorporated by the order confirmed by the Church of Scotland Trust Order Confirmation Act 1932.

153

13.— Delivery to a person's order of shares or debentures in fulfilment of a contract for the purchase of them by him or in satisfaction of a right of his to call for their delivery, or failure to deliver shares or debentures in accordance with the terms of such a contract or on which such a right falls to be satisfied, is deemed to constitute an event in consequence of the occurrence of which he ceases to be interested in them, and so is the lapse of a person's right to call for delivery of shares or debentures.

PART II - PERIODS WITHIN WHICH OBLIGATIONS IMPOSED BY SECTION 324 MUST BE FULFILLED

14.—(1) An obligation imposed on a person by section 324(1) to notify an interest must, if he knows of the existence of the interest on the day on which he becomes a director, be fulfilled before the expiration of the period of 5 days beginning with the day following that day.

(2) Otherwise, the obligation must be fulfilled before the expiration of the period of 5 days beginning with the day following that on which the existence of the interest comes to his knowledge.

15.—(1) An obligation imposed on a person by section 324(2) to notify the occurrence of an event must, if at the time at which the event occurs he knows of its occurrence and of the fact that its occurrence gives rise to the obligation, be fulfilled before the expiration of the period of 5 days beginning with the day following that on which the event occurs.

(2) Otherwise, the obligation must be fulfilled before the expiration of a period of 5 days beginning with the day following that on which the fact that the occurrence of the event gives rise to the obligation comes to his knowledge.

16.— In reckoning, for purposes of paragraphs 14 and 15, any period of days, a day that is a Saturday or Sunday, or a bank holiday in any part of Great Britain, is to be disregarded.

PART III - CIRCUMSTANCES IN WHICH THE OBLIGATION IMPOSED BY SECTION 324 IS NOT DISCHARGED

17.—(1) Where an event of whose occurrence a director is, by virtue of section 324(2)(a), under obligation to notify a company consists of his entering into a contract for the purchase by him of shares or debentures, the obligation is not discharged in the absence of inclusion in the notice of a statement of the price to be paid by him under the contract.

(2) An obligation imposed on a director by section 324(2)(b) is not discharged in the absence of inclusion in the notice of the price to be received by him under the contract.

18.—(1) An obligation imposed on a director by virtue of section 324(2)(c) to notify a company is not discharged in the absence of inclusion in the notice of a statement of the consideration for the assignment (or, if it be the case that there is no consideration, that fact).

(2) Where an event of whose occurrence a director is, by virtue of section 324(2)(d), under obligation to notify a company consists in his assigning a right, the obligation is not discharged in the absence of inclusion in the notice of a similar statement.

19.—(1) Where an event of whose occurrence a director is, by virtue of section 324(2)(d), under obligation to notify a company consists in the grant to him of a right to subscribe for shares or debentures, the obligation is not discharged in the absence of inclusion in the notice of a statement of—

    (a)   the date on which the right was granted,

    (b)   the period during which or the time at which the right is exercisable,

    (c)   the consideration for the grant (or, if it be the case that there is no consideration, that fact), and

    (d)   the price to be paid for the shares or debentures.

(2) Where an event of whose occurrence a director is, by section 324(2)(d), under obligation to notify a company consists in the exercise of a right granted to him to subscribe for shares or debentures, the obligation is not discharged in the absence of inclusion in the notice of a statement of—

    (a)   the number of shares or amount of debentures in respect of which the right was exercised, and

    (b)   if it be the case that they were registered in his name, that fact, and, if not, the name or names of the person or persons in whose name or names they were registered, together (if they were registered in the names of 2 persons or more) with the number or amount registered in the name of each of them.

20.— In this Part, a reference to price paid or received includes any consideration other than money.

General

5.20   Schedule 13, Part I, contains complex provisions for determining when a person is interested in shares for the purposes of section 324-326 and other sections.[30] Schedule 13, Parts II and III, deal with when and how an interest is to be notified. Although section 324(3) gives the Secretary of State the power to introduce exceptions to Schedules 13, Parts I and II[31] there is at present no power to enlarge the provisions of Schedule 13.

5.21   The primary purpose of the provisions of Schedule 13, Part 1 is to extend the meaning of interest: for example under paragraph 2 a beneficiary is taken to be interested in shares held on trust even if as a matter of property law he would not normally be deemed to be so, for example because the beneficiary has only a discretionary interest. In this context however it is not clear whether the term "trust" includes a statutory trust such as that arising in English law on an intestacy, bankruptcy or insolvency. In these cases the beneficial interest is not vested in the beneficiary or creditor until the process of administration, winding up or bankruptcy is complete.[32] Again paragraph 3 makes it clear that a person is

---

[30]   Sections 328 and 346.

[31]   This power has been exercised: see the Companies (Disclosure of Direectors' Interests) (Exceptions) Regulations 1985 (SI 1985/802).

[32]   See *Commissioner of Stamp Duty (Queensland) v Livingston* [1965]AC 694; *Ayerst v C & K (Construction) Ltd* [1976] AC 167. A similar doubt may arise in the Scots law of intestate

taken to be interested in shares as soon as he enters a contract to acquire them. It is not necessary to comply with any formalities or (where the shares form part of a larger holding) to wait until the shares to be sold have been identified.[33] Paragraph 4 attributes the interest of a body corporate in which a person has one-third or more of the voting power to that person. Paragraph 6 covers put and call options in shares and this is particularly important if the prohibition on option dealing in section 323 is removed.

5.22   Schedule 13, Part I appears to be very comprehensive but it is likely that from time to time it will be found that there are cases which it does not cover but ought to cover. It is for consideration whether the Secretary of State should have power to vary the provisions of Part I of Schedule 13 by regulation so as to alter the rules as to what is to be treated as an interest in shares. A similar power is conferred by section 210A of the Companies Act 1985 in relation to the meaning of interests in shares required to be notified under Part VI of the Act.[34]

Consultees are asked whether the Secretary of State should be given power by regulation to vary the rules in Part I of Schedule 13 for determining whether a person has an interest in shares or debentures for the purposes of sections 324-326, 328 and 346.

5.23   Schedule 13, Part II deals with the time which a person has to fulfil his obligation to make disclosure under section 324. The obligation does not arise unless the director has knowledge of the interest and the time period is generally five days. If the company is a listed company, the rules of the exchange may require notification within a shorter period.[35]

5.24   There is one instance where the obligation to give notice to the company is dependent not only on knowing that the event giving rise to the duty to notify has arisen, but also on knowing that there is a legal obligation to give notice and that is where section 324(2) applies and the director is aware of the event when it actually happens. Paragraph 15(1) provides that this is the case where section 324(2) applies. Section 324(2) includes the situation where a director or his spouse or child ceases to be interested in shares, or enters into a contract to purchase shares. It is not clear why there should be a special rule in paragraph 15(1).

succession. It is thought unlikely that in Scots law a creditor in a sequestration or in a corporate insolvency would be regarded as a trust beneficiary in terms of para 2 of Sched 13; the creditor would not have the interest of the trust beneficiary which takes the form of the rights of action set out in *Inland Revenue v Clark's Trustee* 1939 SC 11.

[33]   See also para 8. Under the general law, such appropriation is not required for a trust to be completely constituted: *Hunter v Moss* [1993] 1 WLR 934.

[34]   A similar power in relation to Sched 13 might enable the rules in Pt I of Sched 13 to be brought closer to those governing the disclosure of interests in shares under Pt VI of the Act if that is thought desirable. Pt VI is outside this project.

[35]   Under Listing Rule 16.13, the notification must be made to the Stock Exchange without delay (see Appendix E below).

5.25 Part II makes no provision for the time within which a company must fulfil its obligations under section 325(2)-(4). We invite consultees' views on whether a time period should be specified and what that period should be.

Consultees are asked whether the company should be obliged to comply with section 325(2),(3) and (4) within a specified period and if so whether that period should be the expiration of five days beginning with the day on which the event in question occurs or some other and if so what period.

5.26 We have no observations on Schedule 13, Part III. This makes it clear for instance that the director's notice must include details of the price under a contract which he has entered into.

Consultees are asked if there are any other issues for reform arising under Schedule 13, Parts I-III.

THE COMPANY'S REGISTER OF DIRECTORS' INTERESTS: SECTIONS 325 AND 326 AND SCHEDULE 13, PART IV

325. —(1) Every company shall keep a register for the purposes of section 324.

(2) Whenever a company receives information from a director given in fulfilment of an obligation imposed on him by that section, it is under obligation to enter in the register, against the director's name, the information received and the date of the entry.

(3) The company is also under obligation, whenever it grants to a director a right to subscribe for shares in, or debentures of, the company to enter in the register against his name—

    (a)   the date on which the right is granted,
    (b)   the period during which, or time at which, it is execrable,
    (c)   the consideration for the grant (or, if there is no consideration, that fact), and
    (d)   the description of shares or debentures involved and the number or amount of them, and the price to be paid for them (or the consideration, if otherwise than in money).

(4) Whenever such a right as is mentioned above is exercised by a director, the company is under obligation to enter in the register against his name that fact (identifying the right), the number or amount of shares or debentures in respect of which it is exercised and, if they were registered in his name, that fact and, if not, the name or names of the person or persons in whose name or names they were registered, together (if they were registered in the names of two persons or more) with the number or amount of the shares or debentures registered in the name of each of them.

(5) Part IV of Schedule 13 has effect with respect to the register to be kept under this section, to the way in which entries in it are to be made, to the right of inspection, and generally.

(6) For purposes of this section, a shadow director is deemed a director.

326. —(1) The following applies with respect to defaults in complying with, and to contraventions of, section 325 and Part IV of Schedule 13.

(2) If default is made in complying with any of the following provisions—

(a)   section 325(1), (2), (3) or (4), or
(b)   Schedule 13, paragraph 21, 22 or 28,

the company and every officer of it who is in default is liable to a fine and, for continued contravention, to a daily default fine.

(3) If an inspection of the register required under paragraph 25 of the Schedule is refused, or a copy required under paragraph 26 is not sent within the proper period, the company and every officer of it who is in default is liable to a fine and, for continued contravention, to a daily default fine.

(4) If default is made for 14 days in complying with paragraph 27 of the Schedule (notice to registrar of where register is kept), the company and every officer of it who is in default is liable to a fine and, for continued contravention, to a daily default fine.

(5) If default is made in complying with paragraph 29 of the Schedule (register to be produced at annual general meeting), the company and every officer of it who is in default is liable to a fine.

(6) In the case of a refusal of an inspection of the register required under paragraph 25 of the Schedule, the court may by order compel an immediate inspection of it; and in the case of failure to send within the proper period a copy required under paragraph 26, the court may by order direct that the copy be sent to the person requiring it.

SCHEDULE 13, PART IV: PROVISIONS WITH RESPECT TO REGISTER OF DIRECTORS' INTERESTS TO BE KEPT UNDER SECTION 325

21.— The register must be so made up that the entries in it against the several names appear in chronological order.

22.— An obligation imposed by section 325(2) to (4) must be fulfilled before the expiration of the period of 3 days beginning with the day after that on which the obligation arises; but in reckoning that period, a day which is a Saturday or Sunday or a bank holiday in any part of Great Britain is to be disregarded.

23.— The nature and extent of an interest recorded in the register of a director in any shares or debentures shall, if he so requires, be recorded in the register.

24.— The company is not, by virtue of anything done for the purposes of section 325 or this Part of this Schedule, affected with notice of, or put upon enquiry as to, the rights of any person in relation to any shares or debentures.

25.— The register shall—

(a)   if the company's register of members is kept at its registered office, be kept there;

(b) if the company's register of members is not so kept, be kept at the company's registered office or at the place where its register of members is kept;

and shall ... be open to the inspection of any member of the company without charge and of any other person on payment of [such fee as may be prescribed].

26.—(1) Any member of the company or other person may require a copy of the register, or of any part of it, on payment of [such fee as may be prescribed].

(2) The company shall cause any copy so required by a person to be sent to him within the period of 10 days beginning with the day after that on which the requirement is received by the company.

27.— The company shall send notice in the prescribed form to the registrar of companies of the place where the register is kept and of any change in that place, save in a case in which it has at all times been kept at its registered office.

28.—Unless the register is in such a form as to constitute in itself an index, the company shall keep an index of the names inscribed in it, which shall—

(a) in respect of each name, contain a sufficient indication to enable the information entered against it to be readily found; and

(b) be kept at the same place as the register;

and the company shall, within 14 days after the date on which a name is entered in the register, make any necessary alteration in the index.

29.— The register shall be produced at the commencement of the company's annual general meeting and remain open and accessible during the continuance of the meeting to any person attending the meeting.

General

5.27 Section 325 requires companies to maintain a register for the purpose of recording those notifications made to them by their directors under section 324. They must also inscribe in the register particulars of rights to subscribe for shares or debentures of the company granted to a director: he is not required to notify particulars of these. Part IV of Schedule 13 lays down additional requirements for the maintenance and inspection of this register, including the right of the public to require the company to provide a copy of the same for a prescribed fee.

The DTI's August 1996 proposals

5.28 The DTI proposed the retention of the section 325 register. The DTI's proposal that section 324 should be amended by the introduction of a disclosure threshold would, however, have meant that a company's register of directors' interests would not necessarily have accurately reflected the extent of a director's interests at all times.

Consultees' response and the DTI's conclusion

5.29 In light of the view of consultees that section 324 should not be amended, section 325 will not be affected by the DTI's proposals.

Remaining issues for consideration

5.30 It should be noted that issues relating to the impact of information technology on company registers will form part of the DTI's recently announced long-term review of corporate law.[36]

Consultees are asked whether section 325 and Schedule 13, Part IV raise any other issues for reform.

NOTIFICATION TO THE EXCHANGES: SECTION 329

329.—(1) Whenever a company whose shares or debentures are listed on a [recognised investment exchange other than an overseas investment exchange within the meaning of the Financial Services Act 1986] is notified of any matter by a director in consequence of the fulfilment of an obligation imposed by section 324 or 328, and that matter relates to shares or debentures so listed, the company is under obligation to notify [that investment exchange] of that matter; and [the investment exchange] may publish, in such manner as it may determine, any information received by it under this subsection.

(2) An obligation imposed by subsection (1) must be fulfilled before the end of the day next following that on which it arises; but there is disregarded for this purpose a day which is a Saturday or a Sunday or a bank holiday in any part of Great Britain.

(3) If default is made in complying with this section, the company and every officer of it who is in default is guilty of an offence and liable to a fine and, for continued contravention, to a daily default fine.

Section 732 (restriction on prosecutions) applies to an offence under this section.

General

5.31 This section requires companies whose shares are listed or admitted to trading on a UK recognised investment exchange ("RIE") (within the meaning of the Financial Services Act 1986 and other than an overseas investment exchange) to pass the notifications they receive from directors under sections 324 or 328 to the relevant exchange for the listing or trading of those shares. The relevant exchange must be notified by the end of the day following the day of notification.

5.32 The obligation imposed by this section extends only to information of which the company is itself notified by the director. It does not therefore cover, for example, the grant of options to subscribe for securities to a director, which the company is obliged to put into the register but which the director is not bound to notify.[37] Listing Rule 16.13[38] of the Stock Exchange takes account of this but it is for consideration whether the section itself should be amended to make it clear that

---

[36] See the DTI's Consultative Paper, para 3.4.

[37] See ss 324(1), 325(3) and 328(3).

[38] See Appendix E.

the company should transmit this information also.[39] Then the criminal sanctions would be available, but this may be a factor of decreasing significance if the Financial Services Authority are given power to impose civil penalties for breach of such requirements.[40]

The DTI's August 1996 proposals

5.33 The DTI proposed that section 329 might be amended in isolation so as to exempt from immediate disclosure to exchanges those transactions proposed as suitable subjects for the "disclosure threshold" scheme envisaged for section 324 as well as those suggested for outright exemption (as an alternative to reform of the whole disclosure process via reform of section 324 and Schedule 13, which it explicitly favoured). It was noted that if section 329 alone was amended:

> it would only result in a relaxation of the requirements in relation to the information that must be passed to the exchange on which the company's shares or debentures are listed or admitted to trading. It would thus benefit companies and the relevant stock exchanges, but not directors who would still be required to disclose each transaction to the company as it occurred.[41]

5.34 In addition, it was proposed that the section be amended to make it clear that companies need only notify one exchange of changes in directors' interests in the company where its shares or debentures were quoted on more than one domestic exchange.

5.35 The problem here identified was that, as a result of the section having been drafted at a time when the Stock Exchange was the only relevant recognised investment exchange, the drafting thus failed to anticipate the recognition of, for example, Tradepoint as an RIE (the requirements also now cover the AIM). This had led to speculation that the section could be interpreted as requiring companies to notify all RIE's on which their shares were quoted, even if without their knowledge.

Consultees' response and the DTI's conclusion

5.36 Many respondents argued that, although the objectives of the DTI's proposals were to be commended, aggregation would not reduce the overall burden on companies because of the complexity of the thresholds which would have to be monitored. In view of this, many major companies said they would continue to disclose all transactions to the Stock Exchange immediately. They also expressed the view that the aggregation proposals might lead to administrative errors and therefore the failure properly to notify and disclose directors' interests.

---

[39] This would be consistent with the approach taken in relation to Sched 7. Sched 7, which sets out the requirements for the directors' report to be annexed to the annual accounts states that in addition to the information shown the register of directors' interests details of options to subscribe should also be given (para 2B).

[40] Financial Services and Markets Bill: A Consultation Document (July 1998), para 13.4. See para 1.25 n 28 above, and para 10.34 nn 65 and 67 below.

[41] The DTI's Consultative Paper, para 4.44, p 18.

5.37   Some consultees argued that the purpose of notifications under section 329 should be only to ensure the timely disclosure of price-sensitive information. They took the view that the very large number of current disclosures obscures significant transactions which are of interest to investors and shareholders. In light of these concerns, the DTI has concluded that certain types of transactions, including transactions relating to discretionary PEPs and scrip dividends, should be exempted from the section 329 disclosure requirements; all ordinary sales and purchases of the company's shares and other non-exempted types of transaction would, however, have to be disclosed rapidly to the relevant investment exchange. The DTI has suggested that the Secretary of State would have a new power to designate by order the types of transactions which should be exempt. The DTI has relayed these conclusions to us with the request that we take them forward in the context of our wider study.

5.38   Consultees strongly endorsed the proposal to amend the section to make it clear that companies need only notify one exchange of changes in directors' interests.

5.39   In these circumstances it seems to us that the only specific question that we need to ask of consultees is the one identified above regarding options to subscribe.

Consultees are asked if section 329 should be amended so that a company is bound to transmit to the relevant exchange details of information which the company is bound to enter into the register of directors' interests without notification by the director pursuant to section 325(3) and (4).

Consultees are also asked if section 329 raises any issue for reform not mentioned above.

PART 6
SUBSTANTIVE IMPROVEMENTS 3: LOANS AND SIMILAR TRANSACTIONS (SECTIONS 330-342)

INTRODUCTION

6.1 In this part we review sections 330-342, which restrict directors from taking loans from their company or entering into similar transactions. These sections are complex both in their original drafting and their inter-relationship. The scheme of these provisions is of prohibitions with some exemptions. As noted in Part 3, absolute prohibitions are rare in Part X of the Companies Act 1985. It is suggested there that they can be justified if there is a significant risk of third party effect, such as harm to creditors, sufficient to outweigh the gains to shareholders and directors, or a significant public need.[1] As we see it the reason for the prohibition is to protect creditors and minority shareholders from the depletion in corporate assets through the making of loans, which if they were being made on arms length terms, could usually be raised from third parties.

6.2 The basic prohibition prevents companies making loans to their directors or directors of their holding companies. This prohibition was first introduced in 1947 following the recommendation of the Cohen Committee.[2] The Committee said:

> We consider it undesirable that directors should borrow from their companies. If the director can offer good security, it is no hardship to him to borrow from other sources. If he cannot offer good security, it is undesirable that he should obtain from the company credit which he would not be able to obtain elsewhere. Several cases have occurred in recent years where directors have borrowed money from their companies on inadequate security and have been unable to repay the loans. We accordingly recommend that, subject to certain exceptions, it should be made illegal for any loan to be made by a company or by any of its subsidiary companies or by any person under guarantee from or on security provided by the company or by any of its subsidiary companies to any director of the company.[3]

6.3 The amendment made to the Companies Act 1929 by the Companies Act 1947 was replaced by section 190 of the Companies Act 1948. The basic prohibition was as follows:

> (1) It shall not be lawful for a company to make a loan to any person who is its director or a director of its holding company, or to enter into

---

[1]   See para 3.16 and paras 3.54-3.55 above.

[2]   See the Report of the Committee on Company Law Amendment (1945) Cmd 6659.

[3]   *Ibid,* para 94, pp 49-50.

any guarantee or provide any security in connection with a loan made to such a person as aforesaid by any other person ....

6.4 There were a number of exceptions, including an exception for funds to meet expenditure as a director and for loans made in the ordinary course of business.[4]

6.5 The Company Law Committee under the chairmanship of Lord Jenkins, which reported in 1962, took much the same view as the Cohen Committee. It said :

> 98. Section 190 makes it unlawful for a company to make a loan to any of the company's directors. We have had conflicting evidence about this provision. It has been suggested that this restriction may make it difficult for some companies to obtain suitable directors and that, in particular, loans in connection with house purchase to "working" directors should be permitted. On the other hand, it has been suggested that section 190 can be circumvented and the section should be extended so as to prohibit loans by a company to another company in which the directors of the lending company have a majority interest. For the same reasons as the Cohen Committee, which we have quoted in paragraph 58,[5] we think it undesirable that companies should lend to their directors and we recommend below that section 190 should be strengthened.

> 99. We recommend that :-

> ....

> (p) Section 190 should be extended to prohibit loans by a company to another company in which one or more of the directors of the lending company hold singly or collectively, and whether directly or indirectly, a controlling interest.[6]

6.6 No action was taken to implement the recommendation made by the Jenkins Committee until a number of scandals occurred at the end of the 1970s.[7] In consequence, by the Companies Act 1980, Parliament introduced extensive further controls on loan and similar transactions between a company and its directors. With very minor changes these new controls are the provisions now to be found in sections 330-342 of the Companies Act 1985, following the consolidation of the Companies Acts in that year. Sections 330-342 contain: (1) prohibitions, (2) exemptions, (3) civil remedies and (4) criminal penalties. Some of the exemptions contain financial limits, and so there are provisions which explain how these limits are calculated. The prohibitions can be divided according to the type of company to which they apply. Overall the result is complex and

---

[4] Section 190(1) provisos (c) and (d).

[5] The Jenkins Committee quoted part of the passage in para 6.2 above.

[6] Paras 98-99, pp 34-37. See also para 6.22 of the Hong Kong Consultancy Report in Appendix L below.

[7] Relating to secondary banks and also to Peachey Property Corporation, which was the subject of a DTI investigation: see para 1.10, n 7 above.

inaccessible. We propose to go through each section separately and then put forward options for the future of these provisions.

6.7   The principal provisions of the sections can be summarised as follows.

(a) Prohibitions applying to all companies:

All companies are prohibited from making loans to their directors or directors of their holding companies or providing guarantees or security in connection with a loan by a third party to any such director.[8] (section 330(2))

There are exemptions for small transactions, for transactions at the request of the holding company and the funding of a director's expenditure for corporate purposes.

(b) Prohibitions applying to relevant companies:

Relevant companies are companies which are public companies or are members of a group of companies which include a public company. They are subject to further restrictions applying to transactions which are not loans but which are analogous to loans. In the case of relevant companies, the restrictions in each case extend not only to directors of the company and its holding company but also to persons who are connected with any such director. "Connected" persons are defined in section 346.

Transactions which a relevant company is prohibited from carrying out in favour of the above persons are:

- loans;

- quasi-loans (as defined by section 331(3));

- credit transactions (as defined by section 331(7)); and,

- guarantees and security in connection with any of the above.

In addition to the exemptions applying to all companies, there are exemptions for

- short term quasi-loans (section 332);

- inter-company loans and quasi-loans within the same group (section 333);

- small credit transactions (section 335(1)); and

- credit transactions in the ordinary course of business (section 335(2))

---

[8]   The prohibitions do not therefore on their face apply to persons other than directors, but if the loan is made, for example, to a company which is wholly-owned by the director the loan may be treated as made to him: *Wallersteiner v Moir* [1974] 1 WLR 1015.

(c) Money-lending companies:

There is a further exemption for loans, quasi-loans and guarantees entered into by money-lending companies in the ordinary course of business.

(d) Disclosure:

The prohibitions are backed up by requirements in Schedule 6, Part II to the Companies Act 1985 to disclose particulars of transactions in the notes to the annual accounts, but there is an exemption for certain transactions entered into by authorised banks, which may record the relevant transactions in a register instead (sections 343-344). Schedule 6, Part II, and sections 343-344, are discussed in Part 7 below.

6.8   It should be noted that the term "company" as used in these sections means a British registered company[9] and thus the provisions do not catch a loan made (for example) by a foreign subsidiary (including a company formed in Northern Ireland) to its parent company, even if its parent company happens to be registered in England or Scotland. The term "holding company",[10] on the other hand, includes a body corporate other than a company.[11] We do not consider that these restrictions could be applied to transactions by companies incorporated outside England, Wales and Scotland.

6.9   In this part we examine the provisions of sections 330-342 and seek consultees views on various questions that seem to us to arise from these provisions. We also examine a possible new exemption for loans which have shareholder approval. We consider these matters in turn under the following heads:

- Sections 330 and 331: General restriction on loans etc to directors and persons connected with them and definitions for the purposes of section 330 and subsequent sections

- Sections 332-338: Exemptions from prohibitions

- Sections 339 and 340: "Relevant amounts" for purposes of section 334 and other sections and determining the "value" of transactions or arrangements

- Section 341: Civil remedies

- Section 342: Criminal penalties for breach of section 330

- A possible additional exemption available to all companies for loans made with the consent of shareholders

---

[9]   Section 735 (1).

[10]   Section 736.

[11]   However Scottish firms are not included: see s 740.

SECTIONS 330 AND 331: GENERAL RESTRICTION ON LOANS ETC TO
DIRECTORS AND PERSONS CONNECTED WITH THEM AND DEFINITIONS FOR
THE PURPOSES OF SECTION 330 AND SUBSEQUENT SECTIONS

330.— (1) The prohibitions listed below in this section are subject to the exceptions in sections 332 to 338.

(2) A company shall not—

    (a)   make a loan to a director of the company or of its holding company;

    (b)   enter into any guarantee or provide any security in connection with a loan made by any person to such a director.

(3) A relevant company shall not—

    (a)   make a quasi-loan to a director of the company or of its holding company;

    (b)   make a loan or a quasi-loan to a person connected with such a director;

    (c)   enter into a guarantee or provide any security in connection with a loan or quasi-loan made by any other person for such a director or a person so connected.

(4) A relevant company shall not—

    (a)   enter into a credit transaction as creditor for such a director or a person so connected;

    (b)   enter into any guarantee or provide any security in connection with a credit transaction made by any other person for such a director or a person so connected.

(5) For purposes of sections 330 to 346, a shadow director is treated as a director.

(6) A company shall not arrange for the assignment to it, or the assumption by it, of any rights, obligations or liabilities under a transaction which, if it had been entered into by the company, would have contravened subsection (2), (3) or (4); but for the purposes of sections 330 to 347 the transaction is to be treated as having been entered into on the date of the arrangement.

(7) A company shall not take part in any arrangement whereby—

    (a)   another person enters into a transaction which, if it had been entered into by the company, would have contravened any of subsections (2), (3), (4) or (6); and

    (b)   that other person, in pursuance of the arrangement, has obtained or is to obtain any benefit from the company or its holding company or a subsidiary of the company or its holding company.

331.—(1) The following subsections apply for the interpretation of sections 330 to 346.

167

(2) "Guarantee" includes indemnity, and cognate expressions are to be construed accordingly.

(3) A quasi-loan is a transaction under which one party ("the creditor") agrees to pay, or pays otherwise than in pursuance of an agreement, a sum for another ("the borrower") or agrees to reimburse, or reimburses otherwise than in pursuance of an agreement, expenditure incurred by another party for another ("the borrower") —

    (a)   on terms that the borrower (or a person on his behalf) will reimburse the creditor; or

    (b)   in circumstances giving rise to a liability on the borrower to reimburse the creditor.

(4) Any reference to the person to whom a quasi-loan is made is a reference to the borrower; and the liabilities of a borrower under a quasi-loan include the liabilities of any person who has agreed to reimburse the creditor on behalf of the borrower.

(5) ...

(6) "Relevant company" means a company which—

    (a)   is a public company, or

    (b)   is a subsidiary of a public company, or

    (c)   is a subsidiary of a company which has as another subsidiary a public company, or

    (d)   has a subsidiary which is a public company.

(7) A credit transaction is a transaction under which one party ("the creditor")—

    (a)   supplies any goods or sells any land under a hire-purchase agreement or a conditional sale agreement;

    (b)   leases or hires any land or goods in return for periodical payments;

    (c)   otherwise disposes of land or supplies goods or services on the understanding that payment (whether in a lump sum or instalments or by way of periodical payments or otherwise) is to be deferred.

(8) "Services" means anything other than goods or land.

(9) A transaction or arrangement is made "for" a person if—

    (a)   in the case of a loan or quasi-loan, it is made to him;

    (b)   in the case of a credit transaction, he is the person to whom goods or services are supplied, or land is sold or otherwise disposed of, under the transaction;

    (c)   in the case of a guarantee or security, it is entered into or provided in connection with a loan or quasi-loan made to him or a credit transaction made for him;

    (d)   in the case of an arrangement within subsection (6) or (7) of section 330, the transaction to which the arrangement relates was made for him; and

    (e)   in the case of any other transaction or arrangement for the supply or transfer of, or of any interest in, goods, land or services, he is

> the person to whom the goods, land or services (or the interest) are
> supplied or transferred.

(10) "Conditional sale agreement" means the same as in the Consumer Credit Act 1974.

Explanation of the prohibitions

6.10 The word "loan" only covers a situation where a company advances money on terms that it is to be repaid in money or money's worth. Thus in *Champagne Perrier-Jouet SA v Finch*[12] the court held that a company which had paid a director's bills and supplied goods to the company which he controlled, on credit, had not made a "loan" to him and therefore did not have a lien on his shares under the terms of its articles. The concept of the quasi-loan was introduced to bring within the scope of the prohibition on loans this sort of transaction, as well as the case where a director commits the company to an item of personal expenditure for which he ought to reimburse the company.

6.11 The prohibitions are further complicated by the introduction of the concept of credit transactions (basically, the supply of goods or land on credit or on deferred purchase terms).[13] The possibility of the company acquiring the obligation of a third party under an agreement which it could not itself enter is also covered.[14] The section also makes it unlawful for the company to enter into an arrangement whereby another party enters into a transaction which the company could not itself have entered into and obtains a benefit from the company or its holding company.[15] The term "arrangement" is not defined here as it is for example in section 204(5) and (6) of the Companies Act 1985. It is thought that it must be legally enforceable although it may be informally agreed and consist of a series of agreements rather than a single agreement.[16]

Are restrictions other than on making loans to directors necessary?

6.12 We discuss below whether it would be possible to rewrite sections 330-344 in a simplified form[17] or alternatively to adopt the radical solution of removing the whole of sections 330-344 from the Companies Act 1985.[18] At this stage we ask whether the prohibitions, other then the basic prohibition in section 330(2), are needed.

Accordingly, we ask consultees:

---

[12] [1982] 1 WLR 1359, 1363. Although the case concerned the question whether a transaction constituted a "loan" for the purpose of one of the company's articles, Walton J also said that this was the meaning of the term in the context of s 190 of the Companies Act 1948 (now s 330(1)).

[13] Section 330 (4) and s 331 (7).

[14] Section 330(6).

[15] Section 330(7).

[16] See generally *Re British Basic Slag Ltd's Application* [1963] 1 WLR 727.

[17] See paras 9.34-9.43 below.

[18] See paras 9.3-9.7 and 9.22-9.24 below.

(i) Are the restrictions on quasi-loans and related transactions contained in sections 330-331 required, and, if so, should they extend to directors, holding company directors and connected persons?

(ii) Are the restrictions on credit transactions and related transactions contained in sections 330-331 required, and, if so, should they extend to directors, holding company directors and their connected persons?

(iii) Are the additional restrictions in section 330(6) and (7) on indirect arrangements required?

To which companies should the prohibitions extend?

6.13 The restrictions which apply to companies which are not relevant companies are far less onerous than those which apply to relevant companies. Although non-relevant companies will often be small, this is not universally true. Independent private companies can have substantial assets and turnover, whereas a subsidiary of a public company may be quite small in size. The distinction adopted in section 330 is between companies which belong to a group which can raise capital from the public and other companies.

6.14 The distinction adopted between different types of company in the company accounting requirements is between small and medium-sized companies.[19] The principal basis of the distinction between these two types of company is in terms of qualifying requirements related to size as set out below:

Small company

Turnover	[Not more than £2.8 million]
Balance sheet total	[Not more than £1.4 million]
Number of employees	Not more than 50

Medium-sized company

Turnover	[Not more than £11.2 million]
Balance sheet total	[Not more than £5.6 million]
Number of employees	Not more than 250.

The company must have satisfied two or more of these requirements, usually for two consecutive financial years.[20]

---

[19] See s 247. Words in square brackets were substituted by the Companies Act 1985 (Accounts of Small and Medium-Sized Enterprises and Publication of Accounts in ECUs) Regulations 1992, SI 1992/2452, reg 5(1) and (2).

[20] See s 247(1) and (2). There are exceptions for the company's first financial years and for situations where it qualifies in one only of the two years.

Consultees are asked:

(i) whether section 330 should continue to apply as now, with some of the restrictions applying only to relevant companies; or

(ii) whether the same restrictions should apply to all companies; or

(iii) whether some of the prohibitions, now applying only to relevant companies, should additionally be applied to some companies other than relevant companies and, if so:

> (a) whether such companies should be defined in terms of size; and, if so
>
> (b) whether this should be on the same basis as for small and medium sized companies or on some other basis, and if so what basis;

(iv) whether some relevant companies should cease to be subject to the additional restrictions and, if so, in what circumstances.

SECTIONS 332-338: EXEMPTIONS FROM PROHIBITIONS

(1) Short-term quasi-loans (section 332)

332.—(1)Subsection (3) of section 330 does not prohibit a company ("the creditor") from making a quasi-loan to one of its directors or to a director of its holding company if—

> (a)   the quasi-loan contains a term requiring the director or a person on his behalf to reimburse the creditor his expenditure within 2 months of its being incurred; and
>
> (b)   the aggregate of the amount of that quasi-loan and of the amount outstanding under each relevant quasi-loan does not exceed [£5,000].

(2) A quasi-loan is relevant for this purpose if it was made to the director by virtue of this section by the creditor or its subsidiary or, where the director is a director of the creditor's holding company, any other subsidiary of that company; and "the amount outstanding" is the amount of the outstanding liabilities of the person to whom the quasi-loan was made.

6.15   The Secretary of State has power to increase the financial limits under this section under section 345. The object of this exemption is to avoid making illegal the situation where a quasi-loan is incurred for a very short period, perhaps because the director uses his company credit card for expenditure which is personal and he reimburses the company promptly on receipt of the statement by it from the credit card company.

Consultees are asked whether the exemption contained in section 332 is (a) used in practice, and (b) satisfactory.

171

(2) Intra-group loans (section 333)

333.—In the case of a relevant company which is a member of a group of companies (meaning a holding company and its subsidiaries), paragraphs (b) and (c) of section 330(3) do not prohibit the company from—

    (a)   making a loan or quasi-loan to another member of that group; or

    (b)   entering into a guarantee or providing any security in connection with a loan or quasi-loan made by any person to another member of the group,

by reason only that a director of one member of the group is associated with another.

6.16   This exemption is necessary because a company which is a holding company, or a subsidiary, or a fellow subsidiary, may be a connected person of one of its directors, or its holding company directors, if he holds sufficient shares in any of those companies. No financial limit is imposed.

Consultees are asked whether the exemption contained in section 333 is (a) used in practice, and (b) satisfactory.

(3) Loans of small amounts (section 334)

334.— Without prejudice to any other provision of sections 332 to 338, paragraph (a) of section 330(2) does not prohibit a company from making a loan to a director of the company or of its holding company if the aggregate of the relevant amounts does not exceed [£5,000].

6.17   The Secretary of State has power to increase financial limits under this section.[21] This exemption enables a company to make loans (but not quasi-loans or credit transactions) not exceeding the amount stated[22] to a director or holding company director but not a connected person.

Consultees are asked whether the exemption contained in section 334 is (a) needed, and (b) satisfactory

(4) Minor transactions (section 335(1))

335.—(1) Section 330(4) does not prohibit a company from entering into a transaction for a person if the aggregate of the relevant amounts does not exceed [£10,000].

6.18   The Secretary of State has power to increase financial limits under this section.[23] The exemption enables a relevant company lawfully to enter into credit transactions, and give guarantees and security in support of credit transactions,

---

[21]   Section 345.

[22]   To be calculated as provided in ss 339-340.

[23]   Section 345.

provided that the prescribed limit[24] is not exceeded. The expression "for a person" is explained in section 331(9).

Consultees are asked whether the exemption contained in section 335(1) is (a) needed, and (b) satisfactory.

(5) Transactions in the ordinary course of business (section 335(2))

335.—(2) Section 330(4) does not prohibit a company from entering into a transaction for a person if—

> (a) the transaction is entered into by the company in the ordinary course of its business; and
>
> (b) the value of the transaction is not greater, and the terms on which it is entered into are no more favourable, in respect of the person for whom the transaction is made, than that or those which it is reasonable to expect the company to have offered to or in respect of a person of the same financial standing but unconnected with the company.

6.19   It is to be noted that this exemption, again for credit transactions, and guarantees and security in support of credit transactions, contains two hurdles: first, the transaction must be in the ordinary course of the company's business and second, the terms of the transaction must not discriminate in favour of directors or persons connected with them.

6.20   Under section 335(2)(a), the court looks at the ordinary course of the particular company's business. This means that if, for example, it habitually made loans on the same scale and for the same purposes it could nonetheless satisfy the first requirement by entering into another one of the same scale and for the same purpose[25] even if this was not usual among other companies in the same circumstances. Section 335(2) introduces an objective test with regard to the value of the transactions and its terms. Both tests in section 335(2) involve questions of fact and degree and therefore involve some uncertainty in their application.

Consultees are asked whether the exemption contained in section 335(2) is (a) used in practice, and (b) satisfactory

(6) Transactions at the behest of the holding company (section 336)

336.— The following transactions are excepted from the prohibitions of section 330—

---

[24]   To be calculated in accordance with ss 339-340.

[25]   See generally *Steen v Law* [1964] *AC 303,* which concerned the Australian equivalent of s 54(1)(a) of the Companies Act 1948, and *Fowlie v Slater,* 23 March 1979 (unreported, Divisonal Court) which concerned s 54(1) (a) of the Companies Act 1948. A distinction is to be drawn between the phrase found in s 335(2)(a) and the expression "in the ordinary course of business", which requires an objective examination by reference to the standard of the ordinary course of business and could result in a transaction, exceptional so far as the particular company was concerned, nonetheless being "in the ordinary course of business": see, for example, *Countrywide Banking Corpn Ltd v Dean* [1998] 2 WLR 441.

(a)   a loan or quasi-loan by a company to its holding company, or a company entering into a guarantee or providing any security in connection with a loan or quasi-loan made by any person to its holding company;

(b)   a company entering into a credit transaction as creditor for its holding company, or entering into a guarantee or providing any security in connection with a credit transaction made by any other person for its holding company.

6.21   As already explained, intra-group transactions may be caught by the prohibitions in section 330 where the company making the loan or quasi-loan or entering into the credit transaction, guarantee or security, or its holding company, has a director with respect to whom the company with whom the transaction is made is connected for the purposes of section 346. This exemption takes "upstream" loans, quasi-loans and credit transactions (that is prohibited transactions from a subsidiary to a parent company) outside the scope of prohibitions. There is no financial limit on the amount of the transaction where this exemption is relied on.

Consultees are asked whether the exemption contained in section 336 is (a) used in practice, and (b) satisfactory.

(7) Funding of director's expenditure on duty to the company (section 337)

337.—(1) A company is not prohibited by section 330 from doing anything to provide a director with funds to meet expenditure incurred or to be incurred by him for the purposes of the company or for the purpose of enabling him properly to perform his duties as an officer of the company.

(2) Nor does the section prohibit a company from doing any thing to enable a director to avoid incurring such expenditure.

(3) Subsections (1) and (2) apply only if one of the following conditions is satisfied—

(a)   **the thing in question is done with prior approval of the company given at a general meeting at which there are disclosed all the matters mentioned in the next subsection;**

(b)   **that thing is done on condition that, if the approval of the company is not so given at or before the next annual general meeting, the loan is to repaid, or any other liability arising under any such transaction discharged, within 6 months from the conclusion of that meeting;**

but those subsections do not authorise a relevant company to enter into any transaction if the aggregate of the relevant amounts exceeds [£20,000].

(4) The matters to be disclosed under subsection (3)(a) are—

(a)   **the purpose of the expenditure incurred or to be incurred, or which would otherwise be incurred, by the director,**

(b)   **the amount of the funds to be provided by the company, and**

(c)   **the extent of the company's liability under any transaction which is or is connected with the thing in question.**

6.22 This exemption is very similar to that contained in section 190(1)(c) and (2) of the Companies Act 1948, except that it extends to transactions other than loans and contains a financial limit.

6.23 In general companies must hold an annual general meeting each year.[26] There is nothing to stop shareholders agreeing to deal with the business of the annual general meeting informally and by unanimous consent and without the holding of an actual meeting. Moreover, since the Companies Act 1989, it has been possible for shareholders of a private company to dispense with the holding of annual general meetings.[27] Shareholders of a company can give their approval under section 337(3)(a) informally without holding a meeting, provided that the matters required to be disclosed by section 337(4) are disclosed to each member by whom or on whose behalf the resolution is required to be signed under section 381A.[28]

Consultees are asked whether they consider that the exemption contained in section 337 is (a) used in practice, and (b) satisfactory.

(8) Loan or quasi-loan by a money-lending company (section 338)

338. —(1) There is excepted from the prohibitions in section 330—

> **(a)** **a loan or quasi-loan made by a money-lending company to any person; or**
> **(b)** **a money-lending company entering into a guarantee in connection with any other loan or quasi-loan.**

(2) "Money-lending company" means a company whose ordinary business includes the making of loans or quasi-loans, or the giving of guarantees in connection with loans or quasi-loans.

(3) Subsection (1) applies only if both the following conditions are satisfied—

> **(a)** **the loan or quasi-loan in question is made by the company, or it enters into the guarantee, in the ordinary course of the company's business; and**
> **(b)** **the amount of the loan or quasi-loan, or the amount guaranteed, is not greater, and the terms of the loan, quasi-loan or guarantee are not more favourable, in the case of the person to whom the loan or quasi-loan is made or in respect of whom the guarantee is entered into, than that or those which it is reasonable to expect that company to have offered to or in respect of a person of the same financial standing but unconnected with the company.**

(4) But subsection (1) does not authorise a relevant company (unless it is [a banking company]) to enter into any transaction if the aggregate of the relevant amounts exceeds [£100,000].

---

[26] Except that it may hold its first annual general meeting at any time within 18 months of its incorporation: see generally, s 366 of the Companies Act 1985.

[27] Section 366A.

[28] Schedule 15A, Para 8.

175

(5) In determining that aggregate, a company which a director does not control is deemed not to be connected with him.

(6) The condition specified in subsection (3)(b) does not of itself prevent a company from making a loan to one of its directors or a director of its holding company—

(a) for the purpose of facilitating the purchase, for use as that director's only or main residence, of the whole or part of any dwelling-house together with any land to be occupied and enjoyed with it;

(b) for the purpose of improving a dwelling-house or part of a dwelling-house so used or any land occupied and enjoyed with it;

(c) in substitution for any loan made by any person and falling within paragraph (a) or (b) of this subsection,

if loans of that description are ordinarily made by the company to its employees and on terms no less favourable than those on which the transaction in question is made, and the aggregate of the relevant amounts does not exceed [£100,000].

6.24   Section 338(3) is very similar to section 335(2), as to which see paragraphs 6.19-6.20 above. Section 338(5) was considered necessary to prevent a money-lending company from having to keep track of a large number of customers who happened to be connected persons of a director.

6.25   Section 338(6) enables a money-lending company to give house purchase loans to its directors on favourable terms. We do not know the extent to which this exception is actually used in practice.

Consultees are asked:

(i) With regard to the exemption in section 338(3) (taken on its own):

(a) should this exemption be retained;

(b) is this exemption used in practice;

(c) is this exemption satisfactory?

(ii) With regard to the exemption in section 338(3) taken with section 338(6) (house purchase loans):

(a) should this exemption be retained;

(b) is this exemption used in practice;

(c) is this exemption satisfactory?

SECTIONS 339-340: "RELEVANT AMOUNTS" FOR PURPOSES OF SECTION 334 AND OTHER SECTIONS AND DETERMINING THE "VALUE" OF TRANSACTIONS OR ARRANGEMENTS

339.—(1) This section has effect for defining the "relevant amounts" to be aggregated under sections 334, 335(1), 337(3) and 338(4); and in relation to any

176

proposed transaction or arrangement and the question whether it falls within one or other of the exceptions provided by those sections, "the relevant exception" is that exception; but where the relevant exception is the one provided by section 334 (loan of small amount), references in this section to a person connected with a director are to be disregarded.

(2) Subject as follows, the relevant amounts in relation to a proposed transaction or arrangement are—

    (a)   the value of the proposed transaction or arrangement,

    (b)   the value of any existing arrangement which—

        (i)   falls within subsection (6) or (7) of section 330, and

        (ii)   also falls within subsection (3) of this section, and

        (iii)   was entered into by virtue of the relevant exception by the company or by a subsidiary of the company or, where the proposed transaction or arrangement is to be made for a director of its holding company or a person connected with such a director, by that holding company or any of its subsidiaries;

    (c)   the amount outstanding under any other transaction—

        (i)   falling within subsection (3) below, and

        (ii)   made by virtue of the relevant exception, and

        (iii)   made by the company or by a subsidiary of the company or, where the proposed transaction or arrangement is to be made for a director of its holding company or a person connected with such a director, by that holding company or any of its subsidiaries.

(3) A transaction falls within this subsection if it was made—

    (a)   for the director for whom the proposed transaction or arrangement is to be made, or for any person connected with that director; or

    (b)   where the proposed transaction or arrangement is to be made for a person connected with a director of a company, for that director or any person connected with him;

and an arrangement also falls within this subsection if it relates to a transaction which does so.

(4) But where the proposed transaction falls within section 338 and is one which [a banking company] proposes to enter into under subsection (6) of that section (housing loans, etc), any other transaction or arrangement which apart from this subsection would fall within subsection (3) of this section does not do so unless it was entered into in pursuance of section 338(6).

(5) A transaction entered into by a company which is (at the time of that transaction being entered into) a subsidiary of the company which is to make the proposed transaction, or is a subsidiary of that company's holding company, does not fall within subsection (3) if at the time when the question arises (that is to say, the question whether the proposed transaction or arrangement falls within any relevant exception), it no longer is such a subsidiary.

(6) Values for purposes of subsection (2) of this section are to be determined in accordance with the section next following; and "the amount outstanding" for purposes of subsection (2)(c) above is the value of the transaction less any amount by which that value has been reduced.

340.—(1) This section has effect for determining the value of a transaction or arrangement for purposes of sections 330 to 339.

(2) The value of a loan is the amount of its principal.

(3) The value of a quasi-loan is the amount, or maximum amount, which the person to whom the quasi-loan is made is liable to reimburse the creditor.

(4) The value of a guarantee or security is the amount guaranteed or secured.

(5) The value of an arrangement to which section 330(6) or (7) applies is the value of the transaction to which the arrangement relates less any amount by which the liabilities under the arrangement or transaction of the person for whom the transaction was made have been reduced.

(6) The value of a transaction or arrangement not falling within subsections (2) to (5) above is the price which it is reasonable to expect could be obtained for the goods, land or services to which the transaction or arrangement relates if they had been supplied (at the time the transaction or arrangement is entered into) in the ordinary course of business and on the same terms (apart from price) as they have been supplied, or are to be supplied, under the transaction or arrangement in question.

(7) For purposes of this section, the value of a transaction or arrangement which is not capable of being expressed as a specific sum of money (because the amount of any liability arising under the transaction or arrangement is unascertainable, or for any other reason), whether or not any liability under the transaction or arrangement has been reduced, is deemed to exceed [£100,000].

6.26 It would appear that section 339(1) should also refer to section 338(6) as well as section 338(4).

6.27 Section 340(7) creates a rule to govern the situation where value is unquantifiable. It is automatically deemed to exceed £100,000 so that none of the exceptions which impose financial limits are available. This rule also applies in Schedule 6, and we consider its function there separately below.[29]

6.28 These provisions are clearly very complex.

Consultees are asked if they have any comment on sections 339-340 apart from their complexity.

---

[29] See paras 7.5-7.6 below.

SECTION 341: CIVIL REMEDIES

341.—(1) **If a company enters into a transaction or arrangement in contravention of section 330, the transaction or arrangement is voidable at the instance of the company unless—**

    (a)   **restitution of any money or any other asset which is the subject matter of the arrangement or transaction is no longer possible, or the company has been indemnified in pursuance of subsection (2)(b) below for the loss or damage suffered by it, or**

    (b)   **any rights acquired bona fide for value and without actual notice of the contravention by a person other than the person for whom the transaction or arrangement was made would be affected by its avoidance.**

(2) Where an arrangement or transaction is made by a company for a director of the company or its holding company or a person connected with such a director in contravention of section 330, that director and the person so connected and any other director of the company who authorised the transaction or arrangement (whether or not it has been avoided in pursuance of subsection (1)) is liable—

    (a)   **to account to the company for any gain which he has made directly or indirectly by the arrangement or transaction; and**

    (b)   **(jointly and severally with any other person liable under this subsection) to indemnify the company for any loss or damage resulting from the arrangement or transaction.**

(3) Subsection (2) is without prejudice to any liability imposed otherwise than by that subsection, but is subject to the next two subsections.

(4) Where an arrangement or transaction is entered into by a company and a person connected with a director of the company or its holding company in contravention of section 330, that director is not liable under subsection (2) of this section if he shows that he took all reasonable steps to secure the company's compliance with that section.

(5) In any case, a person so connected and any such other director as is mentioned in subsection (2) is not so liable if he shows that, at the time the arrangement or transaction was entered into, he did not know the relevant circumstances constituting the contravention.

6.29   The code of remedies created by this section is very similar to that created by section 322[30] save that there is no provision for loss of the right of rescission if the transaction is affirmed. As the transaction is prohibited, it cannot be affirmed.[31] Section 341(3) preserves any liability arising under the general law. A director who receives a loan prohibited by section 330 will be liable for breach of fiduciary duty and to compensate the company.[32]

6.30   We are not aware of any defects in this section.

---

[30] Para 6.15 above.

[31] See para 11.41 below..

[32] See *A F Budge (Contractors) Ltd v Budge*, (unreported) 17 July 1995.

Consultees are asked whether they have any comments on section 341.

SECTION 342: CRIMINAL PENALTIES FOR BREACH OF SECTION 330

342.—(1)A director of a relevant company who authorises or permits the company to enter into a transaction or arrangement knowing or having reasonable cause to believe that the company was thereby contravening section 330 is guilty of an offence.

(2) A relevant company which enters into a transaction or arrangement for one of its directors or for a director of its holding company in contravention of section 330 is guilty of an offence.

(3) A person who procures a relevant company to enter into a transaction or arrangement knowing or having reasonable cause to believe that the company was thereby contravening section 330 is guilty of an offence.

(4) A person guilty of an offence under this section is liable to imprisonment or a fine, or both.

(5) A relevant company is not guilty of an offence under subsection (2) if it shows that, at the time the transaction or arrangement was entered into, it did not know the relevant circumstances.

6.31   We discuss the question whether provisions of Part X should carry criminal sanctions more fully in Part 10 of this consultation paper. At this stage:

Consultees are asked whether, if criminal penalties are to be imposed for breach of section 330, they should cover offences by relevant companies (and their officers), or all companies (and their officers).

6.32   The question is raised in Part 3[33] whether there might exist circumstances, in addition to those already permitted by the Act,[34] in which it could be justified for the company rather than a third party to give a loan to a director or a connected person of his with shareholder approval, though any such exemption would have to be subject to strict limits and the present prohibition should be maintained if the interests of creditors would be adversely affected. The following paragraphs of this part discuss the possibility of a new additional exemption for loans made with the consent of shareholders.

A POSSIBLE ADDITIONAL EXEMPTION FOR LOANS MADE WITH THE CONSENT OF SHAREHOLDERS

6.33   The decision whether to make a loan is normally taken by the directors.[35] The prohibitions discussed above mean that directors in many situations cannot lawfully authorise loans in favour of either themselves or their holding company directors or any of their connected persons. These rules protect shareholders. They also protect creditors who might otherwise find that the assets of the

---

[33]   Para 3.54 above.

[34]   See s 337.

[35]   Depending on the terms of the company's constitution.

180

company to which they could look for payment had been lent to directors and persons connected with them.[36] However there are situations in which it can be said the prohibitions have no purpose. Most obviously this occurs where the directors are the shareholders and there are no creditors or the company is fully able to meet all its liabilities.

6.34 We seek consultees' views on the question whether there is any need in practice to create an exemption from all or any of the transactions prohibited by section 330 to meet this kind of case and whether it is desirable to introduce a yet further exemption for this purpose. Any new exemption would have to contain appropriate safeguards for minority shareholders and creditors.

Safeguards for shareholders

6.35 As we see it, the most appropriate safeguard for shareholders would be either a special resolution or unanimous consent. It would not be practicable to use, say, the model of section 337(3) because the loan may be irrecoverable as soon as it is made. Another safeguard that should be considered is a financial limit applying to, say, transactions made by virtue of this new exemption within the same financial year.

6.36 Unanimous consent is a possibility suggested in Part 3 above,[37] but it would be unusual for the Companies Act to require the unanimous consent of members.[38] Unanimous consent is usually permitted as an alternative to a meeting.[39] If a special resolution is required, it is for consideration whether the votes of any shareholder who will benefit under the transaction should be disregarded as they would be under section 174 if they would cause the resolution to pass when it would not otherwise have done so and whether there should be a requirement for disclosure of the statutory declaration to members both before and at the meeting.[40]

Safeguards for creditors

Option (1):The company must have to provide for the whole of the value of the transaction out of its distributable profits

6.37 The effect of this option would be that the company would have to transfer an amount equal to the loan from its distributable reserves to its undistributable reserves. Where a private company gives financial assistance, for the purposes of an acquisition of its shares it must provide for that assistance out of its distributable profits where the net assets are reduced.[41] Where a loan, quasi loan

---

[36] See paras 3.54-3.55 above.

[37] See para 3.55 above.

[38] Section 125(5) requires the consent of all the members to a variation of class rights where the rights are attached by the memorandum and there is no provision for their variation.

[39] See *Cane v Jones* [1981] 1 WLR 1451; and see ss 381A and 381C of the Companies Act 1985.

[40] As in s 174 .

[41] Section 155(2) of the Companies Act 1985.

or credit transaction is made, or a guarantee or security is given, net assets ought not to be thereby reduced immediately after the transaction. If they were, it is difficult to see why the transaction was made.

Option (2): The company's directors must make a statutory declaration as required by section 173 of the Companies Act 1985

6.38   Section 156 provides that where a private company wishes to give financial assistance for the purposes of an acquisition of its shares, its directors must make a statutory declaration.[42] Likewise, where a private company wishes to make a payment out of capital for the redemption or purchase of its shares, its directors must make a statutory declaration. The forms of statutory declaration are similar but not identical. In both cases the directors must state that they have enquired into the company's affairs (and also, where section 173 applies, its prospects) and that they are satisfied that there is no ground on which the company could then be found unable to pay its debts. The statutory declaration under section 156 then contemplates that the company might either carry on business or be wound up in the next 12 months. Only the former possibility is contemplated by the statutory declaration under section 173, and that seems the more appropriate precedent where loans are made under this new exemption. The declaration requires the directors to state that, having regard to their management intentions during the year after the date of the transaction and the company's resources in that period they are of the opinion that the company will be able to carry on in business as a going concern and will accordingly be able to pay its debts as they fall due throughout that year. The directors must take into account the company's prospective and contingent liabilities. The statutory declaration must have annexed to it a report from the auditors stating that they are not aware of anything to indicate that the directors' opinion in the statutory declaration is unreasonable.[43]

6.39   If a statutory declaration is required it would have to be given within a short period of the special resolution as otherwise the statutory declaration may become out of date.[44] If rights are given to members or creditors to object to the proposed payment, no action can be taken on the proposed resolution until the period for such an application has expired. We suggest that a period of six weeks in total should suffice for this.

To what types of transactions and companies should the new exemption refer?

6.40   The new exemption could apply only to loans in favour of directors and/or directors of their holding company, or it could extend to any transaction that would otherwise be prohibited by section 330.

---

[42]   *Ibid*, s 156.

[43]   Section 173(5).

[44]   Section 174 requires the capital payment to be made no earlier than five weeks and no later than seven weeks after the date of the resolution. The statutory declaration must be made on the day the special resolution is passed or within the preceding week (s 174).

6.41   A further question is whether the new exemption should apply to all companies, or only non-relevant companies,[45] or some other class of companies. We consider that the new exemption should not be available where the company is a relevant company since in those companies there are likely to be larger numbers of shareholders who could be adversely affected by the transaction. However as indicated above,[46] the class of non-relevant companies may itself be too wide. We discuss above the possibility of companies being classified according to size, but in this particular context it may be more appropriate to see whether there is an identity between ownership and control, so that an objection to actions of directors in authorisung transactions for their or their connected persons' benefit would be less likely. One of the recommendations in the Law Commision's report on Shareholder Remedies[47] was limited to this class of company, which was in essence a private company in which all or substantially all the members were directors.

Publicity requirements

6.42   Section 175 imposes new rules for publicity to be given to the payment out of capital, including

(1)   a notice in the Gazette and a national newspaper informing creditors of the intention to make the payment and of their right to apply to the court;

(2)   making the statutory declaration available for inspection; and

(3)   filing a copy of the statutory declaration and auditors' report with the registrar.

Objections by members or creditors

6.43   Where a payment is to be made out of capital using the procedure described above, a member or creditor may, within five weeks of the date of the passing of the special resolution approving the payment apply to the court for an order cancelling it.[48] The court can adjourn the proceedings to see if arrangements can be made for the purchase of the member's shares. It can confirm or cancel the resolution.[49]

Consultees are asked:

(i) Is there any need in practice to create a new exemption to meet the case where directors hold all or a majority of the shares and creditors are not prejudiced?

(ii) Is it desirable to create a new exemption for this situation?

---

[45]   Relevant companies are defined by s 331(6) above.

[46]   Paras 6.13-6.14 above.

[47]   Law Com No 246, para 8.3.

[48]   Section 176.

[49]   Section 177.

(iii) Do they consider that there should be safeguards for shareholders and, if so, which do they consider to be the best option:

> (a) a special resolution; or

> (b) unanimous approval by the members?

If they think that some other option is preferable, they are asked to state what that option comprises and why they prefer it.

(iv) Do they consider that there should be safeguards for creditors and, if so, which of the options discussed in paragraphs 6.37-6.39 do they consider to be the best option:

> (a) option 1: the company must have to provide for the whole of the value of the transaction out of its distributable profits; or

> (b) option 2: the company's directors must make a statutory declaration as required by section 173 of the Companies Act 1985?

If they think that some other option is preferable, they are asked to state what that option comprises and why they prefer it.

(v) Should the new exemption apply to:

> (a) loans to directors;

> (b) loans to holding company directors;

> (c) guarantees or security in support of the above;

Or, in the case of relevant companies:

> (d) loans in favour of connected persons;

> (e) quasi-loans in favour of directors or their connected persons;

> (f) credit transactions in favour of directors or their connected persons;

> (g) guarantees or security in respect of any of the above;

In the case of all companies:

> (h) indirect arrangements caught by section 330(6) or (7) of the Companies Act 1985?

(vi) Should the new exemption apply to:

> (a) all companies;

(b) only companies which are not relevant companies as defined by section 331(6);

(c) only another class of companies (please describe)?

(vii) Do consultees think that if this new exemption is adopted:

(a) there should be the same arrangements for publicity as for payment out of capital and as described in paragraph 6.42 above;

(b) there should be power for the court to cancel the approval given by the shareholders on the application of a member or creditor as described in paragraph 6.43 above?

(viii) Do consultees think that if this new exemption is adopted, shareholders who may benefit from the transaction should have their votes disregarded if the resolution would not have been passed without them?

(ix) Do consultees think that if the new exemption is adopted members should have the right to inspect the statutory declaration and the auditors' report?

PART 7
SUBSTANTIVE IMPROVEMENTS 4: DISCLOSURE OF TRANSACTIONS IN WHICH DIRECTORS AND THEIR CONNECTED PERSONS ARE INTERESTED IN THE ANNUAL ACCOUNTS (SCHEDULE 6, PART II) AND THE SPECIAL PROVISIONS FOR BANKS (SECTIONS 343 AND 344)

INTRODUCTION

7.1 This part deals with the disclosure which the Act requires in the annual accounts and elsewhere of the transactions and arrangements in which directors or their connected persons are interested. In Part 2, we provisionally identified a general principle of ample but efficient disclosure.[1] Disclosure is a crucial part of the Act's system of regulating these transactions. The fact that self-dealing transactions have to be disclosed will often act as a brake on directors entering into them or approving them. Their disclosure also enables shareholders to assess the actions of management and to take action against them, whether by removing them as directors or pursing legal remedies against them or, in the case of annual accounts, declining to approve the accounts. As Part 3 states,[2] subject to questions of cost and confidentiality,[3] it is important that each organ in the company receives the information which it needs to perform its role in the company properly.

7.2 The requirements for disclosure in the annual accounts are underpinned by a range of differing sanctions in the Act. Section 232(1) states that the information specified in Schedule 6 must be given in notes to the company's annual accounts. Section 233(5) states that if annual accounts are approved which do not comply with the requirements of the Act, every director of the company who was party to their approval and knew that they did not comply, or is reckless as to whether they comply, is guilty of an offence and liable to a fine. There are provisions which enable the Secretary of State to request a company to revise accounts which do not comply with the Act and whereby the court can order accounts to be revised.[4]

---

[1] See para 2.17(9) above.

[2] See para 3.92(7) above.

[3] Sched 6, Pt II deals with completed transactions, or agreements to enter transactions. It is not thought that these raise any question of confidentiality.

[4] See generally ss 245-245C of the Companies Act 1985. This power has also been conferred on the Financial Reporting Review Panel, to which, like the Accounting Standards Board, the Financial Reporting Council is "parent and mentor" (Financial Reporting Council, Progress Report (1997)).

7.3 The notes to a company's annual accounts must give extensive information about directors' and related party benefits. The Act's requirements are to be found in section 232 of the Companies Act 1985, and Schedule 6. We are not here concerned with Part I of that Schedule (which deals with emoluments, compensation for loss of office and pension payments) or with Part III of the Schedule (which deals with the disclosure of transactions in which officers other than directors are interested). Directors have an obligation to provide information required by Part I of Schedule 6, but not, it appears, that required by Part II of the Schedule.[5]

7.4 The regime regarding disclosure is different in relation to authorised banking institutions and their holding companies. This is dealt with by sections 343 and 345. In this part we look first at Schedule 6, Part II and then go on to consider sections 343-344.

SCHEDULE 6, PART II: DISCLOSURE IN ANNUAL ACCOUNTS OF TRANSACTIONS IN WHICH DIRECTORS ARE INTERESTED

[15.] [The group accounts of a holding company, or if it is not required to prepare group accounts its individual accounts,] shall contain the particulars required by this Schedule of—

(a)   any transaction or arrangement of a kind described in section 330 entered into by the company or by a subsidiary of the company for a person who at any time during the financial year was a director of the company or its holding company, or was connected with such a director;

(b)   an agreement by the company or by a subsidiary of the company to enter into any such transaction or arrangement for a person who was at any time during the financial year a director of the company or its holding company, or was connected with such a director; and

(c)   any other transaction or arrangement with the company or a subsidiary of it in which a person who at any time during the financial year was a director of the company or its holding company had, directly or indirectly, a material interest.

[16.] The accounts prepared by a company other than a holding company shall contain the particulars required by this Schedule of—

(a)   any transaction or arrangement of a kind described in section 330 entered into by the company for a person who at any time during the financial year was a director of it or of its holding company or was connected with such a director;

(b)   an agreement by the company to enter into any such transaction or arrangement for a person who at any time during the financial year was a director of the company or its holding company or was connected with such a director; and

(c)   any other transaction or arrangement with the company in which a person who at any time during the financial year was a director of

[5] Section 232(3) of the Companies Act 1985.

the company or of its holding company had, directly or indirectly, a material interest.

[17.] **(1)** For purposes of paragraphs [15](c) and [16](c), a transaction or arrangement between a company and a director of it or of its holding company, or a person connected with such a director, is to be treated (if it would not otherwise be so) as a transaction, arrangement or agreement in which that director is interested.

(2) An interest in such a transaction or arrangement is not "material" for purposes of those sub-paragraphs if in the board's opinion it is not so; but this is without prejudice to the question whether or not such an interest is material in a case where the board have not considered the matter.

"The board" here means the directors of the company preparing the accounts, or a majority of those directors, but excluding in either case the director whose interest it is.

[18.] Paragraphs [15] and [16] do not apply in relation to the following transactions, arrangements and agreements—

    (a)   a transaction, arrangement or agreement between one company and another in which a director of the former or of its subsidiary or holding company is interested only by virtue of his being a director of the latter;

    (b)   a contract of service between a company and one of its directors or a director of its holding company, or between a director of a company and any of that company's subsidiaries;

    (c)   a transaction, arrangement or agreement which was not entered into during the financial year and which did not subsist at any time during that year.

[19.] Paragraphs [15] and [16] apply whether or not—

    (a)   the transaction or arrangement was prohibited by section 330;

    (b)   the person for whom it was made was a director of the company or was connected with a director of it at the time it was made;

    (c)   in the case of a transaction or arrangement made by a company which at any time during a financial year is a subsidiary of another company, it was a subsidiary of that other company at the time the transaction or arrangement was made.

[20.] Neither paragraph [15](c) nor paragraph [16](c) applies in relation to any transaction or arrangement if—

    (a)   each party to the transaction or arrangement which is a member of the same group of companies (meaning a holding company and its subsidiaries) as the company entered into the transaction or arrangement in the ordinary course of business, and

    (b)   the terms of the transaction or arrangement are not less favourable to any such party than it would be reasonable to expect if the interest mentioned in that sub-paragraph had not been an interest of a person who was a director of the company or of its holding company.

[21.] Neither paragraph [15](c) nor paragraph [16](c) applies in relation to any transaction or arrangement if—

(a)   the company is a member of a group of companies (meaning a holding company and its subsidiaries), and

(b)   either the company is a wholly-owned subsidiary or no body corporate (other than the company or a subsidiary of the company) which is a member of the group of companies which includes the company's ultimate holding company was a party to the transaction or arrangement, and

(c)   the director in question was at some time during the relevant period associated with the company, and

(d)   the material interest of the director in question in the transaction or arrangement would not have arisen if he had not been associated with the company at any time during the relevant period.

[22.] (1) Subject to the next paragraph, the particulars required by this Part are those of the principal terms of the transaction, arrangement or agreement.

(2) Without prejudice to the generality of sub-paragraph (1), the following particulars are required—

(a)   a statement of the fact either that the transaction, arrangement or agreement was made or subsisted (as the case may be) during the financial year;

(b)   the name of the person for whom it was made and, where that person is or was connected with a director of the company or of its holding company, the name of that director;

(c)   in a case where paragraph [15](c) or [16](c) applies, the name of the director with the material interest and the nature of that interest;

(d)   in the case of a loan or an agreement for a loan or an arrangement within section 330(6) or (7) of this Act relating to a loan—

(i)   the amount of the liability of the person to whom the loan was or was agreed to be made, in respect of principal and interest, at the beginning and at the end of the financial year;

(ii)   the maximum amount of that liability during that year;

(iii) the amount of any interest which, having fallen due, has not been paid; and

(iv)   the amount of any provision (within the meaning of Schedule 4 to this Act) made in respect of any failure or anticipated failure by the borrower to repay the whole or part of the loan or to pay the whole or part of any interest on it;

(e)   in the case of a guarantee or security or an arrangement within section 330(6) relating to a guarantee or security—

(i)   the amount for which the company (or its subsidiary) was liable under the guarantee or in respect of the security both at the beginning and at the end of the financial year;

(ii)   the maximum amount for which the company (or its subsidiary) may become so liable; and

189

(iii) any amount paid and any liability incurred by the company (or its subsidiary) for the purpose of fulfilling the guarantee or discharging the security (including any loss incurred by reason of the enforcement of the guarantee or security); and

(f) in the case of any transaction, arrangement or agreement other than those mentioned in sub-paragraphs (d) and (e), the value of the transaction or arrangement or (as the case may be) the value of the transaction or arrangement to which the agreement relates.

[23.] In paragraph [22](2) above, sub-paragraphs (c) to (f) do not apply in the case of a loan or quasi-loan made or agreed to be made by a company to or for a body corporate which is either—

(a) a body corporate of which that company is a wholly-owned subsidiary, or

(b) a wholly-owned subsidiary of a body corporate of which that company is a wholly-owned subsidiary, or

(c) a wholly-owned subsidiary of that company,

if particulars of that loan, quasi-loan or agreement for it would not have been required to be included in that company's annual accounts if the first-mentioned body corporate had not been associated with a director of that company at any time during the relevant period.

[24.] (1) In relation to a company's accounts for a financial year, compliance with this Part is not required in the case of transactions of a kind mentioned in the following sub-paragraph which are made by the company or a subsidiary of it for a person who at any time during that financial year was a director of the company or of its holding company, or was connected with such a director, if the aggregate of the values of each transaction, arrangement or agreement so made for that director or any person connected with him, less the amount (if any) by which the liabilities of the person for whom the transaction or arrangement was made has been reduced, did not at any time during the financial year exceed £5,000.

(2) The transactions in question are—

(a) credit transactions,

(b) guarantees provided or securities entered into in connection with credit transactions,

(c) arrangements within subsection (6) or (7) of section 330 relating to credit transactions,

(d) agreements to enter into credit transactions.

[25.] In relation to a company's accounts for a financial year, compliance with this Part is not required by virtue of paragraph [15](c) or [16](c) in the case of any transaction or arrangement with a company or any of its subsidiaries in which a director of the company or its holding company had, directly or indirectly, a material interest if—

(a) the value of each transaction or arrangement within paragraph [15](c) or [16](c) (as the case may be) in which that director had (directly or indirectly) a material interest and which was made

190

after the commencement of the financial year with the company or any of its subsidiaries, and

(b)   the value of each such transaction or arrangement which was made before the commencement of the financial year less the amount (if any) by which the liabilities of the person for whom the transaction or arrangement was made have been reduced,

did not at any time during the financial year exceed in the aggregate £1,000 or, if more, did not exceed £5,000 or 1 per cent of the value of the net assets of the company preparing the accounts in question as at the end of the financial year, whichever is the less.

For this purpose a company's net assets are the aggregate of its assets, less the aggregate of its liabilities ("liabilities" to include any provision for liabilities or charges within paragraph 89 of Schedule 4).

[26.] Section 345 of this Act (power of Secretary of State to alter sums by statutory instrument subject to negative resolution in Parliament) applies as if the money sums specified in paragraph [24] or [25] above were specified in Part X.

[27.] [(1)] The following provisions of this Act apply for purposes of this Part of this Schedule—

(a)   section 331(2), and (7), as regards the meaning of "guarantee", and "credit transaction";

(b)   section 331(9), as to the interpretation of references to a transaction or arrangement being made "for" a person;

(c)   section 340, in assigning values to transactions and arrangements, and

(d)   section 346, as to the interpretation of references to a person being "connected with" a director of a company.

[(2) In this Part of this Schedule "director" includes a shadow director.]

General

7.5   Schedule 6, Part II was derived from sections 56, 64 and 65 of the Companies Act 1980.[6] It specifies the particulars of transactions in which directors[7] were interested that need to be disclosed in the accounts. The transactions in question are:

(a)   "section 330-type" transactions, that is transactions or arrangements of the kind described in section 330 (whether prohibited or not), and agreements to enter such transactions or arrangements;[8] and

---

[6]   As amended by Sched 3, para 52 of the Companies Act 1981.

[7]   And where applicable, connected persons.

[8]   Paragraphs 15(1)(a), (b), 19(a). Paras 15 and 16 deal with group accounts, and individual company accounts respectively.

(b) other transactions or arrangements in which a director has a material interest.[9]

It is sufficient if the director or connected person involved was a director or connected person at any time during the financial year, and thus, for example, a loan to a director before his appointment is included.[10] The transaction or arrangement need not have been made in the financial year in question, but must have been in force at some point during the year in question.[11]

Materiality

7.6 As already stated,[12] paragraphs 15(c) and 16(c) of Schedule 6 require disclosure (in group and entity accounts respectively) of the particulars of transactions or arrangements in which directors had a direct or indirect material interest. A number of exceptions are included:

(a) transactions, arrangements or agreements where a director is interested by virtue of a common directorship;

(b) contracts of service;

(c) intragroup transactions in the ordinary course of business on arms' length terms; and

(d) transactions in which a director is intended by reason only of the director being associated with the company provided that (a) the company is a member of a group of companies and (b) either it is a wholly owned subsidiary or no other member of the group (apart from a subsidiary of the company) is a party to the transaction or arrangement.

Paragraphs 22 and 23 deal with the particulars to be disclosed. Paragraphs 24 and 25 contain exemptions for minor transactions.

7.7 From such enquiries as we have made it appears that there are few transactions which are disclosable under Schedule 6, Part II which are not required to be disclosed under FRS 8.[13] A possible reason for this is that paragraph 17 of Schedule 6 enables directors to take the decision that a particular interest is not material. In many cases, what is material involves an evaluation of the facts and the directors are well-placed to know the relevant facts. On the other hand, it is possible that this provision leads to a degree of subjective judgment which tends to weaken the effectiveness of Schedule 6. It is for consideration whether a provision

---

[9] Paras 15(1)(c), 16(1)(c).

[10] Paras 15, 16, 19(6).

[11] Paras 18(c).

[12] See para 7.5 above.

[13] See Appendix N.

on these lines should be retained as one way in which materiality can be determined.

7.8 Apart from paragraph 17, "material interest" is not defined in the Schedule and it is unclear, as a matter of construction, whether it bears one or two meanings. The first is that a material interest is one which is likely to be of relevance to shareholders or creditors if it could influence decisions taken by them on the basis of the financial statements. Thus the fact that a transaction was of low value may not be decisive if its circumstances reveal a threat to future profitability, for example, because intellectual property rights were transferred. The second approach is to measure materiality in terms of the extent of a director's interest in a transaction. A material interest would arise here if the director's interest was a substantial one. This means that it is the size of the director's interest, not the value of the transaction which is the starting point. Thus the purchase by a director of a Mars Bar from the company's canteen would be disclosable on this construction but not his 1 per cent interest in a larger contract. Indeed this test is often called the Mars Bar test. However the company may derive more value from the Mars Bar approach as an indicator of potential conflicts of interest.

7.9 The DTI's consultative document in 1991 suggested that an interest in a transaction should be treated as material unless disclosure of the interest would be of no significance to the company's members or creditors, including prospective creditors, and that in determining whether disclosure would be of no significance regard should be had to any other transaction or arrangement entered into during the financial year in question in which the director concerned was directly or indirectly interested.[14] FRS 8 on the other hand applies materiality to the transaction and not to the interest. For the purpose of FRS 8,[15] materiality of a transaction is to be determined by reference to both the reporting entity and to the related party. A transaction of small significance to the company issuing the accounts may be of major importance to the individual director concerned. This is also the view expressed in a recent technical release[16] of the Institute of Chartered Accountants in England and Wales, which says that materiality depends not just on a quantitative judgment as to the transaction's size, but also on a qualitative judgment. It states that ultimately materiality depends on how information could influence the economic decisions of users of the accounts. This is similar to the definition put forward by the DTI in 1991, except that the latter starts with an assumption that all transactions are material. By itself, however, this definition does not explain how it is to be decided whether a transaction is likely to be of significance to users of accounts, and in those circumstances the preferable course may be to provide that references to materiality are to be construed in accordance with accounting standards for the time being.

Consultees are asked:

[14] See para 1.17 above.

[15] See para 20 in Appendix N below.

[16] TECH 32/96 on The Interpretation of Materiality in Financial Reporting (May 1996).

(i) whether Schedule 6 should contain a definition of materiality for the purposes of paragraphs 15(c) and 16(c); and

(ii) if so, how materiality should be defined.

7.10   The discussion of materiality leads to the further question whether it would be possible for Schedule 6, Part II to be repealed and reliance placed on FRS 8. It would obviously be easier for preparers of accounts if they did not have to look at both accounting standards and the Act. However as we see it there are a number of possible difficulties with this course. The Schedule is drafted in more precise terms than FRS 8[17] and carries criminal sanctions.[18] The Act is administered by the DTI whereas the Financial Reporting Review Panel is concerned with material departures from accounting standards. There are differences between the two regimes: for instance Schedule 6 exempts intra-group arms' length transactions in the ordinary course of business[19] whereas FRS 8 does not, and FRS 8 contains exemptions for all transactions between 90 per cent controlled subsidiaries and members of their group or investees of the group qualified as related parties.[20] Under the Financial Reporting Standard for Smaller Entities, smaller companies are permitted to make fewer disclosures than those which FRS 8 requires of larger companies.[21] Schedule 6, Part II could not be repealed in its entirety because the Fourth EC Directive on company accounts[22] requires the notes to the accounts to give certain particulars of "advances and credits" granted to directors.[23]

7.11   There is accordingly likely to be a separate role for Schedule 6, Part II. In those circumstances a number of questions arise concerning Schedule 6, Part II, many of which were raised by the DTI in 1991. It may be however that the need to take any action has changed since that time, particularly in view of the introduction of FRS 8. We seek consultees' views on this question below. Most of these amendments are designed to rationalise and simplify Schedule 6, Part II. But in some instances they also involve policy decisions about the breadth of disclosure of transactions in which directors are interested, in particular whether disclosure should be required even if they are arms' length transactions in the ordinary course of business (question (iii) below). One possible reason for disclosure in this situation is that the terms of a transaction might be altered more easily if the director has an interest in it. On the other hand, in 1991 the DTI proposed

---

[17]   See the discusion below on "connected person" at para 8.5 *et seq* below.

[18]   Section 233(5), but only if the director knows that they do not compy or is reckless as to whether they comply.

[19]   See Sched 6, para 20.

[20]   FRS 8, para 17; cf Sched 6, Pt II.

[21]   In particular, materiality is judged in terms of signifance to the reporting entity.

[22]   1978 OJ L 222/11.

[23]   Art 43.1(13). The prescribed particulars are the amounts, indications of the interests rates, main conditions, any amounts repaid, commitments to give guarantees and an indication of the total for each category. This requirement is extended by the Seventh EC Directive on consolidated accounts (1983 OJ L193/1) to similar transactions entered into by subsidiaries (see art 34.13).

extending this exemption to all transactions in the ordinary course of business.[24] The points raised in relation to questions (iv)-(vi) appear to be drafting omissions. As respects question (vii), it may be of little assistance to the user of accounts to tell him that the value of a transaction is over £100,000 when it is clear that it must have a very much greater value.

Consultees are asked:

(i) whether Schedule 6, Part II should be retained notwithstanding the introduction of FRS 8;

(ii) whether a director should have a duty to give notice to the company of such matters relating to himself and (so far as known to him) his connected persons as may be necessary for the purposes of that part;[25]

(iii) whether the exception for transactions in the ordinary course of business in paragraph 21 should be retained and if so whether it should be extended to apply to transactions which are not intra-group;

(iv) whether the details of the value required to be given in relation to loans (and related guarantees and security) under paragraph 22(d) and (e) should be the same in relation to quasi-loans and credit transactions (including related guarantees and security) or vice-versa;

(v) whether the exemption in paragraph 23 should extend to credit transactions;

(vi) whether there should be an exemption like paragraphs 24 and 25 for loans and quasi-loans;

(vii) whether, where the deemed value provision in section 340(7) applies,[26] the directors should be required if possible to give some estimate of the value;

(viii) whether a transaction should be outside paragraphs 15(c) and 16(d) simply because the director is a common director of both parties to the transaction;[27]

(ix) whether there is any other change to Schedule 6 which should be considered.

SECTIONS 343-344: SPECIAL PROVISIONS FOR BANKS

343. —(1) The following provisions of this section—

---

[24] See Amendments to Schedule 6 of the Companies Act 1985: Disclosure by Companies of Dealings in Favour of Directors, A Consultative Document, DTI (October 1991). But see now FRS 8, Appendix N below.

[25] Cf s 232(3).

[26] Schedule 6, para 26.

[27] See para 18(a) cf FRS 8.

(a) apply in the case of a company which is [a banking company, or is the holding company of a credit institution,] and

(b) are subject to the exceptions provided by section 344.

[(2) Where such a company takes advantage of the provisions of paragraph 2 of Part IV of Schedule 9 in relation to a financial year, that company shall keep a register containing a copy of every transaction, arrangement or agreement of which particulars would, but for that paragraph, be required to be disclosed in the company's accounts or group accounts for that financial year and for each financial year in the preceding 10 in relation to which the company has taken advantage of the provisions of that paragraph.]

(3) In the case of a transaction, arrangement or agreement which is not in writing, there shall be contained in the register a written memorandum setting out its terms.

[(4) Where such a company takes advantage of the provisions of paragraph 2 of Part IV of Schedule 9 in relation to the last complete financial year preceding its annual general meeting, that company shall before that meeting make available at its registered office for not less than 15 days ending with the date of the meeting a statement containing the particulars of transactions, arrangements and agreements which the company would, but for that paragraph, be required to disclose in its accounts or group accounts for that financial year.]

(5) The statement shall be so made available for inspection by members of the company; and such a statement shall also be made available for their inspection at the annual general meeting.

(6) It is the duty of the company's auditors to examine the statement before it is made available to members of the company and to make a report to the members on it; and the report shall be annexed to the statement before it is made so available.

(7) The auditors' report shall state whether in their opinion the statement contains the particulars required by subsection (4); and, where their opinion is that it does not, they shall include in the report, so far as they are reasonably able to do so, a statement giving the required particulars.

(8) If a company fails to comply with any provision of subsections (2) to (5), every person who at the time of the failure is a director of it is guilty of an offence and liable to a fine; but—

(a) it is a defence in proceedings against a person for this offence to prove that he took all reasonable steps for securing compliance with the subsection concerned, and

(b) a person is not guilty of the offence by virtue only of being a shadow director of the company.

(9) For purposes of the application of this section to loans and quasi-loans made by a company to persons connected with a person who at any time is a director of the company or of its holding company, a company which a person does not control is not connected with him.

344.—(1) Section 343 does not apply in relation to—

    (a)   **transactions or arrangements made or subsisting during a financial year by a company or by a subsidiary of a company for a person who was at any time during that year a director of the company or of its holding company or was connected with such a director, or**

    (b)   **an agreement made or subsisting during that year to enter into such a transaction or arrangement,**

if the aggregate of the values of each transaction or arrangement made for that person, and of each agreement for such a transaction or arrangement, less the amount (if any) by which the value of those transactions, arrangements and agreements has been reduced, did not exceed [£2,000] at any time during the financial year.

For purposes of this subsection, values are to be determined as under section 340.

(2) Section 343(4) and (5) do not apply to [a banking company] which is the wholly-owned subsidiary of a company incorporated in the United Kingdom.

7.12   As indicated above, the regime regarding disclosure is different in relation to authorised banking institutions and their holding companies.[28] In this situation the company which prepares its accounts in accordance with Schedule 9 and takes advantage of Part IV, paragraph 3 of that Schedule shall make the register, containing directors' transactions,[29] available at its registered office 15 days prior to the annual general meeting. The register contains a copy of every transaction, arrangement or agreement which other companies would disclose in their accounts. Section 344 disapplies this regime in relation to a transaction for a person who, never owed more than £2000 at any time during the financial year.

7.13   In practice what the shareholders are entitled to see is laid down in paragraphs 22 and 29 of Schedule 6, Part II. The accounts must contain a statement detailing the total amounts outstanding at the end of the financial year for these particular transactions, and the number of officers for whom the transactions were made. The statement should be examined by the company's auditors who should make a report to the members on it.[30] The Register contains the name of each person entering into a transaction and the amounts of liability and unpaid interest.

7.14   These sections were first enacted in the Companies Act 1980. When they were introduced, three reasons were advanced for differential treatment.[31] Firstly, to avoid the disruption of perfectly proper commercial business between companies associated with a director and the bank. Second, that a prohibition would be likely to cut off an important source of potential directors from the bank; the example mentioned being large-scale farmers who may require sizeable loans from time to time. Thirdly, that none of the clearing banks had been implicated in any scandal

---

[28]   Sections 343 and 344 implement article 40(7) of the Bank Accounts Directive.

[29]   Loans, quasi-loans and credit transactions.

[30]   Section 343(6).

[31]   *House of Commons Official Report: Standing Committees* (1979-80) HC 1, col 450 .

during the secondary banking crisis, the consequences of which were keenly felt at the time of debate.

7.15   The fact that a director has to borrow from his company, may indicate that he is not creditworthy. On the other hand, it may be said that greater scrutiny might apply in relation to a bank making a loan to its director than to a company in some other business making a loan. However, the question at issue is whether banks should be treated differently from other companies. This question becomes more acute when it is considered that supermarkets and building societies now offer banking facilities including loans. A further issue is whether the provisions in the sections provide sufficient protection to shareholders, and whether they are aware of their rights under 343(4).

7.16   It is clearly desirable that loans between directors and banks be disclosed. The issue is what level of disclosure should be required. Section 343 in not applying the same level of disclosure for other companies, but requiring a register to be maintained may provide a sufficient safeguard. However, in practice, this form of disclosure may not be sufficiently stringent. It may be said that those bank directors who are not creditworthy may be more inclined to seek advantage from their own companies. A question is whether, in this situation, section 343 encourages banks to enter into transactions without applying the same level of scrutiny as those companies who must provide fuller details on the face of their accounts.

7.17   There would seem to be no reason why the register referred to in section 343 could not be kept in an electronic form.[32]

Consultees are asked:

(i) Are sections 343 and 344 necessary or desirable?

(ii) On the basis these sections are retained, are consultees aware of any deficiency in these sections which are required to be addressed?

---

[32]   Section 723A.

PART 8
SUBSTANTIVE IMPROVEMENTS 5: CONNECTED PERSONS (SECTION 346) AND REMAINING SECTIONS OF PART X OF THE COMPANIES ACT 1985

INTRODUCTION

8.1 In this part we review section 346 (meaning of connected person), and then consider the remaining sections of Part X, namely section 345 (power to increase financial limits) and section 347 (transactions under foreign law).[1]

SECTION 346: THE MEANING OF CONNECTED PERSON

346.—(1) This section has effect with respect to references in this Part to a person being "connected" with a director of a company, and to a director being "associated with" or "controlling" a body corporate.

(2) A person is connected with a director of a company if, but only if, he (not being himself a director of it) is—

    (a)   that director's spouse, child or step-child; or

    (b)   except where the context otherwise requires, a body corporate with which the director is associated; or

    (c)   a person acting in his capacity as trustee of any trust the beneficiaries of which include—

        (i)   the director, his spouse or any children or step-children of his, or

        (ii)   a body corporate with which he is associated,

or of a trust whose terms confer a power on the trustees that may be exercised for the benefit of the director, his spouse, or any children or step-children of his, or any such body corporate; or

    (d)   a person acting in his capacity as partner of that director or of any person who, by virtue of paragraph (a), (b) or (c) of this subsection, is connected with that director; or

    (e)   a Scottish firm in which—

        (i)   that director is a partner,

        (ii)   a partner is a person who, by virtue of paragraph (a), (b) or (c) above, is connected with that director, or

        (iii)   a partner is a Scottish firm in which that director is a partner or in which there is a partner who, by virtue of paragraph (a), (b) or (c) above, is connected with that director.

---

[1]   Section 311 is considered in Part 9: see para 9.29 *et seq* below.

(3) In subsection (2)—

    (a)   a reference to the child or step-child of any person includes an illegitimate child of his, but does not include any person who has attained the age of 18; and

    (b)   paragraph (c) does not apply to a person acting in his capacity as trustee under an employees' share scheme or a pension scheme.

(4) A director of a company is associated with a body corporate if, but only if, he and the persons connected with him, together—

    (a)   are interested in shares comprised in the equity share capital of that body corporate of a nominal value equal to at least one-fifth of that share capital; or

    (b)   are entitled to exercise or control the exercise of more than one-fifth of the voting power at any general meeting of that body.

(5) A director of a company is deemed to control a body corporate if, but only if—

    (a)   he or any person connected with him is interested in any part of the equity share capital of that body or is entitled to exercise or control the exercise of any part of the voting power at any general meeting of that body; and

    (b)   that director, the persons connected with him and the other directors of that company, together, are interested in more than one-half of that share capital or are entitled to exercise or control the exercise of more than one-half of that voting power.

(6) For purposes of subsections (4) and (5)—

    (a)   a body corporate with which a director is associated is not to be treated as connected with that director unless it is also connected with him by virtue of subsection (2)(c) or (d); and

    (b)   a trustee of a trust the beneficiaries of which include (or may include) a body corporate with which a director is associated is not to be treated as connected with a director by reason only of that fact.

(7) The rules set out in Part I of Schedule 13 apply for the purposes of subsections (4) and (5).

(8) References in those subsections to voting power the exercise of which is controlled by a director include voting power whose exercise is controlled by a body corporate controlled by him; but this is without prejudice to other provisions of subsections (4) and (5).

General

8.2   Section 346 sets out the definition of "connected person" which is used in many of the sections in Part X.[2] The principal persons who are "connected" for this purpose with a director are:

(1)   his spouse and infant children;[3]

(2)   a body corporate with which the director is associated;[4]

(3)   trustees of a trust under which the director or his family or his associated companies are beneficiaries;[5] and

(4)   partners (and any Scottish firm of which, or with which, the director is a partner).[6]

8.3   However this is not an exhaustive list and there are complicated provisions for determining whether a body corporate is "associated" with a director. Broadly speaking, he and his connected persons must be interested in 20% of the equity share capital[7] or control (directly or indirectly through another associated body corporate) 20% of the voting power exercisable at any general meeting.[8] The definition of "interest" in Schedule 13, Part I applies for the purpose of section 346[9] so that if the Secretary of State is given power to extend the meaning of interest, it will have effect for the purposes of this section also.

8.4   Although section 346 is complex we are not aware that there are any particular difficulties in its interpretation or application as it stands.

8.5   In the main, Part X adopts a principled approach to the legal consequences of the involvement in transactions in breach of Part X of "connected persons". The position of the following may arise:

(1)   counterparties;[10]

(2)   the connected person;

---

[2]   Ie ss 317, 320-322, 322A, 329, 330, 337, 338, 341, 343 and 344. In addition the options for reform considered above would entail extending the following section to include connected persons: ss 312 and 317.

[3]   Sections 346(2)(a) and 346(3)(a).

[4]   Section 346(2)(b).

[5]   Section 346(2)(c).

[6]   Section 346(2)(d) and (e).

[7]   Defined in s 744 as excluding share capital which carries limited dividend or capital rights.

[8]   Subsection (6) is designed to eliminate circularity.

[9]   Section 346(7).

[10]   By counterparty in this connection we mean another party to the transaction eg a tenant who takes a lease from the company jointly with a connected person of a director and the lease meets the financial threshold in s 320.

(3) the director with whom the person is connected; and

(4) the other director who approved the transaction.

8.6 Counterparties are affected if as a result of the participation the transaction becomes voidable. This can happen under section 320, section 322A and section 341. Those sections give the company the right to avoid the contract even if the counterparty did not know the facts constituting the breach of the relevant section. Thus Part X prefers the rights of the company to those of the counterparty in this respect. The counterparty is not without a remedy since he can sue the directors who represented that the transaction would be binding for breach of warranty of authority.[11]

8.7 In some cases Part X imposes liability on the connected person: this happens in section 322(3), 322A(3) and 341(2).[12] Again the connected person may not know the relevant facts. In each case he is given a defence to the statutory claim for an account or an indemnity if he can show that he did not know the relevant circumstances: see section 322(6), 322A(6) and 341(5).

8.8 The director with whom he is connected is treated more strictly. In two cases, he has a defence to a statutory claim for an account or an indemnity if he can show that he took all reasonable steps to ensure compliance by the company with the relevant provision: sections 322(5) and 341(4). In the case of section 322A, he has no such defence, no doubt because he is expected to know when the board are exceeding their powers (though if he acted reasonably in forming the contrary conclusion he might be entitled to relief under section 727). In the case of section 317 he may find himself in breach of duty even if he did not know about the interest and could not reasonably have done so. We have dealt with this in Part 4 above.[13]

8.9 There are similar definitions to that in section 346 in related areas. These approach the matter differently and the question arises whether the tests and section 346 should be assimilated. Section 346 is an example of prescriptive legislation, namely legislation which seeks so far as possible to set out a comprehensive list of the matters to be included. It does not for instance seek to set out a principle nor does it contain a sweep up clause at the end to cover other people with whom in a particular case a director may have a sufficient connection to make it right that that person be treated as a connected person of his. This approach may have been deliberately adopted so that a counterparty dealing with a director is able to tell whether the party with whom he is dealing is a connected person of that director.[14] If so, the approach in section 346 would be an

---

[11] See generally *Chitty on Contracts* (27th ed, 1994) vol 2, paras 31-093-31-100.

[12] Criminal liability may also be imposed on, in the case of s 323, a spouse or infant child but they have a defence if they prove that they had no knowledge that the spouse/parent was a director of the company in question. See further para 4.216 above and s 327(1).

[13] Para 4.105 above.

[14] The definition in s 346 is to be contrasted with the wider definition of associate in s 435 of the Insolvency Act 1986.

application of the certainty principle which we have provisionally identified above.[15]

8.10   Section 346 may be compared with other similar lists, in particular the definition of "associate" in section 435 of the Insolvency Act 1986 and the definitions of "related party" in the Listing Rules and in FRS 8.[16]

8.11   It may well be inconvenient and inefficient to have several different definitions, and so we have considered whether section 346 could be more closely aligned to any of them. The definition of associate in the Insolvency Act 1986 is wider than the definition of connected person, especially in relation to close family members. Grandparents, brothers, sisters, adult children, former spouses and reputed spouses are included. This definition applies for the purpose of ascertaining whether a longer period should apply for looking at transactions which might be voidable preferences in England and Wales under section 239 of the Insolvency Act 1986.[17] There is no reason why section 346 should be the same as that in section 435 and indeed as we see it the policy considerations may be very different when the question is whether the fund of assets available for creditors can be increased.

8.12   The definition in the Listing Rules is relevant to Part X but only where the company is a listed company and it is proposing to enter into a transaction which requires shareholder approval under section 320. Again the definition is in some respects wider: it includes for example persons who have been directors in the last 12 months, and it has a different focus since it also covers shareholders of the company (shareholders having more than 10% of the votes). There is little reason therefore to consider whether section 346 should be adapted to follow this model. The definition of "related party" in FRS 8 applies for the purposes of disclosure in company accounts and it might therefore be more closely connected with Part X. The definition is set out in full in Appendix N. The definition there states that parties such as directors and group companies are "related parties". Another group is presumed to be related unless it can be shown that they do not exercise influence over each other: it must be shown "that neither party has influenced the financial and operating policies of the other in such a way as to inhibit the pursuit of separate interests". Another group are deemed to be related parties because of their personal relationship, for example close family members of directors and any company in which a director had a controlling interest.[18] Control is however defined not by reference to legal rights to control but by reference to "the ability to direct operating and financial policies of the entity with a view to gaining economic benefits from its activities".

8.13   One of the principles that we provisionally identified in Part 2 was the certainty principle. It is important that company, directors and others should be able, so far

---

[15]   See para 2.17(7) above.

[16]   See Appendix N.

[17]   This section has no application in Scotland.

[18]   Cf s 346, under which it is sufficient if the director has an interest of 20%. FRS 8 also differs from s 346 with respect to partnerships and trusts.

as possible, to tell who is a connected person and the tests quoted above involve a high degree of judgment. It must be borne in mind that the contractual rights of a counterparty will be put aside in favour of those of the company if the transaction does not satisfy the procedural rules in Part X and this is another reason why it might be thought preferable not to adopt a judgmental test.

Consultees are asked:

(i) whether section 346 gives rise to difficulties in practice;

(ii) whether they consider that the test of "connected person" should be closer to any of the definitions of "associate" or "related party" considered above.

Option for reform (1): Make specified additions to the list of connected persons

8.14   As already pointed out, section 346 does not include cohabitants and it is for consideration whether such persons should be included and if so how they should be defined. Cohabitants are now included as persons who may make claims under the Fatal Accidents Act 1976 and under Law Reform (Succession) Act 1995. In both cases the cohabitant is defined as a person who for the whole of the immediately preceding two years lived in the same household as the deceased as husband or wife of the deceased. This definition would exclude same sex cohabitants and imposes a two-year rule to exclude frivolous claims. In Scotland patrimonial damages (that is damages for pecuniary loss) can be awarded to a person, not being the spouse of the deceased, who immediately before the deceased's death was living with the deceased as man and wife.[19]

8.15   Again consistently with the certainty principle mentioned above it seems desirable that there should be a qualifying period of cohabitation before a person had to be treated as a connected person so that persons dealing with the company and indeed fellow directors might be better placed to identify the connected person. However, that period should not be too long because then it would deprive the company of important protection under Part X. Bearing in mind those considerations, consultees may feel that a period of one year would be sufficient.

8.16   It is for consideration whether infant children of the cohabitant who are not children of the director should also be covered if they live with the cohabitant and the director. Children of the director who are born outside marriage would already be included.[20]

---

[19]   See the Damages (Scotland) Act 1976, s 1(1) and Sched 1, para 1(aa).

[20]   Section 346(3)(a). There might also be an argument for including adult children within the definition. It seems somewhat anomalous that a director should be prohibited from, for example, giving a loan to his sixteen year old child, but not his twenty year old child.

8.17 Finally the question arises whether section 327[21] or section 328[22] should be extended to include cohabitants, and children of the cohabitant who are living with the director and the cohabitant, on the same basis.

Consultees are asked:

(i) Should cohabitants, defined as persons who have for a specified period been living with a director of the company in the same household and as man and wife, be connected persons for the purposes of:

(a) section 346;

(b) section 327;

(c) section 328?

(ii) Should the specified period be a continuous period of one year, or some other period (and if so what), or should there be no period?

(iii) Should infant children of the cohabitant be treated as connected persons if they live with the director and the cohabitant and the cohabitant has himself or herself become a connected person and if so should that be for the same purposes?

(iv) Are there any other persons who should be connected persons who are not already covered by section 346?

Option for reform (2): Give the Secretary of State power to vary the list by regulation

8.18 Section 346 will always be subject to the defect that another class of person may need to be included or excluded from the list. It is therefore for consideration whether the Secretary of State should have power to add to the list of connected persons by regulation.

Consultees are asked whether the Secretary of State should be given power to vary the list of connected persons in section 346 by regulation.

THE REMAINING SECTIONS OF PART X

8.19 The sections in Part X which we have not yet considered in this consultation paper are sections 345 and 347.

345(1) The Secretary of State may by order in a statutory instrument substitute for any sum of money specified in this Part a larger sum specified in the order.

(2) An order under this section is subject to annulment in pursuance of a resolution of either House of Parliament.

---

[21] See para 4.216 above.

[22] See para 5.7 above.

(3) Such an order does not have effect in relation to anything done or not done before its coming into force; and accordingly, proceedings in respect of any liability (whether civil or criminal) incurred before that time may be continued or instituted as if the order had not been made.

347   For purposes of sections 319 to 322 and 330 to 343, it is immaterial whether the law which (apart from this Act) governs any arrangement or transaction is the law of the United Kingdom, or of a part of it, or not.

8.20   Section 345 deals with the power of the Secretary of State to increase financial limits in Part X, and raises no points for review.

8.21   Section 347 states that for specified purposes, it is immaterial whether the proper law is English or Scottish or some other law. This provision is necessary to prevent parties seeking to avoid the application of sections 319-322 and 330-343 by choosing a foreign law. But for section 347, sections 319-322 would not apply where the proper law of a transaction was not English or Scottish law, and the prohibitions in section 330 would not apply unless again the proper law of the transaction was English or Scottish law or the transaction was to be performed within the jurisdiction.[23]

8.22   There is a presumption that, in the absence of a contrary intention express or implied, United Kingdom legislation does not apply to the acts of foreign persons or UK persons outside the United Kingdom. The Companies Act 1985 draws a distinction between UK registered companies[24] and other companies. Most of its provisions apply only to UK registered companies, but many of those provisions by their nature apply whether or not the act is done in the jurisdiction.[25] Part X of the Companies Act 1985, other than section 323, applies only to UK registered companies. The provisions are not limited to acts done within the jurisdiction. Section 347 emphasises this point by preventing parties from contracting out of certain sections by choosing a foreign law.

8.23   There is an issue whether it is necessary for the Companies Act to go that far. A comparison can, for instance, be made with the Employment Rights Act 1996, which covers wage protection and other employment rights. An employee cannot contract out of these rights.[26] The major substantive rights apply, whatever the law governing the employment contract, unless he ordinarily works outside Great

---

[23]   *Dicey and Morris, The Conflict of Laws* (12th ed, 1993).

[24]   See the definition of "company" in s 735 of the Companies Act 1985. See also *Arab Bank plc v Mercantile Holdings Ltd* [1994] Ch 71.

[25]   See, eg, s 121 (alteration of share capital). However, where the company has no real connection with the jurisdiction the court may decline jurisdiction on the grounds of forum non conveniens: see eg *Re Harrods (Buenes Aires) Ltd* [1991] BCLC 666. There are examples in the Act of provisions expressly applying to acts of UK companies abroad: see, eg, s 398 (verification of charge on property outside the United Kingdom). Some provisions of the Act apply only to foreign companies: see, eg, s 409 of the Companies Act 1985, which requires overseas companies to register charges over property within England and Wales.

[26]   Section 203(1)(a) provides that any contractual provision which seeks to limit or exclude the operation of the Act is void.

Britain.[27] There is no similar restriction in Part X so that its provisions can apply even though the company does not carry on business here, has no assets located here, and has no creditors or members domiciled or resident here. It can be argued that there is no need for the UK to regulate such a case. On the other hand the situation where a company has no business, assets, creditors or members here will be rare, and it would be difficult to draw up a satisfactory statutory exclusion for it.[28] Part X is concerned with the conduct of directors and the safeguarding of its assets. To achieve its purpose it is difficult to see that it can be restricted in its operation except in this very rare case: if there are assets here or persons here who can be prejudiced by corporate self-dealing of the kind restricted by Part X, Part X ought to apply to a transaction even though that transaction is entered into and is to be performed abroad and to the activities of the directors wherever they take place.[29] Moreover, even if at the date of the transaction there is no connection with this jurisdiction a liability may be incurred within the jurisdiction shortly after say a loan to a director has been made and before it is repaid. For these reasons we are provisionally against any territorial restriction being placed on the operation of Part X.

Consultees are asked if they agree with our provisional view that Part X should apply to acts done outside the jurisdiction. If they disagree with this view, they are asked to state what restrictions should be imposed.

8.24 There is a minor additional question about the sections to which section 347 itself applies. The section identifies the sections in Part X which are transaction-based, but makes no mention of section 322A or section 322B, which are also transaction based. We provisionally consider that they should do so and provisionally so recommend.

Consultees are asked whether they agree with our provisional view that section 347 should be amended to include references to sections 322A and 322B.

---

[27] Section 196(1) and (2) and s 204.

[28] For instance, it may be difficult to define when assets are located here particularly if they are intangible or are moveable, like aircraft.

[29] Compare the position under the Company Directors Disqualification Act 1996. Proceedings can be taken against the director even though the acts relied upon as constituting unfitness occurred outside the jurisdiction: *Re Seagull Manufacturing Co Ltd (No 2)* [1994] Ch 91. The Court noted that if the position were otherwise, it could lead to anomalous results since it would mean that disqualification proceedings could not be brought against a foreign director whose activities, conducted exclusively abroad, had shown him unfit to be a director, even though he might seek to expand his activities and to act as a director in England. *Ibid,* at 104-105.

PART 9
FURTHER OPTIONS: (1) CAN SECTIONS IN PART X BE REPEALED? (2) WOULD PART X BE IMPROVED IF IT WAS REWRITTEN?

INTRODUCTION

9.1 In this part, we consider some more radical solutions than we have considered so far. We consider the repeals of certain provisions in Part X. In the Parts 4 to 8, we considered a number of detailed substantive improvements that might be made to Part X. There were many possibilities, some of which we provisionally recommended. Even if only some of the possible amendments considered in Parts 4 to 8 are in due course recommended in our final report, it is clear that Part X will not decrease in size or become less complex. On the contrary, it will increase in size and complexity significantly. In those circumstances, careful thought has to be given to seeing whether at least some of the provisions in Part X can be repealed. We do this under Option 1 below. We first consider whether groups of sections[1] could be removed and reliance placed on more general principles. We then consider whether two further specified sections should in any event be repealed, sections 311 and 323. Under Option 2 below, we consider the question whether there would be an improvement in Part X if it were rewritten more simply.

9.2 In Part 2 we identified as a potential guiding principle for reform a principle of "enough but not excessive" regulation. We suggested that Part X of the Companies Act 1985 should provide the right balance between regulation and freedom for directors to make business decisions. The application of that aspect of the principle may be regarded as especially challenging in the context of legislation as detailed as Part X. We also said that Part X should not be criticised for failing to deal with every eventuality. Dependent on how complex it was thought that the Companies Act should be, a line can be drawn between those matters which the sections should cover and those which can be left to be dealt with in some other way. In Part 3 we saw that the provisions in Part X have an economic rationale, for instance in protecting third parties (for example creditors) from the prejudice as a result of the ability of others (for example directors) being able to use their powers in a certain way: that consideration might constitute a reason against any move to simplify Part X by removing certain provisions from it. The questions as to whether large parts of Part X should be repealed or disapplied because sufficient self-regulation exists were identified as central general questions in Part 1.[2] In this part, aspects of those two questions will be found to be interlinked. One of the reasons, but not the sole reason for seeking the repeal of certain provisions of Part

---

[1] Sections 312-316, 320-322, and 330-342.

[2] See para 1.13(2) and (3).

208

X is that there is now sufficient self-regulation. With that introduction we turn to consider the question of repealing sections in Part X.

OPTION 1: REPEALING SECTIONS IN PART X

Repealing groups of sections and relying on the general law

9.3 The question which we consider here is whether there are sections in Part X which could be wholly repealed, leaving transactions in which directors are interested to be regulated by simpler more general principles. The sections which might be dealt with in this way are:[3]

(1) Sections 312-316 (compensation for loss of office etc);

(2) Section 319 (Directors' service contracts);

(3) Sections 320-322 (substantial property transactions); and

(4) Sections 330-344 (loans and similar transactions).

9.4 These sections are set out in Part 4, where there is a detailed commentary on them. Sections 312-316 deal with compensation for loss of office received in different circumstances. We suggest some 11 ways in which the sections might be reformed.[4] Section 319 deals with the length of a director's service contract where it has not been approved by the company in general meeting. We made three suggestions here for the reform of this section.[5] Sections 320-322 deal with substantial property transactions involving the company and a director or a connected person. Some eight suggestions were made for amending these sections.[6] Sections 330-344 deal with loans and related transactions in favour of directors or their connected persons. We made only a small number of suggestions as to how these sections might be reformed but we also invited views as to whether the sections were working satisfactorily.[7]

9.5 It is notable that in relation to sections 312-316, 319 and 320-322 there is now considerable self-regulation. This has developed since these provisions were introduced so that the regulatory landscape for transactions where directors have a conflict of interest is now very different from what it was when they were first enacted. In the case of listed companies, the Combined Code seeks to promote a more principled approach to directors' remuneration, including compensation for loss of office.[8] There is no longer a concern that shareholders in publicly-owned companies will find that the directors have entered into arrangements to compensate them from loss of office in anticipation of a foreseeable takeover being

---

[3] We discuss the question of partial repeal of ss 312-316 in paras 9.22-9.24 below.

[4] (Excluding the option of no change); see paras 4.42-4.61.

[5] (Excluding the option of no change); see paras 4.163-4.171.

[6] (Excluding the option of no change): see paras 4. 190-4.204.

[7] See Part 6 above.

[8] See paras 4.30-4.32 above.

successful, without full disclosure to the offeree shareholders. The length of service contracts for listed companies is now governed by the Combined Code, which seeks adherence to much shorter service contracts than would be permitted without shareholder consent under section 319 and does not run into the difficulty that affects the efficacy of the statutory rule, namely that it can be circumvented by the device of the rolling contract.[9] The Listing Rules and the AIM rules contain detailed provisions on transactions between companies and related parties which extend beyond the transactions which sections 320-322 seek to regulate.[10] It can be argued that it is the shareholders in companies subject to these self-regulatory rules that most need to be protected against abuse by directors of their position, and that accordingly if the position is that they are adequately protected by the system of self-regulation the statutory rules may well no longer be necessary. On the other hand, for private companies and the many public limited companies which are not subject to the Listing Rules nor the AIM rules, the balance between the interests of directors and the interests of shareholders is set not by self-regulatory rules but by the provisions of the Companies Act (particularly Part X) and by the general law.

9.6   If, for those companies to which they apply, reliance were to be placed on self-regulatory rules then a number of considerations arise. First, is there evidence that the rules will be complied with? This issue arises mainly in connection with the provisions of the Combined Code and its predecessors dealing with the length of service contracts.[11] The Hampel Committee[12] considered that it was too soon to reach a considered assessment of the long-term impact of the Cadbury Code, and that it was even more difficult to reach a definitive conclusion on the Greenbury Code, and our position is little better. We have discussed in Part 4 some of the evidence available as to the increasing level of compliance with the various codes dealing with the length of directors' service contracts.[13] Second, is self-regulation backed up by adequate sanctions? The Listing Rules and the City Code are backed up by non-legal remedies as explained in Part 1.[14] As we have also explained in that part, a major difference between self-regulation and Part X lies in the lack of legal remedies for enforcement.[15] This would include criminal sanctions, which we discuss in the next part. The question whether any legal underpinning is required for self-regulatory rules on corporate governance is outside this project but is one of the issues for the DTI's wider review.[16]

9.7   In summary, if sections 312-316, 319, 320-322 and 330-342 were repealed:

---

[9]   See paras 4.161-4.169 above.

[10]   See paras 4.182-4.186 above.

[11]   Para 4.158-4.160 above.

[12]   Final Report (January 1998) paras 1.8 and 1.9.

[13]   See para 4.165 above.

[14]   See para 1.25 above.

[15]   See para 1.38-1.44 above.

[16]   DTI Consultative Paper, paras 3.5-3.7.

(1) the criminal sanctions now available under sections 314(3)[17] and 342[18] would no longer be available;

(2) the civil remedies which are specifically provided for in sections 315[19], 322[20] and 341[21] would no longer be available; and

(3) a person wishing to make a claim in the same circumstances would have to rely on the general law or the remedies provided by any relevant self-regulatory rule.

Practical consequences of relying on the general duties

9.8   If these provisions were repealed, then in addition to any relevant self-regulatory rule, the general law would continue to apply. Moreover, if the case for a statutory statement of directors' duties is adopted, it will be easier for people to know what the duties of directors are under the general law. We set out the law in Part 11 below. As that part demonstrates, directors owe a number of fiduciary duties, including the duty to act in good faith in the interests of their company and the duty not to obtain secret profits from their connection with the company.[22] Reliance could be placed on these principles alone as a means of regulating transactions in which directors are interested. We will seek to explain how the general law would operate and then to draw attention to some possible arguments for and against reliance on it alone.

9.9   If there was no statutory restriction on the payment of compensation for loss of office, then the shareholder who discovered that it had been paid and wanted to recover it for the benefit of the company would have to establish that the payments infringed the rule against secret profits described below.[23] If they were duly authorised contractual payments they would not be caught by this rule. He might also find that the articles gave the directors a discretion to make gratuitous payments: for example regulation 87 in Table A authorises the company to pay gratuities on retirement to executive directors. If the directors were not authorised by the articles to make the payment in question, the claim would lie against the directors who authorised the payment for failure to observe the terms of the company's constitution[24] and against the director who received the payment with knowledge that this was the case.

9.10   The directors usually have power to approve contracts of service in favour of other directors.[25] If the contract which they approve exceeds five years without being

---

[17]   See para 10.13 below.

[18]   See para 10.22 below.

[19]   See para 4.40 above.

[20]   See paras 4.177-4.181 above.

[21]   See para 6.29 above.

[22]   See paras 11.5 and 11.13-11.17 below.

[23]   See para 11.13.

[24]   See para 11.18 below.

[25]   See for example regulation 84 in Table A.

terminable by the company, a claim against them would succeed only if the directors had acted otherwise than in the best interests of the company, for example if their intention was to benefit one of their number rather than the company. But the directors when challenged are likely to say that they had to agree to this length of contract or the director would have refused to take up the executive appointment. If this evidence was believed then there would be no uniform restriction on the contractual period.

9.11   Sections 320-322 restrict substantial property transactions in favour of directors or their connected persons without shareholder approval. If the approval is not obtained the contract can be set aside (unless the right to rescission has been lost) and the directors can be called upon to indemnify the company against loss or to account for any profit which they make. Without sections 320-322, the shareholder can only claim that the transaction was entered into in breach of the duty of loyalty or alternatively that a director failed to disclose some interest in the contract in breach of the no-conflict rule described below.[26] But the articles may well make it impossible to bring a claim under the no conflict rule: for example, if the director's interest was through a company then regulation 84(2)(d) would apply.

9.12   If sections 330-342 were repealed, and there were no prohibitions on making loans or quasi-loans, or entering into credit transactions, it would have to be shown that the directors who approved the transactions acted in breach of duty, for example by approving the transactions, not because they were in the company's best interests, but in order to confer a benefit on the person in whose favour the loan was made. Alternatively the facts might permit a claim on the basis that the director had approved the transaction negligently.[27] But there would be no automatic invalidity or liability to make good any loss suffered by the company.

9.13   Assuming that the claim overcame the hurdles mentioned above, such as the absence of a special statutory remedy and the terms of some enabling provision in the articles, the question would arise whether any claim would lie against a third party who participated in the breach of duty or who received company property. Such actions will lie in the former case only where the third party acted dishonestly.[28] In the latter case the third party must again have knowledge of the breach of duty, but in this case it is probably sufficient that there was a breach of duty of which the third party knew or ought to have known.[29] If the property with which the company parted in the course of the breach of duty can still be identified the court may allow the company to recover that property or to trace it into an asset into which it has been substituted.[30]

---

[26]   See para 11.13.

[27]   See below para 12.8-12.10.

[28]   *Royal Brunei Airlines Bhd v Tan* [1995] 2 AC 378, PC.

[29]   See eg *Eagle Trust plc v SBC Securities (No 3)* [1996] I BCLC 121.

[30]   See generally *Re Diplock* [1951] AC 251.

9.14　In Scotland actions will lie against a third party who assists a director in a breach of his duty or who receives benefit from that breach of duty. In the former case a third party is liable only if he was dishonest or lacking in probity, in the sense that he had actual knowledge of or was wilfully blind to the breach of trust.[31] In the latter case the third party who has given value for the benefit must have acted in bad faith. In other words the third party must have had knowledge or have been put on notice that the benefit was given to him in breach of fiduciary duty.[32] Claims against a third party in possession of company funds or property which have been transferred in breach of duty may be advanced on the ground of unjustified enrichment.[33] There is also authority that where company funds have been alienated in breach of fiduciary duty and converted into assets, those assets can be traced on the basis that the circumstances have given rise to a constructive trust.[34]

9.15　In the above paragraphs we have discussed claims for breach of duty under the general law. The same facts might, if they involved a breach of duty by the directors, also constitute grounds for proceedings for relief under section 459 of the Companies Act 1985 for unfair prejudice.[35] If the proceedings succeeded the court would be able to make a range of orders, including an order that the wrongdoers purchase the shares of the applicant at a value adjusted to take account of the wrongful acts.[36] Likewise if the company went into liquidation or administration, the liquidator or administrator might be able to use the statutory remedies available to them under, for example, section 238 of the Insolvency Act 1985 (transactions at an undervalue).

Substantive differences between sections 312-316, 319, 320-322 and 330-342 and the general law

9.16　If sections 312-316, 319, 320-322 and 330-342 were repealed, a party wishing to bring proceedings would not only find himself entitled to different remedies, he would also find that there were material differences in the substantive law. While there is an overlap between these sections and the general law, there are also some significant differences. The sections are generally wider and thus the benefit of this additional protection would be lost if the sections were simply to be repealed.

9.17　The principal differences between sections 312-6 and the general law are as follows:

---

[31]　*Bank of Scotland v Macleod Paxton Woolard & Co* 1998 SLT 258.

[32]　*Style Financial Services Ltd v Bank of Scotland* 1998 SLT 851. *Thomson v Clydesdale Bank* (1891) 18 R 751, (1893) 20 R (HL) 59.

[33]　*Style Financial Services Ltd and Thomson v Clyesdale Bank Ltd* 1998 SLT 851.

[34]　*Sutman International Inc v Herbage* (unreported) 2 August 1991. Lord Cullen.

[35]　See Shareholder Remedies, Law Commision Consultation Paper No 142, paras 9.21-48.

[36]　*Ibid*, para 10.21

(1) sections 312 and 313 require *prior* disclosure.[37] Under the general law, the secret profit could be ratified after the event;

(2) sections 312 and 313 require disclosure to *all* members.[38] Under the general law, on a resolution, whether for approval or ratification, only shareholders having the right to vote could vote on the resolution;

(3) sections 312 and 313 make the payment unlawful. The consequences of this are discussed in Part 10 below. Under the general law, where the payments constitute a breach of trust, they are not for that reason unlawful;

(4) section 314 creates a trust in favour of former members: Under the general law the secret profit belongs to the company even if its shares have changed hands;[39]

(5) sections 314(3) contains a criminal offence;[40] and

(6) section 314 creates a statutory duty of disclosure.

However we consider that the payments which sections 312-314 seek to prohibit would be recoverable as secret profits under the general law.[41]

9.18 The principal difference between section 319 and the general law is that section 319 by stipulating a period of five years lays down a benchmark for the acceptable length of service contract (where stricter voluntary codes of conduct do not apply) so that it is not necessary to reinvent the wheel on this point in each new case.

9.19 The principal difference between sections 320-322 and the general law is that under most articles directors are able to approve transactions in which one of their number is interested. However in listed companies, and many other companies, directors are not permitted to vote on transactions in which they are interested with specified exceptions.[42] Nonetheless the point remains that a resolution of the company in general meeting would not be required. There are differences between the remedies given by section 322 and the general law, in particular affirmation is only permitted within a reasonable time (ratification could take place under the general law at any time), and under the general law the right of rescission may be

---

[37] See Part 3 above, in particular para 3.57.

[38] See *Re Duomatic Ltd* [1969] 2 Ch 365.

[39] See *Regal (Hastings) v Gulliver* [1967] 2 AC 134 n.

[40] Discussed in Part 10 below.

[41] See for example *Gaskell v Chambers (No 3)* (1858) 26 Beav 360, *Attorney-General v Reid* [1994] 1 AC 324. In Scotland the director would hold the payments as constructive trustee. See W A Wilson and A G M Duncan *Trusts, Trustees and Executors* (2 ed, 1995) 6-63f; and *Stair Memorial Encyclopaedia* vol 24 "Trusts, Trustees and Judicial Factors" para 20.

[42] See para 4.93 above.

available when the third party has constructive as opposed to actual notice of the contravention of the Act.[43]

9.20   The principal differences between sections 330-342 and the general law are as follows:

(1)   under the general law it would have to be shown that the transaction, for example of loan, was not entered into bona fide in the interests of the company. Section 330 creates absolute prohibitions on the type of transactions to which it applies;

(2)   section 342 creates criminal offences for breach;

(3)   section 341 (civil remedies) does not permit ratification or affirmation, which would be defences to a claim for breach of duty under the general law;

(4)   under section 341, rescission is barred by the intervention of a third party who acquires rights in the transaction bona fide and for value only if he has no actual notice of the contravention. Under the general law rescission may be available if the third party has constructive knowledge.

9.21   It would follow if sections 330-342 were repealed that sections 343-344 (record to be maintained by certain banks of transactions and arrangements of the kind described in section 330) would have to be repealed. There would also need to be changes to Schedule 6. On the basis that it was still thought right to require disclosure of loans, quasi-loans and other dealings, the disclosure requirements for the annual accounts would need to be rewritten.

Reasons for repealing sections 312-316, 319, 320-322 and 330-342

9.22   We have referred above to the complexity of these provisions. We have also shown in Part 4 that loopholes exist.[44] The most obvious example of this is in section 319 which fails to prohibit rolling contracts.[45] Section 314 applies only to a limited number of takeover offers and the rules allow an offeror to vote shares which have been assented to his offer in favour of the payment. Section 320 only catches the transfer or acquisition of assets: it does not cover other benefits such as the entry into a contract for the provision of services which confers a substantial benefit on the director. The provisions fail to achieve coherent regulation of self-dealing; for instance it is anomalous that section 319 should single out just one term in a service contract, namely a term about the length of a director's service contract and require it to be approved by the shareholders when it exceeds what is considered desirable for management to have discretion to fix without shareholder approval, when other terms in such a contract, notably those as to the period of

---

[43]   Cf s 322(2)(b).

[44]   See eg, para 4.17 above.

[45]   See paras 4.161-4.162 above.

notice required for termination on notice or predetermined compensation clauses[46] are not subject to shareholder approval.

9.23 Part X would of course be greatly simplified if these provisions were removed.

9.24 There are also possible reforms which would address certain arguments against repeal:

(1) It would be possible to strengthen the no conflict rule under the general law and thus increase the power of shareholders. We have also seen how the general law failed to provide adequate protection to shareholders because the no conflict rule could be modified by the articles.[47] However statute could provide that the shareholders had to approve modifications of this kind to the articles at regular intervals. This would give them the opportunity to consider what restriction on such matters were appropriate for the company on an up to date basis.

(2) If it was felt that the only objection to the repeal of these sections was that the duty to act in the company's best interests, and not to obtain secret profits, was only to be found in the case law, and was therefore not particularly accessible to directors, the introduction of a statutory statement of the duties of directors might address this objection by making the law more accessible and comprehensible.[48]

Reasons for retaining these sections

9.25 The principal reasons for retaining these sections is of course that as shown above they provide protection, in terms of substantive law and remedies, which is superior to that offered by the general law. There is no evidence that such protection is no longer required though in many respects its importance is eclipsed in the case of listed companies by self-regulation. But as we have said, self-regulation rules do not apply to private companies and many public limited companies.[49] Moreover in the case of section 319 the Cadbury Committee considered this was an area for statutory control,[50] and the Greenbury and Hampel Committees did not argue to the contrary. The whole or the majority of the board may have a vested interest. In the case of sections 330-342 the protection the sections provide is not merely for the benefit of members. It is also for the benfit of creditors.

9.26 A system for renewing at regular intervals articles which modify the no conflicts rule might well not work in practice and therefore would not necessarily materially alleviate the present situation. There is considerable shareholder apathy and

---

[46] As to this, see para 4.15 *et seq* above, regarding ss 312-316 of the Companies Act 1985.

[47] See paras 11.49-11.51 for a discussion as to whether this modification is affected by s 310 of the Companies Act 1985.

[48] See Part 14 below.

[49] See para 9.5 above.

[50] See para 4.14, p 31 of its report, quoted at para 4.158 above.

individual shareholders may well have insufficient votes to have any real effect on the voting. It is difficult, therefore, to see that the idea of renewable articles would materially enhance the shareholder's position. Moreover there would have to be a complex statutory scheme worked out so that the consequences of non-compliance with the procedure were readily apparent.

9.27   It is of course correct that the scheme in Part X is not complete and coherent. This is one of the conclusions on the economic considerations in Part 3.[51] This may however be consistent with the "enough but not excessive" principle which we have provisionally identified above.[52] The alternative suggested in Part 3 is that there should be a move to a general principle of disclosure to the shareholders of information concerning self-dealing and other conflicts of interest and directors' interests, with shareholder approval being required only where there was a danger of depletion of corporate assets from particular types of transactions or where the agreed division of powers between the board and the shareholders was in danger of being undermined. It can be said that it is desirable to identify the policy which should apply in the regulation of self-dealing situations. Part 3 can be seen as offering a means of doing this without necessarily increasing the burden of regulation. In this it differs from, for instance the approach in the Principles of Corporate Governance published by the American Law Institute.[53] These identify a duty of fair dealing which imposes a duty upon a director who is materially interested in a transaction to make disclosure to the appropriate organ of the company[54] and the option of obtaining the approval of the company in general meeting or of an independent quorum of the board; in the latter case the terms of the transaction have to be fair (or reasonably be considered fair) to the company. That would be one possible model if it was desired to have a coherent system of regulation for transactions in which a director was interested, but it would involve applying a general rule across all situations in which a director was interested and this may impede commercial affairs and increase the risk of litigation. An 'across the board' approach is not necessarily consistent with the principles which we have provisionally identified in Part 2.

9.28   In approaching the repeal of sections 312-316, 319, 320-322 and 330-342, it is arguably more profitable to ask whether the legislature has required the right level of disclosure and to the right persons and imposed an appropriate approval requirement than treat the question as simply one of repeal or no repeal. In any event the arguments against repeal appear to outweigh those in favour. We would nevertheless welcome consultees' views on this issue.

[51]   See para 3.92(8) above.

[52]   See para 9.2 above.

[53]   Principles of Corporate Governance: Analysis and Recommendations published by the American Law Institute (2 vols, 1994); and see generally para 6.21 of the Hong Kong Consultancy Report in Appendix L below.

[54]   This depends on the organ whose approval is sought.

Consultees are asked whether they consider that sections 312-316, 319, 320-322 and 330-342 should be repealed and reliance placed on the general law.

9.29   We now turn to consider the case for repealing sections 311 and 323 in any event.

Repeal of section 311 (Prohibition on tax-free payments to directors)

311.—(1) It is not lawful for a company to pay a director remuneration (whether as director or otherwise) free of income tax, or otherwise calculated by reference to or varying with the amount of his income tax, or to or with any rate of income tax.

(2) Any provision contained in a company's articles, or in any contract, or in any resolution of a company or a company's directors, for payment to a director of remuneration as above mentioned has effect as if it provided for payment, as a gross sum subject to income tax, of the net sum for which it actually provides.[55]

9.30   This prohibition was introduced by the Companies Act 1947 following a recommendation of the the Cohen Committee.[56] The concern expressed by the Cohen Committee was that shareholders should be able to estimate "the total amount of remuneration before deduction of tax as the amount of tax would vary according to the total income of the director"[57] where companies had agreed to pay them their remuneration as directors free of tax. The Cohen Committee's concerns are difficult to follow. Under general principles of tax law it has been clear at least since decisions of the House of Lords in the 1920s that the tax agreed to be paid by the company would itself be taxable.[58] Moreover, the company's promise to pay the director's tax would appear to be a "benefit received by him otherwise than in cash" for the purposes of Schedule 6, paragraph 1(3)(a), and thus the estimated money value would have to be included in the emoluments of directors required to be disclosed in the notes to the annual accounts.

9.31   The existence of section 311 has arguably become at one and the same time an inconvenient anachronism and an irrelevance. There may be perfectly sensible situations which the section renders illegal, as where an employer wishes to

---

[55]   The predecessor of s 311(2), s 189(2) of the Companies Act 1948, was applied in the Scottish case of *Owens v Multilux Ltd* 1974 SLT 189.

[56]   The Cohen Report, para 88. A similar recommendation had been made by the Company Law Amendment Committee in 1918 (the Wrenbury Committee) on the basis that it was not possible for shareholders to find out how much remuneration was payable by the company (Report of the Company Law Amendment Committee, Cd 9138, para 60) but no action was taken to implement this recommendation. The Greene Committee questioned the need for a prohibition as the tax so paid would be additional remuneration but recommended that there should be obligatory disclosure, on the request of holders of shares carrying 25% of the votes, of the aggregate amount of directors' remuneration, including tax paid where remuneration was agreed to be paid tax-free: Report of the Greene Committee, paras 51 and 52. This recommendation was implemented by ss 128 and 147 of the Companies Act 1929, the sections being repealed and replaced by s 196 of the Companies Act 1948.

[57]   Cohen Report, para 88.

[58]   See *North British Railway Co v Scott* [1923] AC 37, *Hartland v Diggines* [1926] AC 289.

compound a claim to PAYE without involving the director.[59] Increasingly remuneration is given to directors in the form of shares so that the provision has no impact and in addition entitlements to benefits are often measured by reference to the tax rate.

9.32   We provisionally consider shareholders are adequately protected in this matter by the disclosure provisions of Schedule 6 to the Companies Act 1985 and that section 311 should be repealed. Obviously it would generally be imprudent for a board to pay themselves salaries on this basis because of the damage it would do to relations with staff who did not receive this benefit but there are other remedies available to deal with this situation.

Consultees are asked whether they agree with our provisional view that section 311 of the Companies Act 1985 should be repealed.

Repeal of section 323 (Option dealing by directors)

9.33   We set out this section and described its history in paragraphs 4.214-4.218 above. The argument for repeal of section 323 is that the mischief which this section addresses is now adequately dealt with by the provisions of the Criminal Justice Act 1993[60] and the Stock Exchange Model Code.[61] Unlike the Criminal Justice Act 1993, section 323 applies to dealings otherwise than on the basis of unpublished price-sensitive information and to off-market dealings but the fact that section 323 has wider application in these ways is not necessarily a reason for retaining it. It would be open for companies to restrict the option dealing which they permit their directors to do by contract and if institutional investors in listed companies or the Stock Exchange are not satisfied that companies are taking a line on this which sufficiently protects the interests of investors they could require companies to cause their directors to observe some uniform code on option dealings by directors and their families: option dealing may be a matter which is now better regulated by a voluntary code. If a company does not approve of option dealing by any of its directors it would in the last resort be in a position to remove him from office under section 303 of the Companies Act 1985, although it may be difficult to gain the support necessary to pass such a resolution. Our provisional view is that section 323 should be repealed.

Consultees are asked whether they agree with our provisional view that section 323 should be repealed in its entirety.

OPTION 2: CAN PART X BE IMPROVED BY REWRITING?

9.34   Some of the provisions of Part X were drafted in haste, when they were first introduced, to meet particular problems that had arisen. This is particularly the

---

[59]   Discharge of the director's liability for unpaid PAYE would constitute "emoluments" for the purposes of disclosure in the annual accounts under Sched 6, but would not require shareholder approval under s 320 because it would not be a non-cash asset for the purposes of s 739. See para 4.189 above.

[60]   See Sched 2, para 5.

[61]   See para 4.223 above.

case with sections 320-322 and 330-347. Some improvements were made when the Companies Acts were consolidated in 1985.[62] In this option we consider whether sections 318 and 330-344, and 347 (in part) might be improved if they were rewritten more simply.

9.35 There have been a number of developments in legislative drafting since 1985. In particular in November 1995 a project was set up to simplify tax legislation.[63] This project is now underway and a number of documents have been published seeking views on how such simplification would be best achieved. No simplification bills have yet been introduced, but the techniques that can be used to simplify legislation are being identified and refined. It is clear that this project will provide instructive material for other areas of statute law in need of simplification. The Tax Rewrite Project's methods include among other things:

- using a more logical structure;

- using shorter sentences; and

- using modern language.

9.36 In the field of company law Australia has been experimenting with simplifying its Corporations Law using many of the same techniques as the Tax Law Rewrite.

9.37 Another major development has been the decision by the United Kingdom Parliament to introduce explanatory notes with Bills.[64] These will be an expanded and improved version of the old explanatory memoranda and notes on clauses and they will be made publicly available. They will be amended as the Bill goes through Parliament and they will present the main points in the Bill in an objective way.

9.38 This development means that if there is a new Bill to give effect to our recommendations at the end of this project, they will probably be introduced with the new Explanatory Notes, which could be accessible to companies and their advisers when the Bill becomes law. This development taken on its own should lead to some improvement in the comprehensibility of legislation to the layman. It will also mean that there will be less cause to have in a Bill material which is merely narrative to help the reader know where to go in the Act. The introduction of notes however may still leave a role for redrafting the statute.

---

[62] For example, minor amendments to ss 320, 322, 343 and 346. This limited revision was achieved through the mechanism of two Orders in Council (SI 1984/134 and SI 1984/1169), short-circuiting the normal parliamentary procedure applicable to consolidating bills, on the basis that the consolidating Act would incorporate any amendments jointly recommended by the Law Commission and Scottish Law Commission. See Law Commission Report No 126 and Scottish Law Commission Report No 83 (1983) Cmnd 9114; and Law Commission Report No 136 and Scottish Law Commission Report No 87 (1984) Cmnd 9272. See also the Companies Act 1981, s 116 (repealed).

[63] The project was initiated pursuant to s 160 of the Finance Act 1995: see generally, The Path to Simplification, A Background Paper (December 1995).

[64] See the second report of the Select Committee on Modernisation of the House of Commons HC (1997-98) 389, 3 December 1997.

9.39   Parliamentary Counsel has prepared a redraft of the provisions of sections 330-344 and part of section 347 using:

- shorter sentences;

- more logical structure;

- provisions to guide the reader;

- formulae;

- splitting up more complex propositions; and

- more modern language.

Counsel's draft may be found in Appendix B below. This draft is purely for illustrative purposes. Considerable further work would be required before it could be introduced into Parliament.[65]

9.40   Consultees will notice that the provisions of the draft are not simpler in substance than those in the existing Act. It is only the language which is simplified. To achieve simplicity in this area there would have to be a decision that some of the restrictions or exemptions could be made more simple or be dispensed with altogether. Only in that way will any substantial progress be made towards cutting back on the sheer volume of regulation in the Companies Acts.

9.41   We now give an example of how the sections might be simplified if the policy itself were simplified.

9.42   Section 318 could be dramatically reduced in length by, for example, the following steps:

(1)   redrafting section 318(1) so that in lieu of paragraphs (a) to (c) it simply requires the company to keep at its registered office copies of its directors' contracts of service (whether with the company itself or a subsidiary) or to the extent that they were not written, memoranda of their terms;

(2)   removing the choice given by the existing section to companies to keep the necessary copies and memoranda at places other than their registered office. This would eliminate the need for subsections (2), (3) and (4); and

(3)   deleting subsections (5) and (11).[66]

9.43   These amendments may reduce the section to about one-third of its present length. Further reduction would be achieved by amalgamating the provisions for inspection of the register in subsection (8) and (9) with the comparable provisions for inspection of the register of debenture holders (section 191(4) and (5)); the

---

[65]   In particular, no account has been taken of consequential amendments or transitional provisions.

[66]   See paras 4.140-4.147 above.

register of interests in shares (section 219(3) and (4)); the register of directors and secretaries (section 288(4) and (5)); the register of members (section 356(5) and (6))[67] and the register of charges (section 423(3) and (4)). The reader would then have to look at more than one section: section 318 would not be a self contained code dealing with all aspects of disclosure of service contracts. Accordingly, the issues for consideration are (a) would the section, as simplified, still be clear to users? and (b) is it acceptable to dispense with the choice of location given by section 318(3), at least for the purpose of simplifying the Act?

Consultees are thus asked:

(i) to consider carefully the re-draft of sections 330-344 (and part of section 347) set out in Appendix B, and to give their views on the re-draft generally;

(ii) whether they consider that the provisions of Part X are now familiar to users so that it would be better not to disturb the existing layout and language;

(iii) whether they consider that redrafting in this manner represents a significant and worthwhile improvement in the existing text;

(iv) whether section 318 should be simplified in the manner indicated in paragraphs 9.42-9.43 above.

---

[67] In this case the court can also order that the company gives a copy of the register or index of members to the party seeking inspection.

PART 10
SHOULD PART X OF THE COMPANIES ACT 1985 BE DECRIMINALISED?

INTRODUCTION

10.1 The view was expressed in Part 3 that there is a role for criminal sanctions where, for instance, there are high costs in detecting wrongdoing and where there are limited incentives for private parties to pursue litigation, perhaps because litigation is too costly in time and effort. It was also said that if criminal sanctions were brought into being for these reasons they should not be disproportionately severe, since this might discourage regulatory authorities from seeking them and courts from imposing them, which would in turn diminish their deterrent value. Excessive severity should therefore be avoided, and to this end a provision which is criminalised should normally be tightly drawn rather than open-textured.[1]

10.2 The contrary view on the usefulness of criminal sanctions has also been expressed. The DTI's Consultative Paper records that it is a common suggestion that the existing Companies Act too readily invokes criminal penalties, when civil remedies would be more appropriate.[2] Others point to the absence of prosecutions under Part X. This is borne out by our enquiries which show that in the period 1990/6, practically no prosecutions are recorded under this Part of the Act.[3]

10.3 The object of this Part is to pursue these issues in more detail and to look at other arguments for or against decriminalising Part X. One of the aims of our review of Part X[4] is to see if Part X can be simplified; and it clearly would be simplified if the criminal sanctions were removed.

10.4 We have first to define our benchmarks for criminalisation in Part X. The mere fact that there are no prosecutions does not mean that the sanctions serve no purpose or, of course, that breaches do not occur. To define our benchmarks we have started from the proposition that these offences are "regulatory offences", that is offences designed to help enforce the rules in this Part of the Act.[5] Whether

---

[1] Paras 3.79-3.84 above.

[2] Para 6.6.

[3] The Home Office keeps records of 'principal offences' under a particular section where the offence committed is an indictable one. A 'principal offence' is the most serious of a number of offences charged. The Home Office has no such recorded prosecutions in relation to offences under Part X during the period January 1990 to December 1996 (the latest date for which figures are available). Prosecutions for summary offences under Part X are kept by the Home Office only as part of a global figure relating to all summary offences under the Companies Acts. The DTI, on the other hand, keeps figures for all offences committed under each section of the Companies Acts. In their records, dating back to 1991, they have just one recorded prosecution under the sections in Part X, which was for a summary offence under s 326(2).

[4] See para 1.11 above.

[5] There is useful discussion of regulatory offences in general and in other fields in the literature: see for example AI Ogus, *Regulation: Legal Form and Economic Theory* (1994); G

those rules are justified is considered elsewhere in this consultation paper.[6] Accordingly in this part we proceed on the basis that the rules which the offences criminalise are appropriate rules in themselves. If that turns out not to be the view reached in our final recommendation, then it follows that no question of criminalising that rule arises.

10.5 Our provisional view is that there are two benchmarks against which regulatory offences should be tested. The first is *proportionality*. A balance has to be struck between the interests of the individual and the interests of the State. A person should not be subject to criminal sanctions for his actions except and to the extent that it is necessary to impose such sanctions for the public good. If for instance there are adequate civil or other sanctions available, criminal sanctions are not justified. But they are justified for instance where the civil sanctions are not effective or there is a public interest in punishing the breach which means that the victim should not have the right to decide whether sanctions should be sought. Or there may be no identifiable victim so that unless criminal proceedings are available there is in fact no sanction.

10.6 The second benchmark, in our provisional view, is *efficiency*. If there is a role for a criminal sanction,[7] it must be one that works and makes a tangible contribution to enforcement of the law. It is not efficient to make an offence so sophisticated that proceedings are never brought because of the difficulty in obtaining evidence or because of the cost in bringing the proceedings. It must be one that the prosecuting authorities can use without excessive administrative cost. This is particularly so in the case of proceedings under Part X. Though we know from the statistics that prosecutions are extremely rare, we are told by the DTI that if minor infringements are discovered, they are able as the law stands to indicate that a prosecution might be brought in future if a further infringement occurs. Also, where a Part X infringement emerges in the course of investigation of more serious criminal conduct, the usual practice would be to charge the more serious offences and not pursue the Part X offences.

10.7 This demonstrates another important point, which is that the mere fact that an offence exists on the statute book does not mean that the prosecuting authorities are bound to pursue criminal proceedings in respect of every breach that they discover. In England and Wales, prosecuting authorities follow the code for Crown prosecutors,[8] which sets out an evidential test and a public interest test. If a case

---

Richardson, "Strict Liability for Regulatory Crime" [1987] Crim LR 295; Rowan-Robinson and others, "Crime and Regulation" [1988] Crim L R 211; Coffee, "Does unlawful mean criminal? Reflection on the Disappearing Tort/Crime Distinction in America Law," in *Foundations of Corporate Law*, R Romano ed (1993).

[6] For instance, we consider in Part 9 whether s 323, for which the Act imposes a criminal sanction, should be repealed: see para 9.33 above.

[7] Its role may be as a deterrent; see para 10.7 below.

[8] Issued by the Director of Public Prosecutions under the Prosecution of Offences Act 1985, s 10. The DTI, which follows the Code, is able to prosecute all offences under Part X. In Scotland, where prosecutions are controlled by the Lord Advocate, the Procurator Fiscal is responsible to the Lord Advocate for dealing with alleged offences in the most appropriate way, having regard to the public interest. He can decide to take no proceedings or he can select one of a number of alternatives to prosecution. It is neither necessary nor appropriate

passes the evidential test it must still pass the public interest test before criminal proceedings can be brought. The relevant factors to be considered in the case of a Part X offence would include the question whether the defendant was in a position of authority or trust and whether the offence was likely to be repeated. The fact that the penalty is likely to be small or that the defendant acted under a misunderstanding are some of the factors that would be taken into account in deciding whether to bring a prosecution. There is a distinct overlap between these factors going to fairness to the individual (which is an aspect of proportionality) and efficiency, since there may be little purpose from the economic point of view in prosecuting a person whom it is reasonably clear will not commit the offence again. Public resources for enforcement of regulatory offences must necessarily be finite. Likewise a criminal sanction is not efficient if it covers ground well covered by civil sanctions already. However, a criminal sanction can still be efficient even if its principal function is as a deterrent.

10.8   On the basis that the question of removing the criminal sanctions will involve the application of the considerations outlined above we turn to examine the following matters

(1)   the various specific criminal offences in Part X;[9]

(2)   the alternative sanctions for these breaches;[10]

(3)   whether civil penalties would be appropriate;[11]

(4)   the arguments for and against attaching criminal penalties to breaches of Part X;[12] and

(5)   whether there should be a new criminal offence for breach of section 312.[13]

We then ask consultees whether Part X should be decriminalised and whether, if the criminal sanctions are retained, changes should be made.

10.9   We point out at the outset that (with one exception) we are concerned only with the existing criminal offences in Part X. We are also not concerned with the issue

for the Procurator Fiscal to institute court proceedings in every case reported to him, even though there may be sufficient evidence that a crime has been committed. The Procurator Fiscal is entrusted by the Lord Advocate with considerable discretion and uses his professional judgment in the light of his knowledge of the particular problems or features of his own jurisdiction, the Lord Advocate's policy in respect of certain classes of case and Crown Counsel's instructions in respect of individual cases when deciding whether to institute criminal proceedings or to take alternative actions. See the statement of the Lord Advocate, Lord Mackay of Drumadoon to the Scottish Grand Committee (1996 SLT (News) 51) and Renton & Brown *Criminal Procedure* (6th ed) para 4.01.

[9]   See paras 10.13-10.23 below.

[10]   See paras 10.24-10.33 below.

[11]   See paras 10.34-10.36 below.

[12]   See paras 10.37-10.39 below.

[13]   See para 10.40 below.

of enforcing other obligations in the Companies Acts or the wider issue of preventing or punishing fraud.[14] As explained, we also proceed in this part on the basis that the prohibitions which Part X criminalises are appropriate as prohibitions in themselves and in addition that there is no regulatory body[15] charged with monitoring or enforcing them. We have not reviewed the punishment that can be given for commission of these offences.[16] We refer below to the effect on civil rights and remedies of the criminal offences but we do not see this as an argument for or against decriminalisation since the civil consequences can if thought appropriate be replicated in the section even if the criminal sanction is removed.

(1) DESCRIPTION OF THE VARIOUS OFFENCES IN PART X

Introduction - mens rea and the concept of "officer in default"

10.10   In paragraphs 10.13-10.23, we set out the criminal offences specifically created by Part X.[17] Several of the offences refer to the expression "officer in default". This is defined in section 730(5) as follows:

> (5) For the purpose of any enactment in the Companies Acts which provides that an officer of a company or other body who is in default is liable to a fine or penalty, the expression "officer who is in default" means any officer of the company or other body who knowingly and wilfully authorises or permits the default, refusal or contravention mentioned in the enactment.

10.11   To fall within this definition the officer must have acted "knowingly" and "wilfully". For the purpose of the first requirement it is sufficent if the defendant knew the facts which constitute the offence:[18] there is no need to show that he knew that he was committing an offence or that he was acting with any dishonest intent. To have acted "wilfully", the officer must have acted "deliberately and

---

[14]   Had we been so concerned, we might have wished to seek consultees views on whether there should be separate offences in the same circumstances but with the added ingredient of intention to defraud.

[15]   Such as the new Financial Services Authority.

[16]   As to which see Sched 24. Ignoring the impact of daily default fines, the offences which Sched 24 treats as most serious are those created by ss 323(2), 324(7), 328(6), 342(1), 342(2) and 342(3) where the maximum penalty is two years' imprisonment.

[17]   Sections 311-313 make payments unlawful but in our view breach of these sections does not, in the context of Part X, constitute an offence at common law. This is because Part X contains a number of specific offences for which the mode of trial and punishment is set out in Sched 22: see eg, *R v Lennox-Wright* [1973] Crim LR 529 (a case under the Human Tissue Act 1961).

[18]   *Burson v Bevan* [1908] 2 Ch 240, 247, per Lord Parker CJ (the case concerned civil proceedings under the Companies Act 1900, section 5). Nelsonian knowledge may suffice: see *Mallon v Allon* [1964] 1 QB 385 at 394, per Lord Parker CJ (a case under the Betting and Gaming Act 1960).

intentionally, not by accident or inadvertence, but so that the mind of the person who does the act goes with it".[19]

10.12   In the case of the remaining offences in Part X, where the concept of "officer in default" is not used, the offences are not offences of strict liability but require similar mens rea.[20] Section 323 requires the wrongdoer to "purchase" options. Section 314(3) and 317(5) create offences if a director fails to do that which it is his duty to do. It seems to us in these cases that the law requires the prosecution to show that the alleged offender knew the facts which constitute the wrongful act or omission. In the usual way, ignorance of the law would be no defence.

Summary of specific offences in Part X

Section 314(3): Director's duty of disclosure on takeover etc[21]

10.13   This section renders a director, who fails to take reasonable steps to ensure disclosure to offeree shareholders of any loss of office payment to be made to him on the takeover of a company, liable to a fine.[22] Moreover, any person properly required by the director to include those particulars in or send them with the notice of offer sent to offeree shareholders, who fails to do so, is also liable to a fine.

Section 317(7): Directors to disclose interest in contracts[23]

10.14   A director who fails to declare an interest in a contract or proposed contract[24] with the company is liable to a fine.[25]

Section 318(8): Directors' service contracts to be open to inspection[26]

10.15   A company or every officer of it who is in default[27] is liable to a fine if it fails to:

(a)   keep copies or particulars of all directors service contracts as required by section 318(1) and (5);

(b)   permit inspection of these copies;[28] and

---

[19]   *R v Senior* [1893] 1QB 283, 291 (a case under the Prevention of Cruelty to Children Act 1894).

[20]   Sections 324(7), 342 and 343.

[21]   See para 4.33 above.

[22]   Section 314(3).

[23]   See para 4.62 *et seq* above.

[24]   Including any transaction or arrangement (whether or not constituting a contract) made after 22 December 1980: s 317(5).

[25]   Section 317(7).

[26]   See para 4.119 above.

[27]   Section 730(5).

[28]   Section 318(7).

(c)   advise the registrar of companies of the place where the copies are kept, or any change in that place, (if not the registered office of the company). [29]

Section 322B(4): Contracts with sole members who are directors[30]

10.16   The terms of an unwritten contract between the sole member of a company and the company itself must be set out in a written memorandum or recorded in the minutes of a directors' meeting. The company and every officer of it who is in default[31] is liable to a fine.[32]

Section 323(1): Prohibition on directors dealing in share options[33]

10.17   A director who purchases put or call options in listed shares or debentures of his company, or any body corporate in the same group, is guilty of an offence.[34]

Section 324(7): Duty of director to disclose shareholdings in own company[35]

10.18   Under section 324, a director is required to notify the company in writing of prescribed details of his interests in shares or debentures of his company, or any company in its group and any change in those interests. Section 328 extends the interests which must be disclosed to those of the spouse and infant children of the director.

10.19   A person who fails duly to discharge these obligations, or in purported discharge makes a statement to the company which he knows to be false, or recklessly makes a statement which is false, commits an offence.[36] The offence created by section 324 can only be prosecuted in England and Wales with the authority of the Secretary of State or the Director of Public Prosecutions.[37]

Section 326(2): Sanctions for non-compliance with section 325 etc[38]

10.20   Section 326 provides sanctions in relation to failures to maintain an accurate register of those directors' interests. Failure to comply with specified provisions of this section and Schedule 13 renders the company and every officer of it who is in default liable to a fine.

---

[29]   Section 318(8).

[30]   See para 4.210 above.

[31]   Section 730(5).

[32]   Section 322B(4). Compare ss 382A(3) and 382B(3) of the Companies Act 1985.

[33]   See para 4.214 above.

[34]   Section 323(2).

[35]   See para 5.6 above.

[36]   Section 324(7); s 328(7).

[37]   Sections 324(8) and 732. See n 8 above for the position in Scotland.

[38]   See para 5.27 above.

Section 329(3): Duty to notify stock exchange of matters notified under preceding section[39]

10.21 If a company fails to notify any recognised stock exchange,[40] other than an overseas investment exchange on which its shares or debentures are listed, of any matter notified to it under sections 324 and 328, the company and every officer of the company in default is guilty of an offence. In England and Wales, the offence created by section 329 can only be prosecuted with the authority of the Secretary of State or the Director of Public Prosecutions.[41]

Section 342(1)-(3): Criminal penalties for breach of section 330 in relation to prohibited loans[42]

10.22 This section relates to transactions in breach of section 330[43] entered into by a "relevant company." This is defined as a public company, but also applies to private companies where there is a public company in the group.[44] An offence is committed:

(a) by a director who authorises or permits such a company to enter into a transaction or arrangement knowing or having reasonable cause to believe that section 330 (general restriction on loans to directors) was being breached;[45]

(b) by a relevant company which enters into a transaction or arrangement for one of its directors or a director of its holding company knowing or having reasonable cause to believe that the company was breaching section 330, unless it can show that at the time the transaction or arrangement was entered into it did not know the relevant circumstances.;[46] or

(c) by a person who procures a relevant company to enter into a transaction or arrangement knowing or having reasonable cause to believe that the transaction or arrangement was in breach of section 330.[47]

Section 343: Record of transactions not disclosed in company accounts

10.23 Certain requirements exist in relation to the disclosure (in the form of a statement available for inspection by members of the company) of loans, quasi-loans and

---

[39] See para 5.31 above.

[40] Within the meaning of the Financial Services Act 1986.

[41] Sections 329(3) and 732. See n 8 above for the position in Scotland.

[42] See para 6.31 above.

[43] See paras 6.10-6.12 above.

[44] Section 331(6).

[45] Section 342(2).

[46] Section 342(2) and (5).

[47] Section 242(3).

credit transactions for banks.[48] Failure to comply with this renders the company and its directors guilty of an offence.[49] It is a defence if all reasonable steps were taken to secure compliance.[50] Moreover a person is not guilty of the offence purely due to being a shadow director.[51]

(2) ARE THERE ALTERNATIVE SANCTIONS FOR THESE BREACHES?

10.24 The criminal sanctions discussed above are but part of a range of sanctions available for breach of the above provisions, and the range of sanctions should be seen as a whole. The main alternative sanctions are the civil sanctions. There are however circumstances in which other remedies apply, and we discuss below the interaction of the criminal sanctions with winding up, director's disqualification, unfair prejudice and breaches of the self-regulatory rules discussed in relation to the relevant sections in Part 4. There would be less need for criminal sanctions in Part X if adequate alternative sanctions exist.[52]

(i) Civil remedies for breach of those provisions of Part X which also involve criminal sanctions

10.25 For the purpose of civil remedies, the sections in Part X with which we are here concerned fall into three groups:

(1) those for which the Act provides a code of civil remedies (sections 314-315 and 330-341);

(2) those for which the Act does not provide any remedies over and above the general law (sections 317 and 323); and

(3) those for which the question of civil remedies does not usually arise because they are obligations to give notice, put documents on display etc (sections 318, 322A, 326, 329 and 343).

As to the first group, civil proceedings will lie for breach of section 314 (director's duty of disclosure on takeover, etc). Indeed the principal remedy is set out in section 315(1) and comprises a statutory trust of the payment that should have been disclosed in favour of former shareholders. The Act also sets out the civil remedies which will lie if a company enters into transactions or arrangements in breach of section 330: if the company is a relevant company the offences specified in section 342 will be committed.

10.26 As to the second group, comprising section 317 and section 323, we have noted in paragraphs 4.62 and 4.214 above the position under the general law. In short, if a director fails to comply with this duty under section 317, he will probably also fail to comply with this duty to disclose secret profits to the company in the general

---

[48] Section 343(2) to (5).

[49] Section 343(8).

[50] Section 343(8)(a).

[51] Section 343(8)(b).

[52] See para 3.84 above.

meeting and in those circumstances he will be liable for breach of duty. Indeed as noted in Part 3[53] the liability of the fiduciary is in many situations not just compensatory; the law removes the profit that the fiduciary may get. As regards section 323, the counterparty will not be bound as the contract is unlawful.[54] Property transferred will normally be irrecoverable.

10.27   As to the third group, civil remedies to enforce a right to inspect a service contract and to enforce a right to inspect and receive a copy of the register of directors' interests are given by section 318(9) and 326(6) respectively. But in the remaining provisions an individual complainant is unlikely to want a remedy to compel compliance (see eg section 322B) or he is unlikely to know about the information which ought to have been disclosed in any event (sections 324, 322B, 326, 329 343).

(ii) Winding up by the court

10.28   Persistent non-compliance could provide grounds for winding up under the Insolvency Act 1986 on the "just and equitable" ground.[55]

(iii) Company Directors Disqualification Act 1986

10.29   Persistent default in compliance with a director's obligations under Part X could result in the court finding that the director was unfit to be a director.[56] Although disqualification proceedings are not penal, the making of a disqualification order does involve a substantial interference with the freedom of the individual and penal consequences for the director.[57] In the context of a breach of statutory provisions regarding accounting records, Sir Donald Nicholls V-C observed:[58]

> It may be that, despite the disqualification provisions having been in operation for some years, there is still a lingering feeling in some quarters that a failure to file annual accounts and so forth is a venial sin. If this is still so, the sooner the attitude is corrected the better it will be. Judicial observations to this effect have been made before, but they bear repetition.

---

[53]   Paras 3.73-3.78 above.

[54]   The rights of a person who is a party to an illegal contract will be considered in the Law Commission's forthcoming consultation paper on illegal transactions.

[55]   Section 122(1)(g).

[56]   Namely under s 6 of the Act. Section 3 of the Act gives the court power to disqualify a person who has been in persistent breach of filing requirements under the Act: see eg *Re Artic Engineering Ltd* [1986] 1 WLR 686. Mithani and Wheeler, *The Disqualification of Company Directors* (1996) contains a very full analysis of the law. 1219 disqualification orders were notified to the Secretary of State in 1996-7 arising under the CDDA 1986.

[57]   See *Re-Lo Line Electric Motors Ltd* [1988] Ch 477.

[58]   *Secretary of State for Trade and Industry v Ettinger and another; Re Swift 736 Ltd* [1993] BCLC 896, 900.

10.30   However, it would probably be unusual for a director to be disqualified on the ground of unfitness solely on the basis of a failure to file returns or accounts.[59]

(iv) Section 459 unfair prejudice remedy.

10.31   In a serious case, non-compliance with Part X could amount to the conduct of a company's affairs in an unfairly prejudicial manner. This would enable the court to grant relief under section 461 of the Companies Act 1985, including an order for the purchase of the applicant's shares at their fair value.[60]

(v) Self-regulatory rules

10.32   Failure to put a service contract on display may result in a breach of the Listing Rules.[61] The consequences of a breach of the Listing Rules are set out in paragraph 1.25 above. With this exception, while provisions of the self-regulatory rules back up the provisions of the Act which carry criminal penalties, they do not in general cover the same ground.

(vi) Investigation

10.33   If there are circumstances suggesting possible contravention of sections 323, 324 or 328, the Secretary of State may appoint inspectors to carry out an investigation.[62]

(3) ARE CIVIL PENALTIES APPROPRIATE?

10.34   Under section 242A a company is liable to a civil penalty where accounts are not delivered in time.[63] The penalty is recoverable by the registrar without an order of the court. The question arises whether this civil penalty approach would be of value in connection with reform of the Part X criminal provisions.[64] A similar approach is proposed in the context of financial services. On 6 May 1998 the Chief Secretary to the Treasury announced a package of measures to tackle market abuse, by means of providing the Financial Services Authority (FSA) with

---

[59]   Lord Hoffmann, in "The Fourth Annual Leonard Sainer Lecture" (1998) Co Law 194 stated: "I cannot say I have ever heard of a director being disqualified solely on the basis of a failure to file accounts".

[60]   Shareholder Remedies, Law Com No 246, para 3.30.

[61]   See para 4.125 above.

[62]   Section 446 of the Companies Act 1985.

[63]   In 1996-7, 50,846 private companies and 657 public companies were up to 3 months late in England and Wales, and a total of £5.41m was levied. A further £12.88m was levied on other firms in 1996-7 for longer periods of late filing. In the same year in Scotland, 3,350 private companies and 35 public companies were up to 3 months late and a total of £335,000 was levied. A further £740,750 was levied on other firms in 1996-7 for longer periods of late filing. The costs incurred by Companies House in 1996-7 for administering the system of late filing penalties for the whole of the UK was £1.52m.

[64]   It would not be possible to obtain punitive damages. The circumstances of a breach of Part X would not satisfy the conditions laid down by Lord Devlin in *Rookes v Barnard* [1964] AC 1129 because it would fail the cause of action test, which restricts the award of damages to those situations where punitive damages were awarded pre *Rookes*. See Aggravated, Exemplary and Restitutionary Damages, Law Com No 247 (1997) pp 53-63.

additional powers.[65] These include giving the FSA the power to make rules and levy fines where breaches occur.[66] The legislative proposals to achieve this have now been published.[67]

10.35　A similar approach has been taken in the Social Security Act 1998 in relation to the recovery of unpaid national insurance.[68] Where it appears to the Secretary of State that the failure to make payment is attributable to the fraud or neglect of an officer of the company which ought to have made payment, he can serve a personal liability notice on the officer requiring him to pay a specified sum and interest. If there is more than one officer considered to be at fault the total amount is to be apportioned between them by the Secretary of State. There is a limited right of appeal against the Secretary of State's findings to the appeal tribunal set up under the Social Security Act 1998. It will be noted that the object of this provision is not to punish but to secure the recovery of unpaid national insurance.

10.36　Our provisional view is that there are clear advantages from the point of view of efficiency in having civil penalties in some cases, for instance where, as with the late filing of accounts, the facts do not admit of dispute, and where it is thought necessary to step up enforcement. On the other hand civil penalties would not be efficient if they depended on questions of fact of a wide variety so that in fairness the individual concerned would have to be given a right of appeal. (While there is no equivalent of the appeal tribunal established by the Social Security Act 1998, there could be a right of appeal to any court having jurisdiction to deal with application under the Companies Acts).[69] Likewise, it is unlikely to be efficient to have civil penalties if public resources would be involved in enforcing them disproportionate to the benefit to be obtained. If civil penalties were more widely imposed under Part X, there would have to be resources allocated to serving the notices and dealing with any right of appeal. At this stage, we are not aware that there is any need to do this but would be grateful for consultees' views.

(4) THE ARGUMENTS FOR AND AGAINST ATTACHING CRIMINAL SANCTIONS TO BREACHES OF PART X

10.37　We take first the arguments against criminalisation of Part X:

---

[65]　Written Answer, *Hansard* (HC), 6 May 1998, vol 311, cols 383-384.

[66]　Criminal offences for market manipulation and insider dealing will however be retained. See further Market Abuse Part 1: Consultation on a draft Code of Market Conduct; Part 2: Draft Code of Market Conduct published by the Financial Services Authority, June 1998.

[67]　Financial Services and Markets Bill: A Consultation Document (July 1998), para 13.4. See paras 1.25, n 28 and para 5.32, n 39 above.

[68]　Section 64, which inserts ss 121C and 121D into the Social Security Administration Act 1992.

[69]　Section 744 of the Companies Act 1985 defines "the court" in relation to a company as any court having jurisdiction to wind up the company. In England and Wales this includes the High Court and any county court having bankruptcy jurisdiction over the company in question. In Scotland this would include the Court of Session and any Sheriff Court having bankruptcy jurisdiction over the company in question. See ss 117 and 120 of the Insolvency Act 1986.

- The criminal offences are rarely enforced, and this is evidence that the offences are not required.

- It would greatly simplify Part X if these various offences were removed.

- It is not right or fair to subject conduct to criminal penalties if those offences are not required in the public interest and are not enforced.

- The offences have no deterrent value.

10.38 We now turn to the arguments in favour of criminalisation. First the fact that the offences are not prosecuted does not mean that the existence of the offences serves no purpose. We know that the prosecuting authorities do threaten prosecutions. It is also clear that the existence of a criminal penalty will often concentrate the mind of a director who might be tempted to disregard the fact that he was breaching the law. The proposed empirical survey may throw some light on the behavioural effect of criminal sanctions in Part X. In addition, when the DTI consulted on the question whether the criminal sanctions should be removed from section 151 of the Companies Act 1985 (prohibition on financial assistance, which, in many situations, unlike the offences in Part X, does not create a bright-line criminal offence)[70] many respondents favoured retaining the criminal sanctions for the company's officers (as opposed to the company itself). Several respondents expressly said that the criminal sanctions acted as a deterrent.[71]

10.39 Second, even where alternative civil sanctions exist, there are grounds for retaining each of the criminal offences in Part X. In the case of sections 314(3) and 318(5) they underpin the director's duty to disclose information which it may well be he is the only person within the company to have. In the case of the offences created by sections 318, 322B, 324, 326 and 329 which involve disclosure of information, there may well be no individual who is concerned to take civil proceedings to enforce compliance. In the case of section 323, the real victims (if there are any) are the company and other users of the market. Their interests in the observance of the section can really only be reflected by imposing criminal sanctions. That leaves section 342; the Act gives substantial civil remedies in the event of the prohibitions on loans and similar transactions. However the victims here will often be creditors in a subsequent insolvency. By that time the civil sanctions are equivalent to shutting the stable door after the horse has bolted. Therefore, given the scale of the loss that can be inflicted on creditors, a criminal offence is arguably appropriate.

---

[70] Phrase taken from para 3.82 above.

[71] The British Venture Capital Association, the Law Society, the Law Society of Scotland, the Institute of Chartered Accountants in Scotland, the Stock Exchange and Osborne Clark all considered that criminal sanctions acted as an important deterrent. Only two respondents, Professor Sealy and Michael Wyatt, argued that they were not.

(5) SHOULD A NEW OFFENCE BE CREATED WHERE PAYMENTS ARE MADE IN BREACH OF SECTIONS 312–316 OF THE COMPANIES ACT 1985?

10.40 We have referred in paragraph 4.25 to the concern that companies are paying compensation for loss of office ostensibly using the exemption section 316(3) when they were not entitled to it. We have sought consultees' views and evidence on this. We have suggested a new disclosure requirement for the annual accounts.[72] The question arises whether if consultees consider that there is significant non-compliance with the section, a new criminal offence should be created for breach of section 312. The offence would be committed by the company which made the payment, any director who knew the facts which gave rise to the need for disclosure and approval of the payment under section 312 and that such disclosure and approval had not taken place, and the director who (with the same knowledge) received the payment.

Consultees are asked:

(i) whether they agree with our provisional view that the two benchmarks to be applied in determining whether there should be criminal liability for breaches of Part X are proportionality and efficiency;

(ii) whether any of the criminal offences in Part X should be repealed;

(iii) whether, if any provision of Part X is decriminalised, the civil remedies should remain as if the provision had not been decriminalised;

(iv) whether, if any provision of Part X is decriminalised, civil penalties along the lines of section 242A should replace any of the existing offences;

(v) whether a new offence should be created where payments are made in breach of sections 312–316 of the Companies Act 1985 along the lines described in paragraph 10.40 above.

---

[72] See para 4.60 above.

235

SECTION B
THE CASE FOR A STATUTORY STATEMENT OF DIRECTORS' DUTIES UNDER THE GENERAL LAW

PART 11
FIDUCIARY DUTIES: THE CURRENT LAW

INTRODUCTION

11.1   In this part we examine the fiduciary duties of directors under the general law, the persons to whom those duties are owed and the circumstances in which the company in general meeting can ratify a breach of those duties. We then examine the ways in which the liabilities of directors can be capped, and describe D&O insurance which can be used to protect directors.[1]

DIRECTORS AS FIDUCIARIES

11.2   A director is not strictly a trustee but in respect of the company's property he may come under the same liabilities as a trustee. In *Re Lands Allotment Co*[2] Lindley LJ said:

> Although directors are not properly speaking trustees, yet they have always been considered and treated as trustees of money which comes to their hands or which is actually under their control; and ever since joint stock companies were invented directors have been held liable to make good moneys which they have misapplied upon the same footing as if they were trustees ...

11.3   It is well established that directors are fiduciaries. That term is not capable of comprehensive definition but the characteristics of the fiduciary relationship can be identified and the principal duties stated:

> A fiduciary is someone who has undertaken to act for or on behalf of another in a particular matter in circumstances which give rise to a relationship of trust and confidence. The distinguishing obligation of a fiduciary is the obligation of loyalty. The principal is entitled to the single-minded loyalty of his fiduciary. This core liability has several facets. A fiduciary must act in good faith; he must not make a profit out of his trust; he must not place himself in a position where his duty and his interest may conflict; he may not act for his own benefit or the benefit of a third person without the informed consent of his principal. This is not intended to be an exhaustive list, but it is sufficient to indicate the nature of fiduciary obligations. They are the

---

[1]   The discussion on capping liabilities and D&O insurance applies also to liability for breach of the duty of care, which we examine in the next part.

[2]   [1894] 1 Ch 616 at p 631; cf [1891–94] All ER 1032 at p 1034.

236

defining characteristics of the fiduciary. As Dr Finn pointed out in his classic work *Fiduciary Obligations* (1977) p 2, he is not subject to fiduciary obligations because he is a fiduciary; it is because he is subject to them that he is a fiduciary.[3]

The classification of directors' fiduciary duties

11.4   We consider the fiduciary duties of directors under the following headings: loyalty,[4] proper purpose,[5] no fetters on discretion,[6] the no-conflict and no-profit rules,[7] the duty to act in accordance with the company's constitution,[8] and the duty to deal fairly as between different classes of shareholders.[9] There are other views as to how they should be classified.[10] For instance, one textbook[11] states that there is one fundamental duty - the duty to act in good faith for the benefit of the company - and that conduct which is in breach of the other duties which we have identified is conduct which causes the director to be likely to be in breach of that fundamental duty. It is further said that a breach of duty can be ratified unless it is a breach of the fundamental duty to act in good faith in the interests of the company. However, the way in which we have classified the duties follows the more conventional approach in this field.[12]

Loyalty

11.5   Directors must act bona fide in what they consider is in the best interests of the company, and those are the words used by Lord Greene MR in *Re Smith and Fawcett Ltd*.[13] Directors therefore cannot use their powers to benefit third parties or themselves. The duty is a subjective one, which is not broken merely because the court would not have reached the same conclusion as the directors as to what was in the company's interests. Provided that the directors act in good faith in what they believe to be the company's interests, it does not matter that their decision also promotes their own interests.[14]

---

[3]   *Bristol and West Building Society v Mothew* [1998] Ch 1 per Millett LJ.

[4]   See para 11.5 below.

[5]   See paras 11.6-11.10 below.

[6]   See paras 11.11-11.12 below.

[7]   See paras 11.13-11.17 below.

[8]   In many cases, this will involve a misapplication of company assets and thus a breach of fiduciary duty. In other circumstances, the directors may simply be liable for breach of the terms of their contract of appointment.

[9]   See paras 11.19-11.20.

[10]   On the classification of fiduciary duties generally, see Finn, *Fiduciary Obligations* (1997).

[11]   Dine, *Company Law* (3rd ed, 1998) pp 189-198.

[12]   Eg *Gower's Principles of Modern Company Law* (6th ed, 1997); and see s 232 of the Australian Corporations Law (Appendix H) and ss 131-134 of the Companies Act 1993 of New Zealand (Appendix I).

[13]   [1942] Ch 304, at 306.

[14]   *Hirsche v Sims* [1894] AC 654.

Proper purpose

11.6   Directors must exercise their powers for the purpose for which those powers are conferred. This is a different and additional requirement from the first. It has been applied, for example, in relation to the power to allot shares. It is not enough that the directors consider that the allotment of shares will be in the company's interests. The allotment must be for one of the purposes for which the power is permitted to be exercised under the company's constitution.

11.7   This particular duty has long been part of our law. It was analysed by the Privy Council in *Howard Smith Ltd v Ampol Petroleum Ltd.*[15] In that case there were two shareholders, Ampol and Bulkships, who held 55 per cent of the shares of Millers Limited. Ampol made an offer for the issued shares of Millers. Howard Smith announced its intention to make a higher offer. The board of Millers quickly allotted shares to Howard Smith with the result that the 55 per cent majority shareholding of Ampol and Bulkships was reduced to 36 percent. Ampol Ltd sought a declaration that this allotment was invalid.

11.8   The Privy Council rejected the argument that, once it was shown that the directors had acted in good faith in what they considered to be the company's interests, that was the end of the matter. Before it could be said that a fiduciary power had been properly exercised, the purpose for which it might be exercised had first to be investigated.

> Having ascertained, on a fair view, the nature of this power, and having defined as best as can be done in the light of modern conditions, the, or some, limits within which it may be exercised, it is then necessary for the court, if a particular exercise of it is challenged, to examine the substantial purpose for which it was exercised and to reach a conclusion as to whether that purpose was proper or not. In doing so it will necessarily give credit to the *bona fide* opinion of the directors, if such is found to exist, and will respect their judgment as to matters of management; having done this, the ultimate conclusion has to be as to the side of a fairly broad line on which the case falls.[16]

11.9   This passage shows that on commercial issues, the courts defer to the judgment of directors.[17] Furthermore, the courts do not seek to test what directors do by reference to what objectively speaking is in the interests of the company. Courts cannot effectively test what is or is not objectively, speaking in the interests of the company. But they can scrutinise what directors do by such matters as proper purpose.[18]

---

[15]   [1974] AC 821; see also *Re a Company* (No 00370 of 1987), *ex p Glossop* [1988] BCLC 570, 577; and *Re BSB Holdings Ltd* (No 2) [1996] 1 BCLC 155, at pp 243-246.

[16]   [1974] AC 821 at p 835.

[17]   *Ibid,* at p 832E-F and at pp 835G to 836A.

[18]   See further R C Nolan, "The Proper Purpose Doctrine and Company Directors" in *The Realm of Company Law* (1998), which contains an analysis of the proper purpose doctrine and draws parallels with the judicial review of administrative action, and examines how the doctrine might be developed in the future.

11.10   The proper purposes principle has been applied to the exercise by directors of a range of discretionary powers, for example, the power to forfeit shares,[19] to make calls,[20] to refuse to register a transfer of shares,[21] or to allot shares. It is with respect to the last power, the power of allotment that the proper purposes principle is most frequently invoked. Thus the power of allotment cannot be used to entrench the directors in office or to deprive an existing majority of its majority position.[22] What constitutes a proper purpose cannot be stated in advance but must be ascertained in the context of the specific sitiuation under consideration, and once ascertained the court has to determine the substantial purpose for which the power was exercised in order to determine the validity of its exercise.[23]

No fetters on discretion

11.11   Directors must in general not fetter their discretion. This means that they must not enter into an agreement with a third party as to how they will exercise their discretion. To do so would prevent them from exercising an independent judgment at the appropriate time. An exception to this is where directors decide that it is in the best interests of the company to enter into a contract and to carry it into effect. In this situation they can themselves enter into any undertaking to exercise their powers in a particular way if it is necessary for them to do so to effectuate the contract. In *Fulham Football Club Ltd v Cabra Estates plc*,[24] the Court of Appeal stated:

> It is trite law that directors are under a duty to act bona fide in the interests of their company. However, it does not follow from that proposition that directors can never make a contract by which they bind themselves to the future exercise of their powers in a particular manner, even though the contract taken as a whole is manifestly for the benefit of the company. Such a rule could well prevent companies from entering into contracts which were commercially beneficial to them.[25]

11.12   The Court of Appeal went on to hold:

> The true rule was stated by the High Court of Australia in *Thorby v Goldberg*.[26] The relevant part of the headnote reads:
>
> > If, when a contract is negotiated on behalf of a company, the directors bona fide think it in the interests of the company as a whole that the transaction should be entered into and carried into effect they may

---

[19]   *Spackman v Evans* (1868) LR 3 HL 171, 186.

[20]   *Alexander v Automatic Telephone Co* [1890] 2 Ch 233.

[21]   Pennington, *Company Law* (7th ed) pp 998-1002.

[22]   The cases are collected and analysed in *Howard Smith Ltd v Ampol Ltd* [1974] AC 821.

[23]   *Ibid*, at 835.

[24]   [1994]1 BCLC 363.

[25]   *Ibid*, at p 392.

[26]   (1964) 112 CLR 597.

bind themselves by the contract to do whatever is necessary to effectuate it.

The no-conflict and no-profit rules

11.13 Under the no-conflict rule certain consequences can flow if directors place themselves in a position where their personal interests or duties to other persons are liable to conflict with their duties to the company unless the company gives its informed consent.[27] This consent may be given in the company's articles or in a resolution of the company in general meeting. If the necessary consent is not obtained, the contract is voidable at the instance of the company unless the right to rescind has been lost under the general law. There is a second "no-profit" rule under which, directors cannot keep secret profits which they make by using information or property or opportunities which belong to their company.

11.14 There are many cases which illustrate these rules. In *Industrial Development Consultants Ltd v Cooley*,[28] for example, the defendant was the former managing director of the plaintiffs. He resigned his office in order to enable him to take up in his own name a valuable contract which had previously been sought by his own company. The company's approach had been rejected. The defendant then learnt that there was a possibility of getting the contract himself and so he resigned as managing director. Subsequently he indeed got the contract. It was held that he was accountable to the plaintiff company for all the profit that he made on the contract, because he had allowed his interest and duty to conflict and had failed to disclose to the company the information which he had obtained before he resigned. Roskill J (as he then was) referred to well known authorities such as *Keech v Sandford*,[29] *Regal (Hastings) Ltd v Gulliver*[30] and *Phipps v Boardman*[31] and he also cited the following passage from the judgment of James LJ in *Parker v McKenna*:[32]

> I do not think it is necessary but it appears to me very important that we should concur in laying down again and again the general principle that in this court no agent in the course of his agency, in the matter of his agency, can be allowed to make any profit without the knowledge and consent of his principal; that that rule is an inflexible rule, and must be applied inexorably by this court, which is not entitled, in my judgment, to receive evidence, or suggestion or argument as to whether the principal did or did not suffer any injury in fact by reason of the dealing of the agent; for the safety of mankind requires that no

---

[27] The directors do not have a duty not to place themselves in a position of conflict; the no-conflict rule imposes a disability and not a duty: see *Movitex Ltd v Bullfield* [1988] BCLC 104. Moreover, a director cannot be restrained from acting as a director of a competing company on the ground that he is in the position of a partner: *London & Mashonaland Exploration Co v New Mashonaland Exploration Co* [1891] WN 165.

[28] [1972] 1 WLR 443; more fully reported in [1972] 2 All ER 162.

[29] (1726) Sel Cas Ch61.

[30] [1967] 2 AC 134n.

[31] *Ibid*, at p 46.

[32] (1874) 10 Ch App 96, 124-125.

agent shall be able to put his principal to the danger of such an inquiry as that.

11.15 Roskill J continued:

> In the nuclear age that last sentence may perhaps seem something of an exaggeration, but, nonetheless it is eloquent of the strictness with which throughout the last century, and indeed in the present century, courts of the highest authority have always applied this rule.[33]

11.16 The defendant had to account for all the profit that he had received notwithstanding that the court found that there was only a 10 percent chance that the company could have got the contract itself. This case accordingly demonstrates the fact that the remedies for breach of fiduciary duty go further than simply compensating the company. The reason for this as a matter of legal analysis is that the court's reasoning was that the defendant had misappropriated the company's property, namely the information which ought to have been reported to it.[34] As we saw in Part 3,[35] the economic justification is that the severe liabilities imposed by law operate as an incentive to directors to comply with their duties and (in this case) to convey information to shareholders. Another way of analysing *Cooley* is to see it as a conflict of interest situation: once Cooley decided to seek to obtain the contract for himself and not the company, this resulted in a conflict between his interests and those of the company which entitled the company to oblige him to account.[36]

11.17 The *Cooley* case should be contrasted with *Island Export Finance Ltd v Umanna*.[37] In that case the company had a business in providing postal caller boxes and the defendant had been its managing director. However he resigned because he was dissatisfied with the company. Subsequently he obtained two new contracts for postal caller boxes. The possibility of these contracts had been known to him when he was a director. His resignation had been for independent reasons and at the time of his resignation the company was not searching for new business. The court held that a director could be liable for misappropriating a business opportunity of the company even after he ceased to be a director. However in this case the claim for an account against the director failed on the basis that the chance to obtain the contracts in question was not a sufficiently maturing business opportunity at the time he ceased to be a director. Moreover, the defendant had not improperly exploited any confidential information which the company could prevent him from using.

---

[33] [1972] 1 WLR 443, 452.

[34] The reasoning that information is property was doubted before *Cooley* in *Boardman v Phipps* [1967] 2 AC 67, and has been rejected in Australia since then; see *Bream v Williams* (1996) 186 CLR 71.

[35] See para 3.34 above. Cf Hong Kong Consultancy report, para 6.23, Appendix L.

[36] See Prentice (1972) 50 Can B Rev 623.

[37] [1986] BCLC 460.

Duty to act in accordance with the company's constitution

11.18   Directors must act in accordance with the company's constitution.[38] So, for example, if the articles say that dividends must not be paid otherwise than out of revenue profits, it will be a breach of duty for directors to pay dividends out of capital profits. Section 35A of the Companies Act 1985 protects third parties who deal with the company in good faith by deeming the directors' powers to be free of any limitation under the company's constitution. Section 322A[39] deals with the consequences of this provision where one of the parties to the transaction is a director of the company or a connected person of his or a company with which he is associated.

Duty to deal fairly as between different shareholders

11.19   In *Mutual Life Insurance v Rank Organisation Ltd*,[40] the directors of Rank had given shareholders, other than North American shareholders, the right to subscribe for new shares of the same class. There was evidence that the North Americans had been excluded because the company did not wish to comply with the requirements for registration of the Securities and Exchange Commission in the United States and comparable commissions in Canada. The directors had had advice from merchant bankers, which they had accepted, and which was in turn based on an investigation by accountants, that to register with the SEC would not be in the interests of the company. The plaintiffs were North Americans. They owned shares in Rank and they claimed that Rank had acted in breach of the membership contract contained in the articles. They claimed that their shares entitled them to equal treatment without discriminating one from another. Goulding J rejected the argument. In the light of the wide powers which the directors had under the articles he held that the directors' power of allotment was only to be cut down by two implied terms:

> First, the time honoured rule that the directors' powers are to be exercised in good faith in the interests of the company, and secondly, that they must be exercised fairly as between different shareholders. I doubt whether it is possible to formulate either of these stipulations more precisely because of the infinity of circumstances in which they may fall to be applied.[41]

11.20   On the facts of the case, Goulding J held that it was abundantly clear that the directors had indeed acted in the best interests of Rank and that there had been no unfairness between the two groups of shareholders.

---

[38]   The company's constitution includes its memorandum and articles of asscoiation (cf s 322A of the Companies Act 1985).

[39]   Considered at paras 4.205-4.209 above.

[40]   [1985] BCLC 11. Applied in *Re BSB Holdings Ltd* (No 2) [1996] 1 BCLC 155.

[41]   *Ibid*, at p 21g-h.

TO WHOM DO THE DIRECTORS OWE THEIR FIDUCIARY DUTIES?

11.21 The duties of a director discussed above are owed to the company.[42] The question is whose interests constitute the company's interests for this purpose? The company is an artificial entity. In reality it has no interests of its own. In *Greenhalgh v Arderne Cinemas*[43] the issue was whether a special resolution has been passed bona fide for the benefit of the company. Sir Raymond Evershed MR said:

> the phrase, "the company as a whole," does not (at any rate in such a case as the present) mean the company as a commercial entity as distinct from the corporators. It means the corporators as a general body. That is to say, you may take the case of an individual hypothetical member and ask whether what is proposed is, in the honest opinion of those who voted in its favour, for that person's benefit.

11.22 On the other hand, regard should not be had only to present members. Regard should also be had to the interests of future members (or the long-term interests of the present members). In an appropriate case, the interests of the company may mean the interests of its creditors. The directors must have regard to the interests of the company's creditors where there is a danger of the company becoming insolvent because they are then the persons interested in the company's assets. In *Winkworth v Edward Baron Development Co Ltd*[44] a man and his wife occupied a property which their company owned. The company became heavily insolvent and the wife sought to argue that the company had agreed to sell her an interest in the property, and that that arose when she paid money to the company which was used to pay off the overdraft which had been incurred to buy the property in the first place. It was argued on her behalf that there was a resulting trust. The House of Lords refused to hold that there was a resulting trust in her favour. Lord Templeman was particularly influenced by the fact that the company was insolvent. He held:

> A duty is owed by the directors of the company to the company and the creditors of the company to ensure that the affairs of the company are properly administered and that its property is not dissipated or exploited for the benefit of the directors themselves to the prejudice of the creditors.[45]

11.23 Far from holding, therefore, that the wife had a share in the property which she and her husband occupied, their Lordships held that since she and her husband had committed a misfeasance towards the company in withdrawing from the company monies to pay for their shares in it, the money which she paid in simply went to pay off some of the amount that she owed the company as the result of her misfeasance. The House of Lords recognised in this case that in some

---

[42] There can however be special circumstances in which directors can come under a fiduciary duty of disclosure to shareholders: see *Re Chez Nico (Restaurants) Ltd* [1992] BCLC 192, 208.

[43] [1951] Ch 286.

[44] [1986] 1 WLR 1512.

[45] *Ibid*, at 1516E-F.

circumstances the duty to the company becomes in reality a duty to the creditors.[46] However, the duty continues to be one owed to the company and not to the creditors.[47]

11.24   As with creditors, the case law also establishes that directors must take account of the interests of employees where that is in the best interests of the company. In a passage often quoted, Bowen LJ said:[48]

> A railway company, or the directors of the company, might send down all the porters at a railway station to have tea in the country at the expense of the company. Why should they not? It is for the directors to judge, provided it is a matter which is reasonably incidental to the carrying on of the business of the company, and a company which always treated its employees with Draconian severity, and never allowed them a single inch more than the strict letter of the bond, would soon find itself deserted - at all events, unless the labour was very much more easy to obain in the market than it is. The law does not say that there are to be no cakes and ale, but there are to be no cakes and ale except such as are required for the benefit of the company. ... It is not charity sitting at the board of directors, because as it seems to me charity has no business to sit at boards of directors *qua* charity. There is, however, a kind of charitable dealing which is for the interest of those who practise it, and to that extent and in that garb (I admit not a very philanthropic garb) charity may sit at the board, but not for any other purpose.

11.25   The City Code requires directors of an offeree company to have regard to the interests of employees as well as shareholders and creditors when advising shareholders on the merits of a bid.[49]

11.26   In relation to employees the Act now makes special provision in section 309 in these terms:

> (1) The matters to which the directors of a company are to have regard in the performance of their functions include the interests of the company's employees in general, as well as the interests of its members.

> (2) Accordingly, the duty imposed by this section on the directors is owed by them to the company (and the company alone) and is enforceable in the same way as any other fiduciary duty owed to a company by its directors.

---

[46]   See also *Facia Footwear Ltd v Hincliffe* [1998] BCLC 218.

[47]   *Yukong Line Ltd v Rendsburg Investments Corporation (No 2)* [1998] 1 WLR 294.

[48]   *Hutton v West Cork Railway Co* (1883) 23 Ch D 654, 672-673.

[49]   General Principle 9. The Amended Proposal for a Thirteenth EC Directive on Takeover Bids (COM (97) 565 OJC 378/10 13 December 1997) requires Member States to ensure that rules made pursuant to that directive require the board of an offeree company to act in "all the interests of the company, including employment" (see art 5(c)). It is not clear whether this would require any extension of UK law.

(3) This section applies to shadow directors as it does to directors.

11.27 Section 309[50] first appeared in 1980. At the same time section 719 first appeared. The latter section reversed the celebrated case of *Parke v Daily News*[51] and established a procedure which enabled companies to obtain approval for voluntary payments to employees on the cessation or transfer of its business. It provides that this power can be exercised "notwithstanding that its exercise is not in the best interests of the company."[52]

11.28 Section 309 of the Companies Act 1985 has been referred to in a number of cases: *Fulham Football v Cabra Estates;*[53] *Re Saul D Harrison*[54]; and *Re London Life Association Ltd.*[55] However, it has not been fully considered in any of these cases, and in particular the courts have not expressed a view on the question of whether section 309 requires directors in exercising their functions to have regard to the interests of employees in general even if their interests are not the same as those of the company in the sense of the corporators. A possible consequence of this view is that the directors would have a discretion to balance the interests of these various groups appropriately. In the *Fulham Football Club* case, the Court of Appeal obiter were minded to reject an argument that the company was bound by undertakings merely because all the shareholders had signed them on the basis that:

> The duties owed by directors are to their company and the company is more than the sum of its members. Creditors, both present and potential, are interested, while section 309 of the Companies Act 1985 imposes a specific duty on directors to have regard to the interests of the company's employees in general.

This can be read as suggesting that section 309 is not limited to requiring directors to have regard to the interests of employees when to do so is conducive to the interests of the general body of shareholders. But if this is so, then "the company" in section 309 has a different meaning from its meaning in section 719(2). There is accordingly doubt as to what section 309 means, but it is outside the scope of this project to review it and make recommendations as to its reform.[56]

11.29 Where the company is a member of a group of companies, the directors may have regard to the interests of the group if, but only if, it is in the interests of the company so to do. Thus, a director of a subsidiary company is not in breach of

---

[50] As to which see eg *Gore-Browne on Companies* (1998) para 27.2.1; Parkinson, *Corporate Law and Theory* (1993), pp 82-87, Prentice (1980) Ind L J 1; and Pettet (1981) Current Legal Problems 199.

[51] [1962] Ch 927. See also *Gibson's Executor v Gibson* (1980) SLT 2.

[52] Section 719(2). It was for this reason that the court held in *Parke* that such payments could not be made.

[53] [1994] 1 BCLC 363.

[54] [1995] 1 BCLC 14, 33.

[55] Unreported, 21 February 1989 per Hoffmann LJ (Chancery Division, Companies Court)

[56] See para 1.55 above. See generally, *Tomorrow's Company*, published by the Royal Society of Arts (1995), para 3.2.

duty if he fails to consider the interests of the subsidiary separately from those of the group, provided that an intelligent and honest man in the same position could reasonably have come to the same conclusion that the transaction was for the benefit of the subsidiary.[57]

RATIFICATION BY THE COMPANY IN GENERAL MEETING

Where no question of insolvency or illegality arises

11.30　In its consultation paper on shareholder remedies,[58] the Law Commission discussed the circumstances in which a breach of duty by a director could be ratified so as to prevent a minority shareholder's action. The description that follows under this heading is largely based on that paper.[59]

11.31　A classic case on ratification is *North-West Transportation Co Ltd v Beatty*.[60] In that case one of the directors was interested in a contract with the company for the sale to it of a ship. The sale was at a proper price and the company required the ship for the purposes of its business. The transaction was approved by the shareholders, but the directors held a majority of the votes. The Privy Council held that any shareholder could vote at a general meeting as he thought fit. Ratification rendered the transaction binding on the company.

11.32　This case should be contrasted with *Cook v Deeks*.[61] The directors had breached their fiduciary duties by diverting business which belonged to the company for their own benefit. The Privy Council held that such a transaction could not be ratified by a resolution which was carried because the wrongdoing directors held the majority of the votes. Lord Buckmaster referred to earlier authorities on fraud on the minority[62] and commented:

> ... even supposing it be not ultra vires of a company to make a present to its directors, it appears quite certain that directors holding a majority of votes would not be permitted to make a present to themselves. This would be to allow a majority to oppress the minority.[63]

11.33　In *Regal (Hastings) Ltd v Gulliver*,[64] the directors took shares in a subsidiary company when the plaintiff holding company could not afford to take them up. The directors made a profit when both the holding company and the subsidiary were sold to a third party purchaser and they were held liable to account to the plaintiff

---

[57]　*Charterbridge Corporation Ltd v Lloyds Bank* [1970] Ch 62. This is different from the special provision made for directors of subsidiary and joint venture companies by s 131 of the New Zealand Companies Act 1993; see Appendix I below.

[58]　Consultation Paper No 142, paras 5.6–5.17.

[59]　It is outside the scope of this project to propose any changes to these rules.

[60]　(1887) 12 App Cas 589 (PC).

[61]　[1916] 1 AC 554 (PC).

[62]　Including *Menier v Hooper's Telegraph Works* (1874) 9 Ch App 350.

[63]　*Cook v Deeks* [1916] 1 AC 554 (PC), 564.

[64]　[1967] 2 AC 134n.

holding company for that profit on the ground that they were in a fiduciary relationship with the company and had made the profit solely because of their position as its directors and in the course of carrying out their duties as such. Lord Russell suggested, however, that they could have protected themselves "... by a resolution (either antecedent or subsequent) of the Regal shareholders in general meeting".[65]

11.34   Academic writers have questioned why ratification should have been considered effective in *Regal (Hastings) Ltd v Gulliver*[66] but not in *Cooks v Deeks*.[67] However, there are many points of distinction between the two cases, which may explain Lord Russell's statement. *Regal (Hastings) Ltd v Gulliver* was not, like *Cook v Deeks*, a minority shareholder's action. It was not a case of fraud; the directors in the *Regal* case had acted in good faith intending to benefit the company. There is no suggestion that they controlled a majority of the votes in general meeting. They were held liable because of the strict rule of substantive law that makes a fiduciary liable to account for a secret profit that he receives by reason of his fiduciary relationship, but it is a rule that can be displaced by ratification.

11.35   In *Queensland Mines v Hudson*,[68] the Privy Council considered the case of a managing director who, by reason of his position as such, was able to secure and exploit for himself a mining exploration licence. The company itself was not in a position to do this[69] and its board, on which representatives of its two shareholders sat, had, following full disclosure of the nature of the transaction, approved the defendant's actions.[70] The Privy Council held that the director was not liable to account for such benefits to the plaintiff company. It is considered that under UK law a board of directors could not ratify a breach of duty; only the company's general meeting can do.

11.36   *North-West Transportation Ltd v Beatty, Regal (Hastings) Ltd v Gulliver* and *Queensland Mines v Hudson* are distinguishable from *Cook v Deeks*. In the first three cases, a reasonable shareholder could consider that the terms were beneficial to the company. In *Cook v Deeks*, however, the ratification procured by the directors involved a gift by the company to the directors.[71] In *Regal (Hastings) Ltd v Gulliver*

---

[65]   *Ibid,* at p 150. See also n 68 below.

[66]   [1967] 2 AC 134n (PC).

[67]   [1916] 1 AC 554 (PC). *Cook v Deeks* was not referred to in the judgments *in Regal (Hastings) Ltd v Gulliver. Gower's Principles of Modern Company Law* (6th ed, 1997) at p 647 concludes that "[a] satisfactory answer, consistent with common sense and with the decided cases is difficult (and perhaps impossible) to provide". See also L S Sealy, "The Director as Trustee" [1967] CLJ 83,102; and L S Sealy, *Cases and Materials in Company Law* (6th ed 1996) p 296.

[68]   (1978) 52 ALJR 399 (PC).

[69]   See *Regal (Hastings) Ltd v Gulliver* [1967] 2 AC 134n (PC).

[70]   See also dicta in *Bamford v Bamford* [1970] Ch 212.

[71]   The Privy Council in *Cook v Deeks* distinguished *North-West Transportation Co Ltd v Beatty* on the grounds that the asset in that case on which the director had made a profit was his own rather than the company's (see [1916] 1 AC 554 (PC), 563-564). However, it is doubtful whether this point is enough in itself to make the transaction ratifiable.

and *Queensland Mines v Hudson*, the company could not itself benefit from the transaction. In *Queensland Mines v Hudson*, the director made full disclosure of the nature of the transaction and obtained approval from the company.

11.37 In *Hogg v Cramphorn*,[72] the directors had used their powers to issue shares for the purpose of forestalling a takeover bid in breach of the proper purposes principle.[73] A minority shareholder brought a derivative action to have the issue set aside. The exercise of power for this purpose is a breach of fiduciary duty, even if the directors believe it to be in the interests of the company. In *Bamford v Bamford*,[74] there was a point of law argued as to whether ratification in similar circumstances would be effective. In both cases the court held that the allotment could be cured by ratification.[75]

11.38 We have referred above to the need for any circular accompanying a notice of meeting to give full and proper disclosure of the purpose of the meeting.[76] Where the directors have acted in breach of their duty to the company and subsequently seek ratification by the company in general meeting of their wrongful act, they must make full and frank disclosure of the breach of duty. This means where they have wrongfully received a benefit, particulars as to the amount received must be disclosed.[77]

Where the company's solvency is prejudiced

11.39 The company in general meeting cannot ratify a breach of duty if the company is insolvent or may thereby become unable to pay its creditors:

> In a solvent company the proprietary interests of the shareholders entitle them as a general body to be regarded as the company when questions of the duty of directors arise. If, as a general body, they authorise or ratify a particular action of the directors, there can be no challenge to the validity of what the directors have done. But where a company is insolvent the interests of the creditors intrude. They become prospectively entitled, through the mechanism of liquidation, to displace the power of the shareholders and directors to deal with the company's assets. It is in a practical sense their assets and not the shareholders' assets that, through the medium of the company, are under the management of the directors pending either liquidation, return to solvency, or the imposition of some alternative administration."[78]

---

[72] [1967] Ch 254.

[73] See paras 11.6-11.10 above.

[74] [1970] Ch 212.

[75] In both *Hogg v Cramphorn* and *Bamford v Bamford*, ratification defeated the actions, but the votes attached to the "tainted" shares were not exercised.

[76] See para 4.50, n 50 above.

[77] *Baillie v Oriental Telephone and Electric Company, Limited* [1915] 1 Ch 503; see also *Jacobus Marler Estates Ltd v Marler* [1916-17] All ER 291.

[78] Per Street CJ in *Kinsela v Russell Kinsela Pty Ltd (in liq)* (1986) 4 NSWLR 722 at 730, approved by Dillon LJ in *West Mercia Safetywear v Dodd* [1988] 1WLR 250, at pp 251-253.

Where the act is illegal or outside the company's powers

11.40 The company cannot ratify an illegal act by a director or one which is outside its powers and not binding on it.[79]

CAPPING DIRECTORS' LIABILITIES 1: BY ORDER OF THE COURT UNDER SECTION 727 OF THE COMPANIES ACT 1985[80]

11.41 Section 727 provides:

> (1) If in any proceedings for negligence, default, breach of duty or breach of trust against an officer of a company or a person employed by a company as auditor (whether he is or is not an officer of the company) it appears to the court hearing the case that that officer or person is or may be liable in respect of the negligence, default, breach of duty or breach of trust, but that he has acted honestly and reasonably, and that having regard to all the circumstances of the case (including those connected with his appointment) he ought fairly to be excused for the negligence, default, breach of duty or breach of trust, that court may relieve him, either wholly or partly, from his liability on such terms as it thinks fit.

> (2) If any such officer or person as above-mentioned has reason to apprehend that any claim will or might be made against him in respect of any negligence, default, breach of duty or breach of trust, he may apply to the court for relief; and the court on the application has the same power to relieve him as under this section it would have had if it had been a court before which proceedings against that person for negligence, default, breach of duty or breach of trust had been brought.

> (3) Where a case to which subsection (1) applies is being tried by a judge with a jury, the judge, after hearing the evidence, may, if he is satisfied that the defendant or defender ought in pursuance of that subsection to be relieved either in whole or in part from the liability sought to be enforced against him, withdraw the case in whole or in part from the jury and forthwith direct judgment to be entered for the defendant or defender on such terms as to costs or otherwise as the judge may think proper.

11.42 Relief under this section is not lightly given. In the recent decision of *Re Duckwari plc (No 1)*[81] referred to above, the Court of Appeal confirmed that section 727 relief was available for a default under section 320 of the Companies Act 1985, but declined to give relief. The director had been told there was a possibility that certain formalities might be waived, but that it was not enough to show that he

---

[79] Though in either case it may release the claim against the director: *Smith v Croft No 2* [1988] Ch 114, at pp 178-183. As to the circumstances in which a transaction which is outside a company's powers is not binding on it, see ss 35A and 322A. The latter is discussed in paras 4.205-4.209 above.

[80] We have not considered any changes to s 727 for the purpose of this paper. They may fall within the DTI's own review of company law.

[81] [1997] 2 BCLC 713 at 722: see para 4.174, n 270 above.

had acted reasonably and that he ought to be released from his liability to indemnify the company for the loss it suffered by reason of the default. In *Gibson's Executor v Gibson*[82] the directors had made an ex gratia payment to one of their number as the company had not made any provision for a pension for him. They were liable to replace this sum as it was in breach of what is now section 312. Lord Dunpark in the Outer House refused relief to the directors on a misfeasance summons on the basis that it would not be fair to do so, so far as the applicant shareholder was concerned.

11.43 In re *D'Jan of London Ltd*,[83] the question arose whether a director who had been found negligent could indeed be given relief under the section, which requires a director to have acted *reasonably*. Hoffmann LJ (sitting as a judge of the Chancery Division) held that a director can nonetheless be given relief under the section on the grounds that the section clearly contemplated that relief could be so given and that it followed that conduct could be reasonable for the purposes of section 727 despite amounting to a lack of reasonable care at common law.[84]

11.44 The court in *Re D'Jan* actually granted relief under section 727 and the reason for doing so illustrates the width of the jurisdiction. The director held 99 of the issued shares and his wife held the other share. The company was in winding up. The director was also an unsecured creditor of the company. In those circumstances the court held that in consequence of his negligence he was liable in the winding up of the company to pay to the company the amount of any dividends he would receive as an unsecured creditor, but was not otherwise liable to pay sums to the company to compensate it for its loss.

11.45 Theoretically under the section an application can be made to the court before the act in question occurs, but in most situations this is a luxury which neither time nor funds allow. Accordingly this section is scant comfort to a director who is concerned as to whether he will be held liable if he does what he proposes to do. This is unfortunate because in very many situations, a director is forced to take some action unless he resigns. While section 727 of the Companies Act 1985 is an important part of the background to this project,[85] it is not a section which we have reviewed. We have proceeded on the basis that the interpretation given to the section in *Re D'Jan* will be upheld by later decisions. We consider that it will.

---

[82] (1980) SLT 2.

[83] [1994] 1 BCLC 561.

[84] Section 727 was amended following the recommendations of the Greene Committee who "in order to remove any possible hardship" recommended that the court granting relief under section 727 should have regard to all the circumstances relating to the director's appointment, although they thought that the general law of negligence was sufficient to deal with this (para 46).

[85] In Fiduciary Duties and Regulatory Rules (1995) Law Com No 236, para 15.13, The Law Commission expressed the view that there was a need to take a global look at exculpatory clauses, examining s 61 of the Trustee Act 1925 and s 727 of the Companies Act 1925 as well as the position of fiduciaries and others.

CAPPING DIRECTORS' LIABILITES 2: STATUTORY PROHIBITION OF INDEMNITIES UNDER SECTION 310[86] OF THE COMPANIES ACT 1985 AND THE POSSIBILITY OF AD HOC RELEASES

11.46 We start with a description of section 310 of the Companies Act 1985 which prohibits contracts which limit or exclude the liabilities of directors and, because of the wide terms in which it is cast, has resulted in the courts analysing the nature of the no-conflict rule discussed above.

11.47 Section 310 provides:

> (1) This section applies to any provision, whether contained in a company's articles or in any contract with the company or otherwise, for exempting any officer of the company or any person (whether an officer or not) employed by the company as auditor from, or indemnifying him against, any liability which by virtue of any rule of law would otherwise attach to him in respect of any negligence, default, breach of duty or breach of trust of which he may be guilty in relation to the company.
>
> (2) Except as provided by the following subsection, any such provision is void.
>
> [(3) This section does not prevent a company—
>
> (a) from purchasing and maintaining for any such officer or auditor insurance against any such liability, or
> (b) from indemnifying any such officer or auditor against any liability incurred by him—
>
> (i) in defending any proceedings (whether civil or criminal) in which judgment is given in his favour or he is acquitted, or
> (ii) in connection with any application under section 144(3) or (4) (acquisition of shares by innocent nominee) or section 727 (general power to grant relief in case of honest and reasonable conduct) in which relief is granted to him by the court.][87]

History of section 310

11.48 This section was first introduced following a recommendation of the Greene Committee.[88] Prior to the introduction of the predecessor of section 310 in 1928, it was common for companies to have wide exculpatory provisions in their articles.

---

[86] We have not considered any changes to s 310 for the purposes of this project. They may fall within the DTI's own review of company law.

[87] Subsection (3) substituted by CA 1989, s 137(1), as from 1 April 1990.

[88] Para 46. The Greene Committee rejected the argument that the shareholders must be taken to have agreed to the articles. "The articles are drafted on the instructions of those concerned in the formation of the company , and it is obviously a matter of great difficulty and delicacy for shareholders to attempt to alter such an article as that under consideration."

In *Re City Equitable Fire Insurance Co Ltd*[89] the directors and auditors escaped liability because the articles of the company exonerated them for breach of duty unless the breach was wilful. The section now provides an absolute bar on arrangements for capping liabilities of directors, other company officers[90] and auditors to the company. It is considered that, but for subsection (3)(a) (which was introduced by the Companies Act 1989), the section prohibited the purchase by the company of D&O cover since it would then be a party to a contract which indemnified a director in breach of duty, but the Companies Act 1989 amended section 310 so as to permit this.[91] It is to be noted that the section prohibits contractual and other arrangements and not one-off payments as such.

Relationship between section 310 and articles which modify the no conflict rule

11.49   There is little authority on the section but a great deal of academic debate as to how it interrelates with articles which modify directors' fiduciary duties.[92] For instance, there are articles in the current version of Table A which permit directors to receive remuneration and expenses and to be interested in certain transactions with the company, or in any company formed by the company or in which the company is interested, without in either such case being liable to account for the profit to the company and in certain cases allowing them to vote on transactions in which they are interested. In private companies the articles are commonly wider than those in Table A. In practice parties may want to modify fiduciary duties; for instance, the parties to a joint venture agreement may agree that the directors of a joint venture company should be free to pass information to one of the joint venturers, even though this may not be in the interests of the joint venture company.

11.50   The issue of the relationship between section 310 and articles modifying the no conflicts rule was considered by Vinelott J in *Movitex v Bulfield*.[93] Vinelott J held that such articles did not infringe section 310:

> The true principle is that if a director places himself in a position in which his duty to the company conflicts with his personal interest or his duty to another, the court will intervene to set aside the transaction without inquiring whether there was any breach of the director's duty to the company. That is an over-riding principle of equity. The shareholders of the company, in formulating the articles, can exclude or modify the application of this principle. In doing so

---

[89]   [1925] Ch 409.

[90]   The term "officer" is defined in s 744 as including any director, manager or secretary.

[91]   It is doubtful whether despite the wide wording of s 310, contracts to which the company is not a party are caught by s 310: see *Burgorgne v London Borough of Waltham Forest* [1997] BCC 347.

[92]   See eg Baker (1985) JBL 181; Birds [1976] 39 MLR 394; Parkinson (1981) JBL 335; Gregory (1982) 98 LQR 413; and Rogerson, "Modification and Exclusion of Directors' Duties" published in *The Realm of Company Law* (1998).

[93]   [1988] BCLC 403.

they do not exempt the director from or from the consequences of a breach of a duty owed to the company.

11.51 This decision, by establishing that directors are not under a *duty* to avoid placing themselves in a position of conflict, explains as a legal matter why Table A contains clauses which modify the no conflicts rule, and it preserves their effectiveness. However it does not provide a policy reason why the no conflicts rule should be capable of being modified but (as result of the introduction of section 310) other fiduciary duties cannot be modified. It would seem unlikely that any thought was given to the distinction drawn by Vinelott J when section 310 or section 727 were introduced. Nor does the decision explain whether there are other fiduciary duties whose effect can be mitigated or varied in some way without bringing section 310 into operation.[94]

Release of claims arising against directors

11.52 Section 310 clearly prevents a company and a director limiting the latter's liabilities by contract. The question is whether the parties can compromise or release a liability once a breach of duty has occured. There is no authority on the question whether section 310 makes void any resolution that the company in general meeting or the board of directors[95] may pass to release a director from liability for breach of duty. The better view[96] is that section 310 is directed to arrangements which apply to future claims rather than to compromises of claims that have already arisen.[97] Likewise the better view is that section 310 does not prevent a company from entering into a compromise with a director of any claim that it may have against him. However there is no authority on this point.[98] The fact that section 310 does not apply does not of course mean that the transaction cannot be challenged on appropriate facts as having been made by the directors in breach of duty.

D&O INSURANCE

11.53 D&O insurance protects a director or officer against claims that may be made by the company[99] or others[100] for breach of duty to the company. As we explain

---

[94] See the valuable discussion on these and other issues to which s 310 gives rise: eg Rogerson, "Modification and Exclusion of Directors' Duties" published in *The Realm of Company Law* (1998).

[95] The board of directors would require the power to do so in the articles. Otherwise it is only the members who could grant such release.

[96] See eg *Gore-Browne on Companies* (44th ed) at 27.21;

[97] If any resolution is proposed to the company in general meeting for the purpose of releasing directors from liability or ratifying what they have done, there must be full disclosure to the shareholders entitled to vote of the purpose of the meeting: see *Kaye v Croydon Tramways Co* [1989] 1 Ch 358.

[98] In *Gray v New Augarita Porcupine Mines Ltd* [1952] 3 DLR 1, the Privy Council held that a board could release a director from his liability to the company for breach of duty but there is no reference in the case to any equivalent in Canadian law at that time to s 310 of the Companies Act 1985.

[99] But see para 11.55 below.

above,[101] the company itself was apparently prohibited by section 310(1) from purchasing this insurance itself. This was changed by the Companies Act 1989 which added subsection (3)(a). We understand that it is now common for larger public companies to purchase this insurance, particularly if the company has business activities in the USA.[102] Indeed, this is demonstrated by the fact that when the amendment first took effect companies were required to state in their annual accounts whether the company had paid for such insurance.[103] This requirement was later dropped[104] on the grounds that such insurance had become common.[105] This is borne out by our own enquiries in the insurance industry. Exact figures are not available but we further understand that the premium income written in the UK for this type of business in 1997 was approaching £300m.[106] This indicates that a significant amount of D&O insurance is taken up. We also understand that the individual director is not taxed on the benefit of the insurance as a benefit in kind provided that the cover is for a period which does not exceed 24 months and the insurance is not mixed with other cover.[107]

11.54 There is no market standard wording for this type of insurance but we have examined one policy which is available and which we understand to contain reasonably usual terms. There are a number of exclusions but we have been told that it is possible to arrange an extension in respect of many of these. It covers a director for any loss by reason of a wrongful act (which includes breach of statutory or other duty, breach of trust, neglect, error, misleading statement, breach of warranty of authority, or wrongful trading) in the capacity of director or officer; and costs by reason of investigations or disqualification proceedings, except to the extent actually recovered by the director. It will also pay on behalf of the company for these reasons, but only if, and to the extent that, the company is required or permitted to indemnify the director. The policy does not cover fines, penalties or (in general) punitive damages, as it is generally not possible to obtain insurance against these matters.[108]

11.55 The claim must be made against the director within the period of the insurance. There is an exclusion for claims brought by fellow directors and claims brought by

---

[100] Including shareholders, who bring a derivative action to enforce a right of action that the company has, or a liquidator.

[101] Para 11.48.

[102] For a detailed study of D&O insurance with some valuable comparisons with the position in the USA, see Colin Baxter, "Demystifying D&O Insurance" (1995) 15 OJLS 537.

[103] Sched 7, para 5A (as amended).

[104] Companies Act 1986 (Miscellaneous Accounting Amendments) Regulations 1986, SI 1996 No189, reg 14(4)(b), 16(1).

[105] See Accounting Simplifications, DTI consultation document (May 1995) para 42, p 30.

[106] Estimated figure for the Lloyd's and company market. This figure excludes non-UK business written in London.

[107] Income and Corporation Taxes Act 1988, s 201AA.

[108] See generally, Aggravated, Exemplary and Restitutionary Damages (1997) Law Com No 247, paras 5.234-5.273. Nor does insurance cover protect directors who are involved in litigation against harm thereby incurred to their reputation: see para 3.88 above.

the company itself unless the claim is brought by shareholders on behalf of the company (in a derivative action or in Scotland a shareholder's action). The insurer's liability for loss or costs is also excluded inter alia where:

(1) brought about by or consequent upon any circumstance existing prior to a specified date and which the director knew or ought reasonably to have known was likely to give rise to a claim;

(2) resulting from any wrongful act etc subsequent to the effective date on which the company is taken over or merged, unless otherwise agreed by the underwriters; or

(3) where there is dishonesty, fraud or malicious conduct of the director.

Cover is severable so that the policy conditions and exclusions are not applied to deny cover to anyone by imputing a wrong done by any other person in the proposal or in relation to any other claims.

11.56 The insurer is entitled at any time to take over and conduct in the name of the director the defence of any claim, conduct negotiations and (subject to the consent of the director) the settlement of any loss or costs. But no director or officer shall be required to contest or settle a claim unless counsel (mutually appointed) shall otherwise advise.

11.57 There is an expectation that the market for this kind of insurance will increase with greater awareness of the responsibilities of directors.[109]

---

[109] It should be noted, however, that the availability of insurance may, of itself, lead to an increase in the number of claims being brought.

PART 12
DUTY OF CARE: THE CURRENT LAW

12.1   In this part we examine the present law on the duty of care owed by a director to his company. The duty of care is a common law duty, owed by directors to their companies in the performance of their functions. The duty has been described as one in tort, or in Scotland in delict, rather than one in contract arising from a director's voluntary assumption of responsibility for a company's property and affairs.[1] Falling below the standard, where loss results, will expose the director in question to an action in negligence by the company.

12.2   We begin by examining the 'traditional view' of the duty of care which implied a very low standard of care. Next we consider the 'modern view' under which a more exacting standard of care has been imposed by recent cases. We then consider the extent to which directors can place reliance on co-directors, officers, auditors and professional advisers. Next we look at the duties of skill and care in an analogous relationship, namely that of trusteeship. Finally, we look briefly at the duties of directors under German law.

THE TRADITIONAL VIEW

12.3   As indicated above, the traditional view implies generally a low standard of care. In *Overend, Gurney & Co v Gibb*,[2] a test of 'ordinary prudence' was put forward. The question which the court had to answer was:

> whether or not the directors exceeded the powers entrusted to them, or whether, if they did not ... they were cognisant of facts of such a character, so plain, so manifest, and so simple of appreciation, that no men with any ordinary degree of prudence, acting on their own behalf, would have entered into such a transaction as they entered into.

12.4   Where, moreover, a director was not cognisant of relevant facts by reason of inattention to the business of the company and avoidance of situations where they would have been made known to him, he would be excused. So it was that in the *Marquis of Bute's* case[3] an action against the Marquis of Bute, who was appointed bank president at the age of six months and attended only one meeting of the board in 39 years, was unsuccessful.[4]

12.5   In the same vein, a director who failed to attend relevant board meetings, and whose credentials were those of a 'country gentleman not a skilled accountant',

---

[1]   *Henderson v Merrett Syndicates Ltd* [1994] 3 WLR 761, 799, per Lord Browne-Wilkinson.

[2]   (1872) LR 5 HL 40, 486-7.

[3]   *Re Cardiff Savings Bank* [1892] 2 Ch 100.

[4]   Although falling asleep at meetings, having attended them, was viewed differently in *Land Credit Co of Ireland v Lord Fermoy* (1870) LR 5 Ch App 763.

was held not liable for recommending payment of a dividend from capital.[5] In *Re Brazilian Rubber Plantations and Estates Ltd*,[6] Neville J held that a director was:

> not bound to bring any special qualifications to his office and may undertake the management of a rubber company in complete ignorance of everything connected with rubber without incurring responsibility for the mistakes which may result from such ignorance.[7]

12.6 *Re Brazilian Rubber* also laid down that if a director did bring special expertise to his office, he was bound to give the company the advantage of it and would be judged accordingly.[8] The position on general business experience was less clear. Some cases seem to have required that a director exercise his judgment, at such board meetings as he did attend, 'as a man of business'.[9] Others, however, required only that he exercise the skill and care of an ordinary prudent man notwithstanding other business experience.[10]

12.7 The traditional line culminated in the case of *Re City Equitable Fire Insurance Co*[11] where Romer J, while recognising that the authorities were not entirely clear,[12] reviewed and summarised them. He held that:

> (1) A director need not exhibit in the performance of his duties a greater degree of skill than may reasonably be expected from a person with his knowledge and experience ... It is perhaps only another way of stating the same proposition to say that directors are not liable for mere errors of judgment. (2) A director is not bound to give continuous attention to the affairs of his company. His duties are of an intermittent nature to be performed at periodical board meetings...He is not, however, bound to attend all such meetings, though he ought to attend whenever, in the circumstances, he is reasonably able to do so. (3) In respect of all duties that, having regard to the exigencies of a business, and the articles of association, may properly be left to some other official, a director is, in the absence of grounds for suspicion, justified in trusting that official to perform such duties honestly.[13]

---

[5] *Re Denham & Co* (1884) 25 ChD 752.

[6] [1911] 1 Ch 425.

[7] *Ibid*, per Neville J, at p 437.

[8] "If he is acquainted with the rubber business he must give the company the advantage of his knowledge when transacting the company's business." *Ibid*, at p 437.

[9] *Dovey v Corey* [1901] AC 477, per Lord Davey.

[10] *Overend, Gurney & Co v Gib*, loc cit at p 495.

[11] [1925] Ch 407.

[12] *Ibid*, at p 427.

[13] *Ibid*, at pp 428-9.

A stricter duty in negligence

12.8   In *Dorchester Finance v Stebbing*,[14] Foster J accepted that the law in this area could be accurately stated as (i) requiring a director to show the degree of skill as may be reasonably expected from a person with his knowledge and experience, and (ii) requiring a director to take such care as an ordinary man might be expected to take on his own behalf.

12.9   Real developments in the law did not occur until cases such as *Norman v Theodore Goddard*,[15] where it was accepted, Hoffmann J declining to hear argument on the point, that the common law duty was accurately set out in section 214(4) of the Insolvency Act 1986. Two years later, in *Re D'Jan of London Ltd*,[16] Hoffmann LJ (sitting as an additional judge of the Chancery Division) held that the duty of care of a director is accurately set out in section 214(4) and that it was the conduct of "... a reasonably diligent person having both (a) the general knowledge, skill and experience that may reasonably be expected of a person carrying out the same functions as are carried out by that director in relation to the company, and (b) the general knowledge, skill and experience that that director has."

12.10   In *Bishopsgate Investment Management Ltd (in liq) v Maxwell*[17] Hoffman LJ suggested, obiter, that the time may now have come for a more objective approach:

> [I]n the older cases the duty of a director to participate in the management of a company is stated in very undemanding terms. The law may be evolving in response to changes in public attitudes to corporate governance ... Even so, the existence of a duty to participate must depend upon how the particular business is organised and the part which the director could be reasonably expected to play.[18]

12.11   There has been no distinction drawn between care, skill and diligence in more recent cases.[19]

RELIANCE ON CO-DIRECTORS, OFFICERS, AUDITORS AND PROFESSIONAL ADVISERS

12.12   As noted previously, the traditional line taken in *Re City Equitable Fire Insurance* was that:

> In respect of all duties that, having regard to the exigencies of a business, and the articles of association, may properly be left to some

---

[14] *Dorchester Finance Co v Stebbing* [1989] BCLC 498.

[15] [1992] BCC 14.

[16] [1993] BCC 646.

[17] [1993] BCLC 1282.

[18] See para 12.7 above.

[19] See paras 13.18-13.19 and 15.23-15.24 below.

other official, a director is, in the absence of grounds for suspicion, justified in trusting that official to perform such duties honestly.

Co-directors and officers

12.13   On the basis of *Re City Equitable*, a director may, as a statement of general principle, rely on his co-directors to the extent that the matter in question is, in terms of the board's internal 'division of labour', within their remit. A director may thus rely on a co-director appointed to the board by reason of his expertise in a particular area, and is 'entitled to rely upon the advice of his fellow directors in matters in which they are, or should be, experts'.[20]

12.14   *Re City Equitable* itself involved total reliance by two directors appointed to a board finance committee, on a third director, the Chairman. Notwithstanding that he was a person of the highest reputation, it was held that this abdication by the two co-directors of a responsibility with which the board as a whole had been charged by shareholders, would have been found to have constituted a breach of duty, 'however reasonable and however safe it might have seemed to the directors', but for an exculpatory article. There had been a division of labour which had not been adhered to by the two directors in question.

12.15   As far as officers are concerned, the emphasis has been to an even greater extent on business efficacy. In *Dovey v Corey*[21] Lord Halsbury stated that:

> I cannot think it can be expected of a director that he should be watching either the inferior officers ... or verifying the calculations of the auditor himself. The business of life could not go on if people could not trust those who are put into a position of trust for the express purpose of attending to details of management.

12.16   Thus the emphasis is largely on the exercise of proper judgment in selection of matters which it is proper for directors to leave to some only of their number, or some other individual or organisation, rather than on any monitoring which should be undertaken once a delegation has been properly made.

Auditors, solicitors and other outside advisers

12.17   As something of a contrast, directors will in certain circumstances be in breach of their duties if they fail to take appropriate, especially legal, advice.[22] The approach in respect of co-directors and officers, that "business cannot be carried on upon principles of distrust",[23] has been applied in relation to outside advisers, notwithstanding a hardening of attitude in other respects, by Hoffmann J in *Norman v Theodore Goddard*. In that case a director who was a chartered surveyor with no knowledge of company law was entitled to rely on a senior solicitor

---

[20]   *Palmer's Company Law,* para 8.408.

[21]   [1901] AC 477, at p 485.

[22]   See *Re Duomatic* [1969] 2 Ch 365, 377.

[23]   *Re City Equitable Fire Insurance*, at p 429.

administering the company's property, whose conduct had given no, or no sufficient grounds for concern.

12.18 Lord Halsbury's speech in *Dovey v Corey*, insofar as it relates to auditors, has already been noted.[24] An auditor is, however, entitled to rely on the honesty of other company officers in the absence of suspicious circumstances.[25] He is not an insurer and does not guarantee that a company's books correctly show the true state of its affairs.[26] His own duty, however, to exercise 'reasonable skill, care and caution'[27] and the necessarily defined and delegated nature of his duties, will go a long way towards satisfying a director's duty when reliance is placed on him.

12.19 In the case of all outside advice, nonetheless, slavish reliance is not acceptable. The obtaining of outside advice does not absolve directors from the duty of exercising their judgment on such advice:[28] where, for example, a discretion is given, it must be exercised.[29]

TRUSTEES' DUTY OF SKILL AND CARE

12.20 The developments in the law governing the trustees' duties of care are not dissimilar from those that have occurred in relation to directors.

12.21 Under the traditional common law rule:

> [I]t is the duty of a trustee to conduct the business of the trust with the same care as an ordinary prudent man of business would extend towards his own affairs.[30]

12.22 However, higher standards are expected of trustees who hold themselves out as having special expertise. Thus in *Barclays Bank v Bartlett*[31] Brightman J held that:

> a professional corporate trustee is liable for breach of trust if loss is caused to the trust fund because it neglects to exercise the special care and skill which it professes to have.[32]

---

[24] See para 12.14 above.

[25] *Re Kingston Cotton Mill Co (No 2)* [1896] 2 Ch 279 (CA).

[26] *Re London and General Bank (No 2)* [1895] 2 Ch 673 (CA).

[27] *Ibid*, at p 683.

[28] *Palmers Company Law*, para 8.409.

[29] See *Re Faure Electric Accumulator Co* (1880) 40 Ch D 141; *Re New Mashonaland Exploration Co* [1892] 3 Ch 577; and *Leeds Estate Building and Investment Company v Shepherd* (1887) 36 Ch D 787.

[30] *Bartlett v Barclays Bank Trust Co Ltd (No 1)* [1980] Ch 515, at p 531, per Brightman J, on the basis of cases such as: *Speight v Gaunt* (1883) 9 App Cas 1, 19 (HL); *Learoyd v Whitley* (1887) 12 App Cas 727; *Eaton v Buchanan* [1911] AC 253 (HL); and *Raes v Meek* (1886) 16 R HL 31, at p 33.

[31] [1980] 1 Ch 515.

[32] *Ibid*, at p 534.

12.23 There are, however, dicta to the contrary,[33] and recent Commonwealth authority seems to favour a single standard.[34]

12.24 In its recent consultation document on trustees' powers and duties[35] the Law Commission considered whether there should be a statutory statement of the duty of care to be exercised by a trustee when they delegate their powers. Five options for the appropriate test were put forward for consultees' views,[36] namely good faith, strict liability, a statutory statement of specified safe harbour criteria, the conduct of a reasonable prudent person and a dual subjective/objective test based on the Model Trustee Code for Australian States and Territories.[37] The latter requires a trustee to:

> act with care, skill, prudence, and diligence having regard to-
>
> (a) the nature, composition and purposes of the trust; and
>
> (b) the skills which the trustee possesses or ought, by reason of his business or calling, to possess.
>
> Therefore the duty is defined by regard to-
>
> • the characteristics of the particular trust; and
>
> • the skills which the trustee actually has; or
>
> • if he or she is professional, the skills which the trustee ought to have.

12.25 This standard allows greater flexibility, and enables fuller account to be taken of the attributes of the particular trustee.[38] The issue might not simply be whether the trustee was either paid, or held him or herself out as having a particular skill in trust administration in order to secure the trusteeship.[39] The conduct of an unpaid trustee who had a particular expertise would also be judged according to that skill, and not as if he or she was in all respects a lay person. Furthermore professional trustees who hold themselves out as having a particular expertise should be judged according to that standard, even if they do not in fact have it.

DUTIES OF DIRECTORS UNDER GERMAN LAW

12.26 Many countries in the European Union have legal systems which are based on codes and the legal environment is very different from our own. We did not

---

[33] *Jobson v Palmer* [1893] 1 Ch 71, per Romer J.

[34] *Australian Securities Commission v A S Nominees Ltd* (1995) 133 ALR 1; *Fales v Canada Permanent Trustee Co* (1976) 70 DLR (3d) 257.

[35] (1997) Consultation Paper No 146.

[36] *Ibid*, para 6.55. The Law Commission is currently preparing a report on this subject.

[37] (1989) vol 1 pp 24-26.

[38] The court does not take such attributes into account under the common law test of reasonable prudence: see *Learoyd v Whitlely* (1887) 12 App Cas 727, at pp 731-732.

[39] Cf *Bartlett v Barclays Bank Trust Co Ltd* (No 1) [1980] Ch 515, at p 534.

consider that it would be useful to carry out a pan-European survey of the law of other member states of the European Union having such systems, but we have considered the duty of care owed by directors under Article 93 of the German Stock Corporation Act ("AktG").[40] The summary of the position set out in paragraphs 12.26-12.30 is based upon a study of the position by Professor Frank Wooldridge.[41]

Introductory remarks: Director's liability for due care

12.27 Executive board members of a German public company (hereinafter called directors) must exercise the care of a sound and conscientious business manager.[42] The standard is not that of an ordinary business man, but that of a man in a leading and responsible position as the manager of other persons' property in a specific enterprise. The test is an objective one, and individual abilities are not taken account of.[43] Furthermore, unfitness or inexperience is not an excuse. When an action is brought against them, it appears that directors have to show compliance with this strict rule.[44] The general view is that the due care requirement is an absolute one, irrespective of subjective fault involving some degree of blameworthiness (*Vorwerfbarkeit*) and any failure, however slight, may result in a requirement to pay damages. However, the German courts and text writers do not always seem to have adopted this view.

12.28 A higher degree of care may be required from professionally qualified directors, such as lawyers, certified accountants, or bankers. This was made apparent in a case heard by the *Landgericht* of Düsseldorf in 1994,[45] in which the court held that the manager of a private company who was an experienced lawyer and who had also served on the board of a large public company, could not escape liability towards the private company by pleading that he had relied on an expert opinion which he had requested.

12.29 A director is also liable for failure to control his colleagues. If each director has particular functions allocated to him by the statutes of the company, the contract of employment or the company rules (*Geschäftsordnung*),[46] then such a director is in principle liable in respect of his own sphere of activity. However, he may

---

[40] See Appendix K below.

[41] Now Professor at the Notre Dame University in London. Professor Wooldridge has written extensively on German Company Law and we are indebted to him for permission to use this summary. Paras 12.26-12-30 and n 48 below were drawn from the text of an article due to be published in *Amicus Curiae*, the Journal of the Society for Advanced Legal Studies, at the Institute of Advanced Legal Studies, University of London.

[42] AktG, para 93(1) No 1. The management board (vorstand) of a German public company (AG) has the exclusive responsibility for managing the corporation. The company also has a supervisory board (Aufsichstrat) which is elected by the shareholder. This appoints and supervises the management board. No person may be a member of both boards.

[43] See Management and Control of Marketable Share Companies Ch *4 International Encyclopaedia of Comparative Law* at p 50.

[44] AktG, para 93(2) No 2.

[45] *Die Aktiengesellschaft* 1994, p 330.

[46] See AktG, para 77.

become liable for the activities of fellow directors if he has exercised inadequate supervision over them, or has failed to intervene where the wrongful conduct of a director has become known throughout the business, or where such conduct has failed to become public knowledge through his own lack of care. The division of functions between different directors in one of the ways described in this paragraph does not release any of them from their duty of supervision (*Überwachungspflicht*), which may be exercised with the help of agents, where necessary. Many of the decisions of the courts concerning the duties of directors involve this duty of supervision.

12.30 It appears that in the past, the German courts have given insufficient attention to the need for directors faced with difficult choices to exercise their business judgment, but their approach to this question now seems to be changing.

Burden of proof

12.31 In an action under AktG, paragraph 93, the company is required to produce evidence of acts of the directors which have caused damage. As far as the proof of causation is concerned, inference from the surrounding circumstances or the rules of prima facie evidence will support the company's action. Furthermore, the question of causation is left to the discretion of the judge in accordance with the provisions of paragraph 287 of the Civil Procedure Code. Damage is presumed in the special cases mentioned in AktG, paragraph 93(3): a detailed account of which is beyond the scope of this brief overview. The general view is that the burden of proof is placed upon the director to show that he exercised the care of a diligent and conscientious manager.[47] However, it has been argued by some writers that this reversal of the normal civil burden of proof (which has also been held to apply to private companies and co-operative societies), only applies to the extent that a director has to show that he has not been guilty of subjective fault.[48]

---

[47] See Willi Joachim, "Liability of Supervisory Directors in Germany" The International Lawyer vol 25, no 1, p 41, at p 63.

[48] The Supreme Court may have somewhat alleviated the burden of proof placed on the officer of a co-operative society who had delegated duties to a possibly dishonest or incompetent consultant in a recent case: see NJW 1997, 1905. It required the co-operative society to prove that the officer had allowed the consultant to receive payment for advisory services which were not included in the settlement agreed upon, whilst the officer was required to prove that she had made payments to a competent consultant, who had rendered the appropriate services for such payment, which held to concrete results which were beneficial to the co-operative society. Thus in this case, the burden of proving that no breach of duty had occurred in relation to particular matters was laid on each party. Such an approach is perhaps justified in particular cases, especially perhaps where certain duties are delegated. The application of the relevant German rules governing the burden of proof, whatever their precise nature, may well depend upon the facts and circumstances of the particular case and in many cases it may be hard to predict the outcome. Although the German rules would generally seem to impose a greater burden on directors than do those applicable in the United Kingdom, they appear workable, although the operation of para 93(2) No 2 is open to some dispute. In some situations (in which the burden placed on that company is lessened) its effect is easy to understand. Thus, for example, a company might assert that its actual assets and resources were less than those shown in the books. The directors would then be called on to explain this deficiency, the reason for which should be within their knowledge. They might well hope to convince the court that this depletion did not take place through any fault of their own, but resulted from inaccurate bookkeeping, for which they

263

Release from liability

12.32   Directors will not be liable to the company in damages if their action depends on a lawful resolution of the general meeting.[49] Such a resolution may be passed because the directors have referred a question of the management of the company to the general meeting,[50] or because a matter is otherwise within the competence of the general meeting. However, the general view is that subsequent ratification of a breach of duty does not relieve the directors from liability. Such liability is also not precluded by reason of the fact that the supervisory board has approved the transaction.[51] The company may, as a general rule, waive the damage claim or enter into a settlement only after three years, and if a minority representing at least ten per cent of the stated capital does not object.[52] Thus the discharge (*Entlastung*) of the directors by the general meeting only expresses a general approval of the management's performance: it does not effect a waiver of claims for damages.[53] However, it has somewhat controversially been held that there is an exception to this rule if the discharge is voted unanimously by all shareholders.[54] It should be emphasised that no one may exercise voting rights, whether by voting in respect of his own shares or acting as a proxy, or a resolution whereby he is to be discharged or released from an obligation, or on a determination whether the company shall assent a claim against him.[55]

could not be held responsible, the assets having been disposed of in specified ways (see BGH BB95, 1754, a case which concerned a private company).

[49]   AktG, para 93(4) No 1.

[50]   AktG, para 119(2).

[51]   AktG, para 93(4) No 2.

[52]   AktG, para 93(4) No 3.

[53]   AktG, para 1202(2).

[54]   BGHZ 29.385.

[55]   AktG, para 136(1).

PART 13
PREVIOUS PROPOSALS FOR A STATUTORY STATEMENT OF DIRECTORS DUTIES

13.1 Over the last 100 years or so, there have been many views expressed on the case for a statutory statement of the duties of directors and attempts to introduce the same. In this Part we set out some of those views and the arguments that were advanced. We do this under the following heads:

- The Davey Committee

- The Greene Committee

- The Jenkins Committee

- Attempts to introduce statutory statements of the duties of directors

THE DAVEY COMMITTEE

13.2 This Committee, chaired by Lord Davey, was set up by the Board of Trade to enquire what amendments were necessary in the Acts relating to joint stock companies formed with limited liability under the Companies Acts 1862-1890. The Davey Committee recommended that the Companies Act should provide that the director owed a duty to his company to exercise reasonable care and skill. It proposed the following clause for this purpose:

> 10(2) Every director shall be under an obligation to the company to use reasonable care and prudence in the exercise of his powers, and shall be liable to compensate the company for any damage incurred by reason of neglect to use such care and prudence.

The Davey Committee said in their report:

> It may also be thought that the clause which imposes on every director an obligation to use reasonable care and prudence in the exercise of his powers, and gives the company a right of action for neglect to do so, goes beyond any actual decision of the courts. But your Committee think it is right in principle.[1]

13.3 No action was taken on the Davey Committee's recommendation.

13.4 The Davey Committee also recommended that the fiduciary duties of promoters of companies and the duties of directors with prospectuses should be set out in the Companies Acts. The recommendation of the Davey Committee with respect to the fiduciary duties of promoters was not implemented but it is interesting to

---

[1] C 7779, para 32.

read the terms of their recommendation as it echoes many of the concerns that are echoed about a statutory statement of directors' duties:

> 30. Before making their recommendation as to the contents of the prospectus your Committee resolved that it was expedient that clauses should be inserted declaring general law with regard to the duties and liabilities of promoters and directors in respect to the promotion of companies and the issue of prospectuses. They have done so because their experience leads them to believe that the principles of law and commercial morality long since adopted and acted on by courts of law and equity are not generally recognised, or, if known, are frequently overlooked and disregarded. They also think that those principles of law, if thoroughly grasped, leave little to be desired so far as concerns the general principles which should regulate the dealings of men of business in this matter. The incorporation of those principles in an Act of Parliament is more likely to bring home to promoters and directors the obligations they undertake, and to shareholders and others the standard of commercial morality which they have a right to expect in those whom they are invited to trust. Your Committee have framed these clauses with great care, and so far as they purport to express the existing law they believe that they are accurate, but they dare not expect their clauses on so delicate a subject to be free from criticism. Your Committee are fully sensible of the danger incident to partial consolidation of the law, and of the possible loss of elasticity and adaptability involved in any attempt to express principles of law in formal clauses of an Act of Parliament. But they believe that the advantages in this case will outweigh the inconvenience. They have endeavoured to provide, as far as possible, against any danger of limiting the ordinary jurisdiction of the courts by recommending that nothing contained in the clauses shall limit or diminish any liability under the general law except as expressly provided. In this respect they have followed the precedent of the Partnership Act (section 46).

13.5   It is useful to note that the Davey Committee recommended a statutory statement because they felt that the duties of promoters were not well understood. In other words they thought that the purpose of the statement would be to inform and educate rather than to change the law. Moreover the Davey Committee contemplated, as appears from the draft bill annexed to their report, a statutory statement which would not limit or diminish any liability which a person might incur under the general law. In other words the statutory statement would be in addition to the general law.

THE GREENE COMMITTEE

13.6   The Company Law Amendment Committee (the Greene Committee) considered the question of codifying directors' duties in 1926 and concluded succinctly:

To attempt by statute to define the duties of directors would be a hopeless task.[2]

THE JENKINS COMMITTEE

13.7   The question of codifying directors' duties was further considered by the Jenkins Committee in 1962. The Report of the Jenkins Committee[3] dealt with the point as follows. It recorded that the Committee had received arguments for and against codification. It stated that the arguments in favour of codification were twofold. First, the duties of directors were contained in complex case law. The second reason given by the Jenkins Committee was that evidence had been given to that Committee that the law on directors' duties was inaccessible to company directors. It then cited some arguments that it had received against codification. First, it was impossible to define directors' duties exhaustively. Secondly, it was said in evidence to the Committee that there was a danger that there would be lacunae or gaps where it would be more difficult to say what the law was if there was a statutory statement of directors' duties.

13.8   The Jenkins Committee came down between the two views and recommended a non-exhaustive statement of the basic principles underlying the fiduciary duties which a director owed to his company. The statement set out a duty to act in good faith and a duty not to make improper use of money or other property of the company or information obtained while acting as a director. The statement also set out the consequence of a breach of one of these duties. These provisions were replicated with immaterial changes in clause 52 of the Companies Bill 1973, which we set out below. The final provision set out in the Jenkins statement of duties was in these terms:

> (iv) these provisions should be in addition to and not in derogation of any other enactment or rule of law relating to the duties or liabilities of directors of a company.[4]

13.9   It is not clear from this concluding provision, read in the context of the report, what status the Jenkins Committee intended the statement of duties to have. The report expresses the view that "a general statement of the basic principles underlying the relationship between directors and their companies - nowhere explicitly stated in the Act - might be useful to directors and others concerned with company management and we recommend such a provision in paragraph 99(a) below." This passage suggests that the statement was simply to replicate without replacing the core provisions of the general law. The provisions are not however a full or complete statement of the equitable rules: for instance the duty

---

[2]   Report of the Company Law Amendment Committee (1925-26) (Cmd 2657), para 46, p 20. The Chairman of this committee was Sir Wilfred Greene KC, who later became Master of the Rolls and a Lord of Appeal in Ordinary.

[3]   Report of the Company Law Committee (1962) Cmnd 1749, paras 86, 87 and 99(a).

[4]   This is similar to s 317(9) (see para 4.73 above) and s 232(11) of the Australian Corporations Law (Appendix H).

not to use company assets under the general law[5] applies even if the use is not at the expense of the company and the company itself could have made no profit.

13.10   Likewise the statement of the consequences of a breach of duty takes no account of the factors that may result in a reduction of the amount for which a director is liable, such as an order that he is indemnified for the expenses that he incurred in making a profit from the use of company assets. Again, the statement makes no reference to ratification of a breach of duty, though this may be implied, since the use of company assets is not a breach of duty unless "improper advantage" is taken of them; nor does it deal with the possible release of such a claim by the company. If the limitations that apply to the equitable rules under the general law apply to the duties as set out in the Jenkins statement then the effect of the Jenkins statement is merely to create mirror images of the equitable duties. This would probably lead to confusion, because there are further equitable rules not replicated in the statutory statement of which someone who only read the statutory statment would be unaware. It is possible that the Jenkins Committee did not intend to recommend the imposition of new statutory duties co-terminous with the relative equitable duties. It may be that all they were seeking to do was to set out in the statute a statement of directors' duties which would act as a signpost to directors and other users of company law that such duties existed but that they were governed by the general law. As we shall see when steps were taken in 1973 to implement the Jenkins Committee recommendation a different formula was used in place of paragraph (iv) set out above.

ATTEMPTS TO INTRODUCE STATUTORY STATEMENTS OF THE DUTIES OF DIRECTORS

Companies Bill 1973

13.11   Clause 52 of the Companies Bill was introduced to give effect to the recommendation of the Jenkins Committee. It provided:

> 52.—(1) A director of a company shall observe the utmost good faith towards the company in any transaction with it or on its behalf and shall act honestly in the exercise of the powers and the discharge of the duties of his office.
>
> (2) A director of a company shall not make use of any money or other property of the company, or of any information acquired by him by virtue of his position as a director or other officer of the company, to gain directly or indirectly an improper advantage for himself at the expense of the company.
>
> (3) A director of a company who, by any breach of subsection (1) or (2) above, makes a profit or inflicts any damage on the company shall be liable to account to the company for the profit or to compensate it for the damage.

---

[5]   See eg *Regal (Hastings) Ltd v Gulliver* [1967] 2 AC 134n.

(4) This section is without prejudice to any other provision of the Companies Acts and to any rule of law with respect to the duties or liabilities of directors.

13.12   The proposal in 1973 was thus to have a statutory statement of directors' duties which would not be a comprehensive statement. It would merely set out the principal duties. In the event the Companies Bill 1973 was lost due to the first general election of 1974. It may be inferred from the terms of the Bill that it was appreciated that there was an ambiguity in paragraph (iv) of the Jenkins Committeestatement. Clause 52 substitutes a new provision for that paragraph. It is doubtful, however, whether clause 52(4) was any more satisfactory. There are two possible views of the meaning of clause 52(4). One view might be that it made the statutory rules a second set of rules which existed alongside the duties arising in general law. This would mean that directors would be at risk of being held liable under either set of rules. It has been noted above[6] that the Jenkins Committee statement appeared to go further than the general law. On this basis the unsatisfactory result of clause 52, if it had become law, would have been to impose new duties on directors which would appear to be wider than the general law. Another view of clause 52(4) might be that it was intended to displace rules of law in so far as they corresponded to the matters dealt with in clause 52(1)-(3). On this view, the reference to other provisions of the Companies Acts and rules of law would be taken to be a reference to the provisions and rules which do not deal with the matters dealt with in clause 52(1)-(3). In other words, clause 52(4) is intended to confirm that no other duties etc are affected by clause 52(1)-(3).

Companies Bill 1978 clauses 44 and 45

13.13   The Companies Bill 1978 was the next attempt to codify directors' duties. It contained two clauses which aimed to codify directors' fiduciary duties and their duties of skill and care. The Bill was a major departure from the previous proposals because it was intended that the statutory statement of fiduciary duties should replace rather than be in addition to the general law.

13.14   Clause 44 provided:

44.—(1) A director of a company shall observe the utmost good faith towards the company in any transaction with it or on its behalf and owes a duty to the company to act honestly in the exercise of the powers and the discharge of the duties of his office.

(2) A director of a company shall not do anything or omit to do anything if the doing of that thing or the omission to do it, as the case may be, gives rise to a conflict, or might reasonably be expected to give rise to a conflict, between his private interests and the duties of his office.

(3) Without prejudice to subsection (1) and (2) above, a director of a company or a person who has been a director of a company shall not, for

---

[6]   See para 13.10.

the purpose of gaining, whether directly or indirectly, an advantage for himself:

    (a) make use of any money or other property of the company; or

    (b) make use of any relevant information or of a relevant opportunity—

        (i) if he does so while a director of the company in circumstances which give rise or might reasonably be expected to give rise to such a conflict; or

        (ii) if while a director of the company he had that use in contemplation in circumstances which gave rise or might reasonably have been expected to give rise to such a conflict.

(4) In this section—

'relevant information', in relation to a director of a company, means any information which he obtained while a director or other officer of the company and which it was reasonable to expect him to disclose to the company or not to disclose to persons unconnected with the company;

'relevant opportunity', in relation to a director of a company, means an opportunity which he had while a director or other officer of the company and which he had—

    (a) by virtue of his position as a director or other officer of the company; or

    (b) in circumstances in which it was reasonable to expect him to disclose the fact that he had that opportunity to the company.

(5) If any person contravenes any of the foregoing provisions of this section he shall be liable to account to the company for any gain which he has made directly or indirectly from the contravention or, as the case may be, shall be liable to compensate the company for any loss or damage suffered directly or indirectly by the company in consequence of the contravention.

(6) A person shall not be liable under the foregoing provision of this section for any act or omission which is duly authorised or ratified.

(7) This section has effect instead of any rule of law stating the fiduciary duties of directors of companies, but is without prejudice—

    (a) to any remedies which may be available apart from this section for a breach of any such duty; and

(b) to any other provision of the Companies Acts imposing duties or liabilities on such directors or defining their duties or liabilities;

and compliance with any requirement of those Acts shall not of itself be taken as relieving a director of a company of any liability imposed by this section.

13.15 Like clause 52 of the 1973 Bill, clause 44 uses the concept of "utmost good faith", which is not a concept used in this area of law and could if enacted have given rise to doubt and dispute. Clause 44(2) contained no exception for the situation where the interest was a minor kind or consisted of a duty to a third party rather than the private interests of the director. Clause 44(3) and (4) are complex and seem to have been tailored to meet the situation that had arisen in *Industrial Development Consultants Ltd v Cooley*.[7]

13.16 Clause 44(6) dealt with authority and ratification. However, there are many problems which it does not address. In particular, it does not lay down which organ of the company could authorise or ratify, and in what manner and in what circumstances. It was therefore not clear for example whether an act done in bad faith could be ratified or whether ratification was ineffective if it rendered the company insolvent.

13.17 Clause 44(7) was a major departure from the clause that the Jenkins Committee had recommended. The effect of that provision is that the statement of the fiduciary duties of directors would have become a comprehensive statutory code. The clause met a barrage of criticism and did not become law.[8]

13.18 Clause 45 provided as follows:

> 45.—(1) In the exercise of the powers and the discharge of the duties of his office in circumstances of any description, a director of a company owes a duty to the company to exercise such care and diligence as could reasonably be expected of a reasonably prudent person in circumstances of that description and to exercise such skill as may reasonably be expected of a person of his knowledge and experience.
>
> (2) Subsection (1) above shall have effect instead of the rules of law stating the duties of care and diligence and of skill owed by a director of a company to the company.

13.19 Clause 45 thus drew a distinction between care and diligence, and skill.[9] In the former case the standard of care was purely objective whereas in the case of skill it was sufficient if the director showed the skill reasonably to be expected of a person with his particular attributes. This approach has been overtaken by section 214 of

---

[7] [1972] 1 WLR 443, more fully reported at [1972] 2 All E R 162.

[8] See Philip L R Mitchell, *Directors Duties and Insider Dealing* (1982) p 37.

[9] See para 12.11 above, and paras 15.23-15.24 below.

the Insolvency Act 1986 (first enacted in the Insolvency Act 1985) which applies an objective test to skill. This development demonstrates the possible dangers in statutory codification of a duty: it is crystallised and cannot be developed by the courts in accordance with changing social and economic conditions. The movement in the case law setting out the standard of care to be shown by a director - from a subjective test[10] to a dual subjective/objective test[11] - in line with the increasing professionalism of business in the course of the twentieth century - is a remarkable example of the modernisation of the law by the judges, facilitated of course by the changes in insolvency legislation made by Parliament.

13.20   In the event, however, the Companies Bill 1978 was lost when a general election was called in 1979.

---

[10]   See *Re Brazilian Rubber Plantations and Estates Co Ltd* [1911] 1 Ch 425.

[11]   See *Re D'Jan of London Ltd* [1993] BCLC 646.

PART 14
A STATEMENT OF DIRECTORS' DUTIES: OPTIONS FOR REFORM

INTRODUCTION

14.1 The scope of this project includes considering the case for a statutory statement of the duties owed by directors to their company under the general law. In this part we consider criticisms made with regard to the inaccessibility of the present law, and then the various options open with respect to a possible statement of directors' duties, and the advantages and disadvantages of each. We ask consultees' views on these options. The scope of this project does not extend to suggesting any change to directors' fiduciary duties and in particular we have not been asked to consider whether any change should be made to the constituencies to whom directors owe their duties.[1]

14.2 The following possibilities are considered:

Option 1: a comprehensive codification[2]

Option 2: a partial codification[3]

Option 3: a statutory statement for guidance only and not replacing the general law[4]

Option 4: a non-binding statement of the main duties under the general law to be used in certain prescribed forms etc[5]

Option 5: authoritative pamphlets[6]

14.3 A draft **Statement of Duties** for the purposes of option 4 has been prepared and appears in Appendix A below. This statement includes a summary of the duty of care on one of the bases discussed in Part 15 below.[7]

CRITICISMS OF THE INACCESSIBILITY OF THE PRESENT LAW

14.4 It is often said that the law on directors' duties is difficult for directors to find or understand because the principles are to be found in the case law rather than in a provision of the Companies Act, and that the law in this field should be more

---

[1] See para 1.55 above.

[2] Paras 14.8-14.22 below.

[3] Paras 14.23-14.24 below.

[4] Paras 14.25-14.31 below.

[5] Paras 14.32-14.40 below.

[6] Paras 14.41-14.44 below.

[7] Namely, the dual objective/subjective test; see paras 15.20-15.25 below.

transparent. One of the arguments for codifying directors' duties is that it makes the law more accessible. It is said that law should be such that anyone who looks for it will find it and such that it can be explained to him in reasonably comprehensible terms. A layman should not have to look to his lawyer whenever he needs to know the basic principles. What a director needs is to know what to do before he acts, not afterwards, since he may be sued or subject to disqualification proceedings if he fails to comply with his obligations. Also, professionals can benefit from codification since it will reduce the need to examine earlier case law.

14.5 In other words, as the DTI's Consultative Paper states, the arguments for having a statutory statement of the duties of directors are to enable the duties to be more widely known and understood. It was for the same reasons that the Davey Committee recommended that the duties of promoters and directors with respect to company promotion should be codified. The Jenkins Committee too thought that a statement of directors' duties might well be useful to directors and others.

14.6 On the other hand it must be recognised that there are limits to the extent that directors will actually be assisted by reading a statement of their duties. First it must necessarily be expressed in general terms and it may need to be explained in order that they can apply it to their particular case. Second the statement would only cover the fundamental duties owed under the general law. It would not set out all the other duties imposed on directors by the Companies Act and other legislation.

14.7 There is no clear evidence as to the extent to which directors themselves regard this as a problem, though our proposed empirical survey will help to resolve this. For the present time, one can fairly assume that some directors, probably those without qualified company secretaries, find the present law difficult to understand.

OPTION 1: A COMPREHENSIVE CODIFICATION

General

14.8 Under this option we consider the pros and cons of codifying the duties of directors under the general law in the Companies Act.[8] In this consultation paper, we use the term "codification" to mean a statement of law of this kind.[9] The main advantages of codification in general are that :

- it makes the law more consistent;

---

[8] One of the objects of the Law Commissions is to consider whether the law can usefully be codified: Law Commission Act 1965, s 3(1).

[9] There are other meanings of the term "codification". In particular it may mean an authoritative non-binding restatement of the law, such as is found in the American Restatements of Torts, Trusts, Restitution and so on. It can also mean an authoritative model law, developed to give guidance to other law-making bodies to produce uniformity between them. An example of this kind of codification can be found in the Uniform Laws of the United States.

- it makes the law more certain;

- it makes the law more accessible, particularly to lay people: they have less need to have the law mediated for them through professionals; and

- it makes the law more comprehensible.[10]

To achieve these advantages the codification needs to be certain in its effect, clear in its expression and comprehensive in its scope.

Arguments in favour of codification

14.9 First, if codification is successfully achieved with the features identified in paragraph 14.8 above, it can be said to be fairer to the citizen who can find more easily, at least in general terms, what the law is before he does an act.

14.10 Second, it can also be said that codification leads to more predictability and that judges ought not to have the power to develop the law in a way which may result in a person coming under a liability which had not been imposed before and could not reasonably have been predicted.

14.11 Third, as appears from Part 9, it may be desirable to repeal some of the provisions of Part X of the Companies Act 1985 and place reliance on the duties of directors under the general law. The argument for adopting this radical solution would be stronger if the duties in question were set out in the Companies Act 1985 itself.

14.12 Fourth, the duties could be expressed in broad and general language which would be capable of being applied in a very wide range of situations. It would thus be capable of being developed as more and more examples were discovered which fell within the general terms.

Arguments against codification

14.13 There are arguments against codification in the sense given. First, codification is a difficult process and successful codification may not be achieved. Where the law has become settled and can be stated without much difficulty, codification can be achieved and brings benefits. An example of codification of this kind is the Sale of Goods Act 1893. Experience however shows that the success of codification is *subject-specific*: not all codification can be achieved or works. In the early years of the Law Commissions, for instance, much effort was put into producing a contract code but the project proved to be too ambitious. There is therefore a risk that codification may be a lengthy exercise and differences of opinion may emerge as a result of which it is impossible to achieve a consensus. For example, a director is in breach of duty if he misappropriates information which he receives and should have reported to his board,[11] but the circumstances in which he ought to report information he receives to his board have not been defined by the courts

---

[10] See Criminal Law: A Code for England and Wales (1989) Law Com No 177, vol 1, paras 2.1-2.8.

[11] See *Industrial Development Consultants v Cooley* [1972] 1 WLR 443, 451S, para 11.14 above.

and there are likely to be differences of view as to what those circumstances should be.

14.14   As regards the duty of care, the usual difficulty in stating the law is to define the ambit of the duty and to specify the persons to whom the duty is owed. That difficulty does not exist in this case because all that it is desired to state is the duty of directors *to their company*. That leaves the standard of care, which is the only other matter that would have to be covered by the codification. That is unclear under the present law, but once the underlying policy is decided upon, there is no difficulty in stating it.[12] However what is being considered under this option[13] is a total codification of all the duties governed by the general law whether they are the duty of care or the fiduciary duties. Fiduciary duties cannot be codified without either being stated in detailed terms in which case there will be a loss of flexibility, or being stated in general terms in which case the statute may have to be interpreted by the courts and the result is that the law may not be much more accessible than it is at present.

14.15   Second, codification is unlikely to result in a comprehensive statement of the law. There are bound to be cases where the codified law has to be interpreted and is not clear on its face.[14] Accessibility is then only superficially improved since a lay person can never be sure what the law is unless he looks elsewhere or seeks professional advice. If he does proceed on the basis that the codification is complete he may be seriously mistaken and misled.

14.16   Third, codification does not always lead to predictability because judges have to interpret the law. Parliament cannot be expected to foresee every situation that might arise or to pass legislation to cover every case. Even when the law is statutory, there is scope for the courts to fill in gaps in the law. Courts have to supply an answer when they are asked what a statute means in a given situation. The view of the courts as simply giving effect to law made by the Legislature is increasingly unrealistic in modern society due to the complexity and volume of legislation being made.

14.17   Fourth, codification might well lead to a loss in flexibility. This is one of the points that concerned, for instance, the Davey Committee. The law of fiduciaries is dynamic and needs to be adapted to new situations: for instance the law has not yet had to define the connection with the company that is necessary to render a director liable to account to the company for the benefit of an opportunity which he receives for his own account while he is a director of the company. Moreover, when duties are codified, people will tend to ask whether as a matter of statutory construction they apply to a given situation rather than whether the situation is one caught by the policy or principle behind the decided cases. Furthermore, if

---

[12]   See Part 15.

[13]   We consider the option of partial codification, that is codification of what can be stated without difficulty, as option 2.

[14]   This is not a new problem, nor is it one confined to common law systems or to systems where the Westminster style of legislative drafting, rather than the style seen in some Continental codes, is adopted: see for example *Luke, X, 25-37* for a discussion of the term "neighbour" in the Hebrew law.

there is a comprehensive codification there is a real risk that a situation occurs which is outside the statutory code but where the law ought to have applied. The courts cannot rewrite what is there or substitute a provision which they think Parliament should have enacted. Judicial evolution of the law is brought to a stop, and it ceases to be possible without further legislation to bring the law in line with changing social conditions.[15] In addition codification in substitution for the existing law could well lead to uncertainty in what the law is. This would involve directors taking legal advice which is likely to result in an added cost for business. It could also lead to more litigation.

14.18   Loss of flexibility is mitigated if the codification is in broad and general language. However the danger of this is that if the language is truly of this description it would not make the law accessible. The lay person will still need a professional to mediate it for him, and inform him of the decisions of the courts as to what fell within the language.

14.19   This may be less of a problem in a civil law system where the courts, in looking at statutory provisions, can often qualify their application or develop rules or obligations which are additional to those provisions.[16] In English law the method of interpretation traditionally has been more restrictive.

14.20   Fifth, the advantage of improved accessibility, without the disadvantage of loss of flexibility, can be more effectively achieved in other ways, such as options 3, 4 and 5 below.

14.21   And finally, with codification, a difficulty that might arise is in amending it, if the need arose, because this would require primary legislation.

Previous consideration of codification

14.22   It is to be noted that in its consultation paper on *Fiduciary Duties and Regulatory Rules*[17] the Law Commission asked consultees whether they would be in favour of codifying fiduciary duties and expressed the provisional view that it would be impractical and undesirable to do this, given the nature and prophylactic function of fiduciary obligations. This view was virtually unanimously supported on consultation and in its final report[18] the Law Commission concluded that its provisional conclusion was correct and that codification should be rejected. This report of course was directed to the question whether fiduciary duties in general,

---

[15]   An example of judicial evolution of a rule of law to bring it into line with modern conditions is the history of the development of the standard of care to be exercised by a director: compare *Re Brazilian Rubber* [1911] 1 Ch 425 and *Re D'Jan of London* [1993] BCC 646: see paras 12.3-12.10 above.

[16]   An example of this can be seen from the summary of law on art 93 of the German Stock Corporations Code at para 12.26 above. The courts have, for example, imposed on professionally qualified directors a higher duty of care (para 12.28 above) and alleviated the reversal of the burden of proof (para 12.31, n 46 above); and see generally Zweigert and Kotz, *An Introduction to Comparative Law* (2nd ed, 1992) pp 95-99 for the role of the courts in developing the Code Civil.

[17]   Consultation Paper No 124, para 6.23.

[18]   Fiduciary Duties and Regulatory Rules, Law Com No 236, para 17.2.

rather than the duties of directors, should be codified, but the Law Commission did not reject codification on the basis of this distinction. As explained above, two authoritative company law committees, the Greene Committee and the Jenkins Committee, have considered and rejected the idea of a comprehensive codification of fiduciary duties.[19]

Consultees are asked whether there should be a comprehensive statutory codification of the duties owed by directors to their company under the general law.

OPTION 2: PARTIAL CODIFICATION OF DIRECTORS' FIDUCIARY DUTIES

14.23 It is clear that the duties with respect to corporate opportunities are not completely settled and that it might be dangerous for that reason to convert them into statutory duties since a case might arise which could not now be foreseen where they ought to have applied. In those circumstances there is a case for codifying the duties which are not in doubt such as the duty to act in what the director considers to be the company's best interests. This is the course that has been followed in Australia. As can be seen in Appendix H, section 232 sets out the duty of a director to act honestly, to exercise reasonable care and diligence, and not to make improper use of information or his position. Section 232(11) concludes by providing that section 232 is in addition to, and not in derogation of, any rule of law relating to the duty or liability of directors. So far as we can ascertain, this partial codification has not caused difficulties in practice in Australia. We also note that in the Corporate Law Economic Reform Bill 1998, recently published by the Australian Government, it is proposed to replace section 232 with statutory duties to exercise care and diligence, to act in good faith and for a proper purpose, and not to misuse the position of director or information obtained. It is again proposed that these provisions should have effect in addition to, and not in derogation of, any rule of law relating to the duty or liability of a director. This formulation is very similar to that used by the Jenkins Committee in their recommendation on directors' duties, which we have discussed in paragraphs 13.7-13.10 above.

14.24 The argument against this course is that the result may be confusing to the layman when he discovers that there are duties which are not set out in the statute.[20] Uncertainty as to the law will continue, and the aim of improving accessibility to the law will only be partially achieved.

Consultees are asked whether they consider that the duties of directors should be codified in part only and, if so, whether such codification should extend to the duty to act in the company's best interests,[21] or to some other, and if so which, of the duties described in Part 11 above.

---

[19] See paras 13.6-13.10 above. See also the views of the Davey Committee at paras 13.2-13.5.

[20] The statement could, of course, state expressly that it does not set out all of a director's duties.

[21] See para 11.5 above.

OPTION 3: STATUTORY STATEMENT OF DIRECTORS' DUTIES NOT REPLACING THE GENERAL LAW

14.25 Another option would be to have a statutory statement of the main propositions established in the case law in the field of fiduciary duties which, like the statement of directors' duties proposed by the Jenkins Committee,[22] does not replace the general law.[23] On the face of it, the advantage of this course would be that it would make part of the law more accessible but yet would not cause the law to lose any of its flexibility since it would always be open to the court to use the general law.

14.26 As we have pointed out above,[24] there are difficulties in this course. If the general law remains, then the director finds himself subject to two regimes - one under the general law and one under the statute. If the new regime created by statute is in fact wider (in respect of the matters to which it applies) than the relevant general law, his duties are increased.

14.27 A further difficulty with this option is that it could mislead someone who read it into thinking that he could not be liable for doing something not mentioned in the statutory statement. Alternatively he might argue, with some force that if that which he did and which constituted a breach of duty was not mentioned in the statement he ought to be treated more leniently as a result.

14.28 There is a further legislative possibility that consultees may wish to consider if the real reasons for having a statutory statement where the general law is preserved are:

(1) to enable readers of the Act to have a summary of the main duties; and

(2) to make it clear to a reader of the legislation that there are duties imposed on directors by the general law and that they are not to be found in the Act.

14.29 The Act could theoretically provide not merely that the statement does not replace the general law but also, unlike the Jenkins Committee proposals, that it does not impose any liability on a director and only provides information. This would avoid the situation in which directors are exposed to two sets of rules and in which the statutory rules turn out to be wider than the rules under the general law. It would have the advantage that there would be some recognition in the Act, which covers most of the other important areas of company law, that directors owe significant duties under the general law.

14.30 However there are other difficulties in the course under consideration. First, the summary may not represent the law as developed by the courts and so (unless

---

[22] See para 13.8 above .

[23] The Jenkins statement was to be "in addition to and not in derogation of any other enactment or rule of law with respect to the duties or liabilities of directors"; Jenkins Report, para 99(a)(iv). The Jenkins Report does not explain what the words were intended to achieve, but it appears that the duties contained in the Jenkins statement were to be new statutory duties covering the same ground as duties imposed by the general law.

[24] See paras 13.7-13.10 above.

amending legislation is passed) the advantages of increased accessibility to the law and increased transparency will be more apparent than real. Second, it is most unusual for a statute to contain provisions which do not set out the law but merely give guidance. If a statement of duties of directors were set out in the Companies Act 1985, but it was also stated that the statement could not result in the imposition of any liability on a director, the statement would be non-legislative material of this kind. The traditional view is that a statute should not contain material of this nature.[25] We cannot at this stage test whether this traditional approach applies to a statutory statement of duties for directors: indeed the question whether Parliament would entertain any departure from the traditional position may depend on the level of consultees' support for it. In case the traditional approach cannot be distinguished, consultees who opt for this option on this basis may wish to indicate their second choice.

14.31   Another problem with this option is that traditionally a statute has only been used for provisions which have legal effect (this would include converting a rule previously found in case law into a statutory rule), and there may be difficulty in persuading Parliament to permit a statement which in effect is purely for guidance to be inserted into a statute.[26] Most non-legislative material can now be given in explanatory notes, which under a new practice are to be produced with bills and Acts of Parliament.[27] Because of this approach, it is probable that even if this option receives overwhelming support the Commissions would wish to recommend an alternative option as well and so consultees who favour this option are asked to state their views on the other options in case this option proves not to be available.

Consultees are asked whether they would favour a statutory statement of directors' duties in the Companies Act 1985 which does not replace the general law and, if so, whether the statement should impose liabilites on directors in addition to those to which they are subject under the existing law, or merely convey information for guidance.

OPTION 4: A NON-BINDING STATEMENT OF THE MAIN DUTIES OF DIRECTORS TO BE USED IN CERTAIN PRESCRIBED FORMS ETC

14.32   The purpose of this option would be to give the Secretary of State power to insert a succinct statement of the main duties of directors into a number of official documents that the company has to produce or file and to require companies to include the statement as an annexe to their articles of association. To enable consultees to see what the option involves so far as the annual accounts and certain specified prescribed forms are concerned, Parliamentary Counsel has

---

[25]   See n 26 below.

[26]   See eg the report by the Joint Committee on Statutory Instruments on the Judicial Pensions (Contributions) Regulations 1998, which stated that the inclusion of mere explanatory matter was not "in accord with proper legislative practice" and that in its view "non-legislative material should not be included in statutory instruments". (June 1998, HL paper 119, HC 33 - xxxvii, p 4). Although the Committee's remarks related to statutory instruments, the same principles apply to statutes.

[27]   See para 9.37 above.

drafted a section, section 309B, which appears in Appendix A. Under this section the Secretary of State can include the statement in forms and documents prescribed under section 10(2) (statement by first directors and secretary), section 288(2) (consent to act as a director), section 363(2) (annual return) and section 680(1) (application to register a company not formed under the companies legislation).

14.33 We also set out in Appendix A a statement of the duties to illustrate this option. At an early point the Statement makes clear its status: it expressly states that it is not a complete statement of the law and that the law is subject to change.[28] The final paragraph of the statement makes it clear that the statement does not affect the law. It also confirms that the fact that a director signs a document in which such a statement is included, acknowledging that he has read the statement, will not affect the duties he owes.

14.34 The statement of duties summarises the following duties, which we regard as the principal duties which a directors owes to his company:

> paragraph 3 - the duty to act in good faith in what the director considers to be the best interests of the company;[29]
>
> paragraph 4 - the duty to comply with the company's constitution;[30]
>
> paragraph 5 - the duty not to make secret profits;[31]
>
> paragraph 6 - the duty not to fetter any of his discretions;[32]
>
> paragraph 7 - the duty to account for a benefit he receives as a result of a transaction entered into by the company in which he has an undisclosed interest;[33]
>
> paragraph 8 - the duty of care skill and diligence;[34]
>
> paragraph 9 - the duty to have regard to the interests of employees;[35] and
>
> paragraph 10 - the duty to act fairly as between different shareholders.[36]

---

[28] Statement of duties, para 2.

[29] See para 11.5 above.

[30] See para 11.16 above.

[31] See paras 11.15-11.16 above.

[32] See para 11.11 above.

[33] See paras 11.13-11.17 above.

[34] On the basis of option 2 considered in Part 15 below.

[35] See para 11.27 above.

[36] See paras 11.19-11.20 above.

14.35 A number of matters about the statement of duties require comment. First, the object has been only to summarise the duties.[38] It does not purport to set them out comprehensively. Second, the statement of duties does not set out the no-conflicts rule,[39] apart from the director's duty to account if he has an undisclosed and unapproved conflict of interest.[40] As we have seen there is no duty as such on a director not to place himself in a position where his duty and interest conflict: rather if he does so, the company may seek to set aside the transaction. Breach of the rule would primarily involve the company being entitled to avoid the resulting contract, but consistently with the statement being a statement of *duties,* and not remedies, the statement of duties only sets out the directors' duty to account for any benefit from the transaction (unless he is permitted to retain it under the company's constitution or the company in general meeting has given its informed consent).[41] Third, nothing is said about the ability of the company to release a claim or to ratify a wrong.[42] Fourth, the statement does not refer, in relation to the duty of care, to the way in which the courts approach questions of commercial judgment.[43] This is important because the view was expressed in Part 3 that any statutory statement of the duty of care should refer to the possibility of release and ratification and incorporate a business judgment defence.[44] The desirability of this is a matter on which the proposed empirical survey may shed light, and on which consultees views would be welcome. Finally in drafting the statement the view has been taken that section 309 of the Companies Act 1985 does no more than set out a duty which directors must perform as part of their duty to act in the company's best interests and that it does not create any duty to consider the interests of the employees in general separate from those interests.[45]

14.36 We envisage that such a statement could be brought to the attention of directors in a number of ways:

---

[38] Inevitably the statement does not cover every aspect of the directors' duties. For instance the statement might have stated that directors should not use the company's assets for purposes not permitted by law and should observe other statutory duties, but the inclusion of this statement might not greatly increase directors' understanding of their duties. The Companies Bills 1973 and 1978 did not include such a statement. See also para 6.13 of the Hong Kong Consultancy Report in Appendix L below.

[39] See para 11.15 above.

[40] Including a conflict of duties, as where a director of another company concerned in the transaction: *Transvaal Lands Co v New Belgium (Transvaal) Land and Development Co* [1914] 2 Ch 488, at p 503.

[41] The nature of the duty to account will depend on the particluar circumstances of the case: see for example *Mahoney v Purnell* [1996] 3 All ER 61 (an undue influence case) where the parties could not be restored to their previous position and the court awarded compensation against the party exercising the undue influence; and see generally Aggravated, Exemplary and RestitutionaryDamages (1997) Law Com No 247, paras 3.28-3.32.

[42] See para 11.30 *et seq* above.

[43] Compare para 2.15(iii) above.

[44] See para 3.91 above, and see paras 15.30-15.41 below. However the statement does refer to the possibility of the company in general meeting permitting a director having a conflict of interest and retaining secret profits, as suggested in Part 3.

[45] For a discussion of the interaction between section 309 and the duty of loyalty, see paras 11.25-11.28 above.

(1) The Secretary of State could make regulations requiring a statement of the duties of directors to appear in the directors' report, just as the Cadbury Code and SAS100 now require a statement of the financial and accounting responsibilities of directors to appear in the accounts.[46] This is provided for in draft section 309B(2) in Appendix A.

(2) The Secretary of State could make regulations inserting the statement into various prescribed returns, such as the annual return and consent to act as a director (draft section 309B(1)). By signing the return, a director would acknowledge that he has read the statement (draft section 309B(3)(b)). The Secretary of State could also be given power to require all directors to sign this statement in the annual return.[47]

(3) The Secretary of State could make regulations requiring companies to annex the statement of duties to their articles of association.[48] The company would not be able to alter the annex because it would not be part of its articles for the purposes of the statutory power to alter the articles by special resolution.[49] If the statement of duties were to be revised the regulations could be amended.

14.37 The Secretary of State would need power to make these regulations. Appendix A sets out by way of illustration a draft section 309B for the purpose of giving the Secretary of State power to make regulations to require the statement of duties to be added to specified prescribed forms or to be inserted into the accounts.[50]

14.38 A similar approach to the suggestion in paragraph 14.36(1) above was recommended by the King Committee in relation to securing compliance with its Code of Corporate Practices and Conduct, which suggested that an appropriate statement in the annual financial statements would read:

> The directors' endorse, and during the period under review, have applied the Code of Corporate Practices and Conduct as set out in the King Report. By supporting the Code the directors have recognised the need to conduct the enterprise with integrity and in accordance with generally accepted corporate practices.[51]

14.39 If the Secretary of State by regulation required the directors' report to include the statement of the duties of directors, and a company produced accounts which did

---

[46] See Appendix G.

[47] Not included in draft s 309B.

[48] Not included in draft s 309B. Compare section 425(3) of the Companies Act 1985, which requires a company to annex to its memorandum of association an order of the court sanctioning a scheme of arrangement under that section. If this is not done, the company and any officer in default is liable to a fine: s 425(4).

[49] Section 9 of the Companies Act 1985.

[50] Section 309B does not provide for the statement of duties to be annexed to a company's articles, or for signature on (say) the annual return other than of the officer submitting the form.

[51] See para 9, Chapter 22.

not comply with this regulation, every person who was director at the relevant time would be guilty of an offence and liable to a fine.[51]

14.40   This option would not make informative pamphlets unnecessary.

Consultees are asked:

(i) whether they consider that the draft statement in Appendix A sets out the principal duties of directors under the general law;[52]

(ii) whether the statement should refer to the possibility of the company in general meeting ratifying the breach of duty or releasing a claim that it may have;

(iii) whether they consider that such a statement should mandatorily be annexed to the company's articles;

(iv) whether they consider that such a statement should be required to be included in the Directors' Report attached to the company's annual accounts;

(v) whether they consider that a director should sign that he has read the statement when he signs a return confirming that he has been appointed a director;

(vi) whether they consider that each director should be required to sign that he has read the statement when the company submits its annual return; and

(vii) whether they think that such a statement should appear in any other statutory return which the company makes.[53]

OPTION 5: AUTHORITATIVE PAMPHLETS

14.41   This option is available whether or not options 2, 3 or 4 are adopted. Authoritative pamphlets summarising the duties of directors may assume greater importance if the law is not to be codified in whole or part. Nowadays there are many booklets issued which seek to explain areas of technical law in layman's terms. Thus for example the Insolvency Service produces a Guide to Bankruptcy. Documents like this play an invaluable role in making the law accessible to laymen.[54]

14.42   Such a booklet would have to be an authoritative document to carry weight. It would therefore have to have the support of the Department of Trade and Industry and bodies such as the Institute of Directors, the Chartered Institute of Secretaries, the Federation of Small Businesses, The Law Society and the

---

[51]   Section 234(5) of the Companies Act 1985. The relevant time would be immediately before the end of the time permitted by the Companies Act 1985 for laying the accounts for the financial year in question before the company in general meeting and filing them with the registrar: see ss 241-242 and 244 of the Companies Act 1985.

[52]   Thus including both the duty of care and fiduciary duties.

[53]   The suggestions made in paragraphs (ii)-(vii) are not achieved by the draft clause and statement in Appendix A.

[54]   See generally the recommendations of the Committee on Standards in Public Life in relation to Public Service Organisations, which may be limited companies: Personal Liability in Public Service Organisations, June 1998.

accountancy bodies etc. The Financial Law Panel[55] in London has started the preparation of a number of pamphlets to offer general guidance on the law of directors' duties. The pamphlets cover directors in different situations including not-for profit companies, small businesses as well as large private companies and public limited companies. The pamphlets focus on practical situations where the way forward is not easily found in a piece of legislation or a text book, but where a director must understand the practical effect of general statements of legal principle. They are designed to be readily understandable to those directors who are not legally qualified.

14.43 Something similar has already been done in Australia. In June 1994 the Australian Securities Commission, the Australian Society of Certified Practising Accountants, and the Institute of Chartered Accountants in Australia jointly published a booklet designed to assist directors in meeting their duties and legal responsibilities called *"The Company Director's Survival Kit. What you need to know about the duties of company directors"*. It was aimed at people becoming directors for the first time, and directors of smaller private companies. It covered the director's duty to act honestly, to exercise care and diligence, not to use inside information, and not to make improper use of their positions. It also dealt with matters such as insolvent trading and the financial responsibilities of directors.

14.44 A means would have to be found of bringing any such pamphlet to the attention of directors. On the face of it, this ought to happen when the company is formed. Companies House could include a copy of the pamphlet when a company is sent formal papers on incorporation.[56] Companies House could also send a copy of the pamphlet to any person whose appointment is notified to it in accordance with section 288 of the Companies Act 1985.

Consultees are asked:

(i) whether they consider that a pamphlet setting out directors' duties – including both the duty of care and fiduciary duties – should be prepared as a means of setting out the duties of directors;

(ii) if so, how they think the pamphlet would be best brought to the attention of directors; and

(iii) whether they consider that a pamphlet of this kind would make it unnecessary to have a statutory statement of directors' fiduciary duties.

---

[55] The Financial Law Panel is an independent body which was formed in 1993 under the sponsorship of the Bank of England and the Corporation of London. The main aims of the Financial Law Panel are to be the central forum for the consideration and practical resolution of legal uncertainties and anomalies as they affect financial markets and services in the United Kingdom. Its role is to give guidance on particular areas of legal uncertainty as they affect financial markets and services; to review and comment on proposals for legislation and regulation in the UK and EC; and to consider and make proposals on such other matters as it considers appropriate relating to the financial markets of the UK. See the City Handbook (June 1998) published by the Bank of England with the support of the Corporation of London.

[56] This may not help people who become directors after the company is bought off the shelf from company formation agents.

PART 15
DUTY OF CARE: OPTIONS FOR REFORM

INTRODUCTION

15.1 In this part, we examine the ways in which the law on the director's duty of care to his company could be reformed. There is no doubt that a director owes a duty to his company to exercise care in carrying out his functions. However, what is not so clear is the *standard* of care which the director must show.

15.2 We begin by summarising the current position in respect of the standard of care which was discussed in detail in Part 12. We then go on to consider whether there should be a statutory statement of the duty of skill and care. Next, we examine what the content of such a statutory statement should be and set out a number of possible options. We then go on to consider the rule that the courts do not investigate bona fide decisions involving matters of business judgment (known as "the business judgment rule") and discuss the question whether there should be a statutory business judgment rule.[1] Next, we consider whether there should be statutory provisions dealing with reliance and delegation.[2] Finally we ask whether there should be a statutory statement of the duty of care even if there is no statutory statement of fiduciary duties.[3]

CURRENT POSITION IN RESPECT OF THE STANDARD OF CARE

15.3 As explained in Part 12 of this consultation paper, the effect of the older cases in this field is that the required standard of care is low: directors discharge their duty if they exercise such care as is reasonably to be expected of them, *having regard to their knowledge and experience*. They are not therefore required to act as (say) reasonably competent directors. If they do not have the knowledge and experience that a reasonably competent director would have, account is taken of that fact and their conduct is judged by reference to the knowledge that they actually have. Furthermore non-executive directors are not required to perform their duties except at board meetings.[4] While all directors should attend board meetings when they reasonably can, the law (as established in the older authorities) does not oblige them to attend.

15.4 However, we also referred in Part 12 to section 214 of the Insolvency Act 1986, which imposes a liability on directors to contribute to the assets of the company if they have caused their company to trade at a time when it could not avoid entering insolvent liquidation. This requires the conduct of directors to be judged both purely objectively and subjectively by reference to their own personal characteristics. Thus, to decide what steps the director ought to have taken, two questions are asked :

---

[1] See paras 15.30-15.41 below.

[2] See paras 15.42-15.50 below.

[3] See para 15.51 below.

[4] See *Gower's Principles of Modern Company Law* (6th ed, 1997), pp 641-4.

(1) what steps would have been taken by a reasonably diligent director who has the knowledge skill and experience reasonably to be expected of a director carrying out the same functions;[5] and

(2) what steps would a reasonably diligent person with this director's knowledge skill and experience have taken?

15.5 More recently the courts have used this section as a basis for saying that the standard of care which a director must now show under the general law requires the director to act as a reasonably diligent person having not only the same general knowledge and experience as the director but also the general knowledge and skill to be expected of a person having the same functions.[6] The better view is that this more modern statement of the duty of care of a director now represents the law and would be followed by the higher courts.

SHOULD THERE BE A STATUTORY STATEMENT OF THE DUTY OF CARE?

15.6 As we see it there are a number of possible purposes to be served by a statutory statement of the director's duty of care to the company:

(1) it would clarify the law and result in certainty as to the effect of the recent decisions;[7]

(2) it would make the law more accessible to directors. Directors may well not have a copy of the Act or be able to find their way around it, but the Act would provide a convenient statement of the law. This could be used by Companies House, representative professional bodies and commercial publishers in books and pamphlets produced for directors; and

(3) by stating the essential proposition of law in more modern language, the law should be more easily understood by directors.

Consultees are asked whether they consider that there are objectives that might be achieved by a statutory statement of the director's duty of care other than those set out in paragraph 15.6.

15.7 A statutory statement of the director's duty of care could set out the standard of care to be exercised by a director comprehensively and accordingly if there were to be a statutory statement of the directors' duty of care it would naturally replace the common law, avoiding the need to define the relationship between it and the common law and difficulties which can arise in doing so.

15.8 However, there is an important question to ask, which is whether this is an area of law where it would be better if development were left to the courts rather than Parliament. The courts could develop the law on a case by case basis. This would be slower and more costly for litigants but it would allow the law to be worked out

---

[5] Or entrusted with the same functions: s 214(5).

[6] See *Gower's Principles of Modern Company Law* (6th ed, 1997) pp 641-4.

[7] See paras 12.8-12.10 above.

in actual situations, thus enabling the law to react to and take account of any problems that arise as it is developed. In this area it is not a question of codifying law that has already become well settled because, as we have seen, the law here has been evolving. On the other hand it is equally clear that at the present moment at least the courts are likely to develop a twofold test on the lines of section 214 of the Insolvency Act 1986. If it is not considered satisfactory to apply a twofold test, then there may be a case for a statutory statement of the duty of care setting a purely subjective standard (option 1 below). If it can be seen that the law is evolving towards a twofold test and it is considered that there is nothing noticeably unsatisfactory about the new standard which the courts are setting, there may be little objection to setting this out in statute (option 2 below).[8] Indeed a statutory statement of the duty of skill and care would help remove uncertainty. It would also make the duties of directors more accessible and comprehensible to directors. However, it is also said that if the duty of care of a director were made statutory, people would be deterred from becoming directors and in particular there would be few who would wish to accept appointment as a non-executive director.[9]

15.9 We explain in this part that we consider that the standard of care to be exercised by a director generally should be no less than that which must be exercised when the company is on the verge of insolvent liquidation - so it should be the same as is required by the courts in interpreting section 214. In our view, this approach would be fair and workable.

Consultees are asked whether or not they favour a statutory statement of the duty of care. Consultees may wish to consider the options for that statement[10] before deciding how to respond.

CONTENT OF A STATUTORY STATEMENT OF THE DUTY OF CARE

15.10 The next issue is the standard by which a director's conduct should be judged in determining whether he has discharged his duty of care. We consider three options:

> Option 1: a subjective test
>
> Option 2: a dual subjective/objective test
>
> Option 3: an objective test only

Option 1: A subjective test

15.11 Under this option, it would be stated that a director owes a duty to his company to exercise the care, diligence and skill that would be exercised by a reasonable person having his knowledge and experience.[11] Account would be taken of the

---

[8] But see para 14.13 above.

[9] See para 15.22 below.

[10] See paras 15.10-15.29 below.

[11] This in effect is the traditional view described at paras 12.3-12.7 above.

responsibilities of the director in question and the circumstances of the particular company.[12] We refer to this as the low standard of care because it will lead to a lower standard of care if the director has inadequate knowledge and experience.

15.12 Various justifications are advanced for a low standard. It is argued that management is not a profession and that directors do not require particular skills to discharge their duties. However, many areas of business now require specialised skills and knowledge beyond those possessed by the layman. The academic literature on management studies is voluminous and various qualifications are available to existing and aspiring managers. Possession of an MBA qualification is becoming increasingly a pre-requisite for recruitment to executive positions or further advancement. Thus, although an Institute of Directors survey in 1990 showed that only a quarter of directors possessed any professional or management qualification,[13] this figure may well rise further in the relatively near future.

15.13 It is also argued that to raise the standard of care may encourage litigation whereas management should be supervised by shareholders, not the courts.[14] As to this argument, to the majority of smaller shareholders in listed or quoted companies, share ownership is simply an investment without the incidents of management control which may have existed formerly. The appointment of directors, although subject to the approval of the company in general meeting, is in reality a matter for the Chairman or board appointments committee, alternative appointments not generally being put to shareholders. Shareholders have, since 1948, had the right to remove directors by ordinary resolution,[15] a power described by Palmer as 'one of the most important principles of modern company law'.[16] The extent to which it is actually used by smaller shareholders is, however, doubtful.[17] Since the beginning of this century, shareholders have had virtually no general supervisory power over the board.[18]

15.14 A further factor is that the power of institutional shareholders to assess and act upon managerial incompetence is often not as strong as may at first appear. Although institutions may be represented on the board:

---

[12] See *Department of Health and Social Security v Evans* [1985] 2 All ER 471, where the question was whether a director could reasonably be expected to know of the failure of his company to pay national insurance contributions for the purposes of section 152(4) of the Social Security Act 1975 (now repealed). The court held that it had to take account of the position held by the director in the company and the responsibilities and duties he in fact discharged.

[13] Professional Development of and for the Board (1990).

[14] *Ibid*, at p 105.

[15] Companies Act 1985, s 303.

[16] *Palmer's Company Law*, vol 2, para 8.032.

[17] See generally the Jenkins Report, paras 103-105.

[18] Article 70 of Table A, which confers on directors the power to manage the company's business, is subject only to the provisions of the Act and to directions given by special resolution. The equivalent power in earlier versions of this article (for example regulation 80 in Table A in the first schedule to the Companies Act 1948) was subject to "regulations" prescribed by the company in general meeting but this was held not to entitle shareholders to control the directors by ordinary resolution: see *Quinn & Axtens v Salmon* [1909] AC 442.

[I]t is difficult for [outside directors] to pose questions of a challenging nature to knowledgeable persons without appearing superficial or incompetent. It is also considered bad form to ask questions that imply doubts about motives and competence... .[19]

15.15 It is also argued with some force that the courts are not well placed to second-guess matters of business judgment:[20]

Directors ... are charged with the responsibility of maximising profits. To do this it will frequently be necessary for them to take risks. Whether a risk is worth running depends on an estimate of its magnitude in the light of the potential reward. Assuming ... that directors have sufficiently researched a project, it is not evident how a court could determine whether the expected profits justify the risks involved, and this is likely to be the case with respect to much business decision-making.[21]

15.16 Another reason is that in some cases a company appoints a person as a director for some attribute that he has, for example he may be a former civil servant or diplomat and the company may wish to take advantage of the knowledge and experience that he has built up in that capacity. Where the candidate was formerly a diplomat in a particular part of the world in which the company is seeking to establish itself it may be useful for the company to have a director who is familiar with the language and culture of that part of the world. He may however have limited knowledge of corporate finance and accounting. It can be argued that the law should take account of his lack of knowledge and skill in this regard.[22]

15.17 As against these points:

(1) The purely subjective test for directors is out of line with the duty generally imposed on persons who agree to provide services. This is especially anomalous where, as is usually the case for executive directors and is often the case for non-executive directors, they are paid.

(2) It is not suggested that the duty of care imposed on directors should be higher than that which is being evolved in the cases in any event.[23]

(3) Insurance cover is marketed to protect directors who do not wish to take the risk of being held liable.[24]

---

[19] Herman, *Corporate Control, Corporate Power* (1981) p 47.

[20] See Shareholder Remedies, Law Com Consultation Paper No 142, paras 9.44-9.48, for discussion of the court's reluctance to hold that anything less than serious mismanagement could amount to unfair prejudice.

[21] Parkinson, op cit, p 109.

[22] It must be borne in mind that it will not be possible for the company either to agree that a director need show some lesser standard of care than that provided for by statute or to agree to limit his liability to the company; on the latter point see Part 11 below. However the court has power to grant relief from liability under section 727 of the Companies Act 1985, which is also discussed in Part 11 below.

[23] See para 12.9 above.

(4)   The present law fails to provide an adequate sanction for mismanagement. Mr Edgar Speyer in a minority report attached to the Report of the Company Law Amendment Committee[25] in 1906 said:

> The suggestion that men will not so easily accept directorships under such conditions[26] is, it is submitted, no answer. It is not directors who need protection, but the public. There is small moral sanction for the position of a man who has ten or more directorships, whose companies go into liquidation through mismanagement and who, apart from what he may have paid for his qualification shares, loses nothing, not even his market value as a director, for he is free to reap an income by joining other boards. A trader who is negligent in the management of his business and ends in bankruptcy has to bear the stigma and the disabilities of the *status* of a bankrupt. I submit that a director ought not to and need not be in any better position than an ordinary trader.

This gap in the law has to some extent been filled by the Company Directors Disqualification Act 1986, which enables the court to disqualify a director whose conduct makes him unfit to be a director. However, a serious case of negligence would have to be made out if the only allegation against him was one of mismanagement. Moreover disqualification serves a different purpose of protecting the public for the future. It does not provide compensation for the company which has lost money through the mismanagement.

(5)   There are many other jurisdictions where directors are bound to act as reasonable competent directors or businessmen.[27]

15.18   Finally, we have pointed out above[28] that it is said that if the duty of care of a director were made statutory, people would be deterred from becoming directors and in particular there would be few who would wish to accept appointment as non-executive directors. It is said that this is less likely to be the case if the standard of care contained in a statutory statement was subjective but this may not turn out to be the case because for some directors with special qualification the subjective standard will be higher than the objective standard.

15.19   Our provisional view is that this option should be rejected. It is out of line with the standard applied to a director's conduct for the purposes of wrongful trading under section 214(4) of the Insolvency Act 1985, and with recent case law.

---

[24]   See paras 11.53-11.57 above.

[25]   Report of the Company Law Amendment Committee (1906) Cd 3052, p 31.

[26]   Ie under conditions similar to those in Germany.

[27]   For example Germany, USA , New Zealand, Australia, Canada (see appendices H-K). In addition, the majority of US States have statutory statements of the director's duty of care.

[28]   See para 15.8.

Consultees are asked whether they consider that the standard of care expected of a director should be judged by a subjective test - so as to be that expected of a reasonable person having the same knowledge and experience that the director has.

Option 2: A dual objective/subjective test

15.20 Section 214 of the Insolvency Act 1986 (Wrongful trading) imposes a dual test. A director can avoid liability if he takes those steps

(1) which would be taken by a reasonably diligent person with the knowledge skill and experience reasonably to be expected of a director carrying out the same functions; and also

(2) which would be taken by a reasonably diligent person with *his* knowledge skill and experience.

15.21 This enables the court to ask what it would be reasonable to expect the director to have done both by reference to the responsibilities that he undertook, and by reference to his own special knowledge and skills, eg as a lawyer. It has been said with reference to section 214(4), that the former is only a minimum standard and "observance of the minimum standard is not necessarily sufficient. The director must also meet such higher standard as is appropriate to his own general knowledge, skill and experience."[29] We provisionally consider that such a dual test is appropriate generally, and not merely where the company is on the verge of insolvency. We do not consider it appropriate for the test to be only subjective, since that would mean that a director could rely on his own particular lack of knowledge or experience. In our view, all directors should be subject to a general standard of care, and a particular director should not be able to rely on his own particular lack of knowledge or experience to avoid being subject to that general

---

[29] Professor R M Goode, *Principles of Corporate Insolvency Law* (2nd ed, 1997). It must be borne in mind that section 214 was highly innovative: never before had a director's conduct been subjected to an objective test. The proposal (then for a purely objective standard) was derived from the Report of the Review Committee on Insolvency Law and Practice under the chairmanship of Sir Kenneth Cork. Section 214 had itself an innovative effect on the general law because it enabled the courts to increase the standard of care to be shown by a director under the general law. See also Prentice, *Corporate Personality, Limited Liability and the Protection of Creditors in Corporate Personality in the Twentieth Century* (1998), ed Grantham and Rickett at p112:"It seems reasonably clear that in this standard [section 214(4)] sub-section(a) set the floor (the objective standard), and sub-section (b) set the ceiling (the subjective standard)." We are aware, however, that the interpretation of that provision has been questioned. And see Wardman, "Directors, Their Duty to Exercise Skill and Care: Do the provisions of the Directors Disqualification Act 1986 provide a basis for the establishment of a more objective standard?" (1994) Business LR 71, at p 75 who states without elaborating the point: "This second assessment [ie what did the past knowledge, skill and experience of the director in question indicate as to what might be reasonably expected of him] could in, theory at least, raise the standard set at the first stage, or, as is more likely to be the case, introduce elements in mitigation where the standard shown falls short of that expected".

standard. On the other hand, we consider it fair that if he has some special expertise, he should have to exercise it.[30]

15.22 On the other hand we are aware that there is anxiety in some quarters that to state the director's duty of care in this way could lead to an increase in the number of claims against directors. It might for instance encourage the company itself or shareholders on its behalf (through the derivative action or in Scotland, the shareholder's action) to bring claims. The statutory statement might also lead to anxiety that that would be the result so that people would decline to act as directors (particularly as non-executive directors) or conduct themselves as a directors in an overcautious way to avoid any claim being mounted against them. There has been a concern along these lines in Australia and we examine that below.[31] Our proposed empirical survey may shed light on this issue. One solution may be the development by private sector bodies of the check lists for compliance with due diligence proposed in paragraph 3.90 above.

15.23 We have considered whether the law should draw a distinction between skill, care and diligence.[32]

15.24 To make a distinction between skill, care and diligence runs the risk that arguments will arise as to whether that which it is alleged the director ought to have done (eg cause the company to diversify into different products) was something which a reasonably careful person in the position of the director would have done or something which the director should have done because the director had some special skill (eg in knowing when the market in the company's existing product line was about to fall). Accordingly, we do not propose to draw a distinction, and instead consider that the same standard should apply to each of skill, care and diligence.

---

[30] Under English law the standard of care which a solicitor is expected to show if he is an expert in a particular branch of the law has been said to be that which "is commensurate with the skill and experience which the solicitor actually has": see *Duchess of Argyll v Beuselinck* [1972] 2 Lloyd's Rep 172, 183. "The uniform standards postulated for the world at large in tort hardly seem appropriate when the duty is not only imposed by the law of tort but arises from a contractual obligation existing between the client and the particular solicitor in question." *Ibid* at p 183. Scots law also requires a professional to exercise the skill and competence which he has. See *Gordon v Wilson* 1992 SLT 849. It is likely that the Scottish courts would adopt the approach taken in *Duchess of Argyll v Beuselinck*. The same applies in the context of a director who has a contract with his company and who was appointed because of the particular skills that he could bring to bear. We considered whether the subjective element of the two fold test was unfair where for example a person had qualified as a barrister but then not practised. We do not consider that this is a difficulty since that person would be judged by the standard to be expected of a barrister who had qualified but had no post-qualification experience.

[31] Section 232(4) of the Australian Corporations Law, which sets out the standard of care to be exercised by directors, only refers to care and diligence and not skill, but s 232(11) states that this provision is in addition to and in derogation of the general law. It is proposed that the Corporate and Economic Reform Bill will clarify this provision so that it is clear that the standard of care must be assessed by reference to the particular circumstances of the director concerned.

[32] As was done in the Clause 46 of the Companies Bill 1978. See also n 31 above.

15.25 It is useful to see how the courts have applied section 214(4) of the Insolvency Act 1986 in practice. The first case to be decided under this section was *Re Produce Marketing Consortium Ltd (No 2).*[33] In that case the company had a small number of directors and shareholders and none of the directors had any special qualification. The company had a large overdraft and its audited accounts showed that it was trading at a loss. Those accounts were late and of course did not show the current position, but the directors knew from their own knowledge of the business that there had been a substantial drop in turnover and Knox J held that they ought to have realised that that meant that they had been trading at a loss. The court was satisfied that this knowledge should be imputed to them. The court however accepted that it should take into account the particular circumstances of the company and that the knowledge skill and experience required in a small company with simple accounting systems would be less than it would be in a larger company. Another case where the court has applied section 214(4) is *Re DKG Contractors Ltd.*[34] The court expressed the view that the directors' skills were "hopelessly inadequate" but that that was insufficient to protect them from liability under section 214.[35]

Consultees are asked whether the standard of care expected of a director should be judged by a twofold subjective/objective test.

15.26 For illustrative purposes a draft clause setting out a director's duty of care skill and diligence has been drafted and appears in Appendix A (draft clause 1 containing a new draft section 309A for the Companies Act 1985). We would draw attention to the following points in particular about the policy which the draft clause is intended to illustrate. First, the intention is to attribute to the director both the notional knowledge and experience which may reasonably be expected of a person in the same position as the director (subsection (1)(a)) and the actual knowledge and experience which the director has (subsection (1)(b)). The intention is that the former would be a minimum standard required by law of all directors. If the particular director possesses greater knowledge or experience than that which may reasonably be expected of directors generally, he would have to meet a higher standard of care, skill and diligence appropriate to *his* knowledge and experience. If he happens to possess less knowledge or experience than that which may reasonably be expected generally of directors, he would nevertheless be required by law to meet the minimum standard applied to all. The intention is that the two tests should be aggregated in this way. A director would not be able to rely on his own particular lack of knowledge or experience to avoid being subject to the general minimum standard of care to be required of all directors.

15.27 The draft clause has been modelled on section 214(4) of the Insolvency Act 1986, which has been interpreted to achieve the desired effect.[36] It can also be said that

---

[33] [1989] BCLC 520.

[34] [1990] BCC 903.

[35] *Ibid*, at p 912.

[36] See para 15.21 above. See Goode, *Principles of Corporate Insolvency Law* (2nd ed, 1997) referred to at para 15.21; and Prentice, *Corporate Personality, Limited Liability and the*

the new section should follow section 214 so as to achieve consistency in the position of directors both during the life of the company and as the company approaches insolvent liquidation, and because the courts have had experience of the wording of section 214 for over 12 years. We are aware, however, that the interpretation of that provision has been questioned.[37] Draft clause 1 in Appendix A is for illustrative purposes only at this stage. We shall return to the detail of the drafting when preparing our Report. Consultees should not assume that if this option is finally recommended, the clause we recommend would necessarily be in this form.

15.28 Secondly, we consider it important that the standard of care set out in statute should take account of the differences of fact between the responsibilities of directors of different types and in different situations,[38] for example between what executive directors and non-executive directors are expected to do. The test at subsection (1)(a) therefore looks at the notional knowledge and experience that may reasonably be expected of a person in the same position as the director, enabling the court to take account of such differences.

Option 3: An objective test only

15.29 A further possibility can be seen in section 137 of the New Zealand Companies Act 1993 which simply applies an objective test to the standard of care to be exercised by a director.[39] The special qualifications that a director has are ignored, even if they were the reason why the company appointed him a director in the first place. This may have merit where the director does not hold himself out as having any additional knowledge skill and experience or is not known to have it, but it may be doubted whether there are many cases where a director has a special skill or special knowledge and experience and this is not known to the company at the time of his appointment and did not constitute one of the reasons for appointing him. Moreover, there are reasons for rejecting this option even if this is a case where the director's special knowledge was not known to the company. If this option were adopted, it would mean that during the life of the company a director's conduct was judged by a purely objective standard, but, once there was a situation in which it was clear that the company would have to go into liquidation and that not all creditors would be paid in full in the liquidation, he was judged by a separate and different standard and that extensive personal liability could be imposed on him under section 214 not merely if he failed to comply with the objective test, but also if he failed to exercise some special skill that he had, for example as an accountant or lawyer. This would not produce a coherent and consistent scheme for imposing liability for negligence on directors.

Protection of Creditors in Corporate Personality in the Twentieth Century (1998) ed Grantham and Rickett, referred to at n 29 above.

[37] See Wardman, "Directors, Their Duty to Exercise Skill and Care: Do the provisions of the Directors Disqualification Act 1986 provide a basis for the establishment of a more objective standard?" (1994) Business LR 71, at p 75 referred to at n 29 above.

[38] See *Re Produce Marketing Consortium Ltd*, and para 15.21 above.

[39] See Appendix I. See also s 232(4) of the Australian Corporations Law, which is set out in Appendix H; and s 122(1) of the Canadian Business Corporations Act 1985, in Appendix J.

Consultees are asked whether they consider that the standard of care expected of a director should be judged solely by an objective test - so as to be that expected of a reasonable person having the knowledge and experience which may reasonably be expected of a person in the same position as the director without taking account of any special expertise that the particular director possesses.

MATTERS OF COMMERCIAL JUDGMENT

15.30   The courts of both Australia and the United Kingdom have expressed an unwillingness to second guess directors on commercial matters. Thus in *Howard Smith v Ampol Petroleum,* Lord Wilberforce, giving the advice of the Privy Council, said:

> it would be wrong for the court to substitute its opinion for that of the management, or indeed to question the correctness of the management's decision ... if bona fide arrived at. [40]

15.31   This approach is comparable to the rule known in the United States as the business judgment rule, which is described in the next paragraphs. The next question is whether, if a statutory duty of care is introduced, there needs to be a statutory statement of the principle of non-interference by the courts in commercial decisions made in good faith. We discuss this question in paragraph 15.41 below. Before that, we examine the business judgment rule in the United States, and recent developments in Australia and South Africa.

The business judgment rule in the United States

15.32   There is in many states of the United States a judge-made rule which prevents directors from being liable for claims for breach of duty/negligence where certain factors are established. [41] Those factors can vary in different states but the American Law Institute endeavoured to distil its principles in their work on the Principles of Corporate Governance:

> 4.01 Duty of care of Directors and Officers; the Business Judgment Rule
>
> (a)   A director or officer has a duty to the corporation to perform the director's or officer's functions in good faith, in a manner that he or she reasonably believes to be in the best interests of the corporation, and with the care that an ordinarily prudent person would reasonably be expected to exercise in a like position and under similar circumstances. This Subsection (a) is subject to the provisions of Subsection (c) (the business judgment rule) where applicable.
>
> The duty in Subsection (a) includes the obligation to make, or cause to be made, an enquiry when, but only when, the circumstances would alert a reasonable director or officer to the need therefor. The extent

---

[40]   [1974] AC 821, at p 832.

[41]   See generally eg M E Eisenberg, "The Duty of Care and the Business Judgment Rule in American Corporate Law" [1997] 2 CFILR 185.

of such enquiry shall be such as the director or officer reasonably believes to be necessary.

In performing any of his or her functions (including oversight functions) a director or officer is entitled to rely on materials and persons in accordance with ## 4.02 and 4.03 (reliance on directors, officers, employees, experts, other persons, and committees of the board).

(b) Except as otherwise provided by statute or by the standard of the corporation [# 1.36] and subject to the board's ultimate responsibility for oversight, in performing its functions (including oversight functions), the board may delegate, formally or informally by course of conduct, any function (including the function of identifying matters requiring the attention of the board or to directors, officers, employees, experts, or other persons: a director may rely on such committees and persons in fulfilling the duty under this Section with respect to any delegated function if the reliance is in accordance with ## 4.02 and 4.03.

(c) A director or officer who makes a business judgment in good faith fulfils the duty under this Section if the director or officer:

(1) is not interested[42] in the subject of the business judgment;

(2) is informed with respect to the subject to the extent the director or officer reasonably believes to be appropriate under the circumstances; and

(3) rationally believes that the business judgment is in the best interests of the corporation.

(d) A person challenging the conduct of a director or officer under this Section has the burden of proving a breach of the duty of care, including the inapplicability of the provisions as to the fulfilment of duty under Subsection (b) or (c), and, in a damage action, the burden of proving that the breach was the legal cause of damage suffered by the corporation.

15.33   For present purposes it is paragraph (c) of the above rule which is of most interest. The commentary states that each of the requirements of this paragraph are supported by authority. The purpose is to protect directors (and officers) from "hindsight reviews of their unsuccessful decisions and to avoid the risk of stifling innovation and venturesome business activity. The business judgment rule (set forth in # 4.01(c)) is a judicial gloss on duty of care standards which sharply reduces exposure to liability."[43] "This standard is intended to provide directors and officers with a wide ambit of discretion."[44] The phrase "rationally believes" in

---

[42]   Because eg he has a financial interest in the transaction which might affect his judgment (Principles of Corporate Covernance, para 1.23).

[43]   American Law Institute Principles of Corporate Governance, Analysis and Recommendations (1992) p 141.

[44]   *Ibid*, at pp 141-2.

#4.01 (c) (3) is intended to bear a wider meaning than "reasonably believes" and "to give a director a safe harbour from liability for business judgments that might arguably fall outside the term 'reasonable' but are not so removed from the realm of reason when made that liability should be incurred."[45] The principle as stated by the American Law Institute is consistent with decisions of the courts which when applying the business judgment rule "have often stated that a "presumption" exists in favour of the propriety or regularity of the actions of directors and officers."[46]

15.34 The business judgment rule will not protect a director who fails to consider exercising his judgment, as opposed to a director who considered whether to take a particular course of action but decided not to do so. The business judgment rule does not protect a director who does not act in good faith or who has a conflict of interest. A director must have the information which he reasonably believes is appropriate before he makes his decision, but he will not be liable for failure to realise that he should have certain information unless he was grossly negligent in reaching the view that he did not require this information.[47] The time available for obtaining the relevant information and the cost of obtaining it are factors which the director can take into account in reaching a view as to what information is appropriate.

The Australian approach

15.35 Different views have been expressed in Australia about the need for a statutory business judgment rule. In its Report No 10, *Company Directors and Officers: Indemnification, Relief and Insurance,* the Companies and Securities Law Review Committee (CSLRC) recommended the enactment of a statutory business judgment rule on the ground that the rule would reinforce directors' ability to make operational decisions which would not be reviewable on their merits in the courts. In 1989, in their *Report on the Social and Fiduciary Obligations of Company Directors,* the Australian Senate Standing Committee on Legal and Constitutional affairs also recommended the introduction of a statutory business judgment rule.

15.36 However the Australian Government rejected the need for a statutory business judgment rule. In 1992 a Corporate Law Reform Bill was introduced which restated the duty of care owed by a director. The Explanatory Memorandum to that Bill stated that the Government considered that the development of a business judgment rule was best left to the courts. The Explanatory Memorandum said that the courts had recognised that directors are not liable for mere errors of judgment and were reluctant to review decisions taken in good faith and not for irrelevant purposes. As a result of the Corporate Law Reform Bill, section 232(4) of the Australian Corporations Code, which is set out in Appendix H, was enacted.

---

[45] *Ibid,* at p 142.

[46] *Ibid,* at p 144.

[47] See *Smith v Van Gorkom* 488 A 2d 858 (Del 1985).

15.37 In November 1997, new proposals for reform were issued for consultation as part of the Corporate Law Economic Reform Program.[48] It was noted that recent case law, in particular the decision in *Daniels v Anderson*,[49] had increased the liability of directors and that subsequent decisions had given rise to uncertainty as to the extent of that liability. The consultation paper stated that

> While it is accepted that directors should be subject to a high level of accountability a failure to expressly acknowledge that directors should not be liable for decisions made in good faith and with due care can have the effect of encouraging business behaviour which is risk-averse.

15.38 The consultation paper noted that the uncertainty might be causing an increase in agency costs,[50] and might also increase the remuneration that had to be paid to directors. An increase could undermine agency costs in company performance. The consultation paper noted that if liability rules were to be "efficient tools of corporate governance, liability rules need to be tempered against the need to ensure that the attention of directors is not significantly diverted from the pursuit of maximising shareholder wealth". The fact that the court had power[51] to relieve directors from liability after the event was insufficient. While the courts already decline to review business decisions, a business judgment rule would create a presumption in favour of a director's judgment and would thus lead to greater certainty. On the other hand the rule should be framed so as to encourage proper corporate practices and not protect directors from ill-informed decisions.

15.39 The draft bill issued for consultation following the issue of the consultation paper contains the following draft business judgment rule:

> (2) A director or other officer of a corporation who makes a business judgment is taken to meet the requirements of subsection (1) [duty of care and diligence], and their equivalent duties at common law and equity, in respect of the judgment if they:
>
> > (a) make the judgment in good faith for a proper purpose; and
> >
> > (b) do not have a material personal interest in the subject matter of the decision; and
> >
> > (c) inform themselves about the subject matter of the decision to the extent they reasonably believe to be appropriate; and
> >
> > (d) rationally believe that the decision is in the best interests of the corporation.

[48] Directors' Duties and Corporate Governance: Corporate Law Reform Program. Proposals for Reform: Paper No 3.

[49] See para 15.45 below.

[50] For an analysis of the economic aspects to this issue, see also Part 3, above paras 3.10-3.14, 3.26 and 3.80.

[51] Under the Australian equivalent of section 727, which is considered in Part 11 below.

The director's or officer's belief that the decision is in the best interests of the corporation is a rational one unless the belief is one that no reasonable person in their position would hold.

Note: This subsection only operates in relation to duties under this section and their equivalent duties at common law or in equity (including the duty of care that arises under the common law principles governing liability for negligence - it does not operate in relation to duties under any other provision of this Law or under any other laws).

(3) in this section:

business judgment means any decision to take or not take action in respect of a matter relevant to the business operations of the corporation.

South Africa

15.40   In South Africa, the King Committee has also recommended that there should be a statutory business judgment rule. It considered that, particularly in the case of non-executive directors, the duty of care and skill was onerous, and that a director should not be liable for breach of the duty of care if he exercised a business judgment in good faith, provided that the decision was an informed one based on all the facts and was a rational decision, and that the director had no self-interest. The King Committee considered that such an approach would encourage the competitiveness of South African companies and therefore recommended that consideration be given to amending the Companies Act so that the duty of skill and care was so limited.[52]

If there is to be a statutory statement of the director's duty of care, should there be a statutory business judgment rule?

15.41   The question arises whether if the director's duty of care is made statutory, the Companies Act should also include a business judgment rule. The courts already adopt the policy of not reviewing commercial decisions or judging directors with the wisdom of hindsight. The Hong Kong Consultancy Report[53] considered that there should be no statutory formulation of the business judgment rule: it did not consider that a case had been made out.[54] The initiatives in Australia seem to be directed at easing uncertainty in the minds of directors about a statutory statement of the duty of care. If any such concern were found in the United Kingdom in the course of the empirical survey, that would be a strong reason for having a business judgment rule. Likewise if there was any evidence that it might lead to a raising of standards of behaviour by directors, for example, by encouraging them to make appropriate enquiries, as opposed to making them more cautious, that too would be a strong reason for having a business judgment rule.

---

[52]   The King Report on Corporate Governance, Institute of Directors in South Africa (November 1994), paras 3.3-3.5.

[53]   Set out in Appendix L.

[54]   Ibid, para 6.20.

Consultees are asked whether they consider that there should be a business judgment rule and if so whether it should be on the lines proposed in Australia or on the lines identified by the American Law Institute or in some other way.

RELIANCE AND DELEGATION[55]

15.42 As noted in paragraph 12.7, it was held in *Re City Equitable Fire Insurance Company Ltd* that a director might delegate matters to one of the company's employees where the articles of association permitted this and the needs of the business required it, in the absence of grounds for suspicion.[56] Likewise, a director might need to rely on information provided to him by employees and others. The question arises whether it is necessary for the Companies Act to state the circumstances in which a director can properly delegate his responsibilities and when he might properly rely on advice from others.

15.43 The present trend in larger companies is towards a monitoring role for company directors. This was highlighted in the recent *AWA* litigation in Australia.

15.44 In *AWA Ltd v Daniels*[57] the court had to decide whether the chief executive and non-executive directors of a company were negligent in the following circumstances. The company and management of AWA Ltd relied on one person and had set in place no system of control of its foreign exchange dealings. The auditors (Daniels) were aware of the weaknesses in the system in this respect but failed to report this to the management, and eventually to report it to the board when it was clear that the management failed to do so. AWA sued its directors and auditors when substantial losses were made. Rogers CJ at trial held that more recent wisdom suggested that it is of the essence of the responsibilities of directors that they take reasonable steps to place themselves in a position to guide and monitor the management of the company:[58] A board's usual functions in addition to the statutory ones were said to be four-fold:

    (a)   to set goals for the corporation;

    (b)   to appoint the corporation's chief executive;

    (c)   to oversee the plans of managers for the acquisition and organisation of financial and human resources towards attainment of the corporation's goals; and

---

[55] For an analysis of economic aspects of this issue, see para 3.11 above.

[56] See also *Dovey v Cory* [1901] AC 477. The reliance must be reasonable and a director who signed share transfers for nil consideration would not have been able to rely on assurances from his fellow directors: *Bishopsgate Investment Managment Ltd v Maxwell No 2* [1994] 1 All ER 261.

[57] (1991-2) 7 ACSR 759.

[58] Cf *Commonwealth Bank v Friedrich* (1991) 5 ASCR 115 at p 187.

> (d) to review, at reasonable intervals, the corporations progress towards attaining its goals.[59]

In relation to the non-executive directors: the court held that they were not bound to give continuous attention to the affairs of the corporation. There is no objective standard as with executive directors. On the facts they were entitled to have confidence in the senior management. As a result, at trial, the non-executive directors were held not liable by the trial judge but the chief executive was found liable in negligence.

15.45 This decision was the subject of an appeal to the New South Wales Court of Appeal, sub nom *Daniels v Anderson*.[60] The Court endorsed the view that the law required directors to take reasonable steps to place themselves in a position to guide and monitor the management of the company.[61] The Court observed a person who accepts the office of director of a particular company undertakes the responsibility of ensuring that he or she understands the nature of the duty a director is called to perform. That duty will vary according to the size and business of the particular company and the experience and skill of a particular director. The duty is a common law duty to take reasonable care owed severally by persons who as fiduciary agents are bound not to exercise the powers conferred upon them for a private purpose or for any person foreign to the power and placed, at the apex of the structure of direction and management. The duty includes that of acting collectively to manage the company.[62] The appeal against the finding of liability on the part of the executive directive was reversed. The appeal against the finding that the non-executive directors were not liable was dismissed.

15.46 The decision on appeal has lead to a certain amount of uncertainty in Australia as to the circumstances in which a director can delegate his responsibilities to others and rely on them. The court stressed that the directors could not blindly rely on the judgments of others and that they needed to take positive steps to satisfy themselves that the company was being properly run. The Companies Act 1993 of New Zealand already contains provisions which provide that directors remain responsible for the exercise of powers they delegate *unless* they believed on reasonable grounds at all times before the exercise of the power that the delegate would exercise the power in conformity with the duties imposed on the directors of the company and have properly monitored the exercise of the power by the delegate.[63] The Companies Act 1993 of New Zealand further provides that a director may rely on information provided by an employee, expert, professional adviser or other directors where the matter falls within their area of responsibility and the director acted in good faith, made proper enquiries and had no grounds

---

[59] (1991-2) 7 ACSR 759, at p 865, line 50.

[60] (1995) 16 ACSR 607.

[61] *Ibid*, at p 664, line 17.

[62] *Ibid*, at p 668, line 14

[63] Section 130, see Appendix I.

for suspicion.[64] These provisions were enacted following recommendations of the New Zealand Law Commission.[65]

15.47 The Australian Government has now issued for consultation draft legislation on the lines of the Companies Act of 1993 of New Zealand. They propose that a director should not be liable for the acts of a delegate[66] if:

> (a) the director believed on reasonable grounds at all times before the exercise of the power that the delegate would exercise the power in conformity with the duties imposed on directors of the company by this Law and the company's constitution (if any); and

> (b) the directors have monitored, by means of reasonable methods properly used, the exercise of the power by the delegate.

15.48 Likewise the Australian Government proposes where reliance permitted by the new legislation occurs, the reliance should be deemed to be reasonable unless the contrary is proved:

10 Reliance on information or advice provided by others

If:

> (a) a director relies on information, or professional or expert advice, given or prepared by:
>
> > (i) an employee of the corporation whom the director believes on reasonable grounds to be reliable and competent in relation to the matters concerned; or
> > (ii) a professional adviser or expert in relation to matters that the director believes on reasonable grounds to be within the person's professional or expert competence; or
> > (iii) another director or officer in relation to matters within the director's or officer's authority; or
> > (iv) a committee of directors on which the director did not serve in relation to matters within the committee's authority; and

> (b) the reliance was made:
>
> > (i) in good faith; and
> > (ii) after making proper inquiry if the circumstances indicated the need for inquiry; and

---

[64] Section 138, see Appendix I. See also s 123(4) of the Canadian Business Corporations Act 1985 in Appendix J and recommendation 6.14 of the Hong Kong Consultancy Report in Appendix L below.

[65] In paras 512 and 513 of Company Law Reform and Restatement, Report No 9 (1989). The report noted that what is now s 128 "establishes a degree of predictability in a difficult area which is productive of disputes."

[66] Under an another draft section directors will be permitted to delegate to a committee of directors, a fellow director, an employee or any other person : s 22.

(c) the reasonableness of the director's reliance on the information or advice arises in proceedings brought to determine whether a director has performed a duty under this Part or an equivalent general law duty;

the director's reliance on the information or advice is taken to be reasonable unless the contrary is proved.

15.49 The reason for the action being taken in Australia is a concern that the present uncertainty could lead to an over-conservative approach to management and impede decision-making by directors. "This is a less than optimal outcome and is not conducive to the development of sound corporate governance practices such as putting in place appropriate board committee systems".[67]

15.50 Again this may be an area where empirical research may throw light whether there is similar uncertainty and a similar tendency in the United Kingdom. If there is not then we consider that there is probably no reason for supposing that the present judge-made law is not working satisfactorily in the area of delegation and reliance by directors.

Consultees are asked whether they consider that there should be a statutory provision which sets out the liability of directors when they delegate their powers to others and the circumstances in which they may rely on information provided by third parties.

STATUTORY STATEMENT OF THE DUTY OF CARE WITHOUT A STATUTORY STATEMENT OF FIDUCIARY DUTIES

15.51 The final issue is this: if it were decided that there should be no statutory statement of the fiduciary duties of directors but it appeared that there were strong arguments for a statutory statement of the duty of care of directors, **do consultees consider that there would be any objection to having a statutory statement of the duty of care on its own?**

---

[67] Consultation Paper No 3, p 46.

SECTION C
MISCELLANEOUS MATTERS

PART 16
EMPIRICAL SURVEY OF DIRECTORS

INTRODUCTION

16.1   As we said above,[1] we intend to carry out an empirical survey as well as seeking the views of consultees by the publication of this Consultation Paper. The survey will be carried out in the consultation period and the results will be made known in and taken into account in the final report. The survey will be carried out by the ESRC Centre for Business Research at the University of Cambridge.

EMPIRICAL RESEARCH

16.2   The analysis of economic considerations in Part 3 indicated a number of issues which would be appropriate for empirical research. Theoretical economic analysis suggests that company law may enhance efficiency by (amongst other things) reducing agency costs, facilitating bargaining between corporate actors, and reducing the effects of externalities (that is to say, the negative, unbargained-for effects of corporate transactions on third parties, such as creditors). Statutory regulation may, in principle, play a useful role in supplementing the general principles of fiduciary law, particularly by providing incentives for the disclosure of certain categories of information by senior managers to other board members and to shareholders.

16.3   However, the efficiency of regulation in this area cannot be assessed unless more is known about how relations between the different corporate actors currently operate in practice. The central aim of empirical research should therefore be to clarify the precise nature of the relationship between shareholders and senior management. Empirical research should aim to build up a more complete picture of how relations between shareholders and managers operate, and, in particular, the role played by representatives of institutional shareholders and by non-executive directors. It will also be necessary to examine the types of relationships which exist in companies of different types (private companies on the one hand, and public and listed companies on the other) and size.

16.4   Empirical research should also seek to ascertain the extent to which bargaining over the form and content of directors' duties in fact takes place. A central contention of the economic theory of the corporation is that legal rules can be used to induce the parties to arrive at efficient allocations of resources through contractual arrangements. However, if, in practice, bargaining is seen as excessively costly or impractical, this potential role for the law may not be capable of being fulfilled. Whether this is the case is a question which cannot be answered

---

[1]   See para 1.15 above.

a priori, but only through empirical investigation. Research here should focus on the forms which such bargaining can take; these include directors' service contracts, the contents of articles of association, shareholders' agreements and shareholders' resolutions.

16.5   In Part 3 it was also noted that that there is some empirical evidence from other jurisdictions (notably Canada) to suggest that if the standard of care for directors' duties of care and skill is raised, directors may be deterred from taking office and may also find it difficult to obtain the necessary liability insurance. We have also noted developments in Australia where the Government has issued for consultation draft legislation to introduce a statutory business judgment rule. Questions have also been raised concerning what the effect upon internal systems of communication, through which company boards ensure internal compliance with their general instructions, would be if the obligations upon directors were increased. These are also issues which can be addressed through empirical analysis. It will be necessary, in this respect, to find out more about the way directors perceive their current legal responsibilities under the duty of care, and how they would regard a possible restatement of the law. It would also be important to obtain evidence concerning the attitudes of commercial creditors, banks, the accounting profession and the insurance industry to these questions

16.6   It is hoped that empirical research will also throw light on the following specific issues:

(1)   whether an authoritative statement of directors' duties would assist directors in practice;

(2)   whether such a statement could most usefully be set out in legislation, or in some other form (such as an annexe to the articles of association);

(3)   whether it would be helpful for such a statement to refer to release, ratification and approval, and to include reference to a business judgment rule;

(4)   the usefulness to directors of non-statutory guidelines specifying what they should do in certain specific situations;

(5)   the role of non-executive directors, and the extent to which they are independent of management;

(6)   whether directors' service contracts which are "rolling contracts" are common;

(7)   the length of directors' service contracts in private companies;

(8)   how section 316(3) (concerning payments to directors for breach of contract) is interpreted and applied in practice;

(9)   the behavioural effect of criminal penalties, and in particular whether they serve a useful purpose in backing up legal advice and making it more likely that rules will be obeyed, even if, in practice, there are no prosecutions;

(10) whether section 317 (concerning disclosure to the board of a contract in which the director has an interest) serves a useful purpose in a sole director company;

(11) whether further disclosure requirements are likely to produce benefits to shareholders;

(12) the costs of calling shareholder meetings; and

(13) the cost and practicability of shareholder-led litigation against directors.

16.7 In order to examine these issues, a dual approach to the research will be undertaken. Firstly, information concerning corporate practices will be obtained through a questionnaire circulated to a representative sample of directors in companies of various types and sizes and in different geographical locations. Secondly, a number of face to face interviews will be conducted with directors, institutional shareholders, members of the accounting profession, lenders and lawyers. Together, these will provide a quantitative and qualitative basis for understanding the nature of current practices and possible effects of changes to the law.

GEOGRAPHICAL CONSIDERATIONS AND ACKNOWLEDGEMENTS

16.8 The survey will be addressed to directors in England, Wales, Scotland and Northern Ireland. The Law Commission, the Scottish Law Commission and the Law Reform Advisory Committee of Northern Ireland consider that the survey will make a valuable contribution to the project. We are very grateful to the Institute of Chartered Accountants in England and Wales, who are sponsoring the survey. We are also grateful to the Institute of Directors for the assistance they are giving in the formulation and distribution of the questionnaire.

PART 17
HOW SHOULD THE LAW APPLY TO DIFFERENT CATEGORIES OF DIRECTOR?

INTRODUCTION

17.1 This part discusses the different types of director for the purposes of Part X and any statement of directors' duties, and the distinction if any to be drawn between executive and non-executive directors. We also mention briefly nominee directors.

THE CLASSIFICATION OF DIRECTORS

17.2 Section 741(1) of the Companies Act 1985 provides a non-exhaustive definition of "director":

> In this Act, "director" includes any person occupying the position of director by whatever name called.

17.3 This does not amount to a complete definition. It merely provides that certain persons are included within the meaning of the term. In *Re Lo-Line Electric Motors Ltd*,[1] Sir Nicholas Browne-Wilkinson VC held that the words "by whatever name called" show that the subsection is dealing with nomenclature, for example where the company's articles provide that the conduct of the company is committed to "governors" or "managers". In practice it is necessary to distinguish, firstly, between a director properly appointed in accordance with the articles of association known as a *de jure* director; secondly, a person who acts without being appointed (either because a purported appointment was invalid or because there never was any appointment) known as a *de facto* director; and thirdly, a category which supposes the existence of a board of directors who act in accordance with the instructions from someone else - the shadow director. It is also relevant to consider alternate directors.

De jure directors

17.4 All registered companies must now have directors and normally there must be at least two, unless the company is a private company.[2] The Act does not however provide for the means of appointing directors, leaving this to the articles of association.[3] Directors so appointed act as directors *de jure* by the authority of their appointment. All the references in Part X to "directors" include de jure directors.

---

[1] [1988] BCLC 698, at p 706.

[2] Although one suffices for a company registered before 1929: see s 282.

[3] However appointed, though, s 303 provides that a director can be removed by ordinary resolution in addition to any other means of removal that may be provided in the articles.

De facto directors

17.5 Directors who have not been legally appointed but nevertheless act as or *assume* the position are *de facto* directors. A *de facto* director openly acts as though he has been validly appointed despite a lack of authority and right to act. A director whose appointment is irregular[4] falls into this category. Equally, a person who is not appointed at all but is held out as a director is also, *de facto*, a director.

17.6 A *de facto* director is *capable* of coming under the definition of director in section 741. But this is not necessarily the case. Ultimately, the meaning of "director" varies according to the context in which it is to be found, and it is a matter of construction whether a particular section covers a person who is a *de facto* director.[5]

17.7 An important question which may arise in practice is what is meant by the description that a *de facto* director is a person who *acts as or assumes* the position of a director. This is particularly important in relation to a person who usurps his position.

17.8 In *Re Hydrodam (Corby) Ltd*[6] Millett J said that:

> It is necessary to plead and prove that ... he undertook functions in relation to the company which could properly be discharged only by a director. It is not sufficient to show that he was concerned with the management of the company's affairs or undertook tasks in relation to its business which can properly be performed by a manager below board level.[7]

17.9 However, in *Re Richborough Furniture Ltd,*[8] despite performing, essentially, the functions of a finance director, it was held that regular negotiations with pressing creditors, though consistent with directorship, could be done by a professional or an employee; and that in a small quasi-partnership type company, decisions which are ordinarily day-to-day matters for the Board could easily be regarded, especially at a time of crisis, as a question for the shareholders to decide, or at least express a view on.[9]

---

[4] For example, where there was not a requisite quorum present at the general meeting purporting to appoint him, this would invalidate the appointing resolution.

[5] See *Re Lo-Line Electric Motors Ltd* [1988] BCLC 698, 705 per Browne-Wilkinson V-C. In that case it was held that as a matter of construction s 300 of the Companies Act 1985 (now repealed) did include a person who was a *de facto* director. See also *Re Hydrodam (Corby) Ltd* [1994] 2 BCLC 180 (concerning wrongful trading under s 214 of the Insolvency Act 1986); and *Re Moorgate Metals Ltd* [1995] 1 BCLC 503, *Re Richborough Furniture Ltd* [1996] 1 BCLC 507 and *Secretary of State v Laing* [1996] 2 BCLC 324 (all of which concerned s 6 of the Company Directors Disqualification Act 1986).

[6] [1994] 2 BCLC 180.

[7] *Ibid*, at p 183.

[8] [1996] 1 BCLC 507.

[9] See also the later cases of *Re Pinemoor Limited* (unreported) 16 January 1996 (Ch D) and *Re Land Travel Limited* 2 May 1997 (Ch D) which interpreted and applied the tests laid down in these cases.

17.10   We consider that the provisions of Part X, and any amendment to the Companies Act to set out the duty of care and any statement of a directors' duties, should apply to both de facto and de jure directors. The provisions regulating conflicts of interest and self-dealing should not (in our provisional view) differ in their effect on directors because of a difference in their manner of appointment.

Do consultees agree with our provisional view that the provisions of Part X, the statutory duty of care and the statement of duties should apply to directors who have not been legally appointed?

Shadow directors

17.11   Since 1917 the Companies Acts[10] have recognised the position of those who, not being directors themselves, exercise control over the management decisions of the directors of the company. Such persons are known as shadow directors.

17.12   The term 'shadow director' is a statutory creation. Section 741(2) states that:

> In relation to a company, "shadow director" means a person in accordance with whose directions or instructions the directors of the company are accustomed to act.[11]

17.13   Many of the modern statutory controls over directors have been applied expressly to shadow directors.[12] The difference between liability as a *de facto* director and a shadow director is that the former has openly acted as if he had been validly appointed, whereas the definition of a shadow director presupposes that there is a board of directors who act in accordance with instructions from someone else, the shadow director. The terms are alternatives and mutually exclusive. The purpose of this provision is plainly to prevent the people who really exercise control from sheltering behind a puppet board.[13]

---

[10]   Companies (Particulars as to Directors) Act 1917.

[11]   However a person is not deemed a shadow director by reason only that the directors act on advice given by him in a professional capacity.

[12]   This is the case, for example, in relation to ss: 288; 305; 309; 317-319; 320-322; 322B; 232-239; 330-346 and 733 (note however, s 741(3) which disapplies treating a body corporate as a shadow director of its subsidiaries for the purposes of specified sections). See also s 214 of the Insolvency Act 1986 (other section of this Act may apply eg ss 212-213; and ss 6-9 and 22(4) of the Company Directors Disqualification Act 1986. A shadow director will also be a director for all the purposes of the Financial Services Act 1986.

[13]   It is important to appreciate that shadow directorship is not prohibited by law and no specific penalty attaches to the status of a shadow director. The most obvious application is to those who choose to act as the corporate governance of a company through nominee directors (see paras 17.29-17.35 below), but the statutory definition is capable of much wider application. In particular, third parties (such as lenders) seeking to protect their own legitimate interests in the context of company rescues may sometimes have little commercial alternative but to become shadow directors.

17.14 The view has been expressed that because the concept of shadow director is a statutory creation it only applies where statutory provisions specify it. Pennington[14] states:

> The Companies Act 1985 merely uses the category of shadow director to impose certain liabilities or prohibitions on persons who would not otherwise be classed as directors, and such persons do not thereby acquire any rights nor powers in connection with the management of the company, nor are they subject to the common law or equitable duties of directors.[15]

17.15 However the better view is that the shadow director is to be regarded as akin to a de facto director and that he can incur the liability of a de jure director under the general law where he effectively acts as a director through the people whom he can influence.[16] So far as statutory liabilities are concerned, the position is clear when a provision expressly states that it includes a shadow director, but where it does not, the question arises whether shadow directors are included. Since the statute contains a large number of references to shadow directors, it is doubtful whether the Companies Act applies to them unless they are expressly mentioned.

17.16 The following provisions of Part X are not expressed to apply to shadow directors: sections 311, 312, 313, 314, 315, 316 and 322A. There appears to be no reason why they should not apply to shadow directors in the same way as the other provisions of Part X. The draft statement of duties does not refer to shadow directors, but it will apply to shadow directors so far as the rules of law which it summarises do so.

Do consultees consider that (a) Part X, and (b) the statutory duty of care[17] should apply to shadow directors?

Alternate directors

17.17 An alternate director may be appointed to act for and on behalf of another director if the other director is unable to act at any time. Such an alternate may be another director, or a third person. The extent of the alternate's powers and the conditions attached to his role, such as whether he is entitled to remuneration from the company or from the director appointing him, depend on the terms of the relevant article. Regulations 65-69[18] of Table A if adopted go far to clarify the alternate's functions.

---

[14] *Pennington's Company Law* (7th ed, 1995), p 712.

[15] This view was also expressed by the Financial Law Panel Report on Shadow Directorships (April 1994).

[16] Thus in *Yukong Line Ltd v Rendsburg Investments Corporation (No 2)* [1998] 1 WLR 294, at p 311, Toulson J proceeded, in our view correctly, on the basis that a shadow director could be in breach of the fiduciary duties as a director. See also Shareholder Remedies (1997) Law Com No 246, para 6.36.

[17] See Part 15 above.

[18] Regulation 69 provides that "an alternate director shall be deemed for all purposes to be a director".

17.18 Whilst the alternate is acting as a director, he stands in a fiduciary position in relation to the company, and accordingly owes the company all the same duties as are owed by a director. Having regard to the statutory definition in section 741,[19] it would appear that he also is subject to the statutory obligations which are imposed on directors. However, he has no legal status when he is not acting as a director.[20]

17.19 It appears that the disqualification of a director from voting in relation to a particular matter does not prevent an alternate director appointed by the disqualified director from voting in relation to that matter.[21]

17.20 The Jenkins Committee[22] took the view that in the eyes of the law an alternate director was in the same position as any other director, and did not consider that special mention needed to be made of alternate directors in the Companies Act.

Do consultees consider that any provision in Part X is difficult to apply in relation to alternate directors so that special provision is needed for them?

EXECUTIVE AND NON-EXECUTIVE DIRECTORS

17.21 Most larger companies now have two types of directors sitting on their board: executive and non-executive directors. Executive directors will generally have extensive powers delegated to them by the articles. They will also have separate service contracts with the company. In contrast, non-executive directors do not have service contracts with the company and are less concerned with the day to day running of the company, but rather bring an outside perspective to the board's deliberations with more concern for general policy and overall supervision, and are compensated by fees for expenses incurred in this role.[23]

17.22 However, both types of directors have overall and equal responsibility for the *leadership* of the company. Traditionally the law has not distinguished between executive and non-executive directors. The Companies Act 1985 also makes no distinction between the two. In practice the functions and duties of directors vary according to their position and day to day management responsibilities. In most larger companies, whose boards comprise both executive and non-executive directors, the executive directors will have additional responsibilities and duties arising out of their executive position as a result of their service contracts. Non-

---

[19] See para 17.2 above.

[20] See *Playcorp Pty Ltd v Shaw* (1993) 10 ACSR 212.

[21] *In Anaray Pty Ltd v Sydney Futures Exchange Ltd* (1982) 6 ACLC 271 Foster J held that an alternate director had not been disqualified from voting since the articles of the company did not make the alternate director the agent of the appointor. Regulation 69 of Table A expressly states that the alternate director shall not be deemed to the agent of the director appointing him and so the same result is likely to apply in the United Kingdom.

[22] Jenkins Report, para 83.

[23] Despite this, however, there is a growing trend towards more formalised letters of appointment, although their status does not change to that of employee under a service contract.

executive directors will not, by definition, owe any additional duties to their companies.

17.23 Non-executive directors are subject to the same legal framework as their executive counterparts. Accordingly, their position can be somewhat invidious in many cases where they are expected to act without the executives day to day decision making power and detailed knowledge of the business.[24] The duty of care owed by non-executive directors would also appear to be the same as that expected of executive directors.[25] However the non-executive is likely to have to do less than an executive director to discharge his duty.

17.24 In *Dorchester Finance Co Ltd v Stebbing*[26] Foster J held that it was unacceptable for even non-executive directors not to attend board meetings or take active interest in the company's affairs. He laid stress on the fact that the two non-executive directors were experienced in accountancy, but made it clear that even directors with no accounting experience were not entitled to blindly accept documents laid before them by auditors:

> For a chartered accountant ... to put forward the proposition that a non-executive director has no duties to perform I find quite alarming. It would be an argument, if put forward by a director with no accountancy experience ... would involve total disregard of many sections of the Companies Act ... In the Companies Act 1948 the duties of a director whether executive or not are the same.

17.25 In *Norman v Theodore Goddard*[27] Hoffmann J said that he was willing to assume that the test of a director's duty of care, in considering what he ought reasonably to have known or inferred, empowered the court to take into account the knowledge, skill and experience which he actually had, in addition to that which a person carrying out his functions should be expected to have.[28]

17.26 The role of non-executive directors and the independence which such individuals were thought to bring to the boardroom was one of the main themes of the Cadbury Report.[29] The London Stock Exchange currently requires UK

---

[24] In performing their duties, non-executive directors often have to rely on the goodwill of executive directors and so it is not uncommon for them to take out insurance policies in addition to any D&O policies taken out by the company.

[25] In the case of executive directors, however, the service contract may impose obligations upon the director that go beyond his duties *qua* director.

[26] [1989] BCLC 498.

[27] [1991] BCLC 1028.

[28] See the further decision of Hoffmann LJ in *Re D'Jan of London* [1994] 1 BCLC 561, at 563f, who held an executive director to have breached both the objective and subjective tests in s 214(4).

[29] The Committee envisaged that "non-executive directors should bring an independent judgment to bear on issues of strategy, performance, resources, including key appointments, and standards of conduct." The Code of Best Practice stated that: "The board should include non-executive directors of 'sufficient calibre and number' for their views to carry significant weight (minimum of 3); the majority should be independent of management and free from any relationship which could materially affect their independent judgment; they should be

companies whose securities are listed on the Exchange to include statements in their annual report as to whether or not they have complied throughout that accounting period with the Code of Best Practice and section A of the best practice provisions annexed to the Listing Rules.[30] Reasons for non compliance must be given.[31] For company reports and accounts published in respect of the year ending 31 December 1998 onwards, the required statement will relate to compliance with provisions of the Combined Code.[32]

17.27 The Hampel Report noted the view that non-executive directors should face less onerous duties than executive directors, since they will inevitably be less well informed about the company's business. However, it supported the retention of common duties "in the interests of the unity and cohesion of the board"[33] and thought that the English Courts' recognition of the practical situation was helpful.[34]

17.28 No distinction has been drawn in the statutory duty of care or statement of duties considered in this consultation paper between an executive and a non-executive director. The court will, however, be able to take into account that a director is only non-executive under our draft section 309A, since the comparator has to be a person "in the same position" as the director in question.

NOMINEE DIRECTORS

17.29 Occasionally, groups or individuals are likely to have the requisite voting power or influence to appoint a director. They may represent a major shareholder, a class of shareholders or debentureholders, a major creditor or an employee group.[35]

appointed for specified periods and be a matter for the board as a whole; and they should be able to consult independent professional advisers as necessary at the company's expense."

[30] See paras 1.34-1.35 above. The Code of Best Practice was published in December 1992 by the Cadbury Committee. The best practice provisions were adopted as an annex to the Listing Rules following publication of the Greenbury Report in July 1995.

[31] Paras 12.43(j) and (w) of the Listing Rules. There is no requirement to explain or justify any areas of non-compliance with section B of the best practice provisions, although paragraph 12.43(x)(ii) of the Listing Rules requires a statement to be made in relation to full consideration being given to the best practice provisions in framing remuneration policy.

[32] See paras 12.43A(a) and (b) of the Listing Rules (introduced on 25 June 1998), which supersede rules 12.43(j) and (w) for company reports and accounts published for the year ending 31 December 1998 onwards.

[33] It stated that what matters in every case is that the non-executive directors should command the respect of the executives and should be able to work with them in a cohesive team to further the company's interests. See para 3.8.

[34] That when called on to decide whether a director has fulfilled his or duty, they have recently tended to take into account such factors as the position of the director concerned and the type of company. In the Australian case *AWA Ltd v Daniels* (1992) 7 ACSR 759, although the judge did not find that a different degree of performance or standard could be expected of non-executive as opposed to executive directors, he did accept that executive directors were required to carry out additional duties and responsibilities arising from their contracts as executives.

[35] Australia is the only jurisdiction where nominee directors are referred to specifically in the companies legislation and even this does little more than assume the existence of nominee

17.30   Nominee directors have been defined as:

> ... persons who, independently of the method of their appointment, but in relation to their office, are expected to act in accordance with some understanding or arrangement which creates an obligation or mutual expectation of loyalty to some person or persons other than the company as a whole.[36]

17.31   As fiduciaries, directors are under a duty to act bona fide in the best interests of the company and not for any collateral purpose. This is a subjective test based on what the director believes in good faith in exercising their power is in the best interest of the company.[37] By definition nominee directors represent sectional interest groups whose interests may differ from the interests of the company as a whole.[38] But they are precluded from placing themselves in a position where their duty to exercise their powers for the company's benefit may be fettered. There is no authority in English law for a nominee to act in the interests of his appointor rather than in the company's interest.

17.32   The English courts have taken a strict view of the duties of nominee directors. *Scottish Co-operative Wholesale Society Ltd v Meyer*[39] confirms the view that a nominated director must not put his principal's interests above those of the company.[40]

17.33   The Australian courts have taken a more liberal approach. In Australia there is authority for the view that although directors must not fetter their discretion or act as mere mouthpieces of another, the fact that they have an extraneous loyalty will not in itself make their acts invalid. Provided that a director has a bona fide belief that promoting the interests of his appointor is consistent with his own appreciation of the interests of the company and provided that belief is not totally unreasonable, the nominee will not be in breach of his fiduciary duty.[41] There is

directors in public companies. Section 317 of the Companies Act 1985 may however apply. There is no judicial authority on this point but it is likely that a nominee director's indirect interest would include an interest of an appointor.

[36] Companies and Securities Law Review Committee (NSW, Australia) Nominee Directors and Alternate Directors: Report No 8, 2 March 1989, at p 7.

[37] *Re Smith & Fawcett Ltd* [1942] Ch 304.

[38] What is encompassed within the "interests of the company as a whole" may vary. Traditionally confined to the interests of members and particular classes of members, directors are also now required to have regard to the interests of creditors and employees in particular situations.

[39] [1959] AC 324.

[40] This was a case under s 210 of the Companies Act 1948 (now s 459 of the Companies Act 1985) in which it was held that a parent company had, via its nominee directors, conducted the affairs of a subsidiary in a manner which was oppressive to the other members of the subsidiary. In pointing out that the directors had done nothing to defend the interests of the subsidiary against the conduct of the parent company, Lord Denning stated: "They probably thought 'as nominees' of the [parent company] their first duty was to [the parent company]. In this they were wrong ...".

[41] See *Re Broadcasting Station 2GB Ltd* [1964-65] NSWR 1662; but cf *Bennetts v Board of Fire Commissioners of New South Wales* (1967) 87 WN (NSW) 307.

also authority that a nominee director's duty may be modified by the company's constituent documents and by the wishes of all those to whom the fiduciary duty is owed, although without denying the general requirement that directors act in the best interests of the company.[42]

17.34 In a number of jurisdictions there is specific legislation which recognises the fact that nominee directors may give special consideration to the interests of their appointor where this is permitted by the company's constitution.[43]

17.35 The issues concerning nominee directors are tied up closely with the whole question of group structures.[44] They must therefore be left to the DTI's wider review of company law and we do not propose to deal with it in the context of this project.

---

[42] See also *Levin v Clark* [1962] NSWR 686. There is support for this approach also in New Zealand: see *Berlei Hestia (NZ) Ltd v Fernyhough* [1980] 2 NZLR 150.

[43] See s 131(2) of the New Zealand Companies Act 1993 and s 203(3) of the Ghana Companies Code.

[44] These include the issue of whether the liability of a nominee director should be extended to his appointor. See *Kuwait Asia Bank EC v National Mutual Life Nominees Ltd* [1990] BCC 567 1 AC 187; cf *Dairy Containers Ltd v NZI Bank Ltd* [1995] 2 NZLR 30.

PART 18
SUMMARY OF QUESTIONS FOR CONSULTATION

INTRODUCTION

18.1   In this part we summarise the issues on which we seek the views of consultees. It would be helpful if, in responding, consultees could indicate either the paragraph of the following summary to which their comments relate, or the paragraph of the paper.

18.2   We have included at the beginning of this part the central general questions which were set out in Part 1. The issues which are raised by these general questions underpin many of the more detailed questions raised in the remainder of the paper and which are brought together below. As we indicated in Part 1, we do not want consultees to lose sight of these more general questions, and it would assist us in analysing the responses to this consultation paper if consultees were able to indicate their views on these central general questions in addition to answering such of the more detailed questions as they wish to or are able to answer.

18.3   In Part 4 we raised in respect of many of the sections of Part X of the Companies Act 1985, a considerable number of different suggestions - which we called "*options*" - as to the way in which the sections might be dealt with or amended. In some cases these are fundamental changes, in others they are small changes designed to deal with specific problems. *Thus it is possible in many cases to choose more than one option.* We have not included in this summary an explanation of those cases where consultees may *not* choose more than one option as we consider that it is apparent from the text of the questions themselves. However, consultees are referred to the earlier explanations given in this respect at paragraphs 4.42, 4.94, 4.132, 4.163, 4.190, and 4.225.

18.4   The consultation questions which have been brought together in this part follow the order in which they appear in the text of the paper and grouped under the following heads:

> Part 1: Central general questions
> Part 2: Guiding principles for reform
>
> SECTION A: PART X OF THE COMPANIES ACT 1985
> Part 4: Substantive improvements 1: Sections 312-323 of the Companies Act 1985
> Part 5: Substantive improvements 2: Disclosure of directors' share dealings (sections 324-326, 328-329 and Schedule 13)
> Part 6: Substantive improvements 3: Loans and similar transactions (sections 330-342)
> Part 7: Substantive improvements 4: Disclosure of transactions in which directors and their connected persons are interested in the annual accounts (Schedule 6, Part II) and the special provisions for banks (sections 343 and 344)

Part 8: Substantive improvements 5: Connected persons (section 346) and remaining sections of Part X of the Companies Act 1985

Part 9: Further options: (1) Can sections in Part X be repealed? (2) Would Part X be improved if it was rewritten?

Part 10: Should Part X of the Companies Act 1985 be decriminalised?

SECTION B: THE CASE FOR A STATUTORY STATEMENT OF DIRECTORS' DUTIES UNDER THE GENERAL LAW

Part 14: A statement of directors' fiduciary duties: Options for reform

Part 15: Duty of care: Options for reform

SECTION C: MISCELLANEOUS MATTERS

Part 17: How should the law apply to different categories of director?

318

PART 1: CENTRAL GENERAL QUESTIONS

Q1   Should detailed substantive amendments be made to Part X?

Q2   Should large parts of Part X be repealed (for example, because they duplicate areas covered by the general law)?

Q3   Should Part X be disapplied where appropriate self-regulatory rules exist?

Q4   Should Part X be rewritten in simple language?

Q5   Should Part X be decriminalised?

Q6   Should directors' duties under the general law be codified? (This involves deciding on the standard of the duty of care).

Q7   Should there be a non-binding but authoritative statement of directors' duties under the general law? (paragraph 1.13)

PART 2: GUIDING PRINCIPLES FOR REFORM

Q8   Consultees are asked whether, in their view, the appropriate principles to guide reform in this area, are those set out at paragraph 2.17 above; and/or whether some other, and if so what, principles should apply for that purpose. (paragraph 2.17)

SECTION A: PART X OF THE COMPANIES ACT 1985

PART 4: SUBSTANTIVE IMPROVEMENTS 1: SECTIONS 312-323 OF THE COMPANIES ACT 1985

Sections 312 - 316: Payments to directors for loss of office, etc

Is section 316(3) properly applied?

Q9   Consultees are asked whether section 316(3) is being properly applied in practice and, if not, to produce, where possible, evidence to support their answer. (paragraph 4.27)

Option 1: No Change

Q10   Consultees are asked whether, if retained, sections 312-316 should be retained without amendment. (paragraph 4.43)

Option 2: Reverse the effect of the decision in Taupo Totara Timber v Rowe

Q11   Consultees are asked whether they agree with our provisional view that sections 312-316 should not apply to covenanted payments. (paragraph 4.46)

Option 3: Amend sections 312-316 to make it clear that they do not apply to covenanted payments

Q12   Consultees are asked whether they agree with our provisional view that sections 312-316 should be amended to make it clear that they do not apply to covenanted payments. (paragraph 4.47)

Option 4: Extend the provisions of sections 312-316 to former directors

Q13   Consultees are asked whether they agree with our provisional view that sections 312-316 should not be amended so as to apply to payments to former directors. (paragraph 4.48)

Option 5: Extend the provisions of sections 312-316 to cover payments to connected persons

Q14   Consultees are asked whether sections 312-316 should cover payments made to connected persons, and, if so, in what circumstances. (paragraph 4.49)

Option 6: Require approvals by company in general meeting under sections 312 and 313 to be by special resolution and where disclosure under those sections or section 314 is required, stipulate that disclosure should cover payments made on the same occasion for which disclosure is not required by those sections.

Q15   Consultees are asked whether they agree with our provisional views that

(i) it should not be a requirement that the approval by the company in general meeting, as required by sections 312 and 313, should be by special resolution;

(ii) it should not be a requirement of approval under those sections or section 314 that there should be a stipulation that details of payments which do not require approval should be disclosed when approval of those which require disclosure is sought. (paragraph 4.50)

Option 7: Non-contractual payments received for loss of other offices

Q16   Consultees are asked:

(i) whether they consider that section 312 should require approval of uncovenanted payments made to a director in respect of the loss of some other position in the company, or its group, apart from that of director (a) if he loses that position at the same time as he loses his office as a director, or (b) whenever he receives such a payment;

(ii) whether they consider that sections 312-316 should apply to any such payments which are covenanted as well. (paragraph 4.53)

Option 8: Deem payments approved if notified and members raise no objection to the proposed payment within a stipulated period

Q17   Consultees are asked whether they agree with our provisional view that sections 312-314 should not be amended so as to permit a company to dispense with approval of the company in general meeting if notice is given to members and there is no objection from a specified proportion of members within a specified period. (paragraph 4.54)

***Option 9: Amend sections 314 and 315 to cover acquisitions by way of a
cancellation of shares under schemes of arrangement etc***

Q18   Consultees are asked whether they consider that sections 314 and 315 should be
amended:

(i) to cover acquisitions by way of a cancellation of shares under a scheme of
arrangement;

(ii) to cover unconditional offers;

(iii) to prevent the offeror or his associates from voting at the meeting convened
pursuant to section 315;

(iv) in any other way to remove deficiencies in their application to takeovers in
accordance with modern practice. (paragraph 4.55)

***Option 10: Amend sections 312-314 to provide civil remedies against the
directors and section 315 so that a claim under this section has priority
where the amount paid to the director was taken into account in
determining the price to offeree shareholders***

Q19   Consultees are asked:

(i) whether they agree with our provisional view that sections 312 and 313 should
be amended to provide for civil remedies on the lines suggested in paragraph 4.50;

(ii) whether section 315 should be amended so as to provide that, unless the court
otherwise orders, the claim of former shareholders under section 315 should
prevail over that of any of the company in section 312 in respect of the same
payment. (paragraph 4.59)

***Option 11: Reinforce section 316(3) by requiring companies to disclose in
their annual accounts particulars of the calculation of compensation paid
to a director***

Q20   Consultees are asked whether they consider that particulars of a severance
payment made to a director should be included in the annual accounts and, if so,
what in their view those particulars should cover and when the disclosure
requirement should arise. (paragraph 4.60)

***Option 12: Extend section 312 to cover the situation where the payment is
made by a company to a director of its holding company in connection
with loss of office as such director***

Q21   Consultees are asked whether section 312 should apply to payments made by a
company to a director of a holding company in connection with his loss of office
as such director and, if so, whether the requirement for disclosure and approval
should be satisfied in both companies (other than a wholly-owned subsidiary).
(paragraph 4.61)

Generally

Q22 Consultees are asked whether any further reform of sections 312-316 should be considered. (paragraph 4.61)

Section 317: Disclosure by directors to their board

Option 1: No change

Q23 Consultees are asked whether section 317 should be retained as it is. (paragraph 4.95)

Option 2: Limit the duty of disclosure to material interests only

Q24 Consultees are asked whether they consider that section 317 should only apply to material interests in a contract; and if so (a) whether "material" should be defined by statute, and (b) if so, whether it should mean those interests whose disclosure might reasonably be expected to affect the decision of the board or some other meaning. (paragraph 4.97)

Option 3: Exempt from the obligation of disclosure transactions or arrangements which either do not come before the board or a committee of the board, or do not require approval by the board or a committee of the board

Q25 Consultees are asked whether they agree with our provisional view that section 317 should not exempt directors from the need to disclose their interests in transactions or arrangements which either do not come before the board, or a committee of the board, or do not require approval by the board, or a committee of the board. (paragraph 4.99)

Option 4: Exempt sole director companies

Q26 Consultees are asked whether they agree with our provisional views that:

(i) section 317 should not apply where there is only one director; and

(ii) if the suggestion put forward at paragraph 4.118 is not adopted, there should be a requirement that where there is only one director, the director should disclose interests to the company in general meeting, unless this requirement is waived by shareholders or varied by resolution or in the articles. (paragraph 4.101)

Option 5: Exempt from the obligation of disclosure interests in director's own service agreement

Q27 Consultees are asked whether they agree with our provisional view that section 317 should exempt directors from the need to make formal disclosure of their interest in their own service contracts. (paragraph 4.102)

***Option 6: Exempt from the obligation of disclosure executive directors'
interests in contracts or arrangements made for the benefit of all
employees***

Q28   Consultees are asked whether there should be an exemption from disclosure
under section 317 for benefits which a director receives which are ordinarily made
to employees on terms no less favourable. (paragraph 4.103)

***Option 7: Exempt from the obligation of disclosure interests arising by
reason only of a directorship of, or non-beneficial shareholding in,
another group company***

Q29   (i) Consultees are asked whether they agree with our provisional view that there
should not be excepted from disclosure under section 317 interests which a
director has by reason only that he is a director of another company in the same
group or has a non-beneficial shareholding in it.

(ii) If consultees disagree, do they consider that this exception should only apply
to directorships and shareholdings in (a) wholly-owned subsidiaries, or (b) all
subsidiaries (whether or not wholly-owned)?[1] (paragraph 4.104)

***Option 8: Exempt from disclosure an interest of which a director has no
knowledge and of which it is unreasonable to expect him to have
knowledge***

Q30   Consultees are asked whether they agree with our provisional view that section
317 should exempt from disclosure an interest of which a director has no
knowledge and of which it is unreasonable to expect him to have knowledge.
(paragraph 4.105)

***Option 9: Make any contract voidable where the requisite disclosure has
not been made and provide a civil remedy for compensation or
disgorgement, or alternatively provide that the section does not affect any
resulting contract***

Q31   Consultees are asked:

(i) whether they agree with our provisional views that:

> (a) a breach of section 317 should automatically result in the contract
> or arrangement being voidable unless the court otherwise directs;

> (b) the contract or arrangement should cease to be voidable in the
> same circumstances as those set out in section 322(2);

> (c) a breach of section 317 should result in the director being
> personally liable (a) to account for any profit he makes, and (b) to
> indemnify the company for any loss it incurs as a result of the breach.

---

[1]   The terms "subsidiary" and "wholly-owned subsidiary" are defined in s 736(2) of the
Companies Act 1985.

(ii) whether, if the answer to (i)(a) is no, section 317 should be amended to state that it has no effect on the contract or arrangement.

(iii) whether, if section 317 is amended so as to require the disclosure of the interests of connected persons, the liability referred to in paragraph (i)(c) above should extend to connected persons, and if so whether connected persons should have a defence if they can show that they did not know of the director's failure to comply with the section. (paragraph 4.113)

Option 10: Disqualify directors of public companies from voting on matters in which they have an interest or a material interest

Q32 Consultees are asked whether they consider that the Companies Act should prohibit directors of public companies from voting on matters in which they have a material interest and, if so, whether there should be any exceptions to this general rule. (paragraph 4.114)

Option 11: Require directors to disclose material interests of their connected persons of which they are aware

Q33 Do consultees agree with our provisional view that section 317 should be amended to provide that a director should disclose the interests of connected persons if he is aware of them and if they would have to be disclosed if they were interests of his? (paragraph 4.115)

Option 12: Require that general notice under section 317(4) include details of the interest concerned

Q34 Consultees are asked whether they agree with our provisional view that a general notice under section 317(3) should be required to state that the nature and extent of the interest, and that the director should give notice amending these particulars if they change. (paragraph 4.116)

Option 13: Require a register of directors interests to be kept which would be open to inspection by members or require a report to be made to shareholders in the annual accounts of the nature of interests which directors had disclosed

Q35 Consultees are asked:

(i) whether a register of directors interests should be required to be kept which would be open to inspection by members;

(ii) whether a report should be required to be made to directors in the annual accounts of the nature of interests which directors had disclosed;

(iii) if the answer to (i) or (ii) is yes

> (a) whether there should be an exemption from disclosure for information which the directors reasonably consider it would be harmful to the company to disclose; and

(b) whether any information disclosed in the register or report should be audited. (paragraph 4.118)

Section 318: Directors' service contracts (1)

Option 1: No change

Q36   Consultees are asked whether section 318 should be retained as it is. (paragraph 4.134)

Option 2: The Secretary of State should have power to disapply section 318 to the extent that, in the Secretary of State's opinion, a company is already bound by sufficient comparable disclosure obligations under the Listing Rules

Q37   Consultees are asked whether the Secretary of State should be able to disapply section 318 to the extent that, in the Secretary of State's opinion, a company is already bound by sufficient comparable disclosure obligations under the Listing Rules. (paragraphs 4.136)

Option 3: Extend section 318 to contracts for services and non-executive directors' letters of appointment

Q38   Consultees are asked whether they agree with our provisional views that:

(i) section 318 should require the disclosure of contracts for services and not just contracts of service; and that

(ii) section 318 should apply to letters of appointment for non-executive directors. (paragraph 4.139)

Option 4: Repeal of subsection (5) (Director to work abroad)

Q39   Consultees are asked:

(i) whether they agree with our provisional view that section 318(5) should be repealed, and, if so, whether the Secretary of State should be given power to exempt prescribed information from disclosure in the case of directors working wholly or mainly abroad; and

(ii) whether, if there continues to be an exemption or a power to give exemption in respect of service contracts which require a director to work wholly or mainly abroad, it should be made clear that, in the case of a contract which requires a director to work abroad and in the UK for different periods of the contract, the exemption or power applies only in relation to the period for which he actually works mainly abroad. (paragraph 4.144)

Option 5: Repeal of subsection (11) (Contract with less than 12 months to run)

Q40   Consultees are asked whether they agree with our provisional view that section 318(11) should be repealed. (paragraphs 4.147)

Option 6: Amend section 318 to require disclosure of particulars of terms collateral to the service contract

Q41   Consultees are asked whether section 318 should require disclosure of particulars of terms collateral to the service contract, and, if so, whether the Secretary of State should have power to exempt prescribed information from disclosure. (paragraph 4.150)

Option 7: Allow inspection of director's service contracts

Q42   Consultees are asked whether the statutory register ought to be open to public inspection (a) in the case of all companies, or (b) in the case of companies listed a the Stock Exchange or AIM only. (paragraph 4.152)

Section 319: Directors' service contracts (2)

Option 1: No change

Q43   Consultees are asked whether section 319 should be retained in its current form. (paragraph 4.164)

Option 2: Reduce the statutory period in section 319(1) from 5 years to 1, 2 or 3 years

Q44   Consultees are asked:

(i) whether the statutory period in section 319(1) should be reduced to (a) one year, (b) two years, or (c) three years;

(ii) whether any reduction of the statutory period should apply either (a) to both listed and unlisted companies, or (b) only to listed companies. (paragraphs 4.168)

Option 3: Amend section 319 to prohibit (without shareholder approval) the creation of "rolling contracts" having a notice or contract period in excess of the period permitted by section 319

Q45   Consultees are asked whether section 319 should be amended to prevent "rolling contracts" for a period exceeding the maximum term permitted by section 319 unless they are first approved by ordinary resolution. (paragraphs 4.169)

Option 4: Deem terms approved if notified and members raise no objection to the proposed term within a stipulated period

Q46   Consultees are asked whether they agree with our provisional view that section 319 should not be amended so as to permit a company to dispense with approval of the company in general meeting[2] if a notice was given to members and there is no objection from a specified proportion of members within a specified period. (paragraphs 4.171)

---

[2]   A like option could be given with respect to approval of the holding company, when that is required.

Sections 320-322: Substantial property transactions involving directors etc

Option 1: No change

Q47   Consultees are asked:

(i) whether they are aware of any difficulties in the operation of these provisions which ought to be addressed; and

(ii) whether they would favour retaining sections 320-322 as they stand. (paragraph 4.191)

Option 2: Amend section 320 so that it does not prohibit a company from making a contract which is subject to a condition precedent that the company first obtains approval under section 320

Q48   Consultees are asked whether they agree with our provisional view that section 320 should be amended so that a company is able to enter into a contract which only takes effect if the requisite shareholder approval is obtained. (paragraph 4.192)

Option 3: Amend section 320 to make it clear that it does not apply to covenanted payments under service agreements with directors or to payments to which section 316(3) applies

Q49   Consultees are asked whether they agree with our provisional view that section 320 should be amended to make it clear that it does not apply to covenanted payments under service agreements with directors or to payments to which section 316(3) applies. (paragraph 4.193)

Option 4: A safe harbour for transactions with administrative receivers and court-appointed administrators

Q50   Consultees are asked whether they consider that an exception should be permitted in section 321 for administrators or receivers. (paragraph 4.194)

Option 5: Give the Secretary of State power to exemption listed companies from section 320

Q51   Consultees are asked whether the Scecretary of State should have the power to exempt listed companies from sections 320-322. (paragraph 4.196)

Option 6: Dispense with the requirement for shareholder approval where the independent non-executive directors approve the transaction

Q52   Consultees are asked whether they agree with our provisional view that section 320 should not be amended so as to provide that alternative approval could be provided by a specified minimum number of non-executive directors of the company. (paragraphs 4.199)

Q53   Consultees are asked whether they agree with our provisional view that section 320 should not be amended so as to permit a company to dispense with approval of the company in general meeting if notice is given to members and there is no objection from a specified proportion of members within a specified period. (paragraph 4.200)

Option 8: Provide that shareholder approval is not required if an expert reports that in his opinion the transaction is fair and reasonable

Q54   Consultees are asked whether they agree with our provisional view that companies should not be able to obtain an independent expert's report as an alternative to having to obtain shareholder approval under section 320. (paragraph 4.202)

Option 9: Provide that the statutory consequences of breach apply only where the company suffers prejudice

Q55   Consultees are asked whether they agree with our provisional view that section 322 should not be amended to the effect that a company will have no remedy under the section where the defendant or defender shows that it was not prejudiced by the transaction. (paragraph 4.204)

Section 322A: Transactions beyond the directors' powers

Q56   Consulteees are asked whether they are aware of any deficiency in section 322A. (paragraph 4.209)

Section 322B: Contracts with sole member directors

Q57   Consulteees are asked whether they are aware of any deficiency in section 322B. (paragraph 4.213)

Sections 323 and 327: Prohibition on option dealing by directors and their near families

Option 1: No change

Q58   Consultees are asked whether section 323 should be left unchanged. (paragraph 4.226)

Option 2: Make off-market dealings in options with inside information an offence

Q59   Consultees are asked whether, if section 323 is not repealed, it should be amended so that it applies only to off market dealings in options on the basis of inside information. (paragraph 4.228)

Option 3: No change, but exempt dealings in options under a scheme for the benefit of employees

Q60 Consultees are asked whether, if section 323 is not repealed, it should be disapplied in relation to the purchase of options under a scheme for the benefit of employees.[3] (paragraph 4.229)

PART 5: SUBSTANTIVE IMPROVEMENTS 2: DISCLOSURE OF DIRECTORS' SHARE DEALINGS (SECTIONS 324-326, 328-329, AND SCHEDULE 13)

The obligation of disclosure: Sections 324 and 328 - Duty of director to notify own and attributed shareholdings in company

Q61 Consultees are asked if non-beneficial holdings should be exempt from section 324 and if so:

(i) whether non-beneficial holdings should be defined as excluding any beneficial interests which the director may have by reason of any right to expenses, remuneration or indemnity;

(ii) whether the exemption should apply irrespective of the size of the transaction or only if the tranaction (when aggregated with other transactions in non-beneficial holdings) does not exceed a certain size;

(iii) if they consider that the exemption should only apply if the transaction does not exceed a certain size, how should such size be ascertained. (paragraph 5.19)

Q62 Consultees are also asked if they consider that there are deficiencies in section 324 not considered above. (paragraph 5.19)

The meaning of "interest" and the mechanics of disclosure: Schedule 13, Parts I-III

Q63 Consultees are asked whether the Secretary of State should be given power by regulation to vary the rules in Part I of Schedule 13 for determining whether a person has an interest in shares or debentures for the purposes of sections 324-326, 328 and 346. (paragraph 5.22)

Q64 Consultees are asked whether the company should be obliged to comply with section 325(2),(3) and (4) within a specified period and if so whether that period should be the expiration of five days beginning with the day on which the event in question occurs or some other and if so what period. (paragraph 5.25)

Q65 Consultees are asked if there are any other issues for reform arising under Schedule 13, Parts I-III. (paragraph 5.26)

---

[3] Including former employees and near relatives as in s 743, see para 4.229, n 353 above.

The company's register of directors' interests: Sections 325 and 326 and Schedule 13, Part IV

Q66 Consultees are asked whether section 325 and Schedule 13, Part IV raise any other issues for reform. (paragraph 5.30)

Notification to the Exchanges: Section 329

Q67 Consultees are asked if section 329 should be amended so that a company is bound to transmit to the relevant exchange details of information which the company is bound to enter into the register of directors' interests without notification by the director pursuant to section 325(3) and (4). (paragraph 5.39)

Q68 Consultees are also asked if section 329 raises any issue for reform not mentioned above. (paragraph 5.39)

PART 6: SUBSTANTIVE IMPROVEMENTS 3: LOANS AND SIMILAR TRANSACTIONS (SECTIONS 330–342)

Sections 330 and 331: General restriction on loans etc to directors and persons connected with them and definitions for the purposes of section 330 and subsequent sections

Are restrictions other than on making loans to directors necessary?

Q69 We ask consultees:

(i) Are the restrictions on quasi-loans and related transactions in sections 330-331 required, and, if so, should they extend to directors, holding company directors and connected persons?

(ii) Are the restrictions on credit transactions and related transactions in sections 330-331 required, and, if so, should they extend to directors, holding company directors and their connected persons?

(iii) Are the additional restrictions in section 330(6) and (7) on indirect arrangements required? (paragraph 6.12)

To which companies should the prohibitions extend?

Q70 Consultees are asked:

(i) whether section 330 should continue to apply as now, with some of the restrictions applying only to relevant companies; or

(ii) whether the same restrictions should apply to all companies; or

(iii) whether some of the prohibitions, now applying only to relevant companies, should additionally be applied to some companies other than relevant companies and, if so:

　　　(a) whether such companies should be defined in terms of size; and if so

(b) whether this should be on the same basis as for small and medium sized companies or on some other basis, and if so what basis;

(iv) whether some relevant companies should cease to be subject to the additional restrictions and, if so, in what circumstances. (paragraph 6.14)

Sections 332-338: Exemptions from prohibitions

(1) Short-term quasi-loans (section 332)

Q71   Consultees are asked whether the exemption contained in section 332 is (a) used in practice, and (b) satisfactory. (paragraph 6.15)

(2) Intra-group loans (section 333)

Q72   Consultees are asked whether the exemption contained in section 333 is (a) used in practice, and (b) satisfactory. (paragraph 6.16)

(3) Loans of small amounts (section 334)

Q73   Consultees are asked whether the exemption contained in section 334 is (a) needed, and (b) satisfactory. (paragraph 6.17)

(4) Minor transactions (section 335(1))

Q74   Consultees are asked whether the exemption contained in section 335(1) is (a) needed, and (b) satisfactory. (paragraph 6.18)

(5) Transactions in the ordinary course of business (section 335(2))

Q75   Consultees are asked whether the exemption contained in section 335(2) is (a) used in practice, and (b) satisfactory. (paragraph 6.20)

(6) Transactions at the behest of the holding company (section 336)

Q76   Consultees are asked whether the exemption contained in section 336 is (a) used in practice, and (b) satisfactory. (paragraph 6.21)

(7) Funding of director's expenditure on duty to the company (section 337)

Q77   Consultees are asked whether they consider that the exemption contained in section 337 is (a) used in practice, and (b) satisfactory. (paragraph 6.23)

(8) Loan or quasi-loan by a money-lending company (section 338)

Q78   Consultees are asked:

(i) With regard to the exemption in section 338(3) (taken on its own):

(a) should this exemption be retained;

(b) is this exemption used in practice;

(c) is this exemption satisfactory?

(ii) With regard to the exemption in section 338(3) taken with section 338(6) (house purchase loans):

> (a) should this exemption be retained;

> (b) is this exemption used in practice;

> (c) is this exemption satisfactory? (paragraph 6.25)

Sections 339-340: "Relevant amounts" for purposes of section 334 and other sections and determining the "value" of transactions or arrangements

Q79 Consultees are asked if they have any comment on sections 339-340 apart from their complexity. (paragraph 6.28)

Section 341: Civil remedies

Q80 Consultees are asked whether they have any comments on section 341. (paragraph 6.30)

Section 342: Criminal penalties for breach of section 330

Q81 Consultees are asked whether, if criminal penalties are to be imposed for breach of section 330, they should cover offences by relevant companies (and their officers), or all companies (and their officers). (paragraph 6.31).

A possible additional exemption available to all companies for loans made with the consent of shareholders

Q82 Consultees are asked:

(i) Is there any need in practice to create a new exemption to meet the case where directors hold all or a majority of the shares and creditors are not prejudiced?

(ii) Is it desirable to create a new exemption for this situation?

(iii) Do they consider that there should be safeguards for shareholders and, if so, which do they consider to be the best option:

> (a) a special resolution;

> (b) unanimous approval by the members?

If they think that some other option is preferable, they are asked to state what that option comprises and why they prefer it.

(iv) Do they consider that there should be safeguards for creditors and, if so, which of the options discussed in paragraphs 6.37-6.39 do they consider to be the best option:

> (a) option 1: the company must have to provide for the whole of the value of the transaction out of its distributable profits;

(b) option 2: the company's directors must make a statutory declaration as required by section 173 of the Companies Act 1985?

If they think that some other option is preferable, they are asked to state what that option comprises and why they prefer it.

(v) Should the new exemption apply to:

> (a) loans to directors;
>
> (b) loans to holding company directors;
>
> (c) guarantees or security in support of the above;

Or, in the case of relevant companies:

> (d) loans in favour of connected persons;
>
> (e) quasi-loans in favour of directors or their connected persons;
>
> (f) credit transactions in favour of directors or their connected persons;
>
> (g) guarantees or security in respect of any of the above;

In the case of all companies:

> (h) indirect arrangements caught by section 330(6) or (7) of the Companies Act 1985?

(vi) Should the new exemption apply to:

> (a) all companies;
>
> (b) only companies which are not relevant companies as defined by section 331(6);
>
> (c) only another class of companies (please describe)?

(vii) Do consultees think that if this new exemption is adopted:

> (a) there should be the same arrangements for publicity as for payment out of capital and as described in paragraph 6.42 above;
>
> (b) there should be power for the court to cancel the approval given by the shareholders on the application of a member or creditor as described in paragraph 6.43 above?

(viii) Do consultees think that if this new exemption is adopted, shareholders who may benefit from the transaction should have their votes disregarded if the resolution would not have been passed without them?

(ix) Do consultees think that if the new exemption is adopted members should have the right to inspect the statutory declaration and the auditors' report? (paragraph 6.43)

PART 7: SUBSTANTIVE IMPROVEMENTS 4: DISCLOSURE OF TRANSACTIONS IN WHICH DIRECTORS AND THEIR CONNECTED PERSONS ARE INTERESTED IN THE ANNUAL ACCOUNTS (SCHEDULE 6, PART II) AND THE SPECIAL PROVISIONS FOR BANKS (SECTIONS 343 AND 344)

Schedule 6, Part II: Disclosure in annual accounts of transactions in which directors are interested

Q83   Consultees are asked:

(i) whether Schedule 6 should contain a definition of materiality for the purposes of paragraphs 15(c) and 16(c); and

(ii) if so, how materiality should be defined. (paragraph 7.9)

Q84   Consultees are asked:

(i) whether Schedule 6, Part II should be retained notwithstanding the introduction of FRS 8;

(ii) whether a director should have a duty to give notice to the company of such matters relating to himself and (so far as known to him) his connected persons as may be necessary for the purposes of that part;

(iii) whether the exception for transactions in the ordinary course of business in paragraph 21 should be retained and if so whether it should be extended to apply to transactions which are not intra-group;

(iv) whether the details of the value required to be given in relation to loans (and related guarantees and security) under paragraph 22(d) and (e) should be the same in relation to quasi-loans and credit transactions (including related guarantees and security) or vice-versa;

(v) whether the exemption in paragraph 23 should extend to credit transactions;

(vi) whether there should be an exemption like paragraphs 24 and 25 for loans and quasi-loans;

(vii) whether, where the deemed value provision in section 340(7) applies,[4] the directors should be required if possible to give some estimate of the value;

(viii) whether a transaction should be outside paragraphs 15(c) and 16(d) simply because the director is a common director of both parties to the transaction;

(ix) whether there is any other change to Schedule 6 which should be considered. (paragraph 7.11)

---

4   Schedule 6, para 26.

Sections 343-344: Special provisions for banks

Q85   Consultees are asked:

(i) Are sections 343-344 necessary or desirable?

(ii) On the basis these sections are retained, are consultees aware of any deficiency in these sections which are required to be addressed? (paragraph 7.17)

PART 8: SUBSTANTIVE IMPROVEMENTS 5: CONNECTED PERSONS (SECTION 346) AND REMAINING SECTIONS OF PART X OF THE COMPANIES ACT 1985

Section 346: The meaning of connected person

General

Q86   Consultees are asked:

(i) whether section 346 gives rise to difficulties in practice;

(ii) whether they consider that the test of "connected person" should be closer to any of the definitions of "associate" or "related party" considered above. (paragraph 8.13)

Option for reform (1): Make specified additions to the list of connected persons

Q87   Consultees are asked:

(i) Should cohabitants, defined as persons who have for a specified period been living with a director of the company in the same household and as man and wife, be connected persons for the purposes of:

(a) section 346;

(b) section 327;

(c) section 328?

(ii) Should the specified period be a continuous period of one year, or some other period (and if so what), or should there be no period?

(iii) Should infant children of the cohabitant be treated as connected persons if they live with the director and the cohabitant and the cohabitant has himself or herself become a connected person and if so should that be for the same purposes?

(iv) Are there any other persons who should be connected persons who are not already covered by section 346? (paragraph 8.17)

Option for reform(2): Give the Secretary of State power to vary the list by regulation

Q88   Consultees are asked whether the Secretary of State should be given power to vary the list of connected persons in section 346 by regulation. (paragraph 8.18)

The remaining sections of Part X

Q89   Consultees are asked whether they agree with our provisional view that Part X should apply to acts done outside the jurisdiction. If they disagree with this view, they are asked to state what restrictions should be imposed. (paragraph 8.23)

Q90   Consultees are asked whether they agree with our provisional view that section 347 should be amended to include references to sections 322A and 322B. (paragraph 8.24)

PART 9: FURTHER OPTIONS: (1) CAN SECTIONS IN PART X BE REPEALED? (2) WOULD PART X BE IMPROVED IF IT WAS REWRITTEN?

Option 1: Repealing sections in Part X

Repealing groups of sections and relying on the general law

Q91   Consultees are asked whether they consider that sections 312-316, 319, 320-22 and 330-342 should be repealed and reliance placed on the general law. (paragraph 9.28)

Repeal of section 311 (Prohibition on tax-free payments to directors)

Q92   Consultees are asked whether they agree with our provisional view that section 311 of the Companies Act 1985 should be repealed. (paragraph 9.32)

Repeal of section 323 (Option dealing by directors)

Q93   Consultees are asked whether they agree with our provisional view that section 323 should be repealed in its entirety. (paragraph 9.33)

Option 2: Can Part X be improved by rewriting?

Q94   Consultees are asked:

(i) to consider carefully the re-draft of sections 330-344 (and part of section 347) set out in Appendix B, and to give their views on the re-draft generally;

(ii) whether they consider that the provisions of Part X are now familiar to users so that it would be better not to disturb the existing layout and language;

(iii) whether they consider that redrafting in this manner represents a significant and worthwhile improvement in the existing text;

(iv) whether section 318 should be simplified in the manner indicated in paragraphs 9.26-9.27 above. (paragraph 9.42-9.43)

PART 10: SHOULD PART X OF THE COMPANIES ACT 1985 BE DECRIMINALISED?

Q95   Consultees are asked:

(i) whether they agree with our provisional view that the two benchmarks to be applied in determining whether there should be criminal liability for breaches of Part X are proportionality and efficiency;

(ii) whether any of the criminal offences in Part X should be repealed;

(iii) whether, if any provision of Part X is decriminalised, the civil remedies should remain as if the provision had not been decriminalised;

(iv) whether, if any provision of Part X is decriminalised, civil penalties along the lines of section 242A should replace any of the existing offences;

(v) whether a new offence should be created where payments are made in breach of sections 312-316 of the Companies Act 1985 along the lines described in paragraph 10.40 above. (paragraph 10.40)

SECTION B: THE CASE FOR A STATUTORY STATEMENT OF DIRECTORS' DUTIES UNDER THE GENERAL LAW

PART 14: A STATEMENT OF DIRECTORS' DUTIES: OPTIONS FOR REFORM

Option 1: A comprehensive codification

Q96 Consultees are asked whether there should be a comprehensive statutory codification of the duties owed by directors to their company under the general law. (paragraph 14.22)

Option 2: Partial codification of directors' fiduciary duties

Q97 Consultees are asked whether they consider that the duties of directors should be codified in part only and, if so, whether such codification should extend to the duty to act in the company's best interests, or to some other, and if so which, of the duties described in Part 11 above. (paragraph 14.24)

Option 3: Statutory statement of directors' duties not replacing the general law

Q98 Consultees are asked whether they would favour a statutory statement of directors' duties in the Companies Act 1985 which does not replace the general law and, if so, whether the statement should impose liabilites on directors in addition to those to which they are subject under the existing law, or merely convey information for guidance. (paragraph 14.31)

Option 4: A non-binding statement of the main duties of directors to be used in certain prescribed forms etc

Q99 Consultees are asked:

(i) whether they consider that the draft statement in Appendix A sets out the principal duties of directors under the general law;[5]

(ii) whether the statement should refer to the possibility of the company in general meeting ratifying the breach of duty or releasing a claim that it may have;

---

[5] Thus including both the duty of care and fiduciary duties.

(iii) whether they consider that such a statement should mandatorily be annexed to the company's articles;

(iv) whether they consider that such a statement should be required to be included in the Directors' Report attached to the company's annual accounts;

(v) whether they consider that a director should sign that he has read the statement when he signs a return confirming that he has been appointed a director;

(vi) whether they consider that each director should be required to sign that he has read the statement when the company submits its annual return; and

(vii) whether they think that such a statement should appear in any other statutory return which the company makes. (paragraph 14.40)

Option 5: Authoritative pamphlets

Q100   Consultees are asked:

(i) whether they consider that a pamphlet setting out directors' duties - including both the duty of care and fiduciary duties - should be prepared as a means of setting out the duties of directors;

(ii) if so, how they think the pamphlet would be best brought to the attention of directors; and

(iii) whether they consider that a pamphlet of this kind would make it unnecessary to have a statutory statement of directors' fiduciary duties. (paragraph 14.44)

PART 15: DUTY OF CARE: OPTIONS FOR REFORM

Should there be a statutory statement of the duty of care?

Q101   Consultees are asked whether they consider that there are objectives that might be achieved by a statutory statement of the director's duty of care other than those set out in paragraph 15.6. (paragraph 15.6)

Q102   Consultees are asked whether or not they favour a statutory statement of the duty of care. Consultees may wish to consider the options for that statement before deciding how to respond.[6] (paragraph 15.9)

Content of a statutory statement of the duty of care

Option 1: A subjective test

Q103   Consultees are asked whether they consider that the standard of care expected of a director should be judged by a subjective test - so as to be that expected of a reasonable person having the same knowledge and experience that the director has. (paragraph 15.19)

---

[6]   See questions 104-106 below.

Option 2: A dual objective/subjective test

Q104　Consultees are asked whether the standard of care expected of a director should be judged by a twofold subjective/objective test. (paragraph 15.25)

Option 3: An objective test only

Q105　Consultees are asked whether they consider that the standard of care expected of a director should be judged solely by an objective test - so as to be that expected of a reasonable person having the knowledge and experience which may reasonably be expected of a person in the same position as the director without taking account of any special expertise that the particular director possesses. (paragraph 15.29)

Matters of commercial judgment

Q106　Consultees are asked whether they consider that there should be a business judgment rule and if so whether it should be on the lines proposed in Australia or on the lines identified by the American Law Institute or in some other way. (paragraph 15.41)

Reliance and delegation

Q107　Consultees are asked whether they consider that there should be a statutory provision which sets out the liability of directors when they delegate their powers to others and the circumstances in which they may rely on information provided by third parties. (paragraph 15.50)

Statutory statement of the duty of care without a statutory statement of fiduciary duties

Q108　Do consultees consider that there would be any objection (not already mentioned) to having a statutory statement of the duty of care on its own? (paragraph 15.51)

SECTION C : MISCELLANEOUS MATTERS

PART 17: HOW SHOULD THE LAW APPLY TO DIFFERENT CATEGORIES OF DIRECTOR?

De facto directors

Q109　Do consultees agree with our provisional view that the provisions of Part X, the statutory duty of care and the statement of duties should apply to directors who have not been legally appointed? (paragraph 17.10)

Shadow directors

Q110　Do consultees consider that (a) Part X, and (b) the statutory duty of care should apply to shadow directors? (paragraph 17.16)

Alternate directors

Q111　Do consultees consider that any provision in Part X is difficult to apply in relation to alternate directors so that special provision is needed for them? (paragraph 17.20)

APPENDIX A

Draft clauses relating to directors' duties and draft statement of directors' duties

Draft section 309A (Duty of care, skill and diligence)

Draft section 309B (Statement relating to directors' duties)

[ON FACING PAGE FOLLOWED BY EXPLANATORY NOTES]

Draft statement relating to directors' duties to their companies

[ON PAGES 344-355]

DRAFT CLAUSES/SCHEDULES

Duty of care, skill and diligence

1. In the Companies Act 1985 this section is inserted after section 309—

Duty of care, skill and diligence.

"Duty of care, skill and diligence.

309A.—(1) A director of a company owes the company a duty to exercise the care, skill and diligence which would be exercised in the same circumstances by a reasonable person having both—

    (a) the knowledge and experience that may reasonably be expected of a person in the same position as the director, and

    (b) the knowledge and experience which the director has.

(2) This section has effect instead of the rules of law stating the duties of care, skill and diligence owed by a director of a company to the company.

(3) References in this section to a director include references to a shadow director."

Statement of duties

2. In the Companies Act 1985 this section is inserted after section 309A—

Statement relating to directors' duties.

"Statement relating to directors' duties.

309B.—(1) In prescribing a form of document falling within this subsection the Secretary of State may include in it a statement containing information about directors' duties; and these documents fall within this subsection—

    (a) a statement referred to in section 10(2);

    (b) a notification referred to in section 288(2) if it is a notification of a person having become a director;

    (c) a return referred to in section 363(2);

    (d) an application referred to in section 680(1).

(2) Regulations under section 257 may require a document to include a prescribed statement containing information about directors' duties.

(3) The enactments and rules of law stating directors' duties are not affected by—

    (a) anything in a statement included in a document by virtue of this section, or

    (b) any acknowledgement by a person (by signing the document) that he has read the statement."

EXPLANATORY NOTES ON DRAFT CLAUSES

Clause 1 inserts a new section 309A into the Companies Act 1985.

Subsection (1) sets out the minimum standard of care, skill and diligence which a director must show to his company. There is some doubt as to the current standard which is required at common law. Traditionally the cases have not required directors to exhibit a greater degree of skill than may reasonably be expected from a person with *their* knowledge and experience (a subjective test) (see paragraphs 12.3-12.7 of the consultation paper). More recently, the courts have been prepared to say that the common law standard now mirrors the tests laid down in section 214(4) of the Insolvency Act 1986, which includes an objective assessment of a director's conduct (see paragraphs 12.8-12.10 of the consultation paper). (Section 214 makes provision (in connection with proceedings under that section to obtain a contribution from a director to a company's losses) as to how a court is to assess the matters which a director ought to have known or concluded about the company's financial position and the steps which he ought to have taken to minimise the loss to creditors). Subsection (1) of section 309A replaces the common law standard of care, skill and diligence (see subsection (2) below) with a dual test which is itself modelled on section 214(4) of the Insolvency Act 1986.

Subsection (1) attributes to the director both the notional knowledge and experience which may reasonably be expected of a person in the same position as the director (subsection (1)(a) - an objective test) and the actual knowledge and experience which the director has (subsection (1)(b) - a subjective test). The court is then required to look at whether the director has exercised the care, skill and diligence which would have been exercised by a reasonable person in the same ciricumstances as the director having both types of knowledge and experience (ie objective and subjective). Subsection (1)(a) is intended to set a minimum standard required by law of all directors. However, where a director possesses particular knowledge or experience over and above that which might otherwise be reasonably expected of a person in his position, then he must meet the higher standard of care, skill and diligence appropriate to *his* knowledge and experience (in accordance with subsection (1)(b)). In considering whether the director has met the appropriate standard, the court must take account of the particular circumstances of the case ("in the same circumstances") and have regard to specific responsibilities that a director either has or has undertaken ("in the same position").

Subsection (2) confirms that the section replaces the common law standard of care, skill and diligence which must exercised by a director. But it does not affect other matters relating to the duty of care, such as remedies.

"Director" is defined in section 741(1) of the Companies Act 1985, and for these purposes is intended to include a de facto director (see the discussion on de facto directors in paragraphs 17.5-17.10 of the consultation paper). Subsection (3) provides that director also includes a "shadow director", as defined in section 741(2) of the Companies Act 1985. "Company" is defined in section 735(1) of the Companies Act 1985.

Clause 2 inserts a new section 309B into the Companies Act 1985.

Subsection (1) permits the Secretary of State to include in certain prescribed forms which must be delivered by a company for registration, a statement containing information about directors' duties. The forms concerned are: (a) the statement of first directors; (b) notice of change of a director; (c) the annual return; and (d) an application by a company not formed under the Companies Acts for registration under the Companies Act 1985.

Subsection (2) gives the Secretary of State power to make regulations under section 257 requiring a statement of directors' duties in prescribed form to be included in any document which is required to be prepared, laid before the company in general meeting or delivered to the Registrar of Companies under Part VII of the Companies Act 1985 (Accounts and Audit). So, for example, regulations could be made requiring the statement of duties to be included in the annual accounts.

The object of both provisions is to enable the relevant documents to be used as a means of bringing these duties to the attention of a company's officers (see the discussion on this point at paragraphs 14.32-14.40 of the consultation paper). The intention is that the statement should set out in simple language the principal duties of a director. A draft of the sort of statement which might be included is set out below and discussed at paragraphs 14.33-14.35 of the consultation paper.

Subsection (3) confirms that any statement included or required to be included in a document by virtue of this section will not have any effect on the duties imposed by law. The statement is for information purposes only. It also confirms that the fact that a director signs a document in which such a statement is included, acknowledging that he has read the statement, will not affect the duties he owes.

343

DRAFT STATEMENT RELATING TO DIRECTORS' DUTIES TO THEIR COMPANIES

General

(1) The law imposes duties on directors. If a person does not comply with his duties as a director he may be liable to civil or criminal proceedings and he may be disqualified from acting as a director.

(2) Set out below there is a summary of the main duties of a director to his company. It is not a complete statement of a director's duties, and the law may change anyway. If a person is not clear about his duties as a director in any situation he should seek advice.

Loyalty

(3) A director must act in good faith in what he considers to be the interests of the company.

Obedience

(4) A director must act in accordance with the company's constitution (such as the articles of association) and must exercise his powers only for the purposes allowed by law.

No secret profits

(5) A director must not use the company's property, information or opportunities for his own or anyone else's benefit unless he is allowed to by the company's constitution or the use has been disclosed to the company in general meeting and the company has consented to it.

Independence

(6) A director must not agree to restrict his power to exercise an independent judgment. But if he considers in good faith that it is in the interests of the company for a transaction to be entered into and carried into effect, he may restrict his power to exercise an independent judgment by agreeing to act in a particular way to achieve this.

Conflict of interest

(7) If there is a conflict between an interest or duty of a director and an interest of the company in any transaction, he must account to the company for any benefit he receives from the transaction. This applies whether or not the company sets aside the transaction. But he does not have to account for the benefit if he is allowed to have the interest or duty by the company's constitution or the interest or duty has been disclosed to and approved by the company in general meeting.

Care, skill and diligence

(8) A director owes the company a duty to exercise the care, skill and diligence which would be exercised in the same circumstances by a reasonable person having both-

(a)   the knowledge and experience that may reasonably be expected of a person in the same position as the director, and

(b)   the knowledge and experience which the director has.

Interests of employees etc

(9)   A director must have regard to the interests of the company's employees in general and its members.

Fairness

(10)   A director must act fairly as between different members.

Effect of this statement

(11)   The law stating the duties of directors is not affected by this statement or by the fact that, by signing this document, a director acknowledges that he has read the statement.

APPENDIX B
Draft provisions on loans to directors

[ON PAGES 347 – 358 FOLLOWED BY EXPLANATORY NOTES]

DRAFT CLAUSES/SCHEDULES

SCHEDULE 13A
Loans to Directors etc

Part I
Index of definitions

5   1. These expressions are defined or otherwise explained by the provisions indicated—

2. Note that other expressions are defined or otherwise explained for more general purposes. For example, section 346 (connected persons etc) has effect for the purposes of Part X of this Act (which includes this Schedule).

Part II
Prohibitions

Prohibitions on all companies

3.—(1) A company must not make a loan to a director of the company or of its holding company.

(2) A company must not enter into a guarantee or provide security in connection with a loan made by any person to a director of the company or of its holding company.

Prohibitions on relevant companies

4.—(1) A relevant company must not make a quasi-loan to a director of the company or of its holding company.

(2) A relevant company must not make a loan or a quasi-loan to a person connected with a director of the company or of its holding company.

(3) A relevant company must not enter into a guarantee or provide security in connection with a loan or quasi-loan made by any person to a

2

SCH. 13A

director of the company or of its holding company or to a person connected with such a director.

(4) A relevant company must not enter into a credit transaction as creditor for a director of the company or of its holding company or for a person connected with such a director. 5

(5) A relevant company must not enter into a guarantee or provide security in connection with a credit transaction made by any person for a director of the company or of its holding company or for a person connected with such a director.

Other prohibitions 10

5.—(1) A company must not arrange to assume or take an assignment of rights, obligations or liabilities under a transaction which would have broken paragraph 3 or 4 if the company had entered into it.

(2) If an arrangement is made in breach of this paragraph, for the purposes of this Schedule the transaction is to be treated as having been 15 entered into on the date of the arrangement.

6. A company must not take part in an arrangement by which—

(a) another person enters into a transaction which would have broken paragraph 3, 4 or 5 if the company had entered into it, and

(b) the other person has obtained or is to obtain a benefit from the 20 company or its holding company or a subsidiary of the company or its holding company.

PART III
PRINCIPAL DEFINITIONS

Introduction 25

7. This Part has effect for the purposes of this Schedule.

Directors

8. References to a director include references to a shadow director.

Relevant companies

9. A relevant company is a company which— 30

(a) is a public company,

(b) is a subsidiary of a public company,

(c) is a subsidiary of a company which has a public company as another subsidiary, or

(d) has a subsidiary which is a public company. 35

Quasi-loans

10.—(1) A transaction is a quasi-loan if a party (the creditor) agrees to pay, or pays otherwise than under an agreement, a sum for another (the borrower)—

(a) on terms that the borrower (or a person on his behalf) will 40 reimburse the creditor, or

(b) in circumstances giving rise to a liability on the borrower to reimburse the creditor.

(2) A transaction is also a quasi-loan if a party (the creditor) agrees to reimburse, or reimburses otherwise than under an agreement, expenditure
5 incurred by another for another (the borrower)—

(a) on terms that the borrower (or a person on his behalf) will reimburse the creditor, or

(b) in circumstances giving rise to a liability on the borrower to reimburse the creditor.

10 (3) A reference to the person to whom a quasi-loan is made is a reference to the borrower.

(4) The liabilities of a borrower under a quasi-loan include the liabilities of any person who has agreed to reimburse the creditor on behalf of the borrower.

15 *Guarantees*

11. A guarantee includes an indemnity, and like expressions must be read accordingly.

Credit transactions etc

12.—(1) A credit transaction is a transaction under which a party (the
20 creditor)—

(a) supplies goods or sells land under a hire-purchase agreement or a conditional sale agreement,

(b) leases or hires land or goods in return for periodical payments, or

(c) otherwise disposes of land or supplies goods or services on the
25 understanding that payment (whether in a lump sum or instalments or by way of periodical payments or otherwise) is to be deferred.

(2) "Conditional sale agreement" has the same meaning as in the
Consumer Credit Act 1974.

1974 c. 39.

30 (3) Services are anything other than goods or land.

Transactions or arrangements made for persons

13.—(1) This paragraph has effect to determine whether a transaction or arrangement is made for a person.

(2) A loan or quasi-loan is made for a person if it is made to him.

35 (3) A credit transaction is made for a person if he is the person to whom goods or services are supplied, or land is sold or otherwise disposed of, under the transaction.

(4) A guarantee or security is made for a person if it is entered into or provided in connection with—

40 (a) a loan or quasi-loan made to him, or

(b) a credit transaction made for him.

(5) An arrangement within paragraph 5 or 6 is made for a person if the transaction to which the arrangement relates was made for him.

SCH. 13A

(6) Any other transaction or arrangement for the supply or transfer of (or of an interest in) goods or land or services is made for a person if he is the person to whom the goods or land or services (or the interest) is or are supplied or transferred.

PART IV

EXCEPTIONS

Small loans

14. Paragraph 3(1) does not stop a company making a loan to a director of the company or of its holding company if the aggregate of the relevant amounts does not exceed £5,000.

Relevant companies: short-term quasi-loans

15.—(1) Paragraph 4(1) does not stop a company (the creditor) making a quasi-loan to a director of the company or of its holding company if the conditions in sub-paragraphs (2) and (3) below are met.

(2) The quasi-loan must require the director (or a person on his behalf) to reimburse the creditor its expenditure within 2 months of it being incurred.

(3) The aggregate of the amount of the quasi-loan and of the amount outstanding under each relevant quasi-loan must not exceed £5,000.

(4) A quasi-loan is relevant if it was made to the director under this paragraph by the creditor or its subsidiary or, if the director is a director of the creditor's holding company, any other subsidiary of that company.

(5) The amount outstanding is the amount of the outstanding liabilities of the person to whom the quasi-loan was made.

Relevant companies: loans in same group

16.—(1) This paragraph applies to a relevant company which is a member of a group of companies (that is, a holding company and its subsidiaries).

(2) Paragraph 4(2) does not stop the company making a loan or quasi-loan to another member of the group, by reason only that a director of one member of the group is associated with another member of the group.

(3) Paragraph 4(3) does not stop the company entering into a guarantee or providing security in connection with a loan or quasi-loan made by any person to another member of the group, by reason only that a director of one member of the group is associated with another member of the group.

Relevant companies: minor transactions

17. Paragraph 4(4) and (5) do not stop a company entering into a transaction for a person if the aggregate of the relevant amounts does not exceed £10,000.

Relevant companies: business transactions

18. Paragraph 4(4) and (5) do not stop a company entering into a transaction for a person if—

(a) the transaction is entered into by the company in the ordinary course of its business,

(b) the value of the transaction is not greater (in respect of the person for whom it is made) than that which it is reasonable to expect the company to have offered to or in respect of a person of the same financial standing but unconnected with the company, and

(c) the terms on which the transaction is entered into are no more favourable (in respect of the person for whom it is made) than those which it is reasonable to expect the company to have offered to or in respect of a person of the same financial standing but unconnected with the company.

Transactions at request of holding company

19. These transactions are excepted from the prohibitions in Part II—

(a) a loan or quasi-loan by a company to its holding company;

(b) a company entering into a guarantee or providing security in connection with a loan or quasi-loan made by any person to its holding company;

(c) a company entering into a credit transaction as creditor for its holding company;

(d) a company entering into a guarantee or providing security in connection with a credit transaction made by any person for its holding company.

Director's expenditure for company

20.—(1) Part II does not stop a company doing anything to provide a director with funds to meet expenditure incurred or to be incurred by him for the purposes of the company or for the purpose of enabling him properly to perform his duties as an officer of the company.

(2) Part II does not stop a company doing anything to enable a director to avoid incurring expenditure for those purposes or that purpose.

(3) However, sub-paragraphs (1) and (2) are subject to sub-paragraphs (4) and (5).

(4) Sub-paragraphs (1) and (2) do not authorise a relevant company to enter into a transaction if the aggregate of the relevant amounts exceeds £20,000.

(5) Sub-paragraphs (1) and (2) apply only if one of these conditions is satisfied—

(a) the thing in question is done with prior approval of the company given at a general meeting at which all the matters mentioned in sub-paragraph (6) are disclosed;

(b) the thing in question is done on condition that, if the approval of the company is not so given at or before the next annual general meeting, the loan is to be repaid within 6 months from the conclusion of the meeting or any other liability arising under the transaction is to be discharged within that period.

6

SCH. 13ASCH. 13A

(6) The matters to be disclosed are—

(a) the purpose of the expenditure incurred or to be incurred by the director, or which would otherwise be incurred by him;

(b) the amount of the funds to be provided by the company;

(c) the extent of the company's liability under any transaction which is connected with the thing in question. 5

Money-lending companies

21.—(1) These transactions are excepted from the prohibitions in Part II—

(a) a loan or quasi-loan made by a money-lending company to any person; 10

(b) a money-lending company entering into a guarantee in connection with a loan or quasi-loan made otherwise than by the company.

(2) However, sub-paragraph (1) is subject to sub-paragraphs (3) to (5); 15
but sub-paragraph (4) is itself subject to sub-paragraph (6).

(3) Sub-paragraph (1) does not authorise a relevant company (unless it is a banking company) to enter into a transaction if the aggregate of the relevant amounts exceeds £100,000; but in determining the aggregate a company which a director does not control is to be treated as not 20
connected with him.

(4) Sub-paragraph (1)(a) applies only if these conditions are satisfied—

(a) the loan or quasi-loan is made by the company in the ordinary course of its business,

(b) the amount of the loan or quasi-loan is not greater (in the case of 25
the person to whom it is made) than that which it is reasonable to expect the company to have offered to a person of the same financial standing but unconnected with the company, and

(c) the terms of the loan or quasi-loan are not more favourable (in the case of the person to whom it is made) than those which it is 30
reasonable to expect the company to have offered to a person of the same financial standing but unconnected with the company.

(5) Sub-paragraph (1)(b) applies only if these conditions are satisfied—

(a) the company enters into the guarantee in the ordinary course of its business, 35

(b) the amount of the guarantee is not greater (in the case of the person in whose respect it is entered into) than that which it is reasonable to expect the company to have offered in respect of a person of the same financial standing but unconnected with the company, and 40

(c) the terms of the guarantee are not more favourable (in the case of the person in whose respect it is entered into) than those which it is reasonable to expect the company to have offered in respect of a person of the same financial standing but unconnected with the company. 45

(6) If sub-paragraph (7) is satisfied the conditions in sub-paragraph (4)(b) and (c) do not of themselves stop a company making a loan to a

352

director of the company or of its holding company—

    (a) for the purpose of facilitating the purchase, for use as the director's only or main residence, of all or part of a dwelling-house together with any land to be occupied and enjoyed with it;

5   (b) for the purpose of improving a dwelling-house (or part of one) so used or any land occupied and enjoyed with it;

    (c) in substitution for a loan made by any person and falling within paragraph (a) or (b) above.

(7) This sub-paragraph is satisfied if—

10   (a) loans of any description mentioned in sub-paragraph (6) are ordinarily made by the company to its employees and on terms no less favourable than those on which the transaction in question is made, and

    (b) the aggregate of the relevant amounts does not exceed £100,000.

15 (8) A money-lending company is a company whose ordinary business includes the making of loans or quasi-loans, or the giving of guarantees in connection with loans or quasi-loans.

PART V

FURTHER DEFINITIONS

Relevant amounts

20 22.—(1) This paragraph and paragraph 23 have effect to determine the relevant amounts to be aggregated under paragraphs 14, 17, 20(4) and 21(3) and (7).

(2) In relation to a proposed transaction or arrangement and the 25 question whether it falls within an exception under Part IV, for the purposes of this paragraph and paragraph 23 the relevant exception is that exception.

(3) Where the relevant exception is the one provided by paragraph 14 (small loans) references in this paragraph and paragraph 23 to a person 30 connected with a director must be ignored.

(4) The relevant amounts in relation to a proposed transaction or arrangement are these—

A. The value of the proposed transaction or arrangement.

B. The value of any existing arrangement which—

35   (a) falls within paragraph 5 or 6,

    (b) also falls within paragraph 23, and

    (c) was entered into by virtue of the relevant exception by the company or by a subsidiary of the company or (where the proposed transaction or arrangement is to be made for a 40 director of its holding company or a person connected with such a director) by that holding company or any of its subsidiaries.

C. The amount outstanding under any other transaction which—

    (a) falls within paragraph 23,

    (b) was made by virtue of the relevant exception, and

    (c) was made by the company or by a subsidiary of the company or (where the proposed transaction or arrangement is to be made for a director of its holding company or a person connected with such a director) by that holding company or   5 any of its subsidiaries.

  (5) For the purposes of item C in sub-paragraph (4) the amount outstanding is the value of the transaction less any amount by which that value has been reduced.

  23.—(1) A transaction falls within this paragraph if it was made—   10

    (a) for the director for whom the proposed transaction or arrangement is to be made, or for a person connected with that director, or

    (b) where the proposed transaction or arrangement is to be made for a person connected with a director of a company, for that director or any person connected with him.   15

An arrangement falls within this paragraph if it relates to a transaction which does so.

  (2) However, sub-paragraph (1) has effect subject to sub-paragraphs (3) and (4).

  (3) If the proposed transaction —   20

    (a) falls within paragraph 21, and

    (b) is one which a banking company proposes to enter into under paragraph 21(6) (housing loans etc),

any other transaction or arrangement which (apart from this sub-paragraph) would fall within this paragraph does not do so unless it was   25 entered into in pursuance of paragraph 21(6).

  (4) If—

    (a) a transaction is entered into by a company which is (at the time the transaction is entered into) a subsidiary of the company which is to make the proposed transaction, or is a subsidiary of   30 that company's holding company, and

    (b) it is no longer such a subsidiary at the time when the question arises whether the proposed transaction or arrangement falls within any relevant exception,

the transaction first mentioned does not fall within this paragraph.   35

Value of transactions and arrangements

  24.—(1) This paragraph has effect to determine the value of a transaction or arrangement for the purposes of paragraphs 18 and 22.

  (2) The value of a loan is the amount of its principal.

  (3) The value of a quasi-loan is the amount (or maximum amount)   40 which the person to whom it is made is liable to reimburse the creditor.

  (4) The value of a guarantee or security is the amount guaranteed or secured.

(5) The value of an arrangement to which paragraph 5 or 6 applies is value A minus amount B, where—

(a) value A is the value of the transaction to which the arrangement relates, and

(b) amount B is any amount by which the liabilities under the arrangement or transaction of the person for whom the transaction was made have been reduced.

(6) The value of a transaction or arrangement not falling within sub-paragraphs (2) to (5) is the price which it is reasonable to expect could be obtained for the goods or land or services to which the transaction or arrangement relates if they had been supplied (when the transaction or arrangement is entered into)—

(a) in the ordinary course of business, and

(b) on the same terms (apart from price) as those on which they have been supplied, or are to be supplied, under the transaction or arrangement in question.

(7) If the value of a transaction or arrangement is not capable of being expressed as a specific sum of money (because the amount of any liability arising under it is unascertainable, or for any other reason) its value is to be taken to exceed £100,000, whether or not any liability under it has been reduced.

PART VI
SANCTIONS
Civil remedies

25.—(1) If a company enters into a transaction or arrangement in breach of Part II the transaction or arrangement is voidable at the instance of the company; but this is subject to sub-paragraphs (2) to (4).

(2) Sub-paragraph (1) does not apply if restitution of any money or any other asset which is the subject matter of the transaction or arrangement is no longer possible.

(3) Sub-paragraph (1) does not apply if the company has been indemnified under paragraph 26 for the loss or damage suffered by it.

(4) Sub-paragraph (1) does not apply if any rights acquired in good faith for value and without actual notice of the breach by a person other than the person for whom the transaction or arrangement was made would be affected by its avoidance.

26.—(1) This paragraph applies if a transaction or arrangement is made by a company for a director of the company or of its holding company, or for a person connected with such a director, in breach of Part II.

(2) The director and the person so connected (where applicable) and any other director of the company who authorised the transaction or arrangement (whether or not it has been avoided under paragraph 25)—

(a) is liable to account to the company for any gain which he has made directly or indirectly by the transaction or arrangement, and

10

SCH. 13A(b) is liable (jointly and severally with any other person liable under this paragraph) to indemnify the company for any loss or damage resulting from the transaction or arrangement.

(3) Sub-paragraph (2) is without prejudice to any liability imposed apart from it, but is subject to sub-paragraphs (4) and (5). 5

(4) If a transaction or arrangement is entered into by a company and a person connected with a director of the company or of its holding company in breach of Part II, the director is not liable under sub-paragraph (2) if he shows that he took all reasonable steps to secure the company's compliance with Part II. 10

(5) In any case—

(a) a person connected with a director of the company or of its holding company, and

(b) any other director of the company who authorised the transaction or arrangement, 15

is not liable under sub-paragraph (2) if he shows that, at the time the transaction or arrangement was entered into, he did not know the relevant circumstances constituting the breach.

Relevant companies: criminal penalties

27.—(1) A director of a relevant company is guilty of an offence if he 20 authorises or permits the company to enter into a transaction or arrangement knowing or having reasonable cause to believe that the company was thereby breaking Part II.

(2) A relevant company is guilty of an offence if it enters into a transaction or arrangement for a director of the company or of its holding 25 company in breach of Part II.

(3) Sub-paragraph (2) does not apply if the relevant company shows that, at the time the transaction or arrangement was entered into, it did not know the relevant circumstances.

(4) A person is guilty of an offence if he procures a relevant company to 30 enter into a transaction or arrangement knowing or having reasonable cause to believe that the company was thereby breaking Part II.

(5) A person guilty of an offence under this paragraph is liable to imprisonment or a fine or both.

PART VII 35

MISCELLANEOUS

Records

28.—(1) This paragraph—

(a) has effect in the case of a company which is a banking company or is the holding company of a credit institution; 40

(b) has effect subject to the exceptions provided by paragraph 29.

(2) If the company takes advantage of paragraph 2 of Part IV of

Schedule 9 in relation to a financial year it must keep a register containing—

    (a) a copy of every transaction, arrangement or agreement which would (but for that paragraph) have to be disclosed in its accounts or group accounts for the financial year and for each financial year in the preceding 10 in relation to which it has taken advantage of that paragraph;

    (b) a written memorandum setting out the terms of every such transaction, arrangement or agreement (in the case of a transaction, arrangement or agreement not in writing).

(3) If the company takes advantage of paragraph 2 of Part IV of Schedule 9 in relation to the last complete financial year preceding its annual general meeting, it must prepare a statement containing the particulars of every transaction, arrangement or agreement which would (but for that paragraph) have to be disclosed in its accounts or group accounts for the financial year.

(4) The company must make the statement available for inspection by its members—

    (a) at its registered office for at least 15 days ending with the date of the meeting, and

    (b) at the meeting.

(5) The company's auditors must—

    (a) examine the statement before it is made available to the members;

    (b) make a report to the members on it;

    (c) say in the report whether in their opinion the statement contains the particulars required by sub-paragraph (3);

    (d) if in their opinion it does not contain the particulars, set out the particulars in the report (so far as they are reasonably able to do so).

(6) The company must annex the auditors' report to the company's statement before it is made available to the members.

(7) If a company fails to comply with any provision of this paragraph every person who is a director of it at the time of the failure is guilty of an offence and liable to a fine.

(8) However—

    (a) it is a defence for a person to prove that he took all reasonable steps to secure compliance with the provision concerned;

    (b) a person is not guilty of the offence by virtue only of being a shadow director of the company.

(9) For the purposes of the application of this paragraph to loans and quasi-loans made by a company to persons connected with a person who at any time is a director of the company or of its holding company, a company which a person does not control is not connected with him.

29.—(1) Paragraph 28(3) and (4) do not apply to a banking company which is the wholly-owned subsidiary of a company incorporated in the United Kingdom.

12

SCH. 13A (2) If the condition in sub-paragraph (3) below is satisfied paragraph 28 does not apply in relation to—

(a) a transaction or arrangement made or subsisting in a financial year, and made by a company or by a subsidiary of a company for a person who at any time in that year was a director of the 5 company or of its holding company or was connected with such a director, or

(b) an agreement, made or subsisting in that year, for a transaction or arrangement which (if entered into or made) would fall within paragraph (a). 10

(3) The condition is satisfied if A minus B did not exceed £2,000 at any time in the financial year, where—

(a) A is the aggregate of the values of each transaction or arrangement made for the person, and of each agreement for such a transaction or arrangement, and 15

(b) B is the amount (if any) by which the value of those transactions, arrangements and agreements has been reduced.

(4) For the purposes of this paragraph—

(a) the value of a transaction or arrangement is to be determined in accordance with paragraph 24; 20

(b) the value of an agreement for a transaction or arrangement is whatever the value of the transaction or arrangement would be if it were entered into or made and paragraph 24 applied.

Foreign law

30. For the purposes of this Schedule it is immaterial whether the law 25 which (apart from this Act) governs a transaction or arrangement is or is not the law of the United Kingdom or of a part of it.

EXPLANATORY NOTES ON DRAFT SCHEDULE

SCHEDULE

This Schedule would constitute Schedule 13A to the Companies Act 1985 and replace sections 330-344 and part of section 347 of the Companies Act 1985. The sections have been reorganised and rewritten in simpler language (see paragraphs 9.34-40 of the consultation paper) so as to facilitate understanding of them. There have been no changes of substance, except that the definition of relevant amounts previously in section 339 has been applied for the purposes of another provision which uses the phrase (formerly section 338(6)(b)).

Paragraphs 1 and 2

The index of definitions is new and is intended to assist the reader in locating the definitions.

Paragraph 3

This sets out the basic prohibitions applying to all companies (as defined in section 735(1) of the Companies Act 1985). They may not make loans to their directors or directors of their holding companies, or give guarantees or provide security for any loan to any such director. The director involved and others may be guilty of a criminal offence if this prohibition is breached: see paragraph 27 of the Schedule.

Paragraph 4

Four additional prohibitions apply to relevant companies (defined in paragraph 9 of the Schedule). First, a relevant company may not make a quasi-loan to any of its directors (or any directors of its holding company) (paragraph 4(1)). Second, a relevant company may not enter into a credit transaction (as defined in paragraph 12 below) in favour of any of its directors (or any director of its holding company) or connected persons of such directors as defined in section 346 of the Companies Act 1985 (paragraph 4(4)). Third, there is a prohibition on a company making loans or quasi-loans to a connected person of the director (paragraph 4(2)). This mirrors the prohibition imposed in relation to directors by paragraph 3. "Connected persons" include specified family members and companies controlled by the director. Fourth, a relevant company is prohibited from giving any guarantee or providing any security in connection with a loan, quasi-loan or credit transaction entered into by anyone else in favour of the director or a connected person of a director (paragraph 4(3) and (5)).

Paragraphs 5 and 6

These contain anti-avoidance provisions. For instance, a company cannot circumvent a prohibition on making a loan by taking an assignment of the rights under a loan made by a third party (paragraph 5(1)). Likewise, a company (A) cannot avoid the prohibition by, for example, persuading another company (B) to give a loan to one of its (A's) directors on terms that A does the same for a director of B (see paragraph 6).

Paragraph 8

"Shadow directors" are persons (other than professional advisers giving professional advice and parent companies) in accordance with whose instructions directors are accustomed to act (section 741 of the Companies Act 1985). The reference to sections 330-346 in section 741(3) will be substituted, in part, by a reference to this Schedule.

Paragraph 9

This defines "relevant company", which broadly means any company which is a public company, or belongs to a group of companies which includes a public company, to which the additional prohibitions in paragraph 4 apply (and paragraphs 5 and 6 in so far as they relate to paragraph 4).

Paragraph 10

This defines "quasi-loan". The object is to catch transactions which fall outside the narrow legal definition of loan, meaning a transaction whereby a party is lent money for a time which he agrees to repay in money or money's worth: see *Champagne Perrier-Jouet SA v HH Finch Ltd* [1982] 1 WLR 1359. Thus a relevant company would make a quasi-loan if it paid a director's department store account direct to the store.

Paragraph 12

This defines "credit transaction". Under sub-paragraph (1)(a), a relevant company would enter into a credit transaction for a director if it sold him a car on hire purchase. Under sub-paragraph (1)(b), a relevant company would enter into a credit transaction if it gave a director a licence of a company flat, even at a commercial rent. (However it would not be a credit transaction if there was no rent). Under sub-paragraph (1)(c), a relevant company would also enter into a credit transaction for a director if it bought him a season ticket to travel to work and he paid the cost by instalments. A conditional sale agreement, as defined by the Consumer Credit Act 1974, involves a sale under which the price is payable by instalments but the seller retains the property in the goods even if the buyer obtains possession of them.

Paragraph 13

This provision is required in order to identify the person "for" whom a transaction of the kind described in the prohibitions was made. For example, under this paragraph a credit transaction consisting of the sale of a car to a director on hire purchase would be made "for" the director. Under paragraph 17, credit transactions made for a particular director can be added together, and if they fall below £10,000 they are permitted under an exception in that paragraph.

Paragraphs 14 to 21

These contain a series of exceptions from the prohibitions listed above. Many of the exceptions are linked to "relevant" amounts to be calculated in accordance with paragraph 22.

Paragraph 14 contains a "de minimis" exception, available for loans where the aggregate of the relevant amounts does not exceed £5,000.

Paragraph 15 contains an exception for short-term limited value quasi-loans, ie quasi-loans requiring reimbursement within 2 months, where the amount owed by the director at any time under that quasi-loan, and any other quasi-loan entered into under the same exception, does not exceed £5,000.

Paragraph 16 excepts intra-group loans, quasi-loans or the giving of guarantees or security in connection with intra-group loans or quasi-loans. (These might otherwise be prohibited if a director has a sufficient shareholding in the holding company to make that company and every company in the group a connected person of his).

Paragraph 17 contains a de minimis exception available for credit transactions where the aggregate of the relevant amounts does not exceed £10,000.

Paragraph 18 excepts credit transactions on normal commercial terms and in the ordinary course of business.

Paragraph 19 excepts transactions in favour of a holding company.

Paragraph 20 excepts transactions where a company wishes to give a director financial assistance to help him work for the company (for example, a bridging loan to help him relocate to a new area). This is permitted up to a limit (found by aggregating the relevant amounts) of £20,000, but must first either be approved by the company in general meeting (and specified conditions as to disclosure met), or be done on terms that if it is not so approved at or before the annual general meeting the loan will be repaid or the liability discharged within six months of the conclusion of the meeting.

Paragraph 21 contains exceptions for money-lending companies, that is companies whose ordinary business includes the making of loans and quasi-loans and the giving of guarantees in connection therewith. The limit on such transactions is £100,000 if the money-lending company is a relevant company. In addition the transaction must be on normal commercial terms and in the ordinary course of business (except where a special exception for "house purchase" loans applies - see paragraphs 21(6) and (7)).

Paragraphs 22 and 23

These explain how the aggregate of the relevant amounts is found. These are calculated on a per director basis, but where the company is a relevant company, transactions of a director's connected persons are aggregated with those of the director. The amounts to be added together are (a) the value (ascertained under paragraph 24) of the proposed transaction; (b) the value of existing arrangements for that director (or where relevant, his connected persons) falling within paragraphs 5 and 6 which have been entered into by virtue of the same exception; and (c) the amount outstanding under any other transaction or arrangement made by virtue of the same exception. For the purposes of (b) and (c), the transactions and arrangements in question are those which have been made by the company or a subsidiary, or (in the case of a transaction in favour of a holding company director) by the holding company or any subsidiary of its.

There are special provisions for the calculation of the relevant amounts where a house-purchase loan is made under paragraph 21(6) (paragraph 23 (3)).

Paragraph 24

This explains how the value of a transaction is ascertained. For example, the value of a guarantee is the amount guaranteed (paragraph 24(4)). If the transaction is not one of those specified in sub-paragraphs (2) to (5), the value is the price which could reasonably have been expected to have been obtained if the goods were supplied in the ordinary course of business and on normal commercial terms. If the value cannot be expressed as a specific sum of money, the value is automatically taken to exceed £100,000 (paragraph 24(7)).

Paragraphs 25 and 26

These deal with civil remedies. A transaction in breach of the prohibitions can be set aside by the company. Paragraph 25 makes provision as to the circumstances in which the right of rescission may be lost, and this includes the situation where the company has been fully indemnified against loss, for example, because a director who authorised the transaction has indemnified the company under paragraph 26(2)(b). A director who authorises a transaction, and a connected person of a director who is otherwise liable under paragraph 26, may be able to use the defence under paragraph 26(5) where they did not know of the relevant circumstances constituting the breach.

Paragraph 27

This deals with criminal penalties. These do not attach in the case of transactions by non-relevant companies.

Paragraphs 28 and 29

A banking company, or holding company of a credit institution, which takes advantage of the exemption (in paragraph 2 of Part IV of Schedule 9 to the Companies Act 1985) from disclosure of certain transactions in favour of directors, and others, in its annual accounts must keep and make available for inspection information in accordance with paragraph 28. Paragraph 29 contains exceptions from the obligation in paragraph 28.

Paragraph 30

This ensures that the prohibitions in the Schedule cannot be circumvented by contracting under some foreign law.

TABLE OF DERIVATIONS FOR THE SCHEDULE

Paragraph of Schedule	Provision of Companies Act 1985
1	-
2	-
3	330(2)
4	330(3), (4)
5	330(6)
6	330(7)
7	-
8	330(5)
9	331(6)
10	331(3), (4)
11	331(2)
12	331(7), (8), (10)
13	331(9)
14	334
15	332
16	333
17	335(1)
18	335(2)
19	336
20	337
21	338
22	339(1), (2), (6) (part)
23	339(3), (4), (5)
24	340
25	341(1)
26	341(2), (3), (4), (5)

(Note: this Table is prepared for guidance only and does not form part of the Schedule)

APPENDIX C

Table of derivations

Companies Acts referred to by year in this table:

The Companies Act 1928

The Companies Act 1929 (consolidating the Companies Acts 1908 to 1928)

The Companies Act 1947

The Companies Act 1948 (consolidating the 1929 and 1947 Companies Acts)

The Companies Act 1967

The Companies Act 1976

The Companies Act 1980

The Companies Act 1985 (consolidating the Companies Acts 1948 to 1983)

Amending changes introduced by other Acts or statutory measures are referred to in the text of the footnotes.

1985	1980	1976	1967	1948	1947	1929	1928
311(1)				189(1)	34(1)		
311(2)[1]				189(2)	34(2)		
312[2]				191	36(1)		
313(1)[3]				192(1)		150(1)	82(1)
313(2)				192(2)		150(2)	82(1)

[1] See also the Companies Consolidation (Consequential Provisions) Act 1985, s 15 (see further s 189(3) of the 1948 Act and s 34(3) of the 1947 Act).

[2] See also the Friendly Societies Act 1992, s 27, Sched 11, para 8(1); and in relation to a company which is a charity, the Charities Act 1993, s 66.

[3] See also the Charities Act 1993, s 66.

1985	1980	1976	1967	1948	1947	1929	1928
314(1)	80, Sch 2			193(1)		150(3)	
314(1)(a)				193(1)		150(3)	82(2)
314(1)(b),(c)				193(1)	36(2)		
314(1)(d)				193(1)	36(2)#	150(3)#	82(2),(3)#
314(2)				193(1)	36(2)#	150(3)	82(2)
314(3)				193(2)	36(4)[4]	150(4),(4A),(4B)	82(3)
315(1)				193(3)	36(4)	150(4),(4A),(4B)	82(3)
315(1)(b)				193(3)	36(3),(4),(5)#	150(4),(4A),(4B)#	82(3)#
315(2)				193(4)	36(4)		
315(3)				193(5)	36(4)		
316(1)				194(1)	36(6)		
316(2)				194(2)		150(5)	82(4)
316(3)[5]				194(3)	36(7)		
316(4)				194(4)		150(6)	82(5)

[4] Section 36(4) of the 1947 Act inserted subsections (4A) and (4B) into s 150(4) of the 1929 Act.

[5] See, in relation to this subsection, the Friendly Societies Act 1992, s 27, Sched 11, para 8(1).

1985	1980	1976	1967	1948	1947	1929	1928
317(1)				199(1)		149(1)	81(1)
317(2)				199(2)		149(2)	81(2)
317(3)(a)				199(3)		149(3)	81(3)
317(3)(b)	Sch 3, para 25#			199(3)#		149(3)#	81(3)#
317(4)				199(3)	41(5)		
317(5),(6)	60						
317(7)	80, Sch 2			199(4)		149(4)	81(4)
317(8)	63(3)						
317(9)				199(5)		149(5)	81(5)
318(1)(a),(b),(2)⁶		s34, Sch 1	26(1)				
318(1)(b)	61(1)#		26(1)				
318(3)			26(2)-(3A)				
318(4)	61(3)#		26(2)-(3A)				
318(5)	61(2),(3)#		26(2)-(3A)				
318(6)	63(4)						

⁶ Section as amended by s 110, Companies Act 1981.

1985	1980	1976	1967	1948	1947	1929	1928
318(7)-(11)[7]	61(3)#, 80, Sch 2		26(4)-(8)				
319(1)[8]	47(2)						
319(2)	47(3)						
319(3)	47(1)						
319(4)	47(6)						
319(5), (6)	47(4), (5)						
319(7)	47(7), 63(1)						
320(1)[9]	48(1)[10]						
320(2)[11]	48(2)						
320(3)	63(1)						
321[12]	48(6)-(8)[13]						

[7] Subsection (7) amended by Companies Act 1989, ss 143(7), 212, Sched 24.

[8] See further, in relation to a company which is a charity, Charities Act 1993, s 66.

[9] See also s 66 of the Charities Act 1993. Sections in the 1980 Act as amended by s 110(2), Companies Act 1981.

[10] As amended by SI 1984/134, art 46*.

[11] As amended by the Companies (Fair Dealing by Directors) (Increase in Financial Limits) Order, SI 1990/1393, art 2.

[12] Subsection (4) added by the Companies Act 1989, s 145, Sched 19, para 8.

[13] As amended by s 110(3) of the Companies Act 1981.

1985	1980	1976	1967	1948	1947	1929	1928
322(1), (2)	48(3)[14]						
322(3), (4)	48(4)						
322(5), (6)	48(5)						
322A[15]							
322B[16]							
323(1), (2)[17]	80(1), Sch 2	42(1), Sch 2	25(1)				
323(3)-(5)			25(2)-(4)				
324(1), (2)	80, Sch 2	Sch 2	27(1)				
324(3) (a)			28(1)				
324(4)			27(4)				
324(5)			27(9)				
324(6)			27(11), (13)				

[14] As amended by SI 1984/134, art 47*.

[15] Added by s 109(1) of the Companies Act 1989.

[16] Inserted by the Companies (Single Member Private Limited Companies) Regulations 1992, SI 1992/1699, reg 2(b), Sched, para 3(1), pursuant to art 5 of the 12th Company Law Directive [1989] OJ L395/40.

[17] Section as amended by Sched 3, para 28 of the Companies Act 1981.

1985	1980	1976	1967	1948	1947	1929	1928
324 (7)			27(8)				
324(8)[18]			27 (10)				
325(1), (2)			29 (1)[19]				
325(3), (4)			29(2)				
325(6)			29 (14)				
326(2)- (5)	80, Sch 2		29 (12)				
326(6)			29 (13)				
327[20]			30				
328(1), (2)	80, Sch 2		31(1)				
328(3), (5)		24, 25(2)	31(2)				
328(6), (9)[21]			31(3), (6)				

[18] See also s 732, Companies Act 1985.

[19] Sections amended by s 119, Sched 3, para 28, Companies Act 1981.

[20] Subsection (2) as amended by the Age of Legal Capacity (Scotland) Act 1991, s 10, Sched 1, para 39.

[21] Subsection (8) as amended by the Age of Legal Capacity (Scotland) Act 1991, s 10, Sched 1, para 39.

1985	1980	1976	1967	1948	1947	1929	1928
329(1), (2)[22]	80, Sch 2	25(1), (2)					
329(3)[23]		25(3), (4)					
330(1)	49			190	35		
330(2), (3)	49(1)						
330(4)	49(2)						
330(5)	63(1)						
330(6), (7)	49(3), (4)						
331	65, 87 (1)[24]						
331(2), (5)[25],(6)	65(1)						
331(3), (4)	65(2)						
331(7)	65(3)						
331(9)	65(6)						
332[26]	50(2)						
333	50(1)[27]						

---

[22] Section as amended by the Financial Services Act 1986, s 212(2), Sched 16, para 20.

[23] See also s 732 Companies Act 1985.

[24] Sections as amended by s 119, Sched 3, para 56 of the Companies Act 1981.

[25] Subsection (5) repealed by the Bankruptcy Act 1987, s 108(2), Sched 7, Pt I.

[26] Subsection (1)(b) as amended by the Companies Act 1989, s 138.

371

1985	1980	1976	1967	1948	1947	1929	1928
334[28]	50(2A)[29]						
335[30]	50(3)(a),(b)						
336[31]	50(4)(a),(b)						
337(1),(2)	50(4)(c)						
337(3)	50(5)						
338(1)	50(4)(d)						
338(2)	65(1)						
338(3),(5)[32]	50(6)						
338(6)[33]	50(7)						

[27] As amended by the Companies Act 1981, s 119, Sched 3, para 49.

[28] As amended by the Companies Act 1989, s 138.

[29] As amended by the Companies Act 1981, s 111(1).

[30] Subsection (1) amended by SI 1990/1393, art 2.

[31] Subsection (3) amended by SI 1990/1393, art 2. See also, for companies which are also a charity, s 66, Charities Act 1993.

[32] Subsection (4) amended by the Companies Act 1989, s 138 and s 23, Sched 10, Pt I, para 10.

[33] Subsection amended by s 138, Companies Act 1989.

1985	1980	1976	1967	1948	1947	1929	1928
339(1), (2)	51(1), (2)[34]						
339(3)	51(3)						
339(4)[35]	51(2A)						
339(5), (6)	51(4), (5)						
340	65(4)						
340(2)- (6)	65(4)						
340(7)[36]	65(5)						
341(1)	52(1)						
341(2), (3)	52(2)						
341(4), (5)	52(3)						
342(1)- (3)	53(1)- (3)						
342(4)	53(5)						
342(5)	53(4)[37]						

[34] Sections as amended by s 111(2) and s 119 and Sched 3, para 50 of the Companies Act 1981.

[35] Subsection amended by Companies Act 1989, s 23, Sched 10, Pt I, para 10.

[36] Subsection amended by SI 1990/1393, art 2.

[37] As amended by SI 1984/1169, art 6.**

1985	1980	1976	1967	1948	1947	1929	1928
343(1)[38]	57(1)[39]						
343(4)	57(2)						
343(6), (7)	57(3), (4)						
343(8)[40]	57(6), (7)						
343(8)(b)	63(2)						
343(9)	57(8)						
344(1)[41]	58(4)						
344(2)[42]	57(5)						
345	62						
346	64[43]						
346(2)	64(1)						
346(3)	64(2)						
346(4)-(6)	64(3)						

[38] Subsection amended by SI 1994/223, reg 6(2). Subsections (2)-(4) substituted by SI 1994/223, reg 6(3) and (4).

[39] Sections amended by SI 1984/134, art 49.*

[40] Excluding sub-subsection (b).

[41] Subsection amended by SI 1990/1393, art 2.

[42] Subsection amended by s 23, Sched 10, Pt I, para 10, Companies Act 1989.

[43] Section as amended by the Companies Act 1981, s 119, Sched 3, paras 54 and 55 and SI 1984/1169, art 7, (paragraph 64(1)(e) inserted by SI 1984/1169).**

1985	1980	1976	1967	1948	1947	1929	1928
346(7), (8)	64(4)						
347	65(8)						

The following sections and schedules of the Companies Act 1985 form part of the additional background to the review of Part X:

1985	1980	1976	1967	1948	1947	1929	1928
309(1), (2)	46, 63(1)						
310	Sch 3, para 26			205	122(4), Sch VII, (1)(c) (d)	152	78(1), 86(5)
Sch 13			27- 29#[44]				
Sch 6, Pt II	56, 64, 65[45]						

KEY

\#   Part of the section.

*   Companies Acts (Pre-Consolidation Amendments) Order 1984 (SI 1984/134).

**   Companies Acts (Pre-Consolidation Amendments) (No 2) Order 1984 (SI 1984/1169).

---

[44] As amended by Sched 3, paras 28, 29 of the Companies Act 1981.

[45] As amended by Sched 3, para 52 of the Companies Act 1981.

APPENDIX D

Extracts from the Stock Exchange's Combined Code

THE COMBINED CODE

PRINCIPLES OF GOOD GOVERNANCE AND CODE OF BEST PRACTICE

Derived by the Committee on Corporate Governance from the Committee's Final Report and from the Cadbury and Greenbury Reports.

PART 1: PRINCIPLES OF GOOD GOVERNANCE

SECTION 1: COMPANIES

...

B. DIRECTORS' REMUNERATION

...

Disclosure

3.   The company's annual report should contain a statement of remuneration policy and details of the remuneration of each director.

...

D. ACCOUNTABILITY AND AUDIT

Internal Control

2.   The board should maintain a sound system of internal control to safeguard shareholders' investment and the company's assets.

...

PART 2: CODE OF BEST PRACTICE

SECTION 1: COMPANIES

A. DIRECTORS

A.1   The Board

...

Code Provisions

A.1.1 The board should meet regularly.

...

A.1.3 There should be a procedure agreed by the board for directors in the furtherance of their duties to take independent professional advice if necessary, at the company's expense.

...

A.1.5 All directors should bring an independent judgement to bear on issues of strategy, performance, resources (including key appointments) and standards of conduct.

A.1.6 Every director should receive appropriate training on the first occasion that he or she is appointed to the board of a listed company, and subsequently as necessary.

...

A.3 Board balance

...

A.3.2 The majority of non-executive directors should be independent of management and free from any business or other relationship which could materially interfere with the exercise of their independent judgement. Non-executive directors considered by the board to be independent should be identified in the annual report.

A.4 Supply of Information

...

A.4.1 Management has an obligation to provide the board with appropriate and timely information, but information volunteered by management is unlikely to be enough in all circumstances and directors should make further enquiries where necessary. The chairman should ensure that all directors are properly briefed on issues arising at board meetings.

...

A.6 Re-election

...

A.6.1 Non-executive directors should be appointed for specified terms subject to re-election and to Companies Act provisions relating to the removal of a director, and reappointment should not be automatic.

A.6.2 All directors should be subject to election by shareholders at the first opportunity after their appointment, and to re-election thereafter at intervals of no more than three years. The names of directors submitted for election or re-election should be accompanied by sufficient biographical details to enable shareholders to take an informed decision on their election.

B. DIRECTORS' REMUNERATION

...

Remuneration policy

...

B.1.5 Executive share options should not be offered at a discount save as permitted by paragraphs 13.30 and 13.31 of the Listing Rules.

...

Service Contracts and Compensation

B.1.7 There is a strong case for setting notice or contract periods at, or reducing them to, one year or less. Boards should set this as an objective, but they should recognise that it may not be possible to achieve it immediately.

B.1.8 If it is necessary to offer longer notice or contract periods to new directors recruited from outside, such periods should reduce after the initial period.

B.1.9 Remuneration committees should consider what compensation commitments (including pension contributions) their directors' contracts of service, if any, would entail in the event of early termination. They should in particular consider the advantages of providing explicitly in the initial contract for such compensation commitments except in the case of removal for misconduct.

B.1.10 Where the initial contract does not explicitly provide for compensation commitments, remuneration committees should, within legal constraints, tailor their approach in individual early termination cases to the wide variety of circumstances. The board aim should be to avoid rewarding poor performance while dealing fairly with cases where departure is not due to poor performance and to take a robust line on reducing compensation to reflect departing directors' obligations to mitigate loss.

...

B.3 Disclosure

...

B.3.1 The board should report to the shareholders each year on remuneration. The report should form part of, or be annexed to, the company's annual report and accounts. It should be the main vehicle through which the company accounts to shareholders on directors' remuneration.

B.3.2 The report should set out the company's policy on executive directors' remuneration. It should draw attention to factors specific to the company.

B.3.3 In preparing the remuneration report, the board should follow the provisions in Schedule B to this Code.

B.3.4 Shareholders should be invited specifically to approve all new long-term incentive schemes (as defined in the Listing Rules) save in circumstances permitted by paragraph 13.13A of the Listing Rules.

B.3.5 The board's annual remuneration report to shareholders need not be a standard item of agenda for AGMs. But the board should consider each year whether the circumstances are such that the AGM should be invited to approve the policy set out in the report and should minute their conclusions.

C. RELATIONS WITH SHAREHOLDERS

...

C.2.4 Companies should arrange for the Notice of the AGM and related papers to be sent to shareholders at least 20 working days before the meeting.

D. ACCOUNTABILITY AND AUDIT

...

D.2   Internal Control

...

D.2.1 The directors should, at least annually, conduct a review the effectiveness of the group's system of internal controls and should report to shareholders that they have done so. This review should cover all controls, including financial, operational and compliance controls and risk management.

...

SCHEDULE B: PROVISIONS ON WHAT SHOULD BE INCLUDED IN THE REMUNERATION REPORT

1.   The report should include full details of all elements in the remuneration package of each individual director by name, such as basic salary, benefits in kind, annual bonuses and long term incentive schemes including share options.

2.   Information on share options, including SAYE options, should be given to each director in accordance with the recommendations of the Accounting Standards Board's Urgent Issues Task Force Abstract 10 and its successors.

3.   If grants under executive share option or other long-term incentive schemes are awarded in one large block rather than phased, the report should explain and justify.

4.   Also included in the report should be pension entitlements earned by each individual director during the year, disclosed on one of the alternative bases recommended by the Faculty of Actuaries and the Institute of

Actuaries and included in the Stock Exchange Listing Rules. Companies may wish to make clear that the transfer value represents a liability of the company, not a sum paid or due to the individual.

5. If annual bonuses or benefits in kind are pensionable the report should explain and justify.

6. The amounts received by, and commitments made to, each director under 1, 2 and 4 above should be subject to audit.

7. Any service contracts which provide for, or imply, notice periods in excess of one year (or any provisions for predetermined compensation on termination which exceed one year's salary and benefits) should be disclosed and the reasons for the longer notice periods explained.

APPENDIX E
Extracts from the Listing Rules of The Stock Exchange

Rule 12.43A

Chapter 16

The Model Code (Appendix to Chapter 16)

Best practice provisions: Directors' remuneration
Section A: Remuneration Committees (annexed to the Listing Rules)

Best practice provisions: Directors' remuneration
Section B: Remuneration policy, service contracts and compensation (annexed to the Listing Rules)

RULE 12.43A

Chapter 12: Annual report and accounts

...

Corporate governance

12.43A In the case of a company incorporated in the United Kingdom, the following additional items must be included in its annual report and accounts:

> (a) a narrative statement of how it has applied the principles set out in Section 1 of of the Combined Code appended to the listing Rules, providing sufficient explanation to enable its shareholders to evaluate properly how the principles have been applied;

> (b) a statement as to whether or not it has complied throughout the accounting period with the provisions set out in Section 1 of Part 2 of the Combined Code. A company that has not complied with the provisions of the Combined Code, or complied with only some of the provisions or (in the case of provisions whose requirements are of a continuing nature) complied for only part of an accounting period, must specify the provisions with which it has not complied, and (where relevant) for what part of the period such non-compliance continued, and give reasons for any non-compliance; and

Directors' remuneration

> (c) a report to the shareholders by the Board, which must contain:

>> (i) a statement of the company's policy on executive directors' remuneration;

(ii) the amount of each element in the remuneration package for the period under review of each director by bane, including, but not restricted to, basic salary and fees, the estimated money value of benefits in kind, annual bonuses, deferred bonuses, compensation for loss of office and payments for breach of contract or other termination payments, together with the total for each director for the period under review and for the corresponding prior period, and any significant payments made to former directors during the period under review; such details to be presented in tabular form, unless inappropriate, together with explanatory notes as necessary;

(iii) information on share options, including SAYE options, for each director by name in accordance with the recommendations of the Accounting Standards Board's Urgent Issues Task Force Abstract 10; such information to be presented in tabular form together with explanatory notes as necessary;

(iv) details of any long-term incentive schemes, other than share options details of which have been disclosed under (iii) above, including the interests of each director by name in the long-term incentive schemes at the start of the period under review; entitlements or awards granted and commitments made to each director under such schemes during the period, showing which crystallise either in the same year or subsequent years; the money value and number of shares, cash payments or other benefits received by each director under such schemes during the period; and the interests of each director in the long-term incentive schemes at the end of the period;

(v) explanation and justification of any element of remuneration, other than basic salary, which is pensionable;

(vi) details of any directors' service contract with a notice period in excess of one year or with provisions for pre-determined compensation on termination which exceeds one year's salary and benefits in kind, giving the reasons for such notice period;

(vii) the unexpired term of any directors' service contract of a director proposed for election or re-election at the forthcoming annual general meeting and, if any director proposed for election or re-election does not have a directors' service contract, a statement to the effect;

(viii) a statement of the company's policy on the granting of options or awards under its employees' share schemes and other long-term incentive schemes, explaining and justifying any departure from that policy in the period under review and any change in the policy from the preceding year;

(ix) for defined benefit schemes (as in Part 1 of Schedule 6 to the Companies Act 1985:

(a) details of the amount of the increase during the period under review (excluding inflation) and of the accumulated total amount at the end of the period in respect of the accrued benefit to which each director would be entitled on leaving service or is entitled having left service during the period under review;

(b) and either:

(i) the transfer value (less director's contributions) of the relevant increase in accrued benefit (to be calculated in accordance with Actuarial Guidance Note GN11 but making no deduction of any underfunding) as at the end of the period; or:

(ii) so much of the following information as is necessary to make a reasonable assessment of the transfer value in respect of each director:

(a) current age;

(b) normal retirement age;

(c) the amount of any contributions paid or payable by the director under the terms of the scheme during the period under review;

(d) details of spouse's and dependants' benefits;

(e) early retirement rights and options, expectations of pension increases after retirement (whether guaranteed or discretionary); and

(f) discretionary benefits for which allowance is made in transfer on leaving and any other relevant information which will significantly affect the value of the benefits.

Voluntary contributions and benefits should not be disclosed; and

(x) for money purchase schemes (as in Part 1 of Schedule 6 to the Companies Act 1985) details of the contribution or allowance payable or made by the company in respect of each director during the period under review.

Requirements of auditors

A company's statement under 12.43A must be reviewed by the auditors before publication only insofar as it relates to provisions A.2, A.3, A12, D1, D.3 and D.6 of the Combined Code. The scope of the auditors' report on the financial statements must cover the disclosures made pursuant to paragraph 12.43A(c)(ii), (iii), (iv) and (ix) and (x) above. The auditors must state in their report if in their opinion the company has not complied with any of the requirements of paragraph 12.43A(c), (iii), (iv), (ix) and (x) of the listing rules and, in such a case, must include in their report, so far as they are reasonably able to do so, a statement giving the required particulars.

CHAPTER 16

Directors

Scope of chapter

This chapter imposes obligations relating to directors, including rules as to the disclosures a company must make about its directors and about dealings in securities of the company by directors and persons connected with them. Chapter 11 sets out requirements for transactions between a company and any of its directors (and other related parties). The appendix to this chapter contains the Model Code for transactions in securities by directors certain employees and persons connected with them.

Failure by a director to accept and discharge his responsibilities for the company's compliance with the listing rules may lead the Exchange to take one or more of the steps set out in paragraph 1.10 with regard to that director.

Blank directors declaration forms (see paragraphs 16.3 to 16.6) should normally be obtained from a company's sponsor. Completed declarations must be sent to Regulatory Information, The Securities and Futures Authority Limited, Cottons Centre, Cottons Lane, London SE1 2QB who act as agents for the Exchange in this respect.

The main headings are:

16.1 directors' responsibilities

16.3 directors' declarations and board changes

16.9 directors' service contracts

384

16.13 notification of interests of directors and connected persons

16.18 the Model Code.

When notifying interests of directors and connected persons (see paragraphs 16.13 to 16.17) companies are recommended to use the form issued by the Exchange for this purpose (see Schedule 11).

Directors' responsibilities

16.1 Under the FSA, directors and proposed directors are personally responsible for information contained in listing particulars or supplementary listing particulars. In addition paragraph 5.2 requires a declaration by directors accepting responsibility for the information to be included in such particulars (see paragraph 6.A.3 or 6.H.3), and directors must provide the Exchange with an assurance in the terms set out in paragraph 5.5 where listing particulars are prepared.

16.2 A listed company must ensure that its directors accept full responsibility, collectively and individually, for the company's compliance with the listing rules.

Directors' declarations and board changes

Directors' declarations

16.3 A new applicant must submit to The Securities and Futures Authority Limited a formal declaration by each of its directors as to their business activities, past and present, in the form specified in Schedule 7 (a "director's declaration"). Such directors' declarations must be submitted at least 14 days prior to the intended date of publication of listing particulars.

16.4 A listed company must submit a director's declaration in respect of any new director to The Securities and Futures Authority Limited within 14 days of the appointment becoming effective.

16.5 A listed company which becomes aware of any changes to any of the details set out in paragraphs 3 to 12 inclusive of the director's declaration of any director must take reasonable steps to ensure that a new director's declaration in respect of that director is submitted to The Securities and Futures Authority Limited within 14 days of the company becoming aware of the changes unless a director's declaration in respect of that director giving details of the changes has already been submitted by another listed company.

16.6 A listed company must take reasonable steps to ensure that a new director's declaration in respect of each director is submitted to The Securities and Futures Authority Limited within 30 days of the third anniversary of the date when a declaration in respect of that director was last lodged (either by the company itself or by any other listed company) whether or not any of the details contained in that declaration have changed. In addition, the Exchange may at any time require a listed company to submit a director's declaration in respect of any director.

16.6A Subject to the provisions of paragraphs 1.5 and 1.6, the Exchange reserves the right to require publication of any of the information contained in a director's declaration, either in the listing particulars of a new applicant or by notification to the Company Announcements Office in the case of a listed company.

Board changes

16.7 A company must notify the Company Announcements Office without delay (by the end of the business day following the decision) when:

(a)   a new director is appointed;

(b)   a director resigns or is removed; or

(c)   any important functions or executive responsibilities of a director are changed.

16.8 The notification required by paragraph 16.7 must state the effective date of the change it if is not with immediate effect and, in the case of an appointment, whether the position is executive or non-executive and the nature of any specific function or responsibility.

Directors' service contracts

16.9 Copies of each directors' service contract must be made available for inspection by any person:

(a)   at the registered office of the company, or in the case of an overseas company, at the offices of any paying agent in the United Kingdom during normal business hours on each business day; and

(b)   at the place of the annual general meeting for at least 15 minutes prior to and during the meeting.

16.10 Where one directors' service contract covers both directors and executive officers, the company may make available for inspection in accordance with paragraph 16.9 a memorandum of the terms of the contract which relate to the directors only.

16.11 Directors' service contracts available for inspection must disclose or have attached to them the following information:

(a)   the name of the employing company;

(b)   the date of the contract, the unexpired term and details of any notice periods;

(c)   full particulars of the director's remuneration including salary and other benefits;

(d)   any commission or profit sharing arrangements;

(e) any provision for compensation payable upon early termination of the contract; and

(f) details of any other arrangements which are necessary to enable investors to estimate the possible liability of the company upon early termination of the contract.

16.12 Paragraph deleted - September 1997

Notification of interests of directors and connected persons

16.13 A company must notify the Company Announcements Office of the following information:

(a) any information relating to interests in securities that are, or are to be, listed which is disclosed to the company in accordance with section 324 (duty of director to disclose shareholdings in own company) as extended by section 328 (extension of section 324 to spouses and children) of the Companies Act 1985 or entered in the company's register in accordance with section 325(3) or (4) of that Act, together with:

(i) the date on which the disclosure was made to the company;

(ii) the date on which the transaction giving rise to the interest (or cessation of interest) was effected:

(iii) the price, amount and class of securities concerned;

(iv) the nature of the transaction; and

(v) the nature and extent of the director's interest in the transaction;

(b) information (unless notified under (a) above) relating to any interest of a connected person of a director in securities that are, or are to be, listed which, if the connected person were a director, would be required to be disclosed by him to the company or entered in the company's register as referred to in (a) above; the notification by the company must identify the director, the connected person and the nature of the connection between them, give the particulars specified in (a)(i) to (iv) above and state the nature and extent of the director's interest (if any) in the transaction; and

(c) details of (unless notified under (a) or (b) above):

(i) the grant to, or acceptance by, a director or a person connected with a director of any option (whether for the call or put or both) relating to securities of the company or of any other right or obligation, present or future, conditional or unconditional, to acquire or dispose of any securities in the company which are or will be listed or any interest of whatsoever nature in such securities; and

(ii)   the acquisition, disposal, exercise or discharged of, or any dealing with, any such option, right or obligation by a director or a person connected with a director;

the notification by the company must identify the director and, where relevant, the connected person and the nature of the connection between them, give the particulars specified in (a)(i) to (iv) above and state the nature and extent of the directors' interest (if any) in the transaction.

16.14   Any notification required by paragraph 16.13 must be made without delay (by the end of the business day following the receipt of the information by the company).

16.15   A company not subject to the Companies Act 1985 must notify to the Company Announcements Office equivalent information to that required under paragraph 16.13 so far as such information is known to the company. Any notification under this paragraph must be made without delay following the company becoming aware of the relevant information.

16.16   In the case of a dealing during a close period in exceptional circumstances as permitted by paragraph 9 of the Model Code (set out in the appendix to this chapter), the information notified to the Company Announcements Office by the company) pursuant to paragraph 16.13 or 16.15 must also include a statement of the nature of the exceptional circumstances in the light of which dealing was permitted.

16.17   A company must require each of its directors to disclose to it all information which the company needs in order to comply with paragraph 16.13 or 16.15 (so far as that information is known to the director or could with reasonable diligence be ascertained by the director), as soon as possible and not later than the fifth business day following the day on which the existence of the interest to which the information relates comes to the director's knowledge. A company must require each of its directors at such times as it deems necessary or desirable to confirm that he has made all due enquiry of those persons who are connected with him. A company is not required to notify the Company Announcements Office information which, notwithstanding compliance by it with this paragraph, it does not have.

The Model Code

16.18   A company must require:

(a)   its directors; and

(b)   any employee of the company or director or employee of a subsidiary undertaking or parent undertaking of the company who, because of his office or employment in the company or subsidiary undertaking or parent undertaking, is likely to be in possession of unpublished price-sensitive information in relation to the company to comply with a code of dealing in terms no less exacting than those of the Model Code (set out in the appendix to this chapter) and must take all proper and reasonable steps to secure such compliance.

16.19 Companies may impose more rigorous restrictions upon dealings by directors and employees if they so wish.

APPENDIX TO CHAPTER 16

The Model Code

Introduction (not forming part of the Model Code)

The freedom of directors and certain employees of listed companies to deal in their company's securities is restricted in a number of ways - by statute, by common law and by the requirement of the listing rules that listed companies adopt and apply a code of dealing based on the Model Code set out in this appendix. This requirement imposes restrictions beyond those that are imposed by law. Its purpose is to ensure that directors, certain employees and persons connected with them (within the meaning of section 346 of the Companies Act 1985) do not abuse, and do not place themselves under suspicion of abusing, price-sensitive information that they may have or be thought to have, especially in periods leading up to an announcement of results. Company directors, like other individuals, are prohibited from insider dealing by the Criminal Justice Act 1993. Under that Act it is a criminal offence for an individual who has information as an insider to deal on a regulated market, or through or as a professional intermediary, in securities whose price would be significantly affected if the insider information were made public. It is also an offence to encourage insider dealing and to disclose inside information with a view to others profiting from it.

The main headings of the Model Code for transactions in securities by directors, certain employees and persons connected with them are:

definitions

dealings by directors and relevant employees

- purpose of dealing

- dealing in close periods

- dealing in other circumstances

- dealing in another company's securities

- clearance to deal

- circumstances for refusal

- dealing in exceptional circumstances

- director acting as trustee

dealings by connected persons and investment managers

- special circumstances

- grant of options

- exercise of options

- personal equity plans

- savings schemes etc.

- guidance on other dealings

relevant employees.

Definitions

(1) In this code the following definitions, in addition to those contained in the listing rules, apply unless the context otherwise requires:

(a) "close period" means any of the periods when a director is prohibited from dealing as specified in paragraph 3 of this code;

(b) "dealing" includes any sale or purchase of, or agreement to sell or purchase, any securities of the company and the grant, acceptance, acquisition, disposal, exercise or discharge of any option (whether for the call, or put, or both) or other right or obligation, present or future, conditional or unconditional, to acquire or dispose of securities, or any interest in securities, of the company and "deal" shall be construed accordingly;

(c) "prohibited period" means any period to which paragraph 7 of this code applies;

(d) "relevant employee" means any employee of the listed company or director or employee of a subsidiary undertaking or parent undertaking of the listed company who, because of his office or employment in the listed company or subsidiary undertaking or parent undertaking, is likely to be in possession of unpublished price-sensitive information in relation to the listed company;

(e) "securities" means any listed securities and, where relevant, securities which have been listed in a member state or admitted to dealing on, or have their prices quoted on or under the rules of, any regulated market;

(f) "unpublished price-sensitive information" means information which:

390

(i) relates to particular securities or to a particular issuer or to particular issuers of securities and not to securities generally or issuers of securities generally (and, for these purposes, information shall be treated as relating to an issuer of securities which is a company not only where it is about the company but also where it may affect the company's business prospects);

(ii) is specific or precise;

(iii) has not been made public within the meaning of section 58 of the Criminal Justice Act 1993; and

(iv) if it were made public would be likely to have a significant effect in the price or value of any securities

and, without prejudice to the generality of the above, it should be considered whether any unpublished information regarding transactions required to be notified to the Company Announcements Office in accordance with chapter 10 or chapter 11 of the listing rules and unpublished information of the kind referred to in the paragraphs of the listing rules set out below is price-sensitive:

Paragraph

9.1	general obligation of disclosure
9.10(a)	alterations to capital structure
9.11 and 9.12	notification of major interests in shares
15.3. 15.9. 15.13 and 15.15	purchase of own securities
16.13 and 16.15	notification of directors' interests; and

(g) "regulated market" means any regulated market defined as such in the Insider Dealing (Securities and Regulated Markets) Order 1994, as amended or supplemented by any further order made under section 60(1) of the Criminal Justice Act 1993.

Dealings by directors and relevant employees

Purpose of dealing

(2) A director must not deal in any securities of the listed company on considerations of a short term nature.

Dealing in close periods

(3) A director must not deal in any securities of the listed company during a "close period". A close period is:

(a) the period of two months immediately preceding the preliminary announcement of the company's annual results or, if shorter, the period from the relevant financial year end up to and including the time of the announcement; and

(b) if the company reports on a half-yearly basis, the period of two months immediately preceding the publication of the half-yearly report in accordance with paragraph 12.49 of the listing rules or, if shorter, the period from the relevant financial period end up to and including the time of such publication; or

(c) if the company reports on a quarterly basis, the period of one month immediately preceding the announcement of the quarterly results or, if shorter, the period from the relevant financial period end up to and including the time of the announcement (save that for the final quarter paragraph 3(a) of this code applies).

(4) A director must not deal in any securities of the listed company at any time when he is in possession of unpublished price-sensitive information in relation to those securities, or otherwise where clearance to deal is not given under paragraph 7 of this code.

(5) Paragraph deleted - July 1994

Clearance to deal

(6) A director must not deal in any securities of the listed company without advising the chairman (or one or more other directors designated for this purpose) in advance and receiving clearance. In his own case, the chairman, or other designated director, must advise the board in advance at a board meeting, or advise another designated director, and receive clearance from the board or designated director, as appropriate.

Circumstances for refusal

(7) A director must not be given clearance (as required by paragraph 6 of this code) to deal in any securities of the listed company during a prohibited period. A "prohibited period" means:

(a) any close period;

(b) any period when there exists any matter which constitutes unpublished price sensitive information in relation to the company's securities (whether or not the director has knowledge of such matter) and the proposed dealing would (if permitted) take place after the time when it has become reasonably probable that an announcement will be required in relation to that matter; or

(c) any period when the person responsible for the clearance otherwise has reason to believe that the proposed dealing is in breach of this code.

(8) A written record must be maintained by the company of the receipt of any advice received from a director pursuant to paragraph 6 of this code and of any clearance given. Written confirmation from the company that such advice and clearance (if any) have been recorded must be given to the director concerned.

Dealing in exceptional circumstances

(9) In exceptional circumstances where it is the only reasonable course of action available to a director, clearance may be given for the director to sell (but not to purchase) securities when he would otherwise be prohibited from doing so. An example of the type of circumstance which may be considered exceptional for these purposes would be a pressing financial commitment on the part of the director that cannot otherwise be satisfied. The determination of whether circumstances are exceptional for this purpose must be made by the person responsible for the clearance.

Director acting as trustee

(10) Where a director is a sole trustee (other than a bare trustee), the provisions of this code will apply, as if he were dealing on his own account. Where a director is a co-trustee (other than a bare trustee), he must advise his co-trustees of the name of the listed company of which he is a director. If the director is not a beneficiary, a dealing in his company's securities undertaken by that trust will not be regarded as a dealing by the director for the purposes of this code, where the decision to deal is taken by the other trustees acting independently of the director or by investment managers on behalf of the trustees. The other trustees or the investment managers will be assumed to have acted independently of the director for this purpose where they:

(a) have taken the decision to deal without consultation with, or other involvement of, the director concerned; or

(b) if they have delegated the decision making to a committee of which the director is not a member.

Dealings by connected persons and investment managers

(11) A director must (so far as is consistent with his duties of confidentiality to his company) seek to prohibit (by taking the steps set out in paragraph 12 of this code) any dealing in securities of the listed company during a close period or at a time when the director is in possession of unpublished price sensitive information in relation to those securities and would be prohibited from dealing under paragraph 7(b) of this code:

(a) by or on behalf of any person connected with him (within the meaning of section 346 of the Companies Act 1985); or

(b) by an investment manager on his behalf or on behalf of any person connected with him where either he or any person connected with him has funds under management with that investment manager, whether or not discretionary (save as provided in paragraphs 10 and 16 of this code).

(12) For the purposes of paragraph 11 of this code, a director must advise all such connected persons and investment managers:

    (a) of the name of the listed company of which he is a director;

    (b) of the close period during which they cannot deal in the company's securities;

    (c) of any other periods when the director knows he is not himself free to deal in securities of the company under the provisions of this code unless his duty of confidentiality to the company prohibits him from disclosing such periods; and

    (d) that they must advise him immediately after they have dealt in securities of the company (save as provided in paragraphs 10 and 16 of this code).

Special circumstances

Grant of options

(13) The grant of options by the board of directors under an employee share scheme to individuals who are not directors or relevant employees may be permitted during a prohibited period if such grant could not reasonably be made at another time and failure to make the grant would indicate that the company was in a prohibited dealing period.

Exercise of options

(14) The chairman or other designated director may allow the exercise of an option or right under an employees' share scheme, or the conversion of a convertible security, where the final date for the exercise of such option or right, or conversion of such security, falls during any prohibited period and the director could not reasonably have been expected to exercise it at an earlier time when he was free to deal (see also paragraph 20(h)).

(15) Where an exercise or conversion is permitted pursuant to paragraph 14 or 20(h) of this code, the chairman or other designated director may not, however, give clearance for the sale of securities acquired pursuant to such exercise or conversion.

Personal equity plans and authorised unit trusts

(16) A director may enter into a discretionary personal equity plan or deal in units of an authorised unit trust without regard to the provisions of this code. In the case of a personal equity plan investing only in securities of the listed company the provisions of paragraph 17 of this code apply.

(17) A director may enter into a personal equity plan which involves regular payments by standing order or direct debit of sums which are to be

invested only in securities of the listed company if the following provisions are complied with:

(a)   he does not enter into the plan to carry out the first purchase of the securities of the listed company within the plan during a prohibited period;

(b)   he does not cancel or vary the terms of his participation, or carry out sales of the securities of the listed company within the plan during a prohibited period; and

(c)   before entering into the plan or cancelling the plan or varying the terms of his participation or carrying out sales of the securities of the listed company within the plan, he obtains clearance under paragraph 6 of this code.

Savings schemes etc

(18)   A director may enter into a scheme under which securities of the listed company:

(a)   are purchased pursuant to a regular standing order or direct debit arrangement; or

(b)   are acquired by way of a standing election to reinvest dividends or other distributions received:

if the provisions set out in paragraph 17 of this code in relation to personal equity plans investing only in the securities of the listed company are complied with.

Guidance on other dealings

(19)   For the avoidance of doubt, the following constitute dealings for the purposes of this code and are consequently subject to the provisions of this code:

(a)   dealings between directors and/or relevant employees of the company;

(b)   off-market dealings; and

(c)   transfers for no consideration by a director other than transfers where the director retains a beneficial interest under the Companies Act 1985.

(20)   For the avoidance of doubt, and notwithstanding the definition of dealing contained in paragraph 1(b) of this code, the following dealings are not subject to the provisions of this code:

(a)   undertakings or elections to take up entitlements under a rights issue or other offer (including an offer of shares in lieu of a cash dividend);

(b) the take up of entitlements under a rights issue or other offer (including an offer of shares in lieu of a cash dividend);

(c) allowing entitlements to lapse under a rights issue or other offer (including an offer of shares in lieu of a cash dividend);

(d) the sale of sufficient entitlements nil-paid to allow take up of the balance of the entitlements under a rights issue;

(e) undertakings to accept, or the acceptance of, a takeover offer;

(f) dealing by a director with a person whose interest in securities is to be treated by virtue of section 328 of the Companies Act (extension of section 324 to spouses and children) as the director's interest;

(g) transfers of shares arising out of the operation of an employees' share scheme into a personal equity plan investing only in securities of the listed company within ninety days of:

   (i) the date of exercise of an option under a savings related share option scheme; or

   (ii) the date of release of shares from a profit sharing scheme;

(h) with the exception of a disposal of securities received by a director as a participant, dealings in connection with an Inland Revenue approved "Save-as-you-earn" share option scheme, or any other employees' share scheme under which participation is extended, on similar terms to those contained in an Inland Revenue approved "Save-as-you-earn" share option scheme, to all or most employees of the participating companies in that scheme;

(i) with the exception of a disposal of securities received by a director as a participant, dealings in connection with an Inland Revenue approved profit share scheme, or any similar profit share scheme under which participation is extended, on similar terms to those contained in an Inland Revenue approved profit share scheme, to all or most employees of the participating companies in the scheme;

(j) arrangements which involve a sale of securities in the listed company with the intention of making a matched purchase of such securities on the next business day ("bed and breakfast" dealings);

(k) transfers of shares already held into a personal equity plan by means of a matched sale and purchase;

(l) the cancellation or surrender of an option under an employees' share scheme.

Relevant employees

(21)   Relevant employees must comply with the terms of this code as though they were directors.

BEST PRACTICE PROVISIONS: DIRECTORS' REMUNERATION
SECTION A: REMUNERATION COMMITTEES

These provisions do not form part of the listing rules. Under paragraph 12.43(w) of the listing rules, a company must include a statement in its annual report and accounts as to whether or not it has complied with these provisions and must explain and justify any areas of non-compliance.

1.   Boards of directors should set up remuneration committees to determine, within agreed terms of reference, the company's policy on executive directors' remuneration and specific remuneration packages for each of the executive directors, including pension rights and any compensation payments.

2.   Remuneration committees should consist exclusively of non-executive directors with no personal financial interest other than as shareholders in the matters to be decided, no potential conflicts of interest arising from cross-directorships and no day-to-day involvement in running the business.

3.   Remuneration committee chairmen should report to the shareholders through means specified in the listing rules.

4.   The members of the remuneration committee should be listed each year in the committee's report to shareholders. When they stand for election or re-election, the proxy cards should indicate their membership of the committee.

5.   The Board itself, or, where required by the Articles of Association, the shareholders, should determine the remuneration of all non-executive directors, within the limits set out in the Articles of Association.

6.   Remuneration committees should consult the company chairman and/or chief executive about their proposals relating to the remuneration of other executive directors and have access to professional advice inside and outside the company.

7.   The remuneration committee chairman, or other member of the remuneration committee, should attend the company's annual general meeting to answer shareholders' questions about directors' remuneration.

8.   The committee's annual report to shareholders need not be a standard item of agenda for annual general meetings, but the committee should consider each year whether the circumstances are such that the annual general meeting should be invited to approve the policy set out in its report and should minute its conclusions.

BEST PRACTICE PROVISIONS: DIRECTORS' REMUNERATION
SECTION B: REMUNERATION POLICY, SERVICE CONTRACTS AND COMPENSATION

These provisions do not form part of the listing rules. Under paragraph 12.43(x)(ii) of the listing rules a statement must be made in the report by the remuneration committee or by the Board if there is no remuneration committee included in the annual report and accounts that the remuneration committee has given full consideration to these provisions in framing its remuneration policy. There is no requirement to explain or justify any areas of non-compliance.

Remuneration policy

1. Remuneration committees should provide the packages need to attract, retain and motivate directors of the quality required but should avoid paying more than is necessary for this purpose.

2. Remuneration committees should judge where to position the company relative to other companies. They should be aware what comparable companies are paying and should take account of relative performance.

3. Remuneration committees should be sensitive to the wider scheme, including pay and employment conditions elsewhere in the group, especially when determining annual salary increases.

4. The performance-related elements of remuneration should be designed to align the interests of directors and shareholders and to give directors keen incentives to perform at the highest levels.

5. Remuneration committees should consider whether the directors should be eligible for annual bonuses. If so, performance conditions should be relevant, stretching and designed to enhance the business. Upper limits should always be considered. There may be a case for part-payment in shares to be held for a significant period.

6. Remuneration committees should consider whether the directors should be eligible for benefits under long-term incentive schemes. Traditional share option schemes should be weighed against other kinds of long-term incentive scheme. In normal circumstances, shares granted or other forms of deferred remuneration should not vest, and options should not be exercisable, in under three years. Directors should be encouraged to hold their shares for a further period after vesting or exercise subject to the need to finance any costs of acquisition and associated tax liability.

7. Any new long-term incentive schemes which are proposed should be approved by shareholders and should preferably replace existing schemes or at least form part of a well-considered overall plan, incorporating existing schemes. The total rewards potentially available should not be excessive.

8. Payouts or grants under all incentive schemes, including new grants under existing share option schemes, should be subject to challenging performance criteria reflecting the company's objectives. Consideration should be given to criteria which reflect the company's performance relative to a group of comparator companies in some key variables such as total shareholder return.

9. Grants under executive share option and other long-term incentive schemes should normally be phased rather than awarded in one large block.

10. Remuneration committees should consider the pension consequences and associated costs to the company of basic salary increases and other changes in remuneration, especially for directors close to retirement.

11. In general, neither annual bonuses nor benefits in kind should be pensionable.

Service contracts and compensation

12. Remuneration committees should consider what compensation commitments (including pension contributions) the directors' contracts of service, if any, would entail in the event of early termination, particularly for unsatisfactory performance.

13. There is a strong case for setting notice or contract periods at, or reducing them to, one year or less. Remuneration committees should, however, be sensitive and flexible, especially over time. In some cases notice or contract periods of up to two years may be acceptable. Longer periods should be avoided wherever possible.

14. If it is necessary to offer longer notice or contract periods, such as three years, to new directors recruited from outside, such periods should reduce after the initial period.

15. Within the legal constraints, remuneration committees should tailor their approach in individual early termination cases to the wide variety of circumstances. The broad aim should be to avoid rewarding poor performance while dealing fairly with cases where departure is not due to poor performance and to take a robust line on reducing compensation to reflect departing directors' obligations to mitigate damages.

16. Where appropriate, and in particular where notice or contract periods exceed one year, companies should consider paying all or part of compensation in instalments rather than one lump sum and reducing or stopping payment when the former director takes on new employment.

APPENDIX F
Cadbury Code of Best Practice

1   The Board of Directors

1.1   The board should meet regularly, retain full and effective control over the company and monitor the executive management.

1.2   There should be a clearly accepted division of responsibilities at the head of a company, which will ensure a balance of power and authority, such that no one individual has unfettered powers of decision. Where the chairman is also the chief executive, it is essential that there should be a strong and independent element on the board, with a recognised senior member.

1.3   The board should include non-executive directors of sufficient calibre and number for their views to carry significant weight in the board's decisions. (Note 1)

1.4   The board should have a formal Schedule of matters specifically reserved to it for decision to ensure that the direction and control of the company is firmly in its hands. (Note 2)

1.5   There should be an agreed procedure for directors in the furtherance of their duties to take independent professional advice if necessary, at the company's expense. (Note 3)

1.6   All directors should have access to the advice and services of the company secretary, who is responsible to the board for ensuring that board procedures are followed and that applicable rules and regulations are complied with. Any question of the removal of the company secretary should be a matter for the board as a whole.

2   Non-Executive Directors

2.1   Non-executive directors should bring an independent judgement to bear on issues of strategy, performance, resources, including key appointments, and standards of conduct.

2.2   The majority should be independent of management and free from any business or other relationship which could materially interfere with the exercise of their independent judgement, apart from their fees and shareholding. Their fees should reflect the time which they commit to the company. (Notes 4 and 5)

2.3   Non-executive directors should be appointed for specified terms and reappointment should not be automatic. (Note 6)

2.4   Non-executive directors should be selected through a formal process and both this process and their appointment should be a matter for the board as a whole. (Note 7)

3 Executive Directors

3.1 Directors' service contracts should not exceed three years without shareholders' approval. (Note 8)

3.2 There should be full and clear disclosure of directors' total emoluments and those of the chairman and highest-paid UK director, including pension contributions and stock options. Separate figures should be given for salary and performance-related elements and the basis on which performance is measured should be explained.

3.3 Executive directors' pay should be subject to the recommendations of a remuneration committee made up wholly or mainly of non-executive directors. (Note 9)

4 Reporting and Controls

4.1 It is the board's duty to present a balanced and understandable assessment of the company's position. (Note 10)

4.2 The board should ensure that an objective and professional relationship is maintained with the auditors.

4.3 The board should establish an audit committee of at least 3 non-executive directors with written terms of reference which deal clearly with its authority and duties. (Note 1 1)

4.4 The directors should explain their responsibility for preparing the accounts next to a statement by the auditors about their reporting responsibilities. (Note 12)

4.5 The directors should report on the effectiveness of the company's system of internal control. (Note 13)

4.6 The directors should report that the business is a going concern, with supporting assumptions or qualifications as necessary. (Note 13).

APPENDIX G

Cadbury Statement of Directors' Responsibilities[1]

STATEMENT OF DIRECTORS' RESPONSIBILITIES

Company law requires the directors to prepare financial statements for each financial year which give a true and fair view of the state of affairs of the company and the group and of the profit or loss of the group for that period. In preparing those financial statements, the directors are required to -

- select suitable accounting policies and then apply them consistently

- make judgements and estimates that are reasonable and prudent

- state whether applicable accounting standards have been followed, subject to any material departures disclosed and explained in the financial statements[2]

- prepare the financial statements on the going concern basis unless it is inappropriate to presume that the company will continue in business[3]

The directors are responsible for keeping proper accounting records which disclose with reasonable accuracy at any time the financial position of the company and of the group and to enable them to ensure that the financial statements comply with the Companies Act 1985. They are also responsible for safeguarding the assets of the company and hence for taking reasonable steps for the prevention and detection of fraud and other irregularities.

---

[1] The APB's SAS 600 - Auditors' report on financial statements - May 1993 (based on the Cadbury Code of Best Practice).

[2] Large companies only.

[3] If no separate statement of the business as a going concern is made by the directors.

402

APPENDIX H

Extracts from Australian Corporations Law

DUTY AND LIABILITY OF OFFICER OF CORPORATION

Section 232

(1) In this section:

    "officer", in relation to a corporation, means:

        (a)   director, secretary or executive officer of the corporation;

    ...

(2) **[Act honestly]** An officer of a corporation shall at all times act honestly in the exercise of his or her powers and the discharge of the duties of his or her office.

(3) [repealed]

(4) In the exercise of his or her powers and the discharge of his or her duties, an officer of a corporation must exercise the degree of care and diligence that a reasonable person in a like position in a corporation would exercise in the corporation's circumstances.

(4A) [......]

(5) An officer or employee of a corporation, or a former officer or employee of a corporation, must not, in relevant circumstances, make improper use of information acquired by virtue of his or her position as such an officer or employee to gain, directly or indirectly, an advantage for himself or herself or for any other person or to cause detriment to the corporation.

(6) An officer or employee of a corporation must not, in relevant circumstances, make improper use of his or her position as such an officer or employee, to gain, directly or indirectly, an advantage for himself or herself or for any other person or to cause detriment to the corporation.

(6A)-(10) [......]

(11) This section has effect in addition to, and not in derogation of, any rule of law relating to the duty or liability of a person by reason of the person's office or employment in relation to a corporation and does not prevent the institution of any civil proceedings in respect of a breach of such a duty or in respect of such a liability.

APPENDIX I

Extracts from New Zealand Companies Act 1993

The following sections of the New Zealand Companies Act 1993 are set out below: 130 to 131, 133 to 134, and 137 to 146

DELEGATION OF POWERS

Section 130

130.—(1) Subject to any restrictions in the constitution of the company, the board of a company may delegate to a committee of directors, a director or employee of the company, or any other person, any one or more of its powers other than its powers under any of the sections of this Act set out in the Second Schedule to this Act.

(2) A board that delegates a power under subsection (1) of this section is responsible for the exercise of the power by the delegate as if the power had been exercised by the board, unless the board-

    (a)   believed on reasonable grounds at all times before the exercise of the power that the delegate would exercise the power in conformity with the duties imposed on directors of the company by this Act and the company's constitution; and

    (b)   has monitored, by means of reasonable methods properly used, the exercise of the power by the delegate.

DUTY OF DIRECTORS TO ACT IN GOOD FAITH AND IN BEST INTERESTS OF COMPANY

Section 131

131.—(1) Subject to this section, a director of a company, when exercising powers or performing duties, must act in good faith and in what the director believes to be the best interests of the company.

(2) A director of a company that is a wholly-owned subsidiary may, when exercising powers or performing duties as a director, if expressly permitted to do so by the constitution of the company, act in a manner which he or she believes is in the best interests of that company's holding company even though it may not be in the best interests of the company.

(3) A director of a company that is a subsidiary (but not a wholly-owned subsidiary) may, when exercising powers or performing duties as a director, if

expressly permitted to do so by the constitution of the company and with the prior agreement of the shareholders (other than its holding company), act in a manner which he or she believes is in the best interest of that company's holding company even though it may not be in the best interests of the company.

(4) A director of a company incorporated to carry out a joint venture between the shareholders may, when exercising powers or performing duties as a director in connection with the carrying out of the joint venture, if expressly permitted to do so by the constitution of the company, act in a manner which he or she believes is in the best interests of a shareholder or shareholders, even though it may not be in the best interests of the company.

POWERS TO BE EXERCISED FOR PROPER PURPOSE

Section 133

133. A director must exercise a power for a proper purpose.

DIRECTORS TO COMPLY WITH ACT AND CONSTITUTION

Section 134

134. A director of a company must not act, or agree to the company acting, in a manner that contravenes this Act or the constitution of the company.

DIRECTOR'S DUTY OF CARE

Section 137

137. A director of a company, when exercising powers or performing duties as a director, must exercise the care, diligence, and skill that a reasonable director would exercise in the same circumstances taking into account but without limitation,—

   (a) The nature of the company; and

   (b) The position of the director and the nature of the responsibilities undertaken by him or her.

USE OF INFORMATION AND ADVICE

Section 138

138.— (1) Subject to subsection (2) of this section, a director of a company, when exercising powers of performing duties as a director, may rely on reports, statements and financial data and other information prepared or supplied and on professional or expert advice given, by any of the following persons:

   (a) An employee of the company whom the director believes on reasonable grounds to be reliable and competent in relation to the matters concerned;

(b) A professional adviser or expert in relation to matters which the director believes on reasonable grounds to be within the person's professional or expert competence;

(c) Any other director or committee of directors upon which the director did not serve in relation to matters within the director's or committee's designated authority.

(2) Subsection (1) of this section applies to a director only if the director—

(a) Acts in good faith; and

(b) Makes proper inquiry where the need for inquiry is indicated by the circumstances; and

(c) Has no knowledge that such reliance is unwarranted.

Transactions Involving Self-interest

MEANING OF "INTERESTED"

Section 139

139.—(1) Subject to subsection (2) of this section, for the purposes of this Act, a director of a company is interested in a transaction to which the company is a party if, and only if, the director—

(a) Is a party to, or will or may derive a material financial benefit from, the transaction; or

(b) Has a material financial interest in another party to the transaction; or

(c) Is a director, officer, or trustee of another party to, or person who will or may derive a material financial benefit from, the transaction, not being a party or person that is—

(i) The company's holding company being a holding company of which the company is a wholly-owned subsidiary; or

(ii) A wholly-owned subsidiary of the company; or

(iii) A wholly-owned subsidiary of a holding company of which the company is also a wholly-owned subsidiary; or

(d) Is the parent, child, or spouse of another party to, or person who will or may derive a material financial benefit from, the transaction; or

(e) Is otherwise directly or indirectly materially interested in the transaction.

(2) For the purposes of this Act, a director of a company is not interested in a transaction to which the company is a party if the transaction comprises only the giving by the company of security to a third party which has no connection with the director, at the request of the third party, in respect of a debt or obligation of the company for which the director or another person has personally assumed responsibility in whole or in part under a guarantee, indemnity, or by the deposit of a security.

DISCLOSURE OF INTEREST

Section 140

140.—(1) A director of a company must, forthwith after becoming aware of the fact that he or she is interested in a transaction or proposed transaction with the company, cause to be entered in the interests register, and, if the company has more than one director, disclose to the board of the company—

(a) If the monetary value of the director's interest is able to be quantified, the nature and monetary value of that interest; or

(b) If the monetary value of the director's interest cannot be quantified, the nature and extent of that interest.

(2) For the purposes of subsection (1) of this section, a general notice entered in the interests register or disclosed to the board to the effect that a director is a shareholder, director, officer or trustee of another named company or other person and is to be regarded as interested in any transaction which may, after the date of the entry or disclosure, be entered into with that company or person, is a sufficient disclosure of interest in relation to that transaction.

(3) A failure by a director to comply with subsection (1) of this section does not affect the validity of a transaction entered into by the company or the director.

(4) Every director who fails to comply with subsection (1) of this section commits an offence and is liable on conviction to the penalty set out in section 373(2) of this Act.

Cf 1995, No 63, s 199

AVOIDANCE OF TRANSACTIONS

Section 141

141.— (1) A transaction entered into by the company in which a director of the company is interested may be avoided by the company at any time before the expiration of 3 months after the transaction is disclosed to all the shareholders (whether by means of the company's annual report or otherwise).

(2) A transaction cannot be avoided if the company receives fair value under it.

(3) For the purposes of subsection (2) of this section, the question whether a company receives fair value under a transaction is to be determined on the basis of

the information known to the company and to the interest director at the time the transaction is entered into.

(4) If a transaction is entered into by the company in the ordinary course of its business and on usual terms and conditions, the company is presumed to receive fair value under the transaction.

(5) For the purposes of this section—

(a) A person seeking to uphold a transaction and who knew or ought to have known of the director's interest at the time the transaction was entered into has the onus of establishing fair value; and

(b) In any other case, the company has the onus of establishing that it did not receive fair value.

(6) A transaction in which a director is interested can only be avoided on the ground of the director's interest in accordance with this section or the company's constitution.

EFFECT ON THIRD PARTIES

Section 142

142.—The avoidance of a transaction under section 141 of this Act does not affect the title or interest of a person in or to property which that person has acquired if the property was acquired—

(a) From a person other than the company; and

(b) For valuable consideration; and

(c) Without knowledge of the circumstances of the transaction under which the person referred to in paragraph (a) of this section acquired the property from the company.

APPLICATION OF SECTIONS 140 AND 141 IN CERTAIN CASES

Section 143

143. Nothing in section 140 and section 141 of this Act applies in relation to-

(a) Remuneration or any other benefit given to a director in accordance with section 161 of this Act; or

(b) An indemnity given or insurance provided in accordance with section 162 of this Act.

INTERESTED DIRECTOR MAY VOTE

Section 144

144.—Subject to the constitution of the company, a director of a company who is interested in a transaction entered into, or to be entered into, by the company, may—

(a) Vote on a matter relating to the transaction; and

(b) Attend a meeting of directors at which a matter relating to the transaction arises and be included among the directors present at the meeting for the purpose of a quorum; and

(c) Sign a document relating to the transaction on behalf of the company; and

(d) Do any other thing in his or her capacity as a director in relation to the transaction—

as if the director were not interested in the transaction.

USE OF COMPANY INFORMATION

Section 145

145.— (1) a director of a company who has information in his or her capacity as a director or employee of the company, being information that would not otherwise be available to him or her, must not disclose that information to any person, or make use of or act on the information, except—

(a) For the purposes of the company; or

(b) As required by law; or

(c) In accordance with subsection (2) or subsection (3) of this section; or

(d) In complying with section 140 of this Act.

(2) A director of a company may, unless prohibited by the board, disclose information to—

(a) A person whose interests the director represents; or

(b) A person in accordance with whose directions or instructions the director may be required or is accustomed to act in relation to the director's powers and duties and, if the director discloses the information the name of the person to whom it is disclosed must be entered in the interests register.

(3) A director of a company may disclose, make use of, or act on the information if—

      (a) Particulars of the disclosure, use, or the act in question are entered in the interests register; and

      (b) The director is first authorised to do so by the board; and

      (c) The disclosure, use, or act in question will not, or will not be likely to, prejudice the company.

APPENDIX J

Extracts from the Canadian Business Corporations Act 1985

122.—(1) Every director and officer of a corporation in exercising his powers and discharging his duties shall ...

(b) exercise the care, diligence and skill that a reasonably prudent person would exercise in comparable circumstances.

Reliance on statements

123.—(4) A director is not liable under section...122 [the skill and care requirement] if he relies in good faith on

(a) financial statements of the corporation represented to him by an officer of the corporation or in a written report of the auditor of the corporation fairly to reflect the financial condition of the corporation; or

(b) a report of a lawyer, accountant, engineer, appraiser or other person whose profession lends credibility to him.

APPENDIX K

Article 93 of the German Stock Corporation Act

ARTICLE 93

Duty of Care and Responsibility of Members of the Management Board

(1) In conducting business the members of the management board shall employ the care of a diligent and conscientious manager. They shall not disclose confidential information and secrets of the company, in particular trade and business secrets, which have become known to them as a result of their service on the management board.

(2) Members of the management board who violate their duties shall be jointly and severally liable to the company for any resulting damage. They shall bear the burden of proof in the event of a dispute as to whether or not they have employed the care of a diligent and conscientious manager.

(3) The members of the management board shall in particular be liable for damages if, contrary to this act:

1. contributions are repaid to shareholders;

2. shareholders are paid interest or dividends;

3. company shares or shares of another company are subscribed, acquired, taken as a pledge or redeemed;

4. share certificates are issued before the par value or the higher issue price has been fully paid;

5. assets of the company are distributed;

6. payments are made after the company has become insolvent or over indebted [sic];

7. remuneration is paid to members of the supervisory board;

8. credit is extended;

9. in connection with a conditional capital increase, new shares are issued other than for the specified purpose or prior to full payment of the consideration.

(4) The members of the management board shall not be liable to the company for damages if they acted pursuant to a lawful resolution of the shareholders' meeting. However, liability for damages shall not be precluded by the fact that the supervisory board has consented to the act. The company may waive or compromise a claim for damages upon the expiry of three years after the claim has arisen, provided that the shareholders' meeting consents thereto and no minority

whose aggregate holding equals or exceeds one tenth of the share capital records an objection in the minutes. The foregoing period of time shall not apply if the person liable for damages is insolvent and enters into a composition with his creditors to avoid or terminate bankruptcy proceedings.[1]

(5) The claim of the company for damages may also be asserted by the company's creditors if they are unable to obtain satisfaction from the company. However, in cases other than those set out in subsection (3) the foregoing shall apply only if the members of the management board have grossly violated the duty of care of a diligent and conscientious manager; subsection (2) sentence 2 shall apply analogously. Liability for damages to the creditors shall be extinguished neither by a waiver nor by a compromise of the company nor by the fact that the act which caused the damage was based on a resolution of the shareholders' meeting. If bankruptcy proceedings have been instituted over the company's assets, the receiver in bankruptcy shall exercise the rights of the creditors against the members of the management board during the course of such proceedings.[2]

(6) Claims under the foregoing provisions shall be barred after the expiration of a period of five years.

---

[1] Effective as of 1 January 1999 § 93(4) sentence 4 will read as follows:

> The foregoing period of time shall not apply if the person liable for damages is insolvent and enters into a composition with his creditors to avoid insolvency proceedings or if the liability for damages is subject to an insolvency plan.

[2] Effective as of 1 January 1999 § 93(5) sentence 4 will read:

> If insolvency proceedings have been instituted over the company's assets, the receiver or the trustee, as the case may be, shall exercise the rights of the creditors against the members of the management board during the course of such proceedings.

APPENDIX L

Extracts from the Review of the Hong Kong Companies Ordinance - Consultancy Report (March 1997)

6.13 RECOMMENDATION

Statutory statement of directors' duties:

There should be a statutory statement of directors' duties to act honestly and in the best interests of the company and to exercise the care, diligence and skill that a reasonably prudent person would. These duties should also be made applicable to those corporate officers appointed by the board.

Current Ordinance

There is no statutory statement of the directors' and officers' duties to act honestly and in the best interests of the company and to exercise the care, diligence and skill that a reasonably prudent person would.

COMMENTARY

A statutory statement of directors' duties would have the beneficial effect of clearly setting out the standard against which actions by directors would be measured. As in other jurisdictions, there is no doubt that the long history in the case law would continue to inform the statutory language, but the statutory standard would prevail. The duties incumbent upon company directors are the product of a long evolution at common law; their development was also influenced by certain equitable notions. Directors' duties may be classified into two categories: fiduciary duties and the duty of care and skill. Directors' fiduciary duties represent Equity's most significant contribution to company law; they place the directors under a fiduciary obligation to act in the best interests of the company, not to abuse or fetter their powers, and not to place themselves in situations of conflict of interest.

At common law, the duty of care incumbent upon directors was anything but onerous; in *Re Brazilian Rubber Plantations and Estates Ltd.*, Neville J. said the following:

> A director's duty has been laid down as requiring him to act with such care as is reasonably to be expected from him, having regard to his knowledge and experience. He is, I think, not bound to bring any special qualifications to his office. He may undertake the management of a rubber company in complete ignorance of everything connected with rubber, without incurring responsibility for the mistakes which may result from such ignorance; while if he is acquainted with the rubber business he must give the company the advantage of his knowledge when transacting the company's business. He is not, I think bound to take any definite part in the conduct of the company's business, but so far as he does undertake it he must use reasonable care in its despatch.

414

Such reasonable care must, I think, be measured by the care an ordinary man might be expected to take in the same circumstances on his own behalf. His is clearly, I think, not responsible for damages occasioned by errors in judgment... (*Re Brazilian Rubber Plantations and Estates*, [1911] Ch. 425 (C.A. at 437).

The duty of care as it has evolved in the case law is derived from a gross negligence standard.

In counterbalance to this very low standard of care (and partly due to the historical development of the company where directors were originally seen as true "trustees" or fiduciaries), fiduciary duties have been imposed on directors. Initially the fiduciary duties imposed by the courts were quite strict, in keeping with the view that directors were in fact trustees. With time, and in the interests of the promotion of commerce and risk-taking enterprises, these strict fiduciary duties were relaxed by the courts. A more modern view of these new fiduciary-like duties would include some of all of the following:

- to act in good faith

- not to fetter their discretion (such as agreeing to vote in a certain way in future)

- to avoid conflicts of interest (such as interested director transactions)

- not to misuse corporate property, information, or opportunities

- not to compete with the company

There are various statutory formulations of directors' duties but all are derived from the standard of care (essentially a negligence standard) and the fiduciary duty attributed to directors by the courts. Such formulations have become the accepted norm in company statutes. Delaware is a notable exception, relying instead on its highly specialised judiciary to formulate the standards. Until recently, it seemed that the United Kingdom was moving in the direction of statutory standards. According to the U.K. Department of Trade and Industry working group on Directors Duties, there was "support emerging for the codification of directors' duties similar to the approach adopted in other Commonwealth countries. The DTI favours a reduced Part X coupled with a 'statement' of directors' duties" (Great Britain, Department of Trade and Industry, *DTI's Programme for the Reform of Company Law - Progress Report* (London: Department of Trade and Industry, 11 June 1996)). A subsequent Progress Report (October 1996) indicates, however, that such an initiative has been again derailed.

The U.K. Jenkins Committee, in 1962, considered that a general statement of the basic principles underlying the fiduciary relationship of directors towards their companies would be useful to directors and others concerned with company management. The Second Report in Hong Kong in 1973 agreed and so recommended. The SCCLR has also so recommended. Efforts were made to

415

develop a statutory formulation of directors' fiduciary duties in Hong Kong, the most recent being the Companies (Amendment) Bill 1991. The Bill was not enacted due to objections expressed in particular by the Law Society. The Law Society was of the view (among other things) that any attempt to draft a statutory formulation of directors' fiduciary duties would be incomplete and that it was better to continue with the present system where a director should consult his professional advisors whenever a question involving his fiduciary duties to the company arose. When the Bill was withdrawn the Government encouraged the private sector to draft guidelines to better inform directors of their duties. In 1995 the Hong Kong branch of the Institute of Directors published *Guidelines for Directors* which was, in part, intended to be responsive to the need for some private sector guidelines. Of special interest in this area is the SEHK Listing Rules' formulation of directors' duties, which demonstrates its affinity to modem statutory formulations. This is a measure which is long overdue and upon which there was considerable consensus in the working party.

There are several issues associated with the statutory formulation of directors' duties. Under the "negligence" branch (the duty to act with care, diligence and skill), the issues are primarily the level of diligence required and the degree of objectivity of the test. There appears to be a fairly general consensus that the "gross negligence" standard of the common law is too low and that the test should be an objective one, to this extent displacing the case law. On the other hand, setting too high a standard has been resisted on several grounds: commercial expediency and the ability to attract good business people to fill directorships. So that although serious consideration has been given to setting a "professional" standard and in fact encouraging the development of a professional class of directors, these efforts have not materialised. The MBCA rejects the notion of raising the standard to that of professional expertise.

> The reference to 'ordinarily prudent person' embodies long traditions of the common law, in contrast to suggested standards that might call for some undefined degree of expertise, like 'ordinarily prudent businessman'. The phrase recognises the need for innovation, essential to profit orientation, and focuses on the basic director attributes of common sense, practical wisdom, and informed judgment (MBCA, Official Comment, s.8.30 (a)).

As for the "fiduciary" branch of directors' duties, the main issues are the breadth of the duty owed, by whom and to whom it is owed (e.g. does it encompass individual or groups of shareholders). There is little quarrel with requiring directors to act honestly, in good faith and in the best interests of the company. Obvious issues of conflict of interests (which under traditional fiduciary standards are dealt with strictly) or duties to a third person may be addressed separately in the legislation. Although it does appear in the New Zealand legislation, care should be taken not to import the "proper purpose" test into the standards. The "proper purpose" test was not recommended by the New Zealand Law Commission but included in the resulting legislation at the behest of Parliament. The Law Commission in New Zealand correctly noted that the "concept of proper purpose was originally derived from the case law on powers and today arguably there is a lack of underpinning objects against which powers could be assessed. On the other hand, recent cases seem to use 'proper purpose' to impose an objective standard where the good faith of directors is accepted" (NZLRC 9, at 119). A proper purpose test is unnecessary given the statutory statement of directors duties proposed.

Corporate officers are included in the U.S. and Canadian formulation of both branches of the duties, in recognition of the commercial reality of managerial responsibilities. The MBCA makes the duties applicable to, corporate officers with "discretionary authority". This recommendation suggests applying the standards to those corporate officers appointed directly by the board of directors. Where most executive officers are also directors, as is often the case in Hong Kong, there would, in fact, be no extension of duties and liabilities.

In connection with the statutory formulation of directors duties in the United States, there has been a recent flurry of so-called "stakeholder," or "constituency" statutes. These statutes widen the range of factors directors may consider in making decisions to include interests such as those of employees, suppliers, customers, the community in which the corporation is situated, and, in some cases, all other "pertinent factors". By 1995, twenty-nine states had enacted such provisions. However, of these, only one, Connecticut, had made these considerations mandatory, the others were worded in a permissive fashion.

The stakeholder statutes were not designed to widen the range of persons to whom directors owe fiduciary duties; none permit any of the mentioned classes to take action if boards fail to consider their interests. Rather than to cause a sea of change in corporate decision-making, these statutes were actually intended, as transcripts from state legislatures reveal, to be anti-takeover defences; in the event that none of the other legislative or corporate anti-takeover defences prevail, directors can always cite constituency concerns as reason for rejecting a hostile bid. They may also have reduced directors' potential fiduciary liability. There has been little litigation over these provisions and their effect on American corporate law has been non-existent for all practical purposes. For these reasons, stakeholder, or constituency provisions are not being recommended; they are not relevant or appropriate in the Hong Kong context.[1]

6.14 RECOMMENDATION

Reliance on reports:

Directors and executive officers should be able to rely in good faith on financial statements and other reports prepared by officers and employees as well as the professional advice of lawyers, accountants, etc.

Current Ordinance

There are no provisions which allow directors and officers to rely in good faith on financial statements and other reports prepared by officers and employees as well as the professional advice of lawyers, accountants, etc.

---

[1]   DR: paras. 236-242, Draft Act s.9.19. CBCA: s.122. OBCA: S.134. MBCA: 8.30(a). NZLC R9: paras. 184-195,497,504520, Draft Act ss. 100(2),101-107. NZLC R16: para. 55, Draft Acts. 101.

COMMENTARY

The reliance defence reflects commercial reality and should be coterminous with the statutory duties. In the United States, under the MBCA it is available to officers who are subject to statutory duties as well as directors. However, an officer's "ability to rely on information, reports, or statements, may, depending upon the circumstances of the particular case, be more limited than in the case of a director in view of the greater obligation he may have to be familiar with the affairs of the corporation [...] Nondirector officers with more limited discretionary authority may be judged by a narrower standard, though every corporate officer or agent owes duties of fidelity, honesty, good faith, and fair dealing to the corporation" (MBCA, Official Comment, s.8.42).

This reliance defence was previously narrower in Canada; financial statements were the only reports which could be relied upon. However, the CBCA was amended in June 1995 and brought into line with MBCA. Now directors in Canada can rely on reports prepared by other professionals (s. 123(4)(b)).[2]

6.15 RECOMMENDATION

Business judgment rule:

There should be no need of a statutory formulation of the 'business judgment rule'.

Current Ordinance

There is no statutory formulation of the 'business judgment rule'.

COMMENTARY

The business judgment rule is a feature of U.S. corporate law that has no direct Commonwealth equivalent, although Australia has been considering introducing it (see J.H. Farrar, "Corporate Governance, Business Judgment and the Professionalism of Directors" (1993) 6 Corp. and Bus. L.J. 365). It is a jurisprudential rule; none of the U.S. states have attempted to codify it, leaving its formulation up to the courts. It is characterised as the presumption that in any given business decision the board "acted on an informed basis, in good faith, and in the honest belief that the action taken was in the best interest of the company" *(Smith v. Van Gorkom*, 488 A 2d 858 at 872 (Del. S.C. 1985)). Thus, plaintiffs must demonstrate by preponderance of evidence that the board was not in fact acting in such a way before the courts will substitute their judgment for that of the board in relation to the decision being reviewed.

The American Law Institute, after numerous failed attempts, finally produced a codification of the business judgment rule in its *Principles of Corporate Governance: Analysis and Recommendations.*

---

[2]   DR: Draft Act s.9.16(9). CBCA: s.123(4). OBCA: S.135(4). MBCA: 8.30(b). NZLC R9: paras. 520-522. NZLC R16: Draft Act s. 107.

A director or officer who makes a business judgment in good faith fulfils the duty under this Section if the director or officer: (1) is not interested [...] in the subject of the business judgment; (2) is informed with respect to the subject of the business judgment to the extent the director or officer reasonably believes to be appropriate under the circumstances; and (3) rationally believes that the business judgment is in the best interest of the corporation (s. 4.01(c)).

Essentially, the business judgment rule is the jurisprudential expression of the unwillingness of U.S. courts to indulge in *ex post facto* review of the merits of business judgments. It is based on the argument that a greater likelihood of judicial review of business decisions will lead boards to choose overly conservative courses of action instead of making decisions with regard to optimal results, thereby damaging corporate performance.

Another argument is that judicial and business decision-making are different processes taking place in different environments: it is doubtful whether judges, who may lack the business expertise required to appreciate all the factors involved in a complex business decision, and whose methods of analysis are legal rather than commercial, will be able to make a decision superior or even equal to the one made by the board. Even if this were not the case, the fairness of allowing review of business decisions on the basis of perfect judicial hindsight is questionable. It must be noted that much of the U.S. case law in this area has dealt with takeover situations, so that the major issue in these cases has been entrenchment of management by the adoption of certain plans of action such as sales of crown jewels, where the board authorises the sale of the asset or division that is motivating the takeover bidder.

It has been argued that courts in Commonwealth jurisdictions implicitly apply similar reasoning in duty-of-care judgments. Certainly, Commonwealth courts are reticent to review business judgments where gross negligence or self interest are not to be found, and will not find directors liable for mere errors of judgment (see, e.g. *Re City Equitable Fire Insurance Co. Ltd.* [1925] 1 Ch. 407). Professor Ziegel states that:

> To a large extent, Anglo-Canadian courts have given implicit recognition to the concerns expressed by [the business judgment rule] in their duty of care judgments. For instance, Lord Wilberforce, in *Howard Smith Ltd v. Ampol Petroleum Ltd.*, [1974] A.C. 821 at 832, stated that:
>
> > There is no appeal on merits from management decisions to courts of law; nor will courts of law assume to act as a kind of supervisory board over decisions within the powers of management honestly arrived at.
>
> In this respect, rather than being articulated as a clearly identifiable doctrinal rule, the considerations underlying the business judgment rule have simply been imported into the formulation of the final standard of care that governs directorial conduct. Viewed in this way, the integration of the business judgment rule into the relevant standard of care takes Anglo-Canadian courts to the same endpoint as their American counterparts (J.S. Ziegel et al., *Cases and Materials on*

Partnerships and Canadian Business Corporations, 3rd ed. (Toronto: Carswell, 1994) at 478).

Recently, there have been suggestions that Australia enact a statutory equivalent to the business judgment rule. The Australian Government has so far been unwilling to do so for the following reasons: 1) the wisdom of importing an American common law rule into the Australian Corporations Law is questionable (compatibility problems might arise); 2) codification of the business judgment rule had, at the date the objections were made, proved impossible; 3) Australian common law contains a rule, which although expressed differently and occurring as part of the standard of care, produces similar results; 4) the Corporations Law allowed the court to excuse directors from liability where they had acted honestly and ought fairly to be excused; and 5) the precise objective of enacting the business judgment rule was unclear. However, following the recent election in Australia, it would appear that the new government is once again considering the adoption of the business judgment rule (see Hon. Brian Gibson, "The Government's View on the Corporations Law" (speech delivered in Sydney, 14 May 1996)).

6.16 RECOMMENDATION

Indemnifying directors:

Companies should be permitted to indemnify directors and officers in specific circumstances; companies should be required to indemnify directors and officers in specific circumstances.

Current Ordinance

Under the Ordinance a contract indemnifying directors for breach of duty is void, as is any provision to such effect in the company's articles (s. 165). However, a company may indemnify directors for costs incurred while successfully defending themselves against a civil or criminal action (s. 165, art. 137). Furthermore, a court, "having regard to all the circumstances of case", may grant relief to a director who has acted "honestly and reasonably" even though held liable for "negligence, default, breach of duty or breach of trust" (s.358, art. 137).

COMMENTARY

Where a director has behaved properly and faithfully, there should be a claim to indemnification from the company. However, blanket indemnification is undesirable. Indemnification where a director has acted in breach of fiduciary duties would effectively involve a waiver of such duties. The factors to be balanced are the need to recruit qualified directors against the use of corporate funds - by directors to avoid the costs imposed on them for certain forms of misconduct. Indemnification should be permissible where it furthers "sound corporate policies" and should be prohibited where it would "protect or encourage wrongful or improper conduct", according to the MBCA. The CBCA indemnification provisions, upon which this recommendation is based, are quite liberal.

The indemnification provisions should be broadened. Indemnification should be permissible where 1) the liability was reasonably incurred in a proceeding in which the manager was involved by virtue of his position, 2) the manager was not in breach of his fiduciary duty to the company and 3) where there is a monetary penalty, reasonably believed his conduct to be lawful. Where the company itself is the plaintiff in the proceeding, different considerations prevail; judicial approval may be required.

Indemnification should be mandatory where the manager has been substantially successful on the merits of a defence (see CBCA, s. 124).[3]

6.17 RECOMMENDATION

Insuring directors:

Companies should be permitted to insure directors and officers except for a failure to act honestly and in good faith with a view to the best interests of the company.

Current Ordinance

Under the Ordinance a company cannot purchase insurance on behalf of directors (s. 165) although the directors themselves may do so. This is comparable to the position taken in the United Kingdom prior to recent amendments to the U.K. Companies Act.

COMMENTARY

The current prohibition on companies purchasing directors' and officers' liability insurance directly is easily circumvented as was the case in the U.K. prior to recent reforms. Companies increased directorial compensation to cover insurance premiums. This was not an ideal state of affairs, however. The CBCA provisions with respect to insurance are, again, quite liberal, essentially permitting the market to decide what risks will be insurable. The only limitation is with respect to acts which are not done honestly and in good faith with a view to the best interests of the company.

Apart from breach of fiduciary duty, the company should be able to purchase directors' and officers' insurance for any risks which the market is prepared to insure. The Dickerson Committee wrote in 1971: "Until experience shows that this broad power to obtain indemnity insurance from commercial carriers has been abused by directors and officers, there appears no reason to limit the insurance coverage that may be obtained" (Dickerson Report at para. 250).[4]

---

[3]   DR: paras. 243-246, Draft Act s.9.20(1)-(3),(5)-(7). CBCA: s.124. OBCA: s.136. MBCA: 8.50-8.51. NZLC R9: paras. 88,560-563, Draft Acts. 125. NZLC R16 : para. 58, Draft Act s 125. UK Companies Act 1985: ss. 310(3),144,727.

[4]   DR: paras. 249-251, Draft Acts. 9.20(4). CBCA: s. 124(4). OBCA: s.136(4). MBCA: 8.57. NZLC R9: paras. 88,560-563, Draft Act s.125. NZLC R16: para. 58, Draft Act s.125. UK Companies Act 1985: s.310. UK Companies Act 1989: s. 137(1).

6.18 RECOMMENDATION

Disqualification of directors:

Disqualification of directors provisions should be eliminated for company law purposes. Those existing provisions relating to securities, insolvency or criminal activity should be re-enacted in appropriate legislation.

Current Ordinance

The provisions governing disqualification orders are long and complex (ss. 168C-S, sch. 15). There are four principal grounds on which a court may make a disqualification order-

- conviction of an indictable offence in connection with the promotion, formation, management, receivership or liquidation of a company or any other indictable offence which involves a finding that he acted fraudulently or dishonestly (s. 168E(l));

- persistent default in relation to filing requirements of the Ordinance requiring any return, account, or other document to be delivered to the Registrar (s. 168F(l));

- fraud in the course of winding up a company or the appearance of guilt for fraudulent trading even if the director has not been convicted (s. 275); and

- unfitness - the court is required to consider the conduct of a person who has been or is a director of an insolvent company (s. 168H).

COMMENTARY

In general, the existing disqualification of directors provisions (drawn from the Company Directors Disqualification Act 1986 in the United Kingdom) are overbroad, for the purposes of core company law. Those provisions dealing with insolvency, capital markets and criminal fraud should be left to other specialised regulatory and enforcement agencies. In addition, the use of director disqualification as an enforcement mechanism for rather mundane administrative offences (such as failure to keep a register of members) may be too draconian. In a new Ordinance, with its simplified structure and emphasis on self-enforcement, there should be fewer administrative offences to police.

The real question is the necessity for broad director disqualification provisions at all. There have been mixed experiences in the jurisdictions which have enacted the U.K. - style provisions.

> It is difficult to reach firm conclusions as to whether disqualification has proved to be an effective device or sanction. Whether disqualification of bankrupt or dishonest persons, of directors whose companies fail to comply with reporting obligations, or those whose companies go into insolvent liquidation has achieved significant protection of the public interest cannot be conclusively ascertained.

All one can say is that disqualification probably has added usefully to the other sanctions and devices enacted by legislation in the public interest (A. Hicks, "Disqualification of Directors - Forty Years On" (1988) J. Bus. L. 27 at 47).

If dishonest or incapable directors are dealt with in the context of insolvency, securities and criminal legislation, is there a need for further more generalised sanction under company law? There may be a certain amount of political expediency behind the U.K. legislation, a public response to perceived abuses in the corporate world in the 1980s. Certainly, there is a strong argument for leaving whatever other situations which might arise to shareholders themselves to police, especially if shareholders possess a broad unfairly prejudicial remedy as part of their arsenal. This would be consistent with the objective of creating a self-enforcing regime for companies.

The CBCA (which preceded the UK director disqualification legislation) does not contain director disqualification provisions, although they do appear in some provincial securities laws and the new Quebec Civil Code. The CBCA, however, does create a very broad statutory duty on directors and officers to act in compliance with the statute and the company constitution. It also provides shareholders with a broad assortment of remedies, including an extremely open ended oppression or unfairly prejudicial remedy.

The MBCA, on the other hand, does provide a form of director disqualification at s. 8.09, "Removal of Directors by Judicial Proceeding". These provisions are much narrower than those in the United Kingdom; a director may be barred from re-election for a period of time, but only to the board of that corporation. The director must have engaged in fraudulent or dishonest conduct or gross abuse of authority or discretion, with respect to the corporation. Removal must be in the best interest of the corporation. Unlike the United Kingdom, where shareholders do not have standing to initiate most forms of disqualification proceedings, the action may be taken by the corporation or shareholders holding at least 10% of the shares. A derivative action for removal may be commenced by a shareholder with less than a 10% share.

The elements of a derivative action are clearly discernible in s.8.09 but the MBCA sees the court ordered removal as being quicker and simpler.

> The purpose of section 8.09 is to permit the prompt and efficient elimination of dishonest directors. It is not intended to permit judicial resolution of internal corporate struggles for control except in those cases in which a court finds that the director has been guilty of wrongful conduct of the type described (MBCA, Official Comment, s.8.09).

New York's variation of the MBCA also permits the state Attorney General (the public official responsible for enforcing corporations legislation) to take an action. Disqualification can thus be seen to be an exceptional recourse.

In the context of the current recommendations, the broad statutory unfairly prejudicial remedy or derivative action should provide the means of removing rogue directors without recourse to specific disqualification provisions.[5]

6.19 RECOMMENDATION

Conflicts of interest:

Consideration should be given to placing directors and executive officers (i.e. those appointed directly by the board) under a duty of fair dealing with respect to transactions they enter into with the company.

Current Ordinance

Not applicable. There is no statutory mechanism through which interested transactions may be upheld. However, a company may provide a procedure by which interested transactions become non-voidable and directors are not liable for any profit realized from such a transaction (Table A, art. 86). In general, companies do not adopt Table A. It is customary for articles to provide for general notice as being sufficient, to require no specific disclosure and to permit interested directors to vote.

COMMENTARY

In the United Kingdom in particular, this is a very unsatisfactory area of the law; there are numerous sections dealing with different varieties of interested director contracts assorted with various sanctions, some of which are criminal. This state of affairs is an indication of the lack of unifying conceptual basis underlying the statutory treatment. At common law, in the mid-nineteenth century, directors were subject to the strict rules of trust law with regards to conflicts of interest such as interested transactions between themselves and their companies. As a result, interested transactions were voidable at the option of the company and the director was accountable for any profit derived from the transaction.

To this day, under trust law, trustees have a fiduciary duty not to place themselves in a conflict of interest in which their personal interests could potentially conflict with their duties as trustees. These rules aim to prevent trustees from misappropriating trust property for their own personal profit instead of managing the property in the best interest of the trust's beneficiaries. The same rules were applied by analogy to directors in order to protect companies from directors who would divert company assets and business opportunities from the company for personal benefit.

The application of this strict trust standard to directors of companies received its clearest expression in *Aberdeen Railway v. Blaikie* (1854) 1 Macq. H. L. 461 (H. L. S. C.). In that case, a contract between the company and a partnership, of which one of the directors was a partner, was made voidable at the instance of the

---

[5]   MBCA: s.8.09.

company notwithstanding that its terms were fair and reasonable. Lord Cranworth L.C. said on that occasion:

> [I]t is a rule of universal application, that no one, having [fiduciary] duties to discharge, shall be allowed to enter into engagements in which he has, or can have, a personal interest conflicting, or which possibly may conflict, with the interests of those whom he is bound to protect. So strictly is this principle adhered to, that no question is allowed to be raised as to the fairness or unfairness of a contract so entered into.

The imposition of the trust standard on directors stems in large part from the history of joint stock companies, which were originally created by trust instruments called deeds of settlement. The use of deeds of settlement finds its origins in the Bubble Act which was enacted in the early 18th century. The Bubble Act aimed to stamp out the outbreak of speculation in freely transferable shares in the 1720's. It took direct aim at unincorporated companies which had freely transferable shares (the objects of speculation). Accordingly, the Act made it very difficult for unincorporated associations to obtain corporate status and enjoy the advantages of incorporation (Gower's at 29-30). Despite the Bubble Act, deeds of settlement enabled unincorporated associations to operate with many of the advantages of incorporation. Under such deeds, company members would agree to be associated in an enterprise with a prescribed joint stock divided into a specified number of shares; management would be delegated to a committee of directors; and the company's property would be vested in a separate body of trustees, some of whom would often also be directors (ibid.).

Under the first Joint Stock Companies Act of 1844, the deed of settlement was recognised to be the joint stock company's constitution; it had to be filed with the Registrar of Companies in order for the company to become incorporated. It was only after the passage of the Joint Stock Companies Act 1856, the first modern Companies Act, that deeds of settlement were superseded by the modern memorandum and articles of association (Gower's at 45). *Thus, at the time Aberdeen was decided, in 1854, many company directors were in effect true trustees, hence the apparently logical conclusion of imposing a trust standard upon them for conflicts of interest.*

These fiduciary duties imported directly from the law of trusts came to be seen as increasingly inappropriate and impractical for corporate directors working in a commercial context. For instance, it became more common for directors to serve on the boards of several companies. This was particularly the case where a company was member of a group of related companies or associated with other companies by means of interlocking directorates. Problems arose because directors owed fiduciary duties to each company of which they were directors and not the group as a whole. It was often in the interests of all companies in a group that they deal with one another (P. Lipton, "Has the 'Interested-Director Cloud' been Lifted? -- A Comparison between the U.S. and Australian Approaches" (1994) 4 Australian Journal of Corporate Law 239 at 242).

As early as the turn of the century, the appropriateness of the trust standard was questioned by Lord Herschell of the Privy Council in *Bray v. Ford*, [1896] A. C. 44 at 51-52:

> It is an inflexible [......] rule of a Court of Equity that a person in a fiduciary position is not entitled to make a profit; he is not allowed to put himself in a position where his interest and duty conflict. It has [...] been deemed expedient to lay down this positive rule. *But I am satisfied that it might be departed from in many cases, without any breach of morality, without any wrong inflicted, and without any consciousness of wrongdoing* [emphasis added].

Uncertainty is the bane of commercial existence and any rule which renders a commercial transaction "voidable" creates undesirable uncertainty.

As noted in the Official Comment to the MBCA, a conflict of interest is not in itself a crime or a tort or necessarily injurious to the company. A "conflict of interest" is not something a director is 'guilty of'; it is simply a state of affairs. It is a state of affairs which can potentially, but not necessarily, lead to an abusive situation. Indeed, in many situations, a company and its shareholders may secure major benefits from a transaction despite the presence of a director's conflicting interest (MBCA, Introductory Comment, s. 8.60).

Given that the imposition of the trust standard was commercially impractical, draftspeople took advantage of the fact that the common law recognised that there was no legal limitation upon what the members of a company could agree to in the articles of association. As a consequence, articles were drafted so that interested transactions would be upheld so long as interested directors disclosed their interest to the board and did not vote. In other cases, articles were widened to such an extent that directors were not required to disclose their interests, were permitted to vote and were absolved altogether of any duty to account for profits derived from an interested transaction.

Such wide articles had become so widespread before 1929 that the Companies Act was amended that year to include what is now section 317 of the U.K. Companies Act 1985. Section 317 of the U.K. Companies Act 1985 and section 162 of the current Ordinance require directors to divulge the nature of their interest in any contract, transaction, or arrangement involving the company to the board of directors. Criminal sanctions apply to non-disclosure, even in the context of one director companies.

Over the last thirty years or so, Commonwealth and U.S. legislatures have come up with various statutory mechanisms through which an interested director or officer transaction may be upheld so as to increase predictability and enhance the practical administration of interested transactions. Third parties and directors cannot function effectively in an environment where companies can challenge and subject interested transactions to *ex post facto* court review years later. To use the language found in the MBCA, these mechanisms have the advantage of providing "safe harbours" and "bright lines" for companies and directors involved in interested transactions; that is to say, they provide clear procedures and criteria by which directors can insulate interested transactions from court review (PE Kay, "Director Conflicts of Interest Under the Model Business Corporation Act: A Model For All States?" (1994) 69 Washington L Rev 207 at 210).

These statutory mechanisms are based on procedural and/or substantive requirements of fairness. In terms of procedural fairness, they often resemble the articles of association drawn up to uphold interested transactions, in that they usually include two requirements. The first requirement is transparency through disclosure - directors in a conflict of interest must disclose both the nature and the extent of their material interest in the transaction. Moreover, directors are generally required to also disclose any material interest they may have in a person who is, or proposes, to be a party to a contract with the company. A material interest is generally defined as an interest that an outside observer would reasonably expect to influence a director's judgment. This objective standard does not require the existence of actual influence upon the director, but only an interest that may be reasonably expected to affect a director's actions (Kay, *supra* at 218). The second requirement is disinterested decision making - the director in a conflict of interest is not allowed to take part in the board's decision making on matters relating to his conflict of interest.

All Commonwealth statutes, the MBCA and s.5.02 of the American Law Institute's *(ALI) Principles of Corporate Governance* require directors to disclose their interests. The MBCA, in subchapter F (ss. 8.60-8.63), requires disinterested decision making at the board level. The New Zealand Companies Act 1993 at s.144 does not require disinterested decision making.

In addition to the requirement of procedural fairness, several jurisdictions have added a requirement of substantive fairness: from an objective standpoint the interested transaction must be reasonable and fair to the corporation. For a transaction to be substantively fair, it must not only have a fair price but also be in the best interests of the corporation. However, in considering the fairness of a transaction, the court will in addition be required to look at not only the price but also whether the transaction provided a benefit to the corporation.(MBCA, Official Comment, s.8.61). The CBCA, the New Zealand Companies Act 1993, the MBCA and s.5.02 of the *Principles of Corporate Governance* all have tests that require interested transactions to be reasonable and fair to the corporation.

It is important to understand the underlying rationales of these requirements. Obviously, the requirement of disclosure aims to make a company board aware that a conflict of interest exists; this allows the company to protect itself against directors acting in their personal interest. For example, they might exclude the interested director from the decision making process, or at least filter the interested directors' pronouncements in light of their personal bias, before arriving at a decision.

Disinterested decision making generally goes hand in hand with the requirement of disclosure, but not necessarily so. The rationale for excluding interested directors is again rather obvious: it allows the board to take a decision without theoretically having the interested director's personal interest coming into play and biasing the board's final decision in his or her favour.

The requirement of substantive fairness is in some ways a final safety net. Although all the requirements of procedural fairness may be respected in terms of disclosure and decision making, the board might still come to a decision that is substantively unfair to the company for various informal reasons -- the interested director is an important and respected director or a personal friend of the other directors, the interested director is the majority shareholder of the corporation, etc. Accordingly, the requirement of substantive fairness is a last stop measure to protect the corporation and its shareholders from a board entering into transactions that are grossly unfair to the corporation.

> Absent the constraints of fiduciary duty [substantive fairness], the majority rule represents a spoils system in which the party that obtains working or numerical voting control has unbundled opportunities for its own self-aggrandisement (D. M. Branson, "Assault on Another Citadel: Attempts to Curtail the Fiduciary Standard of Loyalty Applicable to Corporate Directors" (1988) 57 Fordham L.R. 375 at 394).

The concepts of procedural and substantive fairness are not alien to Hong Kong company and securities law. As noted above, the requirement of disclosure is already a part of the current Ordinance. In terms of disinterested decision making and substantive fairness, companies incorporated under the Ordinance can choose to include such requirements in their articles of association; they are, however, under no obligation to do so. As a matter of practice, articles of Hong Kong companies often provide that interested directors may vote on interested transactions and need not account.

It is noteworthy that Chapter 14 of the SEHK's Listing Rules for "connected transactions" (the SEHK's term for interested transactions) already require disinterested decision making and substantive fairness. For example, Rule 14.26 lays out the circumstances where certain connected transactions are subject to disclosure and disinterested shareholder consent (ie. contrary to *Beatty*, a director cannot vote qua shareholder to uphold an interested transaction). It is also noteworthy that Rule 14.31 states that the primary objective of the circular sent to shareholders should be to demonstrate the reasonableness and fairness of the proposed connected transaction.

Moreover, Rule 14.23(2) gives the Exchange the power to grant a waiver from the requirement to obtain shareholders' approval; instead, the Exchange may require a letter from the company's auditors or financial advisors stating that in their opinion the transaction is fair and reasonable so far as the shareholders of the company are concerned ("fairness" opinions are found in other jurisdictions as well). However, one should take note that these rules do not apply to public companies that are not listed.

At present, the current Ordinance contains only the requirement of disclosure. The other important procedures governing interested transactions are found in the articles of association and case law, which in many important respects, is in an unsatisfactory state. As noted above, much of the case law supposedly applicable to interested transactions and directors' conflict of interest is drawn from a now inappropriate line of trust law cases. Modern directors are not trustees and the role of a corporate manager is not the same as that of a trustee. The trustee's role of preserving the trust capital while investing conservatively to produce income is fundamentally at odds with the risk-taking required of corporate directors and officers in search of profit maximisation (see Welling at 379).

A statutory mechanism that allows interested transactions to be upheld not only enhances predictability and practical administration of interested transactions but is more in keeping with the commercial context in which directors function. Generally speaking, the standard governing commercial relations is one based on good faith and fair dealing. The fiduciary standard for directors has evolved more toward this commercial standard based on honesty and fair dealing; it has been reflected in the CBCA's statutory formulation of directors' duties at s. 122(l): "Every director and officer of a corporation in exercising his powers and discharging his duties shall (a) act honestly and in good faith with a view to the best interests of the corporation ...".

The recommendation made here that directors and officers be placed under a duty of fair dealing with respect to interested transactions flows logically from the duty found at s. 122(l) CBCA, but is a further refinement of it. The s. 122(l) statutory formulation of directors' duties has been heavily interpreted in light of the fiduciary duty line of cases (which obviously import variations on the trust standard). The specific duty of fair dealing in interested director transactions finds its source in the 1994 ALI Principles of Corporate Governance at s. 5.02. It is a statutory expression of the commercial, standard which has in fact evolved in this area, away from the commercially impracticable trust standard. The imposition of an impracticable standard prompted the search for a means of validating commercially reasonable transactions. By stating a duty of fair dealing, the commercial nature of the standard should be made readily apparent and distinguished from stricter fiduciary duties.

The ALI Principles explain the evolution of this duty of fair dealing in the United States.

Many states have "safe harbour" statutes relating to transactions between directors and the corporation. These statutes have generally approached conflict-of-interest transactions in terms of the voidability of transactions and the effect of approval by disinterested directors or shareholders, rather than imposing an affirmative duty of fair dealing. This may reflect the evolution of the law in this area from a rule that originally permitted all transactions with directors to be set aside without regard to fairness, and a tendency to leave the development of affirmative duties of fair dealing to the case law (Comment, s 5.02).

The creation of a statutory duty of fair dealing in interested transactions is a new approach but one which is consistent with the underlying principles in the case law in this area. Further research and careful consideration should be given to introducing this concept.

It is also consistent with concerns expressed by many working party members that shareholders in Hong Kong required greater statutory protections, especially minority shareholders.[6]

6.20 RECOMMENDATION

Qualification of interested transactions:

Interested transactions should be upheld if (i) directors disclose to the board their material interest in the transaction; (ii) do not vote as a director on any resolution to approve the transaction; and (iii) the transaction was reasonable and fair to the corporation at the time it was approved. In the alternative, such transactions could also be approved by unanimous shareholder consent.

Current Ordinance

Article 86 of Table A allows a company to provide a procedure by which interested transactions can be upheld and directors are not liable for any profit realized from such a transaction. Under this procedure a director must 1) disclose the nature of their interest in accordance with s.162 of the Ordinance - the company's articles of association cannot eliminate the s. 162 disclosure requirement: and 2) not vote on the interested transaction nor be counted in the quorum present at the meeting that considers the transaction (art. 86).

COMMENTARY

The CBCA requires that an interested transaction be both procedurally and substantively fair while the MBCA requires such transaction to be either procedurally or substantively fair. There has been some debate in the literature as to the value of a disjunctive or conjunctive scheme. In particular, the MBCA's disjunctive approach has been criticised as being too lax, in that it may allow directors to engage in substantively unfair transactions by simply following the MBCA's requirements of procedural fairness (see generally M.A. Eisenberg, "Self-Interested Transactions in Corporate Law" (1988) Journal of Corporation Law 997; Kay, *supra)*.

However, the difference between a disjunctive test and conjunctive test is arguably more one of form than substance. Commenting on the "reasonable and fair" branch of their draft act which eventually became the CBCA, the Dickerson Report underlined that this branch served only to give content and substance to the directors' general duty to act in the corporation's best interest.

> Particularly noteworthy is the overriding criterion that the contract be "reasonable and fair to the corporation", which is necessary to preclude mutual 'back-scratching" by directors who might otherwise tacitly agree to approve one another's contracts with the corporation.

---

[6] DR: para. 228, Draft Act s.9.17(3)(c). OBCA: s.13.2(7). MBCA: S 8.60-8.63. NZLC R9: paras. 193, 523-542, Draft Act ss. 108-113.

Of course directors who indulge in such conduct will be liable under the general provisions of s. 9.19 [the draft act's provision laying out the directors' general duty to act in the corporation's best interest] in any event [...] *The 'reasonable and fair' standard set out in subsection (3)(c) serves only to underline the director's specific duties in the circumstances* [emphasis added] (Dickerson Report at para. 228).

Likewise, the Official Commentary to the MBCA in discussing its safe harbour procedures (disclosure and disinterested decision making) made a similar observation:

... neither the transaction nor the director is legally vulnerable if the procedures of section 8.62 [disclosure and disinterested decision making] have been properly followed. Subsection (b)(1) is, however, subject to a critically important predicate condition... The condition -- an obvious one-- is that *the board's action must comply with the care, best interests and good faith criteria prescribed in section 8.30(a) for all directors' actions* [emphasis added] (MBCA, Official Comment s. 8.61).

Working party members were generally in favour of tightening the rules in this area provided there was a manner by which transactions could be upheld by shareholder approval (see Recommendation 6.21). The working party members thus supported the conjunctive test which, on balance, is being recommended here.

Professor Sealy noted that the disclosure and disinterested voting procedures were too formalistic for many private companies and suggested the approach adopted in the New Zealand Companies Act 1993 at s. 107(3). If all "entitled persons", essentially shareholders, agree to or concur in a company entering into a transaction in which a director is interested, no further formalities would be required.[7]

6.21 RECOMMENDATION

Shareholder approval of interested transactions:

Shareholders should be able to vote to uphold a transaction by special resolution in certain circumstances.

Current Ordinance

There is no statutory mechanism through which disinterested shareholders may vote to uphold an interested transaction.

COMMENTARY

This recommendation aims to provide another mechanism by which interested transactions, may be upheld. Under s.242 of the CBCA, shareholder ratification

---

[7]   DR: paras. 226-32, Draft Act s.9.17. CBCA: s.120(7). OBCA: s.132(7). MBCA s.8.61. NZLC R9: paras. 193,523-542, Draft Act ss. 108-113 (but note voting by interested directors is permitted).

serves only an evidentiary purpose and not a curative one. Under this provision, a legal action (such as an oppression or unfairly prejudicial action) cannot be stayed or dismissed by reason only that an alleged breach of the director's fiduciary duty has been approved by the shareholders; however, evidence of shareholder approval may be taken - into account - by the court in making an order under the CBCA'S oppression remedy or derivative action. Commenting on this provision, the Dickerson Committee stated:

> ... we think it better to characterise shareholder ratification or waiver as an evidentiary issue, which in effect compels the court to go behind the constitutional structure of the corporation and examine the real issues. If, for example, the alleged misconduct was ratified by majority shareholders who were also the directors whose conduct is attacked, evidence of shareholder ratification would carry little or no weight. If, however, the alleged misconduct was ratified by a majority of disinterested shareholders after full disclosure of the facts, that evidence would carry much more weight indicating that the majority of disinterested shareholders condoned the act or dismissed it as a mere error of business judgment... By giving the court wide discretion to consider the pertinent facts and by barring the court from following a simplistic path such as applying the shareholder ratification rule, we in effect compel the court to adjudge the issue on its merits (Dickerson Report at para. 487).

Although the approach taken in the CBCA definitely has its merits, the Ontario Business Corporations Act (OBCA) and Alberta Business Corporations Act (ABCA), which are in many ways more modern updates of the current CBCA, allow for shareholder ratification by special resolution of interested transactions upon disclosure at sections 132(8) and 115(7), respectively. There was general support for this approach in the working party; in some circumstances, a director may inadvertently fail to make proper disclosure. This defect could be cured by special resolution.[8]

6.22 RECOMMENDATION

Loans to directors:

Transactions involving loans to directors should continue to be prohibited subject to certain exceptions.

Current Ordinance

The Ordinance lays down a general prohibition on loans to directors subject to certain exceptions (s. 157H).

COMMENTARY

At present, s. 157H of the Ordinance lays down a general prohibition of loans to directors. This general prohibition is subject to certain exceptions such as:

---

[8]   OBCA: s.132(8). MBCA: s.8.63.

shareholder approved loans in private companies; loans made by a company whose ordinary course of business includes lending money and giving guarantees; or loans for house purchases, etc; transactions for the purposes of the company; and transactions within a group of companies. There is a cap on the aggregate of some of these exceptions.

The MBCA treats loans to directors no differently from any other interested director transaction. Therefore, loans, guarantees, pledges, or other forms of assistance to directors are permitted and enforceable so long as the disclosure and disinterested approval requirements are observed and the solvency requirements pertaining to a "distribution" are met. This approach is similar to the SEHK's rules for listed companies in Hong Kong; Rule 14.26(6) requires financial assistance to connected persons which is not upon normal commercial terms in the ordinary and usual course of business to be disclosed and approved by a disinterested shareholder vote.

Although this approach was discussed in the working party meetings, loans to directors were viewed as particularly open to abuse in Hong Kong. "Why should companies be providing their directors with loans in the first place?" was the comment of one working member. For this reason, the working party was inclined to retain the existing prohibition and narrow the exceptions somewhat. An issue to be resolved is whether private companies should be able to provide such loans with shareholder approval. Some jurisdictions (such as Singapore) provide for this while others (such as the U.K., in following a recommendation of the Jenkins Committee) do not.

Unfortunately, retention of the prohibition and exceptions will add complexity to the drafting and, in the opinion of Professor Sealy, risks being ineffective. Directors and their counsel can show great ingenuity in structuring transactions to avoid the prohibition.[9]

6.23 RECOMMENDATION: Use of Corporate Information and Opportunity. Directors and officers should not disclose or use for their benefit a corporate opportunity or information that they obtain by reason of their position or employment except (i) with consent of disinterested board members, (ii) where disclosure is required by law or otherwise or (iii) where it is reasonable to assume that the disclosure or use of the information or opportunity will not be likely to prejudice the corporation.

Current Ordinance

There is no statutory scheme to deal with the use of corporate information or the diversion of corporate opportunity.

COMMENTARY

At present, Hong Kong has no statutory scheme to deal with the acquisition or diversion of "corporate opportunities" by directors. As a consequence, this area is

---

[9]   DR: Draft Acts s 5.16(2). CBCA: s 44. OBCA: s 20. MBCA: ss.8.60-8.63. NZLC R9: see generally Draft Act ss 108-113.

governed by the same strict trust standard that governs interested transactions. The general rule established in *Regal (Hastings) v Gulliver,* that any party acting in a fiduciary capacity may not enter into any engagement in which he might have an interest conflicting with that of the beneficiary, and this irrespective of the absence of bad faith, has been accepted in much of the Commonwealth. The law is somewhat different in Canada because of the leading Canadian case of *Peso Silver Mines Ltd v Cropper* [1966] SCR 673. Canadian courts are unwilling to find a director in breach of his or her duties where both good faith is shown, and where no special or privileged information was delivered from the Position as a director.

Both Australia and New Zealand have innovated in this area by introducing statutory provisions to deal with the problem of corporate opportunities by way of rules regulating the use of company information. Under section 232(5)-(6) of the Australian Corporations Law, directors must not make improper use of their position, or information acquired by virtue of their position, to gain, directly or indirectly, an advantage for themselves or for any other person, or to cause detriment to the corporation. Section 232 is in addition to, and not in derogation of, any other law relating to the duty of a director (eg under the common law a director is liable to account even where he has not improperly used the position of director).

However, New Zealand has gone one step further than Australia. At s.145 of the Companies Act 1993, directors may disclose or make use of information obtained in course of their employment, if they disclose to, as well as receive consent from, the board and the disclosure or use of the information will not prejudice the company. Disclosure is also recorded in an "interest register" which is available to shareholders. The emphasis on disclosure in New Zealand is based on pragmatic considerations. There is greater tolerance of situations of potential conflict of interest given the commercial reality of a small, close-knit business community with a high degree of cross-shareholdings in a small number of large companies.

The better approach to yet another register is simply to note the disclosure in the minutes of meeting.[10]

---

[10] MBCA: ss 8.60-8.63. NZLC R9: paras. 92,536-539, Draft Act s.112.

APPENDIX M

Extracts from the City Code on Takeovers and Mergers

THE CITY CODE ON TAKEOVERS AND MERGERS

The City Code on Takeovers and Mergers is issued by the Panel on Takeovers and Mergers. The following extracts are taken from the Code updated on 23rd July 1998.

INTRODUCTION

1 The Code

...

(c) Enforcement of the Code

The Code has not, and does not seek to have the force of law. It has, however, been acknowledged by both government and other regulatory authorities that those who seek to take advantage of the facilities of the securities markets in the United Kingdom should conduct themselves in matters relating to takeovers in accordance with best business standards and so according to the Code.

...those who do not so conduct themselves may find that, by way of sanction, the facilities of those markets are withheld.

...

3 The Code in Practice

(a) General Principles and Rules

The Code is based upon a number of General Principles, which are essentially statements of good standards of commercial behaviour. These General Principles apply to all transactions with which the Code is concerned ... They are applied by the Panel in accordance with their spirit to achieve their underlying purpose, the Panel may modify or relax the effect of their precise wording accordingly.

In addition ... the Code contains a series of Rules ... their spirit must be observed as well as their letter and the Panel may modify or relax the application of a Rule...

...

(d) Disciplinary proceedings

If the Panel finds that there has been a breach of the Code, it may have recourse to:

(i)   private reprimand;

(ii) public censure;

(iii) reporting the offender's conduct to another regulatory authority (eg the Department of Trade and Industry, the Stock Exchange, FSA or the relevant SRO or RPB);

(iv) taking action for the purpose of the requirements of FSA, relevant SROs and certain RPBs which oblige their members not to act for the offender in a takeover or in certain other transactions; and/or

(v)   requiring further action to be taken as the Panel thinks fit.

GENERAL PRINCIPLES

...

9. Directors of an offeror and the offeree company must always, in advising their shareholders, act only in their capacity as directors and not have regard to their personal or family shareholdings or to their personal relationships with the companies. It is the shareholders' interests taken as a whole, together with those of employees and creditors, which should be considered when the directors are giving advice to shareholders. Directors of the offeree company should give careful consideration before they enter into any commitment with an offeror (or anyone else) which would restrict their freedom to advise their shareholders in the future. Such commitments may give rise to conflicts of interest or result in a breach of the directors' fiduciary duties.

...

RULE 21:

Restrictions on frustrating action

During the course of an offer, or even before the date of the offer if the board of the offeree company has reason to believe that a bona fide offer might be imminent, the board must not, except in pursuance of a contract entered into earlier, without the approval of the shareholders in general meeting:–

(a) issue any authorised but unissued shares;

(b) issue or grant options in respect of any unissued shares;

(c) create or issue, or permit the creation or issue of, any securities carrying rights of conversion into or subscription for shares;

(d) sell, dispose of or acquire, or agree to sell, dispose of or acquire, assets of a material amount; or

(e) enter into contracts otherwise than in the ordinary course of business.

The notice convening such a meeting of shareholders must include information about the offer or anticipated offer.

Where it is felt that an obligation or other special circumstance exists, although a formal contract has not been entered into, the Panel must be consulted and its consent to proceed without a shareholders' meeting obtained.

Notes on Rule 21

1. Consent by the offeror.

Where the Rule would otherwise apply, it will nonetheless normally be waived by the Panel if this is acceptable to the offeror.

2. "Material amount"

For the purpose of determining whether a disposal or acquisition is of "a material amount" the Panel will, in general, have regard to the following:–

> (a) the value of the assets to be disposed of or acquired compared with the assets of the offeree company;
>
> (b) where appropriate, the aggregate value of the consideration to be received or given compared with the assets of the offeree company; and
>
> (c) where appropriate, net profits (after deducting all charges except taxation and excluding extraordinary items) attributable to the assets to be disposed of or acquired compared with those of the offeree company.

For these purposes, the term "assets" will normally mean fixed assets plus current assets less current liabilities.

Subject to Note 4, the Panel will normally consider relative values of 10% or more as being of a material amount, although relative values lower than 10% may be considered material if the asset is of particular significance.

If several transactions relevant to this Rule, but not individually material, occur or are intended, the Panel will aggregate such transactions to determine whether the requirements of this Rule are applicable to any of them.

The Panel should be consulted in advance where there may be any doubt as to the application of the above.

...

6. Service contracts

The Panel will regard amending or entering into a service contract with, or creating or varying the terms of employment of, a director as entering into a contract "otherwise than in the ordinary course of business" for the purpose of this Rule if the new or amended contract or terms constitute an abnormal increase in the emoluments or a significant improvement in the terms of service.

This will not prevent any such increase or improvement which results from a genuine promotion or new appointment but the Panel must be consulted in advance in such cases.

...

RULE 25. OFFEREE BOARD CIRCULARS

25.4 Directors' service contracts

(a) The first major circular from the offeree board advising shareholders on an offer (whether recommending acceptance or rejection of the offer) must contain particulars of all service contracts of any director or proposed director of the offeree company with the company or any of its subsidiaries where such contracts have more than 12 months to run. If there are none, this should be stated.

(b) If such contracts have been entered into or amended within 6 months of the date of the document, particulars must be given in respect of the earlier contracts (if any) which have been replaced or amended as well as in respect of the current contracts. If there have been none, this should be stated.

Notes on Rule 25.4

1. Particulars to be disclosed

The particulars required in respect of existing service contracts and, where appropriate under Rule 25.4(b), earlier contracts are:–

(a) the name of the director under contract;

(b) the expiry date of the contract;

(c) the amount of fixed remuneration payable under the contract (irrespective of whether received as a director or for management, but excluding arrangements for company payments in respect of a pension or similar scheme); and

(d) the amount of any variable remuneration payable under the contract (eg commission on profits) with details of the formula for calculating such remuneration.

Where there is more than one contract, a statement of the aggregate remuneration payable is normally regarded as fulfilling the requirements under (c) above, except to the extent that this method would conceal material anomalies which ought to be disclosed (eg because one director is remunerated at a very much higher rate than the others). In cases where contracts have been replaced or amended, however, the particulars of remuneration payable under both the existing and the earlier contracts must relate to each individual separately.

It is not acceptable to refer to the latest annual report, indicating that information regarding service contracts may be found there, or to state that the contracts are open for inspection at a specified place.

2. Recent increases in remuneration

The Panel will regard as the amendment of a service contract under this Rule any case where the remuneration of an offeree company director (with a service contract with more than 12 months to run) is increased within 6 months of the date of the document. Therefore, any such increase must be disclosed in the document and the current and previous levels of remuneration stated.

APPENDIX N
Financial Reporting Standard 8 (Related party disclosures) (FRS 8)

The following note appears in a preamble to FRS 8:[1]

Financial Reporting Standard 8 is set out in paragraphs 1-7.

The Statement of Standard Accounting Practice set out in paragraphs 3-7 should be read in the context of the Objective as stated in paragraph 1 and the definitions set out in paragraph 2 and also of the Foreword to Accounting Standards and the Statement of Principles for Financial Reporting currently in issue.

The Explanation set out in paragraphs 8-23 shall be regarded as part of the Statement of Standard Accounting Practice insofar as it assists in interpreting that statement ...

OBJECTIVE

1. The objective of this FRS is to ensure that financial statements contain the disclosures necessary to draw attention to the possibility that the reported financial position and results may have been affected by the existence of related parties and by material transactions with them.

DEFINITIONS

2. The following definitions shall apply in this FRS and in particular in the Statement of Standard Accounting Practice set out in paragraphs 3-7.

2.1 Close family:-

Close members of the family of an individual are those family members, or members of the same household, who may be expected to influence, or be influenced by, that person in their dealings with the reporting entity.

2.2 Control:-

The ability to direct the financial and operating policies of an entity with a view to gaining economic benefits from its activities.

2.3 Key management:-

Those persons in senior positions having authority or responsibility for directing or controlling the major activities and resources of the reporting entity.

2.4 Persons acting in concert:-

Persons who, pursuant to an agreement or understanding (whether formal or informal), actively co-operate, whether by the ownership by any of them of shares

---

[1] Issued by the Accounting Standards Board in October 1995.

in an undertaking or otherwise, to exercise control or influence[2] over that undertaking.

2.5 Related parties:-

(a)   Two or more parties are related parties when at any time during the financial period:

(i)   one party has direct or indirect control of the other party; or

(ii)   the parties are subject to common control from the same source; or

(iii)   one party has influence over the financial and operating policies of the other party to an extent that that other party might be inhibited from pursuing at all times its own separate interests; or

(iv)   the parties, in entering a transaction, are subject to influence from the same source to such an extent that one of the parties to the transaction has subordinated its own separate interests.

(b)   For the avoidance of doubt, the following are related parties of the reporting entity:

(i)   its ultimate and intermediate parent undertakings, subsidiary undertakings, and fellow subsidiary undertakings;

(ii)   its associates and joint ventures;

(iii)   the investor or venturer in respect of which the reporting entity is an associate or a joint venture;

(iv)   directors[3] of the reporting entity and the directors of its ultimate and intermediate parent undertakings; and

(v)   pension funds for the benefit of employees of the reporting entity or of any entity that is a related party of the reporting entity;

(c)   and the following are presumed to be related parties of the reporting entity unless it can be demonstrated that neither party has influenced the financial and operating policies of the other in such a way as to inhibit the pursuit of separate interests:

---

[2]   In terms of para 2.5(a)(iii).

[3]   Directors include shadow directors, which are defined in companies legislation as persons in accordance with whose directions or instructions the directors of the company are accustomed to act.

       (i)   the key management of the reporting entity and the key management of its parent undertaking or undertakings;

       (ii)   a person owning or able to exercise control over 20 per cent or more of the voting rights of the reporting entity, whether directly or through nominees;

       (iii) each person acting in concert in such a way as to be able to exercise control or influence[4] over the reporting entity; and

       (iv) an entity managing or managed by the reporting entity under a management contract.

   (d)   Additionally, because of their relationship with certain parties that are, or are presumed to be, related parties of the reporting entity, the following are also presumed to be related parties of the reporting entity:

       (i)   members of the close family of any individual falling under parties mentioned in (a)-(c) above; and

       (ii)   partnerships, companies, trusts or other entities in which any individual or member of the family in (a)-(c) above had a controlling interest.

Sub-paragraphs (b), (c) and (d) are not intended to be an exhaustive list of related parties.

2.6 Related party transaction:-

The transfer of assets or liabilities or the performance of services by, to or for a related party irrespective of whether a price is charged.

STATEMENT OF STANDARD ACCOUNTING PRACTICE

Scope

3.   Financial Reporting Standard 8 applies to all financial statements that are intended to give a true and fair view of a reporting entity's financial position and profit or loss (or income and expenditure) for a period. The FRS does not, however, require disclosure:

   (a)   in consolidated financial statements, of any transactions or balances between group entities that have been eliminated on consolidation;

   (b)   in a parent's own financial statements when those statements are presented together with its consolidated financial statements;

   (c)   in the financial statements of subsidiary undertakings, 90 per cent or more of whose voting rights are controlled within the group, of transactions with entities that are part of the group or investees of

---

[4]   In terms of paragraph 2.5(a)(iii).

the group qualifying as related parties, provided that the consolidated financial statements in which that subsidiary is included are publicly available;

(d)   of pension contributions paid to a pension fund; and

(e)   of emoluments in respect of services as an employee of the reporting entity.

Reporting entities taking advantage of the exemption in (c) above are required to state that fact.

4.   The FRS does not require disclosure of the relationship and transactions between the reporting entity and the parties listed in (a)-(d) below simply as a result of their role as:

(a)   providers of finance in the course of their business in that regard;

(b)   utility companies;

(c)   government departments and their sponsored bodies,

even though they may circumscribe the freedom of action of an entity or participate in its decision making process; and

(d)   a customer, supplier, franchiser, distributor or general agent with whom an entity transacts a significant volume of business.

Disclosure of control

5.   When the reporting entity is controlled by another party, there should be disclosure of the related party relationship and the name of that party and, if different that of the ultimate controlling party. If the controlling party or ultimate controlling party of the reporting entity is not known, that fact should be disclosed. The information should be disclosed irrespective of whether any transactions have taken place between the controlling parties and the reporting entity.

Disclosure of transactions and balances

6.   Financial statements should disclose material transactions undertaken by the reporting entity with a related party. Disclosure should be made irrespective of whether a price is charged. The disclosure should include:

(a)   the names of the transacting related parties;

(b)   a description of the relationship between the parties;

(c)   a description of the transactions;

(d)   the amounts involved;

(e)   any other elements of the transactions necessary for an understanding of the financial statements;

(f)   the amounts due to or from related parties at the balance sheet date and provisions for doubtful debts due from such parties at that date; and

(g)   amounts written off in the period in respect of debts due to or from parties.

Transactions with related parties may be disclosed on an aggregated basis (aggregation of similar transactions by type of related party) unless disclosure of an individual transaction, or connected transactions, is necessary for an understanding of the impact of the transactions on the financial statements of the reporting entity or is required by law.

Date from which effective

7.   The accounting practices set out in the FRS should be regarded as standard in respect of financial statements relating to accounting periods commencing on or after 23 December 1995. Earlier adoption is encouraged but not required.

EXPLANATION

The effect of related parties

8.   In the absence of information to the contrary, it is assumed that a reporting entity has independent discretionary power over its resources and transactions and pursues its activities independently of the interests of its individual owners, manages and others. Transactions are presumed to have been undertaken on an arm's length basis, ie on terms such as could have obtained in a transaction with an external party, in which each side bargained knowledgeably and freely, unaffected by any relationship between them.

9.   These assumptions may not be justified when related party relationships exist, because the requisite conditions for competitive, free market dealings may not be present. Whilst the parties may endeavour to achieve arm's length bargaining the very nature of the relationship may preclude this occurring. Sometimes the nature of the relationship between the parties is such that the disclosure of the relationship alone will be sufficient to make users aware of the possible implications of related party transactions. For this reason, transactions between subsidiary undertaking, 90 per cent or more of whose voting rights are controlled within the group, and other members and investees of the same group are not required to be disclosed in the separate financial statements of the subsidiary undertaking.

10.   Even when terms are arm's length, the reporting of material related party transactions is useful information, because the terms of future transactions are more susceptible to alteration as a result of the nature of the relationship than they would be in transactions with an unrelated party. Although the existence of a related party relationship sometimes precludes arm's length transactions, non-independent parties can deal with each other at arm's length, as in the situation where a parent undertaking places no restrictions on two subsidiaries, giving them complete freedom in deciding whether to deal with each other and on what terms. However, assertions in financial statements about transactions with related parties should not imply that the related party transactions were effected on terms equivalent to those that prevail in arm's length transactions unless the parties have conducted the transactions in an independent manner.

Applying the definition of 'related party'

Party

11. The definition of a related party encompasses both an individual or an entity, such as a company or unincorporated business, and a group of individuals or entities acting in concert. Groups of individuals or entities are include in this definition because although a single individual or entity (having, for example only a small shareholding) might not be able to divert a particular reporting entity from pursuing its own separate interests, this could be achieved by the individual or entity acting in concert with others.

Relationship

12. The definition is limited to parties having a relationship with a reporting entity that affects the pursuit of separate interests of either the reporting entity or the other party, since transactions with such parties could have a significant effect on the financial position and operating results of the reporting entity. Consequently, subsidiary undertakings and associates are related parties of the investor. The reporting entity and a major customer or supplier are not related parties by virtue of that connection alone because the reporting entity still retains the freedom to make decisions in its own separate interests.

Common control

13. Entities subject to common control are included in the definition of a related party because the controlling entity could cause such entities to transact particular terms. The relationship could therefore have a material effect on the performance and financial position of the reporting entity. Common control is deemed to exist when both parties are subject to control from boards having a controlling nucleus of directors in common.

Common influence

14. The difference between control and influence is that control brings with it the ability to cause the controlled party to subordinate its separate interests whereas the outcome of the exercise of influence is less certain. Two related parties of a third entity are not necessarily related parties of each other. For example:

   (a) entities are not related parties by reason only of their being associated companies of the same investor. The parties are subject only to influence rather than common control, hence the relationship between them is normally too tenuous to justify their being treated as related parties of each other;

   (b) similarly when one party is subject to control and another party is subject to influence from the same source, those two parties are not necessarily related parties of each other. Since one of the parties is subject only to influence rather than control, the relationship between them would not normally justify their being treated as related parties of each other; and

(c) two entities are not related parties simply because they have a director in common.

In all circumstances, however, it will be appropriate to consider whether one or both transacting parties, subject to control and influence from the same source or common influence, have subordinated their own separate interests in entering into that transaction.

Pension funds

15. The fact that certain pension funds are related parties of the reporting entity is not intended to call into question the independence of the trustees with regard to their fiduciary obligations to the members of the pension scheme. Transactions between the reporting entity and the pension fund may be in the interest of members but nevertheless need to be reported in the accounts of the reporting entity.

Scope

16. Related party disclosure provisions do not apply in circumstances where to comply with them conflicts with the reporting entity's duties of confidentiality arising by operation of law (although operation of law would not include the effects of terms stipulated in a contract). For example, banks are obliged by law to observe a strict duty of confidentiality in respect of their customers' affairs and the FRS would not override the obligation to preserve the confidentiality of customers' dealings.

Exempt subsidiary undertakings

17. The FRS grants certain exemptions to subsidiary undertakings 90 per cent or more of whose voting rights are controlled within the group. These subsidiaries do not have to disclose transactions with other group companies and investees of the group qualifying as related parties. The latter includes associates and joint ventures of other group companies with whom the reporting subsidiary has transacted in circumstances falling under paragraph 2.5(a)(iv). Disclosure would, however, be required of transactions with related parties of the reporting subsidiary other than those that are excluded by the exemption.

Disclosure of control

18. If the reporting entity is controlled by another party, that fact is relevant information, irrespective of whether transactions have taken place with that party, because the control relationship prevents the reporting entity from being independent in the sense described in paragraph 8. Indeed, the existence and identity of the controlling party may sometimes be at least as relevant in appraising an entity's prospects as are the performance and financial position presented in its financial statements. The controlling party may establish the entity's credit standing, determine the source and price of its raw materials, determine the products it sells, to whom and at what price, and may affect the source, calibre and even the primary concern and allegiance of its management.

Disclosure of transactions

Transactions

19. Disclosure is required of all material related party transactions. As transactions include donations to or by the entity, related party transactions are required to be disclosed whether or not a price is charged. The following are examples of related party transactions that require disclosure by a reporting entity in the period in which they occur:

- purchases or sales of goods (finished or unfinished);

- purchases or sales of property and other assets;

- rendering or receiving of services;

- agency arrangements;

- leasing arrangements;

- transfer of research and development;

- licence agreements;

- provision of finance (including loans and equity contributions in cash or in kind);

- guarantees and the provision of collateral security; and

- management contracts.

Materiality

20. Transactions are material when their disclosure might reasonably be expected to influence decisions made by the users of general purpose financial statements. The materiality of related party transactions is to be judged, not only in terms of their significance to the reporting entity, but also in relation to the other related party when that party is:

(a) a director, key manager or other individual in a position to influence, or accountable for stewardship of, the reporting entity; or

(b) a member of the close family of any individual mentioned in (a) above; or

(c) an entity controlled by any individual mentioned in (a) or (b) above.

Aggregation

21. Disclosure of details of particular transactions with individual related parties would frequently be too voluminous to be easily understood. Accordingly, similar transactions may be aggregated by type of related party. For example, in the individual accounts of a group company, purchases or sales with other group companies can be aggregated and described as such. However, this should not be done in such a way as to obscure the importance of significant transactions. Hence

purchases or sales of goods should not be aggregated with purchases or sales of fixed assets. Nor should a material related party transaction with an individual be concealed in an aggregated disclosure.

Other elements of the transaction

22.   Paragraph 6(e) requires disclosure of 'any other elements of the [related party] transactions necessary for an understanding of the financial statements'. An example falling within this requirement would be the need to give an indication that the transfer of a major asset had taken place at an amount materially different from that obtainable on normal commercial terms.

Relationship with statutory and London Stock Exchange requirements

23.   There are extensive statutory and London Stock Exchange requirements and reliefs regarding disclosure of related party transactions and relationships. In certain instances, the FRS will extend existing disclosure requirements; in other instances, the statutory and London Stock Exchange disclosure requirements go beyond those of the FRS. The location of the principal statutory and London Stock Exchange requirements is given in Appendices I and II respectively.

APPENDIX O

List of Individuals and Organisations who have assisted with the project

The Accounting Standards Board

John Aldis, KPMG

Mark Ashworth, Assistant Company Secretary, NatWest Group plc

The Association of British Insurers

The Australian Law Commission

Robert Ayling, Chief Executive, British Airways plc

Colin Bamford, Financial Law Panel

Alan Barr, Burges Salmon

Jonathan Bates, The British Petroleum Company plc

Martin Beagley, ABI

Beaufort Management Consultants Ltd

Robert Bertram, Edinburgh and Heroit-Watt Universities

The Board of Directors, British Airways plc

R E Brown & Others, Syndicate 702 at Lloyd's

Anthony Carey, The Institute of Chartered Accountants in England & Wales

The Centre for Tomorrow's Company

Martin Chester, Theodore Goddard

Alastair Clark, Executive Director, Bank of England

Brian Cleave CB, Solicitor for the Inland Revenue

Allan Cook, Accounting Standards Board

Companies House

Confederation of British Industry

Harriet Creamer, Freshfields

The Crown Office in Scotland

Professor Paul Davies, Balliol College, University of Oxford

Andrew Davison, Eversheds

Dr Simon Deakin, The ESRC Centre for Business Research and Peterhouse College, University of Cambridge

Department of Trade and Industry

Clive Edrupt, CBI

The ESRC Centre for Business Research, University of Cambridge

Financial Law Panel

Financial Services Authority

The Federation of Small Businesses

Ronald D Fox, Fox Williams

The General Council of the Bar, Law Reform Committee

The Hon Mr Justice Girvan

Peter Graham, Norton Rose

Philip Goldenberg, S J Berwin & Co

David Gould, NAPF

Anthony Hammond CB QC, HM Procurator General and Treasury Solicitor

Sir Ronald Hampel, Chairman, ICI plc

Ian Hanford, Federation of Small Businesses

John Harper, Institute of Directors

David Harris, Lovell White Durrant

Neil Harvey, Clifford Chance

John Healey, The Stock Exchange and the Hampel Committee

Giles Henderson CBE, Slaughter & May

Andrew Hicks, University of Exeter

Peter Holgate, Coopers & Lybrand

The Home Office, Research and Statistics Directorate

Dean Horton, Chubb Insurance

Alan Hughes, The ESRC Centre, University of Cambridge

Tim Humphreys, ABI

Rodney Insall, Controller, Company Secretary's Office, British Petroleum Company plc

The Insolvency Service

The Institute of Chartered Accountants in England and Wales

The Institute of Chartered Secretaries and Administrators

Institute of Directors

John Jackson, ICSA

Barry Johnson, Coopers & Lybrand

Helen Jones, Company Secretary, Kingfisher plc

Martyn Jones, Deloitte & Touche

Alan Keat, Travers, Smith Braithwaite

The Law Reform Advisory Committee for Northern Ireland

The Law Society, Company Law Committee

The London Stock Exchange

John Lowry, Brunel University

Kelly Lyles, AIG Europe (UK) Limited

Roger Lyons, TUC and General Secretary of the MSF

Lord Marshall, Chairman, British Airways plc

Michael McKersie, ABI

Adrian J Mezzetti, Gregory, Rowcliffe & Milners

Robin Michaelson, ABI

The National Association of Pension Funds Ltd, Investment Committee

The National Audit Office

Maureen Nolan, ICSA

Richard Nolan, St John's College, University of Cambridge

The Occupational Pensions Regulatory Authority

Stephen Page, Barclays Bank and British Bankers' Association

The Panel on Takeovers and Mergers

The Hon Mr Justice Park

Caroline Phillips, ICSA

Tom Preece, Federation of Small Businesses

Professor Dan Prentice, Erskine Chambers and Pembroke College, University of Oxford

John Quarrell, the NAPF and Nabarro Nathanson

Gail Redwood, Company Secretary, British Airways plc

Jonathan Rickford, Project Director, The Company Law Review (DTI)

Jane Ridley, Financial Services Authority

Ken Rushton, Company Secretary, ICI Plc

The Serious Fraud Office

Isobel N Sharp, Arthur Andersen

The Society of Practitioners of Insolvency

Sir Thomas Stockdale Bt., Erskine Chambers

John Thirlwell, British Bankers' Association

Mia Thomas, CBI

The Trades Union Congress

Treasury Solicitor's Office

HM Treasury & Cabinet Office, Library and Information Service

Mark Watson, Institute of Directors

Ian West, R E Brown & Others, Syndicate 702 at Lloyd's

Ken Wild, Deloitte & Touche

Janet Williamson, TUC

Giles Wintle, ICA

Malcom Woodford, Price Waterhouse

Professor F Wooldridge, Notre Dame University in London

Robert Wright QC, Erskine Chambers